GEORGE STEINER: A READER

Born in Paris in 1929, George Steiner is Extraordinary Fellow of Churchill College, Cambridge, and Professor of English and Comparative Literature at the University of Geneva. After taking degrees at the universities of Chicago and Harvard, where he won the Bell Prize in American literature, Professor Steiner was a Rhodes Scholar at Oxford. He served on the editorial staff of the *Economist* in London from 1952 to 1956. At that time he became a member of the Institute for Advanced Study in Princeton. His books, which have been translated into many languages, include *Tolstoy or Dostoevsky, The Death of Tragedy, Language and Silence, In Bluebeard's Castle, Extraterritorial, After Babel, Heidegger, On Difficulty and Other Essays* and *Antigones*. He has published verse and fiction, and edited *The Penguin Book of Modern Verse Translation*. His novel *The Portage to San Cristobal of A.H.* (1979) was awarded a P.E.N./Faulkner Fiction Stipend and has been dramatized by Christopher Hampton. Professor Steiner's many honours include an O. Henry Short Story award, Fulbright and Guggenheim Fellowships, the first award of the Morton Zabel Prize by the National Institute of Arts and Letters of the United States in 1970, and honorary doctorates from the universities of East Anglia and Louvain. He lists as his passions: music, chess, and mountain-walking.

GEORGE STEINER
A Reader

OXFORD UNIVERSITY PRESS • NEW YORK

Copyright © 1984 by George Steiner

First published in Great Britain in 1984 by Penguin Books Ltd.

First published in the United States in 1984 by Oxford University Press, Inc.

Library of Congress Cataloging in Publication Data

Steiner, George, 1929-
George Steiner.
1. Philology—Addresses, essays, lectures.
I. Title.
P49.S75   1984   410   84-12214
ISBN 0-19-520458-1
ISBN 0-19-505068-1 (PBK.)

Selections from George Steiner, *Language and Silence*, copyright © 1963, 1967 by George Steiner, are reprinted with the permission of Atheneum Publishers.

'"Critic"/"Reader"', copyright © 1979 by George Steiner, was first published in *New Literary History*, a publication of Johns Hopkins University Press.

Selections from *Tolstoy or Dostoevsky* by George Steiner, copyright © 1959 by George Steiner, are reprinted by permission of the author.

Selections from *The Death of Tragedy* by George Steiner, copyright © 1961, 1980 by George Steiner, are reprinted by permission of Oxford University Press, Inc.

The selection from George Steiner, *Extraterritorial*, copyright © 1971 by George Steiner, is reprinted with the permission of Atheneum Publishers.

'The Cleric of Treason,' copyright © 1980 by George Steiner, was first published in *The New Yorker* Magazine.

The selection from *Martin Heidegger* by George Steiner, copyright © 1978 by George Steiner, is reprinted with the permission of Viking Penguin Inc. and Collins Publishers.

'Lieber's Lament' and 'The Defence of A.H.' from *The Portage to San Cristobal of A.H.*, copyright © 1979, 1981 by George Steiner, are reprinted by permission of Simon & Schuster, Inc.

Selections from *On Difficulty* by George Steiner, copyright © 1972, 1975, 1976, 1978 by George Steiner, are reprinted by permission of Oxford University Press, Inc.

Selections from *After Babel* by George Steiner, copyright © 1975 by George Steiner, are reprinted by permission of Oxford University Press, Inc.

The selection from *In Bluebeard's Castle* by George Steiner, copyright © 1971 by George Steiner, is reprinted by permission of Yale University Press and Faber and Faber Publishers.

Printing (last digit):   9 8 7 6 5 4 3 2

Printed in the United States of America

✦ Contents ✦

MATTERS GERMAN

LANGUAGE AND CULTURE

✦ Introduction ✦

To be invited to look back at one's own work in order to make a selection of this kind is an ambiguous privilege. The element of pride, of flattery, is there, of course. But so is a sense of embarrassment, even of anger, at what one now perceives to be the inadequacies, the opportunities missed, in early books and essays. The impulse to rewrite, to alter and amend in the colder light of hindsight and maturity, is all but irresistible. Such up-dating and 'improvement' would, however, not only be transparently dishonest; it could, I suspect, prove self-defeating.

I put single quotes around 'improvement' because it is not at all certain that revision after the fact, after the passage of time, will always produce positive results. The correction of *errata* is one thing; the amendment, the purposed amelioration of argument and judgement, are quite another. There are 'errors' of insight, improprieties of presentation, there are unripe persuasions, which can only be committed and put forward when one is young, when thought and composition are of the morning. There are errors one *ought* to commit at the unguarded outset. Too poised a beginning, the production of first writings that bear only on exact targets and go armoured against the objections of the established or the academic, do not, I think, hold much promise of original development. There are early indiscretions of spirit, magnitudes in the questions posed and the themes chosen, which are an essential, though subsequently vulnerable, prelude to getting things right. Miniaturists and precisians of the middle ground tend to stay themselves. They may never, as Nietzsche's imperative bids us, 'become what one is'.

To have written *Tolstoy or Dostoevsky* (1959) without knowing Russian was hazardous enough; to (partially) justify this risk by citing such sovereign precedents as those of Thomas Mann or André Gide, who had also written about the Russian masters without being able to read them in the original, may have been even more parlous. But I remain unrepentant. Though I could not know it at the time, the conviction from which this first book sprang, namely that serious literary and philosophic criticism comes from 'a debt of love', that we write about books or about music or about art because 'some primary instinct of communion' would have us share with and communicate to others an overwhelming enrichment, was to be the root of all my subsequent work and teaching. Moreover, re-reading *Tolstoy or Dostoevsky* nearly thirty years after I began writing it, I find in it the explicit conviction that great literature, music, art, possess a twofold transcendence. At one level, works of the order of the *Oresteia*, of *King Lear*, of *Anna Karenina* and *The Brothers Karamazov*, express a more or less articulate consciousness of the presence or absence of God in and from human affairs. At another level, the sheer impact of such books on our lives, their mastering seizure of our thoughts, feelings and, indeed, conduct, compels the question of creation (*poiesis*). We ask ourselves whether there is in the genesis of great art and in its effects upon us some analogy to the coming into being of life itself. Theology tells of 'the real presence' in the symbolic object, of the 'mystery' in the form. Today, more and more of my work is an attempt to clarify these concepts, to discover whether and in what rational framework it is possible to have a theory and practice of understanding (hermeneutics) and a theory and practice of value-judgements (aesthetics) without a theological re-insurance or underwriting. *Tolstoy or Dostoevsky* already asked and, in some sense, answered this very question.

The book is sub-titled 'An Essay in the Old Criticism'. This phrasing aimed at the then-dominant ideals and techniques of the 'New Critics' (Allen Tate and R. P. Blackmur were among my teachers; I. A. Richards was to become a friend). The new-critical isolation of the literary text from its historical, ideological, social and biographical context seemed to me didactically in-genious, but essentially false. This first book, therefore, argues the central role of metaphysical, religious, political concerns in literature. It calls for the observance of the organic relations between a poem, play or novel and the social, temporal and linguistic (in the sense of the history of the language) realities which are its matrix. One need not subscribe to romantic 'personal-ism' in order to know that it is mere artifice to seek to immunize the meanings of a work of literature from the life and milieu of the writer. Hence my plea for an 'old criticism', for a perception of literature as a 'central humanity' — a perception which drew simultaneously on philosophic and linguistic models of a traditional kind, notably in Coleridge and Roman Jakobson, and on the Marxist-existentialist views of Lukács and of Sartre.

The polemic aspects of *Tolstoy or Dostoevsky* were, at the time, argued within a larger climate of humanistic consensus. Criteria of intelligibility still obtained. Today, this is no longer the case. The methodological, qualified 'isolationism' of the New Critics has been succeeded by such phenomena as 'post-structuralism' and 'deconstruction'. The conception of *auctoritas*, of the poet's privileged or legitimate intentionality in respect of the meanings of his poem, the postulate of the ultimate stability of these meanings in the text – even where such stability is regarded as an ideal never fully arrived at, always susceptible to challenge and revision by an evolving community of readers in what F. R. Leavis called 'the common pursuit' – are now being erased. With the deconstructive abolition of the subject and of external reference, 'meaning' is, as it were, a momentary weakness in the self-mirroring play of semantic masks and markers. The text itself is, in fact, a 'pre-text', a contingent occasion for decomposition.

My dissent from these Byzantine acrobatics on *moral* as well as on philosophic and linguistic grounds, my belief that the current subversions of the true relations between poem and commentary (they are *not* of the same specific gravity), between literature and literary criticism, must end in sterile obscurity, are set out, summarily at least, in ' "Critic"/"Reader" ', an essay of 1979 included in this collection. The foundation for this dissent and a certain foresight into what must lie ahead when the study and reading of literature cut themselves off from history, from the history of language and from the ethics of common sense, are already manifest in *Tolstoy or Dostoevsky*. This may have become the most timely of my books.

Like *Tolstoy or Dostoevsky*, *The Death of Tragedy* (1961) has been widely translated. Made use of in schools and universities, the book has had influence. In retrospect, I note a major failing. The argument throughout focuses on 'a tragic vision of man and the world' in the strict sense. It deals with a view, held conceptually or metaphorically, of a world in which man moves as an unwelcome, hunted guest. He is subject either to the wanton malignity of elemental forces, of a 'dark God' or 'gods', or to the constant reprisals of evil and mischance in a precariously divided realm (the manichaean model). This is the world-view tested and dramatized in such plays as Sophocles' *Oedipus Tyrannus* and *Antigone*, as Euripides' *Bacchae*, the *Phèdre* of Racine and Büchner's *Wozzeck*. Only those dramas which reach and remain at the heart of the night, which abstain from the promise of hope or of compensation – as in the 'compensatory heaven' of Goethe's *Faust* – are, in the rigorous definition of the term, 'tragedies'.

Because a view of the human condition along these lines is almost un-endurably difficult to think through and to sustain aesthetically, there are, in point of fact, very few absolute tragedies in world literature. More specifically, the notion of absolute tragedy, as we find it in classical Greece and in seventeenth-century France, is alien to the pluralistic, fundamentally tragi-comic bias of Shakespeare (where it occurs in Jacobean drama, it takes the minor key of horror). At the very core of the Shakespearean enterprise is the ironic, forgiving knowledge that at the moment in which Agamemnon falls under the blood-axe, a wedding is being celebrated down the road or, indeed, in the servants' quarters of the palace of Atreus. With the sole exception, it seems to me, of *Timon of Athens*, the mature Shakespeare refuses to compact the universe into a 'black hole'. But it is precisely this compaction, this suspension of relativity and hope, that define the supreme formal expressions of human nothingness and despair in pure tragedy. In *King Lear*, Shakespeare confronts us with the torture of Gloucester and the arbitrary, dog-like slaughter of Cordelia; but the counter-current of humane reconquest, the hint of dawn, is there from the moment in which the servant turns on Cornwall.

This distinction is implicit in *The Death of Tragedy*. But it is not hammered out and applied with sufficient clarity. The *Oresteia* in particular ought to be seen as a motion of spirit through night towards morning of exactly the kind which my book itself defined as 'melodrama'.

It has also been urged that a study of this sort should, by 1961, have included the so-called 'theatre of the absurd', that it should have concluded not with Brecht and Claudel but with a just estimate of playwrights such as Ionesco, Beckett or Pinter. On this point, I remain unconvinced. If there has been any recent advance into authentic tragedy, it is, very probably, that of Edward Bond's dramatic parables. Nor is it an accident that Bond should have chosen Shakespeare as his theme and target. The undoubted genius of Beckett, the talents of Pinter, still strike me as essentially formal. In their plays, we find an internalized epilogue to an eroded tragic vision. The brilliance and the grief lie in the language.

This *Reader* contains the fictional coda to *The Death of Tragedy*. These few pages (from which Barry Collins constructed a dramatic monologue first staged in London in 1976) turn directly to the theme of political inhumanity in our time. Discussing modern drama, I had asked whether *any* art-form could reflect responsibly, could, in the full connotations of the term, be answerable to, the political terror of the century. The background to this question is, of course, that of my own life. Even before I began writing, let alone teaching or publishing, it seemed to me that the problem of the relations between culture and politics, between humane literacy and the politics of torture and mass-murder, was such as to put in question every aspect of the life of the mind. Educated in the classical framework of 'the humanities', feeling myself utterly drawn to the life of intellectual argument and the arts, of philosophy and poetics, I was confronted by an overwhelming, brutal paradox. The edifice of total warfare and of the death-camps, of totalitarian torture and 'the big lie', had its base, had its contemporary triumphs, in the heart-lands of western culture. The spheres of Auschwitz-Birkenau and of the Beethoven recital, of the torture-cellar and the great library, were contiguous in space and time. Men could come home from their day's butchery and falsehood to weep over Rilke or play Schubert. The Jeffersonian, the Arnoldian promise that the spread of education, together with the cultivation of the arts and sciences, would humanize man, would bring with them a civilization of politics had proved illusory. How could this be?

It might be that the two categories of experience, that of literacy and cultural pursuits on the one hand, that of power and politics on the other, had never been congruent. It might be that no genuine interaction could be assumed to exist between them, either in the individual psyche or in the community at large. This possibility, which entails a drastic refutation of much of Hellenism, of the Renaissance doctrine of man's potential for excellence, of the Enlightenment and of the liberal meliorism of the nineteenth century, was grave enough. But I sensed worse. It might be that there *were* actual relations – of the contrastive yet interactive kind expressed by the word 'dialectical' – between certain energies in 'high culture' and barbarism. It might be that high culture, abstract speculation, the obsessive practice and study of the arts, could infect human consciousness with a virus of *ennui*, of febrile tedium, from which, in turn, would grow a fascination with savagery (this is the hypothesis set out in *In Bluebeard's Castle* in 1971). Instead of being an insurance against inhumanity, the humanities and the ideals of disinterested abstraction taught by the humanistic and scientific disciplines might, in fact, make us more prone to political-social indifference – are we not accomplices to all that leaves us indifferent? – and might, in fact, make us fellow-travellers to barbarism. I asked myself whether my entire schooling and the intellectual and formal values which it embodied had not made the cry in the poem, the desolation in the sonata, come to seem more real, more immediate to my imaginings, than the cry in the street.

Those who found this question irrelevant to their spiritual and pedagogic pursuits, those who dissociated the practice and study of the humanities from the facts of the age, seemed to me profoundly irresponsible. How can a man 'teach literature' (itself a highly problematic concept), how can he engage the best of his capacities in the explication and transmission of philosophic or aesthetic values, if he does not seek to know what the effects, if any, will be on the quality and survival of society? How can scholarship and criticism be divorced from the crisis of the humane without, by this' very divorcement, being reduced to academic trivia? I cannot think of any serious work which I have done, as writer of fiction, as critic, as scholar and teacher, in which this has not been the cardinal issue.

In the essay 'To Civilize our Gentlemen' (1965), I sought to apply the notion of a responsible humanism to English studies, and to what was already being widely perceived as a crisis of morale and of standards in the study and teaching of English literature. The alarm, the unctuous evasions, which this and related essays and lectures provoked among senior members of the Faculty of English at Cambridge University are on record. A man indelicate enough to take literature and the university *that* seriously, who believed with Kafka that the 'books we must have' and attempt to read together 'are those books which come upon us like ill-fortune, and distress us deeply, like the death of one we love better than ourselves', because 'A book must be an ice-axe to break the sea frozen inside us', had to be dispensed with.

The Lukács essay of 1960, the consideration of some of the ways in which 'para-Marxist' thinkers and critics (the Frankfurt School) were seeking to incorporate history into aesthetic judgement, go back even earlier. There is much here with which I am no longer satisfied and which would have to be re-thought in the light of a quarter century of new material. The case of Georg Lukács, in particular, is even more ambiguous and, in some respects, tragic than I first made out. But I persist in the belief that the Marxist assignment to philosophic debate, to literature and the arts, to criticism and scholarship, of a pivotal place and function in society, and the Marxist attempts to situate consciousness and form within history, hold vital lessons for the anti-Marxist and liberal imagination. A good deal, furthermore, that is modish and mendacious in our own privileged Arcadias can be seen and felt more honestly under pressure of the Marxist challenge.

To have been acquainted with Lukács personally, to have studied his writings, is to confront – this time on the plane of individual behaviour – the paradox of the co-existence, of the interpenetration, of the highest intellectual distinction and of moral terrorism. What enables a man to illuminate Goethe or Balzac in the morning and to be an out-rider to Stalinism in the afternoon? In the studies of Martin Heidegger (the deepest reader of poetry and language in our time) and of Anthony Blunt, both published in 1980 and represented in this selection, I come back to this antinomy. It haunts me.

The question of the relations between politics and culture, between the humanities and the humane, can be addressed to any political system or historical epoch. A large portion of my own work bears on the phenomenon of Nazism and on the role of German culture and society in the destruction of European Judaism. This is because I happen to be, first and foremost, 'A Kind of Survivor' (1965). I come from the singularly productive world of emancipated Central European Judaism. In its sciences, schools of psychology, in its sociologies and climate of nervous sensibility (now transferred to New York, Chicago or San Francisco), the twentieth century in the west has, in the main, been heir to this world. The reflexes of consciousness, the styles of articulacy which had generated messianic Marxism, Freudian psychoanalysis, the philosophies of discourse of Wittgenstein, the art of Mahler and of Kafka, were almost immediate to my childhood and upbringing. The polyglot habits in this background, the peregrine ironies and premonitions, the scarcely examined investment of familial energies and pride in the intellect and the arts, make up what I am. Without pretence to comparison, I can say that books such as *Language and Silence* (1979), *In Bluebeard's Castle, Extraterritorial* (1975), *After Babel* (1975) or *On Difficulty* (1978) – all of which are present in this *Reader* – take their substance, and much of their 'voice', from the legacy of Ernst Bloch, of Adorno, of Walter Benjamin and from the inheritance of Jewish poetic-philosophic investigations of the word as it is evident in Roman Jakobson, in Karl Kraus, in Fritz Mauthner and Noam Chomsky. The mapping of my identity, the inward orientations, remain those circumscribed by Leningrad, Odessa, Prague and Vienna on the one side, and by Frankfurt, Milan and Paris on the other.

To a degree which numbs understanding, this entire crucible of creation and of hope now lies in ash. And each day oblivion buries it deeper. Even where the houses endure, as in Cracow or Prague, they appear to be casting vacant shadows (had space allowed, I would have wanted to include in this volume one of the novellas from *Anno Domini, 1964*, which deals specifically with this after-life of shadows). Several of the texts in this *Reader* constitute an act of remembrance (a *kaddish*). This is, above all else, the meaning and purpose of Lieber's lament at the heart of the novel, *The Portage to San Cristobal of A.H.*, published in 1979. These texts endeavour to wrest from forgetting one of the very great periods in the history of human thought, of language and of dreams, and to recall the crimes committed upon millions. It is, I believe, the task and dignity of those who, by miracle or chance dispensation, have survived to make of themselves remembrancers against time. It has, in large measure, been Israel's *necessary* disclaimer of this task, it has been the *necessary* commitment of Zionism to present and future, which have made me choose Europe in which to live and work. Surely there must be men and women, however inadequate, to say the names and mark the places after 'the Whirlwind' – the Hebrew term, much preferable to 'Holocaust', a Greek designation, misleading in our context, of sacrifice and ceremonious offering.

The recurrent approach I have taken to these themes and compulsions has been 'linguistic'. This is to say that I have treated, notably in 'The Hollow Miracle' (1959) as well as in *After Babel*, the corrosion of the German language and of language in general by political enormity and lies. Nazism found its instruments within the German language and, in turn, infected that language with political obscenity and the jargon of homicide. Understandably, 'The Hollow Miracle' evoked an extensive, often acrimonious, spate of commentary and polemic. I believe still that my historical-semantic diagnosis is accurate, and that the method of analysis used in this essay has proved fruitful. But the part of prophecy was, fortunately, myopic. German prose has come to aggressive life in Günter Grass. Paul Celan is one of the great lyric poets in western literature after Hölderlin and Rilke. Yet the very case of Celan bids one pause. Here was a polyglot survivor out of the death-camps writing a wholly new German. To use two of his own images: Celan's later poems seem to be harvesting 'silent stones' towards the reconstruction of a language laid waste by sadistic falsehood. This reconstruction lies 'north of the future'; only there shall these mute stones and the German language return to authentic saying.

My approach has also been 'linguistic' in a second sense. I ask in the essay on Schoenberg's *Moses und Aron* (1965), in 'Postscript' (1966), in the monograph on Heidegger, whether language itself can justly communicate, express, give rational or metaphoric constructs to the realities of modern torture and extermination. Ought we to acquiesce in Adorno's famous dictum: 'No poetry after Auschwitz'? What price (it proved literally suicidal) is exacted from the poetry of a Paul Celan and, on a lesser level, of a Sylvia Plath, in exchange for the claim of this poetry to the speech and images of the death-camps? Repeatedly, I asked whether language, being the quintessence of our humanity, must not, indeed ought not, to fall silent at the boundaries of the monstrous.

But this inquiry extends beyond the phenomenologies of Nazi and Stalinist totalitarian systems and their victims. In 'The Retreat from the Word', one of the early papers in this anthology, first published in 1961, I argue that the growing incapacity of common discourse, of the vulgate as we have inherited and practised it, to encompass, to convey generally, to metaphorize for the needs of art and the common imagination, the domains of the exact sciences, the proceedings of mathematical discovery and logical symbolism, the truths of technology, would profoundly restrict the once central authority of literature, of rhetoric, of narrative and verbal description. When I wrote this essay, I was only vaguely aware of the imminence of the computer, of the new sciences of information and encoding, and of the semantic revolutions which these are now bringing with them.

None the less, the intimation of a failure of nerve in speech and writing was such as to direct me to that 'frankness as never before' – Ezra Pound's clairvoyant phrase – which, from the early 1960s onward, has characterized both oral and written language. In successive essays, from 'Night Words' (1965) to 'Eros and Idiom' ten years later (both are to be found in this *Reader*), I tried to interpret and to dissent from the new licence, the new ubiquity of sexuality and sadistically tinged eroticism in our arts and culture. Here, again, ripostes were numerous and often scornful. Nowhere, however, have I seen any reply to my two principal worries. By stripping the speech and physical gestures of his *personae* of all sexual privacy, the novelist, the playwright, the film-maker, after *Lady Chatterley's Lover*, has largely destroyed the autonomy, the mystery of autonomous life, in the imagined character. The knowingness of the novelist in this second half of the twentieth century, his literal 'publication' of sex, render impossible the creation of character as we find it in the novels of George Eliot or of Balzac, in the integral life-force of an Anna Karenina or a Dimitri Karamazov. Nor have my critical respondents paused long enough to consider the very real, though frequently oblique, affinities between the sexual exposure and exploitation of language and gesture in current literature, on the stage, on the screen, and the sexual exposure and exploitation of living men and women in every repressive political and social apparatus east or west. Cruelty flourishes first in the imagination of the *voyeur*.

To put it summarily: what is being taken from us is the ballast of privacy, the 'reserve', in both senses of the word, of inner freedom, inherent in more classical conventions of language and of depiction (cf., in this book, 'The Distribution of Discourse', 1978). We now speak more and louder to say less.

Having been brought up tri-lingually, in a community and culture of the written word, having tried to add some small acquaintance with the languages of mathematics and of physics to my classical training, I did know early on that the study of language, of language in philosophy, literature and politics, would occupy much of my existence. But one of the many differences between genius and the ordinary lies in waste motion. Genius economizes from its outset. It was not until I put together *The Penguin Book of Modern Verse Translation* in 1966, and wrote its preface, that I came upon ground both new and centrally my own. It was only then that I understood that a study of the phenomenon of Babel – the magnificently prodigal, redundant multiplicity of mutually incomprehensible human tongues – might provide a decisive approach to the nature both of speculative thought and of poetic invention.

The writing of *After Babel* took many years. It may be that the book is too long (but ought one not, at least once in the course of work, write a book which *is* too long?). Not only had the fields of reference to include anthropology, linguistics, history, aesthetics and psychology as well as literary studies; I found myself having to define my topics and the methods appropriate to them as I proceeded. With the exception of a numinous but esoteric paper by Walter Benjamin, and of hints thrown out from, say, Saint Jerome to Mandelstam and Ivor Richards, I came across few genuine precedents. For what is at stake in *After Babel* is nothing less than a 'poetics of meaning', an attempt to propose a model for the act of understanding itself via an investigation into the motions of meaning inside and between languages.

Orthodox as well as transformational-generative linguists and grammarians have given *After Babel* an uneasy reception. One mandarin luminary accused me, not altogether unfairly, of wanting to do what only 'a team of scholars and specialists should undertake'; another began his review by describing 'this bad book which is also, alas, a classic' (a condemnation to be gratefully borne). But the secondary literature around the work is growing, and I imagine that the defects and merits of my attempt will take time to sort out.

It is difficult to excise independent yet representative sections from a book of this kind. The interwoven organization in *After Babel* is itself meant to illustrate, to enact, the underlying theme of metamorphic transformation and semantic transfer. What I hope to show, in this 'portable', are some of the dominant motifs and manners of argument. These include the thesis whereby processes of translation, in the strongest sense, occur in *all* acts of comprehension; together with a brief look at the problem, vexatious in Wittgenstein and crucial to any understanding of modernism in literature and the arts, of 'private language' or 'languages', of experience and perceptions only partially communicable. The selections also illustrate something of the treatment of 'lies' and 'misdirections' as elements decisive to linguistic creation – a theme initiated by Plato and touched on by Nietzsche; and a brief, closing conjecture as to the future of English as 'the world language'. But at no other point in this *Reader* do I feel as strongly that a selection or even a sequence of selections can reflect only very inadequately the design and presence of a unified text.

In the wake of the Kabbala and of the language-ontologies of Jacob Boehme and of Heidegger, *After Babel* looks at the concept of the *Logos*, of 'the Word' as force and medium of creation. But if the Word can create, can it not, by the same token, unmake and annihilate? It is this conceit which is expounded, both seriously and parodistically, in the monologue of 'A.H.' at the end of *The Portage*. Reprinted here, this speech-act, this assault of words on the Word, benefited from by Alec McCowen's overwhelming delivery in Christopher Hampton's dramatization of the novel, first produced in London in the winter of 1982. With a symmetry of which I have only now become aware, the text reaches back, across *After Babel*, to the beginnings of my work in 'The Retreat from the Word'.

Constraints on space allow certain passions to be shown here only cursorily; others have had to be left out altogether.

Music plays a large part in my life, and the short piece on Schoenberg is only one among those I would have wished to include. Any thinking about the forms of meaning must grapple with music. Whereas advances in the neuro-physiology of vision, in the understanding of symbolic codes, in the sociology of aesthetic genres, have greatly increased and refined our response to the plastic arts, it is fair to say that our insights into the nature of music, our analyses of the ways in which music comes to 'possess' and affect our psyche, have not progressed decisively beyond Plato. Lévi-Strauss has called the invention of melody 'the supreme mystery in the science of man'. On a more concrete level, it seems to me that the problem of whether or not one can write at all sensibly about the meanings of music, of whether or not linguistic means can be applied to a medium in which content and form are one, is a matter of paramount interest. A verbally intelligible yet truly penetrative hermeneutic of music would, I have a hunch, help to break down the Cartesian mind-body dualism, the abstract classifications and dissociations in our model of the psycho-somatic, which seem to be inhibiting us from a better grasp of ourselves.

Had I the capability, it is to some more satisfactory account of the relations between key, pitch, rhythm, tonality in music on the one hand, and the tenor and flux of the listener's consciousness on the other, that I should most like to contribute. Personally I find myself *needing* music more and more. The number of books one feels one *must* read diminishes; it is re-reading that matters. Music, on the contrary, grows indispensable, as if it had become the elect companion of identity, the homecoming to that inside oneself which time has in its keeping.

Several pieces in this *Reader* allude to the deep-seated, but hardly understood, affinities between music and chess. I have been an inexcusably amateurish but impassioned player and student of chess since boyhood. The elaboration of a human activity inexhaustible in its formal elements and variants, intellectually profound and beautiful, but at the same time strictly trivial in any moral, social, existential sense, demands careful notice. I suspect that the historical thinness of the contributions made by women to chess – as to metaphysics, musical composition, mathematical logic – offers a vital clue to the differences-of-being and differences-in-being of the two sexes. For in each of these pursuits there is an express negation of the external and material world, a negation which, in the final analysis, the common sense of woman, the rootedness of woman in total reality, rebukes as puerile (itself a telling word). The eros of chess is, despite the usual involvement of two persons, autistic.

I have not found room in this collection for anything out of my small book on the Fischer–Spassky world championship match (*The White Knights of Reykjavik*, 1972). But my addiction can be seen in 'A Death of Kings' (1968).

I am a 'mountain-person' as distinct from one who finds echo and mirror in the sea. I feel myself really at home in my own skin only when I am near or among mountains. This, together with its natural multilingualism, has made of Geneva and its University a fortunate base for me. The mountains stand at the door. It seems to me certain that there are connections of consciousness between a love of the mountains and the choices which an individual makes among philosophic, aesthetic, musical options. These links of spirit also touch on politics. Egalitarianism, populism, the utopias of fraternity, are of the sea and its open harbours. The mountains take a darker, more selective view of man. Once or twice, I have contributed, as an outsider, to the rich literature of mountaineering and of mountain-walking. I should have liked to include here one or another of these articles.

Languages have, self-evidently, crowded my life and study. Verbal expressiveness and suppleness have been an incessant pursuit. But there are other modes of communication. There are 'dictions of silence' as intense, as eloquent perhaps, as any afforded by speech. Our relations to animals offer a crucial instance. It is near animals that I have known totalities of reciprocal recognition and exchanges of peace, such as human dialogue yields only rarely, if at all. Thus there is in this *Reader* a central absence. It would be filled only if I reprinted a contribution to the *Yearbook and Guide of the Old English Sheepdog Club* for 1976!

One further omission needs to be mentioned. A book on the encounters between Antigone and Creon in Sophocles and thereafter is now in the press. But my interest and work in the classics have been constant. Space permitting, I would have put in this collection an essay on 'Homer and the Scholars', first published in 1962. In it, three suppositions are put forward. Homer's epics seem to coincide fairly closely with the transition from oral poetry to written 'literature'. They invent 'literature' because they mark the exact point at which the triumph of the (written) word over time and oblivion comes in actual reach of the poet. Homer's 'blindness' would, therefore, be the marker and symbolic embodiment of his illiteracy, of his dictation to the new artificers of the enduring script. Thirdly, I suggest that we might most accurately gauge the interrelations between the *Iliad* and the *Odyssey* if we think of 'Homer' as the assembler and redactor of the oral material in the first epic, and as the author of the second. The *Odyssey* would then be the very first of those literary variants and (in part critical) meditations on the matter of the *Iliad* as these extend across western art and literature from the sixth century B.C. to Joyce and to Pound. These several conjectures might still be worth a look.

A preface should be kept short. Anything like an attempt on my part at a balance-sheet would be pretentious. Looking back, however, I do feel a sadness.

Essays I wrote and published from the late 1950s to the late sixties initiated new areas of awareness, certainly so far as the English-speaking public goes. If the bibliographies are exact, the name of Walter Benjamin had appeared only once in an English-language context before I began writing about the 'para-Marxist' thinkers and critics (in a footnote to a translation of a book on the sociology of art, soon remaindered). 'Night Words' was quickly followed by a spate of symposia, debates and tracts on pornography, censorship and the new totalities of linguistic and representational licence. Outside professional anthropological and ethnographic material, there had, before articles I contributed to the *Times Literary Supplement*, been little reference to Claude Lévi-Strauss and to the impact structuralism would have on other humanistic disciplines. Together with John Wain, I may have been among the first to be fascinated and warily persuaded by certain aspects of Marshall McLuhan's early books (*The Mechanical Bride* remains his finest).

In each case, others took the hint. There is, today, a deluge of articles and monographs on Benjamin, Adorno, Horkheimer and their constellation. Innocent of the determinant background in German philosophic Idealism and of the Judaic endeavours to make of this Idealism its own, most of what is now said and written about the Frankfurt School, notably in Britain, be it academic or 'New Left', is intellectually shallow and politically opportunistic. The debate on pornography has withered into naive sociology on the one hand – can one quantify the amount of mimetic violence triggered by sado-masochistic fiction and film? – and smart gossip on the other. The underlying issues of human creativity and the state of the language persist essentially untouched. Explications and discussions of structuralism and the new semantics have, on the contrary, been often authoritative and helpful. *The Penguin Book of Modern Verse Translation* has, for its part, found numerous well-qualified imitators (*The Oxford Book of English Verse Translation* does not conceal its indebtedness in approach, method and, at many points, content). But only in this last case – *After Babel* followed – did I fully press home my 'openings'. Elsewhere, I left it to others to publicize and harvest each successive sowing.

I have not written the book we still require on the tragic intellectual epilogue to Jewish messianic humanism and utopian criticism, the book we need on Prague–Vienna–Frankfurt as the inner capitals of the twentieth century. I have not written the very necessary book on freedom and censorship in the arts, on the servitude which comes of total permissiveness. Many of my essays tell of the 'language turn' or 'revolution' so pivotal to our current sensibility; but the statements remain fragmented. Under compulsion of this preface, I ask myself: Why?

Various answers suggest themselves. There must have been a culpable impatience in my outlook, an odd irritation in the face of that which I had recognized as of the first significance and, to some modest degree, mastered for myself, but did not want to expound methodically. There was, I distinctly recall, a certain anguish, arrogant perhaps, at what seemed to be, throughout those years, British isolation from the great currents of intellectual discovery and argument on the European continent and, to some extent, in the United States. The Cambridge climate sharpened this sense of parochial isolation and complacency. Consciously or not, I thought of myself as some kind of courier carrying urgent letters and signals to those few who might respond with interest and, in their turn, pass on the challenging news. Pushkin speaks of translators as the post-horses of culture. The critic's truest claim to attention is his occasional capacity to announce, to prepare the reception for, 'the news which stays new'. A third reason may well have been my unreadiness to join in collaborative enterprises. In the humanities, as distinct from the sciences and from such technical pursuits as editorial recension or lexicography, the quality of thought and style is, I remain convinced, directly proportionate to the aloneness of the writer.

But be this as it may, this *Reader* cannot but leave me with a clearer view of occasions missed.

However, if it is representative, this collection will point to work ahead. As I already mentioned, what needs to be thought through and stated unambiguously is the 'underwriting' of our interpretations and judgements of language. The two master-readers in this century, Walter Benjamin and Heidegger, drew heavily, in their metaphoric idiom, in their hermeneutic practice and translations, on an undeclared theology. In an arresting simile, Benjamin compares this theology to a 'blotter' which both underlies and threatens to absorb each of his writings. But so far as I can make out, neither man has made any clear deposit to cover his borrowings. The critic, the interpreter, the committed reader draws, as it were, on the bank-credit of theology, on the ultimately theological re-insurance of the very concept of meaningfulness, without offering in return the collateral of an avowed faith. Can we get much further in our poetics of understanding, in our common pursuit of the identification, interpretation and transmission of that which is indispensable in literature and the arts without an acknowledged transcendence? Or are the Narcissistic sports of deconstruction the necessary and honest consequence of the passage of our culture into agnosticism (atheism rebels with mortal seriousness, it does not play with words)?

As one seeks to elucidate this problem, central to the humanities and to education, the place of Shakespeare in western culture becomes an exemplary challenge. In the wake of Kierkegaard and Tolstoy, Wittgenstein had the absolute honesty to confess that he could make little of Shakespeare, that the plays seemed to him to be the achievement of the most gifted 'word-creator' among recorded men, rather than those of a *Dichter*, of a perceiver and, indeed, begetter of truths. The categories of the transcendent seem to relate closely to his use of the term *Dichter* or 'poet'. To Wittgenstein, it seems manifest that supreme art requires an overtly ethical-metaphysical dimension. How, then, and in what crucial ways, do the art and vision of Shakespeare differ from those of Aeschylus, of Sophocles, of Dante or of Racine? Sovereign over language, Shakespeare crowds the known world of our experience with words. Does this plenitude exclude certain magnitudes? The in-dwelling of Shakespeare's voice and invention in every fibre of Anglo-Saxon consciousness makes it difficult to pose such a question seriously. It carries an aura of mere provocation. Yet there is a sense in which the philosophic-religious reach of, say, Sophocles' *Antigone*, Euripides' *Bacchae*, that most flawless of tragedies which is Racine's *Bérénice*, or Wagner's *Tristan und Isolde*, is not only non-Shakespearean, but anti-Shakespearean. Dare one try and get this question right?

The alert, the generous reader (they are one and the same) will find in this book an interim statement, a report on work in progress.

G.S.

June 1983

❧ *The Critical Act* ❧

To Civilize our Gentlemen

A man would have to be an outright optimist or gifted with self-deception to argue that all is well in the study and teaching of English literature. There is a distinct *malaise* in the field, a sense of things going wrong or by default. The quality of students in respect of intellectual rigour and independence of mind is not always very impressive, compared, say, with the man coming up to read economics, or the good historian, let alone the natural scientist. Motives are unclear or faintly hypocritical. A man reads English because he wants time in which to write fiction or verse, to act or produce plays, or simply because English looks like the soft option before he enters business and begins serious life. Reading a number of good books which an educated man should have read anyway is a pleasant enough way of spending three years at a university, pleasanter than learning a lot of mathematics needed for economics or irregular verbs in a foreign tongue.

The *malaise* in research studies is of a different nature, but no less disturbing. The entire notion of research, when applied to literature, is problematic. As there are fewer and fewer really significant texts to edit, and this is what doctoral research in literature originally meant, as the historical or technical problems to be cleared up grow less and less substantial, the whole thesis business grows more tenuous. And already the hunt for genuine subjects is a difficult one. Many dissertations, particularly the safe ones, deal with trivia or with matters so restrictive that the students themselves lose respect for what they are doing.

The contrasting notion that a dissertation should be a piece of literary criticism, that a young man or woman in the very early twenties should have something fresh or profound or decisive to say about Shakespeare or Keats or Dickens is equally perplexing. Few people are ever able to say anything very new about major literature, and the idea that one can do so when one is young is almost paradoxical. Literature takes a great deal of living with and living by. So which is it to be? The combing of increasingly barren ground for some tiny fragments, or the large, uneasy vagueness of premature generality and judgement? Is either a genuine discipline? Indeed is 'English Lit.' in its academic guise? Exactly what is happening, what is being achieved, when a man reads novels, poems, or plays which he might well have read in the course of ordinary life and certainly ought to have read if he regards himself as a literate member of his society?

English is not the only field in which such questions can be put. The problem of research, of what graduate study means, pertains to the arts as a whole. But the restiveness of many who are engaged in the teaching and study of English literature and the peculiar public acrimony which seems to characterize their professional disagreements suggest that the difficulties have reached a fairly acute stage. All I want is to try to put the question in some kind of historical and moral focus, to try to point to some of the roots of our present dilemmas. In fact these go back almost to the beginning of English Literature as an academic pursuit. Much of what needs saying today is already implicit in William Morris's well-known dissent from the establishment of a chair of English Literature at Oxford. It dates to the 1880s when Morris spoke, and to the late 1860s when Farrar edited the *Essays on a Liberal Education* and Matthew Arnold produced his *Culture and Anarchy*. We must look there for the assumptions on which faculties of English Literature were founded.

What were these assumptions? Do they still hold good? Are they relevant to our present needs? In method and intellectual organization, the academic study of modern languages and literature reflects the older tradition of classical studies. The critical, textual, historical study of Greek and Latin literature not only gave precedent and justification for a similar study of the European vulgate; they were foundations on which that study was built. Behind the analysis of Spenser or Pope, of Milton or Shelley lay an assumed classic literacy, a natural familiarity with Homeric, Virgilian, Horatian or Platonic models and energies. The classic background and interests of Matthew Arnold, Henry Sidgwick, Saintsbury, are representative. The notion that a man could study modern literature, could study or edit it honestly without having the classical background, would have seemed shocking and implausible.

The second major assumption was nationalism. It is no accident that German philology and Germanic textual criticism coincided with the dynamic rise of the German national consciousness (and let us not forget that it was on the genius of the German scholars that the rest of Europe, England, and America drew so heavily). As Herder, the Grimm brothers, and the whole lineage of German literary teachers and critics were frank to proclaim, the study of one's own literary past was a vital part in affirming national identity. To this point of view Taine and the historical positivists added the theory that one gets to know the unique racial genius of a people, of one's own people, by studying its literature. Everywhere the history of modern literary studies shows the mark of this nationalist ideal of the mid- and late nineteenth century.

The third major body of assumption is even more vital, but I find it difficult to analyse briefly. Perhaps I could put it this way: behind the formation of modern, literary analysis, editorial scholarship, and literary history lies a kind of rational and moral optimism. In its philological and historical methods the field of literary study reflects a large hope, a great positivism, an ideal of being something like a science, and we find this all the way from Auguste Comte to I. A. Richards. The brilliant work of the classical and semitic philologists and textual analysts in the nineteenth century, which is one of. the chapters of intellectual glory in Europe, seemed to give warrant for the use of similar means and standards in studying a modern text. The variorum, the concordance, the rigorous bibliography — all these are a direct inheritance of this positivist tradition. But the optimism lay much deeper. The study of literature was assumed to carry an almost necessary implication of moral force. It was thought self-evident that the teaching and reading of the great poets and prose writers would enrich not only taste or style but moral feeling; that it would cultivate human judgement and act against barbarism.

There is a remark by Henry Sidgwick which is typical. He wants us to study English Literature so that our views and sympathies may be enlarged and expanded, 'by apprehending noble, subtle and profound thoughts, refined and lofty feelings', and he sees in literature the 'source and essence of a truly humanizing culture' — I think that is the key phrase. And this high claim extends from Matthew Arnold's idea of poetry as a vital substitute for religious dogma to Dr Leavis's definition of the study of English Literature as the 'central humanity'. Here again we should note the carry-over from the Renaissance and eighteenth-century view of the role of the classics.

Do these assumptions — the classic background, the nationalist consciousness, and the rational, moralizing hope — these habits and traditions of feeling still hold today? In regard to the classics our condition has formidably altered. Consider two passages from Shakespeare. The first is the celebrated nocturne of love between Lorenzo and Jessica:

LORENZO: The moon shines bright ... In such a night as this,
        When the sweet wind did gently kiss the trees,
        And they did make no noise, in such a night
        Troilus methinks mounted the Troyan walls,

And sighed his soul towards the Grecian tents,
Where Cressid lay that night.
JESSICA: In such a night
Did Thisbe fearfully o'ertrip the dew,
And saw the lion's shadow ere himself,
And ran dismayed away.
LORENZO: In such a night
Stood Dido with a willow in her hand
Upon the wild sea banks, and waft her love
To come again to Carthage.
JESSICA: In such a night
Medea gathered the enchanted herbs
That did renew old Aeson.

The second is a brief passage from Berowne's mockeries in Act IV of *Love's Labour's Lost*:

O me, with what strict patience have I sat
To see a king transformed to a gnat!
To see great Hercules whipping a gig,
And profound Solomon to tune a jig,
And Nestor play at push-pin with the boys,
And critic Timon laugh at idle toys!

The classical references in these two passages, as in countless others in Shakespearean drama, were most probably immediately familiar to a large part of Shakespeare's audience. Troilus, Thisbe, Medea, Dido, Hercules, Nestor, would be part of the repertoire of recognition to anyone with a measure of Elizabethan grammar schooling, having come down as living resonance from Plutarch and Ovid's *Metamorphoses* through Chaucer's *Legend of Good Women*. And these allusions are no mere ornament; they organize the essential focus of Shakespeare's text (the partially comic, partially sinister precedents invoked by Lorenzo and Jessica beautifully articulate the impulsive, somewhat frivolous quality of their infatuation). The worthies cited by Berowne reflect ironically on his own role and image of himself.

These several references would have been eloquent to an Augustan with any serious claim to literacy, to a Victorian public school boy, to much of the educated European and English bourgeoisie until, say, 1914. But what of today? Hercules, Dido, and Nestor, probably. What of critic Timon and

Medea's murderous rejuvenation of Aeson, with its grim hint of Jessica's view of old Shylock? Difficult for those without a classical education.

The point is not trivial. As footnotes lengthen, as glossaries become more elementary (right now it might still be 'Troilus: Trojan hero in love with Cressida, daughter of Calchas, and betrayed by her', but in a few years the *Iliad* itself may require identification), the poetry loses immediate impact. It moves out of any direct line of vision into a place of special learning. This fact marks a very large change in the consensus assumed between poet and public. The world of classical mythology, of historical reference, of scriptural allusion, on which a preponderant part of English and European literature is built from Chaucer to Milton and Dryden, from Tennyson to Eliot's *Sweeney Agonistes*, is receding from our natural reach.

Take the second assumption, the glorious, hopeful view of national genius. From being a nineteenth-century dream, nationalism has grown to a present nightmare. In two world wars it has all but ruined western culture. It may end by driving us like crazed lemmings to destruction. In the case of England's political and psychological position the change has been particularly drastic. The implications of the supremacy of the English language, of the exemplary moral and institutional authority of English life, which we see everywhere in the treatment of English literature before the First World War, are no longer tenable. The centre of creative and linguistic gravity has begun to shift. Thinking of Joyce, Yeats, Shaw, O'Casey, T. S. Eliot, Faulkner, Hemingway, Fitzgerald, one makes a commonplace observation. The great energies of the language now enter into play outside England. Only Hardy, John Cowper Powys and Lawrence can be compared to these major writers. The American language is not only asserting its autonomous power and showing far greater facilities of assimilation, of innovation than is standard English, but it is more and more pressing on England itself. American words express economic and social realities attractive to the young in England, to the hitherto under-privileged, and these words are becoming part of the dream-life and vulgate of the post-war English scene. African English, Australian English, the rich speech of West Indian and Anglo-Indian writers, represent a complicated, polycentric field of linguistic force, in which the language taught and written on this island is no longer the inevitable authority or focus.

If these new literacies are to be excluded from our curriculum, will that curriculum become almost wholly historical? Will the student of English literature be taught in a kind of museum? But if we are to include these new literacies, and this is particularly relevant with respect to American literature, what is to be dropped? How are lines of continuity to be drawn? Less Dryden, so we can have more Whitman? Miss Dickinson instead of Mrs Browning?

To the historian and literary scholar of the late nineteenth century the tremendous advance of the sciences was no threat. He looked on it as a glorious parallel adventure. I think this is no longer the case. I have tried to outline the new situation in 'The Retreat from the Word'.

The bearing of the multiplication and scattering of literacies on the entire shape, on the integrity of literary studies seems to me to be profound and far-ranging. Until now it has hardly been understood or brought into rational perspective.

If the relationship of literary studies and literary awareness to the ensemble of knowledge and expressive means in our society has radically altered, so surely has the confident link between literature and civilized values. This, I think, is the key point. The simple yet appalling fact is that we have very little solid evidence that literary studies do very much to enrich or stabilize moral perception, that they *humanize*. We have little proof that a tradition of literary studies in fact makes a man more humane. What is worse – a certain body of evidence points the other way. When barbarism came to twentieth-century Europe, the arts faculties in more than one university offered very little moral resistance, and this is not a trivial or local accident. In a disturbing number of cases the literary imagination gave servile or ecstatic welcome to political bestiality. That bestiality was at times enforced and refined by individuals educated in the culture of traditional humanism. Knowledge of Goethe, a delight in the poetry of Rilke, seemed no bar to personal and institutionalized sadism. Literary values and the utmost of hideous inhumanity could co-exist in the same community, in the same individual sensibility; and let us not take the easy way out and say 'the man who did these things in a concentration camp just said he was reading Rilke. He was not reading him well.' I am afraid that is an evasion. He may have been reading him very well indeed.

Unlike Matthew Arnold and unlike Dr Leavis, I find myself unable to assert confidently that the humanities humanize. Indeed, I would go further: it is at least conceivable that the focusing of consciousness on a written text which is the substance of our training and pursuit diminishes the sharpness and readiness of our actual moral response. Because we are trained to give psychological and moral credence to the imaginary, to the character in a play or a novel, to the condition of spirit we gather from a poem, we may find it more difficult to identify with the real world, to take the world of actual experience to heart – 'to heart' is a suggestive phrase. The capacity for imaginative reflex, for moral risk in any human being is not limitless; on the contrary, it can be rapidly absorbed by fictions, and thus the cry in the poem may come to sound louder, more urgent, more real than the cry in the street outside. The death in the novel may move us more potently than the death in the next room. Thus there may be a covert, betraying link between the cultivation of aesthetic response and the potential of personal inhumanity. What then are we doing when we study and teach literature?

It seems to me that the wide gap between the orthodox academic formulation of 'Eng. Lit.' as it is still so largely prevalent in this country and the realities of our intellectual and psychological situation may account for the general *malaise* in the field. There are questions we must be tactless and undiplomatic enough to raise if we are to stay honest with ourselves and our students. But I have no answers; only suggestions and further queries.

The profusion and stylishness of modern poetic translations from the classics, during two generations from Pound to Lattimore and Robert Fitzgerald, are comparable to those of the age of Tudor and Elizabethan translation. But this tells not so much of a return to traditional humanism as of the fact that even the better schooled among us can no longer cope with Greek and Latin. These translations are often superb and should be used, but they cannot replace that immediacy of response, that natural background, which Milton, Pope, and even Tennyson assumed in their readers. It is therefore possible that such works as Dryden's *Absalom and Achitophel*, a good deal of *Paradise Lost*, of *The Rape of the Lock*, of Shelley's Aeschylaean and Platonic verse will pass increasingly into the custody and delight of the specialist. Milton's *Lycidas* is perhaps a test case; there is scarcely a passage to which the generally educated modern reader has *immediate* access.

I am not saying that we must abandon our classic legacy; we cannot. But I do wonder whether we must not recognize its limited, difficult survival in our culture, and whether that recognition should not lead us to ask whether there may be other co-ordinates of cultural reference that touch more urgently on the present contours of our lives, on the way we now think and feel and try to find our way. This is quite simply a plea for modern comparative studies. M. Etiemble in Paris may be right when he says that an acquaintance with a Chinese novel or a Persian lyric is almost indispensable to contemporary literacy. Not to know Melville or Rimbaud, Dostoevsky or Kafka, not have to read Mann's *Doktor Faustus* or Pasternak's *Doctor Zhivago* is a disqualification so severe from the notion of a vital literacy that we must raise, if not answer, the entire question of whether the close study of one literature makes good sense. Is it not as important for the survival of feeling today for a man to know another living language as it was once important for him to be intimate with the classics and Scripture?

M. Etiemble argues that the Anglo-Saxon and western-European sensibility, the way we in the West think and feel and imagine the present world, will remain largely artificial and dangerously obsolete if we do not make the effort of learning one of the major languages outside the park – say Russian or Hindi or Chinese. How many of us have tried to acquire even the most preliminary knowledge of Chinese, of the oldest of all literate cultures – a culture which is borne by the energies of the largest nation on earth and many features of which are certain to dominate the next era of history? Or, less ambitiously, is a man who has spent his last years of school and his university career in the study of English literature, to the exclusion of nearly every other language and tradition, an educated man? Many reorientations, many ways of ordering and choosing are available to scholarship and the imagination. English literature can be taught in its European context: an awareness of George Eliot implying a simultaneous response to Balzac; Walter Scott being seen in relation to Victor Hugo, Manzoni and Pushkin, as part of that great turn of the human imagination towards history which takes place after the French Revolution. English literature can be seen in its increasingly reciprocal relationship to American literature and the American language. An inquiry can be made into the fascinating divisions of meaning and imaginative connotation which the two communities are making today while still preserving largely a common vocabulary.

Why not study the history of English poetry in close comparison with that of another expansionist and colonizing tradition, say Spanish? How have the characteristics of the language in far places developed in relation to the home tradition? Are the problems of form and consciousness met by the Spanish poet in Mexico comparable to those of the Anglo-Indian; are certain languages better media of cultural exchange than others? The directions of vision are manifold. The alternative is parochialism and retrenchment from reality. The almost total lack of comparative studies in English academic circles – and I open parentheses here to acknowledge that in the new universities such comparative studies are being undertaken but to note my fear that what does not originate at the centre of England, at the top of the academic establishment, does not always have much chance of life – may in itself be a very small thing. But it may also be a symptom of a more general withdrawal, of the fist closing tight against an altered, uncomfortable world. This would be alarming because in culture, no less than in politics, chauvinism and isolation are suicidal options.

The displacement of traditional linguistic modes from an essentially dominant function in our civilization has consequences so intricate and large that we have not even begun to take stock.

It is naive to suppose that a little teaching of poetry to the biophysicist or a little mathematics for the student of English literature will solve the problem. We are in mid-tide of divisive energies too new, too complicated, to allow of any confident remedy. Ninety per cent of all the scientists in human history are now living. Scientific publications over the next twenty-five years, if laid next to each other on an imaginary shelf, would reach to the moon. The shapes of reality and of our imaginative grasp are exceedingly difficult to foresee. Nevertheless, the student of literature now has access to and responsibility towards a very rich terrain, intermediate between the arts and sciences, a terrain bordering equally on poetry, on sociology, on psychology, on logic, and even on mathematics. I mean the domain of linguistics and of the theory of communication.

Its expansion in the post-war period is one of the most exciting chapters of modern intellectual history. The entire nature of language is being re-thought and re-examined as it has not been since Plato and Leibniz. The questions being asked about the relations between verbal means and sensory perception, about the way in which syntax mirrors or controls the reality-concept of a given culture, about the history of linguistic forms as a record of ethnic consciousness – these questions go to the very heart of our poetic and critical concern. The precise analyses of verbal resources and grammatical changes over any period of history which may soon be feasible by means of computers – these may have bearing on literary history and interpretation. We are within reach of knowing the rate at which new words enter a language. We can discern graphic contours and statistical patterns relating linguistic phenomena to economic, sociological changes. Our whole sense of the medium is being revalued.

Let me give only two examples which are familiar to any student of modern linguistics. There is a Latin-American Indian language, indeed there are a number, in which the future – the notion of that which is yet to happen – is set at the back of the speaker. The past which he can see, because it has already happened, lies all before him. He backs into the future unknown; memory moves forward, hope backwards. This is the exact reversal of the primary co-ordinates by which we ourselves organize our feelings in root metaphors. How does such a reversal affect literature or, in a larger sense, to what extent is syntax the ever renewed cause of our modes of sensibility and verbal concept? Or take the well-known instance of the astounding range of terms – I believe it is in the region of one hundred – by which the gauchos of the Argentine discriminate between the shadings of a horse's hide. Do these terms in some manner precede the perception of the actual nuance of colour, or does that perception, sharpened by professional need, cause the invention of new words? Either hypothesis throws a rich light on the processes of poetic invention and on the essential fact that translation means the meshing of two different world images, of two different patterns of human life.

To a contemporary student of literature the latest recension of Dryden or essay on the point of view in *Nostromo* are certainly of interest. But is the work of Jakobson on the structure of speech or of Lévi-Strauss on the relations between myth, syntax, and culture not as important, or dare I say even more so? The theory of communications is a branch of linguistics peculiarly enriched by advances in mathematical logic. The advance since I. A. Richards began his work on the nature of poetic statement, and Wittgenstein inquired into the structure of meaning has been dramatic. I am thinking of the work being done on the relations between visual, auditive, and verbal communications and impulses in Russia, at M.I.T., in the Centre of Culture and Technology at the University of Toronto – particularly at Toronto under Marshall McLuhan. The reception accorded to McLuhan's work by the 'Eng. Lit.' establishment is one of the most disturbing of recent symptoms of parochialism and laziness of mind. *The Gutenberg Galaxy* is an irritating book, full of wildness and imprecision, full of unnecessary gesture, egotistical, almost at certain points megalomaniac; but so of course is Coleridge's *Biographia Literaria* or Blake's *Descriptive Catalogue*. And like Blake, who has greatly influenced his thought, McLuhan has the gift of radical illumination. Even when we cannot follow his leap of argument, we are made to re-think our basic concepts of what literature is, what a book is, and how we read it. Together with Sartre's *Qu'est-ce que la littérature?*, *The Gutenberg Galaxy* should stand on the shelf of anyone who calls himself a student or teacher of writing and of English literature. Are these directions not as exciting, as demanding of stringency as the latest edition of yet another minor poet or the fiftieth analysis of Henry James's narrative style?

The last point I want to touch on is the most difficult to put, even in a provisional way. We do not know whether the study of the humanities, of the noblest that has been said and thought, can do very much to humanize. We do not know; and surely there is something rather terrible in our doubt whether the study and delight a man takes in Shakespeare make him any less capable of organizing a concentration camp. Recently one of my colleagues, an eminent scholar, inquired of me, with genuine bafflement, why someone trying to establish himself in an English literature faculty should refer so often to concentration camps; why they were in any way relevant. They are profoundly relevant, and before we can go on teaching we must surely ask ourselves: are the humanities humane and, if so, why did they fail before the holocaust?

It is at least possible that our emotion in the written word, in the detail of the remote text, in the life of the poet long dead, blunts our sense of present realness and need. One recalls Auden's prayer at the grave of Henry James: 'Because there is no end to the vanity of our calling: make intercession for the treason of all clerks.' Because this is so our hopes should be uneasy yet tenacious, and our claims to relevance modest, yet at all times urgently pressed. I believe that great literature *is* charged with what grace secular man has gained in his experience, and with much of the harvest of experienced truth at his disposal. But to those who challenge, who query the pertinence of my calling, I must more than ever before give scrupulous hearing. In short, I must at every point be ready to answer to them and to myself the question: What am I trying to do? Where has it failed? Can it succeed at all?

If we do not make our humanistic studies responsible, that is if we do not discriminate in our allocation of time and interest between that which is primarily of historical or local significance and that which has in it the pressure of sustained life, then the sciences will indeed enforce their claim. Science can be neutral. That is both its splendour and its limitation and it is a limitation which makes science in the final analysis almost trivial. Science cannot begin to tell us what brought on the barbarism of the modern condition. It cannot tell us how to salvage our affairs though it has made the immediate menace to them more precise. A great discovery in physics or biochemistry can be neutral. A neutral humanism is either a pedantic artifice or a prologue to the inhuman. I cannot put it more exactly or in a succinct formula. It is a matter of seriousness and emotional risk, a recognition that the teaching of literature, if it can be done at all, is an extraordinarily complex and dangerous business, of knowing that one takes in hand the quick of another human being. Negatively I suppose it means that one should not publish three hundred pages on some sixteenth- or seventeenth-century writer without expressing any opinion of whether he is worth reading today. Or, as Kierkegaard memorably said: 'It is not worth while remembering that past which cannot become a present.'

To teach literature as if it were some kind of urbane trade, of professional routine, is to do worse than teach badly. To teach it as if the critical text were more important, more profitable than the poem, as if the examination syllabus mattered more than the adventure of private discovery, of passionate digression, is worst of all. Kierkegaard made a cruel distinction, but we could do worse than bear it in mind when we enter a room to give a lecture on Shakespeare or Coleridge or Yeats: 'There are two ways,' he said; 'one is to suffer; the other is to become a professor of the fact that another suffers.'

In I. A. Richards's *Practical Criticism* we find the following: 'The question of belief or disbelief, in the intellectual sense, never arises when we are reading well. If unfortunately it does arise, either through the poet's fault or our own, we have for the moment ceased to be reading and have become astronomers, or theologians, or moralists, persons engaged in quite a different type of activity.' To which the answer should be: No, we have become men. To read great literature as if it did not have upon us an urgent design, to be able to look untroubled on the day after reading Pound's LXXXIst *Canto*, is to do little more than to make entries in a librarian's catalogue. When he was twenty, Kafka wrote in a letter: 'If the book we are reading does not wake us, as with a fist hammering on our skull, why then do we read it? So that it shall make us happy? Good God, we would also be happy if we had no books, and such books as make us happy we could, if need be, write ourselves. But what we must have are those books which come upon us like ill-fortune, and distress us deeply, like the death of one we love better than ourselves, like suicide. A book must be an ice-axe to break the sea frozen inside us.'

Students of English literature, of any literature, must ask those who teach them, as they must ask themselves, whether they know, and not in their minds alone, what Kafka meant.

➥ Marxism and the Literary Critic ➥
'... Difficulties encountered when writing the truth'

At the origins of the Marxist theory of literature there are three celebrated and canonic texts. Two of them are citations from Engels's letters; the third is contained in a short essay by Lenin. Engels wrote to Minna Kautsky in November 1885:

> I am by no means an opponent of tendentious, programmatic poetry (*Tendenzpoesie*) as such. The father of tragedy, Aeschylus, and the father of comedy, Aristophanes, were both strong *Tendenzpoeten* no less than Dante and Cervantes; and it is the finest element in Schiller's *Kabale und Liebe* that it is the first German political *Tendenzdrama*. The modern Russians and Norwegians, who produce excellent novels, are all *Tendenzdichter*. But I believe that the thesis must spring forth from the situation and action itself, without being explicitly displayed. I believe that there is no compulsion for the writer to put into the reader's hands the future historical resolution of the social conflicts which he is depicting.

Writing in English to Margaret Harkness, at the beginning of April 1888, Engels was more emphatic: 'I am far from finding fault with you for not having written a point-blank socialist novel, a "Tendenzroman" as we Germans call it, to glorify the social and political views of the author. That is not at all what I mean. The more the opinions of the author remain hidden, the better for the work of art.' By virtue of this principle, Engels defends his preference of Shakespeare over Schiller, of Balzac over Zola. The third text, however, is altogether different. In his essay on 'Party Organization and Party Literature', published in *Novaia Jizn* in November 1905, Lenin wrote:

> Literature must become Party literature ... Down with unpartisan *littérateurs*! Down with the supermen of literature! Literature must become a part of the general cause of the proletariat, 'a small cog and a small screw' in the social-democratic mechanism, one and indivisible – a mechanism set in motion by the entire conscious vanguard of the whole working class. Literature must become an integral part of the organized, methodical, and unified labours of the social-democratic Party.

These injunctions were put forward as tactical arguments in the early polemic against aestheticism. But cited out of context, Lenin's call for *Tendenzpoesie* in the most naked sense has come to be regarded as a general canon of the Marxist interpretation of literature.

Clearly, there is between Engels's pronouncements and the Leninist conception a profound divergence in bias and drift of argument – if not a formal contradiction. The kinds of critical response and sensibility engaged by the literary work are, in the respective instances, wholly different. This disparity has not escaped the awareness of Marxist theoreticians. Georg Lukács has twice attempted to reconcile Engels's defence of the poet's uncommitted integrity with Lenin's demand for total partisanship and aesthetic discipline. In his major essay on Engels as a theoretician and critic of literature (1935), Lukács quotes from the letter to Minna Kautsky and proposes an intricate gloss. He argues that the type of *Tendenz* (Edmund Wilson renders this crucial term by 'tendency' but 'thesis' and 'programmatic bias' are closer) which Engels would find acceptable is, at bottom, 'identical with that "Party element" which materialism, from the time of Lenin on, encloses in itself'. According to this analysis, Engels is not objecting to a *littérature engagée* as such but rather to the mixture 'of mere empiricism and empty subjectivity' in the bourgeois novel of the period. Obviously dissatisfied with this treatment of the problem, Lukács reverted to it in 1945, in his 'Introduction to the Writings on Aesthetics of Marx and Engels'. Here he contends that Engels was distinguishing between two forms of *littérature à thèse* (it is significant that the English language and its critical vocabulary have developed no precisely equivalent expression). All great literature, in Lukács's reading, has a 'fundamental bias'. A writer can only achieve a mature and responsible portrayal of life if he is committed to progress and opposed to reaction, if he 'loves the good and rejects the bad'. When a critic of Lukács's subtlety and rigour descends to such banalities – banalities which directly challenge his own works on Goethe, Balzac and Tolstoy – we know that something is amiss. The attempt to reconcile the image of literature implicit in Lenin's essay with that put forward by Engels is a rather desperate response to the pressures of orthodoxy and to the Stalinist demand for total internal coherence in Marxist doctrine. Even the most delicate exegesis cannot conceal the plain fact that Engels and Lenin were saying different things, that they were pointing towards contrasting ideals.

This fact is of signal importance in the history of Marxist literature and Marxist literary criticism. Time and again the ideal of a literature in which 'the opinions of the author remain hidden' has clashed with the Leninist formula of militant partiality. According to the choice which they were compelled to make, even unconsciously, between Engels's aesthetics and Lenin's, Marxist critics have split into two principal camps: the orthodox group and those whom Michel Crouzet has aptly called the 'para-Marxists'. Zhdanovism and the First Soviet Writers' Congress of 1934 rigorously proclaimed the orthodox position. In his address to the Congress, Zhdanov deliberately chose Engels's own terms but rejected Engels's meaning in the name of Leninism: 'Our Soviet literature is not afraid of the charge of being "tendentious". Yes, Soviet literature is tendentious, for in an epoch of class struggle there is not and cannot be a literature which is not class literature, not tendentious, allegedly non-political.' Bukharin followed suit and declared that *Tendenzpoesie* and poetry recognized as of the first rank on purely formal grounds would, more often than not, prove to be one and the same. In evidence, he cited names which recur incessantly in Marxist poetics: 'Freiligrath and Heine, Barbier and Béranger.'

The orthodox school, orthodoxy being in this case a political rather than a historical notion, has its journals both in Russia and in the West (*Soviet Literature* and *La nouvelle critique* are prominent examples). It has its primers such as André Stil's *Vers le réalisme socialiste*, Howard Fast's *Literature and Reality*, and the compendious theoretical pronouncements of Aragon. In England it has found expression in some of the writings of Jack Lindsay and Arnold Kettle. The purest strain of orthodoxy in German Marxism has been embodied in the poems and essays of Johannes Becher. Becher stated in 1954: 'Primarily I owe it to Lenin that I gradually learned to see things as they really are.' The invocation of Lenin is, indeed, the invariable talisman of the orthodox critic.

In the Soviet Union itself, orthodoxy assumed the dour and turgid guise of Zhdanovism and Stalinist aesthetics. To it we owe the most consequent and tragically successful campaign ever waged by a political régime to enlist or destroy the shaping powers of the literary imagination. Only those impelled by professional interest to wade through the official critical journals and state publications of the Stalinist era can fully realize to what levels of inhumanity and mere verbiage, *belles-lettres* and the art of the critic can descend. The pattern is one of desperate monotony: interminable discussions as to whether or not this novel or that poem is in accord with the party line: strident exercises in self-denunciation by authors who have, through some momentary failure of agility, taken an 'incorrect' position on some aspect of socialist realism; incessant demands that fiction, drama and poetry be forged into 'weapons for the proletariat'; glorifications of the 'positive hero' and condemnations, at times hysterical in their puritanism, of any hint of eroticism or stylistic ambiguity. The ideal of Zhdanovism was, precisely, the reduction of literature to 'a small cog and a small screw' in the mechanism of the totalitarian state. By hazard of genius or partisan anger, such a literature could (though, in fact, it did not) produce something of the order of *Uncle Tom's Cabin*. Any work of more genuine complexity or impartiality constitutes a potential threat to 'the organized, methodical, and unified labours' of the party. Under such circumstances a critic has only two functions: he is an interpreter of party dogma and a discerner of heresy. This, precisely, was the inglorious and ultimately suicidal role of Fadeyev.

But neither imprimatur nor anathema are the critic's job of work. What authentic critical impulses did survive went underground into scholarship. Remnants of the liberal imagination took refuge in the craft of the editor and the translator. Thus we find, even during spells of ideological terror, competent translations and discussions of Shakespeare and Dickens, of Molière and Balzac. The war somewhat attenuated the dreariness of the Soviet literary scene. Private anguish and patriotic fervour coalesced with the political necessities of the moment. But there was no evolution in criticism to match the achievements of novelists and poets. The war, in fact, reinforced the Leninist-Zhdanovite thesis that literature is an instrument of battle, that its ultimate values lie in the rhetoric of persuasion and total commitment.

Essentially, therefore, the orthodox wing of Marxist literary criticism and theory, the Leninist espousal of *Tendenzpoesie* as the ideal for both writer and party, has proved barren. There are very few examples of wholly orthodox, yet valid and creative, applications of Leninist principles to a literary text. Perhaps the most distinguished occur among the critical writings of Brecht. These writings should be considered apart from his plays across which there usually falls the brightening shadow of heresy. Brecht's 'Five Difficulties Encountered when Writing the Truth' (1934) has real urgency and conviction. It exemplifies the dictum of another Marxist critic that literary criticism and the study of poetics is the 'act of strategy in the literature-battle (*im Literaturkampf*)'. Brecht's most fascinating exercise in critical orthodoxy, however, came much later, in 1953. It is a dialectical examination (presented in the guise of a discussion between producer and actors) of Act I of Shakespeare's *Coriolanus*. The problem is posed in Leninist terms: how should the scene of the plebeians be interpreted and acted so as to yield the fullest measure of political insight – of insight compatible with a dialectical interpretation of history? In the course of discussion, a high degree of critical intelligence and an acute awareness of theatrical means are brought to bear on the Shakespearean text. The final exchanges are particularly illuminating:

> R. Do you believe that all this and more may be 'read out' of the play?
> B. Read out of and read into.
> P. Do we propose to perform the play because of these insights?
> B. Not for that reason alone. We want to have the pleasure and convey the pleasure of dealing with a piece of illuminated (*durchleuchteter*) history. We wish to experience, to live, a piece of dialectic.
> P. Is that not a somewhat esoteric notion, reserved to the initiate?
> B. By no means. Even at the panoramas shown at public fairs and when hearing popular ballads, simple folk, who are in so few respects simple, enjoy stories of the rise and fall of the mighty, of the cunning of the oppressed, of the potentialities of men. And they seek out the truth, that which 'lies behind it all'.

But this 'living of the dialectic' and the free play of irony and sensibility over the literary text are exceedingly rare among those Marxists who have adopted Lenin's response to literature – as set forth in *Novaia Jizn* – rather than Engels's. (The restriction is necessary, for elsewhere – in the two short essays on Tolstoy and in remarks made to Gorky – Lenin took a subtler and more tolerant view of poetic freedom.)

 2

Of far greater importance, both with respect to past accomplishment and future influence, is the work of the para-Marxist school of criticism and aesthetic theory. It embraces a wide range of attitudes and values – from those of the early Edmund Wilson, whose Marxism was in essence an extension of Taine's historical and social determinism, to those of Theodor Adorno, a critic at times on the verge of orthodoxy. What do the para-Marxists (or we might call them, the 'Engelians') share in common? The belief that literature is centrally conditioned by historical, social and economic forces; the conviction that ideological content and the articulate world-view of a writer are crucially engaged in the act of literary judgement; a suspicion of any aesthetic doctrine which places major stress on the irrational elements in poetic creation and on the demands of 'pure form'. Finally, they share a bias towards dialectical proceedings in argument. But however committed they may be to dialectical materialism, para-Marxists approach a work of art with respect for its integrity and for the vital centre of its being. They are at one with Engels in regarding as inferior the kinds of literature which, in Keats's phrase, have a palpable design upon us. Above all – and it is this which distinguishes them from the orthodox – para-Marxists practise the arts of criticism, not those of censorship.

For evident reasons, these critics have flourished principally outside the immediate orbit of Soviet power. The one exception is, however, decisive. Georg Lukács stands as a lone and splendid survivor in midst the landscape of eastern European and communist intellectual life. His stature as a critic and theoretician of aesthetics is no longer in question. In capaciousness of intellect and breadth of performance, he ranks with the master-critics of our age. No contemporary western critic, with the possible exception of Croce, has brought to bear on literary problems a philosophic equipment of comparable authority. In no one since Sainte-Beuve has the sense of history, the feeling for the rootedness of the imagination in time and in place, been as solid and acute. Lukács's writings on Goethe and Balzac, on Schiller and Hegelianism, on the rise of the historical novel and the dark upsurge of irrationalism in German poetry, are classics. Few have spoken with finer discrimination of Tolstoy and Thomas Mann. The very massiveness of his labours – a collected edition would run to more than twenty volumes – constitutes something of a miracle: the growth and endurance under communist rule of an independent aesthetics, of a large body of practical criticism which diverges time and again from Leninist and Stalinist orthodoxy. The end of Lukács's personal odyssey is, at present, in tragic doubt.[1] But his accomplishments lie beyond the reach of political attainder. They demonstrate that Marxism can yield a poetics and a metaphysic of a high order.

Any consideration of the 'Engelian' strain in Marxist literary criticism leads inevitably to Lukács. Much of his work may indeed be regarded as a broadening and defence of the famous distinction between Balzac and Zola which Engels proposed to Miss Harkness. But I want to consider Lukács's complex and voluminous criticism in another essay. I draw attention, here, to a number of lesser-known critics all of whom are Marxists in substance and

1. This is, fortunately, no longer the case. Lukács survived the aftermath of the Hungarian rising and has lived to see eastern Europe assume new and complex shapes of national feeling. Whether this resurgence of energies founded, essentially, in the nationalist, agrarian past brings him comfort is, of course, another matter.

methodology, yet none of whom would subscribe to the Leninist image of literature as a cog and screw in the Juggernaut of the proletariat.

Around the hard core of French Stalinism, a harsh and disciplined *cadre* oddly untouched by the 'thaw' of 1953–4, there has always flourished a large and animated world of intellectual Marxism. Its leading figures, such as Merleau-Ponty and Sartre, have often inclined towards the vortex of total adherence. But they draw back in the final moment, seeking to establish an ideological position which will be outside the party – but not hostile to it. From both the dialectical and the practical point of view, such an attempt is doomed to ambivalence and failure. But the making of it charges French intellectual life with rare intensity and gives to abstract argument the strong pertinence of conflict. In France, even old men are angry.

There are significant elements of the para-Marxist position in Sartre's writings on literature. But the work of Lucien Goldmann offers a purer and more stringent example of dialectical criticism. His massive treatise, *Le dieu caché* (1955), has led to a major revaluation of the role of Jansenism in seventeenth-century literature. If there has, during the past three years, been an *affaire Racine* in French criticism and scholarship, Goldmann is in part responsible. His gnarled and intricate argument (due in part to the fact that his French is not native) seeks to relate the 'tragic vision' of Pascal's *Pensées* and Racine's dramas to an extremist faction in the Jansenist movement. Goldmann's view of religion, theology and literature is that of a classical Marxist. He sees in a philosophy or a poem an ideological edifice – what Marx called *ein Ueberbau* – whose foundations are economic, political and social. He demonstrates, with a wealth of textual erudition, how elements of class strategy entered into even the most subtle and unworldly of seventeenth-century theological conflicts. But like Engels, and Marx himself, Goldmann insists on the radical complexity of the ideological structure, on the fact that relationships between economic forces and philosophic or poetic systems are never automatic and unilinear. This gives to his treatment of Racine's career a persuasive subtlety. The Racine who emerges from *Le dieu caché* is a poet anchored in history. It is no longer possible, for example, to ignore the relations between the darkening of his world-view and the period of disillusion which seized on French Jansenism after 1675. Frequently, moreover, Goldmann arrives, through a process of dialectical analysis, at conclusions sanctioned by scholars of a wholly different conviction. Thus he sees in the problem of the chorus in neo-classical tragedy a direct reflection of the fragmentation of post-feudal society, the metamorphosis of a unified community into an aggregate of *monades sans portes ni fenêtres*. This accords precisely with the views of Tillyard and Francis Fergusson. At his finest, Goldmann is simply a critic responding with mature admiration to a great text. Commenting on Phèdre's decision to rise from her chair (Act I, scene iii), he observes: 'One approaches the universe of tragedy on one's feet.' Quite so, and Bradley might have said it.

At times, however, Goldmann's Marxism or, more strictly speaking, his materialist left-Hegelianism, does obtrude on the integrity of his judgement. He oversimplifies the structure of Racinian drama by seeking to impose on it a constant pattern – the triad of hero, society and 'hidden God':

> The *solitaires* and nuns of Port-Royal, in effect, conceived of life as a spectacle enacted before God; the theatre was in France, until Racine's arrival, a spectacle enacted before men; it sufficed to achieve a synthesis, to write for the stage the spectacle performed before God and to add to the habitual human audience the mute and hidden spectator who devalues and replaces that audience, for Racinian tragedy to be born.

It is interesting to note that Goldmann's orthodox opponents have rejected his treatment of Racine as excessively schematic. Writing in *La nouvelle critique* (November 1956), Crouzet points out that Goldmann has neglected the question of genre and poetic diction in neo-classicism. In so doing, he has reduced complex poetry to the bare bones of prose content. 'Form and content constitute a unity, but a unity of contradictions,' said Bukharin in a notable aphorism. Authentic Marxist criticism, says Crouzet, 'could not lead to such a desiccation of art'. He goes on to claim that in para-Marxism two vices necessarily coalesce: subjectivism and a mechanistic view of literature. Yet even in making these charges, Crouzet and his Leninist colleagues are ill at ease. They ask, with genuine worry – where is the true Marxist interpretation of Racine? Why has critical orthodoxy produced so little of value? Constantly, the party intellectuals, of whom H. Lefebvre is easily the most eminent,[2] have to admit to their own failings. Outside Lefebvre's works on Pascal and Diderot, official French Marxism has produced little of critical substance. Pierre Albouy's *Victor Hugo, essai de critique marxiste* (*La nouvelle critique*, June–August 1951) is tedious and inferior work. Though they deplore its heresies, French communists recognize in *Le dieu caché* one of the most

---

2. On 22 June 1958, Lefebvre was 'temporarily' expelled from the party. He was accused of 'revisionism' and he is now an independent Marxist.

distinguished attempts yet made to apply dialectical materialism to the best of French literature.

Nothing in Goldmann's book caused greater concern among orthodox Marxists than an entry on the *errata et addenda* page. In it, Goldmann declares that when referring to Lukács (which he does consistently), he has in mind Lukács's *History and Class Consciousness*, a famous essay published in 1923 but long since condemned as erroneous by the Communist Party of the U.S.S.R. and by the author himself. It is to this very same essay, however, that Walter Benjamin, the most gifted of the German 'Engelians', owed his conversion to Marxism in 1924.

Both as a stylist and thinker, Benjamin is difficult to characterize. In him, more perhaps than in any other Marxist, the texture of language precedes and determines the contours of argument. His prose is close-knit and allusive; it lies in ambush, seizing on its subject by indirection. Walter Benjamin is the R. P. Blackmur of Marxism – but of a Marxism which is private and oblique. Like Rilke and Kafka, Benjamin was possessed by a sense of the brutality of industrial life, by a haunted, apocalyptic vision of the modern metropolis (the *Grossstadt* of Rilke's *Malte Laurids Brigge*). He found his feelings verified and documented by Marx's theory of 'dehumanization' and Engels's account of the working class. Thus, Benjamin's essay 'On Certain Motifs in Baudelaire' (1939) is, essentially, a lyric meditation on the brooding immensity of nineteenth-century Paris and the concordant solitude of the poet. The same impulse underlies his admiration of Proust – an admiration obviously suspect from the point of view of the party. Benjamin's two principal essays, 'Goethe's *Elective Affinities*' (1924–5) and 'The Origin of German Tragedy' (1928), are among the most difficult and closely argued in modern European criticism. But if there is in them anything dialectical, it pertains to what Adorno, Benjamin's friend and editor, has called 'the dialectics of fantasy'.

Only once did he approach a problem from a thoroughly Marxist bias. The result is of extreme interest. In a paper entitled 'The Work of Art in the Era of its Technical Reproducibility' (1936), Benjamin proposed to consider neither proletarian art nor art in a classless society, but rather the evolution of art 'under prevailing modes of production'. The ambiguity in the word 'production' – the industrial process in general and the 'reproduction' of art works in particular – is relevant to his theme. Benjamin clearly preceded Malraux in recognizing the 'materiality' of art, the dependence of aesthetic sensibility on changes in the setting and reproduction of painting and sculpture. He wonders, as did Schiller, whether the history of technology might not be matched by a corresponding 'history of perception'. The essay contains yet another seminal idea. Benjamin refers to the strident support which Marinetti and Italian Futurism gave to the invasion of Ethiopia. He suggests that it is of the essence of fascism to beautify the outward trappings and actual inhumanities of political life. But all efforts towards the 'beautification of politics' (*die Aesthetisierung der Politik*) lead fatally to the image of 'glorious war'. Communism, on the other hand, does not render politics artistic. It makes art political. That way, according to Benjamin, lie sanity and peace.

This is a complex notion, either to understand or to refute. Benjamin did not live to clarify it further. Like Christopher Caudwell, whose work does by comparison strike one as rather drab, he fell victim to fascism. Theodor Adorno has observed that Benjamin injected dialectical materialism into his own system as a necessary poison; around this foreign body and creative irritant his sensibility crystallized. So far as literature goes, Adorno himself presents a case of lesser interest. His importance lies in the application of Marxist principles to the history and aesthetics of music.

Sidney Finkelstein, one of a small yet fascinating group of American Marxists, is also primarily a critic and sociologist of music. 'The forms of music,' he writes, 'are a product of society ... The validity of a musical form does not rest upon its "purity", but upon the easy communication it offers, in its time, for stimulating ideas.' In *Art and Society*, however, Finkelstein has ranged more widely, and his book is illustrative of a classical strain in Marxist theory – the alliance between the new culture of the proletariat and ancient folkways. 'I have used a philosophic system,' he declares:

> It is the body of Marxist thought, which can be described simply as springing from the fact that ideas can only be understood in connection with the material realities of life, and the realities of life can only be understood in terms of their inner conflicts, movement and change. Karl Marx and Frederick Engels say, 'Men, developing their material production and their material intercourse, alter, along with their real existence, their thinking and the products of their thinking. Life is not determined by consciousness but consciousness by life.' This is the general approach I have tried to apply to art.

The art forms in which Finkelstein sees the most enduring value are those which are rooted in popular modes. Thus, he argues that Bach's fugal style derived its strength and clarity from the fact that it was based on the division into voices and contrapuntal parts of current folk song. Correspondingly, much of the best in American literature – Mark Twain, Whitman, Sandburg, Frost – would stem from folk rhetoric and the tradition of the popular ballad. Finkelstein discerns in the abstraction and 'difficulty' of modern art a direct consequence of the estrangement between the individual artist and the masses. He concurs with Engels in believing that this estrangement was brought on by the commercial aesthetics of the bourgeoisie. Revolted by the 'tawdry cheapness' (Ezra Pound's phrase) of bourgeois taste, artists of the late nineteenth and early twentieth centuries lifted anchor and put out to sea. There they dwell in a world increasingly private and increasingly divorced from the maturing energies of communal life.

But in stubborn dissent from Zhdanovite orthodoxy, Finkelstein persists in admiring such lone voyagers as Schoenberg, Proust and Joyce. He regards *Ulysses* not as Radek did at the Writers' Congress in 1934 – 'A heap of dung, crawling with worms, photographed by a cinema apparatus through a microscope' – but as a tragic, perhaps self-defeating protest against the 'shallowness and dishonesty of the tons of verbiage' disgorged by the commercial literature of the day. One of Finkelstein's most original notions bears on the nature of romanticism. He seeks to distinguish between negative and positive strains in romantic sensibility. With the former he associates Dostoevsky. This is a point of some importance. The problem of how to approach Dostoevsky is the moment of truth in all Marxist criticism. Not even Lukács has been able to disengage himself from the Leninist and Stalinist condemnation of the Dostoevskyan world view as one implacably hostile to dialectical materialism. A Marxist critic who dealt with the works of Dostoevsky, prior to 1954, was by that mere action giving proof of real courage and independence. In reference to *The Brothers Karamazov*, Finkelstein says of Dostoevsky that 'by emphasizing the irrational over the rational, hinting at subconscious drives which could be neither understood nor controlled, he led to the climax of romanticism in which the artist and human being cut himself off completely from the world as unreal'. In the poetry of Aragon, on the other hand, he sees the 'positive value of romanticism', its kinship with the liberal instincts and sensuous vitality of the masses.

One could examine a host of other figures among critics and historians of literature to illustrate varying strategies within the larger context of the Marxist tradition. But the essential point can be made quite simply: outside the rigid bounds of party ideology, there are numerous critics and philosophers of art whose work is either centrally or in substantial measure conditioned by the dialectical method and historical mythology of Marxism. Among them there are theoreticians and practical critics whom anyone seriously concerned with literature would be wrong to ignore.

 3

The struggle between Leninist orthodoxy and para-Marxism is bitter and incessant. It has compelled Soviet publicists to query the writings of Engels himself. They cannot accept his distinction between Balzac and Zola and yet adhere, at the same time, to Lenin's axiom that the supreme virtue of art lies in its explicit revolutionary bias. Hence Boris Reizov's curious and tormented book, *Balzac the Writer*. Once again, it takes up the vexed problem of the Harkness letter concerning which, as Fadeyev ruefully conceded in his 'Notes on Literature' (February 1956), 'some confusion reigns'. It will be recalled that Engels judged Balzac 'a far greater master of realism than all the Zolas, *passés, présents et à venir'*. He did so despite the fact that Balzac was a Legitimist and a Catholic of a sombre and reactionary cast:

> That Balzac thus was compelled to go against his own class sympathies and political prejudices, that he *saw* the necessity of the downfall of his favourite nobles, and described them as people deserving no better fate; and that he *saw* the real men of the future where, for the time being, they alone were to be found – that I consider one of the greatest triumphs of Realism, and one of the grandest features in old Balzac.

Out of this famous passage has arisen the theory of dissociation between ideology and poetic vision. 'The history of literature', remarks Lucien Goldmann, 'is full of writers whose thought was rigorously contrary to the sense and structure of their work (among many examples, Balzac, Goethe, etc.).' But at the same time, this pronouncement by Engels and its corollary – 'The more the opinions of the author remain hidden, the better for the work of art' – pose a drastic challenge to the Leninist ideal of party literature. If a reactionary novelist, in fact, achieves greater realism than one whose views were explicitly 'progressive', the entire conception of the ideological commitment of art is put in doubt. To resolve this dilemma, Reizov is compelled to infer that Engels may have been mistaken; one need hardly comment on the weight of anxiety behind such a supposition. He perceives in Balzac's worldview 'direct links with the revolutionary philosophy of the French Encyclopedists ... Balzac remains a true successor of the French revolutionary philosophers – whatever his own political declarations.' Historically, of course, this is nonsense. But it does constitute a desperate attempt to reconcile Engels's views, and, *a fortiori*, those of Lukács, with Leninist orthodoxy. For as Valentin Asmus wrote, in an important paper on 'Realism and Naturalism' (*Soviet Literature*, March 1948), Lenin, in contrast to Engels, saw in a 'direct and frank assertion' of tendentiousness 'the chief difference between the proletarian writer and the bourgeois apologist of capitalism'.

That the 'proletarian writer' has, until now, produced little of enduring value, is a fact of which Soviet critics are recurrently aware. In his notorious intervention at the second Congress of Soviet Writers in 1955, Sholokhov ventured to assert that it was the principal task of contemporary Russian literature to escape from official mediocrity and render itself worthy of its inheritance. This has also been Lukács's persistent contention. Hence his unwillingness to deal, at any length, with Russian fiction and poetry of the Stalinist era. But to an orthodox critic such an attitude verges on treason. If Lenin is right, even the most mediocre of post-revolutionary literature is intrinsically more useful to the modern reader than are classics written under feudalism or the rule of the bourgeoisie. As Zhdanov categorically proclaimed: Soviet literature is, by definition, 'the richest in ideas, the most advanced and the most revolutionary'. A critic who devotes the vast majority of his writings to the works of Schiller, Goethe, Balzac, Pushkin and Tolstoy is obviously yielding to counter-revolutionary temptations.

This is the crux of the long-muffled but now open and murderous campaign waged against Lukács by the communist hierarchies of eastern Europe. Lukács's brief role in the Hungarian insurrection merely dramatized or, to use a Marxist term, 'objectified' the inevitable conflict between an orthodox and a para-Marxist interpretation of history. Joseph Revai, the Hungarian Zhdanov, launched the assault on Lukács in 1950. In a pamphlet entitled *Literature and Popular Democracy*, he asks: 'What could Hungarian literature gain from the pass-word given it by Lukács in 1954: "Zola? No, Balzac!"? And what could it gain from the slogan put forward by Lukács in 1948: "Neither Pirandello nor Priestley, but Shakespeare and Molière"? In both instances – nothing.' Lukács's concentration on Balzac and Goethe, suggests Revai, is dangerously obsolete. The dissociation between a writer's ideology and his actual works is no longer admissible. If a novelist seeks to convey an adequate image of reality, he must, indeed he can only, do so within the tenets of Marxist-Leninism. Revai hints that, in the final reckoning, Lukács places 'pure' or 'formalistic' literary canons above party and class interests. From this would logically follow his inability to recognize the pre-eminence of Soviet literature.

On the surface, this might appear as a debate between a Zhdanovite hack and a great critic. But the real conflict lies deeper. It is, once again, a confrontation between the 'Engelian' and the Leninist conceptions of art and the role of the artist in a revolutionary society. Lefebvre saw this as early as 1953. Taking issue with Lukács, he went on to state in his *Contribution à l'esthétique* that Engels had not yet grasped the problem of party literature. The whole debate has been further clarified in the aftermath of the Hungarian uprising. In a recent pronouncement, Revai charges Lukács with being one of those who 'under the guise of the struggle against Zhdanovism', a struggle rendered semi-respectable by the 'thaw' in the Soviet Union, 'in fact are trying to destroy Leninism'. If we understand by 'Leninism' the theory of literature outlined in 1905, Revai is undeniably right. For that is a theory which neither Lukács, nor any other responsible critic, can accept.

In only one domain has there been a *rapprochement* between orthodox and para-Marxist criticism. During the period of 'de-Stalinization', the forbidden ground of Dostoevskyan studies was reopened to Marxist scrutiny. We owe to this fact a serious essay by Vladimir Yermilov (*Soviet Literature*, February 1956). Its critical assumptions are plainly derived from Engels. Yermilov observes a radical dissociation between Dostoevsky's sense of human suffering and his hostility 'to any attempt to find effective ways of struggling for the liberation of man from that injury and insult'. He seeks to substantiate this general interpretation by a close reading of *The Idiot*. Acutely, he sees in that novel a parable on the cruel majesty of money and a 'right-wing critique of capitalism'. In points of detail, Yermilov is often indiscriminate. One relinquishes his essay with the odd feeling that *The Idiot* is a posthumous work by Balzac. But there is no doubt that Yermilov's conclusion represents a notable change in the tone of Soviet criticism: 'Mankind cannot overlook a writer who, in spite of the official lies of his time and reactionary tendencies in his own outlook, found in himself the strength to protest against humiliation and insult.' To find a comparable acknowledgement, one must go back to Lunacharsky and the Dostoevsky centennial of 1920–21.

A few months after the appearance of Yermilov's essay, French orthodox criticism followed suit. G. Fridlander's discussion of *The Idiot* (*La nouvelle critique*, May 1956) contains little of importance. He too believes that the 'progressive reader' will know how to distinguish between Dostoevsky's accurate depiction of social and psychological conflicts in *bourgeois* society and his erroneous, reactionary point of view. The startling element in the piece comes at the outset. Here, Fridlander finds it necessary to inform his communist reader that Dostoevsky was born in such and such a year, that he spent some time in Siberia, and that he wrote a number of novels among which are *Crime and Punishment*, *The Idiot*, and so on. Such candour speaks volumes.

The problems we have touched upon so far are internal; they engage party doctrine and varying modes of dissent. Let us now ask the larger question: what have Marxism, as a philosophy, and dialectical materialism, as a strategy of insight, contributed to the resources of the literary critic? To what aspects of the Marxist performance will a future Saintsbury address himself when writing a history of modern criticism?

First, there is the concept of dissociation – the image of the poet as Balaam speaking truth against his knowledge or avowed philosophy. 'There is nothing absurd', argues Goldmann, 'in the notion of a writer or poet who does not apprehend the *objective* significance of his own works.' Between his explicit ideology and the representation of life which he in fact conveys, there may be a contradiction. Engels put forward this idea with reference to Goethe and Balzac. It throws light also on Cervantes and Tolstoy – whether we approach the latter via Lukács or Isaiah Berlin. Thus, in both *Don Quixote* and *Anna Karenina* the rhetoric of prior intent goes against the grain of the actual narrative. In a good deal of major literature, we are made aware of the latent paradox and tension generated by such internal contrariety. Hence the curious, but suggestive, affinities between a Marxist reading of Balzac and William Empson's recent revaluation of *Tom Jones*. Where Empson perceives the complex play of irony, the Marxist would observe a dialectical conflict between a poet's thesis and his actual vision of things.

Secondly, there is the intricate, yet ultimately persuasive, distinction which Marxist theory draws between 'realism' and 'naturalism'. It goes back to Hegel's reflections on the *Iliad* and the *Odyssey*. Hegel found that in the Homeric epics the depiction of physical objects, however detailed and stylized, did not intrude upon the rhythm and vitality of the poem. Descriptive writing in modern literature, on the other hand, struck him as contingent and lifeless. He threw out the illuminating hint that the industrial revolution and the correlative division of labour had estranged men from the material world. Homer's account of the forging of Achilles' armour or the making of Odysseus' raft presupposes an immediacy of relationship between artisan and product which modern industrial processes no longer allow. Compared to Homeric or even to medieval times, modern man inhabits the physical world like a rapacious stranger. This idea greatly influenced Marx and Engels. It contributed to their own theory of the 'alienation' of the individual under capitalist modes of production. In the course of their debate with Lassalle and of their study of Balzac, Marx and Engels came to believe that this problem of estrangement was directly germane to the problem of realism in art. The poets of antiquity and the 'classical realists' (Cervantes, Shakespeare, Goethe, Balzac) had achieved an organic relationship between objective reality and the life of the imagination. The 'naturalist', on the other hand, looks upon the world as upon a warehouse of whose content he must make a feverish inventory. 'A sense of reality', says a contemporary Marxist critic, 'is created not by a reproduction of all the features of an object but by a depiction of those features that form the essence ... while in naturalistic art – because of a striving to achieve an elusive fullness – the image, also incomplete, places both the *essential* and the *secondary*, the unimportant, on the same plane.'

This distinction is far-reaching. It bears on the decline of French realism after Balzac and Stendhal, and tells us something of Zola's obsessive attempt to make of the novel an index for the world. By virtue of it, we may discriminate between the 'realism' of Chekhov and the 'naturalism' of, say, Maupassant. Through it, also, we may ascertain that *Madame Bovary*, for all its virtues, is a slighter affair than *Anna Karenina*. In naturalism there is accumulation; in realism what Henry James called the 'deep-breathing economy' of organic form.

Thirdly, Marxism has sharpened the critic's sense of time and place. In so doing, it has carried forward ideas initiated by Sainte-Beuve and Taine. We now see the work of art as rooted in temporal and material circumstance. Beneath the complex structure of the lyric impulse lie specific historical and social foundations. The Marxist sensibility has contributed a sociological awareness to the best of modern criticism. It is the kind of awareness realized, for example, in Lionel Trilling's observation that Dostoevskyan plots originate in crises in monetary or class relationships. Through the perspective implicit in Marxism, moreover, historians and critics of literature have been led to a study of the audience. What can be said, historically and socio-logically, of the Elizabethan spectator? In what respect was the Dickensian novel a calculated response to the evolution of a new reading public? Without the presence of the Marxist element in the 'spirit of the age', such critics as L. C. Knights, Q. D. Leavis and Richard Hoggart might not have arrived at their own understanding of the social dynamics of art.

The final point is the most difficult to make. It may give rise to misunderstanding however cautiously I put it. But it is simply this: Marxist-Leninism and the political régimes enacted in its name take literature *seriously*, indeed desperately so. At the very height of the Soviet revolution's battle for physical survival, Trotsky found occasion to assert that 'the development of art is the highest test of the vitality and significance of each epoch'. Stalin himself deemed it essential to add to his voluminous strategic and economic pronouncements a treatise on philology and the problems of language in literature. In a communist society the poet is regarded as a figure central to the health of the body politic. Such regard is cruelly manifest in the very urgency with which the heretical artist is silenced or hounded to destruction. This constant preoccupation with the life of the mind would alone serve to distinguish Marxist autocracy from other species of totalitarianism. To shoot a man because one disagrees with his interpretation of Darwin or Hegel is a sinister tribute to the supremacy of ideas in human affairs – but a tribute nevertheless.

Let us, moreover, distinguish Marxism and the philosophy of art of Marx and Engels from the concrete actualities of Stalinist rule. If we do so, the dread gravity of the Marxist view of literature should remind us of certain truths which few western critics, with the exception of Ezra Pound and Dr Leavis, seem willing to affirm. The health of language *is* essential to the preservation of a living society. It is in literature that language is most truly challenged and guarded. A vital critical tradition, vital even in its polemics, is not a luxury but a rigorous need. The abandonment of values under the pressure of commercialism, the failure of the journalist-critic to discriminate between art and *kitsch*, does contribute to a larger decay. For all its obscurantism and inhumanity, the Marxist conception of literature is neither academic, in the manner of some of the 'New Criticism' practised in America, nor provincial, as is so much of current English criticism. Above all, it is not frivolous. The genuine Marxist critic – as distinct from the Zhdanovite censor – cannot look upon literature in the light of that French idiom, proverbial of frivolity, *ce n'est que de la littérature*.

Georg Lukács
and his Devil's Pact

In the twentieth century it is not easy for an honest man to be a literary critic. There are so many more urgent things to be done. Criticism is an adjunct. For the art of the critic consists in bringing works of literature to the attention of precisely those readers who may least require such help; does a man read critiques of poetry or drama or fiction unless he is already highly literate on his own? On either hand, moreover, stand two tempters. To the right, Literary History, with its solid air and academic credentials. To the left, Book Reviewing — not really an art, but rather a technique committed to the implausible theory that something worth reading is published each morning in the year. Even the best of criticism may succumb to either temptation. Anxious to achieve intellectual respectability, the firm stance of the scholar, the critic may, like Sainte-Beuve, almost become a literary historian. Or he may yield to the claims of the novel and the immediate; a significant part of Henry James's critical pronouncements have not survived the trivia on which they were lavished. Good reviews are even more ephemeral than bad books.

But there is yet another major reason why it is difficult for a serious mind, born into this troubled and perilous century, to devote its main strength to literary criticism. Ours is, pre-eminently, the season of the natural sciences. Ninety per cent of all scientists are alive. The rate of conquest in the sciences, the retreat of the horizon before the inquiring spirit, is no longer in any recognizable proportion to the past. New Americas are found each day. Hence the temper of the age is penetrated with scientific values. These extend their influence and fascination far beyond the bounds of science in the classical sense. History and economics hold that they are, in some central measure, sciences; so do logic and sociology. The art historian refines instruments and techniques which he regards as scientific. The twelve-tone composer refers his austere practices to those of mathematics. Durrell has prefaced his *Quartet* by saying that he endeavours to translate into language and into the manner of his narrative the perspective of Relativity. He sees the city of Alexandria in four dimensions.

This ubiquity of science has brought with it new modesties and new ambitions. Distrustful of mere impulse, science demands a syntax of rigour and proof. In splendid exchange it offers the mirage of certitude, of assured knowledge, of intellectual possession guarded against doubt. The very great scientist will reject this prospect; he will persevere in doubt even at the heart of discovery. But the hope of objective, demonstrable truth is always there and it has drawn to itself the most powerful minds of our time.

In literary criticism there is no promised land of established fact, no utopia of certainty. By its very nature, criticism is personal. It is susceptible neither of demonstration nor of coherent proof. It disposes of no instrument more exact than Housman's beard bristling as the great line of poetry flashed across his mind. Throughout history, critics have sought to show that their *métier* was a science after all, that it had objective canons and means of attaining absolute truths. Coleridge harnessed his intensely personal, often unsteady genius to the yoke of a metaphysical system. In a famous manifesto, Taine proclaimed that the study of literature was no less exact than that of the natural sciences. Dr I. A. Richards has underwritten the hope that there is an objective psychological foundation to the act of aesthetic judgement. His most distinguished disciple, Professor Empson, has brought to the arts of literary criticism the modalities and gestures of mathematics.

But the fact remains: a literary critic is an individual man judging a given text according to the present bent of his own spirit, according to his mood or the fabric of his beliefs. His judgement may be of more value than yours or mine solely because it is grounded on a wider range of knowledge or because it is presented with more persuasive clarity. It cannot be demonstrated in a scientific manner, nor can it lay claim to permanence. The winds of taste and fashion are inconstant and each generation of critics judges anew. Opinions on the merits of a work of art, moreover, are irrefutable. Balzac thought Mrs Radcliffe to be as great a writer as Stendhal. Nietzsche, one of the acutest minds ever to concern itself with music, came to argue that Bizet was a more genuine composer than Wagner. We may feel in our bones that such views are perverse and erroneous. But we cannot refute them as a scientist can refute a false theory. And who knows but that some future age will concur in judgements which today seem untenable? The history of taste is rather like a spiral. Ideas which are at first considered outrageous or *avant-garde* become the reactionary and sanctified beliefs of the succeeding generation.

Thus a modern critic finds himself in double jeopardy. Criticism has about it something of a more leisured age. It is difficult, on moral grounds, to resist the fierce solicitations of economic, social and political issues. If some mode of barbarism and political self-destruction is threatening, writing essays on *belles-lettres* seems a rather marginal pursuit. The second dilemma is intellectual. However distinguished, a critic cannot share in the principal adventure of the contemporary mind – in the acquisition of positive knowledge, in the mastery of scientific fact or the exploration of demonstrable truth. And if he is honest with himself, the literary critic knows that his judgements have no lasting validity, that they may be reversed tomorrow. Only one thing can give his work a measure of permanence: the strength or beauty of his actual style. By virtue of style, criticism may, in turn, become literature.

The masters of contemporary criticism have tried to resolve these dilemmas in different ways. T. S. Eliot, Ezra Pound and Thomas Mann, for example, have made of criticism an adjunct to creation. Their critical writings are commentaries on their own works; mirrors which the intellect holds up to the creative imagination. In D. H. Lawrence, criticism is self-defence; though ostensibly discussing other writers, Lawrence was in fact arguing for his own conception of the art of the novel. Dr Leavis has met the challenge head-on. He has placed his critical powers at the service of an impassioned moral vision. He is intent upon establishing standards of maturity and order in literature so that society as a whole may proceed in a more mature and orderly manner.

But no one has brought to the moral and intellectual dilemmas besetting literary criticism a more radical solution than Georg Lukács. In his works two beliefs are incarnate. First, that literary criticism is not a luxury, that it is not what the subtlest of American critics has called 'a discourse for amateurs'. But that it is, on the contrary, a central and militant force towards shaping men's lives. Secondly, Lukács affirms that the work of the critic is neither subjective nor uncertain. Criticism is a science with its own rigour and precision. The truth of judgement can be verified. Georg Lukács is, of course, a Marxist. Indeed, he is the one major philosophic talent to have emerged from the grey servitude of the Marxist world.

 2

In an essay, dated 1948, Lukács put forward a significant analogy. He said that Newtonian physics gave to the consciousness of the eighteenth century its foremost liberating impulse, teaching the mind to live the great adventure of reason. According to Lukács, this role should be performed in our own time by political economy. It is around political economy, in the Marxist sense, that we should order our understanding of human affairs. Lukács himself came to literature via economics, as we may say that Aristotle approached drama via a systematic inquiry into morals.

Dialectical materialism holds that literature, as all other forms of art, is an 'ideological superstructure', an edifice of the spirit built upon foundations of economic, social and political fact. In style and content the work of art precisely reflects its material, historical basis. The *Iliad* was no less conditioned by social circumstance (a feudal aristocracy splintered into small rival king-doms) than were the novels of Dickens which so strongly reflect the economics of serialization and the growth of a new mass audience. Therefore, argues the Marxist, the progress of art is subject to laws of historical necessity. We cannot conceive of *Robinson Crusoe* prior to the rise of the mercantile ideal. In the decline of the French novel after Stendhal we observe the image of the larger decline of the French bourgeoisie.

But where there is law there is science. And thus the Marxist critic cherishes the conviction that he is engaged not in matters of opinion but in determina-tions of objective reality. Without this conviction, Lukács could not have turned to literature. He came of intellectual age amid the chaotic ferocity of war and revolution in central Europe. He reached Marxism over the winding road of Hegelian metaphysics. In his early writings two strains are dominant: the search for a key to the apparent turmoil of history and the endeavour of an intellectual to justify to himself the contemplative life. One can imagine how Lukács must have striven to discipline within himself his native bent towards literature and the aesthetic side of things. Marxism afforded him the crucial possibility of remaining a literary critic without feeling that he had committed his energies to a somewhat frivolous and imprecise pursuit. In 1918 Lukács joined the Hungarian Communist Party. During the first brief spell of communist rule in Budapest, he served as political and cultural commissar with the Fifth Red Army. After the fall of Belá-Kun, Lukács went into exile. He remained in Berlin until 1933 and then took refuge in Moscow. There he stayed and worked for twelve years, returning to Hungary only in 1945.

This is a fact of obvious importance. German is Lukács's principal language, but his use of it has grown brittle and forbidding. His style is that of exile; it has lost the habits of living speech. More essentially: Lukács's entire tone, the fervent, at times narrow tenor of his vision, mirror the fact of banishment. From Moscow, surrounded by a small coterie of fellow-exiles, Lukács observed the advance of crisis over western Europe. His writings on French and German literature became an impassioned plea against the lies and barbarism of the Nazi period. This accounts for a major paradox in Lukács's performance. A communist by conviction, a dialectical materialist by virtue of his critical method, he has nevertheless kept his eyes resolutely on the past. Thomas Mann saw in Lukács's works an eminent sense of tradition. Despite pressure from his Russian hosts, Lukács gave only perfunctory notice to the much-heralded achievements of 'Soviet realism'. Instead, he dwelt on the great lineage of eighteenth- and nineteenth-century European poetry and fiction, on Goethe and Balzac, on Sir Walter Scott and Flaubert, on Stendhal and Heine. Where he writes of Russian literature, Lukács deals with Pushkin or Tolstoy, not with the poetasters of Stalinism. The critical perspective is rigorously Marxist, but the choice of themes is 'central European' and conservative.

In the midst of the apparent triumph of fascism, Lukács maintained a passionate serenity. He strove to discover the tragic flaw, the seed of chaos, whence had sprung the madness of Hitler. One of his works (in itself a strident, often mendacious book) is entitled *The Destruction of Reason* (1955). It is a philosopher's attempt to resolve the mystery which Thomas Mann dramatized in *Doktor Faustus*. How was the tide of darkness loosed on the German soul? Lukács traces the origins of disaster back to the irrationalism of Schelling. But at the same time he insisted on the integrity and life-force of humane values. Being a communist, Lukács had no doubt that socialism would ultimately prevail. He regarded it as his particular task to marshal towards the moment of liberation the spiritual resources inherent in European literature and philosophy. When Heine's poems were once again read in Germany, there was available an essay by Lukács building a bridge between the future and the scarce-remembered world of liberalism to which Heine had belonged.

Thus Lukács has put forward a solution to the twofold dilemma of the modern critic. As a Marxist, he discerns in literature the action of economic, social and political forces. This action follows on certain laws of historical necessity. To Lukács criticism is a science even before it is an art. His preference of Balzac over Flaubert is not a matter of personal taste or fiat. It is an objective determination arrived at through an analysis of material fact. Secondly, he has given his writing an intense immediacy. It is rooted in the political struggles and social circumstances of the time. His writings on literature, like those of Trotsky, are instruments of combat. By understanding the dialectic of Goethe's *Faust*, says Lukács, a man is better equipped to read the sanguinary riddles of the present. The fall of France in 1940 is writ large in the *Comédie humaine*. Lukács's arguments are relevant to issues that are central in our lives. His critiques are not a mere echo to literature. Even where it is sectarian and polemic, a book by Lukács has a curious nobility. It possesses what Matthew Arnold called 'high seriousness'.

◇ 3 ◇

But in practice, what are Lukács's major achievements as a critic and historian of ideas?

Ironically, one of his most influential works dates from a period in which his communism was tainted with heresy. *History and Class Consciousness* (1923) is a rather legendary affair. It is a *livre maudit*, a burnt book, of which relatively few copies have survived.[1] We find in it a fundamental analysis of the 'reification' of man (*Verdinglichung*), the degradation of the human person to a statistical object through industrial and political processes. The work was condemned by the party and withdrawn by the author. But it has led a tenacious underground life and certain writers, such as Sartre and Thomas Mann, have always regarded it as Lukács's masterpiece.

To my mind, however, his pre-eminence lies elsewhere: in the essays and monographs which he wrote during the 1930s and 1940s and which began appearing in a row of imposing volumes after the end of the war. The essential Lukács is contained in the study of *Goethe and his Time* (1947), in the essays on *Russian Realism in World Literature* (1949), in the volume entitled *German Realists of the XIXth Century* (1951), in the book on Balzac, Stendhal and Zola (1952), and in the great work on *The Historical Novel* (1955). To this should be added a number of massive works of a more strictly philosophic character, such as the *Contributions to a History of Aesthetics* (1954), and what is perhaps Lukács's *magnum opus*, the study of Hegel (the first volume of which appeared in 1948).

It is impossible to give a brief yet adequate account of so great a range of material. But a number of motifs do stand out as classic enrichments of our understanding of literature.

There is Lukács's analysis of the decline of the French novel. He is the

---

1. *History and Class Consciousness* is now available in French [and English]. It has also been republished in the West German edition of Lukács's collected writings, together with other early works. These are among his finest philosophic achievements and show him to be the true predecessor to Walter Benjamin. The cultural authorities in the East allow such western publication of heretical but prestigious Marxist books; a characteristic touch of 'Byzantine' policy.

foremost living student of Balzac and sees in the *Comédie humaine* the master edifice of realism. His reading of *Les Illusions perdues* is exemplary of the manner in which the vision of the historian is brought to bear on the fabric of a work of art. It is this vision which leads directly to Lukács's condemnation of Flaubert. Between Balzac and Flaubert falls the defeat of 1848. The brightness of liberal hopes has faded and France is moving towards the tragedy of the Commune. Balzac looks on the world with the primitive ardour of conquest. The *Comédie humaine* built an empire in language as Napoleon did in fact. Flaubert looks on the world as through a glass contemptuously. In *Madame Bovary* the glitter and artifice of words has become an end in itself. When Balzac describes a hat, he does so because a man is wearing it. The account of Charles Bovary's cap, on the other hand, is a piece of technical bravado; it exhibits Flaubert's command of the French sartorial vocabulary. But the thing is dead. And behind this contrast in the art of the novel, Lukács discerns the transformation of society through mature capitalism. In a pre-industrial society, or where industrialism remains on a small scale, man's relationship to the physical objects that surround him has a natural immediacy. The latter is destroyed by mass production. The furnishings of our lives are consequent on processes too complex and impersonal for anyone to master. Isolated from sensuous reality, repelled by the inhumane drabness of the factory world, the writer seeks refuge in satire or in romantic visions of the past. Both retreats are exemplified in Flaubert: *Bouvard et Pécuchet* is an encyclopedia of contempt, whereas *Salammbô* can be characterized as the reverie of a somewhat sadistic antiquarian.

Out of this dilemma arose what Lukács defines as the illusion of naturalism, the belief that an artist can recapture a sense of reality by mere force of accumulation. Where the realist selects, the naturalist enumerates. Like the schoolmaster in Dickens's *Hard Times*, he demands facts and more facts. Zola had an inexhaustible appetite for circumstantial detail, a passion for timetables and inventories (one recalls the catalogue of cheeses in *Le Ventre de Paris*). He had the gusto to breathe life into a stockmarket quotation. But his theory of the novel, argues Lukács, was radically false. It leads to the death of the imagination and to reportage.

Lukács does not compromise with his critical vision. He exalts Balzac, a man of royalist and clerical principles. He condemns Zola, a progressive in the political sense, and a forerunner of 'socialist realism'. Insight has its scruples.

Even more original and authoritative is Lukács's treatment of the historical novel. This is a literary genre to which western criticism has given only cursory attention. It is difficult to get the range of historical fiction into proper focus. At times, its head is in the mythological stars, but more often the bulk of the thing is to be found in the good earth of commercial trash. The very notion brings to mind improbable gallants pursuing terrified yet rather lightly clad young ladies across flamboyant dust-wrappers. Only very rarely, when a writer such as Robert Graves intervenes, do we realize that the historical novel has distinct virtues and a noble tradition. It is to these that Lukács addresses himself in a major study, *The Historical Novel.*

The form arose out of a crisis in European sensibility. The French Revolution and the Napoleonic era penetrated the consciousness of ordinary men with a sense of the historical. Whereas Frederick the Great had asked that wars be conducted so as not to disturb the normal flow of events, Napoleon's armies marched across Europe and back reshaping the world in their path. History was no longer a matter for archives and princes; it had become the fabric of daily life. To this change the *Waverley* novels gave a direct and prophetic response. Here again, Lukács is on fresh ground. We do not take Sir Walter Scott altogether seriously. That is most probably an injustice. If we care to learn how deliberate an artist Scott was, and how penetrating a sense of history is at work in *Quentin Durward* or *The Heart of Midlothian*, we do best to read a book written in Moscow by a Hungarian critic.

Lukács goes on to explore the development of historical fiction in the art of Manzoni, Pushkin and Victor Hugo. His reading of Thackeray is particularly suggestive. He argues that the antiquarian elements in *Henry Esmond* and *The Virginians* convey Thackeray's critique of contemporary social and political conditions. By taking the periwig off the eighteenth century, the novelist is satirizing the falsehood of Victorian conventions (what a Marxist calls *zeitgenössische Apologetik*). I happen to believe that Lukács is misreading Thackeray. But his error is fruitful, as the errors of good criticism usually are, and it leads to a most original idea. Lukács observes that archaic speech, however deftly handled, does not in fact bring the past closer to our imaginings. The classic masters of historical fiction write narrative and dialogue in the language of their own day. They create the illusion of the historical present through force of realized imagination and because they themselves experience the relationship between past history and their own time as one of live continuity. The historical novel falters when this sense of continuity no longer prevails, when the writer feels that the forces of history are beyond his rational comprehension. He will turn to an increasingly remote or exotic past in protest against contemporaneous life. Instead of historical fiction, we find laborious archaeology. Compare the poetics of history implicit in *The Charterhouse of Parma* with the erudite artifice of *Salammbô*. Amid lesser craftsmen than Flaubert this sense of artifice is re-enforced by the use of archaic language. The novelist endeavours to make his vision of the past authentic by writing dialogue in what he supposes to have been the syntax and style of the relevant period. This is a feeble device. Would Shakespeare have done better to let Richard II speak in Chaucerian English?

Now, as Lukács points out, this decline from the classical conception of the historical novel coincides precisely with the change from realism to naturalism. In both instances, the vision of the artist loses its spontaneity; he is, in some manner, alien to his material. As a result, matters of technique become pre-eminent at the expense of substance. The image of Glasgow in *Rob Roy* is historically perceptive, but more significantly it arises out of the social and personal conflicts of the narrative. It is not a piece of antiquarian restoration. But that is exactly what the image of Carthage in *Salammbô* is. Flaubert has built a sumptuous hollow shell around an autonomous action; as Sainte-Beuve noted, it is difficult to reconcile the psychological motivations of the characters with the alleged historical setting. Sir Walter Scott believed in the rational, progressive unfolding of English history. He saw in the events of his own time a natural consequence of energies released during the seventeenth and eighteenth centuries. Flaubert, on the contrary, turned to antique Carthage or Alexandria because he found his own epoch intolerable. Being out of touch with the present – he saw in the Commune a delayed spasm of the Middle Ages – he failed to achieve an imaginative realization of the past.

Whether or not one agrees with this analysis, its originality and breadth of implication are obvious. It illustrates Lukács's essential practice: the close study of a literary text in the light of far-reaching philosophic and political questions. The writer or particular work are the point of departure. From it Lukács's argument moves outward traversing complex ground. But the central idea or theme is kept constantly in view. Finally, the dialectic closes in, marshalling its examples and persuasions.

Thus the essay on the Goethe–Schiller correspondence deals primarily with the vexed topic of the nature of literary forms. The discussion of Hölderlin's *Hyperion* gives rise to a study of the crucial yet ambiguous role of the Hellenic ideal in the history of the German spirit. In his several considerations of Thomas Mann, Lukács is concerned with what he takes to be the paradox of the *bourgeois* artist in a Marxist century. Lukács argues that Mann chose to stay outside the stream of history while being aware of the tragic nature of his choice. The essay on Gottfried Keller is an attempt to clarify the very difficult problem of the arrested development in German literature after the death of Goethe. In all these instances, we cannot dissociate the particular critical judgement from the larger philosophic and social context.

Because the argument is so close and tightly woven, it is difficult to give representative quotations from Lukács's works. Perhaps a short passage from a paper on Kleist can convey the dominant tone:

> Kleist's conception of passion brings drama close to the art of the short story. A heightened singularity is presented in a manner underlining *its accidental uniqueness.* In the short story this is entirely legitimate. For that is a literary genre specifically designed to make real the immense role of coincidence and contingency in human life. But if the action represented remains on the level of coincidence ... and is given the dignity of tragic drama without any proof of its objective necessity, the effect will inevitably be one of contradiction and dissonance. Therefore, Kleist's plays do not point to the high road of modern drama. That road leads from Shakespeare, via the experiments of Goethe and Schiller to Pushkin's *Boris Godunov.* Due to the ideological decline of the bourgeoisie, it had no adequate continuation. Kleist's plays represent an irrational byway. Isolated individual passion destroys the organic relationship between the fate of the individual person and social-historical necessity. With the dissolution of that relationship, the poetic and philosophic foundations of genuine dramatic conflict are also destroyed. The basis of drama becomes thin and narrow, purely personal and private ... To be sure Kleistian passions are representative of a bourgeois society. Their inner dialectic mirrors typical conflicts of individuals who have become 'windowless monads' in a bourgeois milieu.

The reference to Leibniz is characteristic. The quality of Lukács's mind is philosophic, in the technical sense. Literature concentrates and gives concretion to those mysteries of meaning with which the philosopher is eminently concerned. In this respect, Lukács belongs to a notable tradition. The *Poetics* are philosophic criticism (drama seen as the theoretic model of spiritual action); so are the critical writings of Coleridge, Schiller and Croce. If the going is heavy, it is because the matter of the argument is persistently complex. Like other philosopher-critics, Lukács engages questions that have bedevilled inquiry since Plato. What are the primary distinctions between epic and drama? What is 'reality' in a work of art, the ancient riddle of shadow outweighing substance? What is the relationship between poetic imagination and ordinary perception? Lukács raises the problem of the 'typical' personage. Why do certain characters in literature — Falstaff, Faust, Emma Bovary — possess a force of life greater than that of a multitude of other imagined beings and, indeed, of most living creatures? Is it because they are archetypes in whom universal traits are gathered and given memorable shape?

Lukács's inquiries draw on an extraordinary range of evidence. He appears to have mastered nearly the whole of modern European and Russian literature. This yields a rare association of tough, philosophic exactitude with largeness of vision. By contrast, Dr Leavis, who is no less of a moralist and hard thinker than Lukács, is deliberately provincial. In point of universality, Lukács's peer would be Edmund Wilson.

But there is an obverse to the medal. Lukács's criticism has its part of blindness and injustice. At times, he writes with acrimonious obscurity as if to declare that the study of literature should be no pleasure, but a discipline and science, thorny of approach as are other sciences. This has made him insensible to the great musicians of language. Lukács lacks ear; he does not possess that inner tuning-fork which enables Ezra Pound to choose unerringly the instant of glory in a long poem or forgotten romance. In Lukács's omissions of Rilke there is an obscure protest against the marvel of the poet's language. Somehow, he writes too wondrously well. Though he would deny it, moreover, Lukács does incline towards the arch-error of Victorian criticism: the narrative content, the quality of the fable, influence his judgement. Its failure to include Proust, for example, casts doubt on Lukács's entire view of the French novel. But the actual plot of the *Recherche du temps perdu*, the luxuriance and perversities which Proust recounts, obviously outrage Lukács's austere morality. Marxism is a puritanical creed.

Like all critics, he has his particular displeasures. Lukács detests Nietzsche and is insensitive to the genius of Dostoevsky. But being a consequent Marxist, he makes a virtue of blindness and gives to his condemnations an objective, systematic value. Dr Leavis is evidently ill at ease with the works of Melville. T. S. Eliot has conducted a lengthy and subtle quarrel with the poetics of Milton. But in it, the essential courtesies are observed. Lukács's arguments go *ad hominem*. Infuriated by the world-view of Nietzsche and Kierkegaard, he consigns their persons and their labours to the spiritual inferno of pre-fascism. This is, of course, a grotesque misreading of the facts.

Of late, these defects of vision have become more drastic. They mar *The Destruction of Reason* and the essays on aesthetics which have appeared since that time. Doubtless, there is a question of age. Lukács was seventy in 1955 and his hatreds have stiffened. In part, there is the fact that Lukács is haunted by the ruin of German and western European civilization. He is searching for culprits to hand over to the Last Judgement of History. But above all, there is, I think, an intense personal drama. At the outset of his brilliant career, Lukács made a Devil's pact with historical necessity. The daemon promised him the secret of objective truth. He gave him the power to confer blessing or pronounce anathema in the name of revolution and 'the laws of history'. But since Lukács's return from exile, the Devil has been lurking about, asking for his fee. In October 1956, he knocked loudly at the door.

4

We touch here on matters of a personal nature. Lukács's role in the Hungarian uprising and the subsequent monasticism of his personal life are of obvious historical interest. But they contain an element of private agony to which an outsider has little access. A man who loses his religion loses his beliefs. A communist for whom history turns somersault is in danger of losing his reason. Presumably, that is worse. Those who have not experienced it, however, can hardly realize what such a collapse of values is like. Moreover, the motives of action in the Lukács case are obscure.

He accepted the post of Minister of Culture in the Nagy government. Not, I think, to be among the leaders of an anti-Soviet movement, but rather to preserve the Marxist character of Hungarian intellectual life and to guard its radical inheritance against the reviving forces of the Catholic-agrarian right. More essentially, perhaps, because a Lukács cannot stand to one side of history even when the latter assumes absurd forms. He cannot be a spectator. But on 3 November, one day before the Red Army reconquered Budapest, Lukács resigned from the cabinet. Why? Had he decided that a Marxist should not oppose the will of the Soviet Union in which, for better or worse, the future of dialectical materialism is incarnate? Was he persuaded to withdraw from a doomed cause by friends anxious for his life? We do not know.

After a period of exile in Rumania, Lukács was allowed to return to his home. But he was no longer permitted to teach and his past work became the object of derisive and increasingly fierce attack. This attack actually predates the October rising. Hungary had its miniature version of Zhdanov, a ferocious little man called Joseph Revai. Originally a pupil of Lukács, but later jealous of the master's eminence, he published a pamphlet on *Literature and Popular Democracy* in 1954. In it, he drew up a Stalinist indictment of Lukács's life-work. He accused Lukács of having consistently neglected contemporary Soviet literature. He charged that Lukács's concentration on Goethe and Balzac was dangerously obsolete. Even a mediocre novel by a communist, declares Revai, is infinitely preferable to a great novel by a reactionary or pre-Marxist. Lukács places 'formalistic' literary ideals above class and party interests. His style is inaccessible to a proletarian reader.

After October, these accusations became more strident. Hungarian and East German publicists revived the old charges of heresy made against Lukács's early writings. They recalled his youthful admiration for Stefan George and hunted down traces of 'bourgeois idealism' in his mature works. Yet the old man was not touched and through one of those odd, Solomonic judgements sometimes passed by communist régimes, he was even allowed to publish a small volume of essays with a West German press (*Wider den missverstandenen Realismus*, Hamburg, 1958).

Lukács's relative immunity may have been due to the interest which socialist intellectuals outside the iron curtain have taken in the case. But surely, the more important question is this: how did Lukács himself regard his beliefs and achievements in the light of the October tragedy? Was he drawn towards the great limbo of disillusion? Did his gods fail him at the last?

Such questions cannot be urged very far without impertinence; they involve that inward place of vital illusion which preserves the religious or revolutionary conscience. Lukács's judgement of the Hungarian revolution is contained in a preface which he wrote in April 1957: 'Important events have occurred in Hungary and elsewhere, compelling us to re-think many problems connected with Stalin's life-work. The reaction to the latter, both in the bourgeois world and in socialist countries, is taking the guise of a revision of the teachings of Marx and Lenin. This certainly constitutes the principal threat to Marxism-Leninism.' The words seem desperately beside the point. But let us keep one thing firmly in mind: to men such as Koestler or Malraux, communism was a temporary expedient of passion. Lukács's communism is the root-fibre of his intelligence. Whatever interpretation he puts on the crisis of October 1956 will have been arrived at within the framework of a dialectical vision of history. A man who has lost his sight continues to view his surroundings in terms of remembered images. In order to survive intellectually, Lukács must have hammered out some kind of inner compromise; such punitive forays into one's own consciousness are characteristic of the Marxist condition. His comment about the threat of revisionism gives us a lead. If I interpret him at all accurately, he is saying that the Hungarian episode is a final extension, a *reductio ad absurdum* of Stalinist policy. But that policy was a false departure from Marxist-Leninist doctrine and the violence of its enactment merely proves its bankruptcy. Therefore, the proper response to the Hungarian disaster does not imply an abandoment of Marxist first principles. On the contrary, we must return to those principles in their authentic formulation. Or as one of the insurrectionist leaders put it: 'Let us oppose the Red Army in the name of the Leningrad workers' Soviet of 1917.' Perhaps there is in this idea that old and most deceptive dream: communism divorced from the particular ambitions and obscurantism of Russian domination.

Lukács has always held himself responsible to history. This has enabled him to produce a body of critical and philosophic work intensely expressive of the cruel and serious spirit of the age. Whether or not we share his beliefs, there can be no doubt that he has given to the minor Muse of criticism a notable dignity. His late years of solitude and recurrent danger only emphasize what I observed at the outset: in the twentieth century it is not easy for an honest man to be a literary critic. But then, it never was.

➤ 'Critic'/'Reader' ➤

Some distinctions between *critic* and *reader* may be worth testing on the understanding that, for purposes of focus, these two terms are being used with fictive stringency, that they are being hypostatized.

It may be that the reciprocal relations of the 'critic' and of the 'reader' to the text are not only different but, in certain respects, antithetical. The critic is an epistemologist. This is to say that the distances between himself and the text are of themselves fertile and problematical. Insofar as these distances are made explicit and subject to investigation, they generate intermediate texts, or what are currently known as 'metatexts'. The separation between the critic and 'his' text — in what sense is it 'his'? — is reflexive. It makes sensible, it dramatizes its own inhibitory or translational status. 'Inhibition' and 'translation' are the cardinal and kindred categories of the critic's distancing. There are obstacles and opacities to be overcome or to be sharply delineated in the space between himself and the text. There are, conversely, translations to be made of his text into analogous or parodistic modes of statement (used neutrally, 'parodistic' is a legitimate notion, comprising as it does the whole range of critical restatements and interpretative parallels from punitive dismissal to mimetic enchantment). Inhibition and translation are cognate because it is the obstacle 'in front of' the text which compels circumvention and transfer ('translation'), which prevents the critic's total, exhaustive restatement and repetition of the original text. Such tautologous repetition, on the other hand, is one of the cardinal instances of 'reading'.

The critic argues his distance from and towards the text. To 'criticize' means to perceive at a distance, at the order of remove most appropriate to clarity, to *placement* (F. R. Leavis's term), to communicable intelligibility. The motion of criticism is one of 'stepping back from' in exactly the sense in which one steps back from a painting on a wall in order to perceive it better. But the good critic makes the motion conscious to himself and to his public. He details his recessional steps so as to make the resultant distance, the elucidative measure, the prescriptive perspective — distance entails 'angle' of vision — explicit, responsible, and, therefore, open to argument. It is this activation of distance between critic and object (the 'text' from which he is stepping back and which may, of course, be a painting, a musical composition, a piece of architecture) that makes all serious criticism epistemological. Criticism demands that we ask of and with it: 'How does perception traverse the chosen distance?' 'How was this particular distance chosen?' Examples of what is meant here are so ready as to trivialize the implicit issue. But for the sake of initial argument, consider the contrastive topographies, the contrastive mappings and measurements of a historicist nineteenth-century critic on the one hand, and of a New Critic — whose sight lines are those of the synchronic close-up, of Mallarmé's *distance abolie* — on the other.

Because it purposes adequation to its object, and clarity, because the distance established when the critic 'steps back' invites analysis, apologia, and didactic transmission to others — there are, since antiquity, received methodologies and 'schools' of criticism, manuals of the art, journals in which it is exercised — criticism is simultaneously epistemological and legislative.

The point is a central one, and the uses of *critique* in the Kantian idiom make it succinctly. We have said that the critic steps back from the object of perception in order to 'get closer to it' (focus, clarity, intelligibility are factors of direct access, of nearness to the relevant phenomenon). He establishes and argues distance in order to penetrate. He widens or narrows the aperture of vision so as to obtain a lucid grasp. This motion — we step back to come nearer, we narrow our eyes to see more fully — entails judgement. Why should this be? *Because action* (the critic's motion) *is not, cannot be indifferent.*

The point I am putting forward is not the suspect commonplace whereby there are supposed to be no value-free, no rigorously neutral perceptions — 'suspect' because it is, at least, arguable that one's perception of the correct solution of an equation is not, except in some quasi-mystical sense, a value judgement. No, what is meant here is something different. The critic is an activist of apprehension. His demarcation, his 'pacing' of the elucidative distance between himself and the 'text-object' is operative, instrumental, functional. Operation, instrumentality, or function are not, cannot be indifferent. Indifference does not act. Whether 'disinterestedness' does act is one of the questions ahead. The dynamic distancing of the critic is explicitly intentional. All critics in action are intentionalists whose *modus operandi* performs, emphatically, Husserl's model of cognition ('to perceive' at all is 'to intend'). The critic 'grasps'. He experiences and articulates a *prise de conscience*. His perception is *ein Vernehmen* ('an interpretative taking'). Etymologies are only naively demonstrative; but in these three banal instances, the radical of acquisition, of seizure, is obvious and illuminating. No grasp is indifferent; it assesses the worth of its object.

This allows a first rephrasing of our initial antimony: if critics are Husserlians, 'readers' are Heideggerians (but it is just this which needs to be shown).

It hardly needs saying that refusal, negative intentionality, rebuke, even ridicule are valuations in the full sense. The critic who turns away, who 'overlooks' a given object, is exercising judgement. He empties, he chooses to make inert the potentially vitalized space between perception and perceived. The history of criticism is replete with lifeless, atrophied spaces, even as museums are stocked with 'invisible' pictures. Each invisibility comports an accident or a history of negation. It takes positive inaction to establish, let alone sustain, a vacuum, a zone of unseeing. This inaction also is legislative. Whence a provisional truism: *criticism is ordering sight*. The act of critical viewing takes place in, it delimits and externalizes for argument, an intentional distance from the object. The good critic is one whose stepping back, whose 'making of space', is accountable. The good critic establishes his focal distance in a way which we too can measure, whose angles of incidence we can calibrate. His distance is one which we in turn can pace for ourselves. The underlying scheme of accountable motion is, very likely, geometrical, just as Husserl's scheme of the intentionality and intentional logic of cognition is geometrical. But when we say 'ordering sight', when we say 'placement', when we say *critique*, we say 'judgement'. We very nearly say, having for such assertion a mass of epistemological authority, that all clear seeing is judgement, that every perceptive motion is legislative – because it is act and motion. Can this truism be faulted or, at least, qualified in non-trivial ways? Are there orders of insight which do not 'grasp'? To ask this is to suggest a second way of starting this paper, of testing its conjecture of difference.

Ordering sight ('criticism') objectifies. To make this plain may help to remove the spurious problem of 'critical objectivity'. There never has been, there never can be any *objective criticism* in the proper sense of the term simply because, as we have seen, indifference, non-intentionality, cannot be a property of action. To adduce the patent relativity and instability of 'taste', to cite the historicity of every aesthetic ranking, is a boringly self-evident move. What needs to be understood is the rationale, the integral structure of the arbitrariness of all acts of criticism. No two distancings can be perfectly identical: a photograph can be reproduced, a facsimile can be made of an original, but the particular photographic act – the 'taking' of the picture – cannot be tautologically repeated. A given critical gymnastic – the style of 'the stepping back' from the given object – can methodize itself. It can seek to transmit its practice through didactic exemplification. We saw that there are schools and manuals of criticism. But no critical *reprise*, however scholastic, however servile – e.g. neo-Aristotelianism in the declining Renaissance, the *feuilleton* assembly lines after Sainte-Beuve, the mimes of Parisian semiotics today – is homologous with, is equivalent to the distancing which it seeks to perpetuate. Each and every act of criticism is an intentional specification. It is teleological in respect of the particular case – 'this painting', 'that piece of music', 'this text'. And the category of the teleological, of that which is focused by an act of choosing volition, cannot be 'objective'. It cannot be impartial or take a stance outside itself.

Ecstasy, the capacity or need to stand 'outside oneself', is a theological potential. It may be that the contrast between the teleological and the theological is a third way of phrasing the cut between 'critic' and 'reader'.

Active apprehension and the valuation, the normative placement of the object apprehended which it entails, have no claim to the status of independent facticity. Critical findings are historical facts. They may be psychological facts, though the notion of 'psychological' remains obscure and probably unsatisfactory in this context (as I. A. Richards came to admit). What is certain is that no critical judgement has 'factuality' in any logical, let alone experimentally verifiable, sense. The quest for a verifiable or falsifiable factuality in critical propositions has been a compendious chapter in the history of the art: in Aristotle, in Kant, in Taine, in the earlier Richards. But it remains a chapter of fertile error, of borrowed metaphors. No critical ruling can be refuted. Action knows reaction and counteraction, not refutation. Preference is undecidable. Balzac's suggestion that Mrs Radcliffe was an abler novelist than Stendhal, Tolstoy's considered conclusion that the major tragedies of Shakespeare are 'beneath criticism', the closely argued verdict of a generation of art critics in reference to Rosa Bonheur's superiority to Cézanne – these are not 'eccentricities' or 'lapses'. There can be no eccentricities where there is no stable centre, no 'lapse' where there is no axiomatic paradigm from which to fall. On the contrary: such prescriptive viewings are typological; they are highly instructive, insofar as they make salient the essence of arbitrariness and of free will in every act of ordering vision.

At the risk of repetition: there can be no grammatical, no logical, no statistical cancellation or falsification of the assertion that Shakespeare was a mediocre playwright or Mozart a third-rate composer. Formally and substantively, these are perfectly coherent, intelligible 'positionings' (*prises de position*) towards the relevant object. The fact – and are we always quite certain that it is a general fact? – that these particular postures are chosen or maintained by very few is of no importance. Epistemological spaces are not subject to the ballot. Time, moreover, shifts the statistical balance – essentially irrelevant as that balance may be – between the idiosyncratic and the commonplace. It is the fatality of today's avant-garde to house within itself tomorrow's postcards and art-school plaster casts. In turn, the prognostication that there will be a date at which the 'general consensus' will judge Mozart to have been a third-rate composer is strictly unfalsifiable. But it is a prognostication without inherent interest. It says nothing of the critical act that has judged otherwise. Equally vacant are the demonstrable statements that painters, authors, musicians once held to be mindless charlatans are, now, sanctified (Van Gogh, Joyce, Wagner). Such data belong to the history of criticism. But the critical act, the deed of ordering sight and the space of intentional legislation which it generates, have no history. They are synchronic.

Aristotle's placement of Euripides as 'the most tragic' is fully available and instrumental today. This is to say that implicit distancing, the focus chosen – in this example, it is a focus directed preferentially at the density of relative pathos among the three principal tragedians – can be adopted, can be 'paced out' at present. By the same token, Matthew Arnold on Keats or T. S. Eliot on Baudelaire will be functional tomorrow. Vision has historical, social, local (perhaps even physiological) context: but there is a precise sense in which it does not date. It can be rebuked, countermanded, censored, ridiculed, labelled as statistically null. But it cannot be superseded. To declare that Hanslick was 'wrong' about Wagner, whatever 'wrong' may signify in such an assertion, is not to supersede his finding.

Does this wilful, always singular format of the critical act mean that every sighting is equally worthwhile? Are some valuations more authoritative than others? Or is irrefutability – one cannot conceivably prove that Balzac was mistaken in regard to Stendhal or that abstract art may not be a confidence trick – evidence that all judgement is inherently anarchic? I have never seen a convincing answer to this possibility. The answers given are purely contingent. They tell us what constitutes a 'good critic'. But 'range', 'style', innovative commitment, influence, etc., are merely attributes or *post hoc* ornaments. They are not primaries. They have no probative force. They are opinions on opinion. Perhaps the hoary dilemma can be rephrased.

The useful critic does two things. First, he makes the tenor of his arbitrariness transparent. The angle of his ordering vision is clearly manifest. There are as many rational, arguable spaces as there are geometries. The critic may adopt a posture whose configuration – the word *figura* allows the right overlap between gesture and symbolic code – is mainly moralistic. He can step back from the object and ask: Of what benefit is it to man and society? Is it finally educative? Is it life-enhancing in its implicit or explicit proposals? (*Mutatis mutandis*, Platonism, Tolstoy's position, or that of Leavis exemplify this aesthetic, or more properly speaking, 'anti-aesthetic'.) The critic may function at distances and perspectives which are historicist, biographical in the old sense, psychoanalytic in the new, Marxist, or formalist. His mapping may be largely rhetorical (in a genuinely inventive vein, this would be something like Kenneth Burke's 'space' of ordering sight). He can be – more often than not, he is – eclectic and variable in his adjustments of focus and aperture. 'Critical impressionism' is no less rigorous than 'engagement' or 'determinism' (i.e. Sainte-Beuve is no less rigorous a critic than Lukács or Derrida, if we attach to 'rigorous' any clear connotations of proof or refutability). His is merely a different stylization of the critical exercise, a different 'choreography' and, therefore, distancing between points. But whatever his stance of intentionality, the useful critic offers this stance for identification. He must render unmistakable its partiality (in *parti pris* we again find the key notion of 'seizure'). *Partiality*, in this context, has two main meanings. Every geometry, every argued space of perception, is only one of a set of alternatives which may be formally unbounded (it may well be the case that *anything* can be said of *anything*). It is, therefore, incomplete, 'partial'. Secondly, however catholic the critic's temper, however embracing the largess of his receptivities, his every act of ordering sight is, can only be, 'partial' in the sense of being biased. It stems from one particular angle. As there is no such thing as indifferent action, so there is no such thing as impartial ('objective') criticism. Only immobility is unbiased. But in good criticism, bias is made visible, is made lucid to itself.

The honest critic does a second thing: he ranks (criticism is *ordering* sight). In the arbitrariness which is the epistemological condition of his *métier*, he includes the concept of 'arbiter', of *arbitrage* between values. The intentionality of his vision, the act of assuming a stance in front of one object rather than another, is by definition preferential and discriminatory. Whether explicitly, in the magisterial vein, or implicitly, via the functional trope of an 'epiphany' (the object reveals and imposes itself upon the viewer), the critic's placement is hierarchical. Euripides, rules Aristotle, 'is the most tragic'; it follows necessarily that Aeschylus and Sophocles were less so. 'Dante and Shakespeare divide western literature between them, there is no third', says T. S. Eliot. His verdict is diacritical; it relegates all other poets to a more slender status. The semantics of criticism are inescapably comparative. To perceive normatively is to compare. It is to assay contrastively, a praxis evident in the Arnoldian term *touchstone*.

Thus it is mere cant to profess that a critic ought not to enter the *bourse*, that he ought not to provide market quotations, leaving such concerns to the 'reviewer'. The critic, however eminent, however theoretic in bias, assigns and ascribes valuations every time he views and designates. He may do so with a complexity of motives and with a heuristic care far beyond those of ephemeral marking or fashion. He may, in other words, be an august broker rather than a harried jobber on the floor of the exchange (though the line is always fluid; where, for instance, would we draw it in the works of Hazlitt or of Edmund Wilson?). But no less than the reviewer, the critic is a marker. He marks down – in the 1930s and 1940s the term was 'he dislodges' – Milton, and marks up Donne. He 'rates' Hölderlin above, say, Mörike; he underwrites new issues, such as the modernist movement, as being more productive, as offering a higher yield to attention and sensibility than the late Romantics or Georgians. The instruments of criticism, teaches Coleridge, are 'speculative instruments'. Critical scrutiny values and compares. In 'speculation' inhere perception as well as the forward gamble of conjecture.

And because his 'job of work' (R. P. Blackmur's humbling phrase) is always derivative, because it is often punitive and facile as compared to that of the artist, the good critic is one who will run speculative risks. He will declare his interests and lay himself open to loss. This loss can take various forms: the contempt of the artist whom he is criticizing, the indifference of the market to the values which he proposes, the ridicule or oblivion which later history will visit on his judgements. This declaration of interest and speculative commitment produces a listing (a series of 'quotations' in a sense familiar to both the *bourse* and the life of letters). It produces 'the great tradition', 'the hundred best books', 'the modern masters'. In this ineluctable context vulgarity can be compensated for, and then only in part, by the critic's nerve, by his readiness to invest even more in a sinking share if such investment represents his lucid conviction. The 'classic' in literature is the 'blue chip', 'the gilt-edge', that has long been priced as such by the market. No real critic can or will seek to escape the crassness and fallibilities of choice.

The critic's listing establishes a 'syllabus'. The teleology of a syllabus is economic. It instructs us, even by virtue of omission, on what texts we should expend time and the resources of feeling, and what other texts would constitute waste. The notorious footnote in *The Great Tradition*, cautioning the reader that among all of Dickens's novels only *Hard Times* repays adult interest, is a graphic example of this 'economy of syllabus'. So are the reading lists handed out to generations of undergraduates, lists on which particular chapters are often cited with the manifest inference that the remainder of the book does not merit investment. The apologia for a syllabus is one of purgation: vital space is cleansed and conserved for the 'enduring', for the 'authentic', for the 'classical'. Dead or noxious matter is set aside. Too many canvases, canvases hung too close, inhibit ordering sight. A museum is an ocular syllabus; hence its crowded basements or rummage rooms. The critic selects and 'prices' so as to narrow our options towards excellence, so as to minimize waste motion.

The 'reader' does not aim at a syllabus, but at a 'canon'. This is a fourth stab at articulating the polarity which my argument is testing. 'Canon', of course, remains to be defined.

I have said that ordering sight 'objectifies'. I have tried to show that such objectification in criticism has nothing to do with the phantasm of 'objectivity' — which would be pure stasis, a zero point. What then is meant by 'objectification', by the assertion that it is of the nature of criticism to see that which it sees as an object? It means simply that the *telos*, the thing aimed at by the act of ordering perception, is a datum, a *donné*. It is 'out there', at a distance, at an angle, in a perspective which criticism determines with a view to intelligibility and estimate. This 'givenness' of the object or text as it presents itself for circumspection, elucidation, and judgement, this 'out-thereness', is a definitional platitude. How can there be sight if there is not something 'out there' to be seen, to be stopped, as it were, in front of? But if it is a platitude, it is one of considerable epistemological and ethical consequence.

The fundamental postulate of the critical act is one of realism. The critic cannot operate in a solipsistic, in a rigorously Fichtean, scheme. He cannot collapse subject and object. Were he to do so, there would be no distance at which, 'across which', to exercise ordering sight. Glued to the canvas, the eye would be blind. One can go further: the critical postulate is one of materialism (and it is just this which underlies the discomforts of Platonism when attempting to deal with poetry and the arts). The painting, the piece of music, the text have a material status. They are significant substances. In respect of material artifacts in the 'naive' sense — pictures on wood or canvas, statues hewn of stone or cast in bronze — the primal materialism or substantiality has never been problematic. The art critic finds no handicap in including in the co-ordinates of evaluative reflex such dimensions as pigments, fabric, texture, and so on. It is, moreover, only this epistemological materialism which validates the whole concept, so compelling in western sentiment and in the art market, of some radical difference between the original and even the most faithful of copies or reproductions. Contrastively, we shall see that in the epistemology of 'reading', the copy, the act of copying, may prove to be equivalent to that of creation.

In the case of a language object (a text), the postulate of materiality may seem elusive. And, certainly, the analogies so often drawn between literature on the one hand and painting or sculpture on the other are insipid or inexact. It is only in esoteric or historically decidable instances that the literal substance of the text — epigraphy, watermark, impression — has any immediate critical bearing. Critical grasp does not consider whether its object is quarto or folio size, and the valuation of a text is indifferent as to its first edition or the most mechanical of reproductions. Nevertheless, the language object is an object, a datum 'out there'. This means that the cardinal qualifiers of objective existence do apply to it. The verbal material has been 'produced'; it is, properly, a fabrication. It can, indeed it must, be located in immanence.

The 'reader' is answerable to the possibility of 'transcendence' rather than of immanence. This is, possibly, a fifth way of stating the disjunction which this essay aims at.

The immanent character of the objects of criticism can be categorized variously. The customary rubric is historical. The text was produced, encoded, and made public by this or that author in this or that place and time. It embodies — *embodiment* signifying at this point, and provisionally, not a synonym for but rather a contrary to *incarnation* — a particular selection from the totality of the linguistic raw material and constraints available to the given author. Recent emphasis by Marxist, sociological, or semiotic critics on the economic structures of all 'textuality' — texts are manufactured, they compete for attention in the market, they are objects of merchandising, consumption, and accumulation — only dramatizes an obvious constant. So does the modish notion of *écriture*. However exalted by intent of style and address, a text is indeed an artifact, a 'piece' of language materially cognate with any other piece of language. Thus, when the structuralist-semiotic critic tells us that the poem is part of a seamless continuum with each and every semantic, scriptive act — the bill of lading, the piece of advertisement copy, the most mundane of notations — all of which are, like itself, *écriture*, he is only rephrasing (and trivializing) the postulate of materialism implicit in perceptual objectivization.

He reiterates this same postulate, this time more cogently, when he reminds us that ordering sight (criticism) can be understood as a branch of a more general 'theory of information'. When matter matters, it informs. Hence the critic's legitimate interest in 'how the thing is put together', in the anatomy of its composition and history of its manufacture. The art critic seeks to bring to light the initial sketch, the parts of the canvas painted over in successive manipulations. The literary critic and the critic-musicologist ponder drafts and cancellations. The inherent commitment is that made to temporal, historical substance (to immanence). The postulate is that of the objective reality of compositional process. The critic is a 'geneticist' (where it may be that the 'reader' is an 'ontologist'. This would be a sixth antinomy). In a way which tends to go unnoticed, this compositional perspective is also an assumption of contingency. The art object, the piece of music, the text 'out there', with its historical genesis, might not have been; or it might have been altogether otherwise. It 'happens to be' — which does not mean, to be sure, that its phenomenal emergence in this or that location, at this or that date, in one or another milieu, ought not to be investigated and, so far as is possible, explained. But there is not in the production of artifacts, as the objectivization of the critic's ordering sight perceives them, any formal or substantive imperative of inevitability. There is, even at the 'sublime' reach, a realization of occasion, an occasionality in the strict sense of the term.

So far, I have tried to make arguable and, in consequence, non-trivial, two main propositions. The critic functions at a certain distance. The determination (and honest explication) of this distance, the space in and through which his purposive action is executed, are the integral facts of his ordering, legislative sight. Secondly, I have said that he is distant from and 'distant *to*' an object, a substance which he finds and situates 'out there'. He focuses on, he sights and appraises 'something' which is a particular, contingent presence. In this classical scenario, there is no fusion between perceiver and perceived. The critic after Aristotle is a realist in just that formally elusive but pragmatically unwavering sense in which Kant is a realist when he states in the *Critique of Pure Reason* (sec. 3): 'Our exposition establishes the *reality*, that is, the objective validity, of space in respect of whatever can be represented to us outwardly as object.' Common sense is the working hypothesis, the underwriter of cognitive distance. It authorizes the conviction that the painting will not disappear when the viewer turns away from it, that there is a run-of-the-mill sense in which its existence, if not its cultural status, is independent of notice.

We have seen that there are many and diverse ways in which the critic can assume his stance, and that these ways generate many and diverse 'spaces' or conventions of vision (even as there are many geometries in which the 'same' objects can be diversely situated and described). But whereas, in the case of alternative geometric mappings, such location and description remain formally neutral and, as topology teaches us, interchangeable, the intentionality of the critic's vision, the purposiveness of his act, entail very different relations to the object. The point is an obvious one, but needs to be made carefully. Different critical postures (methodologies, analytical presuppositions, metavocabularies) pertain to practice, to 'how ordering sight' is initiated and performed. Relations, as they are realized within and across the chosen distance, pertain to motive, to 'why it is' that the critic does his essentially derivative, parasitic 'job of work'. Modern physics tells us that we cannot separate the concept of a 'space' from that which takes place in it. And there is a strong sense in which the 'how' and the 'why' of the act of criticism are also conjoined. Nevertheless, the objectivization that comes of the realistic epistemology of criticism is a more general, a more diffuse category than motive. And it is only if we look more closely at motive that we can define more exactly in what way art or literature becomes an object not only 'of' but 'for' criticism.

Patently, there can be as many sorts of motivation as there are critics. There are, however, compendious and usefully vague chapter headings under which the different purposive relations enacted by critical practice can be registered. These would, roughly and readily, include political relations, exemplary-didactic relations, relations whose motor force is primarily philosophically investigative, relations which I would call 'dramatically reproductive', ceremonially propagandistic relations, relations of irony or chastisement. Given the summary scope of this discussion, these and kindred types of critical relation, of the intentionality of different ways of seeing, can only be stenographed – and the citation of names is an unavoidable shorthand.

'Political' is too loose a tag altogether; but one would take it as enveloping those orderings and assessments of the critical object according to its positive or disabling agency in a larger public scheme. Plato would posit this scheme to be the state; for Tolstoy it would be the enforcement of personal and communal altruism; in Lukács's model the scheme is 'history'; in that of Sartre, the realization of 'freedom'. But note that there is, within certain flexible limits, independence as between method and motive: a Platonic purpose can be generated by a New Critical exegesis; 'structuralism' can be either of the 'right' or of the 'left'; Sartre modulates from a historicist to a largely psycho-analytical angle of decipherment. The 'exemplary-didactic' relation overlaps at numerous points with the 'political'; but it shows a more pronounced 'scholastic' edge. I have in mind the Aristotelian programme for the induction and transmission to the audience of states of cognitive and emotive poise (a 'politics of feeling'); Schiller's doctrine of the aesthetic as the principal vehicle of the nurture of civic sensibility; Matthew Arnold's view of high literature as a 'criticism of life' from whose radiant ambience and energies a society acquires moral and executive style.

By 'investigative' in the philosophical vein, one would understand the modes of criticism whose purpose is the explication of an art object or text in terms of its specific nature, operant substance, and phenomenal status. Here the proceedings of the critic belong fairly to the more general class of aesthetics. To divorce the critical motive from the philosophical-theoretic one in, say, Kant, Croce, Walter Benjamin, or Burke would be to urge an empty nomenclature. What I mean by 'dramatically reproductive' relations in criticism are those in which the critic's delineation and judgement of the object are achieved by a kind of mimesis, performative encapsulation, or parallel presentment of that object. The critic's own text is a 'retelling of the thing' with an evaluative appendage. It is the 'summary +' of the plot, the description of the painting or the verbal equivocation – taking this word in its worrying sense – of the piece of music. (When Schumann, on the contrary, offered an explicative critique of a composition by replaying it *in toto* he was, I think, exemplifying the cardinal distinction between 'critic' and 'reader'.) In dramatically reproductive criticism, illustration, quotation, are of the essence. The critic quotes strategically so as to make his point, so as to achieve persuasive economy. His critique is a summation towards judicial ends; quotations are the exhibits it offers in evidence. If philosophical criticism is a branch of aesthetics, performative or mimetic criticism is one of the multiple forms of applied rhetoric. At a guess, one would say that this form comprises nine-tenths of the craft. It stretches from the iceberg mass of daily reviewing – the 'art critic', 'the book critic', 'the music critic' in the media – all the way to such undoubted pinnacles of judicial re-enactment and summation as Samuel Johnson's discourse on Shakespeare or T. S. Eliot's on Dante. But it may be that Eliot on Dante is inspired criticism, whereas Mandelstam on Dante is 'reading'.

Very often this almost ubiquitous order of criticism will have praise as its motive. The aim of the act of ordering sight is to advance the fortunes, to strengthen the impact of a given piece of work or movement. In its hectoring innocence, the communist term *agitprop* strikes the appropriate note. It would characterize Zola's polemics on behalf of Manet, Ezra Pound for modernism, G. Wilson Knight in propagation of Byron's moral fineness. Each of these viewers is, in the given case, a virtuoso of celebration. The contrastive category is that of a critical distancing calculated ('motivated') to diminish, to strip bare, even to eradicate the object – i.e. to bring about its removal from the syllabus, from the public gallery to the basement. This is Apollo's musical critique of Marsyas, Pope's vivisection of Grub Street and his editorial competitors such as Theobald, or Leavis in pursuit of Auden. Though antithetical in purpose, festive advocacy and chastisement are both a part of the general class of 'presentational' or performative critical practice.

Even a thumbnail sketch of these different orders of critical motive raises an obvious question: Can anything useful be said of a phenomenology so various that it includes Aristotle's *Poetics*, Hegel's lessons on the philosophy of art, Baudelaire on Wagner, and I. A. Richards on Coleridge at one end, and the pandemonium of daily academic-journalistic market quotations at the other? The inchoate plurality is undeniable. But so, I believe, is the presence of certain 'primals' and constants. These derive from the epistemology of objectivization.

Distancing objectifies; or to use a term which is in vogue but which is accurate: it *reifies* (*es verdinglicht*). The object of the critical act, be the motives for this act diagnostic or mimetic, laudatory or punitive, is seen as and thus made a 'thing'. Criticism resorts perpetually to the notion of 'living art', of 'vitality', of the 'life-force' in music or poetry. It has, since the *Poetics*, made of the 'organic' both an explicative criterion and an ideal. But these invocations of vitalism are instrumental fictions. For purposes of ordering perception, of placement and verdict, the critical object is reified. One does not anatomize and label living tissue; or, note again the demonstration by Schumann of the antithesis between a musicological presentation, however instinct with approval and analytic authority on the one hand, and the replaying of the piece on the other. Secondly, we have seen that the distance between critic and object is activated by motive. Now whatever the order of intention, the relation established is, in the first place, derivative. The critic, whether he comes to dissect or to mime, to praise or to negate, relates to 'that which is there before him' — in which self-evident proposition 'before' carries both its locative and its temporal meanings. The object existed in time before the critic came upon it, even if this precedence is only one of a few hours as in the case of the journalist-reviewer. Therefore, the ground of being, the raison d'être of even the most formidable and far-reaching of critical arguments is the precedent status of the art object or text. The Sophoclean versions of Oedipus are prior to the *Poetics*; the *Lyrical Ballads* come before the brilliancies of Coleridge's 'practical criticism' in which so much of the modern technique of vision is rooted; Marvell's poems long antedate T. S. Eliot's insights. All criticism is posterior, and this sequent status is not only temporal but existential. The work of art, the text, the musical composition exists not only prior to the ordering sight of the critic; it can exist without it.

No critic is, either formally or in fact, the cause of that which he perceives and relates to.

This existential posteriority, this dependence of the perceptual and normative act on the prior and autonomous nature of the object, signifies that all criticism is, ontologically, *parasitic*. The Platonic paradigm makes graphic the degree of derivation. The carpenter imitates the Idea of the table. The painter mimes this mimesis whose literal form he can neither execute nor judge properly. The critic of the painting expatiates at fourth hand on the mimicry of a shadow. But even in any less caustic model of the orders of executive action and perception, the dependent, ancillary, occasional – because 'occasioned from outside' – nature of all critical vision and utterance is manifest. *The critic is not the maker.* That such a platitude requires emphasis and may even take on polemic resonance is a symptom of the absurdities and reversals of value prominent in today's academy and in the current condition of letters. Sainte-Beuve was morosely right in saying that no one was raising statues to critics; but he may have been a bad prophet.

The reification of the object of criticism and the *necessarily* (not accidentally, not remediably) parasitic nature of the critic's response to this object, determine a fundamental instability in the whole enterprise. Simultaneously criticism judges (even where adjudication is one of hyperbolic acclaim) and knows itself to be a secondhand, an epiphenomenal act. From this asymmetry comes the absolutely central fact that all criticism is, in a certain sense, 'adversative to' its object. This needs to be spelled out clearly. Even where its programme is one of epiphany, of disclosure through placement and praise, even where it seems itself to be the devoted outrider and herald to the work of art, criticism stands not only 'outside' and 'after' its cause: it stands 'against' it. It is, to use Kenneth Burke's pivotal designation, a *counter-statement* to it.

And precisely because it knows itself to be simultaneously magisterial and parasitic, prescriptive and dependent, normative and occasional, criticism harbours inside itself strong solicitations to autonomy. The more lucid it is about its own existential secondhandedness, the more unavoidably will criticism be under pressure of the impulse towards integral status. Implicit in all criticism, not by virtue of historical accident or culpable vanity, but as an ineluctable condition of its being, is the instinct for autonomy. Consciously or not, criticism labours to transcend relation. Criticism contains, at its methodological and intentional core, the potentiality, paradoxical, even absurd in regard to logic, of existing 'beyond' its object. It experiences a constant temptation to make of its object not the necessary and sufficient cause of its own existence, but a mere starting point and receding suggestion. Thus it exhibits a precise drive towards usurpation: it would work away from its own existential derivativeness and take on the ontological primacy of its cause.

This is the aetiology and underlying explanation of the present-day character and hypertrophy of criticism, particularly in reference to literature. The current scene is little short of ludicrous. In the academy and the media, the critic has a prepotent, monumentalized station. Critical methodologies, with spurious claims to theoretical profundity and performative rigour, are multiplied and offered to secondary and tertiary investigation (there are critics of criticism, journals of 'dia'- and 'meta'-criticism in which critics dispute the merits of each other's jargon; there are university qualifications in criticism). In a mode of narcissist terrorism, criticism now proposes to 'deconstruct' and to 'disseminate' the text, to make of the text the labile, ultimately contingent source of its own prepotent display. Such display is sustained by the construction of metalanguages of autistic violence and obscurity. The resultant terror and mist envelop the text object to the point of deliberate effacement. The act of criticism has 'ingested' its object (Ben Jonson's term for parasitic consumption) and now stands autonomous. There are, indeed, specific historical and sociological grounds for this cancerous and inflationary condition. There are local, temporal reasons why criticism today occupies a status unequalled since the Alexandrian scholiasts and grammatologists (there being in both periods a concomitant enfeeblement of literature). But the potentiality of this inversion of values as between the critic and the prior object is implicit in *all* criticism. It has been there from the start. The implication is a necessary and dynamic entailment of the fact that criticism is competitive with the object of its ordering sight, that the critic is not, as the cliché would have it, a failed artist, but a 'counterstater' and rival to the work.

Undoubtedly, moreover, it is the case that a fair amount of criticism takes on autonomy by force of expression. The relevant sections in Coleridge's *Biographia Literaria* are 'literature' in a sense not drastically removed from that which we attach to the poetry they analyse and judge. Criticism can outlast its object by virtue of material hazard: many of the paintings and statues viewed and judged by Vasari have now disappeared. Or criticism may do so because the stature of the critic is, pragmatically, greater than that of the author. Who but the specialist now reads the minor poets about whom Samuel Johnson found memorable points to make? But such supersedures should be accidental, involuntary, arising from factors outside the critic's purpose and control. 'Planned supersession' – the critic's determination to fix his voraciousness on minor or enfeebled objects such as an inferior Balzac novella, the rhapsodies of Lautréamont, a *kitsch* film – is a methodologically and ethically vitiated turn. Subconsciously, perhaps, it seeks compensation, even vengeance for its own parasitism on the object which is, eternally, its precedent and cause of being. Such vengeance can be effective. We are surrounded, currently, by minor or spurious texts which criticism has exploitatively aggrandized, and by major art and texts which criticism has diminished or obscured. We direct students to T. S. Eliot's criticism on Dante; we do not direct them to reading the *Commedia divina*. 'Criticism' and 'reading' grow apart.

Now, unquestionably, parasitism is necessary to life. The bird pecking clean the hide and wounds of the rhinoceros is performing a delicate, vital piece of work. The critic *is* necessary to the life of art and letters. But it is because he is, in significant respects, of an identical species with his host, with his carrier and raison d'être, that this symbiosis breeds ambivalence and usurpation. The solicitation to betrayal, through an act of sight which 'screens' instead of elucidating, through narcissism of theory and idiom, through masked or outright misprision (the critic can bear false witness *and* be hanging judge in a tribunal of his own devising), is always present. It is of the essence of the critical relation. It is, probably, for this reason that great criticism relates to its cause in an intimacy of peculiar sadness.

❖ 2 ❖

Roughly half a dozen contrastive pairings have come up in relation to the initial polarization: 'critic' as against 'reader'. They include the dissociation between an epistemological and an ontological base (a Husserlian bias on the one hand, a Heideggerian one on the other). We saw that there may be a significant difference between the establishment of a 'syllabus' and the acceptance of a 'canon', between objectivizations of the text whose presuppositions are realistic-immanent, and those which draw on a category of transcendence. The teleological motion of criticism, its purposive economies, may differ from the theological tenor of the guarantor or 'third party' implicated in the act of 'reading'. Operative in and through these contrarieties is the intimation of an essential distinction between the judicial authority of the critic, his normative placement of the text or art object at and from an argued distance, and the 'dynamic passivity' or sufferance of the 'reader' who is, where 'reading' achieves its plenitude, the 'one being read'.

These suggestions concerning the 'reader' are admittedly vague and portentous. It is easy to say something about criticism worth looking at and/or disagreeing with. It is difficult to say anything useful about 'reading' in the sense in which this paper seeks to articulate the term. Criticism is discursive and breeds discourse. 'Reading' yields no primary impulse towards self-communication. The 'reader' who discourses is, in a certain manner, in breach of privilege. The surest testimonials we have to major acts of reading tend to be oblique; they tend to be tangential in exactly the sense in which Walter Benjamin, himself a master reader, argues that great translation is tangential to the vulgate meaning of the original. Reading is done rather than spoken about (one of the very few convincing narrations of the act of reading, of *une lecture bien faite et plénière*, that I know of, is to be found in Péguy's *Dialogue de l'histoire et de l'âme païenne*, another in Nadezhda Mandelstam's memoirs; but both of these are narrations, not analyses, not attempts at methodological abstraction 'from outside'). The antinomies, the play of irreconcilable difference, no less than the mystery of interrelation, lie between Narcissus and Echo. Again, this is to invoke the metaphoric. Nevertheless, the diacritical 'cuts' I have listed may, in part at least, be worth arguing more closely.

To the 'reader', in which designation I include whosoever's apprehension of a text, of art, of music, of formed motion is not, is not primarily, that of the critic's legislative sighting, the 'otherness' met with is not 'a thing out there', is not, first and foremost, an 'object'. Now it is perfectly true that criticism also has queried, imaged, metaphorized the 'non-objective' phenomenological status of the poem, the painting, the piece of music. Criticism too will often ascribe to the matter of its speculative and judicial concerns a singular epistemological nature, a kind of 'third realm' in Popper's suggestive terminology. Certain schools of criticism have been more than willing to grant that 'great art' has, by virtue of its inspirational genesis, unrepeatability, formal inexhaustibility, and energies of impact, a substantive mode other than that of, say, natural or manufactured objects. But for the critic this extra-territoriality remains a preliminary concession to be made in respect of aesthetic and psychological unknowns ('unknowns', as it were, yet to be discovered). It is a concession which does not inhibit the exercise of delineation and of judgement.

The 'reader', by contrast, inhabits the provisional — in which manifold term he recognizes as relevant the notions of 'gift', of 'that which serves vision', and of that which 'nourishes' indispensably. He situates himself within, rather than traversing it with conventional concession and lógical embarrassment, the supposition that the text, the work of art, the musical composition are *data* not in the 'scientific' or realistically objectivized sense, but in the primary and archaic signification of 'that which is given to us'. That they are not 'objects' even in a special 'aesthetic' category, but 'presences', 'presentments' whose existential 'thereness' (Heidegger's word) relates less to the organic, as it does in Aristotelian and Romantic poetics and theories of art, than it does to the 'transubstantiational'. The adjective, as well as the concept aimed at, are almost hopelessly pompous and awkward. But the evidence whereby meaning and experience can be attached to them is not negligible. What is implicit is the notion and expression of 'real presence'. The reader proceeds *as if* the text was the housing of forces and meanings, of meanings of meaning, whose lodging within the executive verbal form was one of 'incarnation'. He reads *as if* — a conditionality which defines the 'provisional' temper of his pursuit — the singular presence of the life of meaning in the text and work of art was 'a real presence' irreducible to analytic summation and resistant to judgement in the sense in which the critic can and must judge. But a presentness, a presence of what?

There are different 'as ifs', different modes of provisionality, as there are different configurations and styles of focus in criticism. Authority for the intimation of a 'real presence' can be sought from the Platonic or Romantic trope of 'mantic inspiration'. The art object is *not* an object in any normal sense because it springs out of a mystery of alien ingress, out of the *daimon*'s rush into the momentary vacancy of man's reason and identity. *Poiesis*, the poet's, the singer's inventions, are imperatives from without. The products of true art have in them the live vestiges of transcendent intrusion. A variant on this trope is that of the sacramental as it obtains in the reading and exegesis of 'revealed' texts (where 'revelation' can, but need not be, transmitted by dictation as it is in the paradigmatic account of the rhapsode in Plato's *Ion*). The relevant presumption is that of an inherence, however esoteric, however eroded or possibly falsified by human transcription, of a 'spirit' in, 'behind', the letter. It is just this presumption which underwrites the concept of the 'iconic', the belief that the icon is not so much a representation of the sacred person or scene as it is the immediate manifestation, the epiphany of that person or scene. In other words, the latter are 'really present' to the beholder not by virtue of a voluntary imaginative concession or transposition on the beholder's part, but because *they* have taken dwelling in the icon. A third model of 'inherence' is that provided by the application of an absolute philosophic ontology to aesthetics. It is that which justifies Heidegger's ascription of a total *Dasein*, of a total 'presentness of being', to the worn pair of boots in the Van Gogh painting. As Heidegger urges, the 'real presence' of these boots on or 'within' the canvas is of an order and intensity, of a phenomenological necessity, denied not only to this or that actual pair of boots but denied as well to the most rigorous chemical-functional analysis of 'what it is that boots are made of and for' (a complete reversal of the Platonic scheme of third-hand mimesis and of the naive realism operative in 'criticism').

The enabling models which authorize a reader to assign iconic status to his text vary. But singly or together, they allow him to grasp concretely and to organize his experience of the text in accord with a class of assertions made by writers and artists themselves (assertions to which the 'critic' can only concede a rhetorical validity). In this class, I would include Michelangelo's witness: 'Se il mio rozzo martello i duri sassi forme d'uman aspetto or questo or quello, dal ministro, ch'l guida iscorge e tiello, prendendo il moto va con gli altrui passi.' ('When my rough hammer transforms hard stone to this or that figure of human shape, it moves solely by the volition of Him who guides it; it follows solely in His path.') Or Tolstoy's testimony to Katkov, that Anna Karenina 'had broken away from him', that the imagined persona had taken on autonomous will and being (*va con gli altrui passi*) outside of, indeed against the novelist's design and understanding. Or one might include the arcadian arrogance of Picasso's: 'I never seek, I only find.' In each of these and innumerable analogous cases, the apprehension undergone by the 'begetter' and the reader is of a kind which entails perception and invites terror (both are active in 'to apprehend').

The ascription, even where it remains only a provisional constant, of 'real presence' to the text, means that the reader's engagement with the text is not 'objectifying', that it cannot be a relationship of reification, of competition, and, by logical extension, of supersedure. The reader opens himself to the autonomous being of the text. The dialectic of encounter and of vulnerability (the text can bring drastic hurt) is one in which the ontological core of the text, its presentness of inward being, both reveals and makes itself hidden. This pulsing motion is a familiar one. As we come to know the text, the painting, the piece of music better, as we become more at home in its idiom, there is always more which seems to elude us. Echo draws us inward with a deepening intimation of understanding as yet unfulfilled. Phrased in this way, the observation is routinely psychological. But when the true source of this apparently contradictory pulse of disclosure and concealment is assigned to the text, to the work of art, the presumption is one of 'real presence'. In the iconic text, as this text 'comes upon' the reader, there is both 'sense' and 'force' (*Sinn* and *Kraft* are the two cardinal markers in Frege's theory of meaning, serving to suggest how it is that the sentence carries significations and immediately comprehensible directions much beyond those manifest in the individual, interchangeable word). Such essential excess of meaning characterizes the order of texts or art forms with which the reader engages. All serious aesthetics aims to elucidate what can be termed, to borrow a Marxist econometric vocabulary, the phenomenon of 'surplus value', of the 'forces' in and beyond 'sense' generated by art.

Where the act of reading is sufficiently apprehensive of the ontological pulse in the text, of the concomitant motion of radiance and withdrawal, it will register both the purity and the irreducibility of the pertinent 'force'. *Purity* in this context means essential disinterestedness. The raison d'être of the painting or poem or musical composition being only being, I say 'essential' because, of course, the notion invoked here is, again, a more or less fictive absolute. Even the highest art can involve impurities of motive, such as didacticism, social occasion, public or private record, and so on. But where there is the 'presentness' which I have been implying, these mundanities of motive and performance will not, finally, determine the status and force of the work. Often, in fact, this autonomous force in the work will come to refute the voluntary programme, the temporal meaning with which the artist invested his material. Though he proceeds from an altogether different orientation, Marx seized on precisely this internal dialectic when he noted that the effects, the agencies of survival in Balzac's novels were the ideological negation of those which the writer had purposed.

'Irreducibility' signifies 'non-paraphrasability', the untranslatability of an iconic presence into any other form without loss and estrangement (where 'sense' can be preserved, 'force' cannot). As lived by the true reader, the text is irreducible to, inexhaustible by, even the most penetratively diagnostic, explicative of visions – be they linguistic, grammatological, semiotic, historicist, sociological, 'deconstructive', or what you will. The text can be restated, as Schumann restates the piece of music. There is, in consequence, a sense in which much of 'reading' is reiteration; but the reader's repetition (his 'asking again') is not the critic's quotation. It aims not at illustrative excision from, but at complete re-entry into the text. Whether such re-entry can ever be wholly achieved, whether facsimile is ever total, is a dilemma which long exercised scribes and ministrants. The evident reason for the irreducibility of the iconic is that that which declares and conceals itself in the text or canvas or musical structure is of the order of being rather than of meaning, or, more accurately, that it has force incarnate in but also in excess of sense. It 'is' before it 'means', and the meaning(s) we derive from it are a function of its disinterested autonomy of existence — an existence which does not address itself to any particular beholder but must be met with by him (the Angel was not looking for Jacob). It is this immediate infolding of meaning into force of being which makes of music the most 'iconic', the most 'really present' essent known to man. It follows that music is also that which most absolutely resists paraphrase or translation. But infolding and resistance of this kind characterize all living texts and art.

To summarize: the 'reader's' contiguities to the text are ontological rather than epistemological, as are the 'critic's'. The reader does not encounter or aim at objectivization, but at implication in the possibility, in the 'as if' of a real presence. He knows that the meanings which he obtains from his text are always partial, always ambiguously external, that they are, at best, a bonus of being. René Char puts it more concisely: 'La vitalité du poète n'est pas une vitalité de l'au-delà mais un point diamanté *actuel* de présences transcendantes et d'orages pèlerins.' Authentic reading momentarily fixes transcendence.

'Contiguities', as used above, need to be looked at. The critic keeps his distance. This retention is the condition of his ordering, magisterial focus. The reader attempts to negate the space between the text and himself. He would be penetrated by, immersed in its presentness. The reader strives for fusion with the text via internalization. And here we arrive at a first disjunction in the general category and dialectic of reading. Internalization is eminently feasible in respect of texts and of music; but only partly so in the case of art objects. At its primary and most radical level, the thorough act of reading, the full apprehension of the *présences transcendantes* in language and music, entails memorization. The act of learning *by heart* — an idiom of notable precision — is no technical auxiliary or carry-over from liturgical and pedagogical practice. It is of the essence of the reader's attempt to abolish or sublate that very distance which the critic stakes out. To memorize is, simultaneously, to enter into the text and to be entered into by the text (a process only partly realizable when one 'photographs' a painting or statue mentally). This dual motion of ingress and reception is formally and substantively the analogue of the dual motion of projection and withdrawal in the text or musical composition itself. Commitment to memory is, in the first place, an individual phenomenon. It modifies the spaces and constructs of one's inner being, as does the entrance of a 'high guest' (Hölderlin's simile) into one's house. Very recent work in biochemistry even suggests that such modification has its material counterpart, that the augment of memory leads to delicate ramifications of molecular fabric. But active remembrance is also a collective, a cultural agency. It initiates and preserves a communion of shared echo, of participatory reflex, pertinent to the notion of canon.

An unremembered text or piece of music exists in a penumbra of anticipation as do the volumes currently untouched, where 'currently' can mean centuries, in the patient silences of the great libraries. But a text can only enter into the full life of the canon when it is woken by, housed within, the negated distance of precise memory. It follows that 'total reading' has an inherent logic of dispensation, that it tends towards a condition in which the materiality of the text is no longer required. The icon has been wholly internalized. The executive recollection which makes it present in and to the reader no longer depends on external confirmation. Such orders of internality are no ideal fiction, though they may seem so in our present climate of institutionalized amnesia. In other epochs, societies, or traditions, the commitment to memory, the availability to total recall and reiteration, of massive bodies of texts – epic, ritual, liturgical, historical, taxonomic – was, or still is, routine, as it is routine, even among us, to numerous musicians who dispense with a score and apprehend internally, in the soundless clarity of mastered introspection, great stretches of polyphonic music. (I have seen undergraduates switch off the sound track in a beloved Bogart film and speak in unison long pieces of perfectly remembered dialogue.)

The negation of distance, of which memorization is the final logic, brings on an extreme contraction of focus. Sense and spirit crowd up, as it were, against the actual surface of the text. And here again, instructively, the parallel with the apprehension of art objects begins to break down. In the case of the canvas, statue, or building, we must, to a greater or lesser degree, step back in order to see. But it is in regard to texts precisely this contraction of focus which makes of the single word or short sentence the crucial units of reading, as they are of memorization. The practices of meditation and of commentary on the single word or verse, as they have been developed by exegetes of revealed, of legal, or 'founding' texts – 'founding' in the sense of being the documents of national identity, the epics and chronicles of inception – are not accidental or technical devices. Exegetic meditation on the minimal unit is the ultimate rationale of true reading. Reading and remembrance proceed word by word, a usage implicit in Walter Benjamin's proposal that the genuine translator, the translator who works furthest from the critic's paraphrase, is one who produces a word for word interlinear. With the Scholastics, the reader knows that 'God lies in the detail.'

It is in this entirely practical sense that the most evident records of iconic reading are exegetic: the letter-by-letter hermeneutics of the Kabbalists, the word-by-word commentaries of the Talmudists or Patristic readers, Karl Barth advancing sentence-by-sentence in Romans. But exactly the same contraction of perspective, with its attendant methodological extravagances and myopias, can be brought to bear on the secular poem, the philosophical text (Heidegger on Anaximander or Heraclitus), the legal statute. The difference is simply that the rabbinical exegete or Calvin on the Gospels can proceed without apology or rationalizing metaphor, 'as if' the real presence were unambiguously operative in his text. He can, in short, make explicit the assumption, implicit in all true reading, that the warranty of meaning, that which finally underwrites the capacity of language to have sense and force beyond sense, is of a theological order. The honest realist-critic, on the contrary, operates by virtue of immanent and secular presuppositions. It is these which give him the authority to judge, to consign 'inferior' works to non-remembrance (criticism is one of the means of forgetting).

In both its strengths and potential infirmities, a word-by-word reading will tend to be philological. It is philology, the literal 'love of the *logos*', which has been the natural instrument, the magnifying glass of the exegete. Likewise, musicology can dwell on each note or bar. Textual criticism is sharply 'critical', but in a sense almost antithetical to that of the critic's criticism. Textual criticism is the broom in the house of remembrance, sweeping away accretion of factitiousness in order to make presentness more translucid. It does not judge its text, as the critic must; it labours to restore it to exact mystery. That there are profound mirrorings as between philology and music, that both are disciplines of access to elemental energies of being projected towards and concealed from the intellect, was a fact familiar to Plato and recalled by Nietzsche. Philology and music pertain to the spheres of 'reading' rather than of 'criticism' (how much music criticism is there even worth forgetting?).

The critic prescribes a syllabus; the reader is answerable to and internalizes a canon. In practice, to be sure, the two will overlap. The 'syllabic' in a given culture will select and celebrate, will label as 'classic', the 'great books' around which a language and a society edify their codes of self-recognition. Such 'great books' may indeed be a part of the reader's canon (where criticism also focuses on revealed texts, this will be most obviously the case). But strictly considered, the inclusion in the canon of 'masterpieces' from the syllabus is accidental. Motivations towards the canonic are not, at their source, those of interested and prescriptive activity in the sense in which we found these to be fundamental to the critical exercise of ordering sight. The aim of the canon, and *aim* is precisely the wrong word here, is not that of stylistic exemplarity, in the way in which, for instance, the rhetoric of Boileau and Racine may be seen to have served as official 'weights and measures' for generations of French discourse. It is not nationally didactic in the sense in which much of Shakespeare has been for the Anglo-Saxon political community. In brief, the canon is not a catalogue of magisterially, circumstantially culled and monumentalized pre-eminence. A canon is the individually internalized cluster of crystallization of remembered, exegetically re-enacted texts or text fragments which result from (very often) unsought, unwilled encounter with and answerability to the 'real presence'. The authentic canon is not, or is not in the first place, the product of reasoned intention.

Its crystallization in the reader's inwardness results from a paradox of 'dynamic passivity', from the suspension of self which we experience when we pay utter attention to something, when we make acceptance and apprehension strenuous. This condition can produce a tensed openness which allows, which invites the text 'to read us' as much as we read it. Canonic are the texts and fragments of texts — criticism must seek to view the whole; reading can dwell on the smallest component — whose entrance into the reader's mind, and 'mind' is in this context a wholly inadequate, restrictive designation, whose immediacy to the reader's recall and re-vocation, come to alter the texture of consciousness. The reader revisits, comes back into awareness of the quick of his own augmented being through reference to, through silent colloquy with, through the citation of, texts and pieces of text. The archaic resort to *sortes*, the placing of a blind finger on some passage from a scriptural or poetic book, is an outward dramatization of this inward search for essential insight, for an understanding of one's destiny. The canonic text enters into the reader, it takes its place within him by a process of penetration, of luminous insinuation whose occasion may have been entirely mundane and accidental — decisive encounters so often are — but not, or not primarily, willed. The 'high guests' enter unbidden yet awaited.

There is nothing occult or mystical about this entrance, though psychology has not, until now, given a convincing analysis of its literal mechanism. The occurrence is banal to anyone whose mind and body — both are involved —

have been seized upon by a melody, by a tune, by a verbal cadence which he did not choose by act of will, which has entered into him unawares. It is familiar to whoever has left a room – it need not be a museum gallery – only to discover that there is lodged in his inner eye (the pun on *ego* is not entirely trivial) some detail of an object, of a painting, some configuration of tactile form or colour, which he has no awareness of having fixed upon, of registering consciously. When fully accepted, when made welcome and vital by virtue of precise remembrance and study, such mastering entrants and trespassers take root. They mesh with the fabric of the self; texts become part of the texture of identity. Proust's notation and uses of the 'little theme' from Vinteuil's sonata and of the yellow patch in Vermeer's view of Delft are unsurpassed testimony to the origins and role of the canonic.

This particular set is instructive also in another sense. The Vermeer painting is, by critical consensus, a masterpiece; it figures eminently on the syllabus. The Vinteuil theme, on the other hand, is meant to evoke (so the scholars have found out) a particular motif in a bit of chamber music by Fauré. Even committed Proustians find it difficult to discern any particular excellence or memorability in the original, let alone that central genius of time-annulling beauty and meaning which the narrator attributes to it throughout the novel. Thus, one fundamental element in Proust's canon is of a sort which we would also find in the critical syllabus, whereas the other is idiosyncratic and, by syllabic standards, insignificant, ephemeral, 'third-rate'. But it is to the minor, a classification which it does not, in fact, recognize, that the canonic often pertains. The canon which is the echo chamber of our personal being, which is immediate to and consubstantial with those summonses which give to our identity its individual weight and savour, is like a collage. The 'classic' and the 'syllabic' will figure in it, as the Mona Lisa postcard figures in a surrealist constructivist assemblage. But so will texts, graphic motifs, musical passages which are hardly respectable by the standards of critical judgement. A syllabus is taught; a canon is lived.

Indeed, he is no true reader who has not tasted the drug of the esoteric, who has not discovered that the song of the Sirens, maddening because it ironizes the brevity of personal existence, the insufficiencies of personal memory, is the silent call of the unread book. One would almost say, though this is sophistic hyperbole, of 'any unread book'. Exegesis, philology are, in pure extremity, value blind. Virtuosities of inwardness have been expended on inventories in Leviticus; A. E. Housman's readings, his vitalizing apprehensions, cut deepest in Manilius. The cheap tune haunts us. As Sartre recollects in *Les Mots*, the young person is 'read by', is woken and construed to identity by blood-and-thunder, by near-Valentines, or the memorable purple of travel and romance. (Hérédia's brassy sonnets and the somewhat saccharine memoirs and letters of Renan crystallized my adolescence.)

In turn, this primary inwardness and hybrid character of the canon will inflect the act of reading towards privacy, even secrecy. The critic must declare; this is his public and legislative ordination. The reader will often hold his illuminations mute. Or he will experience a contradictory impetus. He seeks to keep to himself the visitations by and internalizations of those texts or iconic objects which have most intensely affected his being. Yet, possessed of and by his talisman, the reader will want to inform others, where both meanings of *inform*, that of communication and that of shaping, are relevant. In the antiquarian, in the archivist, in the bibliophile and collector of works of art, this radical ambiguity and even duplicity of motives is a familiar trait: The collector conceals his find in order to show it — a psychological reflex (lightly) analogous with what we have seen to be the pulsing dialectic of withdrawal and epiphany in art itself. It is from this divided stance that stem the 'schools of reading', the exegetic and hermeneutic disciplines, be they rabbinical, monastic, academic, or simply familial, whereby a 'master' or first reader attempts to lay his disciples and collaborators open to the text. The opening of the text comes after the laying open of the reader. Literal repetition, transcription, commitment to memory often precede and will, at all times, be co-terminous with exposition. The critic parallels mimetically or by paraphrase; he does not transcribe; he does not memorize the object of his judgement. The Kabbalist, the philologist, the musician, must do so. Thus, when he invites others into the 'inner penetralium' of his sensibility — the phrase was St Augustine's before it was Keats's — when he invites others to make vital the canon which is a constituent of his own being, the reader reads *with* them. In the master critic there is, inherently, the bias to read *for* us.

Other disjunctions follow. The robust critic is a futurist. Whatever the acuity of analysis and judgement which he brings to bear on a past work, his aim, the test of his own antennae, must be the importation into the syllabus of the 'tradition of the new' (Harold Rosenberg's telling expression). He deals, to take up the simile of the *bourse* once again, in 'futures'. We have seen that it is in the measure of speculative risk, in the likelihood that some of his most costly investments will prove abortive, that lies the dignity of his craft. The true reader, on the contrary, is, almost unavoidably, a remembrancer. It is in the ontological 'backwardness' of the canonic, in the fact that so many of the

Eurydices on the reader's pilgrimage (*les orages pèlerins*) are in the shadows behind him, that lie the unworldliness, the dusty sorrows of his calling. This bent towards pastness is both individual and typological: much of the canon is given entrance to, is met with, in childhood or youth, when the inner spaces are as yet uncluttered and memory is rapacious. The great reader, and he is rare, is precisely the one who remains fully vulnerable, fully hospitable to the light and menace of annunciation, in mature age. Much of the canonic is also historical. Therefore, it makes dangerous sense to the reader to intuit, to act on the prejudice, that there will be no texts produced in his lifetime or even thereafter to surpass, perhaps to match, those we attach to the anonymities of Homer or the Book of Job. The modern reader finds himself supposing, almost without examination, that certain 'transcendentals' in the canon, such as Aeschylus, Dante, Shakespeare, Goethe, represent singularities, compactions of totality of a kind which western culture, at least, will not regenerate. The critic's feeling on this must be one of rebellious doubt and contrary hope. When he visits the museum he must be present at the hanging of the new pictures.

 3

The dualities which I have cited, and many others implicit in the argument, can best be subsumed under one fundamental antithesis. The critical act is a function of the ego in a condition of will. The critic wills his praxis. Even where his relation to the object of his focus is most affirmative, elucidative, and heralding, this is to say where it is of the most patent service to the object, this relation is, nevertheless, structurally and dynamically egotistical (using this term in a non-moralistic sense). The yield is, as we saw, a counter-statement, a standing 'over and against' the text or art object which is the occasion of his proposition. The critic signs his perception no less than, often more emphatically than, the begetter of the original object. We saw also that there is in this ineluctable and legitimate egotism the constant potential of rivalry. Consciously or not, the critic competes with the text or art before him. Even celebration can, frequently does, come to eclipse its first cause. This, I suggested, is why the present-day inflation of the critic's status, vocabulary, didactic authority, idiom, media of dissemination, and self-esteem are not accidental by-products of the mandarinization of literature. The prepotence of criticism over original composition, the interposition of the critic's persona between the text and the general light, are betrayals existentially rooted in the critical act. The impulse towards solipsistic sovereignty, towards the finding that there is really little left 'out there' worth serious criticism, or that what there is must be 'deconstructed' by the critic and immersed in Medea's cauldron, is no byzantine paradox. It is a thrust latent in all criticism. Finally, irremediably, the critic is *judge* and *master* of the text.

The reader is *servant* to the text. The genuine teacher, textual editor, scribe are called to a clerisy of service. The text finds out its condign reader. Often he would resist its peremptory ingress, even as the prophet seeks to shut his teeth against the imperatives of his calling (Jonah was a 'reader'). The reader's acceptance of the canon comports a trusteeship, mute and private except in those practices of collaborative reiteration, commitment to memory, and heuristic commentary mentioned above. But whether singular or participatory, unspoken or communicated, the reader is 'in service' to the text. Roy Campbell recounts how the back of his spirit and the back of his body were bent when the text of St John of the Cross 'leapt upon him' from fortunate ambush. He became, as every true reader must become, a shepherd to the being of the text, a doorkeeper at the always closed and always opened gates to meaning. This latter simile is, of course, a borrowing from Kafka's parable of the doorkeeper before the threshold of the Law. In its seeming self-contradiction of closure and aperture, this fable illustrates concretely the process of dialogue with a canonic text. We understand and we do not understand enough; we grasp and that which we grasp eludes us. Again, there is nothing occult about the actual process, though it is difficult to paraphrase. It is the experience of the actor when the part which he has enclosed in memory springs to autonomous, mastering life; it is the ordinary experience of the performing musician in reference to the external or internalized score. Perhaps one might put it this way: *the critic's will acts. The reader's apprehension enacts.*

But if there is nothing occult in this process, there is in its motivation and pursuit a contract with the transcendent. In the final analysis, the reader has subscribed to a contract of implicit presence. He must 'enact as if' the letter is the vessel, however opaque, however fragmented, of the spirit. He must venture a Pascalian wager on the iconic potential of the work. The assumptions of such a contract have often been spelled out: by Novalis, when he urged that the 'true meaning of the World' had been lost but was recapturable in filaments of numinous discourse; by Péguy, when he identified *une lecture bien faite* with the unfolding of the blossom on the silent bough; by Heidegger when he asserted that 'the fate of western man' could well hinge on the right emendation of and answerability to a fragment of Anaximander. Or to put it in shorthand: the reader must suppose and accept that Flaubert was *not* indulging in rhetoric or baseless metaphor when he cried out, in the pain of mortal sickness: 'Why must I die while that tart Emma Bovary lives, and will continue to live?'

The contract with transcendence cannot be empirically validated. Its guarantor is theological, if this word is allowed its widest compass. As is 'theological' the warranty which underwrites the validity of metaphor and analogy (an issue closely argued in Pierre Boutang's key work, *L'Ontologie du secret*). This is the obvious weakness of the reader's theoretical position. The critic owes no hostages to mystery. The reader does. There is a necessary sense for him in the translation chosen by Luther in Revelation when he termed the 'Book of Life' to be an actual book. The reader must give almost literal weight to Mallarmé's conceit that the sum of being is *Le Livre*. This view can be felt to be at once exultant and a little mad – as so often are the practices of textual criticism, epigraphy, philology, heraldry, numismatics, and exegesis in its pure vein. Ecstatic, 'deranged' if you will, servants of the canon stand or dance 'beside themselves' because the text is now the sole and imperious lodger in the house of their being.

Of course, 'critic' and 'reader' as I have sketched them are near-fictions. Neither can be found at all readily in a pure state. There will be in even the most magisterial or narcissist of critics elements of disinterested acceptance, of apprehension beyond judgement. There have been in the most complete readers of whom we have record – an important qualification in view of the privacy of so much reading – critical reflexes, verdicts, impulses towards labelling. Even approximations to absolute types are rare. F. R. Leavis would stand near to the pole of unwavering criticism; Housman comes near to being the total reader (and neither of these two cases is altogether innocent of the pathological). In the ordinary run of things, 'criticism' and 'reading' interpenetrate and overlap. Nonetheless, it may be of some use to bear in mind the fiction of contrastive absolutes.

It is a platitude to observe the dishevelment in today's cultivation of humane letters. The self-satisfactions, assembly-line output of trivia, philosophic vacancy, and histrionics which mark the academic profession of literature and its marriage to journalism are obvious. The debasement of the concept of 'research' in literary studies verges on scandal. Implicit in this essay is the hypothesis that much in this condition derives from a confusion between 'criticism' and the practices of exegetical reading from which the modern study of secular letters sprang. The notion that any but the most exceptional of human beings has anything *critically* new or re-evaluative to say of Dante, or of Shakespeare, or of Kafka, is cant. It is worse cant to institutionalize the belief that such rare ordering sight will manifest itself in the university undergraduate or graduate student. The present edifice of literary-critical studies (gossip in jargon) is a derogation, inevitable in view of the fact that the great majority of texts had been properly edited previously, from the exact arts of philology, historical linguistics, textual criticism, recension, and collation. Today's undergraduate 'critic' and 'researcher in sensibility' is a high-wire acrobat who has not learned to walk.

What we need (I have argued this elsewhere) are not 'programmes in the humanities', 'schools of creative writing', 'programmes in creative criticism' (*mirabile dictu*, these exist). What we need are places, i.e. a table with some chairs around it, in which we can learn again how to read, how to read together. One aims at such a desideratum at the most literal levels. Elementary lexical and grammatical analyses, the parsing of sentences, the scansion of verse (prosody being the inseparable pulse and music of meaning), the ability to make out even the most rudimentary lineaments of those innervations and figures of rhetoric which, from Pindar to Joyce, have been the carriers of felt life – all these are now esoteric or lost skills. We need 'houses of and for reading' in which there is enough silence for the sinews of memory to awake. If language, under the pressure of wonder (the 'surplus value') of multiple meaning, if the music of thought are to endure, it is not more 'critics' we require but more and better 'readers'.

'Great Readers', says Borges, who is himself one, are 'rarer than great writers.' The list would include Montaigne reading Seneca and re-reading himself; Coleridge reading Jacobi and Schelling, a reading whose motion of acquiescence and metamorphic repossession Thomas McFarland has analysed with a tact equalling that of any other study of the stress of influence; Péguy reading Corneille and Victor Hugo; Walter Benjamin reading Goethe's *Elective Affinities*; Heidegger reading Sophocles and Trakl (not Hölderlin, whom he often reads wilfully and with opportunism); Mandelstam reading Dante and Chénier; Alexandre Koyré reading Galileo; Nabokov reading (not translating) Pushkin; Jean Starobinski reading Rousseau; William Empson reading complex words; Gianfranco Contini reading the Provençal poets, Dante, and Montale; Pierre Boutang reading Plato's *Philebus*; Michael Dummett reading Frege, where depth and openness of reading are radically creative; D. Carne-Ross reading Góngora and Ariosto; Gershon Scholem reading the Kabbalists and reading Walter Benjamin ... Servants to the text, scrupulous ecstatics, for in reference to the canonic, scruple and ecstasy are one.

A list of great critics? It would, no doubt, be longer and of greater public lustre. But is there need of such a list? Critics advertise.

← Readings ←

→ Nineteenth-century America →
and Russia

The history of European fiction in the nineteenth century brings to mind the image of a nebula with wide-flung arms. At their extremities the American and the Russian novel radiate a whiter brilliance. As we move outward from the centre — and we may think of Henry James, Turgeniev, and Conrad as intermediary clusters — the stuff of realism grows more tenuous. The masters of the American and the Russian manner appear to gather something of their fierce intensity from the outer darkness, from the decayed matter of folk-lore, melodrama, and religious life.

European observers were uneasily cognizant of what lay beyond the orbit of traditional realism. They sensed that Russian and American imaginings had attained spheres of compassion and ferocity denied to a Balzac or a Dickens. French criticism, in particular, reflects the endeavours of a classical sensibility, of an intelligence attuned to measure and equilibrium, to respond justly to forms of vision that were both alien and exalting. At times, as in Flaubert's acknowledgement of *War and Peace*, this attempt to honour strange gods was tinged with scepticism or bitterness. For in defining the Russian and the American accomplishment, the European critic defined also the incompletions in his own great heritage. Even those who did most to familiarize Europeans with the stars in the eastern and western skies — Mérimée, Baudelaire, the Vicomte de Vogüé, the Goncourts, André Gide, and Valéry Larbaud — might be saddened to discover that in response to a questionnaire circulated in 1957 students at the Sorbonne set Dostoevsky high above any French writer.

In reflecting on the qualities of American and Russian fiction, European observers of the late nineteenth and early twentieth centuries sought to discover points of affinity between the United States of Hawthorne and Melville and pre-revolutionary Russia. The cold war makes this perspective seem archaic or even erroneous. But the distortion lies with us. To understand why it is (to apply Harry Levin's phrase about Joyce) that after *Moby Dick*, *Anna Karenina*, and *The Brothers Karamazov* it became far more difficult to be a novelist at all, one must consider the contrast not between Russia and America, but between Russia and America on the one hand and nineteenth-century Europe on the other. This essay is concerned with the Russians. But the psychological and material circumstances which liberated them from the dilemma of realism were present also on the American scene, and it is through American eyes that some of them may be most clearly perceived.

Obviously this is a vast topic and what follows should be regarded merely as notes towards a more adequate treatment. Four of the acutest minds of their age, Astolphe de Custine, de Tocqueville, Matthew Arnold, and Henry Adams dealt with this theme. Each, from his own specific vantage point, was struck by analogies between the two emergent powers. Henry Adams went further and speculated, with extraordinary prescience, on what the fate of civilization would be once the two giants confronted each other across an enfeebled Europe.

The ambiguous yet determining nature of the relationship to Europe was, during the nineteenth century, a recurrent motif of both Russian and American intellectual life. Henry James made the classic pronouncement: 'It's a complex fate, being an American, and one of the responsibilities it entails is fighting against a superstitious valuation of Europe.'[1] In his tribute to George Sand, Dostoevsky said: 'We Russians have two motherlands – Russia and Europe – even in cases where we call ourselves Slavophiles.'[2] The complexity and the doubleness are equally manifest in Ivan Karamazov's celebrated declaration to his brother:

> I want to travel in Europe, Alyosha, I shall set off from here. And yet I know that I am only going to a graveyard, but it's a most precious graveyard, that's what it is! Precious are the dead that lie there, every stone over them speaks of such burning life in the past, of such passionate faith in their work, their truth, their struggle and their science, that I know I shall fall on the ground and kiss those stones and weep over them; though I'm convinced in my heart that it's long been nothing but a graveyard.

Could this not be the motto of American literature from Hawthorne's *Marble Faun* to T. S. Eliot's *Four Quartets*?

In both nations the relationship to Europe assumed diverse and complex forms. Turgeniev, Henry James, and, later on, Eliot and Pound offer examples of direct acceptance, of conversion to the old world. Melville and Tolstoy were among the great refusers. But in most instances the attitudes were at once ambiguous and compulsive. Cooper noted in 1828, in his

---

1. Henry James, cit. by P. Lubbock in a letter dated early 1872 (*The Letters of Henry James*, New York, 1920).
2. Dostoevsky: *The Diary of a Writer* (trans. by Boris Brasol, New York, 1954).

Gleanings in Europe: 'If any man is excusable for deserting his country, it is the American artist.' On this precise point the Russian intelligentsia was fiercely divided. But whether they welcomed the probability or deplored it, writers from both America and Russia tended to agree that their formative experiences would entail a necessary part of exile or 'treason'. Often the European pilgrimage would lead to a rediscovery and re-valuation of the home country: Gogol 'found' his Russia while living in Rome. But in both literatures the theme of the European voyage was the principal device for self-definition and the occasion for the normative gesture: Herzen's coach crossing the Polish frontier, Lambert Strether (the protagonist of James's *Ambassadors*) arriving in Chester. 'To understand anything as vast and terrible as Russia,' wrote the early Slavophile Kire-evsky, 'one must look on her from afar.'

This confrontation with Europe gives Russian and American fiction something of its specific weight and dignity. Both civilizations were coming of age and were in search of their own image (this search being one of Henry James's essential fables). In both countries the novel helped give the mind a sense of place. Not an easy task; for whereas the European realist worked within points of reference fixed by a rich historical and literary legacy, his counterpart in the United States and in Russia either had to import a sense of continuity from abroad or to create a somewhat spurious autonomy with whatever material came to hand. It was the rare good fortune of Russian literature that Pushkin's genius was of so manifold and classical a cast. His works constituted in themselves a body of tradition. Moreover, they incorporated a large range of foreign influences and models. This is what Dostoevsky meant when he referred to Pushkin's 'universal responsiveness':

> Even the greatest of the European poets were never able to embody in themselves with such potency as Pushkin the genius of an alien, perhaps neighbouring people ... Pushkin alone – among all world poets – possesses the faculty of completely reincarnating in himself an alien nationality.[3]

In Gogol, moreover, the art of the Russian narrative found a craftsman who struck, from the first, the dominant tones and attitudes of the language and the form. The Russian novel did emerge out of his *Cloak*. American literature was less fortunate. The uncertainties of taste in Poe, Hawthorne, and Melville

3. ibid.

and the obscuring idiosyncrasies of their manner point directly to the dilemmas of individual talent producing in relative isolation.

Russia and America lacked even that sense of geographical stability and cohesion which the European novel took for granted. Both nations combined immensity with the awareness of a romantic and vanishing frontier. What the Far West and the Red Man were to American mythology, the Caucasus and its warring tribes, or the unspoiled communities of Cossacks and Old Believers on the Don and the Volga were to Pushkin, Lermontov, and Tolstoy. Archetypal in both literatures is the theme of the hero who leaves behind the corrupt world of urban civilization and enervating passions to affront the dangers and moral purgations of the frontier. Leatherstocking and the hero of Tolstoy's *Tales from the Caucasus* are kindred as they move among the cool pine valleys and wild creatures in melancholy yet ardent pursuit of their 'noble' foe.

The vastness of space brings with it exposures to natural forces at their most grandiose and ferocious; only in the Brontës and, subsequently, in D. H. Lawrence does the European novel show a comparable awareness of nature unleashed. The moody tyrannies of the sea in Dana and Melville, the archaic horrors of the ice-world in Poe's *Narrative of Arthur Gordon Pym*, the image of human nakedness in Tolstoy's *Snowstorm* — all these encounters of man with a physical setting which can destroy him in moments of wanton grandeur lie outside the repertoire of western European realism. Tolstoy's *How Much Land Does a Man Need?* (which Joyce thought the 'greatest literature in the world') could have been written, in the nineteenth century, only by a Russian or an American. It is a parable on the immensity of the earth; it would have made sense neither in Dickens's Kentish landscape nor in Flaubert's Normandy.

But space isolates as much as it enlarges. Common to Russian and American literature was the theme of the artist seeking his identity and his public in a culture too new, too disorganized, and too preoccupied with the demands of material survival. Even the cities, in which the European consciousness perceived the very gathering and transcription of the past, were raw and anonymous in their Russian and American setting. From the time of Pushkin to that of Dostoevsky, St Petersburg stands in Russian literature as a symbol of arbitrary creation; the whole structure had been conjured out of marsh and water by the cruel magic of autocracy. It was rooted neither in the earth nor in the past. Sometimes, as in Pushkin's *Bronze Horseman*, nature took vengeance on the intruder; sometimes, as when Poe perished in Baltimore, the city became a mob — that equivalent of natural catastrophe — and destroyed the artist.

But in the end, the human will triumphed over the gigantic land. Roads were cut through forests and deserts; communities gripped on to the prairie and the steppe. This achievement and the primacy of will that brought it about are reflected in the great lineage of Russian and American classics. In both mythologies what Balzac had described as 'the quest for the absolute' looms large. Hester Prynne, Ahab, Gordon Pym, Dostoevsky's underground man, and Tolstoy himself assailed the will-constraining barriers of traditional morality and natural law. As epigraph to *Ligeia*, Poe chose a passage from the seventeenth-century English divine Joseph Glanvill: 'Man doth not yield himself to the angels, nor unto death utterly, save only through the weakness of his feeble will.' That is Ahab's secret battle-cry and it was Tolstoy's hope when he questioned the need of mortality. In both Russia and America, as Matthew Arnold remarked, life itself had about it the fanaticism of youth.

But in neither instance was it the kind of life on which European fiction drew for its material and on which it built the fabric of its conventions. This is the crux of Henry James's study of Hawthorne. The latter had written, in preface to *The Marble Faun*:

> No author, without a trial, can conceive of the difficulty of writing a romance about a country where there is no shadow, no antiquity, no mystery, no picturesque and gloomy wrong, not anything but a commonplace prosperity, in broad and simple daylight, as is happily the case with my dear native land.

From the author of *The Scarlet Letter* and *The House of the Seven Gables*, one takes this to be a piece of fine-grained irony. But James chose not to do so and elaborated on Hawthorne's 'difficulties'. His discussion, as well as Hawthorne's text, pertain altogether to America. But what James had to say yielded perhaps the most searching analysis that we have of the main qualities of the European novel. By telling us what non-Europeans lacked he tells us also from what impediments they were free. And his treatment is, I submit, as illuminating of the differences between Flaubert and Tolstoy as it is of those between Flaubert and Hawthorne.

Noting the 'thinness' and 'the blankness' of the atmosphere in which Hawthorne worked, James said:

> It takes so many things, as Hawthorne must have felt later in life, when

he made the acquaintance of the denser, richer, warmer European spectacle – it takes such an accumulation of history and custom, such a complexity of manner and types, to form a fund of suggestion for a novelist.

Whereupon follows the famous listing of 'the items of high civilization' absent from the texture of American life and, consequently, from the matrix of reference and emotion available to an American novelist:

> No State, in the European sense of the word, and indeed barely a specific national name. No sovereign, no court, no personal loyalty, no aristocracy, no church, no clergy, no army, no diplomatic service, no country gentlemen, no palaces, no castles, nor manors ... nor ivied ruins ... no Oxford, nor Eton, nor Harrow; no literature, no novels, no museums, no pictures, no political society, no sporting class – no Epsom nor Ascot!

One cannot tell whether this list is to be taken altogether seriously. Neither the court, nor the army, nor the sporting set in James's England was very much concerned with the values of the artist. Oxford's most dramatic association with poetic genius had been the expulsion of Shelley; manors and ivied ruins were the draughty damnation of painters and musicians seeking to entertain their genteel hosts; neither Eton nor Harrow was notable for its encouragement of the gentler virtues. But James's list is relevant none the less. In sharp miniature it conveys the world picture of European realism, what Bergson would have called the *données immédiates* of the art of Dickens, Thackeray, Trollope, Balzac, Stendhal, or Flaubert.

Moreover, given the necessary qualifications and shifts in perspective, this index of deprivation applies equally to nineteenth-century Russia. That too was not a state 'in the European sense of the word'. Its autocratic court, with its semi-Asiatic flavour, was hostile to literature. Much of the aristocracy was steeped in feudal barbarism and only a tiny, Europeanized segment cared for art or the free play of ideas. The Russian clergy had little in common with the Anglican curates and bishops in whose panelled libraries and rook-haunted chambers James passed some of his winter evenings. They were a fanatical and uneducated host in which visionaries and saints neighboured on illiterate sensualists. Most of the other items enumerated by James – the free universities and ancient schools, the museums and political society, the ivied ruins and the literary tradition – were no more present in Russia than in the United States.

And surely in both cases the particular items point to a more general fact:

in neither Russia nor America had there taken place the full evolution of a middle class 'in the European sense of the word'. As Marx pointed out in his later years, Russia was to provide an instance of a feudal system moving towards industrialization without the intermediary stages of political enfranchisement and without the formation of a modern bourgeoisie. Behind the European novel lay the stabilizing and maturing structures of constitutionality and capitalism. These did not exist in the Russia of Gogol or Dostoevsky.

James admitted that there were 'fine compensations' for the thinness of the American atmosphere. He alluded to the immediacy of physical nature in its more eloquent moods, to the writer's contact with a broad range of types, and to the sense of 'wonder' and 'mystery' which comes with meeting men who cannot be placed in any of the distinct categories of a fixed society. But James hastened to add that this absence of hierarchies deprived an artist of 'intellectual standards' and of the touchstones of manner. Instead, it committed him to a 'rather chilly and isolated sense of moral responsibility'.

This is a disturbing sentence even if one takes it to apply solely to Hawthorne. It goes a long way towards explaining how it was that the mature James expended time and admiration on the works of Augier, Gyp, and Dumas *fils*. It casts light on the values which led him to compare *The Scarlet Letter* with Lockhart's *Adam Blair* – not entirely to the latter's detriment. It makes plain why James hoped that American fiction would develop in the image of William Dean Howells, who had started with a 'delightful volume on *Venetian Life*', rather than in that of Poe or Melville or Hawthorne with their 'puerile' experiments in symbolism. Finally, it is an observation which shows why James could make nothing of the Russian contemporaries of Turgeniev.

This 'isolated sense of moral responsibility' (passionate, I should have thought, rather than 'chilly'), this compulsion towards what Nietzsche was to call 'the revaluation of all values', carried the American and the Russian novel beyond the dwindling resources of European realism into the world of the Pequod and the Karamazovs. D. H. Lawrence remarked:

> There is a 'different' feeling in the old American classics. It is the shifting from the old psyche to something new, a displacement. And displacement hurt.[4]

In the American case, the displacement was spatial and cultural; the migration

4. D. H. Lawrence: *Studies in Classic American Literature.*

of the mind from Europe to the new world. In Russia it was historical and revolutionary. In both instances there were pain and unreason, but also the possibility of experiment and the exhilarating conviction that there was at stake more than a portrayal of existing society or the provision of romantic entertainment.

It is true that by Jamesian standards Hawthorne, Melville, Gogol, Tolstoy, and Dostoevsky were isolated men. They created apart from or in opposition to the dominant literary *milieu*. James himself and Turgeniev seemed more fortunate; they were honoured and at home in the high places of civilization without sacrificing the integrity of their purpose. But, in the final analysis, it was the visionaries and the hunted who achieved the 'Titanic' books.

Our imaginary discourse on Russia and America in the nineteenth century, on possible analogues in the achievement of the Russian and the American novel, and on their respective departures from European realism, might speculate on one further point. European fiction mirrors the long post-Napoleonic peace. That peace extended, save for spasmodic and indecisive interruptions in 1854 and 1870, from Waterloo to the First World War. War had been a dominant motif in epic poetry – even when it was war in heaven. It had provided the context for much of serious drama from *Antigone* to *Macbeth* and the masterpieces of Kleist. But it is significantly remote from the preoccupations and themes of the nineteenth-century European novelists. We hear the distant boom of guns in *Vanity Fair*; the approach of war gives the final pages of *Nana* their irony and their unforgettable *élan*; but not until the Zeppelin cruises over Paris, in that despairing night of debauchery which marks the end of the Proustian world, does war re-enter into the main current of European literature. Flaubert, in whom most of these problems are so intensely accentuated, wrote savage and resplendent pages about battle. But it was a battle long ago, in the museum setting of ancient Carthage. Curiously enough, it is to children's and boys' books that we must go to find convincing accounts of men at war – to Daudet and to G. A. Henty, who, like Tolstoy, was profoundly marked by his experiences in the Crimea. European realism, in the adult vein, produced neither a *War and Peace* nor a *Red Badge of Courage*.

This fact enforces a larger moral. The theatre of the European novel, its political and physical matrix from Jane Austen to Proust, was extraordinarily stable. In it, the major catastrophes were private. The art of Balzac, Dickens, and Flaubert was neither prepared nor called upon to engage those forces which can utterly dissolve the fabric of a society and overwhelm private life. Those forces were gathering inexorably towards the century of revolution and total war. But the European novelists either ignored the foreshadowings or misinterpreted them. Flaubert assured George Sand that the Commune was merely a brief reversion to the factionalism of the Middle Ages. Only two writers of fiction clearly glimpsed the impulses towards disintegration, the cracks in the wall of European stability: James in *The Princess Casamassima* and Conrad in *Under Western Eyes* and *The Secret Agent*. It is of the most obvious significance that neither novelist was native to the western European tradition.

The influence of the Civil War, or rather of its approach and aftermath, on the American atmosphere has not, to my mind, been thoroughly assessed. Harry Levin has suggested that the world view of Poe was darkened by a premonition of the impending fate of the South. It is only gradually that we are coming to realize how drastic a role the war played in the consciousness of Henry James. It accounts in part for that susceptibility to the daemonic and the crippling which deepened the Jamesian novel and carried it into areas beyond the confines of French and English realism. But more generally one may say that the instability of American social life, the mythology of violence inherent in the frontier situation, and the centrality of the war crisis were reflected in the temper of American art. They contributed to what D. H. Lawrence termed a 'pitch of extreme consciousness'. He addressed his observation to Poe, Hawthorne, and Melville. It applies equally to *The Jolly Corner* and *The Golden Bowl*.

But what were, in the American case, complex and at times marginal elements were, with respect to nineteenth-century Russia, the essential realities.

◆ *Homer and Tolstoy* ◆

Hugo von Hofmannsthal once remarked that he could not read a page of Tolstoy's *Cossacks* without being reminded of Homer. His experience has been shared by readers not only of *The Cossacks* but of Tolstoy's works as a whole. According to Gorky, Tolstoy himself said of *War and Peace*: 'Without false modesty, it is like the *Iliad*', and he made precisely the same observation with regard to *Childhood, Boyhood and Youth*. Moreover, Homer and the Homeric atmosphere appear to have played a fascinating role in Tolstoy's image of his own personality and creative stature. His brother-in-law, S. A. Bers, tells in his *Reminiscences* of a feast which took place on Tolstoy's estate in Samara:

> a steeplechase of fifty versts. Prizes were got ready, a bull, a horse, a rifle, a watch, a dressing-gown and the like. A level stretch was chosen, a huge course four miles long was made and marked out, and posts were put up on it. Roast sheep, and even a horse, were prepared for the entertainment. On the appointed day, some thousands of people assembled, Ural Cossacks, Russian peasants, Bashkirs and Khirgizes, with their dwellings, koumiss-kettles, and even their flocks ... On a cone-shaped rise, called in the local dialect 'Shishka' (the Wen), carpets and felt were spread, and on these the Bashkirs seated themselves in a ring, with their legs tucked under them ... The feast lasted for two days and was merry, but at the same time dignified and decorous ...[1]

It is a fantastic scene; the millennia dividing the plains of Troy from nineteenth-century Russia are bridged and Book XXIII of the *Iliad* springs to life. In Richmond Lattimore's version:

> But Achilleus
> held the people there, and made them sit down in a wide assembly,
> and brought prizes for games out of his ships, cauldrons and tripods,
> and horses and mules and the powerful high heads of cattle
> and fair-girdled women and grey iron.

Like Agamemnon, Tolstoy thrones upon the hillock; the steppe is dotted with tents and fires; Bashkirs and Khirgizes, like Achaeans, race the four-mile course and take their prizes from the hands of the bearded king. But there is nothing here of archaeology, of contrived reconstruction. The Homeric element was native to Tolstoy; it was rooted in his own genius. Read his polemics against Shakespeare and you will find that his sense of kinship with the poet, or poets, of the *Iliad* and *Odyssey* was palpable and immediate. Tolstoy spoke of Homer as equal of equal; between them the ages had counted for little.

What was it that struck Tolstoy as peculiarly Homeric in his collection of

1. Quoted in D. S. Merezhkovsky: *Tolstoi as Man and Artist, with an Essay on Dostoïevski* (London, 1902).

early memories? Both the setting, I think, and the kind of life he recalled to mind. Take the account of 'The Hunt' in the volume on _Childhood_:

> Harvesting was in full swing. The limitless, brilliantly yellow field was bounded only on one side by the tall, bluish forest, which then seemed to me a most distant, mysterious place beyond which either the world came to an end or uninhabited countries began. The whole field was full of sheaves and peasants ... The little roan papa rode went with a light, playful step, sometimes bending his head to his chest, pulling at the reins, and brushing off with his thick tail the gadflies and gnats that settled greedily on him. Two borzois with tense tails raised sickle-wise, and lifting their feet high, leapt gracefully over the tall stubble, behind the horse's feet. Milka ran in front, and with head lifted awaited the quarry. The peasants' voices, the tramp of horses and creaking of carts, the merry whistle of quail, the hum of insects hovering in the air in steady swarms, the odour of wormwood, straw, and horses' sweat, the thousands of different colours and shadows with which the burning sun flooded the light yellow stubble, the dark blue of the forest, the light lilac clouds, and the white cobwebs that floated in the air or stretched across the stubble – all this I saw, heard, and felt.

There is nothing here that would have been incongruous on the plains of Argos. It is from our own modern setting that the scene is oddly remote. It is a patriarchal world of huntsmen and peasants; the bond between master and hounds and the earth runs native and true. The description itself combines a sense of forward motion with an impression of repose; the total effect, as in the friezes of the Parthenon, is one of dynamic equilibrium. And beyond the familiar horizon, as beyond the Pillars of Hercules, lie the mysterious seas and the untrodden forests.

The world of Tolstoy's recollections, no less than that of Homer, is charged with sensuous energies. Touch and sight and smell fill it at every moment with rich intensity:

> In the passage a samovár, into which Mítka, the postilion, flushed red as a lobster, is blowing, is already on the boil. It is damp and misty outside, as if steam were rising from the odorous manure heap; the sun lights with its bright gay beams the eastern part of the sky and the thatched roofs, shiny with dew, of the roomy pent-houses that surround the yard. Under these one can see our horses tethered to the mangers and hear their steady

chewing. A shaggy mongrel that had had a nap before dawn on a dry heap of manure, stretches itself lazily, and wagging its tail, starts at a jog-trot for the opposite side of the yard. An active peasant-woman opens some creaking gates and drives the dreamy cows into the street, where the tramping, the lowing and the bleating of the herd is already audible ...

So it was when 'rosy-fingered Dawn' came to Ithaca twenty-seven hundred years ago. So it should be, proclaims Tolstoy, if man is to endure in communion with the earth. Even the storm, with its animate fury, belongs to the rhythm of things:

> The lightning flashes become wider and paler, and the rolling of the thunder is now less startling amid the regular patter of the rain ...

> ... an aspen grove with hazel and wild cherry undergrowth stands motionless as if in an excess of joy, and slowly sheds bright raindrops from its clean-washed branches on to last year's leaves. On all sides crested skylarks circle with glad songs and swoop swiftly down ... The delicious scent of the wood after the spring storm, the odour of the birches, of the violets, the rotting leaves, the mushrooms, and the wild cherry, is so enthralling that I cannot stay in the brichka ...

Schiller wrote in his essay *Ueber naive und sentimentalische Dichtung* that certain poets 'are Nature' while others only 'seek her'. In that sense, Tolstoy is Nature; between him and the natural world language stood not as a mirror or a magnifying glass, but as a window through which all light passes and yet is gathered and given permanence.

It is impossible to concentrate within a single formula or demonstration the affinities between the Homeric and the Tolstoyan points of view. So much is pertinent: the archaic and pastoral setting; the poetry of war and agriculture; the primacy of the senses and of physical gesture; the luminous, all-reconciling background of the cycle of the year; the recognition that energy and aliveness are, of themselves, holy; the acceptance of a chain of being extending from brute matter to the stars and along which men have their apportioned places; deepest of all, an essential sanity, a determination to follow what Coleridge called 'the high road of life', rather than those dark obliquities in which the genius of a Dostoevsky was most thoroughly at home.

In both the Homeric epics and the novels of Tolstoy the relationship between author and characters is paradoxical. Maritain gives a Thomist

analogue for it in his study of *Creative Intuition in Art and Poetry*. He speaks
'of the relationship between the transcendent creative eternity of God and
the free creatures who are both acting in liberty and firmly embraced by his
purpose.' The creator is at once omniscient and everywhere present, but at
the same time he is detached, impassive, and relentlessly objective in his
vision. The Homeric Zeus presides over the battle from his mountain fastness,
holding the scales of destiny but not intervening. Or, rather, intervening
solely to restore equilibrium, to safeguard the mutability of man's life against
miraculous aid or the excessive achievements of heroism. As in the detachment of the god, so there is in the clear-sightedness of Homer and Tolstoy
both cruelty and compassion.

They saw with those blank, ardent, unswerving eyes which look upon us
through the helmet-slits of archaic Greek statues. Their vision was terribly
sober. Schiller marvelled at Homer's impassiveness, at his ability to communicate the utmost of grief and terror in perfect evenness of tone. He believed
that this quality – this 'naïveté' – belonged to an earlier age and would be
unrecapturable in the sophisticated and analytic temper of modern literature.
From it Homer derived his most poignant effects. Take, for example, Achilles'
slaying of Lykaon in Book XXI of the *Iliad*:

'So, friend, you die also. Why all this clamour about it?
Patroklos also is dead, who was better by far than you are.
Do you not see what a man I am, how huge, how splendid
and born of a great father, and the mother who bore me immortal?
Yet even I have also my death and my strong destiny,
and there shall be a dawn or an afternoon or a noontime
when some man in the fighting will take the life from me also
either with a spearcast or an arrow flown from the bowstring.'
So he spoke, and in the other the knees and the inward
heart went slack. He let go of the spear and sat back, spreading
wide both hands; but Achilleus drawing his sharp sword struck him
beside the neck at the collar-bone, and the double-edged sword
plunged full length inside. He dropped to the ground, face downward,
and lay at length, and the black blood flowed, and the ground was soaked
       with it.

The calm of the narrative is nearly inhuman; but in consequence the horror
speaks naked and moves us unutterably. Moreover, Homer never sacrifices

the steadiness of his vision to the needs of pathos. Priam and Achilles have met and given vent to their great griefs. But then they bethink themselves of meat and wine. For, as Achilles says of Niobe:

'She remembered to eat when she was worn out with weeping.'

Again, it is the dry fidelity to the facts, the poet's refusal to be outwardly moved, which communicate the bitterness of his soul.

In this respect, no one in the western tradition is more akin to Homer than is Tolstoy. As Romain Rolland noted in his journal for 1887, 'in the art of Tolstoy a given scene is not perceived from two points of view, but from only one: things are as they are, not otherwise.' In *Childhood*, Tolstoy tells of the death of his mother: 'I was in great distress at that moment but involuntarily noticed every detail', including the fact that the nurse was 'very fair, young, and remarkably handsome'. When his mother dies, the boy experiences 'a kind of enjoyment', at knowing himself to be unhappy. That night he sleeps 'soundly and calmly', as is always the case after great distress. The following day he becomes aware of the smell of decomposition:

> It was only then that I understood what the strong, oppressive smell was that mingling with the incense filled the whole room; and the thought that the face that but a few days before had been so full of beauty and tenderness, the face of her I loved more than anything on earth, could evoke horror, seemed to reveal the bitter truth to me for the first time, and filled my soul with despair.

'Keep your eyes steadfastly to the light,' says Tolstoy, 'this is how things are.'

But in the unflinching clarity of the Homeric and Tolstoyan attitude there is far more than resignation. There is joy, the joy that burns in the 'ancient glittering eyes' of the sages in Yeats's *Lapis Lazuli*. For they loved and revered the 'humanness' of man; they delighted in the life of the body coolly perceived but ardently narrated. Moreover, it was their instinct to close the gap between spirit and gesture, to relate the hand to the sword, the keel to the brine, and the wheel-rim to the singing cobblestones. Both the Homer of the *Iliad* and Tolstoy saw action whole; the air vibrates around their personages and the force of their being electrifies insensate nature. Achilles' horses weep at his impending doom and the oak flowers to persuade Bolkonsky that his heart will live again. This consonance between man and the surrounding world extends even to the cups in which Nestor looks for wisdom when the sun is down and to the birch-leaves that glitter like a sudden riot of jewels after the storm has swept over Levin's estate. The barriers between mind and object, the ambiguities which metaphysicians discern in the very notion of reality and perception, impeded neither Homer nor Tolstoy. Life flooded in upon them like the sea.

And they rejoiced at it. When Simone Weil called the *Iliad* 'The Poem of Force' and saw in it a commentary on the tragic futility of war, she was only partially right. The *Iliad* is far removed from the despairing nihilism of Euripides' *Trojan Women*. In the Homeric poem, war is valorous and ultimately ennobling. And even in the midst of carnage, life surges high. Around the burial mound of Patroklus the Greek chieftains wrestle, race, and throw the javelin in celebration of their strength and aliveness. Achilles knows that he is foredoomed, but 'bright-cheeked Briseis' comes to him each night. War and mortality cry havoc in the Homeric and Tolstoyan worlds, but the centre holds: it is the affirmation that life is, of itself, a thing of beauty, that the works and days of men are worth recording, and that no catastrophe – not even the burning of Troy or of Moscow – is ultimate. For beyond the charred towers and beyond the battle rolls the wine-dark sea, and when Austerlitz is forgotten the harvest shall, in Pope's image, once again 'embrown the slope'.

This entire cosmology is gathered into Bosola's reminder to the Duchess of Malfi when she curses nature in agonized rebellion: 'Look you, the stars shine still.' These are terrible words, full of detachment and the harsh reckoning that the physical world contemplates our afflictions with impassiveness. But go beyond their cruel impact and they convey an assurance that life and star-light endure beyond the momentary chaos.

The Homer of the *Iliad* and Tolstoy are akin in yet another respect. Their image of reality is anthropomorphic; man is the measure and pivot of experience. Moreover, the atmosphere in which the personages of the *Iliad* and of Tolstoyan fiction are shown to us is profoundly humanistic and even secular. What matters is the kingdom of *this* world, here and now. In a sense, that is a paradox; on the plains of Troy mortal and divine affairs are incessantly confounded. But the very descent of the gods among men and their brazen involvement in all-too-human passions give the work its ironic overtones. Musset invoked this paradoxical attitude in his account of archaic Greece in the opening lines of *Rolla*:

> Où tout était divin, jusqu'aux douleurs humaines;
> Où le monde adorait ce qu'il tue aujourd'hui;
> Où quatre mille dieux n'avaient pas un athée ...

Precisely; with four thousand deities warring in men's quarrels, dallying with mortal women, and behaving in a manner apt to scandalize even liberal codes of morality, there was no need for atheism. Atheism arises in contrariety to the conception of a living and credible God; it is not a response to a partially comic mythology. In the *Iliad* divinity is quintessentially human. The gods are mortals magnified, and often magnified in a satiric vein. When wounded they howl louder than men, when they are enamoured their lusts are more consuming, when they flee before human spears their speed exceeds that of earthly chariots. But morally and intellectually the deities of the *Iliad* resemble giant brutes or malevolent children endowed with an excess of power. The actions of gods and goddesses in the Trojan War enhance the stature of man, for when odds are equal mortal heroes more than hold their own and when the scales are against them a Hector and an Achilles demonstrate that mortality has its own splendours. In lowering the gods to human values, the 'first' Homer achieved not only an effect of comedy, though such an effect obviously contributes to the freshness and 'fairy-tale' quality of the poem. Rather, he emphasized the excellence and dignity of heroic man. And this, above all, was his theme.

The pantheon in the *Odyssey* plays a subtler and more awesome role, and the *Aeneid* is an epic penetrated with a feeling for religious values and religious practice. But the *Iliad*, while accepting the mythology of the supernatural, treats it ironically and humanizes its material. The true centre of belief lies not on Olympus but in the recognition of *Moira*, of unyielding destiny which maintains through its apparently blind decimations an ultimate principle of justice and equilibrium. The religiosity of Agamemnon and Hector consists in an acceptance of fate, in a belief that certain impulses towards hospitality are sacred, in reverence for sanctified hours or hallowed places, and in a vague but potent realization that there are daemonic forces in the motion of the stars or the obstinacies of the wind. But beyond that, reality is immanent in the world of man and of his senses. I know of no better word to express the non-transcendence and ultimate physicality of the *Iliad*. No poem runs more strongly counter to the belief that 'we are such stuff as dreams are made on'.

And this is where it touches significantly on the art of Tolstoy. His also is an immanent realism, a world rooted in the veracity of our senses. From it God is strangely absent. In Chapter IV [of this book], I shall attempt to show that this absence can not only be reconciled to the religious purpose of Tolstoy's novels but that it is a hidden axiom of Tolstoyan Christianity. All that needs saying here is that there lies behind the literary techniques of the *Iliad* and of Tolstoy a comparable belief in the centrality of the human personage and in the enduring beauty of the natural world. In the case of *War and Peace* the analogy is even more decisive; where the *Iliad* evokes the laws of *Moira*, Tolstoy expounds his philosophy of history. In both works the chaotic individuality of battle stands for the larger randomness in men's lives. And if we consider *War and Peace* as being, in a genuine sense, a heroic epic it is because in it, as in the *Iliad*, war is portrayed in its glitter and joyous ferocity as well as in its pathos. No measure of Tolstoyan pacifism can negate the ecstasy which young Rostov experiences as he charges down on the French stragglers. Finally, there is the fact that *War and Peace* tells of two nations, or rather of two worlds, engaged in mortal combat. This alone has led many of its readers, and led Tolstoy himself, to compare it with the *Iliad*.

But neither the martial theme nor the portrayal of national destinies should blind us to the fact that the philosophy of the novel is anti-heroic. There are moments in the book in which Tolstoy is emphatically preaching that war is wanton carnage and the result of vainglory and stupidity in high places. There are also times at which Tolstoy is concerned solely with seeking to discover 'the real truth' in opposition to the alleged truths of official historians and mythographers. Neither the latent pacifism nor this concern with the evidence of history can be compared to the Homeric attitude.

War and Peace is most genuinely akin to the *Iliad* where its philosophy is least engaged, where, in Isaiah Berlin's terms, the fox is least busy trying to be a hedgehog. Actually, Tolstoy is closest to Homer in less manifold works, in *The Cossacks*, the *Tales from the Caucasus*, the sketches of the Crimean War and in the dread sobriety of *The Death of Ivan Ilych*.

But it cannot be emphasized too strongly that the affinity between the poet of the *Iliad* and the Russian novelist was one of temper and vision; there is no question here (or only in the minute instance) of a Tolstoyan imitation of Homer. Rather, it is that when Tolstoy turned to the Homeric epics in the original Greek, in his early forties, he must have felt wondrously at home.

Tolstoy's Immanence
in the World

I would like to consider three passages from *War and Peace*. The first is the famous portrayal of Prince Andrew in the moment in which he is struck down at Austerlitz:

> 'What's this? Am I falling? My legs are giving way,' thought he, and fell on his back. He opened his eyes, hoping to see how the struggle of the Frenchmen with the gunners ended, and whether the cannon had been captured or saved. But he saw nothing. Above him there was nothing but the sky — the lofty sky, not clear yet immeasurably lofty, with grey clouds gliding slowly across it. 'How quiet, peaceful, and solemn, not at all as it was when I ran,' thought Prince Andrew — 'not as we ran, shouting and fighting, not at all as the gunner and the Frenchman with frightened and angry faces struggled for the mop: how differently do those clouds glide across that lofty infinite sky! How was it that I did not see that lofty sky before? And how happy am I to have found it at last! Yes! All is vanity, all falsehood, except that infinite sky. There is nothing, nothing but that. But even it does not exist, there is nothing but quiet and peace. Thank God! . . .'

The second passage (from the twenty-second chapter of Book VIII) is an account of Pierre's feelings as he drives home in his sledge after assuring Natasha that she is worthy of love and that life lies all before her:

> It was clear and frosty. Above the dirty ill-lit streets, above the black roofs, stretched the dark starry sky. Only looking up at the sky did Pierre cease to feel how sordid and humiliating were all mundane things compared to the heights to which his soul had just been raised. At the entrance to the Arbat Square an immense expanse of dark starry sky presented itself to his eyes. Almost in the centre of it, above the Perchistenka Boulevard, surrounded and sprinkled on all sides by stars but distinguished from them all by its nearness to the earth, its white light, and its long uplifted tail, shone the enormous and brilliant comet of the year 1812 — the comet which was said to portend all kinds of woes and the end of the world. In Pierre, however, that comet, with its long luminous tail aroused no feeling of fear.

On the contrary he gazed joyfully, his eyes moist with tears, at this bright comet which, having travelled in its orbit with inconceivable velocity through immeasurable space, seemed suddenly — like an arrow piercing the earth — to remain fixed in a chosen spot, vigorously holding its tail erect, shining, and displaying its white light amid countless other scintillating stars. It seemed to Pierre that this comet fully responded to what was passing in his own softened and uplifted soul, now blossoming into a new life.

Finally, I want to cite a short passage from the relation of Pierre's capitivity in Book XIII:

The huge endless bivouac that had previously resounded with the crackling of camp-fires and the voices of many men had grown quiet, the red camp-fires were growing paler and dying down. High up in the lit sky hung the full moon. Forests and fields beyond the camp, unseen before, were now visible in the distance. And farther still, beyond those forests and fields, the bright, oscillating, limitless distance lured one to itself. Pierre glanced up at the sky and the twinkling stars in its far-away depths. 'And this is me, and all that is within me, and it is all I!' thought Pierre. 'And they caught all that and put it into a shed boarded up with planks!' He smiled, and went and lay down to sleep beside his companions.

These three passages illustrate how 'in the novel, as elsewhere in the literary arts, what is called technical or executive form has as its final purpose to bring into being — to bring into performance, for the writer and for the reader — an instance of the feeling of what life is about.'[1] In all three the technical form is a great curve of motion speeding outward from a conscious centre — the eye of the character through which the scene is ostensibly perceived — and returning decisively to earth. This motion is allegorical. It communicates plot-values and visual actualities in its own right; but it is at the same time a stylistic trope, a means of conveying a movement of the soul. Two gestures mirror one another: the upward vision of the eye and the downward gathering of the human consciousness. This duality aims at a conceit which is characteristically Tolstoyan: the three passages draw a closed figure, they return to their point of departure — but that point itself has been immensely widened. The eye has returned inward to find that the vast, exterior spaces have entered into the soul.

1. R. P. Blackmur: 'The Loose and Baggy Monsters of Henry James' (*The Lion and the Honeycomb*, New York, 1955).

All three episodes articulate around a separation between earth and sky. The vastness of the sky extends above the fallen prince; 'dark' and 'starry', it fills Pierre's eyes as he tilts his head against his fur collar; the full moon hangs in it and draws his glance into far-away depths. The Tolstoyan world is curiously Ptolemaic. Celestial bodies surround the earth and reflect the emotions and destinies of men. The image is not unlike that of medieval cosmography, with its stellar portents and symbolic projections. The comet is like an arrow transpiercing the earth, and this image hints at the perennial symbolism of desire. The earth is emphatically at the centre. The moon hangs above it like a lamp and even the distant stars appear to be a reflection of the camp-fires. And central to the earth is man. The entire vision is anthropomorphic. The comet, 'vigorously holding its tail erect', suggests a horse in a terrestrial landscape.

The thematic movement, after reaching the 'immeasurably lofty' sky, the 'immense expanse of the night', or the 'oscillating' distances, is brought downward, to earth. It is as if a man had widely cast his net and were drawing it in. The vastness of the sky collapses into Prince Andrew's bruised consciousness, and his physical position is nearly that of burial, of enclosedness in the earth. The same is true of the third example: the 'shed boarded up with planks' stands for more than the hut in which Pierre is being held captive – it evokes the image of a coffin. The implication is reinforced by Pierre's gesture: he lies down beside his companions. The effect of contraction in the second passage is richer and more oblique: we pass rapidly from the comet to Pierre's 'softened and uplifted soul, now blossoming into a new life.' Softened and uplifted like newly turned earth; blossoming like an earth-rooted plant. All the implicit contrasts, between celestial motion and earth-bound growth, between the uncontrollable play of natural phenomena and the ordered, humanized cycles of agriculture, are relevant. In the macrocosm, the tail of the comet is uplifted; in the microcosm, the soul is uplifted. And then, through a crucial transformation of values, we are given to realize that that universe of the soul is the larger.

In each instance, a natural phenomenon moves the observing mind towards some form of insight or revelation. The sky and the grey clouds gliding over Austerlitz tell Prince Andrew that all is vanity; his numbed senses cry out in the voice of Ecclesiastes. The splendour of the night rescues Pierre from the trivialities and malevolence of mundane society. His soul is literally raised to the heights of his belief in Natasha's innocence. There is irony in the motif of the comet. It did portend 'all kinds of woes' to Russia. And yet, though Pierre cannot know it, these woes will prove to be his salvation. He has just told Natasha that if they were both free he would offer her his love. When the comet shall have vanished into the depths of the sky and the smoke have settled over Moscow, Pierre is destined to realize his impulse. Thus the comet has the classical ambiguity of oracles and Pierre is both prophetic and mistaken in his interpretation of it. In the final passage the expanding spectacle of forests and fields and shimmering horizons evokes in him a sense of all-inclusiveness. Outward from his captive person radiate concentric circles of awareness. Momentarily, Pierre is hypnotized by the magic of sheer distance – like Keats in the *Ode to a Nightingale*, he feels his soul ebbing away towards dissolution. The net drags the fisherman after it. But then there flashes upon him the insight – 'all that is within me', the joyous affirmation that outward reality is born of self-awareness.

This progress through outward motion and the threat of dissolution to solipsism is arch-romantic. Byron scoffed at it in *Don Juan*:

> What a sublime discovery 't was to make the
> Universe universal egotism,
> That's all ideal – *all ourselves* . . .

In the art of Tolstoy, however, this 'discovery' has social and ethical implications. The calmness of the cloud-blown sky, the cold clarity of the night, the unfolding grandeur of field and forest reveal the sordid irreality of mundane affairs. They show up the cruel stupidity of war and the cruel emptiness of the social conventions which have brought Natasha to grief. With dramatic freshness they proclaim two ancient pieces of morality: that no man can be altogether another man's captive, and that forests shall murmur long after the armies of invading conquerors have gone to dust. The circumstances of weather and physical setting in Tolstoy act both as a reflection of human behaviour and as a commentary upon it – as do those scenes of pastoral repose with which Flemish painters surrounded their depictions of mortal violence or agony.

But in each of these three passages, so illustrative of Tolstoy's genius and of his principal beliefs, we experience a sense of limitation. Lamb wrote a famous gloss on the funeral dirge in Webster's *The White Devil*:

> I never saw anything like this Dirge, except the Ditty which reminds Ferdinand of his drowned Father in the Tempest. As that is of water, watery; so this is of the earth, earthy. Both have the intenseness of

feeling, which seems to resolve itself into the elements which it contemplates.

War and Peace and *Anna Karenina* are 'of the earth, earthy'. This is their power and their limitation. Tolstoy's groundedness in material fact, the intransigence of his demand for clear perceptions and empirical assurance, constitute both the strength and the weakness of his mythology and of his aesthetics. In Tolstoyan morality there is something chill and flat; the claims of the ideal are presented with impatient finality. This, perhaps, is why Bernard Shaw took Tolstoy for his prophet. In both men there were a muscular vehemence and a contempt for bewilderment which suggest a defect of charity and of imagination. Orwell remarked on Tolstoy's leaning towards 'spiritual bullying'.

In the three examples cited, we come to a point at which the tone falters and the narrative loses something of its rhythm and precision. This occurs as we pass from the portrayal of action to the interior monologue. Every time, the monologue itself strikes one as inadequate. It takes on a forensic note, a neutral resonance, as if a second voice were intruding. The stunned uncertainty of Prince Andrew's consciousness, his attempt to rally the sudden *débâcle* of his thoughts, are beautifully rendered. Suddenly the narrative lapses into the abstract pronouncement of a moral and philosophical maxim: 'Yes! All is vanity, all falsehood, except that infinite sky. There is nothing, nothing but that.' The change of focus is important: it tells much of Tolstoy's inability to convey genuine disorder, to commit his style to the portrayal of mental chaos. Tolstoy's genius was inexhaustibly literal. In the margin of his copy of *Hamlet*, he placed a question mark after the stage direction 'Enter Ghost'. His critique of *Lear* and his presentation of Prince Andrew's collapse into unconsciousness are of a piece. When he approached an episode or condition of mind not susceptible to lucid account, he inclined to evasion or abstraction.

The sight of the comet and the immediate impressions arising out of his meeting with Natasha provoke a complex response in Pierre's mentality and in his vision of things. The proposal of love, which he made out of an impulse at once generous and prophetic, is already exerting influence over Pierre's feelings. But little light is thrown on these changes by Tolstoy's flat assertion that the soul of his hero was 'now blossoming into a new life'. Consider how Dante or Proust would have conveyed the inner drama. Tolstoy was perfectly capable of suggesting mental processes before they reach the simplification of awareness: one need only refer to the famous instance of Anna Karenina's sudden revulsion at the sight of her husband's ears. But in all too many cases he conveyed a psychological truth through a rhetorical, external statement, or by putting in the minds of his characters a train of thought which impresses one as prematurely didactic. The moralizing generality of the image – the soul as a blossoming plant – fails to convey responsibly the delicacy and complication of the underlying action. The technique is impoverished by the thinness of the metaphysics.

Knowing Tolstoy's approach to the theory of knowledge and to the problem of sense perception, we can reconstruct the genesis of Pierre's declaration: 'And this is me, and all that is within me, and it is all I!' But in the narrative context (and the latter alone is decisive), Pierre's assertion has an intrusive finality and a ring of platitude. So great a surge of emotion should, one supposes, culminate in a moment of greater complexity and in language more charged with the individuality of the speaker. This applies to the entire treatment of Pierre's relations with Platon Karataev:

> But to Pierre he always remained what he had seemed that first night: an unfathomable, rounded, eternal personification of the spirit of simplicity and truth.

The weak writing here is revelatory. The figure of Platon and his effect on Pierre are motifs of a 'Dostoevskyan' character. They lie on the limits of Tolstoy's domain. Hence the series of abstract epithets and the notion of 'personification'. What is not altogether of this earth, what is to be found on either hand of normality – the subconscious or the mystical – seemed to Tolstoy unreal or subversive. When it forced itself upon his art, he tended to neutralize it through abstraction and generality.

These failings are not solely, or even primarily, matters of inadequate technique. They are consequential on Tolstoyan philosophy. This can be clearly seen when we examine one of the main objections put forward to Tolstoy's conception of the novel. It is often argued that the characters in Tolstoyan fiction are incarnations of their author's own ideas and immediate reflections of his own nature. They are his puppets; he knew and had mastered every inch of their being. Nothing is seen in the novels that is not seen through Tolstoy's eyes. There are novelists who believe that such narrative omnipotence violates cardinal principles of their craft. One would cite Henry James as the foremost example. In the Preface to *The Golden Bowl*, he recorded his predilection

for dealing with my subject-matter, for 'seeing my story', through the opportunity and the sensibility of some more or less detached, some not strictly involved, though thoroughly interested and intelligent, witness or reporter, some person who contributes to the case mainly a certain amount of criticism and interpretation of it.

The Jamesian 'point of view' implies a particular conception of the novel. In this conception the supreme virtue is dramatization and the author's ability to remain 'outside' his work. In contrast, the Tolstoyan narrator is omniscient and tells his story with unconcealed directness. Nor is this an accident of literary history. At the time when *War and Peace* and *Anna Karenina* were being written, the Russian novel had developed a high sophistication of style and had exemplified various modes of indirection. Tolstoy's relation to his characters arose out of his rivalry with God and out of his philosophy of the creative act. Like the Deity, he breathed his own life into the mouths of his personages.

The result is a matchless amplitude of presentation and a directness of tone which recall the archaic liberties of 'primitive' art. Percy Lubbock, himself an exponent of Jamesian obliquity, writes:

> With less hesitation apparently, than another man might feel in setting the scene of a street or parish, Tolstoy proceeds to make his world. Daylight seems to well out of his page and to surround his characters as fast as he sketches them; the darkness lifts from their lives, their conditions, their outlying affairs, and leaves them under an open sky. In the whole of fiction no scene is so continually washed by the common air, free to us all, as the scene of Tolstoy.[2]

But the cost was considerable, especially in terms of explored depths.

In each of the three passages we have been examining, Tolstoy passes from the exterior to the interior of the particular character; with each inward movement there occurs a loss of intensity and a certain naïveté of realization. There is something disturbing about the effortless manner in which Tolstoy addresses himself to the notion of the soul. He enters too lucidly into the consciousness of his creations and his own voice pierces through their lips. The fairy-tale conceit, 'from that day on he was a new man', plays too broad and uncritical a role in Tolstoyan psychology. We are required to grant a good deal regarding the simplicity and openness of mental processes. On the whole, we do grant it because Tolstoy enclosed

2. Percy Lubbock: *The Craft of Fiction* (New York, 1921).

his characters with such massiveness of circumstance and elaborated their lives for us with such patient warmth that we believe all he says of them.

But there are effects and depths of insight to which these splendidly rounded creations do not lend themselves. Generally, they are effects of drama. The dramatic arises out of the margin of opaqueness between a writer and his personages, out of their potential for the unexpected. In the full dramatic character lurks the unforeseen possibility, the gift for disorder. Tolstoy was omniscient at a price; the ultimate tension of unreason and the spontaneity of chaos eluded his grasp. There is a snatch of dialogue between Pyotr Stepanovich Verkhovensky and Stavrogin in *The Possessed*:

'I am a buffoon, but I don't want you, my better half, to be one! Do you understand me?'

Stavrogin did understand, though perhaps no one else did. Shatov, for instance, was astonished when Stavrogin told him that Pyotr Stepanovich had enthusiasm.

'Go to the devil now, and tomorrow perhaps I may wring something out of myself. Come tomorrow.'

'Yes? Yes?'

'How can I tell! ... Go to hell. Go to hell.' And he walked out of the room.

'Perhaps, after all, it may be for the best,' Pyotr Stepanovich muttered to himself as he hid the revolver.

The intensities achieved here lie outside Tolstoy's range. The tightness, the high pitch of drama, are brought on by the interplay of ambiguous meanings, of partial ignorance with partial insight. Dostoevsky conveys the impression of being a spectator at his own contrivings; he is baffled and shocked, as we are meant to be, by the unfolding of events. At all times he keeps his distance from 'backstage'. For Tolstoy this distance did not exist. He viewed his creations as some theologians believe that God views His: with total knowledge and impatient love.

In the moment in which Prince Andrew falls to the ground, Tolstoy enters into him; he is with Pierre in the sleigh and in the encampment. The words spoken by the characters spring only in part from the context of action. And this brings us once again to the main problem in Tolstoyan criticism — what Professor Poggioli has described as the reflection of Molière's moralizing and didactic Alceste in Tolstoy's own nature.

No aspect of Tolstoy's art has been more severely condemned than its didacticism. Whatever he wrote seems to have, in Keats's phrase, a 'palpable design' upon us. The act of invention and the impulse towards instruction were inseparable, and the technical forms of the Tolstoyan novel clearly reproduce this duality. When Tolstoy's poetic faculties worked at highest pressure, they brought in their wake the abstract generality or the fragment of theory. His distrust of art came sharply to life where the narrative, through its energy or lyric warmth, threatened to become an end in itself. Hence the sudden breaks of mood, the failures of tone, the downgradings of emotion. Instead of being realized through the aesthetic forms, the metaphysics made their own rhetorical demands on the poem.

This occurs in the instances which we are considering. The downward shift is delicate, and the pressure of Tolstoy's imagination is so constant that we scarcely notice the fracture. But it is there — in Prince Andrew's meditations, in the flat assertion about Pierre's soul, and in Pierre's sudden conversion to a philosophic doctrine which, as we know, represented a specific strain in Tolstoyan metaphysics. In this regard the third passage is the most instructive. The outward movement of vision is arrested and drawn back abruptly to Pierre's consciousness. He exclaims to himself: 'And this is me, and all that is within me, and it is all I!' As a piece of epistemology this statement is rather problematic. It expresses one of a number of possible suppositions about the relations between perception and the sensible world. But does it arise out of the imaginative context? I think not, and the proof is that the idea which Pierre expounds runs counter to the general tone of the scene and to its intended lyric effect. This effect is latent in the contrast between the calm eternity of physical nature — the moon in the lofty sky, forests and fields, the bright limitless expanse — and the trivial cruelties of man. But the contrast vanishes if we assume that nature is a mere emanation of individual perception. If 'all that' is inside Pierre, if solipsism is the most legitimate interpretation of reality, then the French have succeeded in putting 'all' into 'a shed boarded up with planks'. The explicit philosophic statement runs against the grain of the narrative. Tolstoy has sacrificed to the speculative bent of his mind the logic and particular colouring of the fictional episode.

I realize that Pierre's language may be read more loosely, that it may be interpreted as a moment of vague pantheism or Rousseauist communion with nature. But the change of pace is unmistakable, and even if we take the end of the passage in the most general sense, the voice would seem to be Tolstoy's rather than Pierre's.

When a mythology is realized in painting or sculpture or choreography, thought is translated from language into the relevant material. The actual medium is radically transformed. But when a mythology is embodied in literary expression, a part of the underlying medium remains constant. Both metaphysics and poetry are incarnate in language. This raises a crucial problem: there are linguistic habits and techniques historically appropriate to the discourse of metaphysics even as there are linguistic habits and techniques more naturally appropriate to the discourse of imagination or fancy. When a poem or a novel is expressive of a specific philosophy, the verbal modes of that philosophy tend to encroach on the purity of the poetic form. Thus we are inclined to say of certain passages in the *Divine Comedy* or *Paradise Lost* that in them the language of technical theology or cosmography overlies the language of poetry and poetic immediacy. It is this kind of interposition which De Quincey had in mind when he distinguished between the 'literature of knowledge' and the 'literature of power'. Such encroachments occur whenever an explicit world-view is argued and set forth in a poetic medium – when one agency of language is translated into another. They occur with particular acuity in the case of Tolstoy.

Didacticism and the bias towards hortatory argument appeared in Tolstoyan fiction from the time that he began writing. Little he wrote later on was more of a tract than *The Morning of a Landed Proprietor* or the early story *Lucerne*. It was scarcely conceivable to Tolstoy that a serious man should publish a piece of fiction for no purpose but entertainment or in the service of no cause better than the free play of invention. That his own novels and tales should convey so much to readers who neither know nor care about his philosophy is an ironic wonder. The supreme and notorious instance of a divergence of attitudes between Tolstoy and his public arises over the parts of historiography and philosophic disquisition in *War and Peace*. In a well-known letter to Annenkov, the literary critic and editor of Pushkin, Turgeniev denounced these sections of the novel as 'farcical'. Flaubert exclaimed: '*Il philosophise*' and suggested that nothing could be more alien to the economy of fiction. And most of Tolstoy's Russian critics, from Botkin to Biryukov, have considered the philosophical chapters in *War and Peace* as an intrusion – valuable or worthless, as the case might be – on the proper fabric of the novel. And yet, as Isaiah Berlin says,

there is surely a paradox here. Tolstoy's interest in history and the

problem of historical truth was passionate, almost obsessive, both before
and during the writing of *War and Peace*. No one who reads his journals
and letters, or indeed *War and Peace* itself, can doubt that the author
himself, at any rate, regarded this problem as the heart of the entire
matter — the central issue around which the novel is built.

Unquestionably this is so. The ponderous and unadorned statements of a
theory of history weary most readers or seem to them extrinsic; to Tolstoy
(at least at the time that he was writing *War and Peace*) they were the pivot
of the novel. As I have mentioned earlier, moreover, the problem of history
is only one of the philosophic questions raised in the work. Of comparable
significance are the search for the 'good life' — dramatized in the sagas of
Pierre and Nicholas Rostov — the gathering of material towards a philosophy
of marriage, the programme of agrarian reform, and Tolstoy's life-long
meditation on the nature of the state.

Why is it, then, that the intrusion of metaphysic practices on literary
rhythms and the consequent failures of realization — such as occur in the
three passages under discussion — do not constitute a more drastic barrier
to the success of the novel as a whole? The answer lies in its dimensions
and in the relation of individual parts to the complete structure. *War and
Peace* is so spaciously conceived, it generates so strong an impetus and
forward motion, that momentary weaknesses are submerged in the general
splendour; the reader can skim over ample sections — such as the essays on
historiography and tactics — without feeling that he has lost the primary
thread. Tolstoy would have regarded such selectivity as an affront to his
purpose even more than to his craft. Much of his later rancour towards his
own novels, the state of mind which induced him to describe *War and Peace*
and *Anna Karenina* as representative instances of 'bad art', reflects his
recognition that they had been written in one key and were being read in
another. They had partly been conceived in a cold agony of doubt and in
haunted bewilderment at the stupidity and inhumanity of worldly affairs; but
they were being taken as images of a golden past or as affirmations of the
fineness of life. In this controversy, Tolstoy may well have been mistaken;
he may have been blinder than his critics. As Stephen Crane wrote in February
1896:

> Tolstoy's aim is, I suppose — I believe — to make himself good. It is an
> incomparably quixotic task for any man to undertake. He will not
> succeed; but he will succeed more than he can ever himself know, and

so at his nearest point to success he will be proportionately blind. This is the pay of this kind of greatness.[3]

Much of the perfection of *Anna Karenina* lies in the fact that the poetic form resisted the demands of the didactic purpose; thus there is between them a constant equilibrium and harmonious tension. In the double plot the duality of Tolstoy's intent is both expressed and organized. The Pauline epigraph initiates and colours the story of Anna but does not utterly control it. Anna's tragic fate yields values and enrichments of sensibility that challenge the moral code which Tolstoy generally held and was seeking to dramatize. It is as if two deities had been invoked: an ancient, patriarchal God of vengeance and a God who sets nothing above the tragic candour of a bruised spirit. Or to put it otherwise: Tolstoy grew enamoured of his heroine, and through the liberality of his passion she achieved a rare freedom. Nearly alone among Tolstoyan characters, Anna appears to develop in directions which point away from the novelist's control and prescience. Thomas Mann was right in asserting that the commanding impulse behind *Anna Karenina* is moralistic; Tolstoy framed an indictment against a society which seized for its own upon a vengeance reserved to God. But for once, Tolstoy's own moral position was ambivalent; his condemnation of adultery was rather close to current social judgement. Like the other spectators at the opera – however mundane or acrimonious they may appear – Tolstoy could not help being shocked by Anna's behaviour, by her tentative advances towards a freer code. And in his own perplexity – in the lack of a perfectly lucid case such as is argued in *Resurrection* – lay opportunities for narrative freedom and for the predominance of the poet. In *Anna Karenina* Tolstoy succumbed to his imagination rather than to his reason (always the more dangerous tempter).

But if the parts of the novel immediately concerned with Anna were freed from the weight of doctrine, it was also because the story of Levin and Kitty acted as a lightning-rod upon which the energies of didacticism were discharged. The balance of the work is, therefore, rigorously dependent on its double plot structure. Without it Tolstoy could not have portrayed Anna with such largess and with the poetic justice of love. But in many respects *Anna Karenina* marks the end of the period in which the contrary impulses in Tolstoy's genius were maintained in creative equilibrium. As

---

3. *Stephen Crane's Love Letters to Nellie Crouse* (ed. by H. Cady and L. G. Wells, Syracuse University Press, 1954).

we have seen, Tolstoy experienced difficulty in completing the book; the artist in him, the technician of fiction, was retreating before the pamphleteer.

After *Anna Karenina*, the moralistic and pedagogic strains in Tolstoy's inspiration, with their attendant techniques of rhetoric, became increasingly dominant. Shortly after its completion, Tolstoy set to work on some of his most urgent tracts in *paideia* and religious theory. When he turned again to the art of the novel, his imagination had taken on the dark fervour of his philosophy. Both *The Death of Ivan Ilych* and *The Kreutzer Sonata* are masterpieces, but masterpieces of a singular order. Their terrible intensity arises not out of a prevalence of imaginative vision but out of its narrowing; they possess, like the dwarf-figures in the paintings of Bosch, the violent energies of compression. *The Death of Ivan Ilych* is a counterpart to the *Letters from the Underworld*; instead of descending into the dark places of the soul, it descends, with agonizing leisure and precision, into the dark places of the body. It is a poem – one of the most harrowing ever conceived – of the insurgent flesh, of the manner in which carnality, with its pains and corruptions, penetrates and dissolves the tenuous discipline of reason. *The Kreutzer Sonata* is, technically, less perfect because the elements of articulate morality have become too massive to be entirely absorbed into the narrative structure. The meaning is enforced upon us, with extraordinary eloquence; but it has not been given complete imaginative form.

The artist in Tolstoy continued to be alive very near the surface; a reading of *The Charterhouse of Parma* in April 1887 re-awoke in Tolstoy the desire to write a major novel. In March 1889, he referred specifically to the thought of composing a 'vast and free' piece of fiction in the manner of *Anna Karenina*. Instead, he went on to write *The Devil* and *Father Sergius*, two of his most sombre parables against the flesh. It was only in 1895, eighteen years after the completion of *Anna Karenina*, that he returned to the grand form.

It is difficult to think of *Resurrection* as a novel in the ordinary sense. The preliminary sketches for it go back to December 1889; but Tolstoy could not reconcile himself to the idea of fiction, particularly on a large scale. It was only when he saw in the work a chance to convey his religious and social programme in an accessible and persuasive form that he could compel himself to the task. Had it not been, finally, for the needs of the Dukhobors (to whom the royalties of *Resurrection* were destined), Tolstoy might never have completed the book. It reflects these changes of mood and a puritanical conception of art. But there are wondrous pages in it, and moments in which Tolstoy gave rein to his unchanging powers. The account of the eastward transportation of the prisoners is handled with a breadth of design and aliveness which transcend any programmatic purpose. When Tolstoy opened his eyes on actual scenes and events, instead of keeping them fixed inward on the workings of his anger, his hand moved with matchless artistry.

This is no accident. In a full-length novel, even the late Tolstoy could allow himself a measure of freedom. Through the repeated exemplifications that a long novel makes possible, abstractions assume a colour of life. Ample flesh surrounds the bones of argument. In a short story, on the contrary, time and space are lacking. The elements of rhetoric cannot be absorbed into the fictional medium. Thus, the didactic motifs, the mythology of conduct in Tolstoy's late stories remain visible and oppressive. Through their sheer length, *War and Peace*, *Anna Karenina*, and *Resurrection* enable Tolstoy to approach that ideal of unity which he pursued with such obstinate passion. In the imaginary landscape of his three principal novels (as Marianne Moore would say) there was room for both a real hedgehog and a real fox.

Perhaps we touch here upon a more general law of literary form – a law of necessary amplitude. Where a complex philosophy is involved, the poetic structure through which it is expressed must be of a certain length. In contrast, Strindberg's late plays suggest that the drama cannot accord its severely contracted forms with the systematic exposition, the 'arguing out', of a metaphysical position. On the actual stage – as distinguished from the ideal theatre of the Platonic dialogues – there is not time or place enough. Only in the long poem or the long novel can 'the element of thought' be allowed an independent role.

Tolstoy has had one student and successor in whom the sense of epic form and philosophic concept were as pronounced and as closely allied as in Tolstoy himself. Thomas Mann was the more sophisticated metaphysician, the more deliberate user of myths. But in his confident use of history and the massive forms, the example of Tolstoy was decisive. Both writers were, to use an ancient and vulnerable distinction, poets of the reasoning mind as well as of the sentient heart. In *Doktor Faustus*, Mann achieved the synthesis of a myth of history, a philosophy of art, and an imagined fable of rare solemnity. In this book, meditation arises wholly out of the fictional circumstance. Tolstoy's transitions from poem to theory were, as we have observed in specific instances, more laboured and more visible to the reading eye. But Tolstoy and Mann stand together in a tradition of philosophic art. They have restored to our awareness an understanding of how the complex structures of metaphysics — the formal mythologies embodying men's beliefs about heaven and earth — are translated into the truths of poetry.

➤ *The Final Comparison* ➤

The contrarieties between Tolstoy and Dostoevsky did not cease with their deaths. Indeed, they were sharpened and dramatized by subsequent events. They had written their works in one of those periods of history which seem particularly favourable to the creation of great art — a period in which a civilization or traditional culture is on the verge of decline. 'Then the vital force of this civilization meets with historical conditions which cease being appropriate to it, but it is still intact, for one moment, in the sphere of spiritual creativity, and it gives its last fruit there, while the freedom of poetry avails itself of the decay of social disciplines and ethos.'[1] Less than forty years after the Grand Inquisitor had prophesied to Christ that the kingdom of man was at hand, some of Tolstoy's hopes and most of Dostoevsky's fears were realized. An eschatological despotism, the lonely, visionary rule foretold by Shigalov in *The Possessed*, was imposed upon Russia.

Dostoevsky and his writings were honoured during the brief dawn of power newly attained and energies newly liberated. Lenin thought *The Possessed* 'repulsive but great', and Lunacharsky described Dostoevsky as 'the most enthralling' of all Russian novelists. The centenary of his birth was marked during 1920–21 by official and critical tributes.[2] But with the triumph of Shigalovism in its radical forms, Dostoevsky came to be recognized as a dangerous foe, as an engenderer of subversion and heresy. The new inquisitors accused him of being a mystic, a reactionary, a sick mind endowed with rare gifts of imagination but crucially devoid of historical insight. They were prepared to tolerate *The House of the Dead* for its portrayal

1. Jacques Maritain: *Creative Intuition in Art and Poetry* (New York, 1953).

2. See Irving Howe: 'Dostoevsky: The Politics of Salvation' (*Politics and the Novel*, New York, 1957).

of tsarist oppression and *Crime and Punishment* for its account of how a revolutionary intellectual may be destroyed by the 'internal contradictions' of a pre-Marxist society. But to Dostoevsky's major works, to *The Idiot*, *The Possessed*, and *The Brothers Karamazov*, the men of the Stalinist era said, as the Inquisitor to Christ: 'Go, and come no more ... come not at all, never, never!' In July 1918, Lenin had decreed that statues should be erected of both Tolstoy and Dostoevsky. By 1932 the hero of Ilya Ehrenburg's *Out of Chaos* had to admit that only Dostoevsky had told the full truth about the people. But it is a truth with which one cannot live. 'It can be given to the dying as formerly they gave last rites. If one is to sit down at a table and eat, one must forget about it. If one is to raise a child, one must first of all remove it from the house ... If one is to build a state one must forbid even the mention of that name.'

Tolstoy, on the contrary, was securely enshrined in the revolutionary pantheon, rather as Rousseau had been sanctified in Robespierre's Temple of Reason. Lenin considered him to be the greatest of all writers of fiction. In the hands of Marxist criticism the difficult aristocrat, the *barin* of whose arrogance Gorky had written with affectionate awe, became the champion of proletarian nationalism. In him the Russian revolution had, according to Lenin, found its true mirror. Dostoevsky, the injured and humbled artisan of letters, the condemned radical and survivor of Siberia, the man who had been familiar with every species of economic and social degradation, was posthumously exiled from the 'homeland of the proletariat'. Tolstoy, the patrician chronicler of high society and rural wealth, the advocate of pre-industrial paternalism, was accorded the freedom of the new millennial city. It is an instructive paradox, suggesting that our interpretation of Ivan Karamazov's poem, however incomplete and metaphoric, is of historical relevance. What the Marxists have discerned in Tolstoy is many of the elements which Dostoevsky imagined in the Inquisitor: a radical belief in human progress through material means, a belief in pragmatic reason, a rejection of mystical experience, and a total absorption in the problems of this world to the near-exclusion of God. They have understood Dostoevsky, on the other hand, very much as the Inquisitor understands Christ, seeing in him the eternal 'disturber', the disseminator of freedom and tragedy, the man to whom the resurrection of an individual soul was more important than the material progress of an entire society.

Marxist literary criticism has dealt richly, though in a selective manner, with the genius of Tolstoy. It has either condemned or ignored the bulk

of Dostoevsky. Georg Lukács is a case in point. He has written extensively
about Tolstoy; in treating of *War and Peace* and *Anna Karenina* his critical
powers are vigorously at ease. But throughout his voluminous pronouncements, Dostoevsky makes only infrequent appearances. Lukács's early book
Die Theorie des Romans refers to him in its final paragraph; we are told in
a burst of obscure rhetoric that the Dostoevskyan novel falls outside the
complex of nineteenth-century problems with which Lukács has been dealing.
In 1943 he at last wrote an essay on the author of *The Brothers Karamazov*.
Significantly, Lukács chose for his motto Browning's verse: 'I go to prove
my soul!' But little came of the venture. The piece is indecisive and
superficial.

It could scarcely be otherwise. Dostoevsky's works embody a total denial
of the world-view held by a Marxist revolutionary. Moreover, they contain
a prophecy which a Marxist must reject if he is to believe in the ultimate
triumph of dialectical materialism. The Shigalovs and the Grand Inquisitors
may, according to Dostoevsky, achieve temporary dominion over the
kingdoms of the earth. But their rule is destined, through its own fatally
determined inhumanity, to end in chaos and self-slaughter. To a perceptive
and believing Marxist, *The Possessed* must read like a horoscope of disaster.

During the Stalinist period, Soviet censorship acted on this insight. The
spell of anti-Stalinism has brought with it a revaluation of Dostoevsky and
a resumption of Dostoevskyan studies. But it is evident that even a liberalized
version of a proletarian and secular dictatorship cannot allow too many of
its subjects to read and ponder the adventures of Prince Muishkin, the
parable of Shigalov and Verkhovensky, or the 'Pro and Contra' chapters in
The Brothers Karamazov. Once again, Dostoevsky's may become the voice
from the underground.

Outside Russia the reverse has, on the whole, been true. Dostoevsky has
penetrated more deeply than Tolstoy into the fabric of contemporary
thought. He is one of the principal masters of modern sensibility. The
Dostoevskyan strain is pervasive in the psychology of modern fiction, in
the metaphysics of absurdity and tragic freedom which emerged from the
Second World War, and in speculative theology. The wheel has come full
circle. The 'Scythian' whom Vogüé introduced to European readers as a
remote barbarian has become the prophet and historian of our own lives.
Perhaps this is because barbarism has drawn so much nearer.

Thus, even beyond their deaths, the two novelists stand in contrariety.
Tolstoy, the foremost heir to the traditions of the epic; Dostoevsky,

one of the major dramatic tempers after Shakespeare; Tolstoy, the mind intoxicated with reason and fact; Dostoevsky, the contemner of rationalism, the great lover of paradox; Tolstoy, the poet of the land, of the rural setting and the pastoral mood; Dostoevsky, the arch-citizen, the master-builder of the modern metropolis in the province of language; Tolstoy, thirsting for the truth, destroying himself and those about him in excessive pursuit of it; Dostoevsky, rather against the truth than against Christ, suspicious of total understanding and on the side of mystery; Tolstoy, 'keeping at all times', in Coleridge's phrase, 'in the high road of life'; Dostoevsky, advancing into the labyrinth of the unnatural, into the cellarage and morass of the soul; Tolstoy, like a colossus bestriding the palpable earth, evoking the realness, the tangibility, the sensible entirety of concrete experience; Dostoevsky, always on the edge of the hallucinatory, of the spectral, always vulnerable to daemonic intrusions into what might prove, in the end, to have been merely a tissue of dreams; Tolstoy, the embodiment of health and Olympian vitality; Dostoevsky, the sum of energies charged with illness and possession; Tolstoy, who saw the destinies of men historically and in the stream of time; Dostoevsky, who saw them contemporaneously and in the vibrant stasis of the dramatic moment; Tolstoy, borne to his grave in the first civil burial ever held in Russia; Dostoevsky, laid to rest in the cemetery of the Alexander Nevsky monastery in St Petersburg amid the solemn rites of the Orthodox Church; Dostoevsky, pre-eminently the man of God; Tolstoy, one of His secret challengers.

In the stationmaster's house at Astapovo, Tolstoy reportedly had two books by his bedside: *The Brothers Karamazov* and the *Essais* of Montaigne. It would appear that he had chosen to die in the presence of his great antagonist and of a kindred spirit. In the latter instance he chose aptly, Montaigne being a poet of life and of the wholeness of it rather in the sense in which Tolstoy himself had understood that mystery. Had he turned to the celebrated twelfth chapter of Book II of the *Essais* while composing his fierce genius to tranquillity, Tolstoy would have found a judgement equally appropriate to himself and to Dostoevsky:

C'est un grand ouvrier de miracles que l'esprit humain . . .

← *Racine* →

Of all modern poets, Racine took most naturally to the closed, neo-classical form of drama. There are biographical and social reasons for it. Like Goethe, Racine was a court poet who accepted the caste values of the aristocratic *milieu*. He worked for the stage, but not with it. There is the immense difference between him and Corneille or Molière. Racine is one of those great dramatic poets (Byron was another) who had no natural liking for the theatre. The history of Racine's relations to the stage is one of increasing fastidiousness. He moved from public drama to private performance and then to silence. In accepting the post of historiographer royal, he followed his own temper and social bias.

Racine chose the purest, most elegant, most uncompromising style of drama so as to achieve the greatest possible independence from the material contingencies of stagecraft. His sensitivity to adverse criticism and his religious scruples regarding the morality of the theatre were a part of his essential fastidiousness. Always in Racine's mind was the ideal of a ritual or court theatre, of a theatre of solemn occasion, as there had been in Athens. He tended to identify himself with the Greek tragedians not because of any particular affinity in world-view, but because the theatre for which he imagined that Sophocles and Euripides had written had possessed a unique dignity. This is the thought expressed in the Preface to *Iphigénie*:

> I have recognized with pleasure, by virtue of the effect which all that I have imitated from either Homer or Euripides has had on our stage, that reason and good sense are the same in all centuries. Parisian taste showed itself to be in accord with that of Athens.

Racine fully realized his ideal in *Esther* and *Athalie*, plays not even intended for performance in the usual sense. Acted by the young ladies of Saint-Cyr in 1689, *Esther* reached the open theatre only in 1721; presented in Madame de Maintenon's rooms at Versailles in 1691, *Athalie* was not publicly performed by the Comédie Française until 1716. Despite their special character, these are the plays in which Racine's art is most deliberately expressed. Their use of the chorus is the outcome of a theory of drama implicit in the entirety of Racine's work.

The art of *Bérénice*, *Iphigénie*, and *Phèdre* solicits perfect attention, not a strong disorder of emotion or the specator's identification with the action. For poor creatures like us to identify ourselves with these royal and ceremonious personages would be psychologically stupid and socially impudent. They are of rarer stuff than we. Thus we may say that Racine, like Brecht, is deliberately seeking to deepen the gulf between audience and stage. 'This is a play', says Brecht when defining his famous concept of alienation (*Verfremdung*); 'it is not real life at all or intended to be.' 'This is a tragic drama', says Racine; 'it is purer and more significant than ordinary life; it is an image of what life might be like if it were lived at all times on a plane of high decorum and if it were at all instants fully responsive to the obligations of nobility.' Both dramatists require a severe distinction between realness and realism.

This is the key to Racine's unworried, persuasive use of the unities. Unity of time and place were to him a natural condition of drama, whereas they had been to Corneille a tightrope on which to perform perilous acrobatics. The disorder of life, the material grossness of things, cannot be excluded from human affairs for more than twenty-four hours at a stretch. Even a Bérénice or a Phèdre must surrender to the vulgarity of sleep. We cannot make of more than one room at a time a place appropriate to the solemnity and purity of tragic action. Take a whole house and somewhere in it there is bound to be laughter. Outside the doors of the Racinian stage life waits with all its chaotic bustle. When the characters walk through those doors, they release their pent-up agony. We may imagine them screaming or weeping. The close of *Bérénice* should be acted quickly, as if in a race against an approaching thunderstorm. The wires are stretched to the breaking point, and at the fall of the curtain they will snap. We cannot conceive of Bérénice enduring an instant longer the suppressed agony of her spirit. She must hurry out.

Or to put it figuratively: the space of action in the dramas of Racine is that part of Versailles in the immediate vision of the king. Here decorum, containment, self-control, ritual, and total attentiveness are enforced. Even the uttermost of grief or hope must not destroy the cadence of formal speech and gesture. But just beyond the door, life plummets back to its ordinary brutishness and spontaneity. Racine is the historian of the king's chamber; Saint-Simon is the historian of the anteroom which is the world. Both are great dramatists.

Bérénice embodies the essential design of Racine's poetics. There occurs in it more than a renunciation of love. The tragedy arises from a refusal of all disorder; a final elegance of action is achieved at the expense of life. The miracle is that so special and closed a view of art and conduct should have produced some of the most superbly exciting drama known to literature. Vast energies are compressed to a flash point and then released with an explosive, murderous finality. The close of *Phèdre* or *Athalie* has in it as much fury as the battle in *Macbeth* or the massacre in *Hamlet*. The difference is simply this: the great bang takes place off stage. It is related to us in the formal *récit* of the messenger or confidant. But that does not make it a jot less exciting. On the contrary; the outward formality of the recital conveys the ferocity of the event. It impels our imaginings toward the scene of disaster:

> Déjà de traits en l'air s'élevait un nuage;
> Déjà coulait le sang, prémices du carnage.[1]

Precisely because Shakespearean and romantic dramas show the deed of violence on stage, they lack this particular mode of conveying the magnitude of a crisis. It is nearly a musical device; the echo suggests the immensity of the distant clamour.

The art of Racine is that of calculated tension. All manner of images spring to mind: the tension between the inherent repose of marble and the swiftness of depicted motion in Greek sculpture, the flying buttress, the in-pent power of a steel spring. Racine is of that family of genius which works most easily within restrictive conventions. The sense of drama we experience when listening to the *Goldberg variations* is of a related order: intense force being channelled through narrow, complex apertures. A controlling poise is maintained between the cool severity of the technique and the passionate drive of the material. Racine poured molten metal into his unbending forms. At every moment, one expects the structure to yield under stress, but it holds, and this expectation is itself conducive to excitement. Sometimes the preoccupation with structure can lead to artifice. The role of Eriphile in *Iphigénie* is rendered necessary by the counterpoint and balance of forces. But it is theatrically and psychologically unconvincing. In Racine, this kind of failure is rare. He is nearly always able to accord the design of tragic action to the demands of classic form.

Racine's four greatest plays are studies of women: *Bérénice, Iphigénie, Phèdre*, and *Athalie. Bérénice* is a magnificent but special case, for in it the

---

1. A cloud of javelins already rose in the air;
   Already blood was flowing, first fruit of carnage.

quality of the tragic is muted. Terror is kept in a minor key. It was in his two Euripidean dramas and in *Athalie* that Racine set himself the most difficult task. In each of these three plays there is tremendous tension between the classic, rational form of the actual drama and the daemonic, irrational character of the fable. Racine opposed a secular mode of art to a world of archaic or sacred myth. It is here, I feel, that his Jansenism is important. At the heart of the Jansenist position is the effort to reconcile the life of reason to the mysteries of grace. This effort, sustained at fearful psychological cost, produced two tragic images of man, that of Racine and that of Pascal. In Pascal, an austere, violent compulsion toward reason plays against a constant apprehension of the mystery of God. In Racine, the language and gestures of a Cartesian society are required to enact sacred and mythological fables. We could not be further from the world of Corneille. The essential myth of Corneillian drama is that of history. Racine invokes the presence of Jehovah and the Minoan sun-god. He releases archaic terrors upon a court theatre.

In *Iphigénie*, there is still a measure of compromise, an attempt to evade some of the implications of irrationalism. Racine suggests that the Athenian view of miracles and supernatural happenings was already conventional, that 'reason' and 'good sense' made the same allowances in Athens as they did in Paris when confronted with the ancient materials of legend. Racine's predilection for Euripides is founded on just this assumption. He supposed that Euripidean *skepsis* and the stylization of mythology in Euripidean drama could be accounted for by the fact that the poet took a rationalistic view of his material. In a very real sense, the distance from the Aeschylean vision of myth to that of Euripides is greater than that which separates Euripides from Racine. Nevertheless, Racine cannot quite evade the root dilemma. He cannot assume in his audience the necessary sophistication of disbelief. Underlying Racine's handling of myth is a complex convention: ritual and action take place without a necessary implication of belief. It is on our acceptance of this convention that *Iphigénie* depends.

The matter of the play is that of legend. We find ourselves in a world of oracles, daemonic winds, and human sacrifice. The traditional *dénouement* (like that of the Medea plays) is wildly fantastic. Operatic composers and choreographers of the baroque and neo-classical period could handle Iphigenia's wondrous rescue from the altar. Diana descending from the clouds is one of the recurrent feats of seventeenth-century stage machinery. The logic of a musical crescendo or ballet finale justified, indeed required, this kind of climax. But for a psychological dramatist such as Racine the problem is far more difficult. In order to avoid it, he departed from the original myth and from Euripides:

> How would it have seemed if I had sullied the stage with the horrid murder of someone whom I had shown to be as virtuous and amiable as Iphigenia? And how would it have seemed if I had resolved my tragedy by means of a goddess and a piece of stage machinery, and by a transformation which may still have found some credence in the age of Euripides but would have appeared to us as too absurd and incredible?

Later in his preface, Racine adds that the modern spectator will not accept miracles. But this evades the issue. If the audience is prepared to accept the mythical conditions of the play as a whole, why should it balk at the final motif of supernatural intervention? Moreover, in Ulysses' narration of Iphigenia's rescue, all the elements of miracle re-enter by the back door:

> Les dieux font sur l'autel entendre le tonnerre,
> Les vents agitent l'air d'heureux frémissements,
> Et la mer leur répond par ses mugissements.
>   . . .
> Le soldat étonné dit que dans une nue
> Jusque sur le bûcher Diane est descendue,
> Et croit que, s'élevant au travers de ses feux,
> Elle portait au ciel notre encens et nos voeux.[2]

Note how adroitly Racine plays the game of reason; the miracle has been reported by a simple soldier. Ulysses, in turn, recounts it. He does not vouch for its veracity. It seems to be a matter of degree of plausibility. Racine retains the substance of the legend and discards some of its more spectacular improbabilities. But at a price; Iphigenia is saved, for what are essentially reasons of decorum and *galanterie*. In her place, Eriphile finds

---

2. The gods make thunder growl above the altar,
    The winds quicken the air to joyous motion,
    And hear the roaring answer of the ocean.
              . . .
    The amazèd soldier says that in a cloud
    Diana lit upon the burning wood,
    And claims that rising through the very fire
    She bore aloft our incense and our prayer.

death. But the consequent absurdities of the plot (Eriphile's descent from Helen and Theseus, her passion for Achilles) are far more disturbing than the affront to reason implicit in Diana's appearance from the clouds. Thus Racine's solution to the problem of the irrational in *Iphigénie* is an unsatisfactory compromise. He was still trying to reconcile the claims of good sense and Cartesian logic to those of mythology. The transition from *Iphigénie* to *Phèdre*, three years later, marks the end of such conciliation.

Phèdre is the keystone in French tragic drama. The best that precedes it seems in the manner of preparation; nothing which comes after surpasses it. It is *Phèdre* which makes one flinch from Coleridge's judgement that Shakespeare's superiority to Racine is a flat truism. The genius of the play is specific to itself (it defines the reaches of its own magnificent purpose), yet it is representative in the highest measure of the entire neo-classic style. The supremacy of *Phèdre* is exactly commensurate to the greatness of the risks taken. A brutal legend of the madness of love is dramatized in theatric forms which rigorously suppress the possibilities of wildness and disorder inherent in the subject. Nowhere in neo-classic tragedy is the contrast between fable and treatment more drastic. Nowhere is the enforcement of style and unity more complete. Racine imposed the shapes of reason on the archaic blackness of his theme.

He took that theme from Euripides, accepting its whole savagery and strangeness. He made only one significant change. In the legend, Hippolytus is consecrated to extreme chastity. He is a cold, pure hunter who spurns the powers of love. Aphrodite seeks vengeance on her disdainer; hence the catastrophe. This is how Euripides and Seneca presented the myth, and in his *Hippolyte* (1573) Garnier followed closely on their example. Racine, on the contrary, makes of the son of Theseus a shy but passionate lover. He repulses the advances of Phèdre not only because they are incestuous but because he loves elsewhere. The original conception of Hippolytus accords perfectly with the dark quality of the legend; Euripides shows him as a forest creature, drawn from covert and enmeshed in human affairs of which he has no complete grasp. Why should Racine have changed him into a courtier and *galant homme*? Mainly, one supposes, because the image of a royal prince fleeing at the approach of women would have struck the contemporary audience as ridiculous. But that is the only concession Racine makes to the claims of decorum. For the rest he lets the furies cry havoc.

He tells us that Phèdre is committed to her tragic course 'by her destiny and by the rage of the gods'. The mechanism of fatality can be variously interpreted; the gods here may be themselves or what later mythologies of consciousness would call heredity. Ibsen speaks of 'ghosts' when he means that our lives may be haunted to ruin by an inherited infection of the flesh. So Racine invokes the gods to account for the eruption in Phèdre of elemental passions more wanton and destructive than those habitual to men. In *Iphigénie*, such invocation gave ground for awkwardness, there being a margin of discord between the presumptions of the fable and the rational bias of the dramatic conventions. In *Phèdre*, Racine avails the imagination of all possible orders of 'truth', allowing the sphere of reason to shade imperceptibly into larger and more ancient apprehensions of conduct. The difference is more than a richening of talent. Behind the tremendous force of the play seems to lie a cruel Jansenist conjecture. The action of *Phèdre* transpires in a time before Christ. Those who then fell into damnation did so in a manner more terrible than any thereafter, having available to them no occasion of redemption. Before Christ's coming, the descent into hell of a being such as Phèdre had a special horror, being irredeemable. Phèdre belongs to the world of those for whom the Saviour had not yet given His life. In that world, tragic personages cast shadows deeper than ours; their solitude is more absolute, being previous to grace. Their blood has not yet mingled in sacrament with that of a Redeemer. In it the taint of original sin burns pure and inhuman. That is the dominant note of the play.

Hippolyte strikes it in the first scene:

> Tout a changé de face
> Depuis que sur ces bords les dieux ont envoyé
> La fille de Minos et de Pasiphaé.[3]

The line is superb not only for its exotic sonority; it opens the gates of reason to the night. Into the courtly setting, so clearly established by the formal notations and cadences of the neo-classic style, bursts something archaic, incomprehensible, and barbaric. Phèdre is the daughter of the inhuman. Her direct ancestor is the sun. In her veins run the primal fires of creation. This fact is deliberately heightened by the tranquil formality, the elegance, of Hippolyte's pronouncement. He goes on to evoke the

---

3.   All things are changed
Since the gods sent to these shores
The daughter of Minos and Pasiphaë.

legendary prowess of his absent father, Theseus. And again, the sense of an archaic, bloodstained, daemonic world is loosed upon the drama:

> Les monstres étouffés et les brigands punis,
> Procruste, Cercyon, et Sciron, et Sinnis,
> Et les os dispersés du géant d'Épidaure,
> Et la Crète fumant du sang du Minotaure.[4]

Smoke, fire, and blood are the dominant images throughout the action.

Phèdre's subjection to the brutish wilfulness of the flesh is perfectly conveyed at her first entrance. There is a famous piece of stage business. Wearied by the weight of her ornaments and of her hair, Phèdre sits down. It is a momentous gesture of submission; the spirit bends under the gross tyranny of the body. Elsewhere in Racine and in neo-classic drama, tragic personages do not sit down. The agonies they suffer are of a moral and intellectual order; they leave the mind bruised or mortally hurt but still in command. Indeed, they seem to lessen the role of the flesh by exalting the outward bearing of the sufferer. If Bérénice sits down under the weight of her grief, it will only be off stage. Phèdre is different. She carries within her an obscure heaviness and fury of blood. It drags at her soul and she sits down. This minute concession spells out her greater yielding to unreason. It is precisely the nakedness of the neo-classic stage, the abstraction of technical form, which allows a dramatist to derive implications so rich and violent from the mere presence of a chair. The stricter a style, the more communicative is any departure from its severity. When Phèdre sits down she lets slip the reins of reason.

In these opening scenes, the word 'blood' is pronounced again and again to accentuate the organic, involuntary nature of her predicament:

OENONE:

Que faites-vous, Madame? Et quel mortel ennui
Contre tout votre sang vous anime aujourd'hui?

PHÈDRE:

Puisque Vénus le veut, de ce sang déplorable
Je péris la dernière et la plus misérable.

. . .

---

4. The monsters strangled and the thieves cast down,
   Procrustes, Sciron, Sinis, and Cercyon,
   The Epidaurian giant massacred,
   Crete smoking with the Minotaur's blood.

OENONE:

Juste ciel! tout mon sang dans mes veines se glace.

. . .

PHÈDRE:

Je reconnus Vénus et ses feux redoutables,
D'un sang qu'elle poursuit tourments inévitables.[5]

The whole blood–fire motif is then contracted into a single image:

De victimes moi-même à toute heure entourée,
Je cherchais dans leurs flancs ma raison égarée.[6]

Phèdre is at the altar (fire) surrounded by sacrificial victims (blood). She seeks reason and foresight in their entrails, the word *flancs* carrying all the relevant weight of erotic and animalistic implication. Again the ornateness and formality of the rhetoric seem to set off, and thereby heighten, the brutish ferocity of the myth.

The discipline imposed on the movement of the play by the solemnity of discourse and the containment of outward action allows the poet to exhibit at the same time the literal and figurative aspects of his material. Racine

5. OENONE:

What are you doing, madam, and what mortal grief
Rouses you today against those of your own blood?

PHÈDRE:

Since Venus will have it so, of that lamentable blood
I shall perish the last and most miserable.

. . .

OENONE:

Just heavens! all my blood is freezing in my veins.

. . .

PHÈDRE:

I recognize Venus and her dreadful fires,
Inescapable torments of those whose blood she pursues.

The meaning throughout hinges on the twofold sense of 'blood': the immediate physiological sense and the meaning 'race', 'lineage', 'family'. Both are implied at the same time, as in the English word 'consanguineous'.

6. Surrounded at every hour by burnt offerings,
I sought out my distracted reason in their entrails.

This is the literal translation. Phèdre is referring, of course, to the Greek and Roman practice of seeking omens and guidance in the entrails of animals sacrificed to the gods. The shock of the image depends on the contrast between 'reason' and the blood-reeking loins of beasts. Racine could make his statement so succinct because he knew that his audience was familiar with classical antiquities.

demands of us a constant awareness of both. Phèdre is possessed by Venus, and Theseus is wandering in the realms of the dead; a woman yields to extremity of love and her husband's absence stands for persistent infidelity. The difference is one of notation. In the first instance, we use the notation of classical mythology; in the latter, that of rational psychology (which is, perhaps, also a body of myths). It is the function of neo-classical rhetoric to keep both conventions of meaning equally in sight. 'Ce n'est plus une ardeur dans mes veines cachée', says Phèdre; 'C'est Vénus toute entière à sa proie attachée.' *Ardeur* is both intensity of passion and material fire; Venus is a metaphor of obsession, but also the literal goddess devouring her prey. The special quality of *Phèdre* derives from the fact that the literal, physical connotations are always somewhat the stronger. Even as Phèdre is compelled to sit down by the mastering weariness of her flesh, so the language of the play seems to bend toward grosser modes of expression such as gesture or outcry. But neo-classical drama allows no such alternatives. The violence is all in the poetry. And it is because the unfolding and containment of it in *Phèdre* are so complete that the economy of Racine has seemed to some even more persuasive than Shakespeare's largess.

Having at his disposal no looseness of form, no adjuncts of pageantry or outward music, Racine makes of his language a constant summation of energy and meaning. Images recur in counterpoint. Phèdre has seen herself as a prey, helpless in the grip of Venus. Having heard the false news of Theseus's death, she declares:

> Et l'avare Achéron ne lâche point sa proie.[7]

As in *Tristan*, the images of love and death are interchangeable; both consume men with similar rapacity. And as the action strides forward, the *leitmotiv* of fire and blood grows more insistent. It is the gods, says Phèdre to Hippolyte, who have kindled 'le feu fatal à tout mon sang'.

When Phèdre learns that her illicit passion has a rival (Hippolyte loves Aricie), the last authority of reason is shattered. We have imagined the theatre of Racine to be an enclosed place, fortified against disorder by the conventions of the neo-classic style. At the start of the play, however, Hippolyte warns us that the atmosphere has altered, as if there was a dimness in the air. The coming to Athens of the daughter of Minos has opened the gates of reason on to an alien and barbaric world. Now they are flung wide. By force of incantation, the maddened queen brings into

7. Greedy Acheron does not release its prey.

the seventeenth-century playhouse presences begotten of chaos and ancient night. She is a daughter of the sun; the whole of creation is peopled with her monstrous and majestic ancestry. Her father holds the scales of justice in hell. In the tremendous closing scene of Act IV, the play shifts into a wilder key. Once more, Phèdre invokes the twin powers of fire and blood:

> Mes homicides mains, promptes à me venger,
> Dans le sang innocent brûlent de se plonger.
> Misérable! et je vis? et je soutiens la vue
> De ce sacré Soleil dont je suis descendue?
> J'ai pour aïeul le père et le maître des dieux;
> Le ciel, tout l'univers est plein de mes aïeux;
> Où me cacher? Fuyons dans la nuit infernale.
> Mais que dis-je? Mon père y tient l'urne fatale;
> Le sort, dit-on, l'a mise en ses sévères mains:
> Minos juge aux enfers tous les pâles humains.[8]

Not since the blood-streaming heavens in Marlowe's *Faustus* has nature presided with more animate fury over a scene of human damnation. If I were to stage the play, I should have the background grow transparent to show us the dance of the Zodiac and Taurus, the emblematic beast of the royal house of Crete.

This unleashing of the forces of myth prepares us for the preternatural fatality of the *dénouement*. There is no need here for the equivocations practised in *Iphigénie*. Every touch adds to our awareness that the action has been invaded by elemental and daemonic presences. Oenone hurls herself into

8. My murdering hands, intent upon vengeance,
   Burn with eagerness to plunge in innocent blood.
   Wretch that I am! yet I live! and bear the sight
   Of that sacred sun from whom I am descended!
   The father and master of the gods is my ancestor;
   The heavens and the entire universe are filled with my forebears;
   Where shall I hide? Let us flee into the night of hell.
   But what am I saying? There my father holds the fatal urn;
   It is said that destiny has placed it in his severe hands:
   In the underworld Minos passes judgement on all pallid mortals.

In the urn of Minos are the lots or tokens that determine whether the dead soul goes to bliss or damnation. Phèdre, contemplating suicide, is terrified at the thought that her guilty shade shall appear for judgement before her own, implacable father.

the sea across which she and her royal mistress came from Crete, and we are reminded of a splendid, barbarous image of Garnier's *Hippolyte*:

> Qu'il t'eût bien mieux valu tomber dessous les ondes,
> Et remplir l'estomac des Phoques vagabondes,
> Lors qu'à ton grand malheur une indiscrète amour
> Te fait passer la mer sans espoir de retour.[9]

As Phèdre enters after Hippolyte's death, Theseus says to her: 'Il est mort, prenez votre victime.' We accept the intimation of inhumanity; a being half-goddess and half-daemon has exacted a blood offering. Dying, Phèdre proclaims her kinship with that other barbarian queen who came from a world of witchcraft beyond the Hellenic pale to wreak havoc in Greece. Phèdre's veins have burnt with the venom of love; now they are consumed by a poison which Medea brought to Athens:

> J'ai pris, j'ai fait couler dans mes brûlantes veines
> Un poison que Médée apporta dans Athènes.[10]

But now, at last, the fire is out, and her closing words tell of light without flame (*clarté, pureté*).

The death of Hippolyte affirms the savage quality of the fable. Theseus, who has rid Greece of wild beasts, summons a monster from the sea for the destruction of his son. The blood and smoke to which Hippolyte refers when recounting the exploits of his father – *Et la Crète fumant du sang du Minotaure* – surround his own hideous death:

> De rage et de douleur le monstre bondissant
> Vient aux pieds des chevaux tomber en mugissant,
> Se roule, et leur présente une gueule enflammée
> Qui les couvre de feu, de sang, et de fumée.[11]

9. 'Twere better you had fallen o'er the rail
   To glut the stomach of a roving seal,
   When careless love, the agent of your ruin,
   Made you cross seas whence there is no return.
10. I have infused into my burning veins
    A poison which Medea brought to Athens.
11. Leaping with pain and rage, the monster falls
    Before the horses' feet, and bellowing rolls
    Around; he fronts them with his flaming throat
    Whence fire, blood, and reeking smoke pour out.

Theseus slew the Minotaur, Phèdre's monstrous half-brother; now a horned beast (in Garnier's version he even has the face of a bull) slays his son. The cycle of horrors is brought to ironic completion.

In these final scenes of the tragedy, the literal violence of the myth carries all before it. It is difficult to interpret these wild, preternatural occurrences as allegories for some more decorous mythology of conduct. The monster springs from the moral blindness of Theseus, but the fire it breathes is real. That we should feel no discord between such realness and the conventions of the neo-classic theatre is supreme proof of Racine's art. The modulation of values, from the figurative to the literal, from the shapes of reason to those of archaic terror, is carefully prepared for. Throughout *Phèdre*, the part of the beast seems to encroach on the fragile bounds of man's humanity. In the end it erupts in a monstrous form, half dragon and half bull, coming from the ungoverned sea to wreck destruction on the ordered, classic land (*Il suivait tout pensif le chemin de Mycènes*).

But the change of key and the descent of the play into a kind of primal chaos are effected entirely inside the closed, neo-classic form. I have spoken of the way in which the rear wall of the stage seems to crumble at the end of Act IV. Actually, of course, it does not. There is not even a change of scene. The infernal presences which darken the air are made real by the sole force of Phèdre's incantation. The monster that slays Hippolyte has a nauseating reality, but, in fact, we see no trace of the beast. The horror is conveyed to us through the formal narration of Théramène (the messenger of Greek and Senecan tragedy making one of his final and most effective appearances in modern drama). All that happens, happens inside language. That is the special narrowness and grandeur of the French classic manner. With nothing but words — and formal, ceremonious words — at his disposal, Racine fills the stage with the uttermost of action. As nothing of the content of *Phèdre* is exterior to the expressive form, to the language, the words come very near the condition of music, where content and form are identical.

Phèdre gives occasion to show this as it is among the few plays which another dramatist of genius did render into his own language:

> Ich Elende! und ich ertrag' es noch,
> Zu dieser heiligen Sonne aufzublicken,
> Von der ich meinen reinen Ursprung zog.
> Den Vater und den Oberherrn der Götter
> Hab ich zum Ahnherrn, der Olympus ist,
> Der ganze Weltkreis voll von meinen Ahnen.

Schiller conveys the outward meaning perfectly, and something of the cadence. But the sense of the violence inside the classic measure is gone. Rob Phèdre's incantation of its music (of the speech uniquely appropriate to it) and the rest is mere outcry.

After *Phèdre*, Racine, so far as drama is concerned, observed twelve years of silence. The poet's fastidiousness toward the ambiguous social status of the theatre deepened and he grew more pious. But a contemporary tells us that the true cause was Racine's unwillingness to jeopardize by any new venture the pre-eminence assured him by *Phèdre*. There may be something in that. It is difficult to conceive how he could have gone beyond *Phèdre* while retaining the conventions of neo-classic drama, how greater risks could have been equally or more finely met. When Racine did return to the theatre, it was in a special and private mode.

In *Esther* and *Athalie* the tension between fable and rational form, which is the mainspring of energy in Racine's previous plays, is resolved. Deriving from Scripture, the truth of the dramatic action is no longer conventional or figurative. It is actual. Racine's notes in the Toulouse copy of *Esther*, and what we have of the preliminary sketches for *Athalie*, show that the poet regarded sacred history as materially true. There are in both plays elements of miracle, but they afford no difficulty of treatment, being rational manifestations of the will of God. Paradoxically, therefore, it is these cantata-dramas, these courtly miracle plays, which most completely embody the stage-craft of the 'theatre of reason'. Written, moreover, for private performance by the young ladies of Saint-Cyr, *Esther* and *Athalie* fulfil an ideal latent in much of Racine's art — that of a festive playhouse of special occasion, removed from the contingencies and vulgarities of commercial drama. In concert with this ideal, Racine for the first time uses a chorus, though the possibilities of that device seem long to have glowed in his imagination.

The two plays are of dissimilar weight. *Esther* is probably unique in that it is a serious, full-length drama intended for presentation by young people and wholly in accord with that intent. (There are remarkable children's operas, but I can think of no comparable children's play.) The softness of tone, the ease with which the tragic crisis is averted, the swift, illustrative punishment of Aman, suggest a Christmas pantomime. One has difficulty in seeing why Racine should entitle *Esther* 'a tragedy'.

Athalie is very different. It is the fourth of Racine's full-length portrayals of women, and not even in *Phèdre* is there a greater mastery of classic form.

The setting of the play is like a parable of enclosedness. The precincts of the Temple are surrounded by a wall on the other side of which lies the corrupt and misgoverned city. The boy-king, Joas, is hidden inside the Temple. Athalie vainly seeks to draw him out on to profane and open ground. At the heart of the sanctuary are the places of high holiness to which only the Levites have access. Formally, the play is surrounded by a chorus, setting it off from more realistic imitations of action. Enclosure within enclosure. The actual dramatic conflict has the linear simplicity of Aeschylus' *Suppliants*. Athalie tries to break through the successive bounds in order to get at her hidden rival and in order to desecrate God's house. The key words of the drama denote the enclosed places (*parvis, limites, enceintes, lieu redoutable*). The angry queen invades the outer defences:

> Dans un des parvis, aux hommes réservé
> Cette femme superbe entre le front levé,
> Et se préparait même à passer les limites
> De l'enceinte sacrée ouverte aux seuls lévites.[12]

In the end, she does invade the sanctuary itself and finds that she has entered a deadly trap. There is no retreat from God's presence:

> Tes yeux cherchent en vain, tu ne peux échapper,
> Et Dieu de toutes parts a su t'envelopper.[13]

It is a simple but marvellously expressive design. Unity of place acquires a double significance: it is both a convention of the neo-classic form and the prime motive of action. In *Athalie*, as in the *Suppliants*, a place of sanctuary is preserved against incursions of violence. One of the last of the great formal tragedies in western literature seems to look back explicitly to the first.

The play is shadowed by the solemnity and half-light of the interior of the Temple. But the language has a rare glitter, as of burnished metal. 'In the gloom,' writes Ezra Pound, 'the gold gathers the light against it.' The entire drama turns on a dialectic of light and darkness. On the plane of appearance there is light in the outside world and darkness inside the Temple. In reality,

12. Into one of the precincts which are reserved to men,
    This haughty woman enters, her head high,
    And was even making ready to transgress the bounds
    Of the holy enclosure to which only Levites are admitted.
13. Thine eyes search vainly, for thou canst not flee,
    On every side God has encompassed thee.

the darkness lies on the idolatrous city, and the Temple is luminous with the radiance of God. Athalie is enveloped in darkness of soul and of royal vestment; the Levites are clothed in white linen. Their weapons blaze with light as they step out of the shadows to surround Athalie. The play is tragic because we know that Joad's vision will be accomplished and Joas will become an evil king. But beyond the blackness of the fate of Israel is the light of the greater redemption. In his prophetic trance, the High Priest sees a new Jerusalem arising from the desert. It is a city of light, 'brillante de clartés'.

After *Athalie* (1691), Racine wrote no more for the theatre. He was only fifty-two, yet his silence had nothing of the quality of defeat which marked the end of Corneille's career. It was the crowning repose of a playwright who had loved drama but never trusted the stage.

Let us return, for a moment, to our initial concern: the 'untranslatability' of Corneille and Racine into any theatrical *milieu* or literary tradition outside France. Given the power and variousness of their work, the parochialism of its reach still seems to me baffling. But part of the answer must, I think, lie with the limitations of the neo-classical ideal. The total action of a neo-classic play occurs inside the language. The elements of stage business and setting are reduced to barest necessity. But it is precisely the sensuous elements in drama that translate best; they belong to the universal language of eye and body and not to any particular national tongue. Where speech has to convey the totality of the intended effect, miracles of translation, or rather of re-creation, are called for. In the case of the French classics, these have not been forthcoming.

But with regard to Corneille, this lack seems a matter of negligence rather than of technical impossibility. We have been kept from Corneille partly because French criticism has itself not taken his full measure. An age that has been roused to the call of Churchillian rhetoric, and which is aware of the cancer of violence endemic in affairs of state, should have an ear for Corneille. The great stride of argument in his plays carries beyond the baroque conventions of the plot. He is one of the very few masters of political drama that western literature has produced. What he can tell us of power and the death of the heart is worth hearing outside the confines of the Comédie Française. And an effective translation is at least conceivable. I imagine it to be a mixture of prose and verse. The parts of intrigue and background matter could be conveyed in a formal and Latinate prose (something in the manner of Clarendon). The flights of rhetoric, the great confrontations of discourse, could be rendered in heroic couplets. This would require a master of that exacting form, one who could give back to the couplet both the pace and the weight which it has in the best of Dryden. Mr Yvor Winters might do it beautifully.

Racine poses a different problem, and it may well be insoluble. Being a presenter of reality in language alone, Racine invested his words with such responsibility that no other words will conceivably do the job. Even the finest translation (Schiller's, for example) brings dispersal and dissolution to the tightness of Racine's style. On the naked stage of *Bérénice* and *Phèdre*, minute shifts in tonality are the prime movers of the drama. The crises which reverberate through the muted air are crises of syntax. It is a change of grammatical number which marks the point of no return in *Phèdre*. The queen has nearly confessed her love to Hippolyte. He shies back in horror:

> Dieux! qu'est-ce que j'entends? Madame, oubliez-vous
> Que Thésée est mon père, et qu'il est votre époux?

PHÈDRE:

> Et sur quoi jugez-vous que j'en perds la mémoire,
> Prince? Aurais-je perdu tout le soin de ma gloire?

HIPPOLYTE:

> Madame, pardonnez. J'avoue, en rougissant,
> Que j'accusais à tort un discours innocent.
> Ma honte ne peut plus soutenir votre vue,
> Et je vais...

PHÈDRE:

>   Ah, cruel! tu m'as trop entendue.
> Je t'en ai dit assez pour te tirer d'erreur.[14]

---

14. HIPPOLYTE:
>   Ye Gods! what do I hear? Madam, do you forget
>   That Theseus is my father, and that he is your husband?
>
> PHÈDRE:
>   And what ground have you to suppose that I forget it,
>   Prince? Could it be that I have abandoned all regard for my place and renown?
>
> HIPPOLYTE:
>   Forgive me, madam. Blushing, I confess
>   That I falsely judged innocent words.
>   My shame no longer can endure your sight,
>   And I go...
>
> PHÈDRE:
>   Ah, cruel one! thou hast understood me all too clearly.
>   I have told thee enough to dispel thy error.

In French, particularly in seventeenth-century usage, *entendre* means both to hear and to understand.

The entire shock of revelation lies in the shift from the formal *vous* to the intimate *tu*. The change is marked three times in the two lines which convey Phèdre's desperate confession. Decorum is gone and with it all possibility of retreat. But the English translator is helpless before the fact, for a change from 'you' to 'thou' renders nearly nothing of the immense crisis. The only counterpart is the way in which a change of key can alter the entire direction of a piece of music.

Or consider Bérénice's question to Titus:

Rien ne peut-il charmer l'ennui qui vous dévore?[15]

It is the fragile tonality of *charmer* and *ennui*, the courtly lilt of the phrase, which communicate the intimations of anguish. But how is one to translate the two words or convey in any other language the ominous cadence of the final vowels? The art of Racine shows us what Valéry meant when he said, 'of two words, choose the lesser.' But nothing in a language is less translatable than its modes of understatement.

This dilemma of translation exists even within French. Racine is studied in the schools and acted in the Comédie. I wonder, however, whether he still speaks to many of his countrymen. The role he plays in French life is monumental rather than vital. You cannot derive from Racine's plays those larger conventions of romantic action or historical pageant which have helped carry over so much of Shakespeare. In no art is the principle of life more completely that of style. What there is in *Andromaque* and *Iphigénie* and *Phèdre*, is totally expressed in the noble intricacy of seventeenth-century speech. That speech does not translate well, either into other languages or even into the loosened fabric of colloquial French.

Italians say this of Leopardi, and Russians of Pushkin. But such judgement carries no diminution. In some poets, universality is a matter of breadth — breadth of range and influence. In others, it is an attribute of intrinsic height. And it may well be the untranslatable poet who strikes nearest the genius of his own tongue.

15. Can nothing soothe the fret that ravens you?

This won't really do. *Charmer* is 'soothe' but also more: it implies relief through elegance and gracious seduction. 'Charm', as the Elizabethans used it, connotes actual magic. Bérénice seeks to dispel Titus's grief only through her entrancing presence. Nor is *ennui* adequately rendered by 'fret'. Used today, the English word seems weak and archaic; in Defoe, it still carries the right overtones of deep-gnawing irritation. Finally, there is *dévorer*, a verb intentionally excessive and out of proportion with *ennui*. What is one to do? But that is my whole point.

➤ Verse in Tragedy ➤

All the plays we have considered so far are written in verse. This has its reasons. For more than two thousand years the notion of verse was nearly inseparable from that of tragic drama. The idea of 'prose tragedy' is singularly modern, and to many poets and critics it remains paradoxical. There are historical reasons for this and reasons of literary technique. But there are also causes deeply rooted in our common understanding of the quality of language. I say verse and not poetry, for poetry can be a virtue of prose, of mathematics, or any action of the mind that tends toward shape. The poetic is an attribute; verse is a technical form.

In literature, verse precedes prose. Literature is a setting apart of language from the requirements of immediate utility and communication. It raises discourse above common speech for purposes of invocation, adornment, or remembrance. The natural means of such elevation are rhythm and explicit prosody. By not being prose, by having metre or rhyme or a pattern of formal recurrence, language imposes on the mind a sense of special occasion and preserves its shape in the memory. It becomes verse. The notion of literary prose is highly sophisticated. I wonder whether it has any relevance before the orations recorded or contrived by Thucydides in his account of the Peloponnesian Wars and before the Dialogues of Plato. It is in these works that we first encounter the feeling that prose could aspire to the dignity and 'apartness' of literature. But Thucydides and Plato come late in the evolution of Greek letters, and neither was concerned with drama.

It is certain that Greek tragedy was, from the outset, written in verse. It sprang from archaic rituals of celebration or lament and was inseparable from the use of language in a heightened lyric mode. Attic drama represents a convergence of speech, music, and dance. In all three, rhythm is the vital centre, and when language is in a state of rhythm (words in the condition of ordered motion), it is verse. In the *Oresteia* no less than in the *Bacchae*, perhaps the last of the great feats of the Greek tragic imagination, the action of the drama and the moral experience of the characters are wholly united to the metric form. Greek tragedy is sung, danced, and declaimed. Prose has no place in it.

Very early, moreover, the mind perceived a relation between poetic forms and those categories of truth which are not directly verifiable. We speak still of 'poetic truth' when signifying that a statement may be false or meaningless by the test of empiric proof, yet possesses at the same time an important, undeniable verity in a moral, psychological, or formal domain. Now the truths of mythology and religious experience are largely of this order. Prose submits its own statements to criteria of verification which are, in fact, irrelevant or inapplicable to the realities of myth. And it is on these that Greek tragedy is founded. The matter of tragic legend, whether it invokes Agamemnon, Oedipus, or Alcestis torn from the dead, cannot be held liable to prosaic inquisition. As Robert Graves says, the imagination has extraterritorial rights, and these are guarded by poetry.

Poetry also has its criteria of truth. Indeed, they are more severe than those of prose, but they are different. The criterion of poetic truth is one of internal consistency and psychological conviction. Where the pressure of imagination is sufficiently sustained, we allow poetry the most ample liberties. In that sense, we may say that verse is the pure mathematics of language. It is more exact than prose, more self-contained, and more capable of constructing theoretic forms independent of material basis. It can 'lie' creatively. The worlds of poetic myth, like those of non-Euclidean geometry, are persuasive of truth so long as they adhere to their own imaginative premises. Prose, on the contrary, is applied mathematics. Somewhere along the line the assertions it makes must correspond to our sensual perceptions. The houses described in prose must stand on solid foundations. Prose measures, records, and anticipates the realities of practical life. It is the garb of the mind doing its daily job of work.

This is no longer entirely the case. Modern literature has developed the concept of 'poetic prose', of a prose liberated from verifiability and the jurisdiction of logic as it is embodied in common syntax. There are prophetic traces of this idea in Rabelais and Sterne. But it does not really assume importance before Rimbaud, Lautréamont, and Joyce. Until their time the distinctions between the role of verse and that of prose were firm.

Verse is not only the special guardian of poetic truth against the critique of empiricism. It is the prime divider between the world of high tragedy and that of ordinary existence. Kings, prophets, and heroes speak in verse, thus showing that the exemplary personages in the commonwealth communicate in a manner nobler and more ancient than that reserved to common men. There is nothing democratic in the vision of tragedy. The royal and heroic characters whom the gods honour with their vengeance are set higher than we are in the chain of being, and their style of utterance must reflect this elevation.

Common men are prosaic, and revolutionaries write their manifestoes in prose. Kings answer in verse. Shakespeare knew this well. *Richard II* is a drama of languages which fail to communicate with each other. Richard goes to ruin because he seeks to enforce the criteria of poetic truth on the gross, mutinous claims of political reality. He is a royal poet defeated by a rebellion of prose.

Like music, moreover, verse sets a barrier between the tragic action and the audience. Even where there is no longer a chorus it creates that necessary sense of distance and strangeness to which Schiller referred. The difference of languages between the stage and the pit alters the perspective and gives to the characters and their actions a special magnitude. And by compelling the mind to surmount a momentary barrier of formality, verse arrests and ripens our emotions. We can identify ourselves with Agamemnon, Macbeth, or Phèdre, but only partially, and after preliminary effort. Their use of a language shaped more nobly and intricately than our own imposes on us a respectful distance. We cannot leap into their skins as we are invited to do in naturalistic drama. Thus verse prevents our sympathies from growing too familiar. At the courts of great monarchs, lesser nobility and the third estate were not allowed too near the royal person. But prose is a leveller and gets very close to its object.

Verse at once simplifies and complicates the portrayal of human conduct. That is the crucial point. It simplifies because it strips away from life the encumbrances of material contingency. Where men speak verse, they are not prone to catching colds or suffering from indigestion. They do not concern themselves with the next meal or train timetables. Earlier in this book, I have cited the opening line of Victor Hugo's *Cromwell*. It infuriated contemporary critics because it used an *alexandrin*, the very mark of high and timeless life, for a precise temporal statement. It drew tragic verse down to the gross world of clocks and calendars. Like wealth, in the poetics of Henry James and Proust, verse relieves the personages of tragic drama from the complications of material and physical need. It is because all material exactions are met by the assumption of financial ease that Jamesian and Proustian characters are at liberty to live in full the life of feeling and intelligence. So it is in tragedy. In a very real sense, the tragic hero lets his servants live for him. It is they who assume the corrupting burdens of hunger, sleep, and ailment. This is one of the decisive differences between the world of the novel, which is that of prose, and the world of the tragic theatre, which is that of verse. In prose fiction, as D. H. Lawrence remarked, 'you know there is a watercloset on the premises.' We are not called upon to envisage such facilities at Mycenae and Elsinore.

If there are bathrooms in the houses of tragedy, they are for Agamemnon to be murdered in.

It is this distinction which lies behind the neo-classic belief that verse should not be made to express menial facts. Since Wordsworth and the romantics, we no longer accept this convention. From the time of the *Lyrical Ballads* to that of *Prufrock*, poetry has appropriated to itself all domains, however sordid or familiar. It is held that all manner of reality can be given suitable poetic form. I wonder whether this is really so. Dryden conceded that verse might be made to say 'close the door', but was dubious whether it should. For in performing such tasks it descends into the chaos of material objects and bodily functions where prose is master. Certain styles of action are more appropriate to poetic incarnation than others. Because we have denied the fact, so much of what passes for modern poetry is merely inflated or bewildered prose. In contemporary verse drama, we see repeated failures to distinguish between proper and improper uses of poetic form. The recent plays of T. S. Eliot give clear proof of what happens when blank verse is asked to carry out domestic functions. It rebels.

But if verse simplifies our account of reality by eliminating life below the stairs, it also immensely complicates the range and values of the behaviour of the mind. By virtue of elision, concentration, obliqueness, and its capacity to sustain a plurality of meanings, poetry gives an image of life which is far denser and more complex than that of prose. The natural shape of prose is linear; it proceeds by consequent statement. It qualifies or contradicts by what comes after. Poetry can advance discordant persuasions simultaneously. Metaphors, imagery, and the tropes of verse rhetoric can be charged with simultaneous yet disparate meanings, even as music can convey at the same moment contrasting energies of motion. The syntax of prose embodies the central role which causal relations and temporal logic play in the proceedings of ordinary thought. The syntax of verse is, in part, liberated from causality and time. It can put cause before effect and allow to argument a progress more adventurous than the marching order of traditional logic. That is why good verse is untranslatable into prose. Consider an example from *Coriolanus* (a play in which Shakespeare's purpose depends heavily on the prerogatives of poetic form):

> No, take more!
> What may be sworn by, both divine and human,
> Seal what I end withal! This double worship —
> Where one part does disdain with cause, the other

> Insult without all reason; where gentry, title, wisdom
> Cannot conclude but by the yea and no
> Of general ignorance – it must omit
> Real necessities, and give way the while
> To unstable slightness. Purpose so barr'd, it follows
> Nothing is done to purpose. Therefore, beseech you –
> You that will be less fearful than discreet;
> That love the fundamental part of state
> More than you doubt the change on't; that prefer
> A noble life before a long, and wish
> To jump a body with a dangerous physic
> That's sure of death without it – at once pluck out
> The multitudinous tongue; let them not lick
> The sweet which is their poison.

No prose paraphrase can give a fair equivalent. Nor can we 'translate' downward Hamlet's soliloquies, Macbeth's meditation on death, or Cleopatra's lament over her fallen lover.

As mathematics recedes from the obvious, it becomes less translatable into anything but itself. As poetry moves further from the prosaic, as it gains in subtlety and concentration, it becomes irreducible to any other medium. Bad verse, verse which is not strictly necessary to the purpose, profits from good paraphrase or even from translation into another language. Witness how much finer Poe sounds in French. But good verse, that is to say poetry, is all but lost.

So far, therefore, as tragic drama is an exaltation of action above the flux of disorder and compromise prevalent in habitual life, it requires the shape of verse. The stylization and simplification which that shape imposes on the outward aspects of conduct make possible the moral, intellectual, and emotional complications of high drama. Poetic conventions clear the ground for the free play of moral forces. The tragic actors in the Greek theatre stood on lofty wooden shoes and spoke through great masks, thus living higher and louder than life. Verse provides a similar altitude and resonance.

This is not to deny that prose has its own tragic register. One would not wish Tacitus to have written in verse, and Keats's letters attain depths of feeling even greater than those of his poetry. But the two spheres are different, and the decision of certain playwrights to carry tragedy from the realm of verse into that of prose is one of the decisive occurrences in the history of western drama.

✦ Tragedy and Myth ✦

We cannot be certain that there is, either in language or in the forms of art, a law of the conservation of energy. On the contrary, there is evidence to show that reserves of feeling can be depleted, that particular kinds of intellectual and psychological awareness can go brittle or unreal. There is a hardening in the arteries of the spirit as in those of the flesh. It is at least plausible that the complex of Hellenic and Christian values which is mirrored in tragic drama, and which has tempered the life of the western mind over the past two thousand years, is now in sharp decline. The history of modern Europe – the deportation, murder, or death in battle of some seventy million men, women, and children between 1914 and 1945 – suggests that the reflexes by which a civilization alters its habits in order to survive mortal danger are no longer as swift or realistic as they once were.

In language this stiffening of the bone is, I submit, clearly discernible. Many of the habits of language in our culture are no longer fresh or creative responses to reality, but stylized gestures which the intellect still performs efficiently, but with a diminishing return of new insight and new feeling. Our words seem tired and shopworn. They are no longer charged with their original innocence or with the power of revelation (think of what light and fire the word *amor* could still cast into the soul as late as the thirteenth century). And because they are weary, words no longer seem prepared to assume the burden of new meaning and plurality which Dante, Montaigne, Shakespeare, and Luther placed upon them. We add to our technological vocabulary by joining together used scraps, like a reclaimer of old metals. We no longer fuse the raw materials of speech into new glory as did the compilers of the King James Bible. The curve of invention points downward. Compare the grey jargon of the contemporary economist to the style of Montesquieu. Set the counting-house prose of the modern historian next to that of Gibbon, Macaulay, or Michelet. Where the modern scholar cites from a classic text, the quotation seems to burn a hole in his own drab page. Sociologists, mass-media experts, the writers of soap operas and politicians' speeches, and teachers of 'creative writing' are the gravediggers of the word. But languages only let themselves be buried when something inside them has, in fact, died.

The political inhumanity of our time, moreover, has demeaned and brutalized language beyond any precedent. Words have been used to justify political falsehood, massive distortions of history, and the bestialities of the totalitarian state. It is conceivable that something of the lies and the savagery has crept into their marrow. Because they have been used to such base ends, words no longer give their full yield of meaning. And because they assail us in such vast, strident numbers, we no longer give them careful hearing. Each day we sup our fill of horrors – in the newspaper, on the television screen, or the radio – and thus we grow insensible to fresh outrage. This numbness has a crucial bearing on the possibility of tragic style. That which began in the romantic period, the inrush of current political and historical emotions on daily life, has become a dominant fact of our own experience. Compared with the realities of war and oppression that surround us, the gravest imaginings of the poets are diminished to a scale of private or artificial terror. In *The Trojan Women*, Euripides had the poetic authority to convey to the Athenian audience the injustice and reproach of the sack of Melos. Cruelty was still commensurate to the scope or response of the imagination.

I wonder whether this is still the case. What work of art could give adequate expression to our immediate past? The last war has had neither its *Iliad* nor its *War and Peace*. None who have dealt with it have matched the control of remembrance achieved by Robert Graves or Sassoon in their accounts of 1914–18. Language seems to choke on the facts. The only array of words still able to get near the quick of feeling is the kind of naked and prosaic record set down in *The Diary of Anne Frank*.

Given the abuses of language by political terror and by the illiteracy of mass consumption, can we look to a return of that mystery in words which lies at the source of tragic poetry? Can the *newspeak* of George Orwell's *1984* (and that year is already upon us) serve the needs of tragic drama? I think not, and this is why T. S. Eliot is so right when he describes the ideal of modern dramatic verse as 'a mirage'.

Naturally such judgement can only be provisional. A master of verse tragedy may arrive on the scene tomorrow. The acclaim given to Archibald MacLeish's *JB* shows that hopes remain high. In English, moreover, there is at least one group of modern verse plays that comes very close to solving the problem of tragic style. Already in *The Countess Cathleen*, Yeats went further than any poet since Dryden in restoring to blank verse the sinews of action:

THE ANGEL: The Light of Lights
                Looks always on the motive, not the deed,
                The Shadow of Shadows on the deed alone.

OONA: Tell them who walk upon the floor of peace
         That I would die and go to her I love;
         The years like great black oxen tread the world,
         And God the herdsman goads them on behind,
         And I am broken by their passing feet.

In *Purgatory*, the mirage of the perfection of dramatic verse is within grasp. Nowhere in the entire play is there a single stopgap or looseness. Every line is held taut, and the cold, luminous power is that of language which has passed through the schooling of the great centuries of prose:

                    Study that tree.
         It stands there like a purified soul,
         All cold, sweet, glistening light.
         Dear mother, the window is dark again,
         But you are in the light because
         I finished all that consequence.
         I killed that lad because had he grown up
         He would have struck a woman's fancy,
         Begot, and passed pollution on.
         I am a wretched foul old man
         And therefore harmless.

But *Purgatory* is a feat which is only briefly sustained, over a single scene involving two voices. Being a vision of an intermediary moment in the proceedings of the soul — a moment between damnation and the greater trial of grace — it is sufficient unto itself. But it offers no solution toward the problem of full-scale drama. And this is true of all of Yeats's best plays. They are glowing embers, as if the virtues of their poetry were too fragile and instantaneous to support the fabric of intrigue and argument required of the normal theatre. *The Dreaming of the Bones* and *Purgatory* are prolegomena to a future drama. Their limitation tells us that a renascence of poetic tragedy demands more than the attainment of style.

It demands that that style be brought into contact with the ordinary everyday world. Such contact does not depend on the degree of realism or modernity which the poet is prepared to allow. The work of art can cross the barriers that surround all private vision — it can make a window of the poet's mirror — only if there is some context of belief and convention which the artist shares with his audience; in short, only if there is in live force what I have called a mythology. Yeats's attempt to create such a mythology is notorious, but inconclusive. The body of myth which he devised for his poems and plays is full of vivid imaginings. In the good poems it shimmers in the far background with a hint of proximate revelation. But often it obtrudes between the reader and the text like stained glass. In reading a poem, there is time and incentive to acquire the esoteric knowledge needed for comprehension; the eye grows used to the darkness and flicker of private meaning. But not in the theatre; our understanding of a stage play must carry instantaneous conviction.

Yeats's failure to construct a mythology for the age is part of that larger failure or withdrawal from imaginative commitment which occurs after the seventeenth century. Greek tragedy moved against a background of rich, explicit myth. The landscape of terror was entirely familiar to the audience, and this familiarity was both a spur and a limit to the poet's personal invention. It was a net to guard from ruin the acrobatics of his fancy. The mythology at work in Shakespearean drama is less formal, being construed of a close yet liberal conjunction of the antique and the Christian world view. But it still gave to reality shape and order. The Elizabethan stage had behind it an edifice of religious and temporal values on whose façade men had their assigned place as in the ranked sculpture of a Gothic portal. The tracery of literal meaning and allegoric inference extended from brute matter to the angelic spheres. The alphabet of tragic drama – such concepts as grace and damnation, purgation and relapse, innocence and corruption through daemonic power – retained a clear and present meaning. There plays around the thoughts and statements of the individual characters in Elizabethan tragedy a light of larger reference. And in varying degrees of immediacy, this light was perceptible to the theatrical audience. No footnote was required to convey the nature of the devilish temptation which ensnares Macbeth; Hamlet's appeal to ministers of grace could strike home without a theological gloss. The playwright depended on the existence of a common ground; a kind of preliminary pact of understanding had been drawn up between himself and his society. Shakespearean drama relies on a community of expectation even as classical music relies on an acceptance of the conventions of interval in the tempered scale.

But the pact was broken during the splintering of the ancient hierarchic world image. Milton was the last major poet to assume the total relevance of classic and Christian mythology. His refusal in *Paradise Lost* to choose between the Ptolemaic and the Copernican accounts of celestial motion is a gesture both serene and sorrowful; serene, because it regards the proposals of natural science as less urgent or assured than those of poetic tradition; sorrowful, because it marks the historical moment in which the forms of the cosmos recede from the authority of humanistic judgement. Henceforth the stars burn out of reach. After Milton the mythology of animate creation and the nearly tangible awareness of a continuity between the human and the divine order – that sense of a relationship between the rim of private experience and the hub of the great wheel of being – lose their hold over intellectual life. Wallace Stevens wrote of 'the gods that Boucher killed'. Rococo painting and the court ballet did worse than kill; they diminished the ancient mysteries and their emblems to ornate trivia. An eighteenth-century pastoral in mythological costume is more than a refusal of myth; it is a parody.

The myths which have prevailed since Descartes and Newton are myths of reason, no truer perhaps than those which preceded them, but less responsive to the claims of art. Yet when it is torn loose from the moorings of myth, art tends toward anarchy. It becomes the outward leap of the impassioned but private imagination into a void of meaning. The artist is Icarus looking for safe ground, and the unsustained solitude of his flight communicates to his work that touch of vertigo which is characteristic of romanticism no less than of modern abstract art. Secure inside the citadel of his persuasions, Chesterton observed how the modern artist lives either by the rags and leavings of old, worn-out mythologies, or seeks to create new ones in their stead. The nineteenth and twentieth centuries have been a classic period for the artist as reviver or maker of myth. *Faust* II is an attempt to fuse Hellenic, Christian, and gnostic elements into a coherent design. Tolstoy and Proust elaborated mythologies of time and of time's governance over man. Zola fell prey to a mystique of the literal fact, constructing his works as do certain modern sculptors when they weld together scrap iron. D. H. Lawrence worshipped the dark gods and the fire in the blood. Yeats strove to persuade himself and his readers (thus making them accomplices to his own doubt) of a mythology of lunar phases and communion with the dead. Blake and Rilke peopled their solitude with angelic hosts.

But where the artist must be the architect of his own mythology, time is against him. He cannot live long enough to impose his special vision and the symbols which he has devised for it on the habits of language and feeling in his society. The Christian mythology in Dante had behind it centuries of elaboration and precedent to which the reader could naturally refer when placing the particular approach of the poet. The cabalistic system invoked by

Blake and the moon-magic of Yeats have only a private or occult tradition. There is outside the poem no stable edifice built on authorities or conventions independent of the poet's assertion (it was the genius of Joyce to observe the need for exterior corroboration when he anchored *Ulysses* to the *Odyssey*). The idiosyncratic world image, without an orthodox or public fabric to support it, is kept in focus only by virtue of the poet's present talent. It does not take root in the common soil.

This is true even in the case of Wagner, although he came closer than anyone else to transforming a private revelation into a public creed. By the enormous strength of his personality and by his cunning rhetoric, he nearly instilled his concocted mythology into the general mind. The Wagnerian note sounded throughout social and political life and had its mad echoes in the ruin of modern Europe. But it is now rapidly fading. Wagnerian symbolism has receded into the limits of the operatic and no longer plays a significant role in the repertoire of feeling.

What I am trying to make clear is a fact which is simple yet decisive toward an understanding of the crisis of modern tragedy. The mythologies that have centred the imaginative habits and practices of western civilization, that have organized the inner landscape, were not the product of individual genius. A mythology crystallizes sediments accumulated over great stretches of time. It gathers into conventional form the primal memories and historical experience of the race. Being the speech of the mind when it is in a state of wonder or perception, the great myths are elaborated as slowly as is language itself. More than a thousand years of reality lay behind the fables of Homer and Aeschylus. The Christian image of the pilgrimage of the soul was ancient before Dante and Milton made use of it. Like a stone that has lain in live water, it had become firm and lustrous to the touch of the poet. When the classic and the Christian world order entered into decline, the consequent void could not be filled by acts of private invention.

Or so it would have seemed until the twentieth century. For we have before us now the startling fact of a mythology created at a specific time by a particular group of men, yet imposed upon the lives of millions. It is that explicit myth of the human condition and of the goals of history which we call Marxism. Marxism is the third principal mythology to have taken root in western consciousness. How long or how deeply it will scar the course of moral and intellectual experience remains uncertain. Perhaps the roots are shallow precisely because the Marxist world-view came into being through political fiat rather than by the ripening of collective emotion. Perhaps it is being maintained only by material power and will prove incapable of inward growth. But at present it is as articulate and comprehensive as any mythology ever devised to order the complex chaos of reality. It has its heroes and sacred legends, its shrines and emblems of terror, its rites of purgation and anathema. It stands as one of the three major configurations of belief and symbolic form available to the poet when he seeks a public context for his art.

But of the three, there is none that is naturally suitable to a revival of tragic drama. The classic leads to a dead past. The metaphysics of Christianity and Marxism are anti-tragic. That, in essence, is the dilemma of modern tragedy.

◆ *Epilogue* ◆

I want to end this book on a note of personal recollection rather than of critical argument. There are no definite solutions to the problems I have touched on. Often allegory will illuminate them more aptly than assertion. Moreover, I believe that literary criticism has about it neither rigour nor proof. Where it is honest, it is passionate, private experience seeking to persuade. The three incidents I shall recount accord with the threefold possibility of our theme: that tragedy is, indeed, dead; that it carries on in its essential tradition despite changes in technical form; or, lastly, that tragic drama might come back to life.

I was taking a train journey through southern Poland not long ago. We passed a gutted ruin on the comb of a hill. One of the Poles in my compartment told me what had taken place there. It had been a monastery, and the Germans had used it as a prison for captured Russian officers. In the last year of the war, when the German armies began receding from the east, no more food reached the prison. The guards pillaged what they could off the land, but soon their police dogs turned dangerous with hunger. After some hesitation, the Germans loosed the dogs on the prisoners, and maddened by hunger, the dogs ate several of them alive. When the garrison fled, they left the survivors locked in the cellar. Two of them managed to keep alive by killing and devouring their companions. Finally, the advancing Soviet army found them. The two men were given a decent meal and then shot lest the soldiers see to what abjection their former officers had been reduced. After that, the monastery was burnt to the ground.

The other travellers in our compartment had listened, and now each in turn recounted some incident comparable or worse. One woman told of what had been done to her sister in the death-camp at Matthausen. I will not set it down here, for it is the kind of thing under which language breaks. We were all silent for a time, and then an older man said that he knew a medieval parable which might help one understand how such events had come to pass:

> In some obscure village in central Poland, there was a small synagogue. One night, when making his rounds, the Rabbi entered and saw God sitting in a dark corner. He fell upon his face and cried out: 'Lord God, what art Thou doing here?' God answered him neither in thunder nor out of a whirlwind, but with a small voice: 'I am tired, Rabbi, I am tired unto death.'

The bearing of this parable on our theme, I take it, is this: God grew weary of the savagery of man. Perhaps He was no longer able to control it and could no longer recognize His image in the mirror of creation. He has left the world to its own inhuman devices and dwells now in some other corner of the universe so remote that His messengers cannot even reach us. I would suppose that He turned away during the seventeenth century, a time which has been the constant dividing line in our argument. In the nineteenth century, Laplace announced that God was a hypothesis of which the rational mind had no further need; God took the great astronomer at his word. But tragedy is that form of art which requires the intolerable burden of God's presence. It is now dead because His shadow no longer falls upon us as it fell on Agamemnon or Macbeth or Athalie.

Or, perhaps, tragedy has merely altered in style and convention. There comes a moment in *Mutter Courage* when the soldiers carry in the dead body of Schweizerkas. They suspect that he is the son of Courage but are not quite certain. She must be forced to identify him. I saw Helene Weigel act the scene with the East Berlin ensemble, though acting is a paltry word for the marvel of her incarnation. As the body of her son was laid before her, she merely shook her head in mute denial. The soldiers compelled her to look again. Again she gave no sign of recognition, only a dead stare. As the body was carried off, Weigel looked the other way and tore her mouth wide open. The shape of the gesture was that of the screaming horse in Picasso's *Guernica*. The sound that came out was raw and terrible beyond any description I could give of it. But, in fact, there was no sound. Nothing. The sound was total silence. It was silence which screamed and screamed through the whole theatre so that the audience lowered its head as before a gust of wind. And that scream inside the silence seemed to me to be the same as Cassandra's when she divines the reek of blood in the house of Atreus. It was the same wild cry with which the tragic imagination first marked our sense of life. The same wild and pure lament over man's inhumanity and waste of man. The curve of tragedy is, perhaps, unbroken.

Finally, there should be present to our minds the possibility – though I judge it remote – that the tragic theatre may have before it a new life and future. I have seen a documentary film showing the activities of a Chinese agricultural commune. At one point, the workers streamed in from the fields, laid down their mattocks, and gathered on the barrack square. They formed into a large chorus and began chanting a song of hatred against China's foes. Then a group leader leapt from the ranks and performed a kind of violent, intricate dance. He was acting out in pantomime the struggle against the imperialist bandits and their defeat by the peasant armies. The ceremony closed with a recital of the heroic death of one of the founders of the local Communist Party. He had been killed by the Japanese and was buried near by.

Is it not, I wonder, in some comparable rite of defiance and honour to the dead that tragedy began, three thousand years ago, on the plains of Argos?

✦ Obsessions ✦

◂ A Death of Kings ▸

There are three intellectual pursuits, and, so far as I am aware, only three, in which human beings have performed major feats before the age of puberty. They are music, mathematics, and chess. Mozart wrote music of undoubted competence and charm before he was eight. At the age of three, Karl Friedrich Gauss reportedly performed numerical computations of some intricacy; he proved himself a prodigiously rapid but also a fairly deep arithmetician before he was ten. In his twelfth year, Paul Morphy routed all comers in New Orleans – no small feat in a city that, a hundred years ago, counted several formidable chess players. Are we dealing here with some kind of elaborate imitative reflexes, with achievements conceivably in reach of automata? Or do these wondrous miniature beings actually create? Rossini's *Six Sonatas for Two Violins, Cello, and Double Bass*, composed by the boy during the summer of 1804, are patently influenced by Haydn and Vivaldi, but the main melodic lines are Rossini's, and beautifully inventive. Aged twelve, Pascal seems in fact to have re-created for and by himself the essential axioms and initial propositions of Euclidean geometry. The earliest recorded games of Capablanca and Alekhine contain significant ideas and show marks of personal style. No theory of Pavlovian reflex or simian mimesis will account for the facts. In these three domains we find creation, not infrequently characteristic and memorable, at a fantastically early age.

Is there an explanation? One looks for some genuine relationship between the three activities; in what way do music, mathematics, and chess resemble one another? This is the sort of question to which there ought to be a trenchant – indeed, a classic – reply. (The notion that there *is* a deep affinity is not novel.) But one finds little except shadowy hints and metaphor. The psychology of musical invention, as distinct from mere virtuosity of performance, is all but non-existent. Despite fascinating hints by the mathematicians Henri Poincaré and Jacques Hadamard, scarcely anything is known about the intuitive and ratiocinative processes that underlie mathematical discovery. Dr Fred Reinfeld and Mr Gerald Abrahams have written interestingly on 'the chess mind', but without establishing whether there is such a thing and, if there is, what constitutes its bizarre powers. In each of these areas, 'psychology' turns out to be principally a matter of anecdotes, among them the dazzling executive and creative showings of child prodigies.

Reflecting, one is struck by two points. It looks very much as if the formidable mental energies and capacities for purposeful combination exhibited by the child-master in music, mathematics, and chess are almost wholly isolated, as if they explode to ripeness apart from, and in no necessary relation to, normally maturing cerebral and physical traits. A musical prodigy, an infant composer, or conductor, may in every other respect be a small child, petulant and ignorant as are ordinary children of his age. There is no evidence to suggest that Gauss's behaviour when he was a young boy, his fluency or emotional coherence, in any way exceeded that of other little boys; he was an adult, and more than a normal adult, solely in respect of numerical and geometric insights. Anyone who has played at chess with a very young and highly gifted boy will have noticed the glaring, nearly scandalous disparity between the ruses and analytic sophistication of the child's moves on the board and his puerile behaviour the moment the pieces are put away. I have seen a six-year-old handle a French Defence with tenacious artistry and collapse a moment after the game was ended into a loud, randomly destructive brat. In short, whatever happens in the brain and nervous synapses of a young Mendelssohn, of a Galois, of Bobby Fischer, that otherwise erratic schoolboy, seems to happen in essential separateness. Now, although the latest neurological theories are again invoking the possibility of specialized location – the idea, familiar to eighteenth-century phrenology, that our brains have different areas for different skills or potentials – we simply do not have the facts. Certain very obvious sensory centres exist, it is true, yet we just do not know how or if the cortex divides its multitudinous tasks. But the image of location is suggestive.

Music, mathematics, and chess are in vital respects dynamic acts of location. Symbolic counters are arranged in significant rows. Solutions, be they of a discord, of an algebraic equation, or of a positional impasse, are achieved by a regrouping, by a sequential reordering of individual units and unit-clusters (notes, integers, rooks or pawns). The child-master, like his adult counterpart, is able to visualize in an instantaneous yet preternaturally confident way how the thing should look several moves hence. He sees the logical, the necessary harmonic and melodic argument as it arises out of an initial key relation or the preliminary fragments of a theme. He knows the order, the appropriate dimension, of the sum or geometric figure before he has performed the intervening steps. He announces mate in six because the victorious end position, the maximally efficient configuration of his pieces on the board, lies somehow 'out there' in graphic, inexplicably clear sight of his mind. In each instance, the cerebral-nervous mechanism makes a veritable leap forward into a 'subsequent space'. Very possibly this is a fiercely specialized neurological – one is tempted to say neuro-chemical – ability all but isolated from other mental and physiological capacities and susceptible of very rapid development. Some chance instigation – a tune or harmonic progression picked out on a piano in the next room, a row of figures set out for addition on a shop slate, the sight of the opening moves in a café chess game – triggers a chain reaction in one limited zone of the human psyche. The result is a beauteous monomania.

Music and mathematics are among the pre-eminent wonders of the race. Lévi-Strauss sees in the invention of melody 'a key to the supreme mystery' of man – a clue, could we but follow it, to the singular structure and genius of the species. The power of mathematics to devise actions for reason as subtle, witty, manifold as any offered by sensory experience and to move forward in an endless unfolding of self-creating life is one of the strange, deep marks man leaves on the world. Chess, on the other hand, is a game in which thirty-two bits of ivory, horn, wood, metal, or (in stalags) sawdust stuck together with shoe polish, are pushed around on sixty-four alternately coloured squares. To the addict, such a description is blasphemy. The origins of chess are shrouded in mists of controversy, but unquestionably this very ancient, trivial pastime has seemed to many exceptionally intelligent human beings of many races and centuries to constitute a reality, a focus for the emotions, as substantial as, often more substantial than, reality itself. Cards can come to mean the same absolute. But their magnetism is impure. A mania for whist or poker hooks into the obvious, universal magic of money. The financial element in chess, where it exists at all, has always been small or accidental.

To a true chess player, the pushing about of thirty-two counters on 8 × 8 squares is an end in itself, a whole world next to which that of mere biological or political or social life seems messy, stale, and contingent. Even the *patzer*, the wretched amateur who charges out with his knight pawn when the opponent's bishop decamps to R4, feels this daemonic spell. There are siren moments when quite normal creatures otherwise engaged, men such as Lenin and myself, feel like giving up everything – marriage, mortgages, careers, the Russian revolution – in order to spend their days and nights moving little carved objects up and down a quadrate board. At the sight of a set, even the tawdriest of plastic pocket sets, one's fingers arch and a coldness as in a light sleep steals over one's spine. Not for gain, not for knowledge or renown, but in some autistic enchantment, pure as one of Bach's inverted canons or Euler's formula for polyhedra.

There, surely, lies one of the real connections. For all their wealth of content, for all the sum of history and social institution vested in them, music, mathematics, and chess are resplendently useless (applied mathematics is a higher plumbing, a kind of music for the police band). They are metaphysically trivial, irresponsible. They refuse to relate outward, to take reality for arbiter. This is the source of their witchery. They tell us, as does a kindred but much later process, abstract art, of man's unique capacity to 'build against the world', to devise forms that are zany, totally useless, austerely frivolous. Such forms are irresponsible to reality, and therefore inviolate, as is nothing else, to the banal authority of death.

Allegoric associations of death with chess are perennial: in medieval woodcuts, in Renaissance frescoes, in the films of Cocteau and Bergman. Death wins the game, yet in so doing it submits, even if but momentarily, to rules wholly outside its dominion. Lovers play chess to arrest the gnawing pace of time and banish the world. Thus, in Yeats's *Deirdre*:

> They knew that there was nothing that could save them,
> And so played chess as they had any night
> For years, and waited for the stroke of sword.
> I never heard a death so out of reach
> Of common hearts, a high and comely end.

It is this ostracism of common mortality, this immersion of human beings in a closed, crystalline sphere, that the poet or novelist who makes chess his theme must capture. The scandal, the paradox of all-important triviality must be made psychologically credible. Success in the genre is rare. Mr James Whitfield Ellison's *Master Prim* (1968) is not a good novel, but there are worthwhile points in it. Francis Rafael, the narrator, is sent by his editor to do a cover story on Julian Prim, the rising star in American chess. At first the middle-aged chronicler, established and suburban to the core, and the nineteen-year-old master don't hit it off. Prim is arrogant and abrasive; he has the manners of a sharp-toothed puppy. But Rafael himself once dreamed of becoming a ranking chess player. In the tautest scene in the novel, a series of 'pots' games at ten seconds a move between Julian and diverse 'pigeons' at the Gotham Chess Club, the novelist and the young killer meet across the board. Rafael almost manages a draw, and there springs up between the two antagonists 'a kind of freemasonry of mutual respect'. By the last page, Prim has won the United States Chess Championship and is engaged to Rafael's daughter. Mr Ellison's story has all the elements of a *roman à clef*. Julian's idiosyncrasies and career seem closely based on those of Bobby Fischer, whose personal and professional antagonism toward Samuel Reshevsky — a conflict unusual for its public vehemence even in the necessarily combative world of chess — is the centre of the plot. Eugene Berlin, Mr Ellison's Reshevsky, is the reigning champion. In a game that provides the all too obvious climax, Julian wrests the crown from his hated senior. The game itself, a Queen's Pawn Opening, though very likely based on actual master-play, is of no deep interest or beauty. Berlin's treatment of the defence is unimaginative, and Julian's breakthrough on the twenty-second move hardly merits the excited response provided by the novelist, let alone the Championship. Minor incidents and personalities are also closely modelled on actuality; no aficionado will fail to recognize the Sturdivant brothers or mistake the location of the Gotham Club. What Mr Ellison does convey is something of the queer, still violence chess engenders. To defeat another human being at chess is to humble him at the very roots of his intelligence; to defeat him easily is to leave him strangely stripped. At a boozy Manhattan soirée, Julian takes on Bryan Pleasant, the English film star, at knight odds and a dollar a game. He wins over and over, double or nothing, his 'queen appearing and slashing at the enemy like a great enraged beast'. In a vindictive display of virtuosity, Julian allows himself less and less time. The naked savagery of his gift suddenly appals him: 'It's like a sickness ... It comes over you like a fever and you lose all sense of the way things are ... I mean who can you beat in fifteen seconds? Even if you're God. And I'm not God. It's stupid to have to say that, but sometimes I have to say it.'

That chess can be to madness close allied is the theme of Stefan Zweig's famous *Schachnovelle* published in 1941 and translated into English as *The Royal Game*. Mirko Czentovic, the World Champion, is aboard a luxurious liner headed for Buenos Aires. For two hundred and fifty dollars a game, he agrees to play against a group of passengers. He beats their combined efforts with contemptuous, maddening ease. Suddenly a mysterious helper joins the browbeaten amateurs. Czentovic is fought to a draw. His rival turns out to be a Viennese doctor whom the Gestapo held in solitary confinement. An old book on chess was the prisoner's sole link with the outside world (a cunning symbolic inversion of the usual role of chess). Dr B. knows all its hundred and fifty games by heart, replaying them mentally a thousand times over. In the process, he has split his own ego into black and white. Knowing each game so ridiculously well, he has achieved a lunatic speed in mental play. He knows black's riposte even before white has made the next move. The World Champion has condescended to a second round. He is beaten in the first game by the marvellous stranger. Czentovic slows down the rate of play. Crazed by what seems to him an unbearable tempo and by a total sense of *déjà vu*, Dr B. feels the approach of schizophrenia and breaks off in the midst of a further brilliant game. This macabre fable, in which Zweig communicates an impression of genuine master-play by suggesting the shape of each game rather than by spelling out the moves, points to the schizoid element in chess. Studying openings and end-games, replaying master games, the chess player is at once white and black. In actual play, the hand poised on the other side of the board is in some measure his own. He is, as it were, inside his opponent's skull, seeing himself as the enemy of the moment, parrying his own moves and immediately leaping back into his own skin to seek a counter to the counter-stroke. In a card game, the adversary's cards are hidden; in chess, his pieces are constantly open before us, inviting us to see things from their side. Thus there is, literally, in every mate a touch of what is called 'suimate' − a kind of chess problem in which the solver is required to manoeuvre his own pieces into mate. In a serious chess game, between players of comparable strength, we are defeated and at the same time defeat ourselves. Thus the taste of ash in one's mouth.

The title of Nabokov's early novel *King, Queen, Knave* refers to a suit of cards. But the primary devices of the book are based on chess. Mr Black and Mr White play chess as the erotic mock melodrama nears its anticlimax. Their game precisely mirrors the situation of the characters: 'Black knight was planning to attack White's king and queen with a forked check.' Chess is the underlying metaphor and symbolic referent throughout Nabokov's fiction. Pnin plays chess; a chance look at the Soviet chess magazine *8 × 8* impels the hero of *The Gift* to undertake his mythical biography of Chernyshevski; the title of *The Real Life of Sebastian Knight* is a chess allusion, and the intimation of master-play between two modes of truth runs through the tale; the duel between Humbert Humbert and Quilty in *Lolita* is plotted in terms of a chess match whose stakes are death. These points and the entire role of chess in Nabokov's opus are set out in Mr Andrew Field's admirably thorough and perceptive *Nabokov: His Life in Art* (1967). But Mr Field rather neglects the masterpiece of the genre. First written in Russian in 1929, *The Luzhin Defence* appeared in English in 1964. The whole novel is concerned with the insubstantial wonders of the game. We believe in Luzhin's chess genius because

Nabokov conveys the specialized, freakish quality of his gift. In all other respects and moves of life, Luzhin is a shambling, infantile creature, pathetically in search of normal human contact. When he thinks of the matter at all, human relations seem to him more or less stylized movements in space; survival in society depends on one's grasp of more or less arbitrary rules, less coherent, to be sure, than those which govern a *prise en passant*. Personal affliction is an unsolved problem, as cold and full of traps as are the chess problems composed by the hated Valentinov. Only a poet himself under the spell of chess could have written the account of the Luzhin–Turati encounter. Here Nabokov communicates, as no other writer has done, the secret affinities of chess, music, mathematics, the sense in which a fine game is a form of melody and animate geometry:

> Then his fingers groped for and found a bewitching, brittle, crystalline combination – which with a gentle tinkle disintegrated at Turati's first reply ... Turati finally decided on this combination – and immediately a kind of musical tempest overwhelmed the board and Luzhin searched stubbornly in it for the tiny, clear note that he needed in order in his turn to swell it out into a thunderous harmony.

Absorbed in the game, Luzhin forgets to apply a lit match to his cigarette. His hand is stung:

> The pain immediately passed, but in the fiery gap he had seen something unbearably awesome, the full horror of the abysmal depths of chess. He glanced at the chessboard and his brain wilted from hitherto unprecedented weariness. But the chessmen were pitiless, they held and absorbed him. There was horror in this, but in this also was the sole harmony, for what else exists in the world besides chess? Fog, the unknown, non being ...

For what else exists in the world besides chess? An idiotic question, but one that every true chess player has at some time asked himself. And to which the answer is – when reality has contracted to sixty-four squares, when the brain narrows to a luminous blade pointed at a single congeries of lines and occult forces – at least uncertain. There are more possible variants in a game at chess than, it is calculated, there are atoms in this sprawling universe of ours. The number of possible legitimate ways of playing the first four moves on each side comes to 318,979,584,000. Playing one game a minute and never repeating it, the entire population of the globe would need two hundred and sixteen billion years to exhaust all conceivable ways of playing the first ten moves of Nabokov's Mr White and Mr Black. As Luzhin plummets to his death, his carefully analysed 'suimate', the chasm of the night and of the chill flagstones below 'was seen to divide into dark and pale squares'.

So does the world in one's recurrent dream of glory. I see the whole scene before me in mocking clarity. The row of tables at Rossolimo's chess café in Greenwich Village or under the greasy ceiling of a hotel lounge in the town of X (Cincinnati, Innsbruck, Lima). The Grand Master is giving a routine exhibition – thirty-five boards in simultaneous play. The rule on such an occasion is that all his opponents play black and move as soon as he steps to the board. The weaker the play, the more rapid his circuit around the room. The more rapid his wolf's prowl, the more harried and clumsy one's answering moves. I am playing a Sicilian Defence, hanging on, trying to parry that darting hand and the punishing swiftness of its visitations. The Grand Master castles on the fifteenth move and I reply Q-QKt5. Once again his step hastens toward my table, but this time, O miracle, he pauses, bends over the board, and, wonder of celestial wonders, calls for a chair! The hall is unbearably hushed, all eyes are on me. The Master forces an exchange of queens, and there surges up in my memory, with daemonic precision, the vision of the Yates–Lasker game in the seventeenth round of the 1924 World Championship in New York. Black won on that March afternoon. I dare not hope for that; I am not mad. But perhaps once, once in my life, a Master will look up from the board, as Botvinnik looked up at the ten-year-old Boris Spassky during an exhibition game in Leningrad in 1947 – look at me not as a nameless *patzer* but as a fellow human being, and say, in a still, small voice, 'Remis'.

✦ *The Cleric of Treason* ✦

In the summer of 1937, the twenty-nine-year-old art critic of the London *Spectator* went over to Paris to see Picasso's newly unveiled *Guernica*. Turbulent acclaim surrounded this great cry of outraged humanity. The critic's finding, which was printed on 6 August, was severely dismissive. The painting was 'a private brain-storm which gives no evidence that Picasso has realized the political significance of Guernica.' In his column for 8 October, the critic, Anthony Blunt, reviewed Picasso's ferocious series of etchings on the *Dream and Lie of Franco*. Again he was negative. These works 'cannot reach more than the limited coterie of aesthetes.' Picasso was blind to the sovereign consideration that the Spanish Civil War was 'only a tragic part of a great forward movement' toward the defeat of Fascism and the ultimate liberation of the common man. The future belongs to an artist like William Coldstream, declared *The Spectator*'s critic on 25 March 1938. 'Picasso belongs to the past.'

Professor Anthony Blunt came back to the study of *Guernica* in a series of lectures he gave in 1966. This time, he conceded the stature of the work and its compositional genius. He located in it motifs from Matteo di Giovanni's *Massacre of the Innocents*, from Guido Reni, from the allegorical paintings of Poussin, on whom he had become the world's foremost authority. Surprisingly, Blunt could show that the apocalyptic terror of *Guernica* was indebted to a passage in Ingres's marmoreal *Jupiter and Thetis*. If there was in Picasso's most celebrated canvas almost no touch of immediate or spontaneous commitment, if all the main themes were already present in the *Minotauromachy* etching of 1935, this was simply a matter of aesthetic economy. This etching had dramatized 'the checking of evil and violence by truth and innocence' in precisely the way that *Guernica* would do, though on a smaller, more playful scale. The artist's underlying attitude concerning the Spanish Civil War was not, as the young Blunt had implied, one of indifference and a refusal to take sides. And in 1945, a few months after he had joined the French Communist Party, Picasso had declared, 'No, painting is not done to decorate apartments. It is an instrument of war for attack and defence against the enemy.'

The art critic for *The Spectator* would not have put it this way. His aesthetics, his sense of the relations between art and society were subtler. The enemy was Matisse, whose vision seemed 'no longer to be one of the real world', and Bonnard, who had chosen formal experiment and colour balance to the detriment of 'human values'. Art, as Blunt saw it in his chronicles from 1932 to early 1939, had one essential and demanding task: to find its way out of abstraction. The Surrealist solution was a spurious one. Reflecting on Max Ernst, in his review for 25 June 1937, Blunt asked, 'Are we to be contented with dreams?' No, the answer lay with a concept that Blunt designated as 'honesty'. The term covers a fair range of meaning. Daumier is obviously honest in his satire on the ruling classes, but even more so in showing the workers that 'their lives could be made the subject for great painting.' But Ingres, purest of draftsmen and most bourgeois of portraitists, is no less honest. The concentration of his technique, the delicate but 'unhesitating realism' of his perception were, indeed, 'revolutionary'. The contrast with Gainsborough is interesting. Here also was a dispassionate portrayer of the fortunate. But it is precisely a lack of technical brilliance that robs Gainsborough's studies of 'condescension', of the honesty to be found in Ingres and in his eighteenth-century predecessors – Fragonard, Watteau, and Lancret. In Rembrandt (7 January 1938), Blunt found 'an honesty so obvious that it strikes one as a moral quality.' The 'honest' road out of the theoretical and pragmatic trap of abstraction could only be a return to some order of realism, but a return that made no concession to technical laxity. Matisse's realism was merely 'empty' and 'smart', like that in the late canvases of Manet.

But as Blunt combed exhibitions and galleries there were signs of a positive turn. They lurked, as it were, in the formalism of Juan Gris; they were evident in the works of a number of English artists, notably Coldstream and Margaret Fitton, whose *Ironing and Airing* was the one submission worth noting in the appalling Royal Academy show in the spring of 1937. And there was, above all, the New Realism of the Mexican masters Rivera and Orozco. It was toward them that Blunt looked with increasing excitement. Here, assuredly, was a body of work that could deal with the realities of the human condition without compromising its aesthetic responsibility, and could, at the same time, profoundly affect the emotions of the common man. The Mexican experience is central to the chapter on 'Art Under Capitalism and Socialism' that Anthony Blunt, art critic and editor of publications at the Warburg Institute, in London, contributed to a volume on *The Mind in Chains*, edited by the poet C. Day Lewis and published in 1937.

Still-life as practised by the masters of later Impressionism embodies an impulse toward flight from the serious issues of personal and social existence, according to Blunt. It 'led to the various forms of esoteric and semi-abstract art which have flourished in the present century.' Art is a complex phenomenon and cannot be judged according to crude psychological and social determinants. Nevertheless, Marxism 'at least gives a weapon for the historical analysis of the characteristics of a style or of a particular work of art.' And it does remind us most usefully that the views of the critic are themselves 'facts' for which historical explanation can be given. Using the instruments of Marxist diagnosis, we arrive at a clear view of the modernist dilemma. Impressionism marked the severance of the major artist from the proletarian world. Daumier and Courbet stayed in imaginative touch with the painful realities of the social condition. Despite its flirtations with political radicalism, Surrealism is *not* a revolutionary art in social terms. Its inherent contempt for the common viewer is matched by the reflex whereby the common viewer, in turn, rejects the Surrealist work, and these attitudes stand in stark contrast to the creative interactions between painter and public in Gothic art and the early Renaissance. The purely abstract artist and his coterie-viewers have cut themselves off 'from all the serious activities of life.' Blunt's conclusion is categorical: 'In the present state of capitalism the position of the artist is hopeless.' But other models of society are emerging from the crucible of revolution. 'A workers' culture' is being built in the Soviet Union. This construction does not entail an annihilation of the past. On the contrary, as Blunt characterizes Lenin's teaching, a true socialist culture 'will take over all that is good in *bourgeois* culture and turn it to its own ends.' Under socialism – and Blunt's dissent from Oscar Wilde's famous essay on the same topic is evident – the modern artist, like his medieval and Renaissance forebears, will be able to develop his personality far more richly than he can under the escapist and trivializing rule of anarchic capitalism. 'He will take a clearly defined place in the organisation of society as an intellectual worker, with a definite function.' It may well be that we in the West do 'not *like* the painting produced in the Soviet Union, but it does not follow that it is not the right kind of art for the Russians at the present time.' And Mexican painting, in its revolutionary and didactic phase, is producing exactly the kind of major, immediately convincing murals and canvases that are so desperately lacking in London, Paris, and New York. Rivera and Orozco are masters who, although members of the middle class and artists first and foremost, are 'helping the proletariat to produce its own culture.' Reciprocally, they benefit from the kind of public scrutiny and support from which the artist under late capitalism has, more or less wilfully, cut himself off. The Soviet and Mexican lessons are clear. Blunt cites with approval Lenin's dictum to Clara Zetkin: 'We communists cannot stand with our hands folded and let chaos develop in any direction it may. We must guide this process according to a plan and form its results.' Art is too serious a matter to be left only to artists, let alone their moneyed patrons.

Throughout 1938, these stern hopes seemed to wither. The choice before the artist grew ever more stark. He could, wrote Blunt in his *Spectator* piece for 24 June, either discipline himself to paint the world as it was, paint something else as mere frivolous distraction, or commit suicide. The Mexican example was being shamefully neglected. 'In the room of every young upper-class intellectual in Cambridge who belonged to the Communist party,' Blunt noted in September, 'there was always to be found a reproduction of a painting by van Gogh', but nothing by Rivera, nothing by Orozco. Obviously, individual exhortation and the play of unforced sensibility were no longer enough. The column dated 8 July had brought an almost desperate gesture: 'Though Hitler's method of regimenting the arts is in every way to be deplored, there is nothing intrinsically wrong in the organisation of the arts by the State.' The Mexican régime had shown the way, 'and let us hope that it may soon happen in Europe.' The hour was late.

The war effort enlisted British artists and art historians in propaganda, in graphic reportage (Henry Moore's famous air raid shelter drawings), and in various arts projects. These represented the planned and militant collaboration between artist and society which Blunt had called for throughout the late nineteen-thirties. Yet it was at this point – in 1939 he became Reader in the History of Art at London University and deputy director of the highly esteemed Courtauld Institute – that Anthony Blunt's writings drew sharply inward. His first learned paper had appeared in the *Journal of the Warburg Institute* for 1937–8, but the great bulk of his published work had been journalistic. After 1938, Blunt's journalism became sparsely occasional, and it was in what was, from 1939 on, the fiercely mandarin *Journal of the Warburg and Courtauld Institutes* and in the *Burlington Magazine*, a venue for fellow experts and connoisseurs, that he issued the unbroken series of scholarly articles that made of him one of the foremost art historians of the age. These articles – on Poussin, on William Blake, on Italian painting and French architecture of the seventeenth and eighteenth centuries, on the relations between the baroque and antiquity – constitute the foundations and, very often, the preliminary form of the more than twenty-five monographs, catalogues, and books that were produced after 1939 by Sir Anthony Blunt (he was knighted in 1956), Slade Professor of Fine Art successively at Oxford and Cambridge, Fellow of the British Academy (1950), Fellow of the Society of Antiquaries (1960), and, above all else, Surveyor of the Queen's Pictures and Adviser for the Queen's Pictures and Drawings (from 1952 and 1972, respectively).

Nicolas Poussin (1594–1665) has been at the centre of Blunt's scholarship and sensibility. More than thirty Poussin studies appeared between 'A Poussin-Castiglione Problem', of 1939–40, and an article on 'Poussin and Aesop', in 1966. Five major papers on the French classical master were published in 1960 alone, three more the following year. It is no exaggeration to say that Blunt is as closely identified with Poussin as another great art historian, Charles de Tolnay, has been with Michelangelo or as Erwin Panofsky was, at certain times in his career, with Dürer. It was via Poussin that Blunt organized and tested his responses not only to classical and neo-classical art and architecture but also to Cézanne's spatial compositions, Rouault's religious art, and the figure groupings and dissemination of light in Seurat. This lifelong passion culminated in a two-volume study of Poussin – incorporating the A. W. Mellon Lectures that Blunt gave in Washington and a catalogue raisonné of the artist's output – which was published by the Bollingen Foundation, in New York, in 1967.

Blunt's scholarly-critical prose is cool to a degree. It seems to repudiate explicitly the dramatized, personal lyricism that marked the writings on art of Pater and Ruskin and of their most fascinating successor, Adrian Stokes. With rare exceptions, Blunt's style avoids even those flashes of impressionism and sinuous rhetoric that ornament the art studies of Kenneth Clark. The lucid unobtrusiveness of the French classical manner, which Blunt has analysed and treasured, has passed into his own idiom. Nevertheless, there are in his reflections on Poussin indices of his central vision. Poussin's art is ennobled by deliberate intent. It embodies 'a carefully thought-out view of ethics, a consistent attitude to religion, and, toward the end of his life, a complex, almost mystical conception of the universe.' Blunt sees in Poussin a master who countered Plato's dismissive finding that the representative arts are merely imitations of reality. A decisive passage on Poussin draws as near as Professor Blunt will allow himself to eloquence:

> His pursuit of a rational form of art was so passionate that it led him in his later years to a beauty beyond reason; his desire to contain emotion within its strictest limits caused him to express it in its most concentrated form; his determination to efface himself, and to seek nothing but the form perfectly appropriate to his theme, led him to create paintings which, though impersonal, are also deeply emotional and, though rational in their principles, are almost mystical in the impression that they convey.

Only disciplined governance, rigorous self-effacement, and absolute technical mastery can lead an artist, a human consciousness, to that immediacy of revelation (the mystical) which reason generates but does not wholly contain. Vehement feeling is guarded by the calm of form. It is with obvious approbation that Blunt cites Poussin's own testimony: 'My nature compels me to seek and love things that are well ordered, fleeing confusion, which is as contrary and inimical to me as is day to the deepest night.' This great tradition of austere nobility is essential to the French genius from Racine to Mallarmé, from the brothers Le Nain to Braque. Very few Englishmen have felt at home in its formality. Blunt, who passed long periods of his youth in France, found in the French tradition the primary climate of his feelings. He came to recognize in Poussin a late Stoic, a Senecan moralist passionate in his very rationality but fastidiously detached from public affairs. Montaigne's, observes Blunt, is the voice — and a voice quintessentially French — of this passionate dispassion. Though these qualities are pre-eminent in Nicolas Poussin, they can be found in other masters and media: in the French architect Philibert de l'Orme (c. 1510–70), to whom Blunt devoted a monograph in 1958; in the great painter Claude Lorrain (1600–1682); in the architect and sculptor Francesco Borromini (1599–1667), of whom Blunt published an incisive, elegant study in 1979. In Borromini's aesthetics, Stoicism joins with Christian humanism to underwrite the view that God is 'supreme reason'. No less than Poussin in his late years, Borromini conceives of man as inevitably puny and miserable but endowed with the capacity for reflection — for translating into disciplined form certain aspects of cosmic energy and order. And this reflection suffuses a Poussin canvas, a Borromini façade, a Fouquet drawing with the light of reasoned mystery.

It is a mark of Blunt's distinction and of the fineness of his antennae that his authority extends to certain artists who at first sight seem contrary to the Gallic ideal. His papers on William Blake go back to 1938. His study *The Art of William Blake* appeared in 1959. Again, the criterion is that of concordance between vision and technique of execution. As in Poussin, though expressed in an altogether different code, there is in Blake's paintings a 'complete integrity of thought and feeling'. In Blake's case, the analysis was fundamentally political. Blake had set his face against materialism — against the money fever of the new industrial age — and against the cant of a sclerotic state religion. He was 'a minority fighter', in severe peril of isolation, of mere eccentricity. His powers as a craftsman, the vital intelligence of his understanding of classic art and modern society enabled him to produce designs of a totally individual character yet of an unmistakable universality of meaning. 'To those who are themselves trying to escape from the dominance of materialism', says Professor Blunt, Blake is of dramatic aid and comfort. And the radicalism of the protest lies in the controlled line of the composition. Such 'extraordinary mixture of severity and fantasy' was to delight Blunt in his study of Borromini's façade for the Collegio di Propaganda Fide in Rome.

To his professional colleagues, Blunt is not only an art historian and an analytic critic of great stature. He is one of the principal cataloguers of our time. The disciplines required, the significance of the product for the study and interpretation of the fine arts as a whole are not easy for the layman to grasp, let alone summarize. As the life-force of speech and writing is, finally, determined by the quality of our dictionaries and grammars, so the access to and valuation of the works of great artists depend on exact attribution and dating. Who painted this canvas? Who drew this drawing? What is the relation of this print to the original plate? When was this statue carved or cast? To what year do we assign this colonnade or that vestibule? Am I looking at individual work or at the product of an atelier working collaboratively with the master or, perhaps, according to his more or less finished maquette? The catalogue raisonné — the chronological listing and precise description of the output of an artist or of his school — is to the historian of art and culture, to the art critic, and to the connoisseur the primary instrument of ordered perception. The means required of the compiler, as of a master lexicographer or grammarian, are of the most stringent and uncommon sort. The cataloguer must, in the first place, be totally versed in the mechanics of the medium he is classifying. He must, for instance, be able to reproduce mentally but also, as it were, at his own fingertips the idiosyncrasies of the etcher's tool if he is to identify the etcher's hand. He must know the metallurgy of the relevant period if he is to judge the state of the plate. The particular texture of the ink used, the exact history of the paper and its watermarks, the aesthetic and commercial considerations that dictated the number of impressions made will be familiar to him. In attributing and dating paintings, the indexer may resort to laboratory techniques: to X-ray and infra-red photography, in order to reveal successive layers of pigment; to the minute analysis of wood, canvas, and metal, in order to fix the chronology and compositional history of the object. Yet mastery of these intricate minutiae is only the preliminary step. The right ascription of a painting, of a statue, of a baptistery to this or that painter, sculptor, or architect, its right dating and placement within the man's work as a whole are, in the last analysis, the result of acute rational intuition. Memory, the retention before the mind's eye of a great range of surrounding, ancillary, comparable, or contrasting art, is indispensable. So is historical imagination, the stab of precise sympathy that enables a historical novelist, a historian, a great stage designer to image the past. Sheer erudition — that is, a voluminous intimacy with the artist's biography, with his professional habits, with the material distribution and the survival of his works as they left his atelier and began their often tortuous journey toward the modern museum, auction room, neglected attic, or private collection – is essential. But these are not the crux. What matters most are 'tactile values' (Berenson's phrase) – requiring an ability to bring taste and sensory awareness to bear unswervingly on the art object both in its minutest detail and in its over-all effect. The master cataloguer has perfect pitch.

Blunt's catalogue of *The Drawings of Nicolas Poussin* began appearing in 1939. *The French Drawings in the Collection of H.M. the King at Windsor Castle* was published in 1945. Nine years later followed *The Drawings of G. B. Castiglione and Stefano della Bella in the Collection of H.M. the Queen at Windsor Castle*. Blunt's descriptive catalogue of seventeenth- and eighteenth-century Venetian drawings in Her Majesty's collection was published in 1957. Three years later came the catalogue of the Roman drawings for this same period in the Sovereign's possession. Anthony Blunt provided the catalogue for the extensive Poussin exhibition in Paris in 1960, and his definitive listing of the artist's paintings came six years later. In 1968, Blunt surveyed the James A. de Rothschild Collection at Waddesdon Manor. In 1971, he published supplements to his previous listings of French and Italian drawings. In all his monographs, moreover, such as the handsome study of *Neapolitan Baroque and Rococo Architecture* (1975) and the Borromini book, attribution, exact description, and datings play a major role. Blunt has literally put in intelligible order central rooms in the house of Western art. As I said, only the expert can fully gauge the labour, the scruple, the degree of flair and concentration involved.

'Scruple' is worth insisting on. The business of attribution, description, dating demands complete integrity on the technical level. Margins must be measured to the millimetre; successive impressions from an original plate or woodblock must be almost microscopically differentiated if the sequence is to be numbered correctly. But in this domain there are also pressures of a moral and economic kind. The outright value of a painting or drawing or engraving, the worth of a sculpture on the crazed art market depend immediately on expert attribution. The temptations are notorious. (Berenson allegedly yielded to them on occasion.) Blunt's austerity was above question. His scholarship, his teaching exemplify formidable standards of technical severity and intellectual and moral rigour. His catalogues, his art history and criticism, the decisions he arrived at in regard to the identification and valuation of pictures and drawings in public and private holding illustrate the motto adopted by Aby Warburg, founder of the institute with which Blunt was closely associated: 'God lurks in the detail.' At this level of learning and connoisseurship, deception and the exposure that follows would be irreparable. There was hardly a day on which Professor Sir Anthony Blunt, Knight Commander of the Royal Victorian Order and honoured guest of the Queen, did not make this clear to his colleagues and to his students.

They responded unstintingly. The *Studies in Renaissance and Baroque Art Presented to Anthony Blunt on his 60th Birthday* (Phaidon, 1967) is more than a ritual gesture. Here some of the most distinguished historians of art and of architecture paid genuine tribute to a master in the field and to an exemplary teacher by publishing essays that mirrored his own high standards and catholicity of insight. But even beyond the honour done to the scholar and the expositor there is the homage to the man. What Professor Blunt's peers and associates throughout the academic world, at the National Art Collections Fund, in the National Trust (the foremost body for the preservation of Britain's historical heritage), in museums, and, one has reason to believe, in the royal entourage wished to express unreservedly was their sense of Sir Anthony's 'qualities of intellect and moral integrity'. The two so obviously went together.

I do not know just when Blunt was recruited into Soviet espionage. It is thought likely that he became actively interested in and sympathetic to Communism as an undergraduate at Trinity College, Cambridge, between 1926 and 1929. Elected a Fellow of the college in 1932, he appears to have acted mainly as a talent spotter and guru for the K.G.B. The evidence points to his extraordinary influence over a circle of young men that included Kim Philby, Guy Burgess, and Donald Maclean, all of whom later took flight to Moscow. Blunt saw service in France in 1939 and 1940 after an attempt, whose details remain murky, to enlist in military intelligence. In 1940, during the chaos and crisis set off by Hitler's breakthrough in the west, Anthony Blunt succeeded in his project. He was now a member of the MI5 branch of the wartime secret service. No outsider seems to know precisely what Blunt's functions were or how senior he became. Initially, he seems to have been monitoring the communications and activities of various foreign embassies and exile governments in London. By passing his findings on to his Soviet control, he would have helped the Russians to plan and carry out their murderous policies in the newly liberated countries of Eastern Europe in 1944 and 1945. Blunt himself has declared that his activities consisted only in keeping the Russians abreast of what MI5 was finding out about German intelligence networks and in passing on occasional routine information about the work and views of his colleagues. Margaret Thatcher, in her statement to the House of Commons in the third week of November 1979 – the statement that revealed Blunt's treason to the public at large – said merely this: 'We do not know exactly what information he passed. We do know, however, to what information he had access.' The implication was that the latter was obviously sensitive. Outwardly, Blunt's membership in MI5 ceased at the end of the war. In reality, of course, the British intelligence community, like its counterpart in every other country, is a kind of permanent club, in which 'old boys' and sometime activists continue on call. In 1950, Blunt seems to have offered his assistance to the security section of the Foreign Office when it was trying to trace a major leakage of classified information from the Washington Embassy. This kind act led Blunt straight to the heart of the Burgess–Maclean file. To this day, the precise mechanism whereby Burgess and Maclean were tipped off seventy-two hours before Maclean was to be interrogated and were thus able to find refuge in the Soviet Union remains known only to a very few. Blunt almost certainly had a hand in the escape. It is not clear whether he acted as initiator and organizer of the operation or merely as a conveyer of urgent signals. What is known is that it was Anthony Blunt who phoned Burgess on the morning of 25 May 1951 – a Friday – to tell him that the net would close in on Maclean on the Monday following. British security services keep the Sabbath. That night, Burgess and Maclean took the ferry from Southampton to Saint-Malo. It was Blunt, moreover, who combed Burgess's London apartment for evidence that might incriminate him and Philby. Philby's nerve held under severe interrogation. According to Mrs Thatcher's Parliamentary statement, Blunt had admitted to helping Philby make contact with Soviet intelligence 'on one occasion' between 1951 and 1956 – the year in which the Queen dubbed Blunt her faithful knight. The evidence suggests, however, that Blunt served as courier between the K.G.B. and the gradually cornered agent. As Philby later put it, from his sunlit bench in a Moscow public park (he was more or less allowed to defect safely in 1963), he received 'through the most ingenious of routes' a message of good cheer from his Kremlin masters and friends. 'It changed the whole complexion of the case. I was no longer alone.'

Nor was Blunt. Needled into action by the Burgess–Maclean farce and by the outrage of the United States intelligence and counter-intelligence agencies, which had vainly sought to alert their British colleagues to the presence of 'moles' at the highest levels of the secret service, interrogators from MI5 saw Blunt eleven times, beginning in 1951. As far as one can gather, Blunt repudiated all suspicions with chill aloofness. Burgess's alleged revelations were the product of an alcoholic notorious for his pranks and fantasies. Some interrogators were convinced that Blunt was lying but could not make the evidence stick. With every year, moreover, Blunt's prestige in public life, his access to royalty and to the near-immunity such access brings were growing. The years from 1952 to 1964 were golden ones for the guardian and surveyor of royal art. But the climate was beginning to sour. The unearthing and trial in 1961 of George Blake, a veteran Soviet spy, Philby's homecoming to Moscow and the spate of revelations that ensued, and the essentially trivial but unnerving scandal of the Profumo affair in the summer of 1963 brought on a general alarm and sense of betrayal. A new round of investigations began. This time, according to the official narrative, Blunt cracked, and made a deal with his hunters. He would confess his treason and co-operate with MI5 as it saw fit in exchange for absolute discretion and personal immunity. The obvious lure lay in the possibility that the K.G.B., not knowing that Blunt had been 'turned', would continue to use his services, and that these would be revealed to British counter-intelligence. This appetizing bargain was to be kept a complete secret. Among the very few who were told was Sir Michael Adeane, the Queen's Private Secretary. He seems to have taken the news with condign aplomb, the more notable because the Assistant Keeper of the Queen's Pictures was one Oliver Miller, a former member of the secret service. As things worked out, the K.G.B. did not take the bait, and Blunt's own co-operation with his new masters was almost non-existent. It looked to his bitterly exasperated controls in MI5 as if he had outplayed them once again. The glitter of Sir Anthony's public honours made matters worse. Leaks and insinuations, very likely planted by the angry intelligence network, began circulating in Fleet Street, in the senior common rooms of Oxford and Cambridge colleges, and through the synapses of establishment gossip. Two journalists, Richard Deacon and Andrew Boyle, were hot on the scent. Threats of prosecution for libel forced Deacon to withdraw the book he had written on the case. Boyle, confident of his facts, and very probably encouraged in certain powerful quarters, published his book (the American edition of which was entitled *The Fourth Man*) on 5 November 1979. The choice of date was a wry hit: to Englishmen, Guy Fawkes Day is an annual reminder of mortal conspiracy. Ten days later, the Prime Minister spoke out.

These, summarily, are the facts as they have been retailed to an avid public by Mr Boyle and other journalists in an avalanche of exposés, by pundits and ex-secret-service figures of every description, by John le Carré acolytes (and, indeed, the Master himself) since Mrs Thatcher's revelations in Parliament. A cursory look at the tale shows that it is so full of gaps, unanswered questions, and implausibilities as to be almost useless. Granted that recruitment in 1940 was chaotic — nevertheless, how was it possible, at the very time of the Hitler–Stalin entente, for MI5 to overlook the political sentiments expounded by Blunt in his *Spectator* art reviews and his 1937 essay? Who buried or withdrew a dossier given to MI5 as early as 1939 by the Soviet defector General Walter Krivitsky — a dossier that all but identified Blunt and his connection with Maclean (though, presumably, in a garbled and fragmentary way)? The implication of efficient protection in very high places is inescapable. Blunt's double life was charmed from the start. How was it that Blunt, who had actually shared a flat with Burgess, was allowed to slip through the net (or was he?) during the 1951 fracas? Everything about the confession and guarantee of immunity in 1964 is implausible. Why should Blunt have caved in just at this time, and of just what category of importance and seniority were his services to the K.G.B. if his interrogators thought him worth sparing public exposure and prosecution for treason? Lord Home, Prime Minister at the time, and Harold Wilson, his successor, have affirmed that they were told nothing, though both were, by virtue of their office, heads of the security services. Why should this have been? And who took the decision, politically trivial but psychologically bizarre in the extreme, either to inform or not to inform Her Majesty that her honour-laden art adviser and regular palace guest was a self-confessed K.G.B. operative? Is it not distinctly conceivable that Blunt's 1964 confession was itself a tactical fraud, and that he continued to do services either as a K.G.B. informant or, more probably, as a classic double agent, 'turned' by both sides but loyal only to one? How else is one to account for the fact, first disclosed in a somewhat oblique statement by Edward Heath, Prime Minister at the time, that the Blunt file had been reopened in 1973 but that three successive attorneys general had, during the ensuing six years, found nothing that was usable as evidence on which to base a prosecution? Evidence supplied by 'moles' and defectors does take a long time to filter through the intelligence channels. But can the information supplied by Anatoli Dolnytsin, a ranking K.G.B. agent who sought cover in the United States in 1962 and appears to have known the entire Philby set-up and Blunt's connection, really have been ignored by

British counter-intelligence? Once more, the suggestion of a guardian angel or coven of angels in very lofty quarters is palpable. A senior Oxford philosopher of impeccable shrewdness, himself a member of the charmed circle of British mandarin socialites, has said to me outright that the Blunt story, as told to the world at large, is in many respects a fabrication. It was devised and revealed precisely in order to lay a smoke screen behind which other eminent characters in the drama could scuttle to safety. Crucial points are 'in fact the exact opposite of what you have been led to believe.' Historians to come will burrow. This or that startling tracer will turn up in as yet unpublished records, letters, personal memoirs. Blunt himself will have his say and rake in the royalties (a predestined pun, that). But it is very doubtful whether any coherent truth will ever emerge. What *is* certain is simply this: Anthony Blunt was a K.G.B. minion whose treason over thirty years or more almost certainly did grave damage to his own country and may well have sent other men – Polish and Czech exiles, fellow intelligence agents – to abject death. The rest is tawdry gossip.

Espionage and treason are, one is given to understand, as ancient as whoredom. And, obviously, they have often engaged human beings of some intelligence and audacity, and, in certain cases, of elevated social standing. Yet the enlistment in this nauseating trade of a man of great intellectual eminence, one whose manifest contributions to the life of the mind are of high grace and perception, and who, as scholar and teacher, made veracity, scrupulous integrity the touchstone of his work – this is indeed rare. I can, with reference to modern times, think of no genuine parallel. Professor Blunt's treason and duplicity do pose fundamental questions about the nature of intellectual-academic obsession, about the co-existence within a single sensibility of utmost truth and falsehood, and about certain germs of the inhuman planted, as it were, at the very roots of excellence in our society. There lies the significance and fascination of the case. I have neither the competence nor the interest to contribute anything to the spate of armchair detection and spy fantasies unleashed by the Blunt affair. But I would like to think for a moment about a man who in the morning teaches his students that a false attribution of a Watteau drawing or an inaccurate transcription of a fourteenth-century epigraph is a sin against the spirit and in the afternoon or evening transmits to the agents of Soviet intelligence classified, perhaps vital information given to him in sworn trust by his countrymen and intimate colleagues. What are the sources of such scission? How does the spirit mask itself?

The Marxist sentiments voiced in Blunt's art reviews and in his contribution to *The Mind in Chains* are banal. They constitute the widespread routine
of anger of a middle-class generation caught up in the threefold context of
western economic depression, rising Fascism and Nazism, and what were
believed to be the dynamic, libertarian successes of the Russian Revolution.
Nothing Blunt writes exhibits any particular grasp either of the philosophical
aspects of Marxist dialectical materialism or of the economic and labour
theory on which this materialism is founded. It is parlour-pink talk in the
approved nineteen-thirties style. Except, perhaps, in one respect. Blunt had
arrived early at the conviction that great art, to which he ascribed pre-eminent
value in human consciousness and society, could not survive the fragmented,
anarchic, and always modish governance of private patronage and mass-
media trivialization. If western painting, sculpture, and architecture were to
regain classic stature, they must do so under the control of an enlightened,
educative, and historically purposeful state. However, as one looks closely at
Blunt's reiterated call for a central authority over the arts, the basis for the
argument is not notably Marxist. The ideal precedent lies much earlier. Like
so many of the 'radical élite', Blunt cherishes two possibly antithetical
persuasions. He holds great art to be of matchless significance to man; and he
would want this significance to be accessible to the community as a whole.
The solution is, more or less unavoidably, Plato's: 'guardians', chosen for their
intellectual force and their probity, are to ensure the positive, life-enhancing
quality of art and are to organize the presentation of such art to their entire
society. And this quality and public presentation will elevate collective
sensibility to a higher plane. Blunt seems to have felt that something very
like this mechanism of authority and diffusion was at work in the autocratic
city-states of Renaissance Italy and, above all, in the century of Louis XIV and
his immediate successor. The patronage of the Medici or of Versailles was at
once centrally authoritarian and progressive. It commanded the production
of pictures, statues, and buildings of enduring merit but made of this production a political-social benefit and stimulus, in which the body politic as a
whole was actively involved. In this way, the individual artists were inte-
grated into the live fabric of society. However private and singular their
inspiration, the canvas, the monument, the loggia or façade that they
designed and produced had come under the rationalizing and humanizing
pressures of public occasion and of the need to communicate both to high
patrons and to the city at large. The art dealer and the private collector, the
tycoon and the journalist-critic, as they mushroom under capitalism, cannot

match such coherence. On the contrary, it is the cash nexus that has fatally split the world of art into the esoteric, at one end, and kitsch, at the other. Blunt seems to locate the crisis somewhere between Ingres, still working under essentially hierarchic and public conditions, and, say, Manet. The available counterpart of the Medici or the ancien régime would be the Leninist commissariat for the fine arts, the revolutionary ministry of culture in Mexico, or, very nearly, as we have seen, the propaganda office and official chamber of art in the Third Reich. Blunt is shrewd enough to know that the price may be steep, at least during a period of historical transition. But how else are the arts, without which man would recede into animality, to be rescued from their isolation, from the prostitution of the money market? It may well be because he found no other answer to this question that Anthony Blunt slid from undergraduate and salon Marxism into the practicalities of treason.

A related, more unusual motive may also have been at work, though I cannot evidence my instinct on this. There is some suggestion that Blunt, when he began serious art studies, was drawn at least as vividly to Claude Lorrain as he was to Poussin. And Lorrain is, arguably, the more original, more haunting master. But, for reasons that involved the very different relations of these two painters to their patrons and public, Poussin's works were largely accessible to students, whereas much of Lorrain was in private and often closed collections at the time. We touch here on a problem about which I feel considerable ambivalence. The private ownership of great art, its seclusion from the general view of men and women, let alone from that of interested amateurs and scholars, is a curious business. The literal disappearance of a Turner or a van Gogh into some Middle Eastern or Latin-American bank vault to be kept as investment and collateral, the sardonic decision of a Greek shipping tycoon to put an incomparable El Greco on his yacht, where it hangs at persistent risk – these are phenomena that verge on vandalism. Ought there to be private possession of great art, with everything that such possession entails of material risk, of greed, of removal from the general currents of thought and feeling? The question is particularly urgent where the painting or statue or architectural motif in question was intended for public display in the first place – as is, of course, the case with the overwhelming majority of medieval, Renaissance, and seventeenth- and eighteenth-century works. To say that private collectors, especially in the United States, have been generous in allowing scholarly guests a look at their treasures (not always, in fact) is no answer. Should mere wealth or the speculative fever of the investor determine the location, the accessibility of universal and always irreplaceable products in the legacy of man? There are times when I feel that the answer ought to be emphatically negative – that great art is not, cannot be, private property. But I am not certain. My conjecture is that Blunt was certain, and that the young scholar-connoisseur, barred from certain paintings and drawings of genius because they were locked up in private keeping, experienced a spasm of contemptuous loathing for capitalism. In the Soviet Union, he knew, great art hangs in public galleries. No scholars, no men and women wanting to mend their souls before a Raphael or a Matisse need wait, cap in hand, at the mansion door.

The second main perspective in which to try and comprehend the Blunt phenomenon is that of homosexuality. Reams have now been written about the incidence of homosexuality in the Cambridge University circles from which the Soviet intelligence services recruited their galaxy of agents. Some of the published information is very likely responsible; much of it is more or less prurient gossip. One of the main witnesses to Blunt's homoeroticism, the late Goronwy Rees, was a brilliant but emotionally erratic and not always impeccable informant. What is not in doubt is the general fact of the strongly homosexual character of the élite in which the young Blunt flourished at Trinity and King's Colleges in Cambridge – and, most especially, of the Apostles, the celebrated semi-secret society of intellectual and aesthetic souls which played so distinctive a role in English philosophical and literary life from the time of Tennyson to that of Strachey and Bertrand Russell. Neither sociology nor cultural history, neither political theory nor psychology has even begun to handle authoritatively the vast theme of the part played by homosexuality in western culture since the late nineteenth century. The subject is so diffuse and of such methodological and emotional complexity that it would require a combination of Machiavelli, de Tocqueville, and Freud to produce the great missing book. There is hardly a branch of literature, of music, of the plastic arts, of philosophy, of drama, film, fashion, and the furnishings of daily urban life in which homosexuality has not been crucially involved, often dominantly. Judaism and homosexuality (most intensely where they overlap, as in a Proust or a Wittgenstein) can be seen to have been the two main generators of the entire fabric and savour of urban modernity in the West. In ways that C. P. Snow did not even hint at in his argument on 'the two cultures', it is, by and large, the striking absence of any comparable homosexual presence in the exact and applied sciences which has helped bring on the widening gap between the general culture and the scientific. This is a vast and as yet only imperfectly understood development, of which the role of homosexuality in politics and in the world of espionage and betrayal is only a specialized, though dramatic, feature. In the case of Blunt and the apostolic youths of Cambridge and Bloomsbury, moreover, homosexuality may be too restrictive a concept.

Until very recently, the more privileged orders in English society were educated in celibate schools and in the celibate colleges of Oxford and Cambridge, which have admitted women only during these last seven or eight years. This education was underwritten by an explicit ideal of masculine friendship, of a masculine intimacy and mutual trust more lasting and radiant than the plebeian values of the outside world. Cyril Connolly's *Enemies of Promise*, Philip Toynbee's exquisite *Friends Apart*, give a classic picture of this adolescent Arcadia, with its overtones of white flannel summer afternoons and heroic deaths in manly wars to come. This masculine code would comprise stages of homosexual encounter ranging all the way from the most platonic (itself an ambiguous term) of schoolboy crushes to full involvement. But even the latter was in many instances only a transitory phase before the fading of the summer light and a man's responsible entry into the colder climate of matrimony and family life. It is, therefore, not the homoeroticism that matters most but the vision of a small constellation of men, their souls attuned by shared schooling and by the shared enchanted setting of Cambridge cloisters and gardens. The strength of elective affinity in such a coterie is twofold: there are the bonds of internal affection, and there is a rejection, more or less conscious, more or less aggressive, of the vulgar usages and philistine values of 'the others', of the banal multitude. The password to this whole complex of attitudes and beliefs is a very famous declaration by E. M. Forster, made first in the late thirties and repeated innumerable times since: 'If I had to choose between betraying my country and betraying my friend, I hope I should have the guts to betray my country.' Much overrated as a novelist – only *A Passage to India* is of absolutely the first rank – Forster was for successive Cambridge generations the tuning fork of conscience. His own homosexuality, the fastidious privacy of his ways, his place among the Apostles made of him very nearly a court of appeals in questions of ethical choice. Incidentally, one cannot but wonder how much Forster may have known of the truth concerning Burgess, Philby, Maclean, Blunt, and their praetorians. Now, there can be no doubt but that his proposition on betrayal is worth close scrutiny. I happen to feel myself strongly drawn to its implicit valuation. Nationalism is the venom of modern history. Nothing is more bestially absurd than the readiness of human beings to incinerate or slaughter one another in the name of nationhood and under the infantile spell of a flag. Citizenship is a bilateral arrangement that is, that ought always to be subject to critical examination and, if need be, abrogation. No city of man is worth a major injustice, a major falsehood. The death of Socrates outweighs the survival of Athens. Nothing dignifies French history more surely than the willingness of Frenchmen to go to the brink of communal collapse, to weaken the bonds of nationhood drastically (as they in fact did) over the Dreyfus case. Long before Forster, Dr Johnson had defined patriotism as the last refuge of a scoundrel. It seems to me doubtful whether the human animal will manage to survive if it does not learn to do without frontiers and passports, if it cannot grasp that we are all guests of each other, as we are of this scarred and poisoned earth. One's homeland is the common patch of space – it can be a hotel room or a bench in the nearest park – that the gross surveillance and harrying of modern bureaucratic régimes, East or West, still allow one for one's work. Trees have roots; men have legs with which to leave after they have, in conscience, said no. Thus, there is in Forster's challenge an ecumenical humanism worth defending. Had Anthony Blunt renounced his gilded career, and sought barren refuge in Moscow or committed suicide rather than inform on his Cambridge brethren, one would condemn him for the traitor he is, but one would acknowledge an enactment of Forster's high paradox and see some logical culmination of a long tradition of boyish fidelity. Blunt, of course, did nothing so quixotic or elegant. He betrayed his country *and* his friends with the same cold gusto.

Nonetheless, the homosexual motif may have counted in two ways. It would have given Soviet intelligence a stranglehold of blackmail over Blunt and his circle at a time when English laws, even in respect of consenting adults, were still draconian. More significant, the homoerotic ethos may have persuaded men such as Blunt and Burgess that the official society around them, whatever prizes it might bestow on their talents, was in essence hostile and hypocritical. It was, consequently, ripe for just overthrow, and espionage was one of the necessary means to this good end. The irony is that the Stalinist Soviet Union, as André Gide reported in bitter disillusion, was far more oppressive of homosexuality than the capitalist West. Blunt, who had in the 1940 preface to his *Artistic Theory in Italy 1450–1600* thanked Guy Burgess for his aid and stimulus on 'all the more basic points' – Burgess's authority in Renaissance aesthetics is not immediately obvious – could flourish both within and outside the British secret service. In Russia, they order these matters differently.

But, crucial as they are, neither Blunt's overt Marxism nor his commitment to the freemasonry of golden lads takes us to the heart of the maze, which is the radical duplicity, the seeming schizophrenia, of the scholar-teacher of impeccable integrity and the professional deceiver and betrayer. When our society troubles to think of the matter at all, it and the conventions of mutual recognition by which it orders its daily affairs take casually for granted the make-up, the status of the scholar. It is only in hoary jokes about the pure pedant's forgetfulness, corporal eccentricities, or inaptitude to the simpler, more basic needs of common existence that some ancient uneasiness and suspicion surface. The absolute scholar is in fact a rather uncanny being. He is instinct with Nietzsche's finding that to be interested in something, to be totally interested in it, is a libidinal thrust more powerful than love or hatred, more tenacious than faith or friendship – not infrequently, indeed, more compelling than personal life itself. Archimedes does not flee from his killers; he does not even turn his head to acknowledge their rush into his garden when he is immersed in the algebra of conic sections. The point of strangeness is this: the conventional repute, the material or financial worth, the sensory attraction, the utility of the object of such interest is utterly irrelevant. A man will invest his sum of living in the study of Sumerian potsherds, in the vertiginous attempt to classify the dung beetles of one corner of New Guinea, in the study of the mating patterns of wood lice, in the biography of a single writer or statesman, in the synthesis of one chemical substance, in the grammar of a dead language. Korean chamber pots of the ninth century, the question of the accent in ancient Greek – witness Browning's ironic but tensed celebration of 'A Grammarian's Funeral' – can compact a man's mental and nervous powers to the pitch of ecstatic fury. Mephistopheles was wasteful when he tempted Faustus with the secrets of the universe: the one *Orchis* missing from his hothouse collection, the torn page in the Laurentian codex of Aeschylus, or the as yet undiscovered proof of Fermat's Last Theorem would have served. The scholar absolute, the mandarin, is a creature cancerous with the blank 'holiness of the minute particular' (William Blake's tag). He is, when in the grip of his pursuit, mono-maniacally disinterested in the possible usefulness of his findings, in the good fortune or honour that they may bring him, in whether or not any

but one or two other men or women on the earth care for, can even begin
to understand or evaluate, what he is after. This disinterestedness is the
dignity of his mania. But it can extend to more troubling zones. The archivist,
the monographer, the antiquarian, the specialist consumed by fires of esoteric
fascination may be indifferent also to the distracting claims of social justice,
of familial affection, of political awareness, and of run-of-the-mill humanity.
The world out there is the formless, boorish impediment that keeps him
from the philosopher's stone, or it may even be the enemy, mocking,
frustrating the wild primacy of his addiction. To the utmost scholar, sleep
is a puzzle of wasted time, and flesh a piece of torn luggage that the spirit
must drag after it. The legendary teacher Alain instructed his French students,
'Remember, gentlemen, that each true idea is a rejection of the human body.'
Hence not only the legends that cluster about Faust, the tale of the man
who sacrifices wife, child, home to the breeding of the perfectly black tulip
(an old story retold by Dumas), and all the terror fables about deranged
cabbalists and scientists but also the sober facts concerning the obsessed,
sacrificial, self-devouring lives of the abstracted ones since Thales of Miletus
fell down the dark well while seeking to calculate the ecliptic conjunction
of sun and moon. It is indeed a haunting and haunted business.

   The more so, I think, when the spell is antiquarian. Even at the sharpest
edge of autistic engagement, the scientist is oriented toward the future, with
what it contains of morning light and positive chance. The numismatician
labouring to identify archaic coinage, the musicologist deciphering medieval
notations, the philologist at his corrupt codex, or the art historian who is
endeavouring to catalogue minor baroque or rococo eighteenth-century
drawings not only has entered into the labyrinth and underworld of the
esoteric but has, necessarily, inverted time. For him, the pulse of most vivid
presence beats from out of the past. This, again, is a social and psychological
estrangement to which we pay too little heed. Today's high-school student
solves equations inaccessible to Newton or to Gauss; an undergraduate
biologist could instruct Darwin. Almost the exact contrary holds true for
the humanities. The proposition that there is to come in the West no writer
to match, let alone excel, William Shakespeare or that music will not produce
again the phenomena of prodigal quality manifest in Mozart and Schubert
is logically undemonstrable. But it carries a formidable weight of intuitive
credibility. The humanist is a rememberer. He walks, as does one troupe of
the accursed in Dante's *Inferno*, with his head twisted backward. He lurches
indifferent into tomorrow. The sixth-century Greek lyric fragment, the Dufay

canon, the drawings by Stefano della Bella are the magnet to his steps — or, as the immemorial myth of fatal retrospection has it, they are his Eurydice. This disorientation (many of us have experienced a subtle pang of nausea and bewilderment on leaving a movie theatre in broad daylight) can generate two reflexes. The first is a hunger for involvement — an attempt, desperate at times, to hook into the warming density of 'the real'. The mandarin reaches out of his retrospective isolation to grab at sexual or social or political life. Except in rare cases — 'As for living, we leave that to our servants', remarked a French aesthete — obsessive scholarship breeds a nostalgia for action. It is 'the deed' that tempts Dr Faustus out of the prison of 'the word'. It was the unhoped-for chance of applying their eerily arcane skills — the analysis of chess problems, epigraphy, number theory, the theory of grammar — that enlisted a peerage of British dons in the brilliant coding and decoding operations during the Second World War. All who look back on the days of 'Ultra' and 'Enigma' at Bletchley Park do so with a sense of holiday. For once, hermetic addiction and the raw needs of the time coincided.

The second reflex lies, I suspect, much nearer to the subconscious. It is one of bizarre violence. The practice of devoting one's waking hours to the collation of a manuscript, to the recension of watermarks on old drawings, the discipline of investing one's dreams in the always vulnerable elucidation of abstruse problems accessible only to a handful of prying and rival colleagues can secrete a rare venom into the spirit. *Odium philologicum* is a notorious infirmity. Scholars will lash out at one another with unbridled malignancy over what appear to the laity to be minuscule, often risible points of debate. The great Lorenzo Valla was not the only Renaissance humanist who ran for his life in the wake of bilious textual controversy. Philology, musicology, and art history, because they hinge on minute niceties of perception and judgement, are especially prone to these gusts of mutual incrimination and loathing. Because their constant focus is antiquarian and archival, they can infect their adepts with a queer, lifeless brand of detestation. In a classic essay on A. E. Housman (1938), Edmund Wilson made the acute suggestion that the macabre violence in *A Shropshire Lad* ought to be seen in conjunction with the jeering savagery of Professor Housman's learned reviews and papers on Greek and Latin philology. Both stem from the cloistered, compressed asceticism of the Cambridge scholar. Like that of T. E. Lawrence, an Oxford variant, such asceticism cuts a writer off from 'the great springs of life' and can nurture a pathological need for cruelty. Today, Edmund Wilson might have felt free to press home his insight by pointing to the shared, clandestine motif of academic homosexuality. Poets such as Pope and Browning have caught the whiff of sadism in academe. So have some playwrights and novelists. Anatole France's *The Crime of Sylvestre Bonnard* handles the theme lightly; it takes on naked terror in Ionesco's playlet *The Lesson*. Fantasizing about action out there in the 'real' world, spinning dreams about the secret centrality, about the occult importance of the labours in which he has interred his existence – labours that the vast majority of his fellow men would deem wholly marginal and socially wasteful if they knew of them at all – the pure scholar, the master of catalogues, can sup on hatred. At the ordinary level, he will exorcize his spleen in the ad-hominem nastiness of a book review, in the arsenic of a footnote. He will vent his resentments in the soft betrayals of an ambiguous recommendation or examination report and in the scorpion's round of a committee on tenure. The violence stays formal. Not, one supposes, in Professor Blunt.

Here the hair-fine exactitudes of scholarship found compensation or parodistic counter-statement – for there are sensibilities both strong and obscurely lamed which demand some kind of mocking self-subversion, which find it compelling to deride something central to their own being, as one's tongue exasperates an aching tooth – in the lies and corruptions of the mole. Here the ascetic scruple of the pedagogue who instructed generations of disciples in the merciless code of documentary truth was counterpoised by the long mastery of falsehood and of forgery. Above all, Professor Blunt was able to translate into clandestine performance, into covert mendacity and, possibly, murderousness (the men and women tagged for Soviet vengeance in Eastern Europe), those fantasies of virile action, those solicitations of violence, which bubble like marsh gas from the deeps of abstruse thought and erudition. Blunt's remark on Borromini's suicide in 1667 sounds as near to self-disclosure as anything we have heard so far:

> To have been under a strain so violent that it drove him to this act of violence – if not of madness – and yet immediately afterwards to be able to dictate such a lucid account of the event, reveals a combination of intense emotional power and rational detachment which are among the qualities which go to make him such a great architect.

'Intense emotional power', though narcissistic, and 'rational detachment', such as the scholar must cultivate in pursuit of his obsession – these seem to characterize the custodian of the Queen's art treasures no less than the K.G.B. intelligencer. The controlled duality is that of a double agent toward himself, of a betrayer of others who feeds, at some last level of irony, at once juvenile and sophisticated, on self-treason. One psychological dividend for Blunt seems to be this: he is simultaneously his own witness and his own judge; the only tribunal he recognizes as competent is that of his own duplicity.

It is Blunt's condescension, the intact carapace of his self-esteem which have struck those who have sought him out since his public exposure. Hardened souls in journalism have recoiled from the man's cold sophistries, from the edge of self-satisfaction with which he savoured the smoked-trout sandwiches thoughtfully put before him by a team of interviewers in the editorial sanctum of the London *Times*. He has depicted his long years of service to the Soviet intelligence organs as marginal, almost amateurish in their insignificance. He has denied handing over information of any real importance. His implication in the Philby–Burgess–Maclean murk was only that of personal amity, of the decent thing done among kindred souls. His television performance in the third week of November 1979 was a classic. It identified not only the tawdriness of Blunt but, even more disturbingly, that of the medium itself. Here was, as one newspaper later put it, 'a man with an infinite capacity for duplicity' doing a silvery, suave little pas de deux before millions. The fine hands wove arabesques suggesting cordial complicities with inquisitors and with a great public that Blunt, fairly enough, must have read as eager and prurient. The mouth moved primly, dropping seemingly hesitant yet elegantly veneered sentences in a minor key characteristic of the Cambridge common rooms of an earlier vintage. But Professor Blunt's eyes remained throughout as flat and chill as glass. It was his younger companion, harried by the press and the vileness of it all, who jumped or fell from the window of Blunt's apartment. Blunt himself, seen in Rome in mid-September, was rumoured to be working on his memoirs and apologia in sunny refuge.

This charade is of no importance. What historians will look at is the gamut of reactions the public unmasking of Blunt provoked in the English social and cultural establishment. For weeks, the letters-to-the-editor page of the *Times* hummed with an agitated chorus. Outright disgust or anathema was sparse. Mandarins and 'top people' (the *Times*'s own half-deprecating phrase) rallied to Blunt's support. Their apologetics took one or a combination of three principal lines. One was that the wretched creature had been sufficiently chastised by Parliamentary exposure and the baying pack of vulgar journalists. Had he not confessed and received assurance of immunity many years before? Should so *distingué* a personage suffer double jeopardy? A second mode of argument was more substantial. Blunt's conversion to Communism, pleaded some of the more representative voices in current English letters, in the arts, and in political thought, had been part of a widespread movement. To turn toward Moscow in the thirties, to flinch from the waste of decaying capitalism and the menace of Mussolini, Franco, and Hitler, was, at the time, to do the decent, the perceptive thing. If Anthony Blunt was to be flayed, who, as Shakespeare phrased it, 'should 'scape whipping'? Why should an Auden depart in the odour of sanctity and a Blunt be hounded? That most of the pro-Soviet intelligentsia had had second thoughts at the time of the Hitler–Stalin alliance and that almost none translated their sympathies into espionage and treason were points conceded but dealt with lightly. The third line of advocacy, expressed by, for example, the historian A. J. P. Taylor, was this: Blunt's exposure was based on tainted evidence, most notoriously the disclosures of an American who was a former C.I.A. agent. Little credibility could be attached to the stuff, and no man should be pilloried on such insubstantial grounds. Taylor is right when he points to the flimsiness and fabricated tenor of the affair as it was officially revealed. Nonetheless, there is no doubt as to Blunt's essential treason. The pressure of sentiment on his behalf, moreover, was not primarily judicial, or even reasoned. It stemmed from the ethos of unyielding friendship as it is proclaimed in E. M. Forster's talismanic aphorism. Roasted half to death, Tom Brown, in the infernal Arcadia of his school days, will not snitch even on the class bully. Henty's midshipmen, Kipling's subalterns, the golden youths of 1914 go to their several deaths in the aura of male fidelity. A gentleman does not tell on his friend; he does not turn on his friend when the latter has, for whatever reason, fallen on hard days. Asked what he would do if Blunt now appeared at his door, one Cambridge don answered for many: 'I would offer him a drink and say, "Bad business. Hard luck, Anthony." I think that in Cambridge personal loyalties and friendships count for a great deal, and very rightly. And that still counts. Certainly nothing has happened that would make him less of a friend.' The schoolboy idiom of the passage – 'bad business,' 'hard luck' – and the mawkish fatuousness of the last sentence come near to exemplifying the prevailing tone.

Having been told beforehand of Mrs Thatcher's impending statement, Professor Blunt resigned from the less prestigious of the two clubs he belongs to in London. He continues a presumably welcome member of the other. His knighthood was withdrawn by royal decree – a very rare move, which was last made, unless I am mistaken, in respect of Sir Roger Casement when he sought to stir up trouble in Ireland during the First World War. (Casement, of course, was hanged.) Under extreme pressure, Blunt resigned his Honorary Fellowship of Trinity College before the college council had to face what would have been an anguished vote. He has neither offered nor been asked to renounce his honorary degrees, most signally at Oxford. When the British Academy met last 3 July, amid considerable public interest, the matter of Blunt's continued membership was discussed. But the august body then moved on to other business. The letters 'F.B.A.' remained after Blunt's name. As it happened, I saw several Academicians the day after the meeting and asked them what their attitudes would have been had Blunt been an agent for the Nazi secret services. No clear answer emerged. Some conceded that they were, in fact, abiding by an ill-defined double standard, that pro-Nazi treason had a simple nastiness that pro-Soviet treason, particularly when embarked upon in the nineteen-thirties, did not. Even the world of the Gulag and of present danger could not wholly efface the almost aesthetic difference. Others found that they would have refused to exclude Blunt from the Academy even if he had spied for Himmler. Queried in turn, I was unable to give a plain answer. Fellowship in the British Academy honours eminent scholarship. Blunt's performance as an art historian stands luminous. Are 'monuments of unageing intellect' – Yeats's proud phrase – susceptible to moral or political denial? I just don't know. I, too, have taken the vows of the cleric. And, opening the *Times Literary Supplement* a day or so later – the *TLS* is the mailbox of the British intelligentsia – I read a compellingly authoritative review by Anthony Blunt of a recent work on French neo-classical architecture. Should the editor not have commissioned it? Should Blunt have had the shame, the need for shadow, not to write it? Again, I don't know. Pressures there must have been. Blunt offered his resignation to the Academy on 18 August.

Huddled in his penal cage at Pisa, Ezra Pound, whose treasons strike one as amateurish and essentially histrionic compared with Blunt's, wrote one of the great laments on man in all literature. Yet, out of lucid abjection, Canto LXXXI leaps toward morning, toward the conviction that there is in art, in high thought, a redemption for the hellish ways of our condition:

> But to have done instead of not doing
> > this is not vanity
> To have, with decency, knocked

> That a Blunt should open
>   To have gathered from the air a live tradition
> or from a fine old eye the unconquered flame
> This is not vanity.

Pound is referring, almost certainly, to Wilfrid Scawen Blunt, the aesthete, traveller, and lyric poet, who died in 1922, and after whom Anthony Blunt's oldest brother, himself an art connoisseur and an addict of Paris, was named. But no matter. Pound meant the name to stand for everything that is radiant and truthful in our love and study of art. For all who have treasured these lines as a touchstone of our hopes, and for all who will read them in generations to come, the damage has been done. As it stands, 'Blunt' burns a derisive hole in the bright fabric of the poem. At the last, this may be Professor Anthony Blunt's strongest claim to remembrance. Damn the man.

‐ *Matters German* ‐

→ *The Hollow Miracle*[1] →

Agreed: post-war Germany is a miracle. But it is a very queer miracle. There is a superb frenzy of life on the surface; but at the heart, there is a queer stillness. Go there: look away for a moment from the marvel of the production lines; close your ears momentarily to the rush of the motors.

The thing that has gone dead is the German language. Open the daily papers, the magazines, the flood of popular and learned books pouring off the new printing presses; go to hear a new German play; listen to the

---

1. Understandably, this essay caused much hurt and anger. Discussion and misquotation of it have continued in Germany to the present time. The journal *Sprache im technischen Zeitalter* devoted a special number to the debate, and controversy arose anew at the meeting in the United States in the spring of 1966 of the German writers known as the *Gruppe 47*. The academic profession took a particularly adverse view of the case.

If I republish 'The Hollow Miracle' in this book, it is because I believe that the matter of the relations between language and political inhumanity is a crucial one; and because I believe that it can be seen with specific and tragic urgency in respect of the uses of German in the Nazi period and in the acrobatics of oblivion which followed on the fall of Nazism. De Maistre and George Orwell have written of the politics of language, of how the word may lose its humane meanings under the pressure of political bestiality and falsehood. We have scarcely begun, as yet, to apply their insights to the actual history of language and feeling. Here almost everything remains to be done.

I republish this essay also because I believe that its general line or argument is valid. When I wrote it, I did not know of Victor Klemperer's remarkable book: *Aus dem Notizbuch eines Philologen*, published in East Berlin in 1946 (now reissued by Joseph Melzer Verlag, Darmstadt, under the title: *Die unbewältigte Sprache*). In far more detail than I was able to give, Klemperer, a trained linguist, traces the collapse of German into Nazi jargon and the linguistic-historical background to that collapse. In 1957, there appeared a small, preliminary lexicon of Nazi German: *Aus dem Wörterbuch des Unmenschen*, compiled by Sternberger, Storz and Süskind. In 1964, suggestions I had made for more detailed study were taken up in Cornelia Berning's *Vom 'Abstammungsnachweis' zum 'Zuchtwart'*. Dolf Sternberger has come back to the whole question in his essay on *'Mass/stäbe der Sprachkritik'* in *Kriterien* (Frankfurt, 1965). In Hochhuth's *The Representative*, particularly in the scenes involving Eichmann and his business cronies, Nazi German is given precise, nauseating expression. The same is true in Peter Weiss's *Interrogation* and, as I try to show in the 'Note on Günter Grass', in the *Hundejahre*.

In these past ten years, moreover, a new chapter has begun in the complex history of the German language and of its articulations of political reality. East Germany is once again developing much of that grammar of lies, of totalitarian simplifications, which was brought to such a high degree of efficiency in the Nazi era. Walls can be built between two halves of a city, but also between words and humane content. [1968]

language as it is spoken over the radio or in the Bundestag. It is no longer the language of Goethe, Heine and Nietzsche. It is not even that of Thomas Mann. Something immensely destructive has happened to it. It makes noise. It even communicates, but it creates no sense of communion.

Languages are living organisms. Infinitely complex, but organisms nevertheless. They have in them a certain life force, and certain powers of absorption and growth. But they can decay and they can die.

A language shows that it has in it the germ of dissolution in several ways. Actions of the mind that were once spontaneous become mechanical, frozen habits (dead metaphors, stock similes, slogans). Words grow longer and more ambiguous. Instead of style, there is rhetoric. Instead of precise common usage, there is jargon. Foreign roots and borrowings are no longer absorbed into the bloodstream of the native tongue. They are merely swallowed and remain an alien intrusion. All these technical failures accumulate to the essential failure: the language no longer sharpens thought but blurs it. Instead of charging every expression with the greatest available energy and directness, it loosens and disperses the intensity of feeling. The language is no longer adventure (and a live language is the highest adventure of which the human brain is capable). In short, the language is no longer lived; it is merely spoken.

That condition can last for a very long time (observe how Latin remained in use long after the springs of life in Roman civilization had run dry). But where it has happened, something essential in a civilization will not recover. And it has happened in Germany. That is why there is at the centre of the miracle of Germany's material resurrection such a profound deadness of spirit, such an inescapable sense of triviality and dissimulation.

What brought death to the German language? That is a fascinating and complicated piece of history. It begins with the paradoxical fact that German was most alive before there was a unified German state. The poetic genius of Luther, Goethe, Schiller, Kleist, Heine, and in part that of Nietzsche, predates the establishment of the German nation. The masters of German prose and poetry were men not caught up in the dynamism of Prussian-Germanic national consciousness as it developed after the foundation of modern Germany in 1870. They were, like Goethe, citizens of Europe, living in princely states too petty to solicit the emotions of nationalism. Or, like Heine and Nietzsche, they wrote from outside Germany. And this has remained true of the finest of German literature even in recent times. Kafka wrote in Prague, Rilke in Prague, Paris and Duino.

The official language and literature of Bismarck's Germany already had in them the elements of dissolution. It is the golden age of the militant historians, of the philologists and the incomprehensible metaphysicians. These mandarins of the new Prussian empire produced that fearful composite of grammatical ingenuity and humourlessness which made the word 'Germanic' an equivalent for dead weight. Those who escaped the Prussianizing of the language were the mutineers and the exiles, like those Jews who founded a brilliant journalistic tradition, or Nietzsche, who wrote from abroad.

For to the academicism and ponderousness of German as it was written by the pillars of learning and society between 1870 and the First World War, the imperial régime added its own gifts of pomp and mystification. The 'Potsdam style' practised in the chancelleries and bureaucracy of the new empire was a mixture of grossness ('the honest speech of soldiers') and high flights of romantic grandeur (the Wagnerian note). Thus university, officialdom, army, and court combined to drill into the German language habits no less dangerous than those they drilled into the German people: a terrible weakness for slogans and pompous clichés (*Lebensraum*, 'the yellow peril', 'the Nordic virtues'); an automatic reverence before the long word or the loud voice; a fatal taste for saccharine pathos (*Gemütlichkeit*) beneath which to conceal any amount of rawness or deception. In this drill, the justly renowned school of German philology played a curious and complex role. Philology places words in a context of older or related words, not in that of moral purpose and conduct. It gives to language formality, not form. It cannot be a mere accident that the essentially philological structure of German education yielded such loyal servants to Prussia and the Nazi Reich. The finest record of how the drill call of the classroom led to that of the barracks is contained in the novels of Heinrich Mann, particularly in *Der Untertan*.

When the soldiers marched off to the 1914 war, so did the words. The surviving soldiers came back, four years later, harrowed and beaten. In a real sense, the words did not. They remained at the front and built between the German mind and the facts a wall of myth. They launched the first of those big lies on which so much of modern Germany has been nurtured: the lie of 'the stab in the back'. The heroic German armies had not been defeated; they had been stabbed in the back by 'traitors, degenerates, and Bolsheviks'. The Treaty of Versailles was not an awkward attempt by a ravaged Europe to pick up some of the pieces but a scheme of cruel vengeance imposed on Germany by its greedy foes. The responsibility for unleashing war lay with Russia or Austria or the colonial machinations of 'perfidious England', not with Prussian Germany.

There were many Germans who knew that these were myths and who knew something of the part that German militarism and race arrogance had played in bringing on the holocaust. They said so in the political cabarets of the 1920s, in the experimental theatre of Brecht, in the writings of the Mann brothers, in the graphic art of Käthe Kollwitz and George Grosz. The German language leapt to life as it had not done since the Junkers and the philologists had taken command of it. It was a brilliant, anarchic period. Brecht gave back to German prose its Lutheran simplicity and Thomas Mann brought into his style the supple, luminous elegance of the classic and Mediterranean tradition. These years, 1920–30, were the *anni mirabiles* of the modern German spirit. Rilke composed the *Duino Elegies* and the *Sonnets to Orpheus* in 1922, giving to German verse a wing-stroke and music it had not known since Hölderlin. *The Magic Mountain* appeared in 1924, Kafka's *Castle* in 1926. *The Threepenny Opera* had its premiere in 1928, and in 1930 the German cinema produced *The Blue Angel*. In the same year appeared the first volume of Robert Musil's strange and vast meditation on the decline of western values, *The Man Without Qualities*. During this glorious decade, German literature and art shared in that great surge of the western imagination which encompassed Faulkner, Hemingway, Joyce, Eliot, Proust, D. H. Lawrence, Picasso, Schoenberg and Stravinsky.

But it was a brief noontime. The obscurantism and hatreds built into the German temper since 1870 were too deep-rooted. In an uncannily prophetic 'Letter from Germany', Lawrence noted how 'the old, bristling, savage spirit has set in'. He saw the country turning away 'from contact with western Europe, ebbing to the deserts of the east'. Brecht, Kafka and Thomas Mann did not succeed in mastering their own culture, in imposing on it the humane sobriety of their talent. They found themselves first the eccentrics, then the hunted. New linguists were at hand to make of the German language a political weapon more total and effective than any history had known, and to degrade the dignity of human speech to the level of baying wolves.

For let us keep one fact clearly in mind: the German language was not innocent of the horrors of Nazism. It is not merely that a Hitler, a Goebbels, and a Himmler happened to speak German. Nazism found in the language precisely what it needed to give voice to its savagery. Hitler heard inside his native tongue the latent hysteria, the confusion, the quality of hypnotic trance. He plunged unerringly into the undergrowth of language, into those zones of darkness and outcry which are the infancy of articulate speech, and which come before words have grown mellow and provisional to the touch of the mind. He sensed in German another music than that of Goethe, Heine and Mann; a rasping cadence, half nebulous jargon, half obscenity. And instead of turning away in nauseated disbelief, the German people gave massive echo to the man's bellowing. It bellowed back out of a million throats and smashed-down boots. A Hitler would have found reservoirs of venom and moral illiteracy in any language. But by virtue of recent history, they were nowhere else so ready and so near the very surface of common speech. A language in which one can write a 'Horst Wessel Lied' is ready to give hell a native tongue. (How should the word *'spritzen'* recover a sane meaning after having signified to millions the 'spurting' of Jewish blood from knife points?)

And that is what happened under the Reich. Not silence or evasion, but an immense outpouring of precise, serviceable words. It was one of the peculiar horrors of the Nazi era that all that happened was recorded, catalogued, chronicled, set down; that words were committed to saying things no human mouth should ever have said and no paper made by man should ever have been inscribed with. It is nauseating and nearly unbearable to recall what was wrought and spoken, but one must. In the Gestapo cellars, stenographers (usually women) took down carefully the noises of fear and agony wrenched, burned or beaten out of the human voice. The tortures and experiments carried out on live beings at Belsen and Matthausen were exactly recorded. The regulations governing the number of blows to be meted out on the flogging blocks at Dachau were set down in writing. When Polish rabbis were compelled to shovel out open latrines with their hands and mouths, there were German officers there to record the fact, to photograph it, and to label the photographs. When the SS élite guards separated mothers from children at the entrance to the death-camps, they did not proceed in silence. They proclaimed the imminent horrors in loud jeers: *'Heida, heida, juchheisassa, Scheissjuden in den Schornstein!'*

The unspeakable being said, over and over, for twelve years. The unthinkable being written down, indexed, filed for reference. The men who poured quicklime down the openings of the sewers in Warsaw to kill the living and stifle the stink of the dead wrote home about it. They spoke of having to 'liquidate vermin'. In letters asking for family snapshots or sending season's greetings. Silent night, holy night, *Gemütlichkeit*. A language being used to run hell, getting the habits of hell into its syntax. Being used to destroy what there is in man of man and to restore to governance what there is of beast. Gradually, words lost their original meaning and acquired nightmarish definitions. *Jude, Pole, Russe* came to mean two-legged lice, putrid vermin which good Aryans must squash, as a party manual said, 'like roaches on a dirty wall'. 'Final solution', *endgültige Lösung*, came to signify the death of six million human beings in gas ovens.

The language was infected not only with these great bestialities. It was called upon to enforce innumerable falsehoods, to persuade the Germans that the war was just and everywhere victorious. As defeat began closing in on the thousand-year Reich, the lies thickened to a constant snowdrift. The language was turned upside down to say 'light' where there was blackness and 'victory' where there was disaster. Gottfried Benn, one of the few decent writers to stay inside Nazi Germany, noted some of the new definitions from the dictionary of Hitler German:

> In December 1943, that is to say at a time when the Russians had driven us before them for 1,500 kilometres, and had pierced our front in a dozen places, a first lieutenant, small as a hummingbird and gentle as a puppy, remarked: 'The main thing is that the swine are not breaking through.' 'Break through', 'roll back', 'clean up', 'flexible, fluid lines of combat' — what positive and negative power such words have; they can bluff or they can conceal. Stalingrad — a tragic accident. The defeat of the U-boats — a small, accidental technical discovery by the British. Montgomery chasing Rommel 4,000 kilometres from el Alamein to Naples — treason of the Badoglio clique.

And as the circle of vengeance closed in on Germany, this snowdrift of lies thickened to a frantic blizzard. Over the radio, between the interruptions caused by air-raid warnings, Goebbels's voice assured the German people that 'titanic secret weapons' were about to be launched. On one of the very last days of Götterdämmerung, Hitler came out of his bunker to inspect a row of ashen-faced fifteen-year-old boys recruited for a last-ditch defence of Berlin. The order of the day spoke of 'volunteers' and élite units gathered invincibly around the Führer. The nightmare fizzled out on a shameless lie. The *Herrenvolk* was solemnly told that Hitler was in the front-line trenches, defending the heart of his capital against the Red beasts. Actually, the buffoon lay dead with his mistress, deep in the safety of his concrete lair.

Languages have great reserves of life. They can absorb masses of hysteria, illiteracy and cheapness (George Orwell showed how English is doing so today). But there comes a breaking point. Use a language to conceive, organize, and justify Belsen; use it to make out specifications for gas ovens; use it to dehumanize man during twelve years of calculated bestiality. Something will happen to it. Make of words what Hitler and Goebbels and the hundred thousand *Untersturmführer* made: conveyors of terror and falsehood. Something will happen to the words. Something of the lies and sadism will settle in the marrow of the language. Imperceptibly at first, like the poisons of radiation sifting silently into the bone. But the cancer will begin, and the deep-set destruction. The language will no longer grow and freshen. It will no longer perform, quite as well as it used to, its two principal functions: the conveyance of humane order which we call law, and the communication of the quick of the human spirit which we call grace. In an anguished note in his diary for 1940, Klaus Mann observed that he could no longer read new German books: 'Can it be that Hitler has polluted the language of Nietzsche and Hölderlin?' It can.

But what happened to those who are the guardians of a language, the keepers of its conscience? What happened to the German writers? A number were killed in the concentration camps; others, such as Walter Benjamin, killed themselves before the Gestapo could get at them to obliterate what little there is in a man of God's image. But the major writers went into exile. The best playwrights: Brecht and Zuckmayer. The most important novelists: Thomas Mann, Werfel, Feuchtwanger, Heinrich Mann, Stefan Zweig, Hermann Broch.

This exodus is of the first importance if we are to understand what has happened to the German language and to the soul of which it is the voice. Some of these writers fled for their lives, being Jews or Marxists or otherwise 'undesirable vermin'. But many could have stayed as honoured Aryan guests of the régime. The Nazis were only too anxious to secure the lustre of Thomas Mann's presence and the prestige that mere presence would have given to the cultural life of the Reich. But Mann would not stay. And the reason was that he knew exactly what was being done to the German language and that he felt that only in exile might that language be kept from final ruin. When he emigrated, the sycophantic academics of the University of Bonn deprived him of his honorary doctorate. In his famous open letter to the dean, Mann explained how a man using German to communicate truth or humane values could not remain in Hitler's Reich:

The mystery of language is a great one; the responsibility for a language and for its purity is of a symbolic and spiritual kind; this responsibility does not have merely an aesthetic sense. The responsibility for language is, in essence, human responsibility ... Should a German writer, made responsible through his habitual use of language, remain silent, quite silent, in the face of all the irreparable evil which has been committed daily, and is being committed in my country, against body, soul and spirit, against justice and truth, against men and man?

Mann was right, of course. But the cost of such integrity is immense for a writer.

The German writers suffered different degrees of deprivation and reacted in different ways. A very few were fortunate enough to find asylum in Switzerland, where they could remain inside the living stream of their own tongue. Others, like Werfel, Feuchtwanger, and Heinrich Mann, settled near each other or formed islands of native speech in their new homeland. Stefan Zweig, safely arrived in Latin America, tried to resume his craft. But despair overcame him. He was convinced that the Nazis would turn German into inhuman gibberish. He saw no future for a man dedicated to the integrity of German letters and killed himself. Others stopped writing altogether. Only the very tough or most richly gifted were able to transform their cruel condition into art.

Pursued by the Nazis from refuge to refuge, Brecht made of each of his new plays a brilliant rearguard action. *Mutter Courage* was first produced in Zurich in the dark spring of 1941. The further he was hounded, the clearer and stronger became Brecht's German. The language seemed to be that of a primer spelling out the A B C of truth. Doubtless, Brecht was helped by his politics. Being a Marxist, he felt himself a citizen of a community larger than Germany and a participant in the forward march of history. He was prepared to accept the desecration and ruin of the German heritage as a necessary tragic prelude to the foundation of a new society. In his tract 'Five Difficulties in the Telling of the Truth', Brecht envisioned a new German language, capable of matching the word to the fact and the fact to the dignity of man.

Another writer who made of exile an enrichment was Hermann Broch. *The Death of Virgil* is not only one of the most important novels European literature has produced since Joyce and Proust; it is a specific treatment of the tragic condition of the man of words in an age of brute power. The novel turns on Virgil's decision, at the hour of his death, to destroy the manuscript of the *Aeneid*. He now realizes that the beauty and truth of language are inadequate to cope with human suffering and the advance of barbarism. Man must find a poetry more immediate and helpful to man than that of words: a poetry of action. Broch, moreover, carried grammar and speech beyond their traditional confines, as if these had become too small to contain the weight of grief and insight forced upon a writer by the inhumanity of our times. Towards the close of his rather solitary life (he died in New Haven, nearly unknown), he felt increasingly that communication might lie in modes other than language, perhaps in mathematics.

Of all the exiles, Thomas Mann fared best. He had always been a citizen of the world, receptive to the genius of other languages and cultures. In the last part of the *Joseph* cycle, there seemed to enter into Mann's style certain tonalities of English, the language in the midst of which he was now living. The German remains that of the master, but now and again an alien light shines through it. In *Doktor Faustus*, Mann addressed himself directly to the ruin of the German spirit. The novel is shaped by the contrast between the language of the narrator and the events which he recounts. The language is that of a classical humanist, a touch laborious and old-fashioned, but always open to the voices of reason, scepticism, and tolerance. The story of Leverkühn's life, on the other hand, is a parable of unreason and disaster. Leverkühn's personal tragedy prefigures the greater madness of the German people. Even as the narrator sets down his pedantic but humane testimony to the wild destruction of a man of genius, the Reich is shown plunging to bloody chaos. In *Doktor Faustus* there is also a direct consideration of the roles of language and music in the German soul. Mann seems to be saying that the deepest energies of the German soul were always expressed in music rather than in words. And the history of Adrian Leverkühn suggests that this is a fact fraught with danger. For there are in music possibilities of complete irrationalism and hypnosis. Unaccustomed to finding in language any ultimate standard of meaning, the Germans were ready for the sub-human jargon of Nazism. And behind the jargon sounded the great dark chords of Wagnerian ecstasy. In *The Holy Sinner*, one of his last works, Mann returned to the problem of the German language by way of parody and pastiche. The tale is written in elaborate imitation of medieval German, as if to remove it as far as possible from the German of the present.

But for all their accomplishment, the German writers in exile could not safeguard their heritage from self-destruction. By leaving Germany, they could protect their own integrity. They witnessed the beginnings of the catastrophe, not its full unfolding. As one who stayed behind wrote: 'You did not pay with the price of your own dignity. How, then, can you communicate with those who did?' The books that Mann, Hesse, and Broch wrote in Switzerland or California or Princeton are read in Germany today, but mainly as valuable proof that a privileged world had lived on 'somewhere else', outside Hitler's reach.

What, then, of those writers who did stay behind? Some became lackeys in the official whorehouse of 'Aryan culture', the *Reichsschrifttumskammer*. Others equivocated till they had lost the faculty of saying anything clear or meaningful even to themselves. Klaus Mann gives a brief sketch of how Gerhart Hauptmann, the old lion of realism, came to terms with the new realities:

> Hitler ... after all ... My dear friends! ... no hard feelings! ... Let's try to be ... No, if you please, allow me ... objective ... May I refill my glass? This champagne ... very remarkable, indeed – the man Hitler, I mean ... The champagne too, for that matter ... Most extraordinary development ... German youth ... About seven million votes ... As I often said to my Jewish friends ... Those Germans ... incalculable nation ... very mysterious indeed ... cosmic impulses ... Goethe ... Nibelungen Saga ... Hitler, in a sense, expresses ... As I tried to explain to my Jewish friends ... dynamic tendencies ... elementary, irresistible ...

Some, like Gottfried Benn and Ernst Jünger, took refuge in what Benn called 'the aristocratic form of emigration'. They entered the German Army, thinking they might escape the tide of pollution and serve their country in the 'old, honourable ways' of the officer corps. Jünger wrote an account of the victorious campaign in France. It is a lyric, elegant little book, entitled *Gärten und Strassen*. Not a rude note in it. An old-style officer taking fatherly care of his French prisoners and entertaining 'correct' and even gracious relations with his new subjects. Behind his staff car come the trucks of the Gestapo and the élite guards fresh from Warsaw. Jünger does not mention any such unpleasantness. He writes of gardens.

Benn saw more clearly, and withdrew first into obscurity of style, then into silence. But the sheer fact of his presence in Nazi Germany seemed to destroy his hold on reality. After the war, he set down some of his recollections of the time of night. Among them, we find an incredible sentence. Speaking of pressures put on him by the régime, Benn says: 'I describe the foregoing not out of resentment against National Socialism. The latter is now overthrown, and I am not one to drag Hector's body in the dust.' One's imagination dizzies at the amount of confusion it must have taken to make a decent writer write that. Using an old academic cliché, he makes Nazism the equivalent of the noblest of Homeric heroes. Being dead, the language turns to lies.

A handful of writers stayed in Germany to wage a covert resistance. One of these very few was Ernst Wiechert. He spent some time in Buchenwald and remained in partial seclusion throughout the war. What he wrote he buried in his garden. He stayed on in constant peril, for he felt that Germany should not be allowed to perish in voiceless suffering. He remained so that an honest man should record for those who had fled and for those who might survive what it has been like. In *Der Totenwald* he gave a brief, tranquil account of what he saw in the concentration camp. Tranquil, because he wished the horror of the facts to cry out in the naked-ness of truth. He saw Jews being tortured to death under vast loads of stone or wood (they were flogged each time they stopped to breathe until they fell dead). When Wiechert's arm developed running sores, he was given a bandage and survived. The camp medical officer would not touch Jews or Gypsies even with his glove 'lest the odour of their flesh infect him'. So they died, screaming with gangrene or hunted by the police dogs. Wiechert saw and remembered. At the end of the war he dug the manuscript out of his garden, and in 1948 published it. But it was already too late.

In the three years immediately following the end of the war, many Germans tried to arrive at a realistic insight into the events of the Hitler era. Under the shadow of the ruins and of economic misery, they considered the monstrous evil Nazism had loosed on them and on the world. Long rows of men and women filed past the bone heaps in the death-camps. Returned soldiers admitted to something of what the occupation of Norway or Poland or France or Yugoslavia had been like – the mass shootings of hostages, the torture, the looting. The churches raised their voice. It was a period of moral scrutiny and grief. Words were spoken that had not been pronounced in twelve years. But the moment of truth was rather short.

The turning point seems to have come in 1948. With the establishment of the new Deutschmark, Germany began a miraculous ascent to renewed economic power. The country literally drugged itself with hard work. Those were the years in which men spent half the night in their rebuilt factories because their homes were not yet inhabitable. And with this upward leap of material energy came a new myth. Millions of Germans began saying to themselves and to any foreigner gullible enough to listen that the past had somehow not happened, that the horrors had been grossly exaggerated by Allied propaganda and sensation-mongering journalists. Yes, there were some concentration camps, and *reportedly* a number of Jews and other unfortunates were exterminated. 'But not six million, *lieber Freund*, nowhere near that many. That's just propaganda, you know.' Doubtless, there had been some regrettable brutalities carried out on foreign territory by units of the SS and SA. 'But those fellows were *Lumpenhunde*, lower-class ruffians. The regular army did nothing of the kind. Not our honourable German Army. And, really, on the Eastern Front our boys were not up against normal human beings. The Russians are mad dogs, *lieber Freund*, mad dogs! And what of the bombing of Dresden?' Wherever one travelled in Germany, one heard such arguments. The Germans themselves began believing them with fervour. But there was worse to come.

Germans in every walk of life began declaring that they had not known about the atrocities of the Nazi régime. 'We did not know what was going on. No one told us about Dachau, Belsen or Auschwitz. How should we have found out? Don't blame us.' It is obviously difficult to disprove such a claim to ignorance. There *were* numerous Germans who had only a dim notion of what might be happening outside their own backyard. Rural districts and the smaller, more remote communities were made aware of reality only in the last months of the war, when battle actually drew near them. But an immense number *did* know. Wiechert describes his long journey to Buchenwald in the comparatively idyllic days of 1938. He tells how crowds gathered at various stops to jeer and spit at the Jews and political prisoners chained inside the Gestapo van. When the death trains started rolling across Germany during the war, the air grew thick with the sound and stench of agony. The trains waited on sidings at Munich before heading for Dachau, a short distance away. Inside the sealed cars, men, women, and children were going mad with fear and thirst. They screamed for air and water. They screamed all night. People in Munich heard them and told others. On the way to Belsen, a train was halted somewhere in southern Germany. The prisoners were made to run up and down the platform and a Gestapo man loosed his dog on them with the cry: 'Man, get those dogs!' A crowd of Germans stood by watching the sport. Countless such cases are on record.

Most Germans probably did not know the actual details of liquidation.

They may not have known about the mechanics of the gas ovens (one official Nazi historian called them 'the anus of the world'). But when the house next door was emptied overnight of its tenants, or when Jews, with their yellow star sewn on their coats, were barred from the air-raid shelters and made to cower in the open, burning streets, only a blind cretin could not have known.

Yet the myth did its work. True, German audiences were moved not long ago by the dramatization of *The Diary of Anne Frank*. But even the terror of the *Diary* has been an exceptional reminder. And it does not show what happened to Anne *inside* the camp. There is little market for such things in Germany. Forget the past. Work. Get prosperous. The new Germany belongs to the future. When recently asked what the name Hitler meant to them, a large number of German schoolchildren replied that he was a man who had built the *Autobahnen* and had done away with unemployment. Had they heard that he was a bad man? Yes, but they did not really know why. Teachers who tried to tell them about the history of the Nazi period had been told from official quarters that such matters were not suitable for children. Some few who persisted had been removed or put under strong pressure by parents and colleagues. Why rake up the past?

Here and there, in fact, the old faces are back. On the court benches sit some of the judges who meted out Hitler's blood laws. On many professorial chairs sit scholars who were first promoted when their Jewish or Socialist teachers had been done to death. In a number of German and Austrian universities, the bullies swagger again with their caps, ribbons, duelling scars, and 'pure Germanic' ideals. 'Let us forget' is the litany of the new German age. Even those who cannot, urge others to do so. One of the very few pieces of high literature to concern itself with the full horror of the past is Albrecht Goes's *The Burnt Offering*. Told by a Gestapo official that there will be no time to have her baby where *she* is going, a Jewish woman leaves her baby carriage to a decent Aryan shopkeeper's wife. The next day she is deported to the ovens. The empty carriage brings home to the narrator the full sum of what is being committed. She resolves to give up her own life as a burnt offering to God. It is a superb story. But at the outset, Goes hesitates whether it should be told: 'One has forgotten. And there must be forgetting, for how could a man live who had not forgotten?' Better, perhaps.

Everything forgets. But not a language. When it has been injected with falsehood, only the most drastic truth can cleanse it. Instead, the post-war history of the German language has been one of dissimulation and deliberate forgetting. The remembrance of horrors past has been largely uprooted. But at a high cost. And German literature is paying it right now. There are gifted younger writers and a number of minor poets of some distinction. But the major part of what is published as serious literature is flat and shoddy. It has in it no flame of life. Compare the best of current journalism with an average number of the *Frankfurter Zeitung* of pre-Hitler days; it is at times difficult to believe that both are written in German.

This does not mean that the German genius is mute. There is a brilliant musical life, and nowhere is modern experimental music assured of a fairer hearing. There is, once again, a surge of activity in mathematics and the natural sciences. But music and mathematics are 'languages' other than language. Purer, perhaps: less sullied with past implications; abler, possibly, to deal with the new age of automation and electronic control. But not language. And so far, in history, it is language that has been the vessel of human grace and the prime carrier of civilization.

✦ *A Kind of Survivor* ✦
For Elie Wiesel

Not literally. Due to my father's foresight (he had shown it when leaving Vienna in 1924), I came to America in January 1940, during the phoney war. We left France, where I was born and brought up, in safety. So I happened not to be there when the names were called out. I did not stand in the public square with the other children, those I had grown up with. Or see my father and mother disappear when the train doors were torn open. But in another sense I am a survivor, and not intact. If I am often out of touch with my own generation, if that which haunts me and controls my habits of feeling strikes many of those I should be intimate and working with in my present world as remotely sinister and artificial, it is because the black mystery of what happened in Europe is to me indivisible from my own identity. Precisely because I was not there, because an accident of good fortune struck my name from the roll.

Often the children went alone, or held the hands of strangers. Sometimes parents saw them pass and did not dare call out their names. And they went, of course, not for anything they had done or said. But because their parents existed before them. The crime of being one's children. During the Nazi period it knew no absolution, no end. Does it now? Somewhere the determination to kill Jews, to harass them from the earth simply because they *are*, is always alive. Ordinarily, the purpose is muted, or appears in trivial spurts — the obscenity daubed on the front door, the brick through the shop window. But there are, even now, places where the murderous intent might grow heavy: in Russia, in parts of North Africa, in certain countries of Latin America. Where tomorrow? So, at moments, when I see my children in the room, or imagine that I hear them breathing in the still of the house, I grow afraid. Because I have put on their backs a burden of ancient loathing and set savagery at their heels. Because it may be that I will be able to do no more than the parents of the dead children to guard them.

That fear lies near the heart of the way in which I think of myself as a Jew. To have been a European Jew in the first half of the twentieth century was to pass sentence on one's own children, to force upon them a condition almost beyond rational understanding. And which may recur. I have to think that — it is the vital clause — so long as remembrance is real. Perhaps we Jews walk closer to our children than other men; try as they may, they cannot leap out of our shadow.

This is my self-definition. Mine, because I cannot speak for any other Jew. All of us obviously have something in common. We do tend to recognize one another wherever we meet, nearly at a glance, by some common trick of feeling, by the darkness we carry. But each of us must hammer it out for himself. That is the real meaning of the Diaspora, of the wide scattering and thinning of belief.

To the Orthodox my definition must seem desperate and shallow. Entire communities stayed close-knit to the end. There were children who did not cry out but said *Shema Yisroel* and kept their eyes wide open because His kingdom lay just a step over the charnel pit (not as many as is sometimes said, but there *were*). To the strong believer the torture and massacre of six million is one chapter — one only — in the millennial dialogue between God and the people He has so terribly chosen. Though Judaism lacks a dogmatic eschatology (it leaves to the individual the imagining of transcendence), the Orthodox can meditate on the camps as a forecourt of God's house, as an almost intolerable but manifest mystery of His will. When he teaches his children the prayers and rites (my own access to these was that of history, not of present faith), when they sing at his side at the high holidays, the pious Jew looks on them not with fear, not as hostages that bear the doom of his love, but in pride and rejoicing. Through them the bread shall remain blessed and the wine sanctified. They are alive not because of a clerical oversight in a Gestapo office, but because they no less than the dead are part of God's truth. Without them history would stand empty. The Orthodox Jew defines himself (as I cannot) in the rich life of his prayer, of an inheritance both tragic and resplendent. He harvests the living echo of his own being from the voices of his community and the holiness of the word. His children are like the night turned to song.

The Orthodox Jew would not only deny me the right to speak for him, pointing to my lack of knowledge and communion; he would say, 'You are not like us, you are a Jew outwardly, in name only.' Exactly. But the Nazis made of the mere name necessary and sufficient cause. They did not ask whether one had ever been to synagogue, whether one's children knew any Hebrew. The anti-Semite is no theologian; but his definition is inclusive. So we would all have gone together, the Orthodox and I. And the gold teeth would have come out of our dead mouths, song or no song.

Two passages from Exodus help the mind grasp enormity. Perhaps they are mistranslations or archaic shards interpolated in the canonic text. But they help me as do poetry and metaphor, by giving imaginative logic to grim possibility. Exodus IV, 24 tells how God sought to kill Moses: 'And it came to pass by the way in the inn, that the Lord met him and sought to kill him.' I gloss this to mean that God suffers gusts of murderous exasperation at the Jews, towards a people who have made Him a responsible party to history and to the grit of man's condition. He may not have wished to be involved; the people may have chosen Him, in the oasis at Kadesh, and thrust upon Him the labours of justice and right anger. It may have been the Jew who caught Him by the skirt, insisting on contact and dialogue. Perhaps before either God or living man was ready for proximity. So as in marriage, or the bond between father and child, there are moments when love is changed to something very much like itself, pure hatred.

The second text is Exodus XXXIII, 22–3. Moses is once more on Sinai, asking for a new set of tablets (we have always been nagging Him, demanding justice and reason twice over). There follows a strange ceremony of recognition: 'And it shall come to pass, while my glory passeth by, that I will put thee in a cleft of the rock, and will cover thee with my hand while I pass by: And I will take away mine hand, and thou shalt see my back parts: but my face shall not be seen.' This may be the decisive clue: God can turn His back. There may be minutes or millennia – is our time His? – in which He does not see man, in which He is looking the *other way*. Why? Perhaps because through some minute, hideous error of design the universe is too large for His surveillance, because somewhere there is a millionth of an inch, it need be no more, out of His line of sight. So He must turn to look there also. When God's back parts are towards man, history is Belsen.

If the Orthodox Jew cannot allow my definition, or this use of the holy word as metaphor and paradox, neither can the Zionist and the Israeli. They do not deny the catastrophe, but they know that it bore splendid fruit. Out of the horror came the new chance. The state of Israel is undeniably a part of the legacy of German mass murder. Hope and the will to action spring from the capacity of the human mind to forget, from the instinct for necessary oblivion. The Israeli Jew cannot look back too often; his must be the dreams not of night but of day, the forward dreams. Let the dead bury the mounds of the dead. His history is not theirs; it has just begun. To someone like myself, the Israeli Jew might say: 'Why aren't you here? If you fear for the lives of your children, why not send them here and let them grow up amid their own kind? Why burden them with your own perhaps literary, perhaps masochistic, remembrance of disaster? This is their future. They have a right to it. We need all the brains and sinews we can get. We're not working for ourselves alone. There isn't a Jew in the world who doesn't hold his head higher because of what we've done here, because Israel exists.'

Which is obviously true. The status of the Jew everywhere has altered a little, the image he carries of himself has a new straightness of back, because Israel has shown that Jews can handle modern weapons, that they can fly jets, and turn desert into orchard. When he is pelted in Argentina or mocked in Kiev, the Jewish child knows that there is a corner of the earth where he is master, where the gun is his. If Israel were to be destroyed, no Jew would escape unscathed. The shock of failure, the need and harrying of those seeking refuge, would reach out to implicate even the most indifferent, the most anti-Zionist.

So why not go? Why not leave the various lands in which we still live, it seems to me, as more or less accepted guests? Many Russian Jews might go if they could. North African Jews are doing so even at the price of destitution. The Jews of South Africa may before too long be forced to the same resolve. So why don't I go, who am at liberty, whose children could grow up far from the spoor of the inhuman past? I don't know if there is a good answer. But there is a reason.

If the way I think of my Jewishness will appear unacceptable or self-defeating to the Orthodox and the Israeli, it will also seem remote and over-dramatized to most American Jews. The idea that Jews everywhere have been maimed by the European catastrophe, that the massacre has left all who survived (even if they were nowhere near the actual scene) off balance, as does the tearing of a limb, is one which American Jews can understand in an intellectual sense. But I don't find that it has immediate personal relevance. The relationship of the American Jew to recent history is subtly and radically different from that of the European. By its very finality, the holocaust justified every previous impulse of immigration. All who had left Europe to establish the new Jewish communities in America were proved terribly right. The Jewish soldier who went to the Europe of his fathers came better armed, technologically more efficient than his murderous enemy. The few Jews he found alive were out of a hideous but spectral world, like a nightmare in a foreign tongue. In America, Jewish parents listen at night for their children; but it is to make sure that the car is back in the garage, not because there is a mob out. It cannot happen in Scarsdale.

I am not sure, not completely (this is precisely where I am an outsider). Most American Jews are aware of anti-Semitism in specialized areas of life – the club, the holiday resort, the residential district, the professional guild. But in comparative terms, it tends to be mild, perhaps because America, unlike Europe or Russia, has no history of guilt towards the Jew. The size and human wealth of the American Jewish community are such, moreover, that a Jew need hardly go outside his own sphere to enjoy American life at its best and freest. The principal dynamism of American life, however, is a middle- and lower-middle-class conformity, an enforcing consensus of taste and ideal. Nearly by definition, the Jew stands in the way of uniform coherence. Economic, social, or political stress tend to make this latent disparity – the hostile recognition and reciprocal self-awareness of 'difference' – more acute. Depression or a drastic increase in unemployment would isolate the status of the Jew, focusing resentment on his prosperity and on the ostentatious forms that prosperity has taken in certain aspects of Jewish life. The struggle over Negro rights, which is coming to overshadow so much of American life, has obvious bearing. Among urban Negroes anti-Semitism is often open and raw. It can be used by the Negro as a basis of temporary alliance with other under-privileged or resentful elements in the white community. Beyond these possibilities lies the larger pattern: the stiffening of consensus, the increasing concentration of American values in a standardized moralistic nationalism.

I agree that American anti-Semitism will stay mild and covert. So long as the economy expands and the racial conflict can be kept in tolerable bounds. So long as Israel is viable and can offer refuge. This is probably the root condition. The support given to Israel by the American Jewish community is both thoroughly generous and thoroughly self-interested. If a new wave of immigration occurred, if the Russian or Tunisian Jew came knocking at America's door, the status of American Jewry would be immediately affected.

These complex safeguards and conditions of acceptance can break down. America is no more immune than any other nationalistic, professedly Christian society from the contagion of anti-Semitism. In a crisis of resentment or exclusion, even the more assimilated would be driven back to our ancient legacy of fear. Though he might have forgotten it and turned Unitarian (a characteristic half-way house), Mr Harrison's neighbours would remind him that his father was called Horowitz. To deny this is to assert that in America human character and historical forces have undergone some miraculous change – a utopian claim which the actual development of American life in the twentieth century has more than once rebuked.

Nevertheless, the sense I have of the Jew as a man who looks on his children with a dread remembrance of helplessness and an intimation of future, murderous possibility, is a very personal, isolated one. It does not relate to much that is now alive and hopeful. But it is not wholly negative either. I mean to include in it far more than the naked precedent of ruin. That which has been destroyed – the large mass of life so mocked, so hounded to oblivion that even the names are gone and the prayer for the dead can have no exact foothold – embodied a particular genius, a quality of intelligence and feeling which none of the major Jewish communities now surviving has preserved or recaptured. Because I feel that specific inheritance urgent in my own reflexes, in the work I try to do, I am a kind of survivor.

In respect of *secular* thought and achievement, the period of Jewish history which ended at Auschwitz surpassed even the brilliant age of co-existence in Islamic Spain. During roughly a century, from the emancipation of the ghettoes by the French Revolution and Napoleon to the time of Hitler, the Jew took part in the moral, intellectual, and artistic noon of bourgeois Europe. The long confinement of the ghetto, the sharpening of wit and nervous insight against the whetstone of persecution, had accumulated large reserves of consciousness. Released into the light, a certain Jewish élite, and the wider middle-class circle which took pride and interest in its accomplishments, quickened and complicated the entire contour of western thought. To every domain they brought radical imaginings; more specifically, the more gifted Jews repossessed certain crucial elements of classic European civilization in order to make them new and problematic. All this is commonplace; as is the inevitable observation that the tenor of modernity, the shapes of awareness and query by which we order our lives are, in substantial measure, the work of Marx, Freud and Einstein.

What is far more difficult to show, though it seems to me undeniable, is the extent to which a common heritage of fairly recent emancipation, a particular bias of rational feeling — specialized in origin but broadening out to become the characteristic modern note — informs their distinct, individual genius. In all three, we discern a mastering impulse to visionary logic, to imagination in the abstract, as if the long banishment of the Eastern and European Jew from material action had given to thought a dramatic autonomy. The intimation of an energy of imagination at once sensuous and abstract, the release of the Jewish sensibility into a world dangerously new, unencumbered by reverence, is similarly at work in the subversions of Schoenberg and Kafka, and in the mathematics of Cantor. It relates Wittgenstein's *Tractatus* to that of Spinoza.

Without the contribution made by the Jews between 1830 and 1930, western culture would be obviously different and diminished. At the same time, of course, it was his collision with established European values, with classic modes of art and argument, which compelled the emancipated Jew to define his range and identity. In this collision, in the attempt to achieve poise in an essentially borrowed milieu, the converted Jew or half-Jew, the Jew whose relation to his own past grew covert or antagonistic — Heine, Bergson, Hofmannsthal, Proust — played a particularly subtle and creative role.

Those who helped define and shared in this *Central European Humanism* (each of the three terms carrying its full charge of implication and meaning) showed characteristic traits, characteristic habits of taste and recognition. They had a quick way with languages. Heine is the first, perhaps the only great poet whom it is difficult to locate in any single linguistic sensibility.

The habits of reference of this European Jewish generation often point to the Greek and Latin classics; but these were seen through the special focus of Winckelmann, Lessing and Goethe. An almost axiomatic sense of Goethe's transcendent stature, of the incredible ripeness and humanity of his art, colours the entire European-Jewish enlightenment, and continues to mark its few survivors (Goethe's fragment *On Nature* converted Freud from an early interest in law to the study of the biological sciences). The Central European Jewish bourgeoisie was frequently intimate with the plays of Shakespeare and assumed, rightly, that the performance of Shakespearean drama in Vienna, Munich or Berlin (often acted and staged by Jews) more than matched what could be found in England. It read Balzac and Stendhal (one recalls Leon Blum's pioneer study of Beyle), Tolstoy, Ibsen and Zola. But it often read them in a special, almost heightened context. The Jews who welcomed Scandinavian drama and the Russian novel tended to see in the new realism and iconoclasm of literature a part of the general liberation of spirit. Zola was not only the explorer of erotic and economic realities, as were Freud, Weininger or Marx: he was the champion of Dreyfus.

The relationship of Jewish consciousness to Wagner was passionate, though uneasy. We see late instances of this duality in the musicology of Adorno and the fiction of Werfel. It recognized in Wagner the radicalism and histrionic tactics of a great outsider. It caught in Wagner's anti-Semitism a queer, intimate note, and gave occasional heed to the stubborn myth that Wagner was himself of Jewish descent. Being new to the plastic arts, hence beautifully free and empiric in its responses, Jewish taste, in the guise of dealer, patron and critic, backed Impressionism and the blaze of the modern. Through Reinhardt and Piscator it renovated the theatre; through Gustav Mahler the relations between serious music and society. In its golden period, from 1870 to 1914, then again in the 1920s, the Jewish leaven gave to Prague and Berlin, to Vienna and Paris a specific vitality of feeling and expression, an atmosphere both quintessentially European and 'off-centre'. The nuance of spirit is delicately mocked and made memorable in the unquiet hedonism, in the erudite urbanity of Proust's Swann.

Almost nothing of it survives. This is what makes my own, almost involuntary, identification with it so shadowy a condition. European Jewry and its intelligentsia were caught between two waves of murder, Nazism and Stalinism. The implication of the European and Russian Jew in Marxism had natural causes. As has often been said, the dream of a secular millennium — which is still alive in Georg Lukács and the master historian of hope, Ernst

Bloch – relates the social utopia of communism to the messianic tradition. For both Jew and communist, history is a scenario of gradual humanization, an immensely difficult attempt by man to become man. In both modes of feeling there is an obsession with the prophetic authority of moral or historical law, with the right reading of canonic revelations. But from Eduard Bernstein to Trotsky, from Isaac Babel to Pasternak, the involvement of the Jewish personality in communism and the Russian revolution follows an ironic pattern. Nearly invariably it ends in dissent or heresy – in that heresy which claims to be orthodox because it is seeking to restore the betrayed meaning of Marx (the Polish Marxist Adam Schaff would be a contemporary instance of this 'Talmudic revisionism'). As Stalinism turned to nationalism and techno-cracy – the new Russia of the managerial middle class has its precise origins in the Stalinist period – the revolutionary intelligentsia went to the wall. The Jewish Marxist, the Trotskyite, the socialist fellow-traveller were trapped in the ruins of utopia. The Jew who had joined communism in order to fight the Nazis, the Jewish communist who had broken with the party after the purge trials, fell into the net of the Hitler–Stalin pact.

In one of the vilest episodes in modern history, the militia and police of European appeasement and European totalitarianism collaborated in handing over Jews. The French delivered to the Gestapo those who had fled from Spain and Germany. Himmler and the G.P.U. exchanged anti-Stalinist and anti-Nazi Jews for further torture and elimination. One thinks of Walter Benjamin – one of the most brilliant representatives of radical humanism – committing suicide lest the French or Spanish border-guards hand him over to the invading SS; of Buber-Neumann whose widow was nearly hounded to death by Stalinist cadres *inside* a Nazi concentration camp; of a score of others trapped between the Nazi and the Stalinist hunter (the memoirs of Victor Serge close with the roll of their several and hideous deaths). Which bestial bargain and exchange at the frontier made eloquent the decision to hound the Jew out of European history. But also the peculiar dignity of his torment. Perhaps we can define ourselves thus: *The Jews are a people whom totalitarian barbarism must choose for its hatred.*

A certain number escaped. It is easily demonstrable that much important work in American scholarship in the period from 1934 to *c.* 1955, in the arts, in the exact and social sciences, is the afterlife of the Central European renaissance and embodied the talent of the refugee. But the particular cast of the American Jewish intelligence on native ground, which I first met at the University of Chicago in the late 1940s, and which now plays so obviously powerful a role in American intellectual and artistic life, is something very different. There is little of Karl Kraus's notion of style and humane literacy in, say, *Partisan Review*. Kraus is very nearly a touchstone. Ask a man if he has heard of him or read his *Literature and Lies*. If so, he is probably one of the survivors.

In Kraus, as in Kafka and Hermann Broch, there is a mortal premonition and finality. Broch, who seems to me the major European novelist after Joyce and Mann, is a defining figure. His *The Death of Virgil*, his philosophic essays, are an epilogue to humanism. They focus on the deed which should dominate our rational lives so far as we still conduct them, which should persistently bewilder our sense of self – the turn of civilization to mass murder. Like certain parables of Kafka and the epistemology of the early Wittgenstein, the art of Broch goes near the edge of necessary silence. It asks whether speech, whether the shapes of moral judgement and imagination which the Judaic-Hellenic tradition founds on the authority of the word, are viable in the face of the inhuman. Is the poet's verse not an insult to the naked cry? Broch died in America in a strange, vital solitude, giving voice to a civilization, to an inheritance of humane striving, already done to death.

The humanism of the European Jew lies in literal ash. In the accent of survivors – Hannah Arendt, Ernst Bloch, T. W. Adorno, Erich Kahler, Lévi-Strauss – whose interests and commitments are, of course, diverse, you will hear a common note as of desolation. Yet it is these voices which seem to me contemporary, whose work and context of reference are indispensable to an understanding of the philosophic, political, aesthetic roots of the inhuman; of the paradox that modern barbarism sprang in some intimate, perhaps necessary way, from the very core and locale of humanistic civilization. If this is so, why do we try to teach, to write, to contend for literacy? Which question, and I know of none more urgent, or the idiom in which it is put, probably puts the asker thirty years out of date – on either side of the present.

As do certain other questions, increasingly muted and out of focus. Yet which cannot go unasked if we are to argue the values and possibilities of our culture. I mean the general complicity in the massacre. There were superb exceptions (in Denmark, Norway, Bulgaria), but the tale is sordid and much of it remains an ugly riddle. At a time when 9,000 Jews were being exterminated *each day*, neither the R.A.F. nor the U.S. Air Force bombed the ovens or sought to blow open the camps (as Mosquitoes, flying low, had broken wide a prison in France to liberate agents of the Maquis). Though the Jewish and Polish underground made desperate pleas, though the German bureaucracy made little secret of the fact that the 'final solution' depended on rail transport, the lines to Belsen and Auschwitz were not bombed. Why? The question has been asked of Churchill and Harris. Has there been an adequate answer? When the *Wehrmacht* and *Waffen-SS* poured into Russia, Soviet intelligence quickly noted the mass killing of the Jews. Stalin forbade any public announcement of the fact. Here again, the reasons are obscure. He may not have wanted a rekindling of separate Jewish consciousness; he may have feared implicit reference to his own anti-Semitic policies. Whatever the cause, many Jews who could have fled eastward stayed behind unknowing. Later on, in the Ukraine, local gangs helped the Germans round up those who cowered in cellars and woods.

I wonder what would have happened if Hitler had played the game after Munich, if he had simply said, 'I will make no move outside the Reich so long as I am allowed a free hand inside my borders.' Dachau, Buchenwald and Theresienstadt would have operated in the middle of twentieth-century European civilization until the last Jew in reach had been made soap. There would have been brave words on Trafalgar Square and in Carnegie Hall, to audiences diminishing and bored. Society might, on occasion, have boycotted German wines. But no foreign power would have taken action. Tourists would have crowded the *Autobahn* and spas of the Reich, passing near but not too near the death-camps as we now pass Portuguese jails or Greek prison-islands. There would have been numerous pundits and journalists to assure us that rumours were exaggerated, that Dachau had pleasant walks. And the Red Cross would have sent Christmas parcels.

Below his breath, the Jew asks of his gentile neighbour: 'If you had known, would you have cried in the face of God and man that this hideousness must stop? Would you have made some attempt to get my children out? Or planned a ski-ing party to Garmisch?' The Jew is a living reproach.

Men are accomplices to that which leaves them indifferent. It is this fact which must, I think, make the Jew wary inside western culture, which must lead him to re-examine ideals and historical traditions that, certainly in Europe, had enlisted the best of his hopes and genius. The house of civilization proved no shelter.

But then, I have never been sure about houses. Perforce, the Jew has often been wanderer and guest. He can buy an old manse and plant a garden. An anxious pastoralism is a distinctive part of the attempt of many American middle-class and intellectual Jews to assimilate to the Anglo-Saxon back-ground. But I wonder whether it's quite the same. The dolls in the attic were not ours; the ghosts have a rented air. Characteristically, Marx, Freud, Einstein end their lives far from their native ground, in exile or refuge. The Jew has his anchorage not in place but in time, in his highly developed sense of history as personal context. Six thousand years of self-awareness are a homeland.

I find that the edge of strangeness and temporary habitation carries over into language, though here again my experience is obviously different from that of the native-born American Jew. European Jews learned languages quickly; often they had to as they wandered. But a final 'at homeness' may elude us, that unconscious, immemorial intimacy which a man has with his native idiom as he does with the rock, earth and ash of his acre. Hence the particular strategies of the two greatest European Jewish writers. Heine's German, as Adorno has pointed out, is a brilliantly personal, European idiom on which his fluent knowledge of French exercised a constant pressure. Kafka wrote German as if it were all bone, as if none of the enveloping texture of colloquialism, of historical and regional overtone, had been allowed him. He used each word as if he had borrowed it at high interest. Many great actors are or have been Jews. Language passes *through* them, and they shape it almost too well, like a treasure acquired, not inalienable. This may be pertinent also to the Jewish excellence in music, physics and mathematics, whose languages are international and codes of pure denotation.

The European Jew did not want to remain a guest. He strove, as he has done in America, to take root. He gave strenuous, even macabre proof of his loyalty. In 1933–4, Jewish veterans of the First World War assured Herr Hitler of their patriotism, of their devotion to the German ideal. Shortly thereafter, even the limbless and the decorated were hauled to the camps. In 1940, when Vichy stripped French Jews of their rights, veterans of Verdun, holders of the *Médaille militaire*, men whose families had lived in France since the early nineteenth century, found themselves harried and stateless. In the Soviet Union a Jew is so designated on his identity card. Is it foolish or hysterical to suppose that, labour as he may, the Jew in a gentile nation-state sits near the door? Where, inevitably, he arouses distrust.

From Dreyfus to Oppenheimer, every burst of nationalism, of patriotic hysteria, has focused suspicion on the Jew. Such statistics probably have no real meaning, but it may well be that the proportion of Jews actually implicated in ideological or scientific disloyalty has been high. Perhaps because they have been vulnerable to blackmail and clandestine menace, because they are natural middlemen with an ancient ease in the export and import of ideas. But more essentially, I imagine, because they are pariahs whose sense of nationality has been made critical and unsteady. To a man who may tomorrow be in desperate flight across his own border, whose graveyard may be ploughed up and strewn with garbage, the nation-state is an ambiguous haven. Citizenship becomes not an inalienable right, a sacrament of *Blut und Boden*, but a contract which he must re-negotiate, warily, with each host.

The rootlessness of the Jew, the 'cosmopolitanism' denounced by Hitler, by Stalin, by Mosley, by every right-wing hooligan, is historically an enforced condition. The Jew finds no comfort in 'squatting on the window sill' (T. S. Eliot's courteous phrase). He would rather have been *echt Deutsch* or *Français de vieille souche* or Minuteman born, than 'Chicago Semite Viennese'. At most times he has been given no choice. But though uncomfortable in the extreme, his condition is, if we accept it, not without a larger meaning.

Nationalism is the venom of our age. It has brought Europe to the edge of ruin. It drives the new states of Asia and Africa like crazed lemmings. By proclaiming himself a Ghanaian, a Nicaraguan, a Maltese, a man spares himself vexation. He need not ravel out what he is, where his humanity lies. He becomes one of an armed, coherent pack. Every mob impulse in modern politics, every totalitarian design, feeds on nationalism, on the drug of hatred which makes human beings bare their teeth across a wall, across ten yards of waste ground. Even if it be against his harried will, his weariness, the Jew — or some Jews, at least — may have an exemplary role. *To show that whereas trees have roots, men have legs and are each other's guests.* If the potential of civilization is not to be destroyed, we shall have to develop more complex, more provisional loyalties. There are, as Socrates taught, necessary treasons to make the city freer and more open to man. Even a Great Society is a bounded, transient thing compared to the free play of the mind and the anarchic discipline of its dreams.

When a Jew opposes the parochial ferocity into which nationalism so easily (inevitably) degenerates, he is paying an old debt. By one of the cruel, deep ironies of history, the concept of a chosen people, of a nation exalted above others by particular destiny, was born in Israel. In the vocabulary of Nazism there were elements of a vengeful parody on the Judaic claim. The theological motif of a people elected at Sinai is echoed in the pretence of the master race and its chiliastic dominion. Thus there was in the obsessed relation of Nazi to Jew a minute but fearful grain of logic.

But if the poison is, in ancient part, Jewish, so perhaps is the antidote, the radical humanism which sees man on the road to becoming man. This is where

Marx is most profoundly a Jew (while at the same time arguing the dissolution of Jewish identity). He believed that class and economic status knew no frontiers, that misery had a common citizenship. He postulated that the revolutionary process would abolish national distinctions and antagonisms as industrial technology had all but eroded regional autonomy. The entire socialist utopia and dialectic of history is based on an international premise.

Marx was wrong; here, as in other respects, he thought too romantically, too well of men. Nationalism has been a major cause and beneficiary of two world wars. The workers of the world did not unite; they tore at each other's throats. Even beggars wrap themselves in flags. It was Russian patriotism, the outrage of national consciousness, not the vision of socialism and class solidarity, which enabled the Soviet Union to survive in 1941. In Eastern Europe, state socialism has left national rivalries fierce and archaic. A thousand miles of empty Siberian Steppe may come to matter more to Russia and China than the entire fabric of communist fraternity.

But though Marx was wrong, though the ideal of a non-national society seems mockingly remote, there is in the last analysis no other alternative to self-destruction. The earth grows too crowded, too harassed by the shadow of famine, to waste soil on barbed wire. Where he can survive as guest, where he can re-examine the relations between conscience and commitment, making his exercise of national loyalty scrupulous but also sceptical and humane, the Jew can act as a valuable irritant. The chauvinist will snarl at his heels. But it is in the nature of a chase that those who are hunted are in advance of the pack.

That is why I have not, up till now, been able to accept the notion of going to live in Israel. The State of Israel is, in one sense, a sad miracle. Herzl's Zionist programme bore the obvious marks of the rising nationalism of the late nineteenth century. Sprung of inhumanity and the imminence of massacre, Israel has had to make itself a closed fist. No one is more tense with national feeling than an Israeli. He must be if his strip of home is to survive the wolf-pack at its doors. Chauvinism is almost the requisite condition of life. But although the strength of Israel reaches deep into the awareness of every Jew, though the survival of the Jewish people may depend on it, the nation-state bristling with arms is a bitter relic, an absurdity in the century of crowded men. And it is alien to some of the most radical, most humane elements in the Jewish spirit.

So a few may want to stay in the cold, outside the sanctuary of nationalism – even though it is, at last, their own. A man need not be buried in Israel. Highgate or Golders Green or the wind will do.

If my children should happen to read this one day, and if luck has held, it may seem as remote to them as it will to a good many of my contemporaries. If things go awry, it may help remind them that somewhere stupidity and barbarism have already chosen them for a target. This is their inheritance. More ancient, more inalienable than any patent of nobility.

✦ *Schoenberg's* Moses und Aron ✦

It is difficult to conceive of a work in which music and language interact more closely than in Arnold Schoenberg's *Moses und Aron*. (The German title has an advantage of which Schoenberg, half in humour, half in superstition, was aware: its twelve letters are a symbolic counterpart to the twelve tones which form a basic set in serial composition.) It is, therefore, impertinent to write about the opera if one is unable to analyse its powerful, intensely original musical structure. This analysis has been undertaken by several musicologists and students of Schoenberg.[1] One would wish that the intrinsic difficulty of the subject had not been aggravated by the 'initiate' technicality of their approach. This is especially true of the account of the music written by Milton Babbit and issued with the only recording so far available of *Moses and Aaron* (Columbia K-31-241).

If I write this programme note, it is because the great majority of those in the audience at Covent Garden will be in my position; they do not have the training or knowledge needed to grasp the technical unfolding of the score. The demands made are, in fact, severely beyond those required by a classical composition, or even by the orchestral density of Mahler. Together we shall have to take comfort in Schoenberg's frequent admonition: 'I cannot often

---

1. The most complete discussion of the work is to be found in Karl H. Wörner: *Schoenberg's 'Moses and Aaron'* (trans. P. Hamburger, London, 1963). Among the most important technical discussions of the music are those by Hans Keller in *The Score* (No. 21, 1957), and W. Zillig in *Melos, Zeitschrift für Neue Musik* (Vol. 3, 1957). A fascinating, though often quirky and unnecessarily obscure survey of the philosophic and historical background of the opera may be found in T. W. Adorno: *'Sakrales Fragment: Ueber Schoenberg's Moses und Aron'* (a lecture delivered in Berlin in April 1963 and reprinted that same year in Adorno's *Quasi una fantasia*).

enough warn against the overrating of analysis since it invariably leads to
what I have always fought against: the knowledge of how something is *made*;
whereas I have always tried to promote the knowledge of what something
is.' And one recalls Kierkegaard's observation at the outset of his discussion
of *Don Giovanni*: 'Though I feel that music is an art which to the highest
degree requires experience to justify one in having an opinion about it, still
I comfort myself … with the paradox that, even in ignorance and mere
intimations, there is also a kind of experience.'

In the case of *Moses and Aaron* I would go further. It belongs to that very
small group of operas which embody so radical and comprehensive an act of
imagination, of dramatic and philosophic argument articulated by poetic and
musical means, that there are aspects of it which go well beyond the normal
analysis of an operatic score. It belongs not only to the history of modern
music – in a critical way, as it exemplifies the application of Schoenberg's
principles on a large, partly conventional scale – but to the history of the
modern theatre, of modern theology, of the relationship between Judaism and
the European crisis. These aspects do not define or in any way exhaust the
meaning of the work; that meaning is fundamentally musical. But an account
of them may prove helpful to those who approach the work for the first time,
and who would place it in its historical and emotional context. Like other very
great and difficult works of art, Schoenberg's opera goes decisively outside
the confines of its genre while giving to that genre a new and seemingly
obvious fulfilment.

In a letter to Alban Berg of 16 October 1933, when he had just returned
formally to Judaism in the face of Nazi anti-Semitism, Schoenberg wrote: 'As
you have doubtless realized, my return to the Jewish religion took place long
ago and is indeed demonstrated in some of my published work (*'Thou shalt
not, thou must'*) as well as in *Moses and Aaron*, of which you have known since
1928, but which dates from at least five years earlier; but especially in my
drama *The Biblical Way* which was also conceived in 1922 or 23 at the latest.'[2]
Der Biblische Weg remains unpublished; but what is known about it points
clearly to the theme of the opera. It tells of a Zionist visionary, in whose name,
Max Arun, there may be a foreshadowing of Moses and Aaron, who fails to
achieve his goal through human imperfection. Equally relevant is the other
piece referred to by Schoenberg, the second of the *Four Pieces* for mixed
chorus, Op. 27. Written in 1925, it sets to music the prohibition of Mosaic

2. All quotations are from the *Letters*, ed. by Erwin Stein (London, 1964).

law against the making of images. 'An image asks for names ... Thou shalt believe in the Spirit; thou must, chosen one.' This injunction, expressed in a cadenced prose which anticipates the 'spoken song' of the opera, summarizes the central dramatic idea and conflict of *Moses and Aaron*. But Schoenberg's interest in the musical statement of religious thought and in the dramatic idiom of the Old Testament goes back even further: to *Die Jakobsleiter*, an oratorio left incomplete in 1917.

This concern persisted throughout Schoenberg's later work: in the *Kol Nidre* of 1938, in the brief, harrowing cantata *A Survivor from Warsaw* (1947), in the setting of Psalm 130 (1950), in Schoenberg's final opus, the unfinished *Modern Psalms*. The last words he set to music were: 'And yet I pray as all that lives prays.' Thus *Moses and Aaron* is thematically and psychologically related to an entire set of works in which Schoenberg sought to express his highly individual, though at the same time profoundly Judaic concept of identity, of the act of spiritual creation, and of the dialogue – so inherent in music – between the song of man and the silences of God. The opera is both Schoenberg's *magnum opus* (What T. W. Adorno calls his *'Hauptwerk quand-même'*) and a composition rooted in the logic and development of his entire musical thought.

Schoenberg began writing *Moses and Aaron* in Berlin in May 1930; he completed Act II in Barcelona on 10 March 1932. Roberto Gerhard, in whose Barcelona flat Schoenberg often worked, tells an instructive anecdote. Schoenberg did not mind friends chatting in the room, even when he was engaged on the fantastically complex score; what he could not tolerate were sudden spells of quiet. The dates of composition are, of course, important. On the one hand they mark Schoenberg's hard-fought professional acceptance, as Ferruccio Busoni's successor at the Prussian Academy of Arts. But they also mark bouts of illness which led Schoenberg to seek refuge in a southern climate, and, above all, the rise of the Nazi menace. A year after he had completed Act II, Schoenberg was compelled to leave Berlin and start a life of exile.

He did not live to complete the opera or hear it performed. An extract was given in concert form at Darmstadt on 2 July 1951 (plans for a production at the *Maggio Musicale* in Florence fell through). Schoenberg died less than a fortnight later. The first complete concert performance was given at the Musikhalle in Hamburg under the direction of Hans Rosbaud in March 1954. On 16 June 1957 Rosbaud directed the stage premiere of *Moses und Aron* at the Stadttheater in Zurich. This was followed by a Berlin production under

Hermann Scherchen in October 1959. Since that time there have been few major opera houses in Europe or the United States which have not expressed the hope of producing the work, and retreated before its formidable exactions.

Karl Wörner says that *Moses and Aaron* 'is without precedent'. This is not so: as opera, it is related to Wagner's *Parsifal,* and there are orchestral anticipations both in Mahler and in Schoenberg's own earlier compositions and in his short operas, *Erwartung* and *Die glückliche Hand.* But it is technically more demanding than any other major opera, and the quality of the religious-philosophic conflict requires from the performers and producer an unusual range of insight and sympathy. Schoenberg has deliberately used a genre saturated with nineteenth-century values of unreality and modish display to express an ultimate seriousness. In so doing he reopened the entire question of opera.

The libretto is organized wholly in terms of musical form and development (if serial music anticipates electronic music it is in the totality of control which the composer aims at in every aspect of the musical experience). As Schoenberg remarked: 'It is only while I'm composing that the text becomes definite, sometimes even after composition.' Nevertheless, the book of *Moses and Aaron* is itself of great fascination. Schoenberg has a distinctive style which one sees in his paintings and theoretical writings no less than in his music. He worked in large strokes, and achieved an effect of clarity and abstract energy by leaving out syntactical qualifications or half-tones. Like much in Schoenberg's musical texts and literary tastes, the libretto shows traces of German expressionism, and of the sources of expressionism. Characteristically, Strindberg plays a part: Schoenberg knew *Wrestling Jacob* when he planned *Die Jakobsleiter,* and was aware of Strindberg's *Moses* when writing his own very different treatment of the theme.

The idiom used in *Moses and Aaron* is highly personal. It is kept apart from the rhythms and tonality of the Luther Bible. Schoenberg wrote to Berg on 5 August 1930: 'I am of the opinion that the language of the Bible is medieval German, which, being obscure to us, should be used at most to give colour; and that is something I don't need.' Above all, each German word, whether in *Sprechgesang,* in direct song or choral declaration, is uniquely and precisely fitted to the musical context. The words are no less *durchkomponiert* ('fully composed, musicalized') than are the notes. This is what makes any decision to produce *Moses and Aaron* in English so wrong-headed. To alter the words — their cadence, stress, tonalities — as must be done in translation, is tantamount to altering the key relations or orchestration in a piece of classical music. Moreover, there is no need to subvert Schoenberg in this way: the story of Exodus is known to everyone, and Schoenberg's presentation of the plot is utterly lucid. A brief outline would give an English-speaking audience all the help it wants.

The relationship of language to music in *Moses and Aaron* is unlike that in any other opera. The problem of that relationship, of how to apportion the stress between word and musical tone, of whether the ideal libretto should not be weak precisely in order to mark the distance between music drama and the spoken play, underlies the whole history of opera. As Joseph Kerman has shown, it is the problematic achievement of Wagner, the late Verdi, and twentieth-century operatic composers to have given the libretto a new seriousness. Hence the marked affinity to modern literature and psychological argument in the operas of Janáček, Berg, and Stravinsky. Hence the ironic allegoric treatment of the debate between poet and composer in Richard Strauss's *Capriccio*.

But *Moses and Aaron* goes much deeper. It belongs to that group of works produced in the twentieth century, and crucial to our present aesthetics, which have their own possibility as essential theme. I mean that it asks of itself – as Kafka does of fiction, as Klee asks of visual form – whether the thing can be done at all, whether there are modes of communication adequate. Kierkegaard wrote of Mozart: 'The happy characteristic that belongs to every classic, that which makes it classic and immortal, is the absolute harmony of the two forces, form and content.' One would say of modern art that what makes it such and unmistakable to our sensibility is the frequent dissonance between moral, psychological content and traditional form. Being a drama of non-communication, of the primal resistance of intuitive or revealed insight to verbal and plastic incarnation (the refusal of the word to be made flesh), *Moses and Aaron* is, on one vital plane, an opera about opera. It is a demonstration of the impossibility of finding an exhaustive accord between language and music, between sensual embodiment and the enormous urgency and purity of intended meaning. By making the dramatic conflict one between a man who speaks and a man who sings, Schoenberg has argued to the limit the paradoxical convention, the compromise with the unreal, inherent in all opera.

The paradox is resolved in defeat, in a great cry of necessary silence. This alone makes it difficult to think of a serious opera coming after or going beyond *Moses and Aaron*. But that was exactly Schoenberg's own problem as a post-Wagnerian, and as an heir to Mahler in artistic morality even more than in orchestral technique. Like Mahler he was proposing to aggravate, in the literal sense, the easy co-existence, the *libertinage* between music and public which obtained in the opera house at the turn of the century and which Strauss, for all his musical integrity, never refuted. As Adorno notes, *Moses and Aaron* can be approached in the same spirit as a major cantata of Bach. But unlike Bach, it is a work which at every moment examines its own validity and expressive means.

The motif of a sharp conflict between Moses and Aaron is, of course, present in the Pentateuch. It may well be that later priestly editors, with their particular professional association with Aaron's priesthood, smoothed away some of the grimmer evidence, and obscured the full, murderous consequences of the clash. Schoenberg made of this archaic, obscure antagonism a conflict of ultimate moral and personal values, of irreconcilable formulations or metaphors of man's confrontation with God. Working on the principle – discernible at the roots of Greek tragic drama – that fundamental human conflict is internal, that dramatic dialogue is in the final analysis between self and self, Schoenberg gathered the entire force of collision into a single consciousness.

This is the drama of Moses. Aaron is one of the possibilities (the most seductive, the most humane) of Moses's self-betrayals. He is Moses's voice when that voice yields to imperfect truth and to the music of compromise. Schoenberg remarked in 1933: 'My Moses more resembles – of course only in outward respect – Michelangelo's. He is not human at all.' So far as the harsh, larger-than-life stature of the personage goes, this may be so. But the poignancy of the opera, its precise focus of emotion and suffering, comes above all from Moses's humanity, from that in him which is riven and inarticulate. It is not of the fiercely contained eloquence of Michelangelo's statue that one thinks when listening to *Moses and Aaron*, but of Alban Berg's *Wozzeck* (written just before Schoenberg started composing his own opera). Moses and Wozzeck are both brilliant studies in dramatic contradiction, operatic figures unable to articulate with their own voices the fullness of their needs and perceptions. In both cases the music takes over where the human voice is strangled or where it retreats into desperate silence.

Schoenberg admitted to Berg: 'Everything I have written has a certain inner likeness to myself.' This is obviously true of Moses, and it is here that Michelangelo's figure, which fascinated Freud in a similar way, may be relevant. To any Jew initiating a great movement of spirit or radical doctrine in a profoundly hostile environment, leading a small group of disciples, some of them perhaps recalcitrant or ungrateful, to the promised land of a new metaphysic or aesthetic medium, the archetype of Moses would have a natural significance. By introducing into music, whose classical development and modes seemed to embody the very genius of the Christian and Germanic tradition, a new syntax, an uncompromisingly rational and apparently dissonant ideal, Schoenberg was performing an act of great psychological boldness and complexity. Going far beyond Mahler, he was asserting a revolutionary – to its enemies an alien, Jewish – presence in the world of Bach and Wagner. Thus the twelve-tone system is related, in point of sensibility and psychological context, to the imaginative radicalism, to the 'subversiveness' of Cantor's mathematics or Wittgenstein's epistemology.

Like Freud, Schoenberg saw himself as a pioneer and teacher, reviled by the vast majority of his contemporaries, driven into solitude by his own unbending genius, gathering a small band around him and going forward, in exile, to a new world of meaning and vital possibility. In Moses's bitter cry that his lessons are not being understood, that his vision is being distorted even by those nearest him, one hears Schoenberg's own inevitable moments of discouragement and angry loneliness. And there is almost too apt an analogy in the fact that he died on the threshold of acceptance, before his stature had been widely acknowledged, before he could complete *Moses and Aaron* or hear any of it performed.

Except for one moment (I, 2, bars 208–17) – and I have never understood just why it should be at *this* particular point in the opera – Moses does not sing. He speaks in a highly cadenced, formal discourse, his voice loud and bitter against the fluencies of the music and, in particular, against Aaron's soaring tenor. (The parodistic yet profoundly engaged treatment of Aaron's vocal score seems to be full of references to traditional operatic *bel canto* and the ideal of the Wagnerian *Heldentenor*.) The fact that the protagonist of a grand opera should not sing is a powerful theatrical stroke, even more 'shocking' than the long silence of Aeschylus' Cassandra or the abrupt, single intervention of the mute Pylades in *The Libation Bearers*. But it is also much more than that.

Moses's incapacity to give expressive form (music) to his vision, to make revelation communicable and thus translate his individual communion with God into a community of belief in Israel, is the tragic subject of the opera. Aaron's contrasting eloquence, his instantaneous translation – hence traduction – of Moses's abstract, hidden meaning into sensuous form (the singing voice), dooms the two men to irreconcilable conflict. Moses cannot do without Aaron; Aaron is the tongue which God has placed into his own inarticulate mouth. But Aaron diminishes or betrays Moses's thought, that in him which is immediate revelation, in the very act of communicating it to other men. As in Wittgenstein's philosophy, there is in *Moses and Aaron* a radical consideration of silence, an inquiry into the ultimately tragic gap between what is apprehended and that which can be said. Words distort; eloquent words distort absolutely.

This is implicit in the first lines of the opera spoken by Moses against the background of the orchestral opening and the murmur of the six solo voices which portray the Burning Bush. The fact that Moses so often speaks simultaneously with Aaron's song, or that we hear his voice in conflict with the orchestra, points to Schoenberg's essential design: Moses's words are internal, they are his thought, clear and integral only before it moves outward into the betrayal of speech.

Moses addresses his God as 'omnipresent, invisible, and inconceivable'. *Unvorstellbar*, that which cannot be imagined, conceived or represented (*vorstellen* means, precisely, to enact, to mime, to dramatize concretely), is the key-word of the opera. God is *because* He is incommensurate to human imagining, because no symbolic representation available to man can realize even the minutest fraction of His inconceivable omnipresence. To know this, to serve a Deity so intangible to human mimesis, is the unique, magnificent destiny which Moses envisions for his people. It is also a fearful destiny. As the Voice out of the Burning Bush proclaims:

> This people is chosen
> before all others,
> to be the people of the only God,
> that it should know Him
> and be wholly His;
> that it undergo all trials
> conceivable to thought
> over the millennia.

The last two lines are eloquently ambiguous: the words can also be read to mean: 'all trials to which this thought – of a God invisible and inconceivable – may be exposed.'

Aaron enters and the misunderstanding between the two brothers is immediate and fatal. Aaron rejoices in the proud uniqueness of Israel's mission, in the grandeur of a God so much more powerful and demanding than all other gods (these other gods continue to be real to Aaron). He exults in *imagining* such a God, in finding words and poetic symbols by which to make Him present to His people. Yet even as he sings, Moses cries out: 'No image can give you an image of the unimaginable.' And when Aaron elaborates, with a rich ease of illusion mirrored in the music, the notion of a God who will punish and reward His people according to their deserts, Moses proclaims a Kierkegaardian God, infinitely, scandalously transcending any human sense of cause and effect:

> Inconceivable because invisible;
> because immeasurable;
> because everlasting;
> because eternal;
> because omnipresent;
> because omnipotent.

To which litany of abstraction, of inexpressible apprehension, Aaron responds with the joyous assurance that God shall bring wonders to pass on behalf of His enslaved people.

He does. Confronted with the rebellious bewilderment of the Jews, with their call for visible signs of the new revelation, Moses retreats into his own inarticulateness. It is Aaron who proclaims himself the word and the deed. It is he who casts Moses's rod to the ground where it turns into a serpent, and shows Moses's hand to be leprous and then miraculously restored. During the entire last part of the act, Moses is silent. It is Aaron who proclaims the doom of Pharaoh and the covenant of the Promised Land. Fired by his eloquence, the people of Israel march forth and the music is exultant with Aaron's certitude. It is through him that God appears to be speaking.

In one sense, in one possible idiom, He is. Moses's understanding of God is much more authentic, much deeper; but it is essentially mute or accessible only to very few. Without Aaron, God's purpose cannot be accomplished; through Aaron it is perverted. That is the tragic paradox of the drama, the metaphysical scandal which springs from the fact that the categories of God are not parallel or commensurate to those of man.

Act II centres on the Golden Calf. With Moses's long absence on Sinai, the Elders and the people have grown rebellious and afraid. The invisibility of God has become an intolerable anguish. Aaron yields to the voices that cry out for an image, for something that eye and hand can grasp in the act of worship. On the darkening stage the Golden Calf shines forth.

What follows is one of the most astonishing pieces of music written in the twentieth century. As musical analysts point out, it is a symphony in five movements with solo voices and choruses. The orchestration is so intricate yet dramatic in its statements and suggestions that it seems incredible that Schoenberg should have *heard* it all inside him, that he should have known exactly (if he did) how these fantastic instrumental and rhythmic combinations would work without, in fact, ever hearing a note played. The pageant of the Golden Calf makes the utmost demands on orchestras, singers, and dancers. Rearing horses, treasure-laden camels, and Four Naked Virgins are requirements which even the most resourceful of opera houses may find difficult to meet.

What Schoenberg had in mind is something very different from an ordinary operatic ballet. It is a total dramatic integration of voice, bodily motion, and orchestral development. Even the most frenzied moments of the idolatrous, sexual orgy are plotted in terms of a rigorous, immensely subtle musical structure. As Schoenberg wrote to Webern: 'I wanted to leave as little as possible to those new despots of the theatrical art, the producers, and even to envisage the choreography as far as I'm able to ... You know I'm not at all keen on the dance ... Anyway so far I've succeeded in thinking out movements such as at least enter into a different territory of expression from the caperings of common-or-garden ballet.'

But these 'caperings' are not wholly irrelevant. In Schoenberg's treatment of the Golden Calf, as in so much of *Moses and Aaron*, there is a revaluation cither straightforward or parodistic – of the conventions of opera. Are these conventions applicable to the modern circumstance? How much seriousness can they sustain? Thus the Golden Calf is both the logical culmination of, and a covert satire on, that catalogue of orgiastic ballets and ritual dances which is one of the distinctive traits of grand opera from Massenet's *Hérodiade* to *Tannhäuser*, from *Aïda* and *Samson et Dalila* to *Parsifal* and *Salome*. Schoenberg is fully aware of the dual quality of the scene. It is at the same time supremely serious and ironic in its exhaustive use of the convention: 'In the treatment of this scene, which actually represents the very core of my thought, I went pretty much to the limit, and this too is probably where my piece is most *operatic*; as indeed it must be.'

With the return of Moses – his indistinct, terrifying figure looms suddenly on the horizon and is seen by one of the exhausted revellers – the drama moves swiftly to its climax. At a glance from Moses, the Golden Calf vanishes: *'Begone, you that are the image of the fact that what is measureless cannot be bounded in an image.'* The two brothers confront each other on the empty stage. And once more it is Aaron who has the better of the argument. He has given the people an image so that Israel may live and not fall into despair. He loves the people and knows that the demands of abstraction and inwardness which Moses makes upon the human spirit are beyond the power of ordinary men. Moses loves an idea, an absolute vision, relentless in its purity. He would make of Israel the hollow, tormented vessel of an inconceivable presence. No people can endure such a task. Even the Tables of the Law which Moses has brought from the mountain are only an image, a palpable symbol of hidden authority.

Baffled, incensed by Aaron's argument, Moses smashes the Tables. Aaron accuses him of faint-heartedness. The tribes of Israel shall continue their march to the Promised Land whether or not they have grasped the full meaning of God's revelation. As if to confirm his words, the Chorus resumes its march across the stage. It is led by a pillar of fire, and Aaron goes forth glorying in the visible wonder of God.

Moses is left alone. Is Aaron right? Must the inconceivable, unimaginable, unrepresentable reality of God diminish to mere symbol, to the tangible artifice of miracle? In that case all he has thought and said (the two are identical to Moses) has been madness. The very attempt to express his vision was a crime. The orchestra falls silent as the unison violins play a retrograde inversion of the basic twelve-tone set. Moses cries out, 'O word, thou word that I lack!' and sinks to the ground, broken.

This is one of the most moving, dramatic moments in the history of opera and of the modern theatre. With its implicit allusion to the *Logos*, to the Word that is yet to come but which lies beyond speech, it gathers into one action both the claims of music to be the most complete idiom, the carrier of transcendent energies, and all that is felt in twentieth-century art and philosophy about the gap between meaning and communication. But Moses's defeat also has a more specific, historical bearing, which may help us understand why Schoenberg did not complete the opera.

The letters of 1932 and 1933 show that he had every intention of doing so. As late as November 1948, Schoenberg could write: 'I should really best like to finish *Die Jakobsleiter* and *Moses and Aaron*.' What intervened?

There is evidence that Schoenberg found it difficult to give the third act a coherent dramatic shape. He wrote to Walter Eidlitz on 15 March 1933 that he had recast Aaron's Death for the fourth time 'because of some almost incomprehensible contradictions in the Bible'. As it stands, the text of Act III is a curious torso, both repetitive and moving. Once more, Moses and Aaron, now in chains, state their opposite conceptions of idea and image. But Moses no longer addresses his brother directly. He is speaking to the Jewish people as it prepares to enter into the mire and compromise of history. He prophesies that Jews will prosper only so long as they dwell in the stern wilderness of the spirit, in the presence of the One and Inconceivable God. If they forget their great act of renunciation and seek an ordinary haven in the world, they will have failed and their suffering shall be the greater. Salvation lies in apartness. The Jew is himself when he is a stranger.

Freed of his chains, Aaron falls dead at Moses's feet. (Is there here, one wonders, a reminiscence of Hunding's death when Wotan glances at him in scorn?) As we have no music to accompany the words, it is difficult to judge their effect. But the third act is essentially static. There is no dramatic justification for Moses's triumph over a prostrate Aaron. Much is missing.

But the real impediment probably lay deeper. As Adorno remarks, *Moses and Aaron* was 'a preventive action against the looming of Nazism'. Yet even as Schoenberg worked on the score, Nazism was moving rapidly to its triumph. The words *Volk* and *Führer* figure prominently in the opera; they designate its supreme historical values, Israel and Moses. Now they were wrestled out of Schoenberg's grasp by a million voices bawling them at Nuremberg. How could he continue to set them to music? As he laboured on the third act in March 1933, Schoenberg must have known that the culture in which he had hammered out his vision of a new music, and for whose opera houses he had conceived *Moses and Aaron*, was heading for ruin or exile – as was his own personal life.

It is this which gives the end of Act II its tremendous authority and logic. The events that were now to come to pass in Europe were, quite literally, beyond words, too inhuman for that defining act of humane consciousness which is speech. Moses's despairing cry, his collapse into silence, is a recognition – such as we find also in Kafka, in Broch, in Adamov – that words have failed us, that art can neither stem barbarism nor convey experience when experience grows unspeakable. Thus *Moses and Aaron* is, despite its formal incompletion, a work of marvellous finality. There was no more to be said.[3]

3. This is why it seems to me that a spoken performance of the third act, which Schoenberg himself envisioned and regarded as permissible, adds nothing and, in fact, weakens the uncanny force and beauty of the musical close.

❧ *Postscript* ❧

Two passages, at random: the first from Chaim Kaplan's Warsaw Diary, the second from Jean-François Steiner's study of Treblinka:

> A rabbi in Lodz was forced to spit on a Torah scroll that was in the Holy Ark. In fear of his life, he complied and desecrated that which is holy to him and to his people. After a short while he had no more saliva, his mouth was dry. To the Nazi's question, why did he stop spitting, the rabbi replied that his mouth was dry. Then the son of the 'superior race' began to spit into the rabbi's mouth, and the rabbi continued to spit on the Torah.

> Despite all the precautions taken by his friends, Professor Mehring was called out of the ranks during roll-call. When the punishment squad, performing its 'exercise', began to thin out, Professor Mehring was seized by an extraordinary will to live and started running like a madman. 'Lalka' observed this and, when a quarter of the prisoners had fallen, made the 'exercise' go on to see how long the old man, running a few yards behind the others, could hold out.
> He yelled – If you catch up with them, your life is saved.
> And gave the order to whip on the survivors.
> The survivors faltered and slowed down in order to help the Professor; but the blows redoubled, making them stumble, shredding their clothes, covering their faces with blood. Blinded with blood, reeling with pain, they again speeded up. The Professor, who had gained a little ground, saw them pull away from him again and threw his arms forward, as if to grasp the other prisoners, as if to plead with them. He stumbled once, then a second time; his tortured body seemed to fall apart; he tried once more to recover his balance, then, all at once, stiffened and collapsed in the dust. When the Germans drew near, they saw a thread of blood flowing from his mouth. Professor Mehring was dead.

Indeed, rather lucky: not hung by his feet and flogged to death like Langner, the lashes being so timed that he would not die until evening. Not thrown alive into the crematoria fire. Not drowned, as were many, by slow immersion in urine and ordure. Principally, perhaps, without having with his own hands hanged his child in the barrack at night, to preserve him from further torture in the morning.

One of the things I cannot grasp, though I have often written about them, trying to get them into some kind of bearable perspective, is the time relation. At a previous point in rational time, Professor Mehring was sitting in his study, speaking to his children, reading books, passing his hand over a white tablecloth on Friday evening. And flayed alive, 'blood splashing slowly from his hair', Langner was, in some sense, the same human being who had, a year earlier, perhaps less, walked the daylight street, done business, looked forward to a good meal, read an intellectual monthly. But in what sense? Precisely at the same hour in which Mehring or Langner was being done to death, the overwhelming plurality of human beings, two miles away on the Polish farms, 5,000 miles away in New York, were sleeping or eating or going to a film or making love or worrying about the dentist. This is where my imagination balks. The two orders of simultaneous experience are so different, so irreconcilable to any common norm of human values, their co-existence is so hideous a paradox – Treblinka *is* both because some men have built it and almost all other men let it be – that I puzzle over time. Are there, as science-fiction and Gnostic speculation imply, different species of time in the same world, 'good times' and enveloping folds of inhuman time, in which men fall into the slow hands of living damnation? If we reject some such module, it becomes exceedingly difficult to grasp the continuity between normal existence and the hour at which hell starts (on the city square when the Germans begin the deportations, or in the office of the *Judenrat* or wherever), an hour marking men, women, children off from any precedent of life, from any voice 'outside', in that other time of sleep and food and humane speech. On the fake station platform at Treblinka, cheerfully painted and provided with window-boxes so as not to alert the new arrivals to the gas-ovens half a mile farther, the painted clock pointed to three. Always. There is an acute perception in this on the part of Kurt Franz, the commander of the extermination camp.

This notion of different orders of time simultaneous but in no effective analogy or communication, may be necessary to the rest of us, who were not there, who lived as if on another planet. That, surely, is the point: to discover the relations between those done to death and those alive then, and the relations of both to us; to locate, as exactly as record and imagination are able, the measure of unknowing, indifference, complicity, commission which relates the contemporary or survivor to the slain. So that, being now instructed as never quite before – and it is here that history *is* different – of the fact that 'everything is possible', that starting next Monday morning at, say, 11.20 a.m. time can change for oneself and one's children and drop out of humanity, we may better gauge our own present position, its readiness for or vulnerability to other forms of 'total possibility'. To make oneself concretely aware that the 'solution' was not 'final', that it spills over into our present lives is the only but compelling reason for forcing oneself to continue reading these literally unbearable records, for going back or, perhaps, forward into the non-world of the sealed ghetto and extermination camp.

Moreover, despite the large amount of work done by historians, despite the mountains of documentation amassed during the trials, very important questions of 'relation' remain obscure or unanswered. There is, first of all, the matter of the unwillingness of European powers and the United States during the late 1930s to make more than token gestures towards the rescue of Jewish children. There is the appalling evidence of the enthusiasm shown in Poland and western Russia by the local population when it came to helping the Germans kill Jews. Of the 600 who succeeded in escaping from Treblinka to the forests, only forty survived, the majority being killed by Poles. 'Go to Treblinka where you Jews belong' was a not uncommon answer to Jewish women and children seeking refuge among Polish neighbours. In the Ukraine, where many Jews remained in the face of the German advance because Stalinist policy carefully prohibited any warning to them of Nazi intentions, matters were, if conceivable, even worse. Had the people of occupied Europe chosen to help the Jews, to identify themselves even symbolically with the fate of their Jewish fellow countrymen, the Nazi massacre could not have succeeded. This is shown by the solidarity and courage of Christian communities helping Jews in Norway, Denmark and parts of Bulgaria.

But what of the outside, what of the powers actually at war with Nazi Germany? Here the evidence is, until now, controversial and full of ugly undertones. Many questions remain almost taboo. There are motives of internal politics, historical prejudice and personal cruelty which may account for the indifference towards and even participation in the destruction of the Jews by Stalinist Russia. The failure of the R.A.F. and U.S. Air Force to bomb the gas-ovens and rail lines leading to the death-camps after substantial information about the 'final solution' had reached London from Poland and Hungary, and after desperate pleas to that effect had been transmitted by elements in the Polish underground, remains an ugly riddle. The absence of any such raids — even *one day* of interruption in the gas-ovens would have meant the life of 10,000 human beings — cannot be accounted for merely on technical grounds. Low-flying R.A.F. planes blew open the door of a prison in France rescuing vital members of the resistance from further torture and execution. Just when did the names Belsen, Auschwitz, Treblinka first turn up in allied intelligence files, and what was done about them?

It has been said that the answer is one of psychological paralysis, of the sheer incapacity of the 'normal' mind to imagine and hence give active belief to the enormities of the circumstance and the need. Even those — and they may have been few — who came to believe that the news out of eastern Europe was authentic, that millions of human beings were being methodically tortured and gassed in the middle of the twentieth century, did so at some abstract remove, as we might believe a piece of theological doctrine or an historical occurrence far in the past. The belief did not relate. We are post-Auschwitz *homo sapiens* because the evidence, the photographs of the sea of bones and gold fillings, of children's shoes and hands leaving a black claw-mark on oven walls, have altered our sense of possible enactments. Hearing whisperings out of hell again we would know how to interpret the code; the skin of our hopes has grown thinner.

This is obviously an important argument, particularly when extended to the problem of German awareness of what was going on and to the even more vexed matter of Jewish unreadiness, disbelief, even in some passive or metaphoric sense, acquiescence in the massacre. The earth at Treblinka contained, in one corner of the camp, 700,000 bodies, 'weighing approximately thirty-five thousand tons and filling a volume of ninety thousand cubic metres'. If the Jews could not, until the closing of the oven door or the stench of the fire-pit, believe this to be true, if the intelligence of a people prepared for apocalyptic anguish by 2,000 years of harrying could not focus on this new and final possibility, how could that of other men? It is one of the daemonic attributes of Nazism (as of sadistic literature) to taint those who accept its imaginings as literally feasible — even when they reject them with loathing — with an element of self-doubt and unbalance. To *believe* the reports on Auschwitz smuggled out by the underground, to credit the statistical facts before such credence had become irrefutable and generally shared throughout the surviving world, was to yield in some measure to the monstrousness of the German intent. Scepticism ('such things cannot happen now, not at this point in man's history, not in a society that has produced Goethe') had its part of humane dignity and self-respect. And tragically so among east

European Jews, with their complex involvement in German culture and western enlightenment.

This is clearly shown both in the fictionalized account of Vilna at the start of Steiner's *Treblinka,* and in the opening pages of Kaplan's diary. Jewish reactions fluctuated wildly between hope that German occupation would bring some rational order to suffering – imprisonment in a ghetto could signify protection from the ever-recurrent if random brutalities of gentile neighbours – and the hope that Hitler would soon allow the departure of the Jews from Europe. What wisps of information did leak through about Nazi mass exterminations were, for a long time, treated either as the natural fantasies of the affrighted or as dangerous falsehoods disseminated by pro-vocateurs to demoralize the Jews or incite them to some act of rebellion. The latter would provide the Nazis with an 'excuse' to act 'more harshly'. Above all, there was the hope that the world outside would come in aid. On 24 January 1940 Kaplan wrote:

> A small ray of light has shone forth from between the clouds that are spread across our skies. The information has reached us that the American Quakers will send a rescue mission to Poland. This time the aid will be offered in American fashion, without regard to race or religion, and even the Jews will be able to benefit from the proffered aid. May they be blessed! For us this is the first time that, instead of 'except the Jews', the expression 'including the Jews' has reached us, and it rings in our ears with a strange sound. Is it really true?

And on 11 June 1940 the Jews of Warsaw took comfort from the firm belief that 'the French are fighting like lions with the last of their strength'. Hope, the radical property of man to regard himself in some kind of mutual relationship to other men, died inch by inch. The memory of hope cries out in one of the last messages received by the outside world during the rising of the Warsaw ghetto: 'The world is silent. The world *knows* (it is inconceiv-able that it should not) and stays silent. God's vicar in the Vatican is silent; there is silence in London and Washington; the American Jews are silent. This silence is astonishing and horrifying.' In fact there was noise just outside the ghetto walls, carefully recorded by German newsreel teams: the frequent laughter and applause of Polish spectators watching men leaping into flames and the houses blowing up.

When did belief darken to certitude? According to J.-F. Steiner (but his account is partially dramatic fiction or rearrangement) it was Langner, dying under the lash, who cried out with his last breath that 'you will all be slain. They cannot let you out of here after what you have witnessed.' In Kaplan's testimony the process of recognition is gradual. Each spasm of tenacious vitality – a joke made, a child fed, a German sentry cajoled or outwitted – seemed to Kaplan a guarantee of survival: 'A nation which can live in such terrible circumstances as these without losing its mind, without committing suicide – and which can still laugh – is sure of survival. Which will disappear first, Nazism or Judaism? I am willing to bet! Nazism will go first!' Thus on 15 August 1940. By June 1942 the possibility of the 'final solution' was becoming plain in Kaplan's mind. Though 'imprisoned within double walls: a wall of brick for our bodies, and a wall of silence for our spirits', Kaplan could state, on 25 June, that Polish Jewry was being totally slaughtered. He even refers to 'lethal gas'. But it was not until the deportation order in late July 1942 that the recognition of doom closed in. Rumour flew about that it had been Himmler's sadistic jest to promulgate the decree on the eve of the Ninth of Av, 'a day of retribution, a day fated for mourning through all generations. But all that is irrelevant. In the last analysis these are accidental, momentary manifestations. They did not cause the decree. The real purpose is deeper and more fundamental – the total destruction of the Jewish nation.' That this purpose has survived Nazism in many individuals and certain societies, even societies where there are scarcely any Jews left alive, that it runs close beneath the surface of many aspects of Soviet life, enforces the need to look back. There are elements of anti-Semitism deeper than sociology or economics or even historical superstition. The Jew sticks like a bone in the throat of any other nationalism. 'God of Gods!' wrote Kaplan as the end drew near, 'shall the sword devour thy sons for ever?'

The diary breaks off in the evening hours of 4 August, with Jewish police under Nazi supervision scouring block after city block. Taken to the *Umschlagplatz* (whose features and tablet of remembrance the present régime in Warsaw has all but obliterated), Kaplan and his wife were deported. They are thought to have been murdered in Treblinka in December 1942 or January 1943. Kaplan's foresight and the help of a Pole outside the ghetto ensured the survival of these small notebooks. Together with Emmanuel Ringelblum's *Notes from the Warsaw Ghetto*, this diary constitutes the only complete record of Jewish life in Warsaw from the outbreak of war to the time of deportation. Over and over Kaplan writes that this diary is his reason for survival, that the record of atrocity must reach the outside world. The last sentence reads:

'If my life ends – what will become of my diary?' He won his desperate, patient gamble; his voice has overcome the ash and the forgetting.

It is the voice of a rare human being. A teacher of Hebrew, an essayist, a scholar of Jewish history and customs, Chaim Aron Kaplan chose to stay in Warsaw in 1941, though his American and Palestinian contacts might have secured him an exit visa. He wrote in Hebrew, but with that erudite, critical background of classical and European humanism characteristic of the modern Jewish intelligentsia. On 26 October 1939 he set down his credo:

> Even though we are now undergoing terrible tribulations and the sun has grown dark for us at noon, we have not lost our hope that the era of light will surely come. Our existence as a people will not be destroyed. Individuals will be destroyed, but the Jewish community will live on. Therefore, every entry is more precious than gold, so long as it is written down as it happens, without exaggerations and distortions.

This latter clause he fulfilled to an almost miraculous degree. In midst of hell, Kaplan discriminates between the horror witnessed and that which is only reported. Through extreme precision he came to a deep, diagnostic perception. As early as 28 October 1939 Kaplan had defined the root condition of the relations between Germans and Jews: 'In the eyes of the conquerors we are outside the category of human beings. This is the Nazi ideology, and its followers, both common soldiers and officers, are turning it into a living reality.' He knew what not very many, as yet, are prepared to see plainly: that Nazi anti-Semitism is the logical culmination of the millennial Christian vision and teaching of the Jew as killer of God. Commenting on the murderous beatings of Jews by German and Polish gangs at Easter 1940, Kaplan adds: 'Christian "ethics" became conspicuous in life. And then – woe to us!' He observed the queer mystery of German culture, the co-existence in the same men of bestiality and eager literacy:

> We are dealing with a nation of high culture, with 'a people of the Book' ... The Germans have simply gone crazy for one thing – books ... Where plunder is based on an ideology, on a world outlook which in essence is spiritual, it cannot be equalled in strength and durability ... The Nazi has both book and sword, and this is his strength and might.

That the book might well be Goethe or Rilke remains a truth so vital yet outrageous that we try to spit it out, that we go on mouthing our hopes in culture as if it was not there to break our teeth. It may do so, if we do not come to understand its meaning with something of Kaplan's calm and precision of feeling.

That precision extends to Kaplan's observation of moments of humanity on the part of the Germans. The flush of embarrassment on the face of a German sentry is gratefully recorded; an officer stopping to help a child trampled by a German soldier, and adding, 'Go and tell your brethren that their suffering will not last much longer!' is remembered as if he were a mysterious harbinger of grace (31 January 1940). At all times there is the effort to understand how 'this pathological phenomenon called Nazism', this 'disease of the soul' can affect an entire people or class of human beings. In Kaplan the very act of truthful observation becomes an exercise in rational possibility, a counter-statement to the madness and degradation in the street. There is scarcely a touch of hate in this book, only the desire to understand, to test insight against reason. Seeing a German whip an old pedlar to death in the open street, Kaplan writes: 'It is hard to comprehend the secret of this sadistic phenomenon ... How is it possible to attack a stranger to me, a man of flesh and blood like myself, to wound him and trample upon him, and cover his body with sores, bruises and welts, without any reason? How is it possible? Yet I swear that I saw all this with my own eyes.' In such labour of understanding lies the only mode of forgiveness. Only those who actually passed through hell, who survived Auschwitz after seeing their parents flogged to death or gassed before their own eyes (like Elie Wiesel), or who found their own kin amid the corpses from which they had to extract gold teeth, a daily encounter at Treblinka, can have the right to forgive. *We* do not have that right. This is an important point, often misunderstood. What the Nazis did in the camps and torture chambers is wholly unforgivable, it is a brand on the image of man and will last; each of us has been diminished by the enactment of a potential sub-humanity latent in all of us. But if one did not undergo the thing, hate or forgiveness are spiritual games — serious games no doubt — but games none the less. The best now, after so much has been set forth, is, perhaps, to be silent; not to add the trivia of literary, sociological debate, to the unspeakable. So argues Elie Wiesel, so argued a number of witnesses at the Eichmann trial. The next best is, I believe, to try and understand, to keep faith with what may well be the utopian commitment to reason and historical analysis of a man like Kaplan.

But as I write this, a minute splinter of the enormity drives home. There is no other man precisely like Chaim Aron Kaplan. This is so of every death; metaphysically an absolute uniqueness passes from the store of human resources. But despite its outward democracy death is not wholly equal. The integrity, the fineness of intelligence, the humane rationalism exhibited on every page of this indispensable book – representing a specific tradition of feeling, of linguistic practice – are irretrievably lost. The particular type of human possibility realized in central and east European Judaism is extinct. We know next to nothing about genetic reserves, about the raw material of diverse inheritance on which the human species draws for its laboured progress. But numerical renewal is only a part of the story. In murdering Chaim Kaplan and those like him, in making certain that their children would be ash, the Germans deprived human history of one of the versions of its future. Genocide is the ultimate crime because it pre-empts on the future, because it tears up one of the roots from which history grows. There can be no meaningful forgiveness because there can be no repair. And this absence from our present needs, from our evolutionary hopes, of the strains of moral, psychological, cerebral quality extinguished at Belsen and Treblinka constitutes both the persistence of the Nazi action and the slow, sad vengeance of the unremembered dead.

A lack of modesty, of the finely shaping ironies which mark the Warsaw Diary, has been notable in the debates over *Treblinka*. Born in 1938, of a Jewish father who was deported and killed by the Germans, and a Catholic mother, Jean-François Steiner did not experience the actual massacre. It was a trip to Israel and the well-known *malaise* felt by younger Jews throughout the Eichmann trial – 'why did Jews in Europe go like lambs to the slaughter?' – that prompted Steiner to interview the handful of survivors of Treblinka (twenty-two in Israel, five in the United States, one in England) and to write an account of 'the revolts in an extermination camp'. Hailed by Madame de Beauvoir as a vindication of Jewish courage and as a pioneer work in the sociological, psychological interpretation of a community in hell, *Treblinka* has been bitterly attacked by others (David Rousset and Léon Poliakov among them) for its alleged inaccuracies, racism, and for what comfort its general thesis of Jewish passivity may give to Miss Hannah Arendt. The recriminations have been ugly, as they were in the Arendt case. And this, though humiliating and subversive to intelligence, is proper. For it is by no means certain that rational discourse *can* cope with these questions, lying as they do outside the normative syntax of human communication, in the explicit domain of the bestial; nor is it clear that those who were not themselves fully involved should touch upon these agonies unscathed. Those who were inside – Elie Wiesel in *La Nuit, Les Portes de la forêt, Le Chant des morts*, Koppel Holzmann in *Die Höhlen der Hölle* — can find right speech, often allegoric, often a close neighbour to silence, for what they choose to say. We who come after are shrill and discomfort each other with claims of anger or impartial perception. M. Poliakov speaks of the successive 'scandals' which attend all books on the murder of the Jews from Schwarz-Bart's *The Last of the Just* to Hochhuth's *The Representative*, and now *Treblinka*. Silence during the murder, but scandal over the books.

Steiner has set himself a difficult, somewhat strange task: to reconstruct the life and insurrection in a death-camp in the form of a fictionalized documentary, of a piece of closely documented reportage using the imaginary dialogues, character sketches and dramatized montage of fiction. The fact that almost all the survivors of the rising of 2 August 1943 were later murdered by Polish peasants, by Ukrainian fascist bands, by right-wing units in the Polish resistance or by the *Wehrmacht*, has meant that Steiner had to rely on the tortured memories of a few individuals for the bulk of his material. His choice of a dramatized genre, which is profoundly honest in so far as it represents the effort of a non-witness to imagine backwards, to enter hell by act of imaginative talent, entails obvious risks. Repeatedly during the Eichmann trial, witnesses blunted the prosecutor's questions saying: 'You cannot understand. Who was not *there* cannot imagine.' And unable to imagine entirely, to translate document into self, into the indelible mark on one's own skin, Jean-François Steiner resorts, probably unconsciously, to the conventions of violence and suspense current in modern fiction and high journalism.

Consequently *Treblinka* uses the cinematic chronology and stills of a *Time* story. It is full of memorable dialogue and dramatic silences. Actual and imagined personages appear in episodes grouped and cut by an obviously skilled eye (a Truman Capote stretched to fury). The mental life of Kurt Franz ('Lalka') is rendered with Dostoevskyan nuance. Now I have no doubt that all these monstrous and heroic scenes took place: that fathers and sons helped one another commit suicide in the barracks, that naked girls offered themselves to *kapos* in a last striving for life, that Ukrainian guards and doomed Jews danced and played music together on hot summer evenings in the bizarre death-village built by Franz. I know from other evidence that Steiner's account of the Treblinka symphonic orchestra is true, that the boxing matches and cabaret he describes did indeed take place, that a small number of Jewish men and women, hunted past endurance, came voluntarily to the gates of Treblinka asking for admission and death. In the great majority of cases, Steiner's narrative and dialogue is firmly grounded in direct and documentary evidence. But because that evidence is mastered by the literary talent of the writer, because a narrative persona full of distinct rage and stylistic force interposes between the insane fact and the profoundly exciting economy, hence order, of the book, a certain unreality obtrudes. Where it is represented with such skill, intricate modulations affect the hideous truth. It becomes more graphic, more terribly defined, but also has more acceptable, conventional lodging in the imagination. We believe; yet do not believe intolerably, for we draw breath at the recognition of a literary device, of a stylistic stroke not finally dissimilar from what we have met in a novel. The aesthetic makes endurable.

But although this is not a book I can unreservedly trust — the pressure it puts on the imagination is not always that which most nearly, most scrupulously relates us to the presence of the dead — many of the charges made against Steiner are unjust.

It is true that insurrection was not as rare as Steiner makes out — witness actions recorded at Bialistok, Grodne, Sobivor, Auschwitz and, above all, in Warsaw itself. Nevertheless, Treblinka was the only death-camp actually destroyed by a Jewish uprising, and the conditions under which that uprising was planned were indeed fantastic.

Treblinka is not the first or most authoritative attempt at a sociology of the damned. Kogon's *SS-Staat* and Bettelheim's *The Informed Heart* are much more reliable. But Bettelheim's observations in particular bear on an earlier, relatively imaginable version of camp life. In Treblinka, with its incessant assembly-line of death and technology of mass disposal, with its fake railway station and teutonic village, with its dogs trained to attack men's private parts and its official Jewish marriages, life had reached a pitch of extreme insanity. Jean-François Steiner conveys this world, extraterritorial to reason, not, I imagine, in its complete, literal truth. How could he? 'I who was there still do not understand,' writes Elie Wiesel. But what he has translated from the silences, necessary forgettings, partial speech of the survivors often rings true. Principally, he makes one grasp something of the deliberate torture of hope and choice by which the Nazis broke the spring of will in men. In a world in which, as in the cruel myth of Plato's *Gorgias*, men constantly had before their eyes the calendar of their own deaths, the Nazis introduced a mechanism of minimal hope. 'You can go on living if you do this or that to our satisfaction.' But the doing almost invariably involved a choice so hideous, so degrading that it further diminished the humanity of those who made it. The father had to choose to let his child die; the *kapo* had to flog harder; the informer had to betray; husband had to let wife go unknowing to the ovens lest he himself be immediately selected. To live was to choose to become less human.

Exactly this same process is analysed by Kaplan. It was the notorious game of yellow or white passes and labour-cards. Which one meant life, which death? Or three cards are issued to a family of four, forcing parents and children to select one of their own number for extermination. Hope mocked can break a human identity more swiftly than hunger. But hunger there was, and continuous physical torment, and the sudden cessation of all human privacy.

Thus the riddle is *not* why the east European Jews failed to offer more resistance, why, thrust out of humanity, deprived of all weapons, methodically starved, they did not revolt (in essence, Hannah Arendt's thesis suffers from a failure of imagining). In fact, this is a radically indecent question, asked as it is so often by those who remained silent during the massacre. The question is how it was possible for Chaim Kaplan to keep his sanity, and how Galewski and his resistance committee were able to rise from amid the stinking mountains of the dead and lead an attack against SS machine-guns. The mystery is that even *one* man should have retained sufficient remembrance of normal life to recognize man in his companions and in his own brutalized image. Only from such recognition can rebellion and that supreme deed of identity which is to give one's life for the survival of others — as the Treblinka committee did to a man — arise.

Certain Jewish mystics have said that Belsen and Treblinka embody a momentary eclipse or madness of God; other have spoken of God's especial, and therefore unfathomable, nearness to His chosen in the gas-oven and at the whipping-block. These are metaphors of reason when reason suffers despair or a hope more grievous than despair. What the documents tell us is that in the dark of God's absence, certain men, buried alive, buried by that silence of Christianity and western civilization which makes all who were indifferent accomplice to the Nazis, rose and destroyed their parcel of hell. For all its unpleasant stylistic virtuosity, for all its contrivances and, perhaps, inaccuracies, *Treblinka* gives us some understanding of how this came about. The charge that J.-F. Steiner has somehow humiliated the Jews by showing them through the eyes of German and Ukrainian torturers, and that his account of the initial paralysis of Jews at Treblinka contributes to a racist myth of Jewish passivity, seems to me unfounded. It overlooks his primary intent which is to imagine for himself and for us the unimaginable, to speak where only silence or the Kaddish for the unnumbered dead have a natural place.

But enough of the debate. These books and the documents that have survived are not for 'review'. Not unless 'review' signified, as perhaps it should in these instances, a 'seeing-again', over and over. As in some Borges fable, the only completely decent 'review' of the Warsaw Diary or of Elie Wiesel's *Night* would be to recopy the book, line by line, pausing at the names of the dead and the names of the children as the orthodox scribe pauses, when recopying the Bible, at the hallowed name of God. Until we knew many of the words by *heart* (knowledge deeper than mind) and could repeat a few at the break of morning to remind ourselves that we live *after*, that the end of the day may bring inhuman trial or a remembrance stranger than death.

In the Warsaw ghetto a child wrote in its diary: 'I am hungry, I am cold; when I grow up I want to be a German, and then I shall no longer be hungry, and no longer cold.' And now I want to write that sentence again: 'I am hungry, I am cold; when I grow up I want to be a German, and then I shall no longer be hungry, and no longer cold.' And say it many times over, in prayer for the child, in prayer for myself. Because when that sentence was written I was fed, beyond my need, and slept warm, and was silent.

◆ *Heidegger's Silence* ◆

Though voluminous, the literature on Heidegger's involvement with Nazism does not seem to press home the two questions that need asking. What, if anything, relates the fundamental ontology of *Sein und Zeit* to this involvement? What, if anything, can be said to account for Heidegger's *total* public silence (with one jejune posthumous exception) *after* 1945, concerning the holocaust and his own attitudes towards the policies and bestialities of the Third Reich? The restriction to 'public' may or may not be relevant; there may or may not be private pronouncements in the archive, for instance in the correspondence with Hannah Arendt.

To wade through the pertinent material is a sickening business. So far as they can be reconstructed, the facts are these:

In April 1933, Professor von Möllendorf, a Social Democrat, is prevented from assuming the rectorship of Freiburg University. He, together with his senior colleagues, asks Heidegger to take on the post. His fame may be of salutary use to the university in threatening times. Heidegger belongs to no party and has taken no role whatever in politics. He hesitates, but is persuaded. Heidegger is elected rector with only one dissenting vote and begins his term of office on 21 April. To do so at all is tantamount to becoming a functionary under the new régime, and he joins the National Socialist Party during the first days of May. At the very start of his rectorship Heidegger prohibits the dissemination of anti-Semitic tracts by Nazi students inside the university building. He forbids a planned book-burning of 'decadent', 'Jewish', and 'Bolshevik' works in front of the university, and tries to prevent the purge of 'undesirable' volumes from the university library. It is roughly at this point that we come to one of the most notorious items in the entire dossier: Heidegger's alleged authorization of the banning from use of the library of his non-Aryan teacher and predecessor, Edmund Husserl. To the best of my knowledge, no such authorization was issued. If the two men did not see one another in those sick days, the reason was that they had already drifted apart on personal and philosophic grounds. (Heidegger's failure to intervene positively and publicly on Husserl's behalf is, of course, another matter altogether.)

Refusing to ratify the dismissal of two anti-Nazi deans of the university, Wolf and von Möllendorf, Heidegger resigns his rectorship in late February 1934. (It is vital to remember that Hitler assumed complete domination only on 19 August 1934, after the death of Hindenburg.) On resigning, or immediately thereafter, Heidegger leaves the party. Nazi hacks, such as Professor Ernst Krieck, now denounce Heidegger as an obscurantist whose world-view is, despite momentary appearances, the very opposite of the Führer's. There is some evidence that Heidegger's courses, particularly on Nietzsche, are placed under surveillance from the winter semester of 1934–5 onward. A new edition of *Sein und Zeit* appears in 1942. The dedication to Edmund Husserl is omitted. To the best of my knowledge, it is the publisher who insists on this omission, without which the book would not have been allowed. All the laudatory references to Husserl, including the famous footnote on page 38, stand as before. In the summer of 1944, the university authorities declare Heidegger to be 'the professor whose services can be most readily dispensed with.' As a result, Heidegger is sent to do a spell of compulsory work on the construction of earthworks on the banks of the

Rhine. He gives his final class on 8 November 1944. The Allied powers forbid Heidegger to teach. This interdict is in force until 1951.

The key texts for this period are Heidegger's address to colleagues and students on the occasion of the loyalty oath pledged to the new régime in March 1933; his rector's address on the 'Self-determination of the German University' in May 1933; his declaration of support for the referendum of 12 November 1933, in which Hitler called on Germany to ratify its exit from the League of Nations; his commemoration, on 1 June 1933, of the death of Albert Leo Schlageter, a nationalist martyr executed by the occupying French forces in the Ruhr; the speech on 'Labour-Service and University' of 20 June 1933; and the loosely related 'Summons to Labour Battalions' of 23 January 1934. A further document is provided by a photograph of Rector Heidegger surrounded by uniformed Nazi officials and thugs at a celebration of refusal and vengeance on Armistice Day 1933.

As one looks at these texts, and the shorter pronouncements that were made during Heidegger's rectorship, there can be no doubt whatever: it is vile, turgid, and brutal stuff in which the official jargon of the day blends seamlessly with Heidegger's idiom at its most hypnotic. The *Volk* has won back the 'truth' of its 'will to be', of its *Daseinswillen*. The genius of Adolf Hitler has led his people out of the idolatries and corruptions of 'rootless and impotent thinking'. It is the National Socialist revolution which will enable philosophers, now reunited to the *Volk* as a whole, to return with 'hard clarity' (a characteristic bit of ontological-Nazi idiom) to the question of the meaning of human existence. It is the 'supreme privilege' of the academic community to serve the national will. The sole justification for 'so-called "intellectual labour"' is the investment of such labour in the historical, national needs and purposes from which it has sprung. For a university student, to enter the labour battalions of the new Reich is not to waste or betray his calling. On the contrary, it is to give that calling its ethical and social foundations without which, as *Sein und Zeit* has shown, there can be no authentic destiny.

By breaking with the past, by smashing the sham brotherhood of the League of Nations, by yielding itself into 'the keeping of the Führer and of that world-historical movement' which he incarnates, Germany is exemplifying, as no other people has ever done, that projection of being toward futurity which is the supreme act of authentication. (The kinship of the vocabulary with that of Part III of *Sein und Zeit* is organic.) A plebiscite for Hitler is 'a vote for the future' – a future which is the 'truer' for being the long-awaited inheritance, the being-past (*Erbe* and *Gewesenheit*) of the German people. 'The Führer himself', proclaims Heidegger in the *Freiburger Studenten Zeitung* for 3 November 1933, 'is the only present embodiment and future embodiment of German action and its law.' To oppose him would be treason against being.

Yet one must note that there are, in the midst of these brutal effronteries and servilities, some covert but tenacious indirections. The address attendant on the loyalty oath speaks of a system that will eschew 'the rule of might'. The notorious *Rektorats-Rede* has in it hints that the revolution which is being hailed is, or must become, one of spiritual essence rather than politics in the normal sense. The attack on the League of Nations urges the need for a much deeper conception of peace among peoples, for the realization that every nation, not Germany alone, must find for itself the grandeur and the truth of its *Bestimmung* (its 'determination', 'its assignment through its calling'). Considered closely, a number of key passages dissolve into a curious mist of quietism somewhere to the other side of politics.

Heidegger's *Introduction to Metaphysics* goes back to lectures given in 1935. Heidegger reissues the text in 1953. He retains the following statement: 'The works that are being peddled about nowadays as the philosophy of National Socialism but have nothing whatever to do with the inner truth and greatness of this movement [namely the encounter between global technology and modern man] have all been written by men fishing in the troubled waters of "values" and "totalities".' Thus the 'inner truth and greatness' of the Nazi movement stands affirmed. As R. Minder has shown, Heidegger's study of Hebbel, *Dichter in der Gesellschaft* (*The Poet in His Society*) of 1966, is replete with Nazi jargon of *Blut und Boden* and the sanctified mission of the *Volk*. On 23 September 1966, Martin Heidegger gave a lengthy interview to the magazine *Der Spiegel* (an oddly trivializing venue) on condition that it appear posthumously. It was published in June 1976. It is masterly in its feline urbanity and evasions. Heidegger acknowledges that he saw no alternative to Nazism in 1933 if Germany were to survive. But before even the crassest of his 1933–4 utterances are to be judged, they must be 'thought through' in depth. Where he called for a self-renewal of the German universities under the aegis of the party, it is not the latter that should be emphasized but the ontological connotations of *self*. Compromises in phraseology and public stance were unavoidable if higher education was to be safeguarded. Whatever their unfortunate personal differences, Heidegger continued to draw on Husserl's teachings in his own expositions of phenomenology. The Hölderlin lectures of 1934–5, the Nietzsche seminar of 1936, 'spied upon by official informants', ought, in essence, to be seen as an encoded counter-statement to and polemical confrontation with Nazism (*eine Auseinandersetzung*). What the demure interviewers did not ask was this: Is there anywhere in Heidegger's work a repudiation of Nazism, is there anywhere, from 1945 to his death, a single syllable on the realities and philosophic implications of the world of Auschwitz? These are the questions that count. And the answer would have to be, No.

My own reading of the evidence is this: Like millions of other German men and women, and a good many eminent minds outside Germany, Heidegger was caught up in the electric trance of the National Socialist promise. He saw in it the only hope for a country in the grip of economic and social disaster. The Nazism to which Heidegger adhered, moreover, was, as yet, masking its essential barbarism. It was Heidegger's error and vanity, so characteristic of the academic, to believe that he could influence Nazi ideology, that he could bring his own doctrine of existential futurity to bear on the Hitlerite programme, while at the same time preserving the prestige and partial autonomy of the scholarly establishment. He was fatuously mistaken. But if the photograph I have referred to is anything to go by, Heidegger was, already by November 1933, acutely uncomfortable among his Nazi colleagues. His official implication in the movement lasted only nine months and he quit – the point is worth reiterating – before Hitler's assumption of total power. Many eminent intellectuals did far worse.

But the spate of articles and speeches of 1933–4 cries out against Martin Heidegger. For here he goes so crassly beyond official obligation, let alone a provisional endorsement. The evidence is, I think, incontrovertible: there *were* instrumental connections between the language and vision of *Sein und Zeit*, especially the later sections, and those of Nazism. Those who would deny this are blind or mendacious. In both – as in so much of German thought after Nietzsche and Spengler – there is the presumption, at once mesmerized by and acquiescent in, of a nearing apocalypse, of so deep a crisis in human affairs that the norms of personal and institutional morality must be and shall inevitably be brushed aside. There was in the pseudo-messianism of the Hitler phenomenon a confirmation of some of Heidegger's most shadowy but deep-seated apprehensions. Both Nazism and the onto-logical anthropology of *Sein und Zeit* stress the concreteness of man's function in the world, the primordial sanctity of hand and body. Both exalt the mystical kinship between the labourer and his tools in an existential innocence which must be cleansed of the pretensions and illusions of abstract intellect. With this emphasis goes a closely related stress on rootedness, on the intimacies of blood and remembrance that an authentic human being culti-vates with his native ground. Heidegger's rhetoric of 'at-homeness', of the organic continuum which knits the living to the ancestral dead buried close by, fits effortlessly into the Nazi cult of 'blood and soil'. Concomitantly, the Hitlerite denunciations of 'rootless cosmopolitans', the urban riffraff, and unhoused intelligentsia that live parasitically on the modish surface of society, chime in readily with the Heideggerian critique of 'theyness', of technological modernity, of the busy restlessness of the inauthentic.

Heideggerian 'resoluteness' (*Entschlossenheit*) has more than a hint of the mystique of commitment, of self-sacrificial and self-projective élan preached by the Führer and his 'hard-clear' acolytes. Both enact that heightening of personal fate into national and ethnic vocation which is analysed in *Sein und Zeit*. In both there is, logically and essentially, an exaltation of death as life's purposed summit and fulfilment. Here again, there is a shared Hegelian and Nietzschean background. If, as Heidegger argues, history in the traditional, critically evaluated sense is meaningless, then that meaning-lessness must be made graphic and shown to be a dead end. In the Hitlerite recomposition of the historical past, in the apocalyptic imperative of a totally new beginning in German destiny, Heidegger could find a confirmation of his own more technical, more esoteric anti-historicism.

But above all, there is the idiom of *Sein und Zeit* and that of the National Socialist jargon. Both, though at obviously different levels, exploit the genius of German for suggestive darkness, its ability to give to (often empty or half-baked) abstractions a physical presence and intensity. There is in Heidegger's supposition, itself at once metaphorical and mesmeric, that it is not man who speaks where language is most fully effective, but 'language itself through man', an ominous hint of Hitler's brand of inspiration, of the Nazi use of the human voice as a trumpet played upon by immense, numinous agencies beyond the puny will or judgement of rational man. This motif of dehumanization is key. Nazism comes upon Heidegger precisely at that moment in his thinking when the human person is being edged away from the centre of meaning and of being. The idiom of the purely ontological blends with that of the inhuman.

But nauseating as they are, Heidegger's gestures and pronouncements during 1933–4 are tractable. It is his complete silence on Hitlerism and the holocaust after 1945 which is very nearly intolerable.

Every mid-twentieth-century body of serious thought, whether libertarian or conservative, secular or theological, social or psychological, has sought to come to grips with the phenomena of genocide and the concentration camp, with the brusque irruption into the calendar of man of the seasons in hell. The postulate that Auschwitz and Belsen signify some zero-point in the condition and definition of man is now a platitude. For a philosopher, for a German witness, for a thinking, feeling human being implicated in at least a part of the relevant events, to say absolutely nothing is tantamount to complicity. For we are always accomplice to that which leaves us indifferent. Is there, then, anything one can argue to account for or to justify the total silence of one whose later works, according to Martin Buber, 'must belong to the ages'?

Only conjecture is possible. Allegations of anti-Semitism are, in respect of the magnitude of the case, trivial, but also, I believe, false. I have been unable to locate anti-Jewish sentiments or utterances in the works of Heidegger, even in those of a public and political nature – a fact which, from the outset, isolates him from the mainstream of Nazism. If Heidegger was, on certain obvious levels, a great man, a teacher whose philosophic-linguistic activity literally towers over various aspects of contemporary speculation, he was, at the same time, a very small man. He led his existence amid a worshipful coterie and, particularly in his later years, behind barriers of adulation. His sorties into the world at large were few and carefully orchestrated. It may well be that he did not have the courage or magnanimity needed to confront his own political past, and the question of Germany's espousal of barbarism. Though engaged in overthrowing traditional meta-physics, though committed to a radical and anti-academic concept of thought, Heidegger was simultaneously a German *Ordinarius*, the lifelong incumbent of a prestigious chair, incapable, either emotionally or intellectually, of facing, of 'thinking through', as he would put it, the easy collapse of German academic and cultural institutions before the Nazi challenge.

Moreover, as one ponders Heidegger's career, with its marvellous economy of motion and capacity to generate legend (there are, here, definite points of contact with Wittgenstein's career), the trait that emerges overwhelmingly is that of cunning, of 'peasant shrewdness'. The pursed mouth and small eyes seem to peer at the questioner out of a millennial legacy of adroit reticence. In view of the facts and of his own part in them, Heidegger may have intuited that a refusal to say anything whatever — even where, especially where he would be pontificating on world politics and American-Soviet materialism — would be, by far, the most effective stance. To which one ought, in fairness, to add the possibility that the enormity of the disaster and of its implications for the continuance of the western spirit may have seemed to Heidegger, as it has to other writers and thinkers, absolutely beyond rational comment. But he could, at the very least, have said *this*, and the interest he took in the poetry of Celan shows that he was fully aware of the option.

One further hypothesis seems worth testing. Heidegger's involvement with Germany and the German language, in what he takes to be their unique affinity with the dawn of man's being and speech in archaic Greece, is all-determining. It governs his life and work. Germany's pre-eminence in just those activities which may be the highest in reach of man, namely philosophy and music, is a constant theme in German thought and self-awareness. From Bach to Webern, from Kant to Heidegger and Wittgenstein, it is in the German sphere that the genius of man would seem to touch the summits and to plumb the last depths. Given this *Geschick*, this 'destined singularity', it could be conceivable that it is from inside the German world also that must spring ultimate inhumanity, the final experiments of man with his own potentiality for destruction. There would be a sense, albeit resistant, indeed offensive, to analytic or pragmatic explanation, in which the possibility of a Bach and of a Beethoven, of a Kant and of a Goethe, would entail — as surely as that of a Wagner and of a Nietzsche — the chance of catastrophe. Embodying 'man and superman' or the phenomenon of human identity in its complete spectrum of dialectical extremities, Germany and German history would have the 'mittence' of self-destruction, of negation (abstractions for which Hegel and Heidegger had found terms of drastic expression). To offer a critique of this vocation 'from beneath', to attempt to circumscribe it within bounds of common sense and morality, would be useless. It would be a trivialization of tragic but exemplary *Dasein*.

Perhaps it was along some such lines (and they are not wholly without force of evidence) that Heidegger thought when he chose to remain mute. Perhaps cunning is a part of fundamental ontology. I do not know. What remains is the cold silence and the abject evasions of Heidegger's followers (among whom Jews are implausibly prominent). What remains, as well, is the question of how this silence, on which Celan seems to touch in his enigmatic poem 'Todtnauberg', is to be accorded with the lyric humanity of Heidegger's later writings.

✦ Lieber's Lament ✦

[This lament over the Holocaust is spoken by 'Lieber', the organizer, the inspirer — real or imagined — of those who are hunting Adolf Hitler in the Amazonian forests. It is the sixth chapter of the novel The Portage to San Cristobal of A.H.]

Ajalon to Nimrud. Message received. Can you hear me? Ajalon to Nimrud. Glory to God. In the highest. And for ever. The sun stood still over Ajalon so that we could prevail. But then the night stood still. For twelve years. Darkness unmoving. Over us and our children. Can you hear me? Over. But now there is light again, at Gilead and in Hebron, and to the ends of the earth. I tell you there is light as never before. And tonight the stars will dance over Arad. And the world stand still to draw breath, and the dew be like cymbals in the grass. Because he is ours. Because he is in the hands of the living. In your hands. Ajalon to Nimrud. Listen to me. You must not let him speak, or only few words. To say his needs, to say that which will keep him alive. But no more. Gag him if necessary, or stop your ears as did the sailor. If he is allowed speech he will trick you and escape. Or find easy death. His tongue is like no other. It is the tongue of the basilisk, a hundred-forked and quick as flame. As it is written in the learned Nathaniel of Mainz: there shall come upon the earth in the time of night a man surpassing eloquent. All that is God's, hallowed be His name, must have its counterpart, its backside of evil and negation. So it is with the Word, with the gift of speech that is the glory of man and distinguishes him everlastingly from the silence or animal noises of creation. When He made the Word, God made possible also its contrary. Silence is not the contrary of the Word but its guardian. No, He created on the night-side of language a speech for hell. Whose words mean hatred and vomit of life. Few men can learn that speech or speak it for long. It burns their mouths. It draws them into death. But there shall come a man whose mouth shall be as a furnace and whose tongue as a sword laying waste. He will know the grammar of hell and teach it to others. He will know the sounds of madness and loathing and make them seem music. Where God said, let there be, he will unsay. And there is *one* word — so taught the blessed Rabbi Menasseh of Leyden — *one* word amid the million sounds that make the secret sum of all language, which if spoken in hatred, may end creation, as there was one that brought creation into being. Ajalon to Nimrud. Are you getting me? Perhaps *he* knows that word, he who very nearly did us to death, who deafened God so that the covenant seemed broken and our children given to ash. Do not let him speak freely. You will hear the crack of age in his voice. He is old. Old as the loathing which dogs us since Abraham. Let him speak to you and you will think of him as a man. With sores on his skin and need in his bowels, sweating and hungering like yourselves, short of sleep. If he asks for water fill the cup. If he asked twice he would no longer be a stranger. Give him fresh linen before he needs it. Those who speak to us of their dirt and the itch in the groin are no longer enemies. Do not listen to his sleep. Over. If you think of him as a man, sodden when the rains come, shaking to the bone when you reach the Cordilla, you will grow uncertain. You will not forget. O I know you will never forget. Rememberers for Jacob. But the memory will turn alien and cold. A man's smell can break the heart. You will be so close now, so terribly close. You will think him a man and no longer believe what he did. That he almost drove us from the face of the earth. That his words tore up our lives by the root. Listen to me. Ajalon calling. Can you hear me? This is an order. Gag him if you must. Words are warmer than fresh bread; share them with him and your hate will grow to a burden. Do not look too much at him. He wears a human mask. Let him sit apart and move at the end of a long rope. Do not stare at his nakedness lest it be like yours. Over to you. Are you receiving me, Simeon? I am not mad. There are thousands of miles to go before he is safely in Jerusalem. You will come to know him as you do your own stench. Look away from his eyes. They say that his eyes have a strange light. Do not leave the boy alone with him. The boy knows but does not remember, not in his own flesh. What this man did. Ajalon calling. Come in, Nimrud. Tell me that you remember. The garden in Salonika, where Mordechai Zathsmar, the cantor's youngest child, ate excrement, the Hoofstraat in Arnheim where they took Leah Burstein and made her watch while her father, the two lime trees where the road to Montrouge turns south, 8 November 1942, on which they hung the meathooks, the pantry on the third floor, Nowy Swiat xi, where Jakov Kaplan, author of the *History of Algebraic Thought in Eastern Europe 1280–1655*, had to dance over the body of, in White Springs, Ohio, Rahel Nadelmann who wakes each night, sweat in her mouth because thirty-one years earlier in the Mauerallee in Hanover three louts drifting home from an SS recruitment spree had tied her legs and with a truncheon, the latrine in the police station in Wörgel which Doktor Ruth Levin and her niece had to clean with their hair, the fire-raid on Engstaad and the Jakobsons made to kneel outside the shelter until the incendiaries, Sternowitz caught in the woods near Sibor talking to Ludmilla, an aryan woman, and filled with water and a piano-wire wound tight around his, Branka seeing them burn the dolls near the ramp and when she sought to hide hers being taken to the fire and, Elias Kornfeld, Sarah Ellbogen, Robert Heimann in front of the biology class, Neuwald Gymnasium lower Saxony, stripped to the waist, mouths wide open so that Professor Horst Küntzer could demonstrate to his pupils the obvious racial, an hour of school which Heimann remembered when at Matthausen naked again, Lilian Gourevitch given two work-passes for her three children in Tver Street and ordered to choose which of the children was to go on the next transport, Lilian Gourevitch given two work-passes, yellow-coloured, serial numbers BJ7732781 and 2, for her three children in Tver Street and ordered to choose, Lilian Gourevitch, the marsh six kilometres from Noverra where the dogs found Aldo Mattei and his family in hiding, only a week before the Waffen-SS retreated northward, thus completing the register of fugitives, five Jews, one Gypsy, one hydrocephalic, drawn up at the *prefettura* in Rovigo, the last Purim in Vilna and the man who played Haman cutting his throat, remember him, Moritz the caretaker whose beard they had torn out almost hair by hair, pasting on a false beard and after the play taking the razor in the boiler-room, Dorfmann, George Benjamin Dorfmann, collector of prints of the late seventeenth century, doctor and player on the viola, lying, no kneeling, no squatting in the punishment cell at Buchenwald, six feet by four and one half, the concrete cracked with ice, watching the pus break from his torn nails and whispering the catalogue numbers of the Hobbemas in the Albertina, so far as he could remember them in the raw pain of his shaven skull, until the guard took a whip, Ann Casanova, 21 rue du Chapon, Liège, called to the door, asking the two men to wait outside so that her mother would not know and the old woman falling on to the bonnet of the starting car, from the fourth floor window, her dentures scattered in the road, Hannah, the silken-haired bitch dying of hunger in the locked apartment after the Küllmans had been taken, sinking her teeth into the master's houseshoes, custom-made to the measure of his handsome foot by Samuel Rossbach, Hagadio, who in the shoe-factory at Treblinka was caught splitting leather, sabotage, and made to crawl alive into the quicklime while at the edge Reuben Cohen, aged eleven, had to proclaim 'so shall all saboteurs and subverters of the united front', Hagadio, Hagadio, until the neighbours, Ebert and Ilse Schmidt, today Ebert Schmidt City Engineer, broke down the door, found the dog almost dead, dropped it in the garbage pit and rifled Küllman's closets, his wife's dressing-table, the children's attic with its rocking horse, jack-in-the-box and chemistry set, while on the railway siding near Dornbach, Hagadio, the child, thrown from the train by its parents, with money sewn to its jacket and a note begging for water and help was found by two men coming home from seeding and laid on the tracks, a hundred yards from the north switch, gagged, feet tied, till the next train, which it heard a long way off in the still of the summer evening, the two men watching and eating and then voiding their bowels, Hagadio, the Küllmans knowing that the smell of gas was the smell of gas but thinking the child safe, which, as the thundering air blew nearer spoke into its gag, twice, the name of the silken-haired bitch Hannah, and then could not close its eyes against the rushing shadow; at Maidanek ten thousand a day, I am not mad, Ajalon calling, can you hear me, unimaginable because innumerable, in one corner of Treblinka seven hundred thousand bodies, I will count them now, Aaron, Aaronowitch, Aaronson, Abilech, Abraham, I will count seven hundred thousand names and you must listen, and watch Asher, I do not know him as well as I do you, Simeon, and Eli Barach and the boy, I will say Kaddish to the end of time and when time ceases shall not have reached the millionth name, at Belzec three hundred thousand, Friedberg, Friedman, Friedmann, Friedstein, the names gone in fire and gas, ash in the wind at Chelmno, the long black wind at Chelmno, Israel Meyer, Ida Meyer, the four children in the pit at Sobivor, four hundred and eleven thousand three hundred and eighty one in section three at Belsen, the one being Salomon Rheinfeld who left on his desk in Mainz the uncorrected proofs of the grammar of Hittite which Egon Schleicher, his assistant newly promoted Ordinarius, claimed for his own but cannot complete, the one being Belin the tanner whose face they sprinkled with acid from the vat and who was dragged through the streets of Kershon behind a dung-cart but sang, the one being Georges Walter who when they called him from supper in the rue Marot, from the blanquette de veau finely seasoned, could not understand and spoke to his family of an administrative error and refused to pack more than one shirt and asked still why why through his smashed teeth when the shower doors closed and the whisper started in the ceiling, the one being David Pollachek whose fingers they broke in the quarry at Leutach when they heard that he had been first violin and who in the loud burning of each blow could think only of the elder-bush in his yard at Slanič, each leaf of which he had tried to touch once more on the last evening in his house after the summons came, the one not being Nathaniel Steiner who was taken to America in time but goes maimed nevertheless for not having been at the roll call, the one being all because unnumbered hence unrememberable, because buried alive at Grodne, because hung by the feet at Bialistok like Nathansohn, nine hours fourteen minutes under the whip (timed by *Wachtmeister* Ottmar Prantl now hotelier in Steyerbrück), the blood, Prantl, reporting, splashing out of his hair and mouth like new wine; two million at, unspeakable because beyond imagining, two million suffocated at, outside Cracow of the gracious towers, the sign-post on the airport road pointing to it still, Oszwiecin in sight of the low hills, because we can imagine the cry of one, the hunger of two, the burning of ten, but past a hundred there is no clear imagining; he understood that, take a million and belief will not follow nor the mind contain, and if each and every one of us, Ajalon calling, were to rise before morning and speak out ten names that day, ten from the ninety-six thousand graven on the wall in Prague, ten from the thirty-one thousand in the crypt at Rome, ten from those at Matthausen Drancy Birkenau Buchenwald Theresienstadt or Babi-Yar, ten out of six million, we should never finish the task, not if we spoke the night through, not till the close of time, nor bring back a single breath, not that of Isaac Löwy, Berlin, Isaac Löwy, Danzig (with the birthmark on his left shoulder), Isaac Löwy, Zagreb, Isaac Löwy, Vilna, the baker who cried of yeast when the door closed, Isaac Löwy, Toulouse, almost safe, the visa almost granted, I am not mad but the Kaddish which is like a shadow of lilac after the dust of the day is withered now, empty of remembrance, he has made ash of prayer, AND UNTIL EACH NAME is recalled and spoken again, EACH, the names of the nameless in the orphan's house at Szeged, the name of the mute in the sewer at Katowic, the names of the unborn in the women ripped at Matthausen, the name of the girl with the yellow star seen hammering on the door of the shelter at Hamburg and of whom there is no record but a brown shadow burnt into the pavement, until each name is remembered and spoken to the LAST SYLLABLE, man will have no peace on earth, do you hear me Simeon, no place, no liberation from hatred, not until every name, for when spoken each after the other, with not a single letter omitted, do you hear me, the syllables will make up the hidden name of GOD.

He did it.

The man next to you now. Whose thirst and sour breath are exactly like yours.

O they helped. Nearly all of them. Who would not give visas and put barbed wire on their borders. Who threw stones through the window and spat. Who when six hundred escaped from Treblinka hunted down and killed all but thirty-nine — Polish farmers, irregulars, partisans, charcoal burners in the forest — saying Jews belong in Treblinka. He could not have done it alone. I know that. Not without the helpers and the indifferent, not without the hooligans who laughed and the soft men who took over the shops and moved into the houses. Not without those who said in Belgravia and Marly, in Stresa and in Shaker Heights that the news was exaggerated, that the Jews were whining again and peddling horrors. Not without D. initialling a memo to B-W. at Printing House Square: *no more atrocity stories. Probably overplayed.* Or Foggy Bottom offering seventy-five visas above the quota when one hundred thousand children could have been saved. Not alone.

But it was he who made real the old dream of murder. Everyman's itch to clear his throat of us. Because we have lasted too long. Because we foisted Christ on them. Because we smell other.

It was he who turned the dream into day. Read what he said to his familiars, what he spoke in his dancing hours. He never alludes to the barracks or the gas, to the lime-pits or the whipping blocks. Never. As if the will to murder and the knowledge were so deep inside him, so much the core of his being that he had no more need to point to them. Our ruin was the air he moved in. We do not stop to count our breaths.

It was he. With his scourge of speech and divining rod. His wrist breaking each time he passed over other men's weakness. With his nose for the bestial and the boredom in men's bones. His words made the venom spill. Over to you, Simeon. Can you hear me?

Do you remember the photograph in the archive in Humboldtstrasse? Munich, August 1914, the crowd listening to the declaration of war. The faces surging around the plinth. Among them, partially obscured by a waving arm, but, unmistakable, his. The eyes upturned, shining. Within twenty-four months nearly every man in the photograph was dead. Had a shell found him out, a bullet, a grenade splinter, one of millions, the night would not have stood still over us. We would have grown old in our houses, there would be children to know our graves.

It was he. The sweating carcass by your side. The man picking his nose as you listen to me or dropping his trousers.

None of the others could have done it. Not the fat bully or the adder.

He took garbage and made it into wolves. Where his words fell lives petty or broken grew tall as hate. He.

Do not listen to him now. Guard him better than eyesight. We must have him alive. Knit the skin to his bones. Carry him if you must. Let him lie in the sun and in dry places. Force his mouth open if he won't eat. Search his teeth for poison and smear ointment on his boils. Tend him more dearly than if he were the last child of Jacob.

Skirt Orosso if you can. The ground is not sure. And keep from men's sight. If it was known that we had him they would snatch him from us. And mock us again.

I shall wait for you in San Cristobal. Send me news of your position. Each day at the agreed hour. I shall leave here in good time. Life is new in me now. I shall wait for you at the edge of the forest. Ajalon calling. Come in Nimrud. Come in. Can you hear me?

Simeon, answer me. Over to you. Over. This is Lieber calling
this is Lieber
this is

➤ *The Defence of A.H.* ➤

[*This is the imaginary defence of Adolf Hitler in front of his captors and the Indian witness, Teku — whose name, transposed into Hebrew, can be read to signify that which 'remains insoluble' till the time of God's judgement. This speech constitutes the closing chapter of* The Portage to San Cristobal of A.H.]

Erster Punkt. Article one. Because you must understand that I did not invent. It was Adolf Hitler who dreamt up the master race. Who conceived of enslaving inferior peoples. Lies. Lies. It was in the doss-house, in the *Männerheim* that I first understood. It was in. God help me, but that was long ago. And the lice. Large as a thumb-nail. 1910, 1911. What does it matter now? It was there that I first understood your secret power. The secret power of your teaching. Of *yours*. A chosen people. Chosen by God for His own. The only race on earth chosen, exalted, made singular among mankind. It was Grill who taught me. Do you know about Grill? No. You know nothing about me.

Jahn Grill. But that wasn't his name. Do you hear me? Called himself Jahn, said he was a defrocked priest. For all I know he may have been. That too. But his real name was Jacob. Jacob Grill, son of a rabbi, from Poland. Or Galicia. What does it matter. One of yours, yours, yours. We lived close. One soap-sliver between us. It was Grill who taught me, who showed me the words. The chosen people. God's own and elect amid the unclean, amid the welter of nations. Who shall be chastised for impurity, for taking a heathen to wife, who shall have bondsmen and bondswomen from among the *goyim*, but stay apart. My promise was only a thousand years. 'To eternity' said Grill; lo, it is written here. In letters of white fire. The covenant of election, the setting apart of the race, *das heilige Volk*, like unto no other. Under the iron law. Circumcision and the sign on your forehead. One law, one race, one destiny unto the end of the end of time. 'And Joshua burnt Ai, and made it an heap for ever, even a desolation unto this day.' 'And Joshua made them that day hewers of wood and drawers of water for the congregation.' All of them. Men, women, children. To serve Israel in bondage. But more often there was no one to enslave. 'And they utterly destroyed all that was in the city, both man and woman, young and old, and ox, and sheep, and ass, with the edge of the sword.' Your holy books. The smell of blood. Jacob Grill, friend Grill, and Neumann, for whom I painted postcards, they smelt of shit. But they taught me. That a people must be chosen to fulfil its destiny, that there can be no other thus made glorious. That a true nation is a mystery, a single body willed by God, by history, by the unmingled burning of its blood. It does not matter what you call the roots of the dream. A mystery of will, of chosenness. To conquer its promised land, to cut down or lay in bondage all who stand in its path, to proclaim itself eternal. 'Let the trumpet blow in Zion. Let the Cherubim of the Lord bring fire and plague unto our enemies.' You could hear the lice crack between Grill's fingers. God how his breath stank. But he read from the book. Your book. Of which every letter is sacred, and every mite of every letter. That's so isn't it? Read till lights out, and after, singsong through the nose, because he knew it by heart, from his schooldays, and had heard his father. The rabbi. 'They utterly destroyed all that was in the city.' In Samaria. Because the Samaritans read a different scripture. Because they had built a sanctuary of their own. Of terebinth. Six cubits to the left. They had made it seven or five or God knows. Put to the sword. The first time. Every man, woman, child, she-ox, the dogs too. No. No dogs. They are of the unclean things that hop or crawl on the earth, like the Philistine, the unclean of Moab, the lepers of Sidon. To slaughter a city because of an

idea, because of a vexation over words. Oh that was a high invention, a device
to alter the human soul. Your invention. One Israel, one *Volk*, one leader.
Moses, Joshua, the anointed king who has slain his thousands, no his ten-
thousands, and dances before the ark. It was in Compiègne, wasn't it? They
say I danced there. Only a small dance.

The pride of it, the brute cunning. Whatever you are, wherever, be it
ulcerous as Job, or Neumann scratching his stinking crotch. You should have
seen the two of us peddling those postcards, like starved dogs. But what does
it matter if you're one of the chosen people? One of God's familiars, above
all other men, set apart for His rages and His love. In a covenant, a singling
out, a consecration never to be lost. Grill told me that. Jahn Jacob Grillschmuhl
Grill or whatever his greasy name was, reeking of piss when he crawled up
the stairs. Even he. The apostate. The outcast from Zion. Was still of the
chosen, a private vexation to the Almighty. 'Listen,' he said, 'listen Adi,' no
man else ever called me that, 'you think you see me as I am, Grill the loser,
the doss-house bum. But you're blind. All you *goyim* are blind. For all you
know, Adi, I am one of the seventy-two chosen, chosen even above the
chosen. One of the secret just ones on whom the earth rests. And while you
snore tonight or swallow your spit, listen to me Adi, here in this barrack, right
here, my blind friend, the Messiah may come to me and know me for his own.'
And he would roll his eyes and give a little laugh, a yellow Jew-laugh. It went
through me like a knife. But I learnt.

From you. Everything. To set a race apart. To keep it from defilement. To
hold before it a promised land. To scour that land of its inhabitants or place
them in servitude. Your beliefs. Your arrogance. In Nuremberg, the search-
lights. That clever beaver Speer. Straight into the night. Do you remember
them? The pillar of fire. That shall lead you to Canaan. And woe unto the
Amorites, the Jebusites, the Kenites, the half-men outside God's pact. My
'Superman'? Second-hand stuff. Rosenberg's philosophic garbage. They
whispered to me that *he* too. The name. My racism was a parody of yours,
a hungry imitation. What is a thousand-year *Reich* compared to the eternity
of Zion? Perhaps I was the false Messiah sent before. Judge me and you must
judge yourselves. *Übermenschen*, chosen ones!

– What my client means, began Asher.

Punkt II. There had to be a solution, a *final* solution. For what is the Jew
if he is not a long cancer of unrest? Gentlemen, I beg your attention, I demand
it. Was there ever a crueller invention, a contrivance more calculated to
harrow human existence, than that of an omnipotent, all-seeing, yet invisible,

impalpable, inconceivable God? Gentlemen, I pray you, consider the case, consider it closely. The pagan earth was crowded with small deities, malicious or consoling, winged or pot-bellied, in leaf and branch, in rock and river. Giving companionship to man, pinching his bottom or caressing him, but of his measure. Delighting in honey-cakes and roast meat. Gods after our own image and necessities. And even the great deities, the Olympians, would come down in mortal visitation, to do war and lechery. Mightier than we, I grant you, but tangible and taking on the skin of things. The Jew emptied the world by setting his God apart, immeasurably apart from man's senses. No image. No concrete embodiment. No imagining even. A blank emptier than the desert. Yet with a terrible nearness. Spying on our every misdeed, searching out the heart of our heart for motive. A God of vengeance unto the thirtieth generation (those are the Jews' words, not mine). A God of contracts and petty bargains, of indentures and bribes. 'And the Lord gave Job twice as much as he had before.' A thousand she-asses where the crazed, boiled old man had had only five hundred to start with. It makes one vomit, doesn't it? *Twice* as much. Gentlemen, do you grasp the sliminess of it, the moral trickery? Cast your guiltless servant into hell, thunder at him out of the whirlwind, draw leviathan by the nose, and then? Double his income, declare a dividend, slip him a lordly tip. Why did Job not spit at that cattle-dealer of a God? Yet the holy of holies was an empty room, a silence in a silence. And the Jew mocks those who have pictures of their god. *His* God is purer than any other. The very thought of Him exceeds the powers of the human mind. We are as blown dust to His immensity. But because we are His creatures, we must be better than ourselves, love our neighbour, be continent, give of what we have to the beggar. Because His inconceivable, unimaginable presence envelops us, we must obey every jot of the law. We must bottle up our rages and desires, chastise the flesh and walk bent in the rain. You call me a tyrant, an enslaver. What tyranny, what enslavement has been more oppressive, has branded the skin and soul of man more deeply, than the sick fantasies of the Jew? You are not Godkillers, but *Godmakers*. And that is infinitely worse. The Jew invented conscience and left man a guilty serf.

But that was only the first piece of blackmail. There was worse to come. The white-faced Nazarene. Gentlemen, I find it difficult to contain myself. But the facts must speak for themselves. What did that epileptic rabbi ask of man? That he renounce the world, that he leave mother and father behind, that he offer the other cheek when slapped, that he render good for evil, that he love his neighbour as himself, no, far better, for self-love is an evil thing to be overcome. Oh grand castration! Note the cunning of it. Demand of human beings more than they can give, demand that they give up their stained, selfish humanity in the name of a higher ideal, and you will make of them cripples, hypocrites, mendicants for salvation. The Nazarene said that his kingdom, his purities were not of this world. Lies, honeyed lies. It was here on earth that he founded his slave-church. It was men and women, creatures of flesh, he abandoned to the blackmail of hell, of eternal punishment. What were our camps compared to *that*? Ask of man more than he is, hold before his tired eyes an image of altruism, of compassion, of self-denial which only the saint or the madman can touch, and you stretch him on the rack. Till his soul bursts. What can be crueller than the Jew's addiction to the ideal?

First the invisible but all-seeing, the unattainable but all-demanding God of Sinai. Second the terrible sweetness of Christ. Had the Jew not done enough to sicken man? No, gentlemen, there is a third act to our story.

'Sacrifice yourself for the good of your fellow man. Relinquish your possessions so that there may be equality for all. Hammer yourself hard as steel, strangle emotion, loyalty, mercy, gratitude. Denounce parent or lover. So that justice may be achieved on earth. So that history be fulfilled and society be purged of all imperfection.' Do you recognize the sermon, gentlemen? The litany of hatred? Rabbi Marx on the day of atonement. Was there ever a greater promise? 'The classless society, to each according to his needs, brotherhood for all mankind, the earth made a garden again, a rational Eden.' In the name of which promise tyranny, torture, war, extermination were a necessity, an historical necessity! It is no accident that Marx and his minions were Jews, that the congregations of Bolshevism — Trotsky, Rosa Luxembourg, Kamenev, the whole fanatic, murderous pack — were of Israel. Look at them: prophets, martyrs, smashers of images, word-spinners drunk with the terror of the absolute. It was only a step, gentlemen, a small, inevitable step, from Sinai to Nazareth, from Nazareth to the covenant of Marxism. The Jew had grown impatient, his dreams had gone rancid. Let the kingdom of justice come here and now, next Monday morning. Let us have a secular messiah instead. But with a long beard and his bowels full of vengeance.

Three times the Jew has pressed on us the blackmail of transcendence. Three times he has infected our blood and brains with the bacillus of perfection. Go to your rest and the voice of the Jew cries out in the night. 'Wake up! God's eye is upon you. Has He not made you in His image? Lose your life so that you may gain it. Sacrifice yourself to the truth, to justice, to the good of mankind.' That cry has been in our ears too long, gentlemen, far too long. Men had grown sick of it, sick to death. When I turned on the Jew, no one came to his rescue. No one. France, England, Russia, even Jew-ridden America did nothing. They were glad that the exterminator had come. Oh they did not say so openly, I allow you that. But secretly they rejoiced. We had to find, to burn out the virus of utopia before the whole of our western civilization sickened. To return to man as he is, selfish, greedy, short-sighted, but warm and housed, so marvellously housed, in his own stench. 'We were chosen to be the conscience of man' said the Jew. And I answered him, yes, I, gentlemen, who now stand before you: 'You are not man's conscience, Jew. You are only his bad conscience. And we shall vomit you so we may live and have peace.' A final solution. How could there be any other?

– The question the defendant is raising, rasped Asher

Do not interrupt. I will not tolerate interruption. I am an old man. My voice tires. Gentlemen, I appeal to your sense of justice, your notorious sense of justice. Hear me out. Consider my third point. Which is that you have exaggerated. Grossly. Hysterically. That you have made of me some kind of mad devil, the quintessence of evil, hell embodied. When I was, in truth, only a man of my time. Oh inspired, I will grant you, with a certain – how shall I put it? – nose for the supreme political possibility. A master of human moods, perhaps, but a man of my time.

Average, if you will. Had it been otherwise, had I been the singular demon of your rhetorical fantasies, how then could millions of ordinary men and women have found in me the mirror, the plain mirror of their needs and appetites? And it was, I will allow you that, an ugly time. But I did not create its ugliness, and I was not the worst. Far from it. How many wretched little men of the forests did your Belgian friends murder outright or leave to starvation and syphilis when they raped the Congo? Answer me that, gentlemen. Or must I remind you? Some *twenty* million. That picnic was under way when I was new-born. What were Rotterdam or Coventry compared to Dresden and Hiroshima? I do not come out worst in that black game of numbers. Did I invent the camps? Ask of the Boers. But let us be serious. Who was it that broke the *Reich*? To whom did you hand over millions, tens of millions of men and women from Prague to the Baltic? Set them like a bowl of milk before an insatiable cat? I was a man of a murderous time, but a small man compared to *him*. You think of me as a satanic liar. Very well. Do not take my word for it. Choose what sainted, unimpeachable witness you will.

The holy writer, the great bearded one who came out of Russia and preached to the world. It is long ago now. My memory aches. The man of the archipelago. Yes, that word sticks in the mind. What did he say? That Stalin had slaughtered *thirty* million. That he had perfected genocide when I was still a nameless scribbler in Munich. My boys used their fists and their whips. I won't deny it. The times stank of hunger and blood. But when a man spat out the truth they would stop their fun. Stalin's tortures worked for the pleasure of the thing. To make men befoul themselves, to obtain confessions which are lies, insanities, obscene jokes. The truth only made them more bestial. It is not I who assert these things: it is your own survivors, your historians, the sage of the Gulag. Who, then, was the greater destroyer, whose blood-lust was the more implacable? Stalin's or mine? Ribbentrop told me: of the man's contempt for *us*. Whom he found amateurish, corrupt with mercy. Our terrors were a village carnival compared to his. Our camps covered absurd acres; he had strung wire and death-pits around a continent. Who survived among those who had fought with him, brought him to power, executed his will? Not one. He smashed their bones to the last splinter. When my fall came my good companions were alive, fat, scuttling for safety or recompense, cavorting towards you with their contritions and their memoires. How many Jews did Stalin kill, your saviour, your ally Stalin? Answer me that. Had he not died when he did, there would not have been one of you left alive between Berlin and Vladivostok. Yet Stalin died in bed, and the world stood hushed before the tiger's rest. Whereas you hunt me down like a rabid dog, put me on trial (by what right, by what mandate?), drag me through the swamps, tie me up at night. Who am a very old man and uncertain of recollection. Small game, gentlemen, hardly worthy of your skills. In a world that has tortured political prisoners and poured napalm on naked villagers, that has stripped the earth of plant and animal. That has done these things and continues to do them quite without my help and long after I, 'the one out of hell' – oh ludicrous, histrionic phrase – was thought to have been extinct.

Asher's breath came loud and empty.

Do not trouble yourself, *Herr Advokat*. I have only one more point to make. The last. That strange book *Der Judenstaat*. I read it carefully. Straight out of Bismarck. The language, the ideas, the tone of it. A clever book, I agree. Shaping Zionism in the image of the new German nation. But did Herzl create Israel or did I? Examine the question fairly. Would Palestine have become Israel, would the Jews have come to that barren patch of the Levant, would the United States *and* the Soviet Union, *Stalin's* Soviet Union, have given you recognition and guaranteed your survival, had it not been for the Holocaust? It was the Holocaust that gave you the courage of injustice, that made you drive the Arab out of his home, out of his field, because he was lice-eaten and without resource, because he was in your divinely-ordered way. That made you endure knowing that those whom you had driven out were rotting in refugee camps, not ten miles away, buried alive in despair and lunatic dreams of vengeance. Perhaps I *am* the Messiah, the true Messiah, the new Sabbatai whose infamous deeds were allowed by God in order to bring His people home. 'The Holocaust was the necessary mystery before Israel could come into its strength.' It is not I who have said it: but your own visionaries, your unravellers of God's meaning when it is Friday night in Jerusalem. Should you not honour me who have made you into men of war, who have made of the long, vacuous day-dream of Zion a reality? Should you not be a comfort to my old age?

Gentlemen of the tribunal: I took my doctrines from you. I fought the blackmail of the ideal with which you have hounded mankind. My crimes were matched and surpassed by those of others. The *Reich* begat Israel. These are my last words. The last words of a dying man against the last words of those who suffered; and in the midst of incertitude must matters be left till the great revelation of all secrets.

Teku had not understood the words, only their meaning. Whose brazen pulse carried all before it. He had leapt up to cry out 'Proven'. To cry it to the earth twice and twice to the north as is the custom. But the air seemed to be exploding around him. Loud drum-beats hammering closer and closer, driving his voice back into his throat. He looked up, his ears pounding.

The first helicopter was hovering above the clearing. The second

✦ *Language and Culture* ✦

✦ The Retreat from the Word ✦

The Apostle tells us that in the beginning was the Word. He gives us no assurance as to the end.

It is appropriate that he should have used the Greek language to express the Hellenistic conception of the *Logos*, for it is to the fact of its Greco-Judaic inheritance that western civilization owes its essentially verbal character. We take this character for granted. It is the root and bark of our experience and we cannot readily transpose our imaginings outside it. We live inside the act of discourse. But we should not assume that a verbal matrix is the only one in which the articulations and conduct of the mind are conceivable. There are modes of intellectual and sensuous reality founded not on language, but on other communicative energies such as the icon or the musical note. And there are actions of the spirit rooted in silence. It is difficult to *speak* of these, for how should speech justly convey the shape and vitality of silence? But I can cite examples of what I mean.

In certain Oriental metaphysics, in Buddhism and Taoism, the soul is envisioned as ascending from the gross impediments of the material, through domains of insight that can be rendered by lofty and precise language, towards ever deepening silence. The highest, purest reach of the contemplative act is that which has learned to leave language behind it. The ineffable lies beyond the frontiers of the word. It is only by breaking through the walls of language that visionary observance can enter the world of total and immediate understanding. Where such understanding is attained, the truth need no longer suffer the impurities and fragmentation that speech necessarily entails. It need not conform to the naive logic and linear conception of time implicit in syntax. In ultimate truth, past, present and future are simultaneously comprised. It is the temporal structure of language that keeps them artificially distinct. That is the crucial point.

The holy man, the initiate, withdraws not only from the temptations of worldly action; he withdraws from speech. His retreat into the mountain cave or monastic cell is the outward gesture of his silence. Even those who are only novices on this arduous road are taught to distrust the veil of language, to break through it to the more real. The Zen *koan* — you know the sound of two hands clapping, what is the sound of one? — is a beginner's exercise in the retreat from the word.

The western tradition also knows transcendences of language towards
silence. The Trappist ideal goes back to abandonments of speech as ancient
as those of the Stylites and Desert Fathers. St John of the Cross expresses
the austere exaltation of the contemplative soul as it breaks loose from the
moorings of common verbal understanding:

> Entréme donde no supe,
> Y quedéme no sabiendo,
> Toda sciencia trascendiendo.

But to the western point of view, this order of experience inevitably carries
a flavour of mysticism. And whatever our lip service (itself a revealing word)
to the sanctity of the mystic vocation, the commanding western attitude is
that of Cardinal Newman's quip, that mysticism begins in mist and ends in
schism. Very few western poets – perhaps only Dante – have persuaded the
imagination of the authority of transrational experience. We accept, at the
lambent close of the *Paradiso*, the blindness of eye and understanding before
the totality of vision. But Pascal is nearer the mainstream of classic western
feeling when he says that the silence of cosmic space strikes terror. To the
Taoist that selfsame silence conveys tranquillity and the intimation of God.

The primacy of the word, of that which can be spoken and communicated
in discourse, was characteristic of the Greek and Judaic genius and carried over
into Christianity. The classic and the Christian sense of the world strive to
order reality within the governance of language. Literature, philosophy,
theology, law, the arts of history, are endeavours to enclose within the
bounds of rational discourse the sum of human experience, its recorded past,
its present condition and future expectations. The code of Justinian, the
Summa of Aquinas, the world chronicles and compendia of medieval
literature, the *Divina Commedia*, are attempts at total containment. They bear
solemn witness to the belief that all truth and realness – with the exception
of a small, queer margin at the very top – can be housed inside the walls of
language.

This belief is no longer universal. Confidence in it declines after the age
of Milton. The cause and history of that decline throw sharp light on the
circumstances of modern literature and language.

It is during the seventeenth century that significant areas of truth, reality
and action recede from the sphere of verbal statement. It is, on the whole,
true to say that until the seventeenth century the predominant bias and

content of the natural sciences were descriptive. Mathematics has its long, brilliant history of symbolic notation; but even mathematics was a shorthand for verbal propositions applicable to, and meaningful within, the framework of linguistic description. Mathematical thought, with certain notable exceptions, was anchored to the material conditions of experience. These, in turn, were ordered and ruled by language. During the seventeenth century, this ceased to be the general case, and there began a revolution that has transformed for ever man's relationship to reality and radically altered the shapes of thought.

With the formulation of analytical geometry and the theory of algebraic functions, with the development by Newton and Leibniz of calculus, mathematics ceases to be a dependent notation, an instrument of the empirical. It becomes a fantastically rich, complex and dynamic language. *And the history of that language is one of progressive untranslatability.* It is still possible to translate back into verbal equivalents, or at least close approximations, the proceedings of classical geometry and classical functional analysis. Once mathematics turns modern, however, and begins exhibiting its enormous powers of autonomous conception, such translation becomes less and less possible. The great architectures of form and meaning conceived by Gauss, Cauchy, Abel, Cantor and Weierstrass recede from language at an ever-accelerated pace. Or rather, they require and develop languages of their own as articulate and elaborate as those of verbal discourse. And between these languages and that of common usage, between the mathematical symbol and the word, the bridges grow more and more tenuous, until at last they are down.

Between verbal languages, however remote in setting and habits of syntax, there is always the possibility of equivalence, even if actual translation can only attain rough and approximate results. The Chinese ideogram can be transposed into English by paraphrase or lexical definition. But there are no dictionaries to relate the vocabulary and grammar of higher mathematics to those of verbal speech. One cannot 'translate' the conventions and notations governing the operations of Lie groups or the properties of n-dimensional manifolds into any words or grammar outside mathematics. One cannot even paraphrase. A paraphrase of a good poem may turn out to be bad prose; but there is a discernible continuity between shadow and substance. The paraphrase of a complex theorem in topology can only be a grossly inadequate approximation or a transposal into another branch or 'dialect' of the particular mathematical language. Many of the spaces, relations and events that advanced mathematics deals with have no necessary correlation with sense-data; they are 'realities' occurring within closed axiomatic systems. You can speak about them meaningfully and normatively only in the speech of mathematics. *And that speech, beyond a fairly rudimentary plane, is not and cannot be verbal.* (I have watched topologists, knowing no syllable of each other's language, working effectively together at a blackboard in the silent speech common to their craft.)

This is a fact of tremendous implication. It has divided the experience and perception of reality into separate domains. The most decisive change in the tenor of western intellectual life since the seventeenth century is the submission of successively larger areas of knowledge to the modes and proceedings of mathematics. As has often been noted, a branch of inquiry passes from pre-science into science when it can be mathematically organized. It is the development within itself of formulaic and statistical means that gives to a science its dynamic possibilities. The tools of mathematical analysis transformed chemistry and physics from alchemy to the predictive sciences that they now are. By virtue of mathematics, the stars move out of mythology into the astronomer's table. And as mathematics settles into the marrow of a science, the concepts of that science, its habits of invention and understanding, become steadily less reducible to those of common language.

It is arrogant, if not irresponsible, to invoke such basic notions in our present model of the universe as quanta, the indeterminacy principle, the relativity constant or the lack of parity in so-called weak interactions of atomic particles, if one cannot do so in the language appropriate to them — that is to say, in mathematical terms. Without it, such words are phantasms to deck out the pretence of philosophers or journalists. Because physics has had to borrow them from the vulgate, some of these words seem to retain a generalized meaning; they give a semblance of metaphor. But this is an illusion. When a critic seeks to apply the indeterminacy principle to his discussion of action painting or of the use of improvisation in certain contemporary music, he is not relating two spheres of experience; he is merely talking nonsense.[1]

1. I am no longer certain that this is so. Obviously most of the analogies drawn between modern art and developments in the exact sciences are 'unrealized metaphors', fictions of analogy which do not have in them the authority of real experience. Nevertheless, even the illicit metaphor, the term borrowed though misunderstood, may be an essential part of a process of reunification. It is very probable that the sciences will furnish an increasing part of our mythologies and imaginative reference. The vulgarizations, false analogies, even errors of the

We must guard against such deception. Chemistry uses numerous terms derived from its earlier descriptive stage; but the formulas of modern molecular chemistry are, in fact, a shorthand whose vernacular is not that of verbal speech but that of mathematics. A chemical formula does not abbreviate a linguistic statement; it codifies a numerical operation. Biology is in a fascinating intermediary position. Classically, it was a descriptive science, relying on a precise and suggestive use of language. The force of Darwin's biological and zoological proposals was founded, in part, on the persuasion of his style. In post-Darwinian biology, mathematics has played an ever more commanding role. The change of stress is clearly marked in D'Arcy Wentworth Thompson's great work, *Of Growth and Form*, a book in which poet and mathematician are equally engaged. Today, large areas of biology, such as genetics, are mainly mathematical. Where biology turns towards chemistry, and biochemistry is at present the high ground, it tends to relinquish the descriptive for the enumerative. It abandons the word for the figure.

It is this extension of mathematics over great areas of thought and action that broke western consciousness into what C. P. Snow calls 'the two cultures'. Until the time of Goethe and Humboldt, it was possible for a man of exceptional ability and retentiveness to feel at home in both the humanistic and the mathematical cultures. Leibniz had still been able to make notable contributions to both. This is no longer a real possibility. The chasm between the languages of words and of mathematics grows constantly wider. Standing on either rim are men who, in respect of each other, are illiterate. There is as great a sum of illiteracy in not knowing the basic concepts of calculus or spherical geometry as there is in not knowing grammar. Or to cite Snow's famous point: a man who has read no Shakespeare is uncultured; *but not more so* than one who is ignorant of the second law of thermodynamics. Each is blind to comparable worlds.

Except in moments of bleak clarity, we do not yet act as if this were true. We continue to assume that humanistic authority, the sphere of the word, is predominant. The notion of essential literacy is still rooted in classic values, in a sense of discourse, rhetoric and poetics. But this is ignorance or sloth of

---

poet and critic may be a necessary part of the 'translation' of science into the common literacy of feeling. And the bare fact that aleatory principles in the arts coincide historically with 'indeterminacy' *may* have a genuine significance. It is the nature of that significance which needs to be felt and shown. [1968]

imagination. Calculus, the laws of Carnot, Maxwell's conception of the electromagnetic field, not only comprise areas of reality and action as great as those comprised by classic literacy; they probably give an image of the perceptible world truer to fact than can be derived from any structure of verbal assertion. All evidence suggests that the shapes of reality are mathematical, that integral and differential calculus are the alphabet of just perception. The humanist today is in the position of those tenacious, aggrieved spirits who continued to envision the earth as a flat table after it had been circumnavigated, or who persisted in believing in occult propulsive energies after Newton had formulated the laws of motion and inertia.

Those of us who are compelled by our ignorance of exact science to imagine the universe through a veil of non-mathematical language inhabit an animate fiction. The actual facts of the case – the space-time continuum of relativity, the atomic structure of all matter, the wave-particle state of energy – are no longer accessible through the word. It is no paradox to assert that in cardinal respects reality now begins *outside* verbal language. Mathematicians know this. 'By its geometric and later by its purely symbolic construction,' says Andreas Speiser, 'mathematics shook off the fetters of language ... and mathematics today is more efficient in its sphere of the intellectual world, than the modern languages in their deplorable state or even music are on their respective fronts.'

Few humanists are aware of the scope and nature of this great change (Sartre is a notable exception and has, time and again, drawn attention to *la crise du langage*). Nevertheless, many of the traditional humanistic disciplines have shown a deep *malaise*, a nervous, complex recognition of the exactions and triumphs of mathematics and the natural sciences. There has taken place in history, economics and what are called, significantly, the 'social sciences', what one might term a fallacy of imitative form. In each of these fields, the mode of discourse still relies almost completely on word-language. But historians, economists and social scientists have tried to graft on to the verbal matrix some of the proceedings of mathematics or total rigour. They have grown defensive about the essentially provisional and aesthetic character of their own pursuits.

Observe how the cult of the positive, the exact and the predictive has invaded history. The decisive turn occurs in the nineteenth century, in the work of Ranke, Comte and Taine. Historians began regarding their material as elements in the crucible of controlled experiment. From impartial scrutiny of the past (such impartiality being, in fact, a naive illusion) should emerge those statistical patterns, those periodicities of national and economic force, which allow the historian to formulate 'laws of history'. This very notion of historical 'law', and the implication of necessity and predictability, which are crucial to Taine, Marx and Spengler, are a gross borrowing from the sphere of the exact and mathematical sciences.

The ambitions of scientific rigour and prophecy have seduced much historical writing from its veritable nature, which is art. Much of what passes for history at present is scarcely literate. The disciples of Namier (not he himself) consign Gibbon, Macaulay or Michelet to the limbo of *belles-lettres*. The illusion of science and the fashions of the academic tend to transform the young historian into a ferret gnawing at the minute fact or figure. He dwells in footnotes and writes monographs in as illiterate a style as possible to demonstrate the scientific bias of his craft. One of the few contemporary historians prepared to defend openly the poetic nature of all historical imagining is C. V. Wedgwood. She fully concedes that all style brings with it the possibility of distortion: 'There is no literary style which may not at some point take away something from the ascertainable outline of truth, which it is the task of scholarship to excavate and re-establish.' But where such excavation abandons style altogether, or harbours the illusion of impartial exactitude, it will light only on dust.

Or consider economics: its classic masters, Adam Smith, Ricardo, Malthus, Marshall, were masters of prose style. They relied upon language to explain and persuade. In the late nineteenth century began the development of mathematical economics. Keynes was perhaps the last to span both the humane and the mathematical branches of his science. Discussing the contributions of Ramsey to economic thought, Keynes pointed out that a number of them, though of signal importance, involved mathematics too sophisticated for the layman or the classical economist. Today the gap has widened tremendously; econometrics is gaining on economics. The cardinal terms – theory of values, cycles, productive capacity, liquidity, inflation, input-output – are in a state of transition. They are moving from the linguistic to the mathematical, from rhetoric to equation. The alphabet of modern economics is no longer primarily the word, but rather the chart, the graph, and the number. The most powerful economic thought of the present is using the analytic and predictive instruments forged by the functional analysts of nineteenth-century mathematics.

The temptations of exact science are most flagrant in sociology. Much of present sociology is illiterate, or more precisely, anti-literate. It is conceived in a jargon of vehement obscurity. Wherever possible, the word and the grammar of literate meaning are replaced by the statistical table, the curve or the graph. Where it must remain verbal, sociology borrows what it can from the vocabulary of the exact sciences. One could make a fascinating list of these borrowings. Consider only the more prominent: norms, group, scatter, integration, function, co-ordinates. Each has a specific mathematical or technical content. Emptied of this content and forced into an alien setting, these expressions become blurred and pretentious. Like mutinous captives, they do ill service to their new masters. Yet in using the gibberish of 'culture co-ordinates' and 'peer-group integrations', the sociologist pays fervent tribute to the mirage that has haunted all rational inquiry since the seventeenth century – the mirage of mathematical exactitude and predictability.

Nowhere, however, is the retreat from the word more pronounced and startling than in philosophy. Classic and medieval philosophy were wholly committed to the dignity and resources of language, to the belief that words, handled with requisite precision and subtlety, could bring the mind into accord with reality. Plato, Aristotle, Duns Scotus and Aquinas are masterbuilders of words, constructing around reality great edifices of statement, definition and discrimination. They operate with modes of argument that differ from those of the poet; but they share with the poet the assumption that words gather and engender responsible apprehensions of the truth. Again, the turning point occurs in the seventeenth century, with Descartes's implicit identification of truth and mathematical proof, and, above all, with Spinoza.

The *Ethics* represents the formidable impact upon a philosophic temper of the new mathematics. In mathematics, Spinoza perceived that rigour of statement, that consistency and majestic certitude of result, which are the hope of all metaphysics. Not even the severest of scholastic arguments, with its array of syllogisms and lemmas, could rival that progress from axiom to demonstration and new concept which is to be found in Euclidean and analytic geometry. With superb naïveté, therefore, Spinoza sought to make of the language of philosophy a verbal mathematics. Hence the organization of the *Ethics* into axioms, definitions, demonstrations and corollaries. Hence the proud *q.e.d.* at the close of each set of propositions. It is a queer, entrancing book, as pellucid as the lenses Spinoza ground for a living. But it often yields only a further image of itself. It is an elaborate tautology. Unlike numbers, words do not contain within themselves functional operations. Added or divided, they give only other words or approximations of their own meaning.

Spinoza's demonstrations merely affirm; they cannot give proof. Yet the attempt was prophetic. It confronts all subsequent metaphysics with a dilemma; after Spinoza, philosophers know that they are using language to clarify language, like cutters using diamonds to shape other diamonds. Language is seen no longer as a road to demonstrable truth, but as a spiral or gallery of mirrors, bringing the intellect back to its point of departure. With Spinoza, metaphysics loses its innocence.

Symbolic logic, a glimpse of which may already be found in Leibniz, is an attempt to break out of the circle. At first, in the work of Boole, Frege and Hilbert, it was intended as a specialized tool designed to test the internal consistency of mathematical reasoning. But it soon assumed a much larger relevance. The symbolic logician constructs a radically simplified but entirely rigorous and self-consistent model. He invents or postulates a syntax freed from the ambiguities and imprecisions which history and usage have brought into common language. He borrows the conventions of mathematical inference and deduction and applies them to other modes of thought in order to determine whether such modes have validity. In short, he seeks to objectify crucial areas of philosophic inquiry by stepping outside language. The nonverbal instrument of mathematical symbolism is now being applied to morals and even to aesthetics. The old notion of a calculus of moral impulse, of an algebra of pleasure and pain, has had its revival. A number of contemporary logicians have sought to devise a calculable theoretic basis for the act of aesthetic choice. There is scarcely a branch of modern philosophy in which we do not find the numerals, italicized letters, radicals and arrows with which the symbolic logician seeks to replace the shop-worn and rebellious host of words.

The greatest of modern philosophers was also the one most profoundly intent on escaping from the spiral of language. Wittgenstein's entire work starts out by asking whether there is any verifiable relation between the word and the fact. That which we call fact may well be a veil spun by language to shroud the mind from reality. Wittgenstein compels us to wonder whether reality can be *spoken of*, when speech is merely a kind of infinite regression, words being spoken of other words. Wittgenstein pursued this dilemma with passionate austerity. The famous closing proposition of the *Tractatus* is not a claim for the potentiality of philosophic statement such as Descartes advanced. On the contrary; it is a drastic retreat from the confident authority of traditional metaphysics. It leads to the equally famous conclusion: 'It is clear that Ethics cannot be expressed.' Wittgenstein would include in the class of inexpressibles (what he calls the mystical) most of the traditional areas of philosophic speculation. Language can only deal meaningfully with a special, restricted segment of reality. The rest, and it is presumably the much larger part, is silence.

Later on, Wittgenstein departed from the restrictive position of the *Tractatus*. The *Philosophic Investigations* take a more optimistic view of the inherent capacities of language to describe the world and to articulate certain modes of conduct. But it is an open question whether the *Tractatus* is not the more powerful and consistent statement. It is certainly deeply felt. For the silence, which at every point surrounds the naked discourse, seems, by virtue of Wittgenstein's force of insight, less a wall than a window. With Wittgenstein, as with certain poets, we look out of language not into darkness but light. Anyone who reads the *Tractatus* will be sensible of its odd, mute radiance.

Though I can only touch on the matter briefly, it seems clear to me that the retreat from the authority and range of verbal language plays a tremendous role in the history and character of modern art. In painting and sculpture, realism in the broadest sense – the representation of that which we apprehend as an imitation of existent reality – corresponds to that period in which language is at the centre of intellectual and emotive life. A landscape, a still-life, a portrait, an allegory, a depiction of some event out of history or legend are renditions in colour, volume and texture of realities which can be expressed in words. We can give a linguistic account of the subject of the work of art. The canvas and the statue have a title that relates them to the verbal concept. We say: this is a portrait of a man with a golden helmet; or, this is the Grand Canal at sunrise; or, this is a portrayal of Daphne turning into a laurel. In each case, even before we have seen the work, the words elicit in the mind a specific graphic equivalent. No doubt this equivalent is less vivid or revealing than the painting by Rembrandt or Canaletto, or the statue by Bernini. But there is a substantive relation. The artist and the viewer are talking about the same world, though the artist says things more profound and inclusive.

It is precisely against such verbal equivalence or concordance that modern art has rebelled. It is because so much eighteenth- and nineteenth-century painting seemed merely to be an illustration of verbal concepts – a picture in the book of language – that post-impressionism broke away from the word. Van Gogh declared that the painter paints not what he sees but what he feels. What is seen can be transposed into words; what is felt may occur at some level anterior to language or outside it. It will find expression solely in the specific idiom of colour and spatial organization. Non-objective and abstract art reject the mere possibility of a linguistic equivalent. The canvas or the sculpture refuses to be entitled; it is labelled *Black and White No. 5* or *White Forms* or *Composition 85*. When there is a title, as in many of De Kooning's canvases, the title is often an ironic mystification; it is not meant to mean but to decorate or bewilder. And the work itself has no subject of which one can render a verbal account. The fact that Lassaw calls his twists of welded bronze *Clouds of Magellan* provides no exterior reference; Franz Kline's *Chief* (1950) is merely a whorl of paint. Nothing that can be *said* about it will be pertinent to the habits of linguistic sense. The patches of colour, the skein of wire or the aggregates of cast iron, seek to establish reference only to themselves, only inwards.

Where they succeed, their assertion of immediate sensuous energy provokes in the viewer a kinetic response. There are shapes by Brancusi and Arp that draw us after them into a counterpart of their own motion. De Kooning's *Leaves in Weehawken* by-passes language and seems to play directly on our nerve-ends. But more often, the abstract design conveys only the rudimentary pleasures of decoration. Much of Jackson Pollock is vivid wallpaper. And in the majority of cases, abstract expressionism and non-objective art communicate nothing whatever. The work stands mute or attempts to shout at us in a kind of inhuman gibberish. I wonder whether future artists and critics will not look back with puzzled contempt upon the mass of pretentious trivia that now fills our galleries.

The problem of atonal, concrete, or electronic music is, obviously, a very different one. Music is explicitly related to language only where it sets a text, where it is music of a specific formal occasion, or where it is programme music seeking to articulate in sound a deliberate scene or situation. Music has always had its own syntax, its own vocabulary and symbolic means. Indeed, it is with mathematics the principal language of the mind when the mind is in a condition of non-verbal feeling. Yet, even within music, there has been a distinct movement away from the reaches of the word.

A classical sonata or symphony is not in any way a verbal statement. Except in very simplified instances ('storm-music'), there is no unilateral equivalent between the tonal event and a particular verbal meaning or emotion. *Nevertheless*, there is in classical forms of musical organization a certain grammar or articulation in time which does have analogies with the processes of language. Language cannot translate into itself the binary structure of a sonata, but the statement of successive subjects, the fact of variation on them, and the closing recapitulation do convey an ordering of experience to which language has valid parallels. Modern music shows no such relationships. In order to achieve a kind of total integrity and self-containment, it departs violently from the domain of intelligible 'exterior' meaning. It denies to the listener any recognition of content, or, more accurately, it denies him the possibility of relating the purely auditive impression to any verbalized form of experience. Like the non-objective canvas, the piece of 'new' music will often dispense with a title lest that title offer a false bridge back to the world of pictorial and verbal imaginings. It calls itself *Variation 42* or *Composition*.

In its flight from the neighbourhood of language, moreover, music has been drawn inevitably to the promise of mathematics. Glancing at a recent issue of the *Musical Quarterly*, one finds a discussion of 'Twelve-Tone Invariants':

> The initial pitch class of S is denoted by the couple (O,O), and is taken as the origin of the coordinate system for both order and pitch numbers, both of which range over the integers O–11 inclusive, each integer appearing once and only once as an order number and a pitch number. In the case of order numbers, this represents the fact that twelve and only twelve pitch classes are involved: in the case of pitch numbers, this is the arithmetical analogue of octave equivalence (congruent mod. 12).

Describing his own method of composition, a contemporary composer, by no means among the most radical, observes: 'The point is that the notion of invariancy inherent by definition to the concept of the series, if applied to all parameters, leads to a uniformity of configurations that eliminates the last traces of unpredictability, or surprise.'

The music that is produced by this kind of approach may be of considerable fascination and technical interest. But the vision behind it is clearly related to the great crisis of humane literacy. And only those committed by profession or affectation to the ultra-modern would deny that much of what passes for music at the present time is brutal noise.

◇ 2 ◇

What I have argued so far is this: until the seventeenth century, the sphere of language encompassed nearly the whole of experience and reality; today, it comprises a narrower domain. It no longer articulates, or is relevant to, all major modes of action, thought, and sensibility. Large areas of meaning and praxis now belong to such non-verbal languages as mathematics, symbolic logic, and formulas of chemical or electronic relation. Other areas belong to the sub-languages or anti-languages of non-objective art and *musique concrète*. The world of words has shrunk. One *cannot* talk of transfinite numbers except mathematically; one *should not*, suggests Wittgenstein, talk of ethics or aesthetics within the presently available categories of discourse. And it is, I think, exceedingly difficult to speak meaningfully of a Jackson Pollock painting or a composition by Stockhausen. The circle has narrowed tremendously, for was there anything under heaven, be it science, metaphysics, art, or music, of which a Shakespeare, a Donne, and a Milton could not speak naturally, to which their words did not have natural access?

Does this signify that fewer words are in actual use today? That is a very intricate and, as yet, unresolved question. Not including taxonomic lists (the names of all species of beetles, for example), it is estimated that the English language at present contains some 600,000 words. Elizabethan English is thought to have had only 150,000. But these rough figures are deceptive. Shakespeare's working vocabulary exceeds that of any later author, and the King James Bible, although it requires only 6,000 words, suggests that the conception of literacy prevailing at the time was far more comprehensive than ours. The real point lies not in the number of words potentially available, but in the degree to which the resources of the language are in actual current use. If McKnight's estimate is reliable (*English Words and Their Background*, 1923), 50 per cent of modern colloquial speech in England and America comprises only thirty-four basic words; and to make themselves widely understood, contemporary media of mass communication have had to reduce English to a semi-literate condition. The language of Shakespeare and Milton belongs to a stage of history in which words were in natural control of experienced life. The writer of today tends to use far fewer and simpler words, both because mass culture has watered down the concept of literacy and because the sum of realities of which words can give a necessary and sufficient account has sharply diminished.

This diminution – the fact that the image of the world is receding from the communicative grasp of the word – has had its impact on the quality of language. As western consciousness has become less dependent on the resources of language to order experience and conduct the business of the mind, the words themselves seem to have lost some of their precision and vitality. This is, I know, a controversial notion. It assumes that language has a 'life' of its own in a sense that goes beyond metaphor. It implies that such concepts as tiredness and corruption are relevant to language itself, not only to men's use of it. It is a view held by De Maistre and Orwell, and it gives force to Pound's definition of the poet's job: 'We are governed by words, the laws are graven in words, and literature is the sole means of keeping these words living and accurate.' Most linguists would regard implications of internal, independent vitality in language as suspect. But let me indicate briefly what I mean.

There is in the handling of the English language in the Tudor, Elizabethan and Jacobean periods a sense of discovery, of exuberant acquisition, which has never been wholly recaptured. Marlowe, Bacon, Shakespeare use words as if they were new, as if no previous touch had clouded their shimmer or muted their resonance. Erasmus tells of how he bent down in a muddy lane ecstatically when his eye lit upon a scrap of print, so new was the miracle of the printed page. This is how the sixteenth and seventeenth centuries seem to look upon language itself. The great treasure of it lies before them, suddenly unlocked, and they ransack it with a sense of infinite resource. The instrument now in our hands, on the contrary, is worn by long usage. And the demands of mass culture and mass communication have made it perform tasks of ever-increasing tawdriness.

What save half-truths, gross simplifications or trivia can, in fact, be communicated to that semi-literate mass audience which consumer democracy has summoned into the marketplace? Only in a diminished or corrupted language can most such communication be made effective. Compare the vitality of language implicit in Shakespeare, in the Book of Common Prayer or in the style of a country gentleman such as Cavendish, with our present vulgate. 'Motivation researchers', those grave-diggers of literate speech, tell us that the perfect advertisement should neither contain words of more than two syllables nor sentences with dependent clauses. In the United States, millions of copies have been printed of 'Shakespeare' and the 'Bible' in the form of comic-strips with captions in basic English. Surely there can be no doubt that the access to economic and political power of the semi-educated has brought with it a drastic reduction in the wealth and dignity of speech.

I have tried to show elsewhere, in reference to the condition of German speech under Nazism, what political bestiality and falsehood can make of a language when the latter has been severed from the roots of moral and emotional life, when it has become ossified with clichés, unexamined definitions, and left-over words. What has happened to German is, however, happening less dramatically elsewhere. The language of the mass media and of advertisement in England and the United States, what passes for literacy in the average American high school or the style of present political debate, are manifest proofs of a retreat from vitality and precision. The English spoken by Mr Eisenhower during his press conferences, like that used to sell a new detergent, was intended neither to communicate the critical truths of national life nor to quicken the mind of the hearer. It was designed to evade or gloss over the demands of meaning. The language of a community has reached a perilous state when a study of radioactive fall-out can be entitled 'Operation Sunshine'.

Whether it is a decline in the life-force of the language itself that helps bring on the cheapening and dissolution of moral and political values, or whether it is a decline in the vitality of the body politic that undermines the language, one thing is clear. The instrument available to the modern writer is threatened by restriction from without and decay from within. In the world of what R. P. Blackmur calls 'the new illiteracy', the man to whom the highest literacy is of the essence, the writer, finds himself in a precarious situation.

What I want to examine, in closing, is the effect on the actual practice of literature of the retreat from the word and the concomitant divisions and diminutions of our culture. Not, of course, on all western literature, nor even on a significant fraction. But only on certain literary movements and individual writers who seem exemplary of the larger withdrawal.

 3 <>

The crisis of poetic means, as we now know it, began in the later nineteenth century. It arose from awareness of the gap between the new sense of psychological reality and the old modes of rhetorical and poetic statement. In order to articulate the wealth of consciousness opened to the modern sensibility, a number of poets sought to break out of the traditional confines of syntax and definition. Rimbaud, Lautréamont and Mallarmé strove to restore to language a fluid, provisional character; they hoped to give back to the word the power of incantation – of conjuring up the unprecedented – which it possesses when it is still a form of magic. They realized that traditional syntax organizes our perceptions into linear and monistic patterns. Such patterns distort or stifle the play of subconscious energies, the multitudinous life of the interior of the mind, as it was revealed by Blake, Dostoevsky, Nietzsche and Freud. In his prose poems, Rimbaud seeks to liberate language from the innate bond of casual sequence; effects seem to come before causes and events unfold in inconsequent simultaneity. That became a characteristic conceit of surrealism. Mallarmé made of words acts not primarily of *communication* but of *initiation* into a private mystery. Mallarmé uses current words in occult and riddling senses; we recognize them but they turn their back on us.

Although they yield superb poetry, these conceptions are fraught with danger. To work at all, the new private language must have behind it the pressure of genius; mere talent, a far more available commodity, will not do. Only genius can elaborate a vision so intense and specific that it will come across the intervening barrier of broken syntax or private meaning. The modern poet uses words as a private notation, access to which is rendered increasingly difficult to the common reader. Where a master is at work, where privacy of means is an instrument of heightened perception and no mere artifice, the reader will be led towards the necessary effort. Even before one has grasped Rimbaud's vision or the eccentric structure of argument in the *Duino Elegies*, one is aware that Rimbaud and Rilke are using language in new ways in order to pass from the real to the more real. But in the hands of lesser men or impostors, the attempt to make language new is diminished to barrenness and obscurity. Dylan Thomas is a case in point. He realized, with the flair of a showman, that a wide, largely unqualified audience could be flattered by being given access to a poetry of seeming depth. He combined a froth of Swinburnean rhetoric with cabbalistic devices of syntax and imagery. He showed that one could have one's Orphic cake and eat it too. But barring certain eloquent exceptions, there is in his poems less than meets the dazzled eye.

Where poetry seeks to dissociate itself from the exactions of clear meaning and from the common usages of syntax, it will tend towards an ideal of musical form. This tendency plays a fascinating role in modern literature. The thought of giving to words and prosody values equivalent to music is an ancient one. But with French Symbolist poetry, it assumes specific force. Implicit in Verlaine's doctrine — *De la musique avant toute chose* — is the attractive but confused notion that a poem should communicate most immediately through its sonorities. This pursuit of the tonal rather than the conceptual mode produced series of poetic works which yield their full implications only when they are actually set to music. Debussy was able to use Maeterlinck's *Pelléas et Mélisande* nearly intact; the same is true of Richard Strauss and Wilde's *Salomé*. In either case, the poetic work is a libretto in search of a composer. The musical values and proceedings are already explicit in the language.

More recently, the submission of literary forms to musical examples and ideals has been carried even further. In Romain Rolland and Thomas Mann, we find the belief that the musician is the artist in essence (he is *more* an artist than, say, the painter or writer). This is because only music can achieve that total fusion of form and content, of means and meaning, which all art strives for. Two of the foremost poetic designs of our time, T. S. Eliot's *Four Quartets* and Hermann Broch's *The Death of Virgil*, embody an idea that can be traced back to Mallarmé and *L'Après-midi d'un faune*: they attempt to suggest in language corresponding organizations of musical form.

The Death of Virgil is a novel built in four sections, each of which is figurative of one of the four movements of a quartet. Indeed, there are hints that Broch had before him the structure of a particular late quartet of Beethoven. In each 'movement', the cadence of the prose is meant to reflect a corresponding musical tempo: there is a swift 'scherzo' in which plot, dialogue and narrative move at a sharp pace; in the 'andante', Broch's style slows down to long, sinuous phrases. The last section, which renders Virgil's actual passage into death, is an astounding performance. It goes beyond Joyce in loosening the traditional bonds of narrative. The words literally flow in sustained polyphony. Strands of argument interweave exactly as in a string quartet; there are fugal developments in which images are repeated at governed intervals; and, at the last, language gathers to a dim, sensuous rush as remembrance, present awareness and prophetic intimation join in a single great chord. The entire novel, in fact, is an attempt to transcend language towards more delicate and precise conveyances of meaning. In the last sentence, the poet crosses into death, realizing that that which is wholly outside language is outside life.

There is a sociological footnote relevant to these turnings of literature towards music. In the United States, and to a growing extent in Europe, the new literacy is musical rather than verbal. The long-playing record has revolutionized the art of leisure. The new middle class in the affluent society reads little, but listens to music with knowing delight. Where the library shelves once stood, there are proud, esoteric rows of record albums and high-fidelity components. Compared to the long-playing record, the paperback book is an ephemeral, lightly discarded thing. It does not lead to the collecting of a real library. Music is today the central fact of lay culture. Few adults read aloud to each other; fewer yet spend a regular part of their spare time in a public library or athenaeum as did the generation of the 1880s. Many gather before the hi-fi set or join in musical performance.

There are complex social and psychological reasons for this. The tempo of urban and industrial life leaves one exhausted at nightfall. When one is tired, music, even difficult music, is easier to enjoy than serious literature. It stirs feeling without perplexing the brain. It allows even those who have little previous training access to classic masterpieces. It does not separate human beings into islands of privacy and silence as does the reading of a book, but conjoins them in that illusion of community which our society strives for. Where Victorian wooers sent garlands of verse to their intended, the modern swain will choose a record explicitly meant as background to reverie or seduction. As one looks at recent album-covers, one realizes that music has become the substitute for the candlelight and dark velvets which our style of life no longer provides.

In short, the musical sound, and to a lesser degree the work of art and its reproduction, are beginning to hold a place in literate society once firmly held by the word.

What is, perhaps, the dominant school in contemporary literature has made a virtue of necessity. The style of Hemingway and of his myriad imitators is a brilliant response to the diminution of linguistic possibility. Sparse, laconic, highly artificial in its conventions of brevity and understatement, that style sought to reduce the ideal of Flaubert — *le mot juste* — to a scale of basic language. One may admire it or not. But, undeniably, it is based on a most narrow conception of the resources of literacy. Moreover, the technical mastery of a Hemingway tends to blur a crucial distinction: simple words can be used to express complex ideas and feelings, as in Tacitus, the Book of Common Prayer, or Swift's *Tale of a Tub*; or they can be used to express states of consciousness that are themselves rudimentary. By retrenching language to a kind of powerful, lyric shorthand, Hemingway narrows the compass of observed and rendered life. He is often charged with his monotonous adherence to hunters, fishermen, bullfighters or alcoholic soldiers. But this constancy is a necessary result of the available medium. How could Hemingway's language convey the inward life of more manifold or articulate characters? Imagine trying to translate the consciousness of Raskolnikov into the vocabulary of 'The Killers'. Which is not to deny the perfection of that grim snapshot. But *Crime and Punishment* gathers into itself a sum of life entirely beyond Hemingway's thin medium.

The thinning out of language has condemned much of recent literature to mediocrity. There are various reasons why *The Death of a Salesman* falls short of the discernible reach of Arthur Miller's talent. But an obvious one is the paucity of its language. The brute snobbish fact is that men who die speaking as does Macbeth are more tragic than those who sputter platitudes in the style of Willy Loman. Miller has learned much from Ibsen; but he has failed to hear behind Ibsen's realistic conventions the constant beat of poetry.

Language seeks vengeance on those who cripple it. A striking example occurs in O'Neill, a dramatist committed, in a sombre and rather moving way, to the practice of bad writing. Interspersed in the sodden morass of *A Long Day's Journey into Night*, there are passages from Swinburne. The lines are flamboyant, romantic verbiage. They are meant to show up the adolescent inadequacies of those who recite them. But, in fact, when the play is performed, the contrary occurs. The energy and glitter of Swinburne's language burn a hole in the surrounding fabric. They elevate the action above its paltry level and instead of showing up the character show up the playwright. Modern authors rarely quote their betters with impunity.

But amid the general retreat or flight from the word in literature, there have been a number of brilliant rearguard actions. I shall cite only a few instances, limiting myself to English.

No doubt the most exuberant counter-attack any modern writer has launched against the diminution of language is that of James Joyce. After Shakespeare and Burton, literature has known no greater gourmand of words. As if aware of the fact that science had torn from language many of its former possessions and outer provinces, Joyce chose to annex a new kingdom below ground. *Ulysses* caught in its bright net the live tangle of subconscious life; *Finnegans Wake* mines the bastions of sleep. Joyce's work, more than any since Milton's, recalls to the English ear the wide magnificence of its legacy. It marshals great battalions of words, calling back to the ranks words long asleep or rusted, and recruiting new ones by stress of imaginative need.

Yet when we look back upon the battle so decisively won, we can attribute to it little positive consequence, and scarcely any wider richening. There have been no genuine successors to Joyce in English; perhaps there can be none to a talent so exhaustive of its own potential. What counts more: the treasures which Joyce brought back to language from his wide-ranging forays remain piled glitteringly around his own labours. They have not passed into currency. They have caused none of that general quickening of the spirit of speech which follows on Spenser and Marlowe. I do not know why. Perhaps the action was fought too late; or perhaps the privacies and parts of incoherence in *Finnegans Wake* have proved too obstructive. As it stands, Joyce's performance is a monument rather than a living force.

Another rearguard action, or raid behind enemy lines, has been that of Faulkner. The means of Faulkner's style are primarily those of Gothic and Victorian rhetoric. Within a syntax whose convolutions are themselves expressive of Faulkner's landscape, ornate, regional language makes a constant assault upon our feelings. Often the words seem to grow cancerous, engendering other words in ungoverned foison. At times, the sense is diluted as in a swamp-mist. But nearly always, this idiosyncratic, Victorian night-parlance *is* a style. Faulkner is not afraid of words even where they submerge him. And where he is in control of them, Faulkner's language has a thrust and vital sensuousness that carry all before them. Much in Faulkner is overwritten or even badly written. But the novel is always *written* through and through. The act of eloquence, which is the very definition of a writer, is not let go by default.

The case of Wallace Stevens is particularly instructive. Here is a poet who was by nature a rhetorician, who saw language as ceremonious and dramatic gesture. He was a lover of the savour and shimmer of words, passing them over his tongue like a taster of rare vintage. Yet the inventions or habits of style most characteristic of his work come from a narrow and brittle source. Consider some of his best-known finds: 'bright nouveautés', 'foyer', 'funeste', 'peristyle', 'little arrondissements', 'peignoir', 'fictive', 'port' (in the sense of posture). Most are Latinizations or naked borrowings from the French. They are conceits superimposed on language, not, as in Shakespeare or Joyce, growths from within the natural soil. Where the intent is one of exotic ornament, as in the 'tambourines' and 'simpering Byzantines' of 'Peter Quince', the effect is memorable. Elsewhere, it is merely florid or rococo. And behind Wallace Stevens's linguistic acquisitiveness, there is a queer streak of provincialism. He borrows French words with obtrusive excitement, rather like a traveller acquiring French bonnets or perfumes. He once declared that English and French are closely related languages. Not only is the proposition shallow, but it betokens a view of his own idiom which a poet should guard against.

Looking at the present scene, I wonder whether there are not signs of a renascence of the word, in the purely literary domain, in the work of an English novelist of Irish descent and Anglo-Indian background:

Frankly Scobie looks anybody's age; older than the birth of tragedy, younger than the Athenian death. Spawned in the Ark by a chance meeting and mating of the bear and the ostrich; delivered before term by the sickening grunt of the keel on Ararat, Scobie came forth from the womb in a wheel-chair with rubber tyres, dressed in a deer-stalker and a red flannelbinder. On his prehensile toes the glossiest pair of elastic-sided boots. In his hand a ravaged family Bible whose fly-leaf bore the words 'Joshua Samuel Scobie 1870. Honour thy father and thy mother.' To these possessions were added eyes like dead moons, a distinct curvature of the pirate's spinal column, and a taste for quinqueremes. It was not blood which flowed in Scobie's veins but green salt water, deep-sea stuff. His walk is the slow rolling grinding trudge of a saint walking on Galilee. His talk is a green-water jargon swept up in five oceans – an antique shop of polite fable bristling with sextants, astrolabes, propentines and isobars ... Now the retreating tide has left him high and dry above the speeding currents of time, Joshua the insolvent weather-man, the islander, the anchorite.

I know the objections to Lawrence Durrell. His style beats against the present tide. Anyone trained on Hemingway will sicken and cloy at it. But perhaps it is he who is at fault, having been long kept on thin gruel. Durrell's masters are Burton, Sir Thomas Browne, De Quincey, Conrad. He stands in the old tradition of the fullness of prose. He is attempting to make language once again commensurate with the manifold truths of the experienced world. His attempt has entailed excesses; Durrell is often precious, and his vision of conduct is more flimsy and shallow than are the technical resources at his command. But what he is trying to do is of real interest: it is no less than an effort to keep literature vocal.

But literature represents, as we have seen, only a small part of the universal crisis. The writer is the guardian and shaper of speech, but he cannot do the job alone. Today, this is truer than ever before. The role of the poet in our society and in the life of words has greatly diminished. Most of the sciences are wholly out of his grasp and he can impose on only a narrow range of the humanities his ideals of clear and inventive discourse. Does this mean that we must abandon to illiterate jargon or pseudo-science those crucial domains of historical, moral and social inquiry in which the word should still be master? Does this mean that we have no grounds for appeal against the strident muteness of the arts?

There are those who hold out small hope. J. Robert Oppenheimer has pointed out that the breakdown of communication is as grave within the sciences as it is between sciences and humanities. The physicist and mathematician proceed in a growing measure of mutual incomprehension. The biologist and the astronomer look on each other's work across a gap of silence. Everywhere, knowledge is splintering into intense specialization, guarded by technical languages fewer and fewer of which can be mastered by any individual mind. Our awareness of the complication of reality is such that those unifications or syntheses of understanding which made common speech possible no longer work. Or they work only at the rudimentary level of daily need. Oppenheimer goes further: he indicates that the very attempt to find bridges between languages is misleading. There is no use trying to explain to the layman the reality-concepts of modern mathematics or physics. It cannot be done in any honest, truthful way. To do it by approximate metaphor is to spread falsehood and to foster an illusion of understanding. What is needed, suggests Oppenheimer, is a harsh modesty, an affirmation that common men cannot, in fact, understand most things and that the realities of which even a highly trained intellect has cognizance are few.

With respect to the sciences, this sombre view seems unassailable. And perhaps it dooms most knowledge to fragmentation. But we should not readily accede to it in history, ethics, economics or the analysis and formulation of social and political conduct. Here literacy must reaffirm its authority against jargon. I do not know whether this can be done; but the stakes are high. In our time, the language of politics has become infected with obscurity and madness. No lie is too gross for strenuous expression, no cruelty too abject to find apologia in the verbiage of historicism. Unless we can restore to the words in our newspapers, laws, and political acts some measure of clarity and stringency of meaning, our lives will draw yet nearer to chaos. There will then come to pass a new dark age. The prospect is not remote: 'Who knows,' says R. P. Blackmur, 'it may be the next age will not express itself in words ... at all, for the next age may not be literate in any sense we understand or the last three thousand years understood.'

The poet of the *Pervigilium Veneris* wrote in a darkening time, amid the breakdown of classic literacy. He knew that the Muses can fall silent:

> perdidi musam tacendo, nec me Apollo respicit:
> sic Amyclas, cum tacerent, perdicit silentium.

'To perish by silence': that civilization on which Apollo looks no more shall not long endure.

⟶ *Night Words*[1] ⟵

Is there any science-fiction pornography? I mean something *new*, an invention by the human imagination of new sexual experience? Science-fiction alters at will the co-ordinates of space and time; it can set effect before cause; it works within a logic of total potentiality — 'all that can be imagined can happen'. But has it added a single item to the repertoire of the erotic? I understand that in a forthcoming novel the terrestrial hero and explorer indulges in mutual masturbation with a bizarre, interplanetary creature. But there is no real novelty in that. Presumably one can use anything from seaweed to accordions, from meteorites to lunar pumice. A galactic monster would make no essential difference to the act. It would not extend in any real sense the range of our sexual being.

The point is crucial. Despite all the lyric or obsessed cant about the boundless varieties and dynamics of sex, the actual sum of possible gestures, consummations, and imaginings is drastically limited. There are probably more foods, more undiscovered eventualities of gastronomic enjoyment or revulsion than there have been sexual inventions since the Empress Theodora resolved 'to satisfy all amorous orifices of the human body to the full and at the same time'. There just aren't that many orifices. The mechanics of orgasm imply fairly rapid exhaustion and frequent intermission. The nervous system is so organized that responses to simultaneous stimuli at different points of the body tend to yield a single, somewhat blurred sensation. The

---

1. Controversy over this article continued for many months, and is continuing still. My knowledge of and interest in pornography are, I would suppose, no greater than the middle-class average. What I was trying to get into focus is the notion of the 'stripping naked' of language, of the removal from private, intensely privileged or adventurous use, of the erotic vocabulary. It does seem to me that we have scarcely begun to understand the impoverishment of our imaginings, the erosion into generalized banality of our resources of individual erotic representation and expression. This erosion is very directly a part of the general reduction of privacy and individual style in a mass consumer civilization. Where everything can be said with a shout, less and less can be said in a low voice. I was also trying to raise the question of what relation there *may* be between the de-humanization of the individual in pornography and the making naked and anonymous of the individual in the totalitarian state (the concentration camp being the logical epitome of that state). Both pornography and totalitarianism seem to me to set up power relations which must necessarily violate privacy.

Though the discussion which followed publication has been heated, neither of these two issues has, I feel, been fully understood or engaged.

notion (fundamental to Sade and much pornographic art) that one can double one's ecstasy by engaging in *coitus* while being at the same time deftly sodomized is sheer nonsense. In short: given the physiological and nervous complexion of the human body, the number of ways in which orgasm can be achieved or arrested, the total modes of intercourse, are fundamentally finite. The mathematics of sex stop somewhere in the region of *soixante-neuf*; there are no transcendental series.

This is the logic behind the *120 Days*. With the pedantic frenzy of a man trying to carry *pi* to its final decimal, Sade laboured to imagine and present the sum-total of erotic combinations and variants. He pictured a small group of human bodies and tried to narrate every mode of sexual pleasure and pain to which they could be subject. The variables are surprisingly few. Once all possible positions of the body have been tried – the law of gravity does interfere – once the maximum number of erogenous zones of the maximum number of participants have been brought into contact, abrasive, frictional, or intrusive, there is not much left to do or imagine. One can whip or be whipped; one can eat excrement or quaff urine; mouth and private part can meet in this or that commerce. After which there is the grey of morning and the sour knowledge that things have remained fairly generally the same since man first met goat and woman.

This is the obvious, necessary reason for the inescapable monotony of pornographic writing, for the fact well known to all haunters of Charing Cross Road or pre-Gaullist book-stalls that dirty books are maddeningly the same. The trappings change. Once it was the Victorian nanny in high-button shoes birching the master, or the vicar peering over the edge of the boys' lavatory. The Spanish Civil War brought a plethora of raped nuns, of buttocks on bayonets. At present, specialized dealers report a steady demand for 'WS' (stories of wife-swapping, usually in a suburban or honeymoon resort setting). But the fathomless tide of straight trash has never varied much. It operates within highly conventionalized formulas of low-grade sadism, excremental drollery, and banal fantasies of phallic prowess or feminine responsiveness. In its own way the stuff is as predictable as a Boy Scout manual.

Above the pulp-line – but the exact boundaries are impossible to draw – lies the world of erotica, of sexual writing with literary pretensions or genuine claims. This world is much larger than is commonly realized. It goes back to Egyptian literary papyri. At certain moments in western society, the amount of 'high pornography' being produced may have equalled, if not surpassed, ordinary *belles-lettres*. I suspect that this was the case in Roman Alexandria, in France during the *Régence*, perhaps in London around the 1890s. Much of this subterranean literature is bound to disappear. But anyone who has been allowed access to the Kinsey Library in Bloomington, and has been lucky enough to have Mr John Gagnon as his guide, is made aware of the profoundly revealing, striking fact that there is hardly a major writer of the nineteenth or twentieth centuries who has not, at some point in his career, be it in earnest or in the deeper earnest of jest, produced a pornographic work. Likewise there are remarkably few painters, from the eighteenth century to post-Impressionism, who have not produced at least one set of pornographic plates or sketches. (Would one of the definitions of abstract, non-objective art be that it cannot be pornographic?)

Obviously a certain proportion of this vast body of writing has literary power and significance. Where a Diderot, a Crébillon *fils*, a Verlaine, a Swinburne, or an Apollinaire write erotica, the result will have some of the qualities which distinguish their more public works. Figures such as Beardsley and Pierre Louÿs are minor, but their lubricities have a period charm. Nevertheless, with very few exceptions, 'high pornography' is not of pre-eminent literary importance. It is simply not true that the locked cabinets of great libraries or private collections contain masterpieces of poetry or fiction which hypocrisy and censorship banish from the light. (Certain eighteenth-century drawings and certain Japanese prints suggest that the case of graphic art may be different; here there seems to be work of the first quality which is not generally available.) What emerges when one reads some of the classics of erotica is the fact that they too are intensely conventionalized, that their repertoire of fantasy is limited, and that it merges, almost imperceptibly, into the dream-trash of straight, mass-produced pornography.

In other words: the line between, say, *Thérèse Philosophe* or *Lesbia Brandon* on the one hand, and *Sweet Lash* or *The Silken Thighs* on the other, is easily blurred. What distinguishes the 'forbidden classic' from under-the-counter delights on Frith Street is, essentially, a matter of semantics, of the level of vocabulary and rhetorical device used to provoke erection. It is not fundamental. Take the masturbating housemaid in a very recent example of the Great American Novel, and the housemaid similarly engaged in *They Called Her Dolly* (n.d., price 6s.). From the point of view of erotic stimulus, the difference is one of language, or more exactly – as verbal precisions now appear in high literature as well – the difference is one of narrative sophistication. Neither piece of writing adds anything new to the potential of human emotion; both add to the waste.

Genuine additions are, in fact, very rare. The list of writers who have had the genius to enlarge our actual compass of sexual awareness, who have given the erotic play of the mind a novel focus, an area of recognition previously unknown or fallow, is very small. It would, I think, include Sappho, in whose verse the western ear caught, perhaps for the first time, the shrill, nerve-rending note of sterile sexuality, of a libido necessarily, deliberately, in excess of any assuagement. Catullus seems to have added something, though it is at this historical distance nearly impossible to identify that which startled in his vision, which caused so real a shock of consciousness. The close, delicately plotted concordance between orgasm and death in Baroque and Metaphysical poetry and art clearly enriched our legacy of excitement, as had the earlier focus on virginity. The development in Dostoevsky, Proust and Mann of the correlations between nervous infirmity, the psychopathology of the organism, and a special erotic vulnerability, is probably new. Sade and Sacher-Masoch codified, found a dramatic syntax for, areas of arousal previously diffuse or less explicitly realized. In *Lolita* there is a genuine enrichment of our common stock of temptations. It is as if Vladimir Nabokov had brought into our field of vision what lay at the far edge (in Balzac's *La Rabouilleuse*, for instance) or what had been kept carefully implausible through disproportion (*Alice in Wonderland*). But such annexations of insight are rare.

The plain truth is that in literary erotica as well as in the great mass of 'dirty books' the same stimuli, the same contortions and fantasies, occur over and over with unutterable monotony. In most erotic writings, as in man's wet dreams, the imagination turns, time and time again, inside the bounded circle of what the body can experience. The actions of the mind when we masturbate are not a dance; they are a treadmill.

Mr Maurice Girodias would riposte that this is not the issue, that the interminable succession of fornications, flagellations, onanisms, masochistic fantasies, and homosexual punch-ups which fill his *Olympia Reader* are inseparable from its literary excellence, from the artistic originality and integrity of the books he published at the Olympia Press in Paris. He would say that several of the books he championed, and from which he has now selected representative passages, stand in the vanguard of modern sensibility, that they are classics of post-war literature. If they are so largely concerned with sexual experience, the reason is that the modern writer has recognized in sexuality the last open frontier, the terrain on which his talent must, if it is to be pertinent and honest, engage the stress of our culture. The pages of the *Reader* are strewn with four-letter words, with detailed accounts of intimate and specialized sexual acts, precisely because the writer has had to complete the campaign of liberation initiated by Freud, because he has had to overcome the verbal taboos, the hypocrisies of imagination in which former generations laboured when alluding to the most vital, complex part of man's being.

'Writing dirty books was a necessary participation in the common fight against the Square World ... an act of duty.'

Mr Girodias has a case. His reminiscences and polemics make sour reading (he tends to whine); but his actual publishing record shows nerve and brilliance. The writings of Henry Miller matter to the history of American prose and self-definition. Samuel Beckett's *Watt* appeared with Olympia, as did writings of Jean Genet (though not the plays or the best prose). *Fanny Hill* and, to a lesser degree, *Candy* are mock-epics of orgasm, books in which any sane man will take delight. Lawrence Durrell's *Black Book* seems to me grossly overrated, but it has its serious defenders. Girodias himself would probably regard *Naked Lunch* as his crowning discernment. I don't see it. The book strikes me as a strident bore, illiterate and self-satisfied right to its heart of pulp. Its repute is important only for what it tells us of the currents of homosexuality, camp, and modish brutality which dominate present 'sophisticated' literacy. Burroughs indicts his readers, but not in the brave, prophetic sense argued by Girodias. Nevertheless, there can be no doubt of the genuineness of Girodias's commitment or of the risks he took.

Moreover, two novels on his list *are* classics, books whose genius he recognized and with which his own name will remain proudly linked: *Lolita* and *The Ginger Man*. It is a piece of bleak irony – beautifully appropriate to the entire 'dirty book' industry – that a subsequent disagreement with Nabokov now prevents Girodias from including anything of *Lolita* in his anthology. To all who first met Humbert Humbert in *The Traveller's Companion Series*, a green cover and the Olympia Press's somewhat mannered typography will remain a part of one of the high moments of contemporary literature. This alone should have spared Mr Girodias the legal and financial harryings by which Gaullist Victorianism hounded him out of business.

But the best of what Olympia published is now available on every drugstore counter – this being the very mark of Girodias's foresight. The *Olympia Reader* must be judged by what it actually contains. And far too much of it is tawdry stuff, 'doing dirt on life', with only the faintest pretensions to literary merit or adult intelligence.

It is almost impossible to get through the book at all. Pick it up at various points and the sense of *déjà-vu* is inescapable ('This is one stag-movie I've seen before'). Whether a naked woman gets tormented in Sade's dungeons (*Justine*), during Spartacus's revolt (Marcus Van Heller: *Roman Orgy*), in a kinky French château (*L'Histoire d'O*) or in an Arab house (*Kama Houri* by one Ataullah Mordaan) makes damn little difference. *Fellatio* and buggery seem fairly repetitive joys whether enacted between Paris hooligans in Genet's *Thief's Journal*, between small-time hustlers and ex-prizefighters (*The Gaudy Image*), or between lordly youths by Edwardian gaslight in *Teleny*, a silly piece attributed to Oscar Wilde.

After fifty pages of 'hardening nipples', 'softly opening thighs' and 'hot rivers' flowing in and out of the ecstatic anatomy, the spirit cries out, not in hypocritical outrage, not because I am a poor Square throttling my libido, but in pure, nauseous *boredom*. Even fornication can't be as dull, as hopelessly predictable as all that!

Of course there are moments which excite. *Sin for Breakfast* ends on a subtle, comic note of lewdness. *The Woman Thing* uses all the four-letter words and anatomic exactitudes with real force; it exhibits a fine ear for the way in which sexual heat compresses and erodes our uses of language. Those (and I imagine it includes most men) who use the motif of female onanism in their own fantasy life will find a vivid patch. There may be other nuggets. But who can get through the thing? For my money, there is one sublime moment in the *Reader*. It comes in an extract (possibly spurious?) from Frank Harris's *Life and Loves*. Coiling and uncoiling in diverse postures with two naked Oriental nymphets and their British procuress, Harris is suddenly struck with the revelation that 'there indeed is evidence to prove the weakness of so much of the thought of Karl Marx. It is only the bohemian who can be free, not the proletarian.' The image of Frank Harris, all limbs and propensities ecstatically engaged, suddenly disproving *Das Kapital* is worth the price of admission.

But not really. For that price is much higher than Mr Girodias, Miss Mary McCarthy, Mr Wayland Young, and other advocates of total frankness seem to realize. It is a price which cuts deep not only into the true liberty of the writer, but into the diminishing reserves of feeling and imaginative response in our society.

The preface to the *Olympia Reader* ends in triumph:

> Moral censorship was an inheritance from the past, deriving from centuries of domination by the Christian clergy. Now that it is practically over, we may expect literature to be transformed by the advent of freedom.

Not freedom in its negative aspects, but as the means of exploring all the positive aspects of the human mind, which are all more or less related to, or generated by, sex.

This last proposition is almost unbelievably silly. What needs a serious look is the assertion about freedom, about a new and transforming liberation of literature through the abolition of verbal and imaginative taboos.

Since the *Lady Chatterley* case and the defeat of a number of attempts to suppress books by Henry Miller, the sluice gates stand open. Sade, the homosexual elaborations of Genet and Burroughs, *Candy*, *Sexus*, *L'Histoire d'O* are freely available. No censorship would choose to make itself ridiculous by challenging the sadistic eroticism, the minutiae of sodomy (smell and all) which grace Mailer's *American Dream*. This is an excellent thing. But let us be perfectly clear why. Censorship is stupid and repugnant for two empirical reasons: censors are men no better than ourselves, their judgements are no less fallible or open to dishonesty. Secondly, the thing won't work: those who really want to get hold of a book will do so somehow. This is an entirely different argument from saying that pornography doesn't in fact deprave the mind of the reader, or incite to wasteful or criminal gestures. *It may, or it may not*. We simply don't have enough evidence either way. The question is far more intricate than many of our literary champions of total freedom would allow. But to say that censorship won't work and should not be asked to, is not to say that there has been a liberation of literature, that the writer is, in any genuine sense, freer.

On the contrary. The sensibility of the writer is free where it is most humane, where it seeks to apprehend and re-enact the marvellous variety, complication, and resilience of life by means of words as scrupulous, as personal, as brimful of the mystery of human communication, as the language can yield. The very opposite of freedom is cliché, and nothing is less free, more inert with convention and hollow brutality than a row of four-letter words. Literature is a living dialogue between writer and reader only if the writer shows a twofold respect: for the imaginative maturity of his reader, and in a very complex but central way, for the wholeness, for the independence and quick of life, in the personages he creates.

Respect for the reader signifies that the poet or novelist invites the consciousness of the reader to collaborate with his own in the act of presentment. He does not tell all because his work is not a primer for children or the retarded. He does not exhaust the possible responses of his reader's own imaginings, but delights in the fact that we will fill in from our own lives, from resources of memory and desire proper to ourselves, the contours he has drawn. Tolstoy is infinitely freer, infinitely more exciting than the new eroticists, when he arrests his narrative at the door of the Karenins' bedroom, when he merely initiates, through the simile of a dying flame, of ash cooling in the grate, a perception of sexual defeat which each of us can re-live or detail for himself. George Eliot is free, and treats her readers as free, adult human beings, when she conveys, through inflection of style and mood, the truth about the Casaubon honeymoon in *Middlemarch*, when she makes us imagine for ourselves how Dorothea has been violated by some essential obtuseness. These are profoundly exciting scenes, these enrich and complicate our sexual awareness, far beyond the douche-bag idylls of the contemporary 'free' novel. There is no real freedom whatever in the compulsive physiological exacti-tudes of present 'high pornography', because there is no respect for the reader whose imaginative means are set at nil.

And there is none for the sanctity of autonomous life in the characters of the novel, for that tenacious integrity of existence which makes a Stendhal, a Tolstoy, a Henry James tread warily around their own creations. The novels being produced under the new code of total statement shout at their person-ages: strip, fornicate, perform this or that act of sexual perversion. So did the SS guards at rows of living men and women. The total attitudes are not, I think, entirely distinct. There may be deeper affinities than we as yet under-stand between the 'total freedom' of the uncensored erotic imagination and the total freedom of the sadist. That these two freedoms have emerged in close historical proximity may not be coincidence. Both are exercised at the expense of someone else's humanity, of someone else's most precious right – the right to a private life of feeling.

This is the most dangerous aspect of all. Future historians may come to characterize the present era in the West as one of a massive onslaught on human privacy, on the delicate processes by which we seek to become our own singular selves, to hear the echo of our specific being. This onslaught is being pressed by the very conditions of an urban mass-technocracy, by the necessary uniformities of our economic and political choices, the new elec-tronic media of communication and persuasion, by the ever-increasing exposure of our thoughts and actions to sociological, psychological, and material intrusions and controls. Increasingly, we come to know real privacy, real space in which to experiment with our sensibility, only in extreme guises: nervous breakdown, addiction, economic failure. Hence the appalling monotony and *publicity* – in the full sense of the word – of so many outwardly prosperous lives. Hence also the need for nervous stimuli of an unprecedented brutality and technical authority.

Sexual relations are, or should be, one of the citadels of privacy, the nightplace where we must be allowed to gather the splintered, harried elements of our consciousness to some kind of inviolate order and repose. It is in sexual experience that a human being alone, and two human beings in that attempt at total communication which is also communion, can discover the unique bent of their identity. That we can find for ourselves, through imperfect striving and repeated failure, the words, the gestures, the mental images which set the blood to racing. In that dark and wonder ever-renewed both the fumblings and the light must be our own.

The new pornographers subvert this last, vital privacy; they do our imagining for us. They take away the words that were of the night and shout them over the roof-tops, making them hollow. The images of our love-making, the stammerings we resort to in intimacy, come pre-packaged. From the rituals of adolescent petting to the recent university experiment in which faculty wives agreed to practise onanism in front of the researchers' cameras, sexual life, particularly in America, is passing more and more into the public domain. This is a profoundly ugly and demeaning thing whose effects on our identity and resources of feeling we understand as little as we do the impact on our nerves of the perpetual 'sub-eroticism' and sexual suggestion of modern advertisement. Natural selection tells of limbs and functions which atrophy through lack of use; the power to feel, to experience and realize the precarious uniqueness of each other's being, can also wither in a society. And it is no mere accident (as Orwell knew) that the standardization of sexual life, either through controlled licence or compelled puritanism, should accompany totalitarian politics.

Thus the present danger to the freedom of literature and to the inward freedom of our society is not censorship or verbal reticence. The danger lies in the facile contempt which the erotic novelist exhibits for his readers, for his personages, and for the language. Our dreams are marketed wholesale.

Because there were words it did not use, situations it did not represent graphically, because it demanded from the reader not obeisance but live echo, much of western poetry and fiction has been a school to the imagination, an exercise in making one's awareness more exact, more humane. My true quarrel with the *Olympia Reader* and the genre it embodies is not that so much of the stuff should be boring and abjectly written. It is that these books leave a man less free, less himself, than they found him; that they leave language poorer, less endowed with a capacity for fresh discrimination and excitement. It is not a new freedom that they bring, but a new servitude. In the name of human privacy, enough!

◆ *Eros and Idiom* ◆

In Chapter XI of Book III of *Emma* the heroine is shocked into a realization of her own condition of feeling:

> Harriet was standing at one of the windows. Emma turned round to look at her in consternation, and hastily said,
> 'Have you any idea of Mr Knightley's returning your affection?'
> 'Yes,' replied Harriet modestly, but not fearfully – 'I must say that I have.'
> Emma's eyes were instantly withdrawn; and she sat silently meditating, in a fixed attitude, for a few minutes. A few minutes were sufficient for making her acquainted with her own heart. A mind like hers, once opening to suspicion, made rapid progress. She touched – she admitted – she acknowledged the whole truth. Why was it so much worse that Harriet should be in love with Mr Knightley, than with Frank Churchill? Why was the evil so dreadfully increased by Harriet's having some hope of a return? It darted through her, with the speed of an arrow, that Mr Knightley must marry no one but herself!

The economy of the passage is all. This economy is the immediate product of a large confidence, of a community of response between Jane Austen and her material and the novelist and her readers. Such community expresses itself in a prose which is, structurally, a shorthand. The words used by the novelist draw on public energies, on areas of meaning and implication which may be wide but whose reach of admissible reference is determined. The idiomatic carries a general charge of required significance. Metaphors are relatively infrequent or when they appear they do so in a condition of eroded vitality. Another way of saying that a language can move richly while 'on the surface' is to say that *Emma* was written in a time, in a moment of culture, in which style and convention were close.

A closeness of this kind usually has behind it a strong literary manner now attenuated and become a part of current speech. Below the concise ease of Emma's self-recognition runs the current, once sharply stylized, of Restoration comedy. It is the established specificity of the terminology of manner and feeling in Restoration comedy and the sentimental novel of the late eighteenth century that enables Jane Austen to proceed with speed and confident exactitude. There is no need of shading or of the vital indeterminacies of the modern tone. *Heart* and *mind* have their own determined valuations in a vocabulary of consciousness no doubt complex and particular in its historical roots but, so far as the novelist is concerned, now available for direct, unencumbered use. The 'evil so dreadfully increased' carries considerable intensity, but it is subverted, to the precise measure of irony required, by the fact that it belongs to an idiom conventionally, fictionally heightened into imperfect gravity. There is no mistaking the gestures, hence no need of elaboration or localized stress. The turn in consternation, the eyes instantly withdrawn, Emma's fixity, are parts of a code of significant manners as declaratory in their simplicity, in their lack of visual rhetoric, as is her diction. And it is precisely the triumph of a mastered conventionality to make its own individual, richly felt point in the most public of ways: that arrow of love darting through Emma. Nothing could be more deliberately worn, more void of its initial, long-forgotten metaphoric vivacity. The shaft of love piercing the unwilling or unknowing maiden's heart had, long before *Emma*, lost even the salience of a cliché. Yet Jane Austen can afford this dead turn and can make it active. The banality of the image qualifies — a qualification urged throughout the novel — the genuine authority and hurt of Emma Woodhouse's feelings. Her vulnerabilities are real but bounded, which defining limitation is beautifully enforced by the very turn of the phrase: 'Mr Knightley must marry no one but herself!' The imperious note, Emma's placing of herself at the centre, the mere setting of the last word, restore to self-confidence, and restore to our own sense of a necessary if gentle irony, the figure of the young woman woken to love. Where conventions of expressive form are so stable and so explicitly associative of writer to reader, syntax comes fully into its own.

The active life of conventionality is notable, principally, in Jane Austen's handling of the implicit sexual material. So direct yet unobtrusively public is the available idiom that we almost overlook the raw facts of the situation:

two women in love and necessarily rival. Both the allusion to Frank Churchill and the predatory, if comic, pulse of the last sentence, sharpen the edge of feeling. It is men and women who are in play and the gamut of possibilities between them from seduction to marriage. Emma is transformed body and soul, within the limitations of crisis allowed by Jane Austen. A few moments later Miss Woodhouse is at the edge of her own sense of being: 'ashamed of every sensation but the one revealed to her – her affection for Mr Knightley. – Every other part of her mind was disgusting.' Yet the sexual turbulence, the implications of action that flow from the muted encounter of Emma and Harriet, cannot, need not be articulated. They are inside the narrative, not in the sense of impulse hidden or unconscious, but as an area of understood meaning so intelligently faced, so publicly acquiesced in – the novelist and her reader having, as it were, negotiated a treaty of mutual intent – that there is no need of localizing articulation. Such a pact, in reference to sexuality, is the underlying condition of Jane Austen's art. Without it she could not proceed as swiftly and with as confidently limited a completeness as she does. The 'negotiation' of that *entente* is a long story. It involves the middle-class rejection of the open eroticism – open in the sense of being pictorial, punning, metaphorically unstable – of Restoration comedy, while at the same time absorbing much of that eroticism into sentimental fiction. In Samuel Richardson eroticism shifts from solicitation to spectacle; a distance of condescension and socially informed sentiment, adroitly varied by the novelist, intervenes between the world of the fiction and that of the reader. Jane Austen is heir to that 'distancing', although in her what had been in *Clarissa* a zone of prurience is now firm, neutral ground. But the most relevant fact is that Jane Austen's conventionality, free and intelligent as it strikes us, was already a rearguard action, an attempt to transmit to a new, splintered society standards, manners of judgement founded in the culture of the age of Johnson and Cowper. By the time of *Mansfield Park* and *Emma* the erotic imagination had broken free on at least two principal lines: in the trashy but often cunningly stylized and 'psychologically underpinned' sexuality of the Gothic novel, and in the lyric concreteness of Romantic poetry. Sixteen years before Emma, in the Preface to the *Lyrical Ballads*, William Wordsworth had firmly related 'the sexual appetite' to 'the great spring of the activity of our minds'. And one need but glance at the 'Lucy' poems to realize how far Wordsworth's terminology had advanced toward a complex, disturbingly penetrative use of sexual symbolism. In their treatment of the relations of feeling and desire between men and women, the novels of Jane Austen represent a rearguard action. They succeed through sheer force of serenity (a serenity obviously related to their total refusal of contemporaneous politics and history). But such leisured progress on a tightrope could not be performed again. In Jane Austen sex is, essentially, gender. The terms were soon to be reversed.

But neither as rapidly nor as generally as might have been expected. Jane Austen's contract had looked to the past. It was based on minority values and a theory of formal expression. The erotic reticence or erosive conventionality of the English novelists of the mid-century had broader motives. The novel had become the principal currency of middle-class feeling with its expectations of entertainment, of unobtrusive instruction, and, above all, of emotional and intellectual 'familiarity'. Both connotations, intimacy and familial tone, are important. The Victorian novel-reader wished to be at home in the world of his reading and demanded that those in his sitting-room be a party to his pleasures. Publishers, home-libraries, periodicals, an entire industry of allowed sensibility, flourished in response to well-established canons of imaginative temperance and domesticity. Economically this helped bring on a formidable expansion of serious if 'middle-brow' literacy. Artistically it necessitated a series of concessions or evasive tactics on the part of the novelists. In no one did necessary concession and bias of temper unite more coherently than in Dickens. His genius and the representative stature he achieved were in large part the result of a vital accord between the taste of the public and Dickens's profound sympathy with that taste.

The complicated energies released in Dickens's work pose many problems. None is more arresting than the fact that no other writer of comparable stature, of even related imaginative multiplicity in any modern literature, has ever been so innocent of stated adult sexuality. To say that this innocence has made of Dickens a classic for children or, more accurately, a classic whom adults re-read in a special ambience of remembered trust (we cannot so re-read *Gulliver's Travels*), is merely to point to an obvious consequence. Dickens's refusal of adult sexuality left clear marks. The symbolic vehemence and scarcely mastered crudity of melodrama in *Bleak House* and *Great Expectations* suggest a subterranean pressure of erotic recognition. The curious flashes of cruelty and hysteria notable as early as the 'black tales' in *Pickwick Papers* persist; they give to *Little Dorrit* much of its disturbing strength. But more often and, so far as Dickens's enormous readership was concerned, more characteristically, the absence of the erotic produced varieties of sentimentality. Dickens created a garden for fallen man, a nursery world from which middle-class optimism and bustle have, temporarily at least, banished the serpent. The Dora–David–Agnes relationship in *David Copperfield* is as deliberate a pastoral as any to be found in the Renaissance trope of the garden of love. It relegates the values of adult sexuality to the 'innocent' eroticism of the child (innocent before Freud). Dickens touches with sure instinct on a chord vibrant even in severe Protestantism: the resistance of the imagination to the thought that children too have been mined by original sin. In *The Turn of the Screw*, Henry James was to create a parody, deliberately sexual in focus, of Dickens's 'juvenile-pastoral'.

Dickens's achievement is formidable, but not all could so readily pay the price. Thackeray's relations with his middle-class audience and the latter's criteria of sexual tameness were unsteady and, at moments, waspish. His recourse, both emotional and strategic, to the eighteenth century points directly towards a lost candour and robustness in the erotic. Hence the famous complaint in the Preface to *Pendennis* that the novelist must drape masculinity and give 'a certain conventional simper' to his depiction of man, that no one since Fielding had been allowed to show man whole. Thackeray's *malaise* is evident in the flawed genius of *Vanity Fair*. Becky Sharp's career, set down by the novelist in precise contemporaneity with Marx's *Communist Manifesto*, illustrates what is probably the foremost insight of the modern novel: the interweaving, the symbolic and structural interchange between economic and sexual relations. It develops Balzac's recognition that class, sex, and money are expressions of more essential, underlying power relations. But, as often in Thackeray, the lack of available frankness induces a satirical, mock-ceremonious tone. Compelled to observe 'family manners' which are at odds with the abrasive candour of his perceptions, Thackeray writes tangentially; being less than 'Man' his personages accept all too easily the designation of puppets.

The case most difficult to account for in terms of middle-class taste and professional response is, of course, that of the Brontës. The depth of sexual commitment in *Wuthering Heights* is disguised or rather stylized by a brilliant recourse to already obsolete Gothic counters. *Jane Eyre* aroused hostility by its assumption of sexual readiness – poised, asking for mature arousal – in a 'decent' woman. But here also an intense stylization occurs. We may observe, in the encounters of the heroine and Rochester, how sexuality is made elemental, how a vocabulary of feverish grandeur effaces specific eroticism. In Charlotte Brontë, as in Lucretius, there is the vision of a world totally, therefore in the last analysis innocently, guiltlessly, informed by desire. Precisely because it is a lesser work, *Villette* proved more indicative of future solutions. The pressure of erotic recollections is intense; but the narrative moves on a level of symbolic realism, of natural incidents symbolically ordered, which was to give prose fiction its full authority. From *Villette* it was but a step to the more confident art of George Eliot.

There are several reasons why *Middlemarch* is pre-eminent among English novels, why it exhibits a cumulative genius of persuasion which, almost inevitably, directs one to Tolstoy. One of the main causes is the quality and extent of George Eliot's information, the sheer pressure of knowledge, exact and imaginatively mastered, she brings to bear on every aspect of her material. It is this particular authority of the thoroughly *known* which gives to the novel — 'vast, swarming, deep-coloured, crowded with episodes', as Henry James termed it[1] — a firm pivot. We do not find before *Middlemarch* (and we scarcely find again in the subsequent history of the English novel) the erudition, the responsible learning dramatically imagined and conveyed, which make possible the treatment of Lydgate's medical work and ambitions in Chapter XV of Book II. The description of Reform Bill agitation and of the role of the new journalism in it — a role ironically yet understandingly located in the novelist's handling of Will Ladislaw — again draws its conviction from a body of knowledge personally gathered, wholly ordered, and in reach of feeling. This same authority informs George Eliot's presentation of the two principal sexual motifs in the book, the Dorothea–Casaubon fiasco and Lydgate's relationship to Rosamond.

The narrative of the Casaubon honeymoon, with its possible reference to the life of Mark Pattison, is so closely meshed that it is difficult to locate in any single passage the full tact and perception of the novelist. The city of Rome is made the direct symbolic counterpart of Dorothea's bewilderment. 'The past of a whole hemisphere seems moving in funeral procession with strange ancestral images and trophies gathered from afar. But this stupendous fragmentariness heightened the dream-like strangeness of her bridal life.' The very season informs against the obscurely woken young woman: 'autumn and winter seemed to go hand in hand like a happy aged couple one of whom would presently survive in chiller loneliness.' Working in this chapter (XX, Book II) at the tense limits of available concreteness, George Eliot does resort to uneasy paraphrase: 'Forms both pale and glowing took possession of her young sense'; 'many souls in their young nudity are

1. Henry James: 'The Novels of George Eliot', in *Views and Reviews* (London, 1908).

tumbled out among incongruities'. The uncharacteristic baroque touch is deeply informative: the 'young nudity' is not primarily that of the soul, a point clarified, if any such clarification is required, by a constant reference to the statues and paintings seen by Dorothea. The 'incongruities' (and 'tumbled' is a beautifully betraying verb) are those of a brutal marital fiasco. But such is the density and strong pulse of the narrative that the local need for paraphrase, with its attendant risk of modish allegory, does not dim the precise, radical truth:

> Now, since they had been in Rome, with all the depths of her emotion roused to tumultuous activity, and with life made a new problem by new elements, she had been becoming more and more aware, with a certain terror, that her mind was continually sliding into inward fits of anger and repulsion, or else into forlorn weariness.

The vocabulary remains 'chaste' in the precise Augustan sense of the word, the chastity being largely a matter of abstraction, of a generalized syntax. But the cumulative intensity of George Eliot's manner, her power to suggest a known particularity, make the full meaning of what she is saying unmistakable. When the physical touch does come, the effect is the more poignant: 'she had ardour enough for what was near, to have kissed Mr Casaubon's coat-sleeve, or to have caressed his shoe-latchet.' The master-stroke, moreover, comes later, when the honeymoon is a sombre recollection. At the close of Chapter XXIX of Book III, Dorothea and Celia are talking of the latter's engagement to Sir James Chettam. Will Dodo be glad to see Sir James and hear him tell of his cottages?

> 'Of course I shall. How can you ask me?'
> 'Only I was afraid you would be getting so learned,' said Celia, regarding Mr Casaubon's learning as a kind of damp which might in due time saturate a neighbouring body.

The image comes through with repellent force. It tells of sexual failure and revulsion. The contrasting note of sentimental fecundity in Celia and the cottages is delicately struck. The rich exactitude of physical implication is achieved through an exercise of narrative truth so complete, so spaciously laid out, that we do not resent or experience as dated the abstraction, the extreme reticence of George Eliot's idiom.

This idiom is, appropriately, somewhat different in the Lydgate–Rosamond strands of the novel. 'There is nothing more powerfully real than these scenes in all English fiction,' wrote Henry James,[2] 'and nothing certainly more *intelligent.*' That reality does not stem from naive verisimilitude. It is, at decisive moments, achieved by means essentially emblematic. As has been repeatedly noticed, Lydgate's courtship of Rosamond and the subsequent crises of their marriage are punctuated by a set of key images. An entire range of dramatic tones is expressed through Rosamond's 'fair long neck' and the submissions or angry turns it performs. A larger nakedness is set out in that 'exquisite nape which was shown in all its delicate curves' (Chapter LVIII, Book VI). The covert echoes of Eve and of the serpent with 'sleek enamelled neck' enforce the gravity of Lydgate's fall. With a degree of control almost Shakespearean, in that it 'misses nothing', the novelist again focuses our attention on Rosamond's neck during the climactic meeting between Rosamond and Dorothea. But here the erotic values are suppressed and the statement is one of agonized candour; what we are directed to now is 'Rosamond's convulsed throat' (the careful imitation of Milton at the end of the chapter clinches the latent identification of Rosamond). Nor ought we to miss the confident, almost theatrical placing of symbolic props in the narrative of Lydgate's proposal (Chapter XXXI, Book III). Lydgate 'moved his whip and could say nothing.' Rosamond 'dropped her chain as if startled, and rose too, mechanically' ('as if' and 'mechanically' alert us to an inevitable artifice). 'When he rose he was very near to a lovely little face set on a fair long neck.' We cannot evade the serpentine note. Lydgate 'did not know where the chain went'; but in half an hour he leaves the house fettered, a man 'whose soul was not his own, but the woman's to whom he had bound himself'.

In what measure is George Eliot conscious of the associations she so exactly invokes, of the symbolic contents, to us so graphically Freudian, of that moving whip and broken chain? She does not need to be conscious of them in our sense of deliberate, 'publicly coded' significance. Her intellectual and psychological awareness is as complete as that of any twentieth-century novelist, as directly germane to the intended effect, but it has a different 'knowingness'. This difference is the key point.

George Eliot's perceptions of sexual feeling, the closeness of observation she brings to bear on erotic sensibility and conflict, yield nothing to that of the moderns. In most instances what passes for characteristic post-Freudian insight is, by comparison, shallow. But these perceptions and the free play of imaginative recognition are immensely in advance of, immensely more

2. *Ibid.*

explicit than, the vocabulary available to a serious novelist of the 1870s. George Eliot knows more, far more, than she says or feels called upon to *say*; but that knowledge, precise, informed by a marvellous grasp of human particularity, gives to what is said an unmistakable authority, an energy of undeclared content felt, registered, though as it were unheard. Between the urgent wealth of felt life and the actual idiom of the novel there is a zone of silence, an area of conventional selection in which the novelist's responses – material, psychologically informed, canny as are any of the moderns – are translated into the temperance and conventional indirection of Victorian public speech. But it is just this distance, this close presence of the known but unstated, that gives to the novel its intensity, its matchless energy of adult life. At every point in the treatment of Dorothea's unsentimental education or of Lydgate's submission to Rosamond, George Eliot's verbal reticence stands not for thinness, for absence of radical intelligence, but on the contrary for a nearness of unwasted resource. This reticence, moreover, this deliberate tact, allow effects of sensibility almost lost to modern fiction. The novelist treats both her characters and her readers as complex beings; she would not search out the last privacy of self. Hence her largess of imaginative acceptance. At the close of Book IV, the darkness of the Casaubon marriage deepens into explicit night. Dorothea watches her ailing husband coming upstairs, a light in hand:

> 'Dorothea!' he said, with a gentle surprise in his tone, 'Were you waiting for me?'
> 'Yes. I did not like to disturb you.'
> 'Come, my dear, come. You are young, and need not to extend your life by watching.'
> When the kind quiet melancholy of that speech fell on Dorothea's ears, she felt something like the thankfulness that might well up in us if we had narrowly escaped hurting a lamed creature. She put her hand into her husband's, and they went along the broad corridor together.

The focus is steady and unswervingly honest: the image of the 'lamed creature' carries all the relevant charge of frustration, of a relationship irreparably crippled (how much we *lose* by our knowingness about the symbolic, almost lexical equivalent between lameness and castration). But the wonder of the thing lies in its generosity, in the realization unfolded in Dorothea and the reader of Casaubon's human complication, of the claims which that complication can make on our response. This brief nocturne, once again rounded with a Miltonic echo, sets the art of George Eliot beside that of Tolstoy. The authority of compassion is as controlling, as humanizing here as it is in Tolstoy's treatment of Alexei Karenin. But note how closely it depends on the reticence of the medium. It would be impossible for George Eliot to evoke this delicacy of response, this completeness of sympathy, had the ugliness, the rot of body and nerve in Dorothea's honeymoon and married life, been made verbally explicit. Chasteness of discourse acts not as a limitation but as a liberating privacy within which the characters can achieve the paradox of autonomous life.

The lag of permissible terminology behind perception, and the narrative poise it made necessary and possible, did not last. The formal conventions and social expectations involved were too manifold to be stable. Henry James's *The Portrait of a Lady* is at significant points a *reprise* of *Middlemarch*. But the intervening years, short as they were, and even more so James's own view[3] of *Middlemarch* as setting a limit 'to the development of the old-fashioned English novel', have brought a difference. The treatment of the corroding marriage of Isabel Archer and Gilbert Osmond is indebted to the Dorothea–Casaubon theme; Florence and the chill discretion of fine art close on Isabel as Rome closed on Dorothea. The 'vivid flash of lightning' which at last brings Dorothea and Ladislaw together strikes again as Casper Goodwood embraces Mrs Osmond. But the inwardness which James aims for, the explicit sophistication of psychological analysis, are such that a generalized, unworried vulgate is no longer adequate. The knowledge possessed by the novelist no longer underlines the narrative; it presses on it and insinuates into the writer's style a new consciousness of symbolism. In Henry James chasteness and reserve are deliberate means; we are meant to observe the strenuous tactics of exclusion. What is left out lies in ambush around the next corner. In the Jamesian novel or in such specific uses of 'mask' as James's ghostly tales, reticence about sexual matters is not a statement of felt life, but a subtle privation. Often the unsaid comes through with a kind of poetic rush. Nothing could surpass the vividness of implied statement about Olive Chancellor's feelings towards Verena Tarrant in *The Bostonians*, a vividness conveyed by the summarizing touch: 'and the vague snow looked cruel'. No more need be said of the relevant sterility and unrealized Lesbian impulse. But too often in James's abundant dramatizations of sexuality the excluded concreteness, the immediacies omitted, lead a subterranean life and proliferate

3. *Ibid.*

in habits of allegory both too oblique and too obtrusive. What presses on James is an alternative convention, the possibility of graphic statement. George Eliot writes as if *Madame Bovary* had not posed the challenge, had not articulated the poetics of a new relationship between language and the sexual imagination. Henry James cannot afford such indifference. The potentiality of Flaubert weighs on him; he rejects it at the price of intricate, self-conscious labour.

Three *causes célèbres* mark the development of the 'new eroticism' in modern literature: the trial of *Madame Bovary* in January 1857, the decision of the United States District Court in the matter of *Ulysses* in 1933, and the unsuccessful prosecution of *Lady Chatterley's Lover* in London in 1962. From the point of view of literary thought, of the argument between public norms and total imaginative possibility, only Judge Woolsey's ruling on *Ulysses* matters. But the dynamism of total explicitness, the attempt in serious literature to achieve a complete verbal re-presentation of sexuality begins with — or, more accurately, can be defined in respect of — Flaubert (and the indictment, shortly after, of Baudelaire's *Les Fleurs du mal*). The confrontation between public censorship and the claims of the responsible erotic imagination was itself the result of specific and by no means self-evident sociological circumstances. The libertine fiction of the eighteenth century had gone well beyond anything we find in Flaubert; a number of Balzac's novels, such as *Le Père Goriot* and *La Rabouilleuse*, had silhouetted if not directly rendered motifs of sexual pathology, of scabrous sexual *malaise* far more lurid than anything in *Madame Bovary*. It was not literature that had changed or swerved to sudden licence; the alteration lay in the consolidation of middle-class taste, in the assumption, so characteristic of the mid-nineteenth century, that bourgeois criteria of allowed sensibility, that the emotional habits and norms of mercantile culture, embodied a controlling ideal. With the spread of cheap printing, moreover, and the new breadth of responding literacy, fiction had come to matter. The erotica of the *ancien régime* was élitist, as was the stylized diction in which it was couched. The art of Flaubert was, potentially at least, open to a much wider audience. Hence the subversive vitality of its challenge to the official community of good taste.

It is, at a distance, difficult to recapture outrage. The prosecution conceded Monsieur Flaubert's eminent talent; it was precisely this talent which made his novel so corrupting. 'A moral conclusion cannot make up for lascivious details.' The corset straps whistling snake-like around Emma Bovary's hips, the suave shudder of abandonment with which the young woman surrenders to Rodolphe – these were images that did not discredit realism but the art of fiction itself. 'To impose on art the single rule of public decency is not to make art subservient – it is to do it honour.' Maître Senard's defence of his client bore entirely on the question of motive. *Madame Bovary* is a profoundly moral work. 'Death is in these pages.' Each moment of erotic ecstasy is paid for a hundred-fold in suicidal disgust. The court agreed; whatever the 'reprehensive vulgarity' of local touches, the novel as a whole aimed at a serious, indeed tragic, indictment of adultery. Looking back, Henry James reflected, 'so far have we travelled since then – that *Madame Bovary* should in so comparatively recent a past have been to that extent a cause of reprobation; and suggestive above all, in such connections, as the large unconsciousness of superior minds.' Unconsciousness, no doubt, to the shallow moralism and officious spleen that would greet the book; but not, one supposes, to the radical issues involved.

Flaubert does no less than assert – an assertion the more trenchant for being wholly a matter of mountainous technical labour, of professional *métier* carried to the verge of personal breakdown – that artistic excellence, the high seriousness of the true artist, carries its own complete moral justification. Even as it comes to active being in a sphere strangely between truth and falsehood, the work of art lies outside any code of current ethical convention. It acts on that code, qualifying and re-shaping it towards a more catholic response to human diversity. But it lies outside, and its true morality is internal. The justification of a work of literature is, in the deep sense, technical; it resides in the wealth, difficulty, evocative force of the medium. Trashy prose, be it humanely purposive and moral in the utmost, merits censorship because its executive means are inferior, because the way in which the thing is done diminishes the reach of the reader's sensibility, because it substitutes the lie of simplification for the exigent intricacy of human fact. Serious fiction and serious poetry cannot be immoral whatever their force of sexual suggestion or savagery of communicated image. Seriousness – a quality demonstrable solely in terms of the fabric itself, of the resources of metaphor drawn upon, of the arduousness and originality of linguistic statement achieved – is the guarantor of relevant morality. Seriously expressed, no 'content' can deprave a mind serious in response. Whatever enriches the adult imagination, whatever complicates consciousness and thus corrodes the clichés of daily reflex, is a high moral act. Art is privileged, indeed obliged, to perform this act; it is the live current which splinters and regroups the frozen units of conventional feeling. That – not some modish pose of abdication, of otherworldliness

— is the core of *l'art pour l'art*. This morality of 'enacted form' is the centre and justification of *Madame Bovary*.

Is this assertion of necessary and sufficient internal morality true? Or, rather, what kind of truth does it argue? This, precisely, is the question which besets us a century after *Madame Bovary*, in a context more perplexing and urgent than any envisaged by Flaubert or his accusers. I will come back to it. What needs clarification here is the theory of language, of the relationships between language and imagination operative in the account of sexual experience in Flaubert's novel.

Recognition of the genius of the work has been accompanied, almost from the start, by a measure of discomfort. James found Emma Bovary 'really too small an affair',[4] a vessel too restricted for the subtle profusion of consciousness posited by the novelist. Taking as starting-point Flaubert's own record of his frenetic quest for *le mot juste*, the sentences re-cast twenty times in an agonized pursuit of uniquely appropriate cadence, Georg Lukács saw in *Madame Bovary* a crisis of confidence, a retreat from that imaginative ease in the real world which distinguishes classic art. Only a sensibility unhoused (which eviction Lukács ascribes to the philistine pressures on the artist of mature capitalism) could invest so passionately, and ultimately despairingly, in the autonomous reality of the word. Sartre's image of Flaubert as literally suffocated in the coils of a perfect style is merely a variant of Lukács's case. Flaubert's chronicle of martyrdom, of the insane pitch of effort at which he laboured to achieve a unique, unflawed authenticity of expressive form, contributes powerfully to the impression of coldness, of still air, many have experienced in reading and re-reading *Madame Bovary*. The death which Flaubert's advocate found in these pages is not merely one of moralizing verdict.

How does Flaubert's ideal of exhaustive explicitness actually work out in regard to the presentment of sexual experience? Going back to the major instances, one realizes by how wide a margin of selective musicality and atmospheric inference Flaubert's narrative departs from any naive *verismo*.

Çà et là, tout autour d'elle, dans les feuilles ou par terre, des taches lumineuses tremblaient, comme si des colibris, en volant, eussent éparpillé leurs plumes. Le silence était partout, quelque chose de doux semblait sortir des arbres; elle sentait son cœur, dont les battements recommençaient, et le sang circuler dans sa chair comme un fleuve de lait. Alors, elle entendit

4. Henry James: 'Gustave Flaubert', in *The Art of Fiction and Other Essays* (Oxford, 1948).

tout au loin, au delà du bois, sur les autres collines, un cri vague et prolongé, une voix qui se traînait, et elle l'écoutait silencieusement, se mêlant comme une musique aux dernières vibrations de ses nerfs émus. Rodolphe, le cigare aux dents, raccommodait avec son canif une des deux brides cassée.[5]

[Here and there around her the leaves were dappled with a flickering brightness as though humming-birds had shed their wings in flight. Silence was everywhere. Sweetness seemed to breathe from the trees. She felt her heart beginning to beat again, and the blood flowing inside her flesh like a river of milk. Then far away beyond the forest, on the other side of the valley, she heard a strange, long-drawn cry that hung on the air, and she listened to it in silence as it mingled like music with the last vibrations of her jangled nerves. Rodolphe, cigar in mouth, was mending one of the bridles with his pocket-knife.]

The Freudian valuations of that 'river of milk' or of that cigar between the lover's teeth are undeniable, as are the allegoric, traditional counters such as the broken bridle. But the specific miracle of the passage lies in Flaubert's simulation of Emma's return to consciousness after the sexual act. It is a simulation achieved by means of rhythm and image. The modulations in the past tenses of the verbs, the utterly deliberate punctuation and adjustment in the lengths of successive clauses, enforce on our own breathing, on the imitative somatic stance by which a reader responds to a suggested series of images, an exact counterpart to Emma Bovary's ebbing sensuality and tranquil, yet delicately haunted, peace. The symbolic properties invoked precisely sustain the intended feeling: that lengthy, vague cry beyond the woods resounds at moments lyric and ominous throughout Romantic litera-ture. We hear a last ironic echo of it in the twang of the broken string in *The Cherry Orchard*. The humming-bird plumage and dim softness out of the trees in the smouldering sunset (*dans la rougeur du soir*) belong to the stylized ecstasies of Romantic verse and fiction. Flaubert's use of them is adroit; they reflect both outward to our own sensibility and inward to the rhetoric of romance on which Emma Bovary feeds — a rhetoric precisely located for us by the fact that Emma, on returning home, immediately falls to dreaming of 'the lyric legion' of adulterous heroines. In short, the reality of the passage is sensuously overwhelming. It elicits from us emotions, a physical and psychological *mimesis*, exactly correspondent to the narrative. But the reality

5. Gustave Flaubert: *Madame Bovary* (Paris, 1857), Pt II, Ch. IX.

is not one of obvious verbal facsimile. The rhythms are vividly, directly suggestive (as they are again in the notorious carriage-ride with Léon), not the actual terms used. Flaubert's eroticism is a matter of cadence. It is the theory of total expression, therefore, rather than the actual practice of *Madame Bovary*, which proved exemplary.

In Flaubert, as in Baudelaire, the pursuit of explicitness was not an end in itself but part of a rigorous morality of aesthetic form. The explicitness achieved was still governed by considerations of stylistic elegance. In Maupassant, Zola, and the naturalistic movement, explicitness of a new, far more literal order breaks through. Integrity of representation came to replace integrity of artistic form as the essential criterion of seriousness. To say less than all was to abdicate from the novelist's intellectual and social function. The naturalistic writer saw himself as the peer of the physical scientist and analytic historian; his novels had to communicate a correspondingly anatomical and unflinching view of human affairs. No less than Symbolism (though the two movements are exactly opposed in their aesthetics) Naturalism moved on a wave of conscious anti-philistinism. To shock the bourgeois, to challenge the taboos of respectable speech, became an obligation. For his part the enlightened reader – 'mon semblable, – mon frère!' – demonstrated his maturity and toughness of sensibility by concealing his shock or, indeed, spurring the artist to new audacities. The passage from *le mot juste* to *le mot exact* in the 1870s and 1880s was the result of a mutually accelerating impulse of both writer and reader. To that impulse increasingly graphic means of reproduction and direct reportage – the modern newspaper story, the photograph – brought a competitive challenge. To keep its grip on a public stimulated by but soon almost immune to all but the grossest intensities of journalistic description, the novel had to pass from image to picture. Hence the photographic insistence of the Goncourts, of Maupassant, and of Zola. A drastic advance toward erotic verisimilitude separates the language of *Nana* from that of Flaubert:

> Nana se pelotonnait sur elle-même. Un frisson de tendresse semblait avoir passé dans ses membres. Les yeux mouillés, elle se faisait petite, comme pour se mieux sentir. Puis, elle dénoua les mains, les abaissa le long d'elle par un glissement, jusqu'aux seins, qu'elle écrasa d'une étreinte nerveuse. Et rengorgée, se fondant dans une caresse de tout son corps, elle se frotta les joues à droite, à gauche, contre ses épaules, avec câlinerie. Sa bouche goulue soufflait sur elle le désir. Elle allongea les lèvres, elle se baisa

longuement près de l'aisselle ... Alors, Muffat eut un soupir bas et prolongé ... Il prit Nana à bras le corps, dans un élan de brutalité, et la jeta sur le tapis.[6]

[Nana gathered herself into a ball. A shiver of tenderness seemed to have passed through her limbs. Moist-eyed, she made herself small so as to feel her body more closely. Then she unclasped her hands and slid them down her body as far as her breasts, which she crushed in a nervous embrace. Her throat out-thrust and as if melting into a caress of her entire body, Nana cuddled her cheeks, first right then left, against her shoulders. Her greedy mouth breathed desire across her own flesh. She pointed her lips and kissed herself, unhurriedly, near her armpits ... Muffat breathed a low, prolonged sigh ... He seized Nana, in a brutal rush, and threw her on to the carpet.]

Flaubert saw in *Nana* the triumphant culmination of an ideal of sexual candour which he himself had initiated and enforced on a hypocritical society: 'que la table d'hôte des tribades "révolte toute pudeur," je le crois! Et bien! Après! merde pour les imbéciles.'

Changes in the middle-class tolerance of sexual shock, the reluctance of the *imbéciles* to reveal themselves as such, whatever their private feelings, were hastened by an almost automatic linguistic mechanism. From *Nana* to *Ulysses* and *Lady Chatterley's Lover*, from *Lady Chatterley* to *Last Exit to Brooklyn*, a constant progression toward the limits of sexual explicitness is at work. Each advance brings with it, by a compulsive logic of formal structure, the need to take the next step, to bring verbal means another bit closer to complete erotic re-enactment (even as each increase of nakedness and allowed posture in the cinema or photography has brought us nearer to the open representation of intercourse). Flaubert and his naturalistic successors had set off a self-perpetuating dynamic inside the idiom of the novel. Often writer and audience exaggerate the spontaneity, the deliberate moral courage of the latest frankness. In the whole process a powerful linguistic automatism is manifest.

Since about 1890 homosexuality has played a vital part in western culture and, perhaps even more significantly, in the myths and emblematic gestures which that culture has used in order to arrive at self-consciousness. Artists

6. Émile Zola: *Nana* (Paris, 1880), Ch. VII.

who have covertly or publicly practised paederasty and/or various modes of
adult homoeroticism hold an important, at certain points predominant place
in modern literature, art, music, ballet, and in the minor or decorative arts.
The tonality of the 'modern movement', the theories of the creative act
implicit in important branches of twentieth-century arts and letters, cannot
be dissociated from the lives and work of Oscar Wilde, Proust, André Gide,
Stefan George, and Cocteau. From early rhapsodies or masques of Gide to
the poetry of Allen Ginsberg and the fiction of James Purdy, James Baldwin,
and William Burroughs, explicit homosexuality or homosexuality symbolically declared, activates much that is most distinctive of the sensibility of the
age. Why?

The phenomenon itself has been extensively studied; its causes and central
energies remain obscure. It can be argued that the problem is one of optics,
that homosexuality played no less of a role in Periclean Athens or Renaissance
Florence, that the cultural élite of the rococo was no less inclined to homosexuality than the world of Diaghilev: the difference being, simply, one of
the data available. But although there is something in this and although the
salience of modern homosexuality is in part a visual effect – the surrounding
medium of middle-class norms and a simultaneous loosening of verbal and
legal taboos have made homosexuality more prominent – the facts are more
stubborn and intricate. From *art nouveau* to 'camp' and Gay Lib, homosexual
codes and ideals are a major force. They seem to underlie, as if re-enacting
their own solipsism, their own physiological and social enclosedness, that
most characteristic of modern strategies: the poem whose real subject is the
poem, art that is about self-possibility, ornament and architecture that have
as their main referent not some grid of actual human use but other ornament
or other form. So far as much of the best, of the most original in modern art
and literature is autistic, i.e. unable or unwilling to look to a reality or
'normality' outside its own chosen rules, so far as much of the modern genius
can be understood from the point of view of a sufficiently comprehensive,
sophisticated theory of games, there is in it a radical homosexuality. In other
words, homosexuality could be construed as a creative rejection of the
philosophic and conventional realism, of the *mundanity* and extroversion of
classic and nineteenth-century feeling. That feeling produces works of art and
literature which 'look outward' for their meaning and validity, which accept
authorities and solicit approvals outside themselves. The painting aims to
'look like something in the real world', the poem has a final basis of verification in prose paraphrase or common sense, music has structures powerfully

analogous to the syntax of common discourse. Heterosexuality is the very essence of such classic realism, of art and language that are centrally acts of communication, of relationship to the 'outside'. Where poetics after Mallarmé turn inward, where the subject of a painting becomes painting, where music and dance reject translation into any alphabet of exterior meaning, they seem to express needs and conceptions of self-sufficient form deeply related to homosexuality or to that abstraction of homosexuality which is narcissism. The mirrors of the modern shine inward in a probing, tormenting meditation on the self or on that 'other' like enough to be its shadow (in Proust and Cocteau the iconography of 'enclosedness' and the rules of the mirror-game are most consciously worked out).

On a simpler level, the homosexual current in post-Symbolist literature may be understood as a strategy of opposition, as the artist's most emphatic stance against philistinism. Such a stance, which the artist himself often finds indispensable to sustain his creative solitude, became increasingly difficult to adopt as puritanism weakened. In the Romantic period the mere choice of art or literature as a mode of life had been enough to assert a rebellious eccentricity, a dissent from the social norm. Flaubert already found the process of necessary dissociation more difficult and made a constant, if muted, rebellion of the obsessive mania of his work. In Poe and Baudelaire drugs provide a haven, which is also an exile, outside the frontiers of the bourgeois order. As the artist became accepted, his rebellions blunted by the indifference or conventionalized shock of the now sophisticated public, his task of self-definition grew more arduous. Where could he find a genuine extraterritoriality, a posture genuinely offensive (in the sense both of attack and of provoked outrage)? The Verlaine–Rimbaud scandal and the career of Oscar Wilde gave to homosexuality representative, strategic values. The homosexual overlapped with the artist in being an outsider, a 'grand refuser' of those standards of creativity and utilitarian relationship which define middle-class, industrial, post-Puritan civilization. Homosexuality in part made possible that exercise in solipsism, that remorseless mockery of philistine common sense and bourgeois realism which is modern art. As the twentieth century progresses other externalities, other 'offending/offensive exiles' such as those of the Jew and of the Negro come to serve as strategic functions for the writer and artist. A common narcissism and subversion relates these different creative masks. But whatever its sources, the homosexual current has produced much, one is tempted to say a major part, of what will stand in the treatment of love in modern literature.

Looking back at *Death in Venice* from the vantagepoint of present overt-
ness, one is struck by the hushed ceremony of the story, by Thomas Mann's
unworried exploitation of allegoric pointers – the Wagnerian reference of the
title, Aschenbach's name, the death-ship, the orgiastic nightmare, naked *amor*
risen from the sea – no longer available to our 'knowingness' (it is in the
passage from knowledge to 'knowingness' that I am trying to locate our
theme). The tale looks back to civilizing encumbrances and dreams of reason
which Mann knew to be doomed. Nevertheless it would be myopic to
underestimate its sexual audacity. In a manner comparable to the love poetry
of Donne, *Death in Venice* articulates, perhaps rediscovers, a death-haunted
eroticism, a *morbidezza* in which a crisis of desire is made expressive of a far
wider disorder of human values. The master of style discovers the intrusive
inadequacy of speech: 'Aschenbach understood not a word he said; it might
be the sheerest commonplace, in his hearing it became mingled harmonies.'
The naked radiance of the boy liberates the great writer from 'the marble mass
of language'. Eros overwhelms him: 'Mind and heart were drunk with passion,
his footsteps guided by the daemonic power whose pastime it is to trample
on human reason and dignity.' The betraying egoism of Aschenbach's experience, the fact that it is on Tadzio's mere shadow that he lavishes 'lover-
like, endearing terms' – there is never between the old man and the boy either
touch or speech – only reinforces the mortal intensity of lust. Though
explicitly linked to the poetic, partially allegoric paedophilia of the Platonic
dialogues and the Socratic myth of *eros*, Mann's novella seems to initiate a
series of similar narratives. From Gide's *Les Faux-monnayeurs* to Nabokov's
Lolita, modern fiction has produced a number of remarkable realizations of an
adult's sexual relation to a child or group of children. These encounters are
almost invariably homoerotic and it may be Nabokov's reversal that gives
to *Lolita* some of its unsettling sparkle.

The case of Marcel Proust can hardly be touched on in a brief survey. But
it is striking how largely Proust studies, voluminous and often intelligent as
they are, have failed to grasp the nettle. The affair between the narrator and
Albertine is one – and there are obviously not many in the history of art and
literature – that literally enlarges the resources of our sensibility, that actually
educates our recognitions to new possibilities of feeling. Proust has widened
the repertoire of sexual consciousness. Areas of adolescent sexuality, of
imaginary possession, of jealousy, of sexual loss have, through Proust's
formulation, become larger or newly accessible. As is the uncanny case with
very great art, *À la recherche du temps perdu* has acted as a prescriptive

mythology, calling into being nuances of emotion, twists of being and pretence, which were, somehow, a *terra incognita* of the self. Biographical information, in the matter of Proust over-abundant and therefore obscuring, leads one to suppose that Albert lives formidably in Albertine. The young woman, feminine and rounded as she is, masks what is, in some sense, the subterranean, more direct truth of homosexual love. So André Gide felt in his strictures on Proust's 'insincerity'. But the facts are even more tangled. We know that Albertine does incorporate the traits of women whom Proust knew and who, at some level of perceptual enchantment, meant much to him. Thus the foremost celebration of love in twentieth-century literature is ambiguous to the core. But not ambiguous in any shallow, tactical sense manipulated by a critic. The Albert–Albertine figure, the narrator's trans-positions between heterosexual and homosexual codes, belong to that strange suspension of sexual difference or rather to that fusion of erotic being which we find at certain particular summits in the western tradition. The mysterious completeness of Proust's eroticism, mysterious because it is also an artifice, relates to the myth of sexual unison in the *Symposium*, to the androgynous conceit in some of Leonardo da Vinci's representations of the human figure, to the interchangeability and co-presence of masculine and feminine in some of the poetry and drama of Marlowe, of Shakespeare, and of Goethe's amorous elegies. Where our imagination moves deepest it strives beyond sexuality, which is, inevitably, division, to an erotic whole.

It is precisely against this wholeness, not against any simple hetero-sexuality, that Proust sets off the torturing incompletion of Sodom and Gomorrah. His detailed mapping of homosexual and Lesbian life and society has within it a moralizing, damning force. Charlus has an immensity of presence denied to Vautrin not only because Proust can go further than Balzac – he can detail the world of perversion in a way unavailable to the idiom of the 1830s – but because he is making a persistent tragic statement about the nature of human love itself. Because he is setting out, as Plato and Shakespeare did, the dialectic of identity and desire: how may we reach the beloved without destroying something of that principle of self from which love springs? In the homosexual and the Lesbian that paradox is frozen to sterile acceptance. The broken sphere of Plato's myth is made a treadmill. One need only re-read the close of the first chapter of *Sodome et Gomorrhe* to experience the underlying grimness of Proust's vision of Sodom and why total (therefore unattainable) communication with, total (therefore unattainable) possession of the beloved, becomes to the narrator the very meaning of life. Thus

Proust's homosexuality, though vitally significant, animates, as Gide's or Cocteau's does not, imagined, a poetically experienced, completeness of love.

In Jean Genet there is no such completeness. On the contrary, there is a fierce striving for partiality, for the special point of view. The homosexual, criminal underground of Genet's novels defines itself by its derisive 'otherness' (*altérité*). Its relation to established society is one of subversive travesty. Hence the dominant function of disguise, charades, masks, and transvestism in Genet's art. Above all, this travesty inspires Genet's talent for high rhetoric, his use of the French language at its most formal, of French prosody where it is most like Victor Hugo, to brazen the unspeakable. Genet makes every brutality and obscenity of homosexual relations explicit, but in a special highly original way. By spelling out *everything* in a style of lyric declamation, he creates a kind of solid, graphic unreality — as does a painting by Cara-vaggio. In Genet homosexuality becomes a 'garden of love', divorced from ordinary society less by its bestial violence and elaborate slang than by its intense stylization, by the terrain it affords for play-acting, festive ceremonies, and unbridled pathos. Genet is heir to Maeterlinck and Yeats, to those who have sought a stage for action more formal, more rigorously aesthetic than that provided by realism. Reticence is one kind of stylization; total explicit-ness is another:

> Élève-toi dans l'air de la lune, o ma gosse.
> Viens couler dans ma bouche un peu de sperme lourd
> Qui roule de ta gorge à mes dents, mon Amour,
> Pour féconder enfin nos adorables noces.
>
> Colle ton corps ravi contre le mien qui meurt
> D'enculer la plus tendre et douce des fripouilles.
> En soupesant charmé tes rondes, blondes couilles,
> Mon vit de marbre noir t'enfile jusqu'au cœur.

[Rise in the moonlight, my sweet jocko. Come and let a little heavy semen drip into my mouth, rolling from your throat to my teeth, Beloved, so as to make fruitful at last our adorable wedding. Glue your ravished body against my dying flesh, dying to bugger the most tender and sweet of rogues. While charmed I weigh your round, blond balls, my black marble prick shafts you to the heart.]

It is impossible to 'go further' than does *Le Condamné à mort*. Yet such is the elevation of tone — with its echoes, at once parodistic and scholastic, of Victor

Hugo, Rimbaud, and even Péguy — that the category of obscenity does not seem to fit. It is where the brazen singularity of vision falters, where naturalism and mere reportage corrupt style, that the matter of obscenity or motive arises (as it does in John Rechy's *City of Night* and Hubert Selby's *Last Exit to Brooklyn*, two books very probably inspired by Genet). Genet has made of violent, totally promiscuous buggery a world, a dramatic form, fantastic yet relevant by virtue of ironic mime to the mendacities and savageries of our normal, respectable condition.

Homosexuality has not been the only indirection of love explored by modern literature. The rapid erosion of verbal and representational taboos that follows on the work of Havelock Ellis, Krafft-Ebing, and Freud has brought types of erotic behaviour previously restricted to straight pornography, to the twilit zone of *curiosa* and popular ethnography, or to forensic medicine into the repertoire of serious literature. It is difficult to think of any mode of sexual action — bestial, fetishistic, sadomasochistic, incestuous — that has not been shown in modern fiction or drama. Incest is, in the Freudian reading, a primary structure in evolving human consciousness. It has a dim but unmistakable centrality in Greek tragic mythology. In the return to Greek motifs of modern drama, incest has figured prominently. The richest, most humanely serious treatment of a brother-sister passion may be seen in Robert Musil's novel *Der Mann ohne Eigenschaften*. The work is incomplete and we cannot be certain that Ulrich and Agathe would have consummated their tense, searching need of each other. But what fragments we have of a third volume, especially the broken, dance-like exchange by moonlight, suggest Musil's broad grasp of the theme, his aim to make of it, as often in contemporary literature, a symbol of love seeking total communion, total privacy from the 'otherness' of the world. A comparable equivalence between brother-sister incest and the general drama of human isolation can be seen, though on a slighter scale, in Cocteau's *Les Enfants terribles* and Sartre's *Les Séquestrés d'Altona*.

Clearly, however, it is in its uses of cruelty, of the sadistic components or aberrations of sexuality, that modern literature has gone furthest. Sadistic motifs and their interweaving with the erotic are perennial in art and literature; they play a pronounced role in the baroque and Gothic sensibilities. The image of love as a torturer, of a secret analogy between lover and beloved and torturer and tortured, seems archetypal to human consciousness. We find it memorably enacted in Hieronymus Bosch's gardens of delight. But the modern focus is different, at once more diffuse and more specific in its concentration on sadism in sexual phantasy and private life. From, say, Zola's *L'Assommoir* (1878) to Pauline Réage's *L'Histoire d'O* (1954) and William Burroughs's *The Naked Lunch* (1959), the explicitness of sadistic action has increased continually. Phantasies and presumed realities which had been the stock-in-trade of pornography have passed intact into serious literature. Sade has become both a dramatic emblem of man 'at the outer edge' and the object of a modish philosophic and literary cult. I have written elsewhere of some aspects of this obsessive imaginative exploitation of cruelty and erotic humiliation. Only the main points can be referred to here. Few topics provoke a more confident display of liberal cant. We simply *do not know* whether or to what degree sadistic literature initiates or quickens imitative behaviour (work under way on this question in clinical psychology is, as yet, rudimentary but results suggest that there *may* be a relationship between sadistic suggestion and subsequent conduct). The claim that sadistic literature merely induces masturbation and thus diminishes the individual or social potential for sadistic action may or may not be valid. It cannot, in either case, be naively generalized. The impact of sadistic proposals on the literate, otherwise engaged or furnished sensibility is wholly different from such impact on those whose imaginative lives are barren, hollowed by monotony, or ill-equipped to handle the conventions of unreality in a printed text (here the evidence of the Moors murder case seems pertinent).

The literary historian asks a different question: is the theme of cruelty and the associated obsession with violence in some way related to the political character of the age? Genet, Norman Mailer, William Burroughs have said that the bestialities recounted in their work mirror the crisis of inhumanity through which we appear to be living since 1914. A literature which failed to reflect modern barbarism, the widespread return of torture in political life, the programmatic degradation of the human person in concentration camps and colonial wars, would be a lie. There is unquestionably a truth in this argument. But it is not easy to judge whether the literature of violence does not at times anticipate, almost conjure up the facts (Céline would be a case in point), and whether anything is gained by adding, even in phantasy, to the energies of the inhuman.

Where the modern imagination *has* gone deeper than that of any previous age (though the recognition itself is as old as Aeschylus) is in its depiction of love and sexual encounter as power relations. We know more plainly than before, because Strindberg, Proust, D. H. Lawrence, and Beckett have taught us, that sexual relations are, in the sphere of intimacy, a reproduction of conflicts, alliances, strategic manoeuvres as we find them in social and economic relations. The symbolic, psychosomatic links between sexuality and money are foreshadowed in Ben Jonson and explicit in Swift. But the close cross-hatching of social or economic metaphors with the 'spontaneities' of love is very much a part of the development of the modern novel. We locate it first in Balzac and George Eliot; it is superbly exploited in James's *The Wings of the Dove* and *The Golden Bowl*. Where erotic codes become more problematic, where power relations and the struggle for sexual domination sharpen, the sadistic motif — at its serious, tragic level — arises. Nowhere is the theme of erotic torment, this 'daily pathology' of love, more powerfully dramatized, more illuminatingly related to economic and class conflicts, than in John Cowper Powys's *A Glastonbury Romance*. The *Romance* and *Wolf Solent* mark perhaps the only 'advance', if such a term can be used, of the sexual imagination beyond Dostoevsky and Proust. The eroticism of Powys is at once more extreme and more delicate than anything we find in Lawrence, but it is obscured by a private, often portentous rhetoric. If it were better known, 'The River' chapter in the *Romance*, with its display of a 'cold-blooded and elemental lechery', would have focused many of the wonders and outrages lavished on the naiveties of *Lady Chatterley's Lover*. Like the famous suppressed chapter of *The Possessed*, 'The Iron Bar' in the *Romance* seeks out the dark common root of the nerve of cruelty and the nerve of desire. Owen Evans, like Powys himself, is half-crazed with sadistic imaginings. Cordelia Geard announces that she is with child:

> 'What shall we call him if he's a boy, Owen?' Her voice just then was more than he could bear. Nothing makes human nerves dance with such blind fury as a voice piercing the hollow of the ear at the moment when the will is stretched out like a piece of India rubber on the rack of indecision.
>
> 'Torture!' he shouted, sitting up in the purple chair and clutching its elbows furiously, while the rim of her hat was now completely crushed beneath him. 'We'll call him Torture; and if she's a girl we'll call her Finis, the End. For she'll *be* the end. And all is the end.'

There ensues one of the strangest, most compelling scenes of love-making in modern fiction. Ungainly, bewildered, yet instinctively clairvoyant, Cordy pulls off her clothes. She stirs 'some deep chord of excited desire in the man with the burning eyes'. Sexuality triumphs over sadism by enclosing it, by touching a common root, deep as life, inextricable as are within us the need to possess and the need to destroy.

It is not, however, in the treatment of deviance or sexual pathology that common sense would locate the most obvious, prodigal element of the new literary freedom. It is in the explicit rendition, particularly in the novel, of heterosexual intercourse. In a hundred years we have moved from the suggestive paraphrase of *Madame Bovary* – suggestive mainly in its hints of imitative cadence and in its invocation of symbolic props – to the following (two passages representative, current enough to have been chosen almost at random):

> It turned into a very serious session, no memorable jokes or clever ideas. He just stayed on top of her, embracing her buttocks to get her pressed against him and opening her cunt with his broad stiff staff. He got the head of his cock into the centre of her sex, and stayed on it, rubbed on it, without mercy ... Her spread legs pulled together and locked him to her, and her perspiring body got ready for the second time ... He fucked her until she was a hot river, until he could feel her not knowing or caring who or what the thing inside of her was ...[7]

> ... I turned her over suddenly on her belly, my avenger wild ... holding her prone against the mattress with the strength of my weight, I drove into the seat of all stubbornness, tight as a vice, and I wounded her, I knew it, she thrashed beneath me like a trapped little animal, making not a sound, but fierce not to allow me this last of the liberties, and yet caught, forced to give up millimetre by millimetre the bridal ground of her symbolic and therefore real vagina. So I made it, I made it all the way – it took ten minutes and maybe more, but as the avenger rode down to his hilt ... she gave a last little cry of farewell, and I could feel a new shudder which began as a ripple, and rolled into a wave, and then it rolled over her ...[8]

The chronology of the change, of the successive advances toward total explicitness, is complex and would repay detailed study. The work of Zola and Maupassant marked a deliberate expansion of sexual designation. In so far as it addressed itself to the physicality of man, to society as biologically determined, the entire naturalistic movement – Gorky, Dreiser, Hauptmann – tended to a new erotic frankness. When the 'breakthrough' comes, in *Ulysses*, in *Lady Chatterley's Lover*, in the writings of Céline and Henry Miller,

---

7. Harriet Daimter (pseud.): 'The Woman Thing', in *The Olympia Reader* (New York, 1965).

8. Norman Mailer: 'The Time of Her Time', in *Advertisements for Myself* (New York and London, 1959).

it does so on an explicitly linguistic level. The turn of sensibility toward a complete probing of sexual experience, the conviction that such experience is inseparable from the felt life of fiction, are manifest in Flaubert. The steps taken by Joyce or D. H. Lawrence are 'technical', though in a sense that involves an entire philosophy of language and literary form. The taboos challenged and exorcized are those of vocabulary. What passes in the 'place of excrement' and love itself are seen to be four-letter words, and are spelt out. What follows on Molly Bloom's reveries and the bucolics of Lady Chatterley is strictly inevitable, a *passage à la limite* in an almost algebraic sense. Given the new dispensation, each generation of fiction has gone a step further toward totality, towards *saying all* in words as graphic, as exact as the language can provide. There are stages on this *via amorosa*. William Faulkner's *Sanctuary* (1931) and realistic crime fiction, related as they are to film and pulp writing, introduce a new authenticity of erotic slang and a cold, precise bawdy. The American novel comes out of World War II charged with a graphic economy of speech. By the late 1950s the semantic battles fought by Joyce and Lawrence had been won. No word, no turn of phrase was inviolate or exempt from public use. In Doris Lessing's *The Golden Notebook*, one of the finest novels written in English since the war, Ella is shown in a mood not wholly unlike Jane Austen's Emma:

> Now she cannot sleep, she masturbates, to accompaniment of fantasies of hatred about men. Paul has vanished completely: she has lost the warm strong man of her experience, and can only remember a cynical betrayer. She suffers sex desire in a vacuum. She is acutely humiliated, thinking that this means she is dependent on men for 'having sex', for 'being serviced', for 'being satisfied'. She uses this kind of savage phrase to humiliate herself.[9]

The delicate comedy of the passage, a comedy distinctly akin to *Emma*, lies precisely in the fact that these phrases are not 'savage', that they echo a lost gentility, or rather a phase of mere 'adult frankness' before total explicitness.

The sociological and psychological correlatives of this 'frankness as never before' lie outside the scope of this essay. They are very large. What failures of nerve in humane literacy, what distrust of the imagination, has brought on this obsessive, philosophically naive investment in the word? How does the common use, and hence devaluation, of what were, for a long time, the

9. Doris Lessing: *The Golden Notebook* (London, 1962).

'private parts' of speech, the taboo idiom of intimacy or subterranean argot, relate to the much larger political, commercial, scientific assaults on privacy that mark our century? Or is there, on the contrary, an endeavour to strip such words of their numinous force, to bring language to daylight as Freud had brought the symbolic vocabularies of the unconscious? And in what way would such 'enlightenment' relate to mass democracy, to a society intent on levelling taste? For the sense of audacity registered by the writer — when and especially when he insists on breaking a previous verbal taboo — is not one felt by the less educated, less privileged classes. To them the discourse of love has long been monosyllabic. To what extent is the accelerated movement toward complete explicitness in literature only a logical consequence of a movement of all narrative forms toward the techniques of the cinema? In other words, is sexual frankness in prose fiction merely another attempt at 'verbal photography', at competing in language with the total *verismo* available to the camera and the tape-recorder? (In which context it is worth noting how closely the sexual revelations of such documentary records as Professor Oscar Lewis's *La Vida* now seem to resemble those imagined by novelists. The tape starts imitating the cliché of fiction.) What bearing has all this on the life of the imagination, a concept which has, I believe, a politically relevant and verifiable meaning? Already there is some evidence, though difficult to assess, of a standardization in sexual behaviour, of a decline from individuality and private discovery in this most inward, most vulnerable of psychic resources. Banality and brutality of idiom diminish the reach, the wondrous specificity of individual human consciousness. At the same time the new mythology of orgasm, of sexual prowess and ardent receptivity, may be setting standards of expectation, routines of high hope, in fact realizable by no more than a minority of human beings. So far as most ordinary men and women are concerned, the largesse and publicized splendours of the new sexuality are a lie, perhaps as corrosive as were the repressive daemonologies of puritanism or the cant (often exaggerated) of the Victorians.

The literary historian deals with smaller questions, though anyone seriously engaging problems of language touches on the human fact in its widest implications. How may one assess the effect of the new total freedom on the state of literary form, particularly of the novel?

In the art of Jane Austen a stylized idiom — stylized most coherently by what it excluded — served as a contract of permissible expectation between novelist and reader. The stability of vision which such a contract affords enabled the writer to work both economically and exhaustively; the area defined for imaginative penetration could be superbly exploited. But it was a limited terrain, better suited to the framework of stage comedy, with its necessarily public standards of speech, than to the new means and opportunities of the novel. Too much was left unsaid and, therefore, unrealized; or, more precisely, that which was excluded from the available vocabulary entailed additional omissions even wider in scope. Jane Austen's notorious indifference to the fierce historical, social crises which surround her life and her fiction is no accident, no contingent convention. It relates immediately to the exclusion of the new sense, so actively developing in the early nineteenth century, of the erotic and the unconscious. Jane Austen applies the same excluding idiom to the power relations of politics, class, and money as she does to those of sexuality — an idiom no longer consonant with the demands and possibilities of insight as we find them, say, in Stendhal. She keeps at bay, through a specific code of permissible expression, disorders of sensibility — erotic, financial, political — which would have marred the profound discipline and fineness of her design, but made of it a larger thing. The arrow that strikes Emma hits clean and sharp but passes too easily through a medium as thin and unambiguous as are the silhouettes prized by Jane Austen's genteel contemporaries.

The major, the 'classic' phase of the novel, as it extends from George Eliot to Conrad, the early D. H. Lawrence, and Thomas Mann, seems to me inseparable from a definite creative tension between idiom and consciousness in the erotic domain. When we consider *Middlemarch*, *The Portrait of a Lady*, *Anna Karenina*, *Nostromo*, *The Rainbow*, *The Magic Mountain*, we are made aware of a distinctive completeness of erotic intelligence. The novelist's view of the human person, of psychic processes, of the centrality of sexual experience, comes through to us at every point. Nothing germane to the psychological, social context need be omitted. The language of the novelist is comprehensive of all requisite perception; we sense immediately 'behind' or within it a formidable, entirely verifiable, gathering of felt knowledge.

'Behind' or within it; this is my point. The explicitness is complete but *internal*. The failure of the Karenin marriage is drastic; the hurt and specificity of sexual crisis presses on the reader. But such are the authority and density of the medium, of the world which Tolstoy builds around each imaginative fact, that the crisis is conveyed to us through the simplest of images — a fire dying in the grate. The threefold relationship of Isabel Archer, Madame Merle, and Gilbert Osmond draws on elements of sadism, of sexual torment, of voyeurism as raw as any in present fiction. We are allowed no escape from the cruel insistence of James's understanding. But again, the relevant statements are made 'internally'; it is the fullness and clear focus of invoked imagery, the control of relevant tone which informs, not the use of sexual terminology. The pathology of sex in Mann's novel is exact and pervasive. But the 'facts' about Claudia Chauchat or Mynheer Peeperkorn are communicated to us inside, as it were, the clarity, the strange cruel innocence of myth. No semantic 'photography' is required. Undeniably, this distance between sexual awareness and idiom did pose problems for the novelist. I have suggested that the proliferating symbolism and paraphrases of James point to an unresolved inadequacy of expressive means; a similar *malaise* may be accountable for the portentous lyricism and obliquity of some of Conrad. But in *Middlemarch*, in *Anna Karenina*, in *The Bostonians*, in *Sons and Lovers*, the tension between the known and the 'out-spoken' produces a shapely stress and poise of imagination. And it is, by necessary extension, a poise and stress which allows, indeed compels the inclusion in the novel of political, economic, social reality. If the classic novel has produced an image of society more adequately complex and informed than any other in literature or history, it is precisely because it extends to society, to life as a whole, the organic view it takes of human love or human hatred. Sexual intelligence, kept so by avoidance of the falsifications of gross, explicit vocabularies, becomes political intelligence in the truest sense – in the sense of Stendhal, George Eliot, Tolstoy and the early Lawrence.

The change to a new verbal freedom, the drive for complete designation, as it leads from *Lady Chatterley's Lover* to Norman Mailer, has brought changes to the metaphysic, if that term is allowed, of the novel – changes first discernible in Flaubert's view of *Madame Bovary*. The contemporary novelist controls his characters as the classic novelist does not. This is a difficult point to make clearly, but its meaning – as Tolstoy has testified when noting the autonomous, scandalous vitality and 'resistance' of his personages – is more than metaphoric. Every writer 'invents' and thus governs the agents of his fiction, but George Eliot, Henry James, and Tolstoy seem to leave around men and women a zone of unexplored freedom, a kind of inviolate spring of independent life. This effect derives, I believe, from a crucial notion of privacy. There are elements, particularly sexual elements, in their personages which the great novelists fully realize but do not verbalize. They seem to accord to their own imaginings a certain privilege of discretion. It is by virtue of a discretion closely similar to that which we show towards other human beings that the fictions of *Middlemarch* or *War and Peace* – complex, rounded, never wholly known or mastered – stay with us. George Eliot, Henry James, and Tolstoy allow us, demand from us, a serious collaboration, because they signify completely but do not say, let alone shout, all. They draw our sensibility into a collaborative response. We imagine and, in some modest degree, we 'create with them'. We are neither found out nor expertly embarrassed in the act of reading (such embarrassment of the reader being a characteristic tactic of the new eroticism). The novelist guards our freedom of imaginative life as he does that of his characters. In the 'new freedom' there is more than a touch of bullying. Our imaginings are programmed, obscene words are shouted at the inner ear. The new idiom has made it difficult to distinguish between integrity and mendacity. Of two passages quoted earlier, which is by a master of contemporary prose, which by a pseudonymous hack? Audacity, four-letter eloquence has rapidly become a cliché, a formulaic gesture as predictable as Petrarchan love-rhetoric and less varied. Loudness is poverty. *Doctor Zhivago* is not, at every point, a persuasive novel; we are asked to extend to the hero assumptions of poetic genius and corresponding political insight in fact appropriate only to Pasternak himself. Nevertheless, the relationship of Zhivago and Lara has assumed an almost magical authority in the modern poetics of love. Readers have felt here a maturity, a complete-ness of sexual realization hardly to be found elsewhere. Yet Pasternak's treatment is reticent in the extreme. His silences, like those of Tolstoy or Mann, seem to create meaning. The violences, the gusts of terror which surround Zhivago and Lara are as radical as any invoked in Mailer's *The American Dream* or in *Last Exit to Brooklyn*. We emerge from both shaken, and, perhaps, instructed. But by calling on us to imagine, to give echo from the experienced if unspoken truths of our own privacies, Pasternak leaves us freer than he found us. A sexual idiom free from compulsive literalness is, I think, vital to this liberating effect.

The present code of sexual explicitness may be related to the general *malaise* of the novel. The inhumanities of speech and action so obsessively reproduced in many important contemporary novels have, as their natural counterpoint, the 'non-humanity' of the *nouveau roman*. The human person is as splintered, as used and deformed in many modern novels as it is in certain schools of twentieth-century painting and sculpture. It is as absent from the *nouveau roman* (or at least its theories) as from non-representational art. We have added many words to the vocabulary of fiction and drama. We say and show all (or will do so next month, next week). Have we lost the curious wonder of an imagined living presence, the paradox of reality by which Anna Karenina or Isabel Archer outlive their begetters and will outlive us? The 'sexual revolution' in twentieth-century speech, literature, and graphic representation may, in the final analysis, be rooted in a much deeper transformation of values. It is the nature of the individual, of identity as a sustained act of privacy, and the relationship of the individual to the fact of death which may be altering profoundly as we move out of the middle-class phase of western history. The criteria of private sensibility, of literary survival, as they are implicit in post-Renaissance poetry and fiction, of a literate exchange between writer and reader, may belong to a receding, perhaps inevitably élitist past. The collective, cinematic future, the new codes of indifference now developing in regard to individual death or artistic fame, may render obsolete the conventions of literature as we have known them. These questions arise directly from any consideration of eros and idiom, but go far beyond it.

At the present juncture it would appear that 'total emancipation' has in fact brought a new servitude, that literature, and especially prose fiction, is less free, less confident than it was. The collapse of taboos has led to a frenetic search for new shocks, for extremes of speech or behaviour as yet unexploited.

This is an unfashionable view. And I reject – though very uneasily when it comes to sadistic writing – any form of imposed censorship. But one contemporary master, at least, is in favour of censorship, precisely on grounds of poetic freedom. Jorge Luis Borges writes:

> In distinction from mathematical or philosophical language, the language of art is indirect; its essential, most necessary instruments are illusion and metaphor; not explicit declaration. Censorship impels writers to use procedures which are of the essence ... A writer who knows his craft can say all he wishes to say without affronting the good manners or infringing the conventions of his time. One knows full well that language itself is a convention.[10]

The question is a difficult one, and censorship only a minor aspect. What is at stake is the education, the quickening of human feelings as against their diminution through simplification and brutality. Because it lies at the heart of consciousness, sexual experience offers both a denial and a challenge to the genius of language. It is through that genius that men have, at least until now, principally defined their humanity.

10. Jorge Luis Borges: 'Pornographie et censure', in *L'Herne* (Paris, 1964).

The Distribution of Discourse

Lévi-Strauss and other anthropologists conjecture that there are loquacious, word-spendthrift cultures, and cultures which are avaricious of speech and hoard language. This hypothesis is nearly impossible to verify. But obvious as they are, the obstacles to verification point to significant concepts and composites of opaque material. How would one define, for purposes of quantification, the sum of speech, of linguistic communication, of enunciatory action by verbal means, in a given society and at a given moment? What is the word-count of articulate exchange or discourse during a twenty-four-hour period for any 'speech-unit' or 'social-semantic cluster' of two or more human beings? Suppose we devised acoustic and tabulatory equipment capable of registering all speech-sounds in a determined time and place (such equipment has in fact been used to study some of the temporal variables in the flow of telephone messages). Would the numerical result be of any significance? There might be non-trivial points of comparison, as between social classes, the conspicuous consumption or retention of words as between men and women, the differing economics of verbal investment and output as between age-groups. Though it would pose delicate problems of interpretation (are the time and place chosen representative of the standard of speech-habitats, what corrective or constant ought one to introduce into the speech-curve in order to adjust to the differential weight of a highly developed, polysemic or allusive idiom as compared with more rudimentary monosyllabic conventions of diction, and so on?), the evidence might be well worth having. Yet even with the most sophisticated controls, such a summation and distributive analysis of verbal events would be radically incomplete. The most sensitive electronic count would register and tabulate only *external* speech.

With the exception of L. S. Vygotsky (whose investigations bear essentially on the genesis of linguistic competence in the very young child), linguists have given almost no thought to the formal characteristics, statistical mass, psychological economy or social specificities of *internal* speech. How often, under what lexical, grammatical and semantic categories and constraints, at what rate of flow, in which language (where the polyglot is concerned) do we speak to ourselves? Are there meaningful discriminations to be made between those modes of soliloquy in which there is a greater or lesser degree of attendant labial motion and those in which there is no such motion, at least at the observable level? Merely to pose these questions is to realize that inward speech is the *terra incognita* of linguistic theory and of psycholinguistic and sociolinguistic positivism. It is precisely the absence of a competing linguistic theory or body of experimental data which has provided the psychoanalytic language-model of Freud and of Lacan with a crucial area of contrivance. A reflection on the nature and history of human speech, a theoretical-statistical account of semantic totality, could well begin with the premise that the major portion of all 'locutionary motions', this is to say of all intentionalities of verbalization, whether audible or not, is *internalized*. This premise would lead to a number of fruitful inquiries.

The initial area would be genetic and motivational (the two being inseparable). The large majority of mythological and scientific conjectures on the origins of language posit the unexamined axiom of inter-personal communication. Whether in Hesiod, Humboldt or J. Monod, we find the implicit or enunciated supposition that the evolution of human speech is concomitant with, generated by, or creative of trans-individual societal behaviour. Through speech men communicate with one another, and such communication is the indispensable requisite and motor of all social or higher forms of action. The mutation to speech, with its reciprocal interactions as between function and capacity in the cortex, establishes man's humanity and pre-eminence in the organic order. The development of language would thus have been, in the Darwinian sense, the supreme adaptive advantage. Verbal exchanges between human speakers construct an informational environment more powerful and dynamic than that of nature. Indeed we have seen recently the growth of the concept of 'informational thermodynamics' in which the informational 'bit', with its analogues all the way from the alphabet, phrasing and punctuations of the genetic code to the most complex forms of language, would constitute the prime unit of energy.[1] Again the underlying axiom or model is societal, the current of articulate energy is outer-directed.

This need not be the case. It is entirely possible to envisage an evolutionary scenario in which the dynamics of survival would entail the early development of inner-directed and intra-personal address. Myths of mutual nomination, such as that of Jacob and the Angel, or of ordeals of self-identification and designation, such as that of Oedipus (both types being, I believe, variants on the same motif), seem to point towards a problematic,

---

1. cf. L. Brillouin: *Science and Information Theory* (London, 1962); *Scientific Uncertainty and Information* (London, 1964).

possibly millennially prolonged development of and struggle towards a working notion of singular identity (in schizophrenia, in the numerous pathologies of *dédoublement*, this notion is again subverted or made recessive). The confident scission between self and other, between 'I' and 'you', may well be an arduous, late achievement whose underlying economics are dialectical. Autonomy is diacritical to reciprocity. So that there can be semantic exchange distinguishable from echo there must be a determination of integral source. It may be that such determination is underwritten by speaking to oneself before, during or after linguistic encounter with another. Such monologue need not be unvoiced. The self-oriented or apparently objectless chatter of the very young and the very old may be a recapitulation of primal patterns of address. A whole range of causalities or conditions is conceivable: we speak to ourselves in answer to a limitless variety of external or somatic stimuli (hope, fear, self-castigation, self-encouragement); we speak to ourselves in order *not* to speak to others (the ubiquitous fairy-tale motif of those who whisper their compelling secrets into mute wells or under rocks illustrates one of the relevant mechanisms); we speak to ourselves to anchor our own presentness, to ground the threatened or elusive sense of self (soliloquy in the dark, in shock); we speak to ourselves to store the acquisitions of experience, to hoard and make inventory (to what degree is the history of the evolution and incision of memory, in its early stages at least, a history of self-address, of literal deposit by articulate import? The *ars memoriae* of the Renaissance is a branch of rhetoric); we speak to ourselves when engaged in language-play, this is to say in any of the manifold and disinterested – non-utilitarian, non-focused – modes of phonetic, lexical, syntactic experiment and transformation which are characteristic of the child, of 'automatic speech', or of poetry (a poem is first said inward). Each of these orders of motive or occasion is complexly functional in respect of the origins and conservation of the ego. In evolutionary terms, internal speech, in some probationary guise possibly related to the slow development of the neurophysiological instrumentalities of articulation, may have preceded external vocalization. Or it may have evolved as a necessary correlative to it. Or it may have come *after* public utterance as an absolutely essential safeguard of identity and of the private spaces of being (we will return to this point). Whatever the evolutionary chronology and intricacies of interaction, internal speech-acts are as important as external, societal speech-acts, and it is very likely that they represent the denser, statistically more extensive portion of the total distribution of discourse.

Can one trace this polarization in the growth of the individual? The most stimulating discussion on this point remains that between Vygotsky[2] and Piaget, who replied to Vygotsky's critique in 1936. Vygotsky held that in their ontogenetic development thought and speech have different roots. In the linguistic growth of the child, he found a pre-intellectual stage; correspondingly, there is a pre-linguistic stage in thought development. Up to a certain point in time, the two follow different and independent lines. It is when these lines converge that thought becomes verbal and speech rational. Differently from Watson,[3] Vygotsky found no evidence that inner speech develops in some mechanical way through a gradual decrease in the audibility of external utterance (the child's resort to whispering in his third or fourth year). Instead he proposed a three-phase model: external speech, egocentric speech, inner speech. In the latter 'the external operation turns inward and undergoes a profound change in the process. The child begins to count in his head, to use "logical memory", that is, to operate with inherent relationships and inner signs. In speech development this is the final stage of inner, soundless speech'. This development necessarily depends on outside factors. It is the child's exploration of the social aspects and functions of language that leads to the development of logic on which inner speech is based. Hence Vygotsky's conclusion that 'verbal thought is not an innate, natural form of behaviour but is determined by a historical-cultural process and has specific properties and laws that cannot be found in natural forms of thought and speech'. All our observations, argues Vygotsky,

> indicate that inner speech is an autonomous speech function. We can confidently regard it as a distinct plane of verbal thought. It is evident that the transition from inner to external speech is not a simple translation from one language into another. It cannot be achieved by merely vocalizing silent speech. It is a complex, dynamic process involving the transformation of the predicative, idiomatic structure of inner speech into syntactically articulated speech intelligible to others.

Thus inner speech is not the interior aspect of external speech. In it, according to Vygotsky, words die as they bring forth thought. It is a 'thinking in pure meanings. It is a dynamic, shifting, unstable thing, fluttering between word and thought, the two more or less stable, more or less firmly delineated components of verbal thought'. Below and beyond it lies the plane of 'thought

2. L. S. Vygotsky: *Thought and Language* (Cambridge, Mass., 1934, 1962).
3. J. Watson: *Psychology from the Standpoint of a Behaviourist* (New York, 1919).

itself'. In his concluding remarks, Vygotsky calls for an as yet unformulated 'historical theory of inner speech'.

One need not accept the entirety of Vygotsky's paradigm, with its methodologically and evidentially vulnerable emphasis on preverbal, pre- and extralinguistic 'thought', to appreciate the value of his focus on inner speech and the importance of the notion of a 'historical theory of inner speech'. The present essay is intended as a provisional and rudimentary contribution towards such a theory. It elides the substantive and terminological issues raised by Vygotsky's binary scheme of 'thought' and 'language'. It takes 'inner speech', the unvoiced soliloquy, the silent monologue, to signify and include all internalized motions of statement, whether these derive from a simple suppression of outward vocalization ('I am saying to myself that which I wish not or dare not say out loud') or from subconscious, 'pre-verbal' sources. What it seeks to stress is the application to internal speech-phenomena of the concept of historicity.

Merely to say this is to perceive that if we have histories of *la langue*, this is to say histories of the lexical and grammatical features which constitute the diachronic morphology of a human tongue, we have none of *la parole*. We know next to nothing of the genesis, institutionalization, transformations in the speech-conventions and habits of historical societies except in those highly specialized cases in which such conventions and habits are codified by writing (leaving aside, for the moment, the difficult question of the degree to which written forms ever codify the speech *milieu* in which they are composed). We do not know, or know only through the distorting glass of the written text, what men and women in a given historical time and place regarded as comprised in the areas of articulate verbal communication or what they regarded as 'inexpressible' for reasons which can range the whole way from mystical illumination to social taboo. What could one talk about or not talk about? If we seek to compare two communities or historical epochs, what can we surmise of their respective speech prodigalities or parsimonies? In the antique Mediterranean world, the Greeks were a byword for loquaciousness. It was said of the Romans (but the sources here may be suspect precisely because they are mostly Roman) that they cultivated laconic modes of utterance and prized taciturnity. What is the contrastive evidence worth, and would it allow even the crudest of quantifications (just how many more words 'flowed' in a Greek house or in the *agora* than in a Roman domestic setting or in the *forum*?). To stick with this one example for reasons of illustration: suppose the general report to have been valid, what of the crucial phenomena of repartition as between sexes, age-groups or social classes? Certain Greek women — precisely those few of whom literary and social anecdote has record — were celebrated for their eloquence. The Roman code, on the contrary, is that crystallized in Shakespeare's rendition of Coriolanus's greeting of Virgilia: 'My gracious silence, hail'. Recent scholarship, however, suggests that there were key spheres of activity — economic, familial, even religious — in which Roman women exercised a more forceful, more articulate role than did their Attic counterparts, and Juvenal's Sixth Satire does not seem to point to feminine quietness in the imperial city (we possess no history of noise-levels, of the decibels of word-volume in which different generations, societies and communities within the same societies have conducted their daily lives). What of children? Rule-of-thumb testimony, memoirs, the tales of travellers, adduce a mass of evidence on the subject. We are told of societies in which the child is incited to speak early and copiously, in which the babble of children is a source of adult satisfaction and amusement. Other periods and societies (the Lutheran manse, the Victorian brownstone) are characterized as repressive in respect of children's speech and voices. Here the rewards of adult approval go to extreme sparseness of response or silence. Chateaubriand's memoirs tell of an atavistic feudal *milieu* in which young children and even adolescents were bound to strict silence between late afternoon and the ritual, monosyllabic reply to parental benediction and dismissal at bedtime. How much temporal and geographical ground does such an account comprise? What of the servants' quarters? Quite obviously the statistics of speech-production and distribution have social determinants. It is in the nature of the case that almost all written records of linguistic behaviour stem from the literate and the privileged. 'History' has made mute the preponderant part of mankind. But in at least one cardinal domain, that of sexual speech, what evidence we have strongly suggests that the less literate and underprivileged classes of society, both urban and rural, knew a licence and wealth of accepted expression entirely inadmissible in middle- and upper-class contexts. Erotic taboos in language are class-bound. A laconic surface or ideal of linguistic consumption can have beneath it a spendthrift argot. Reciprocally, periods and societies whose literary achievements imply a formidable resource of lexical, grammatical and semantic means, may in fact be founded on under-pinnings of inarticulacy and even silence. What were the contrasts of articulacy as between the Elizabethan élite and the *beau monde* of the French eighteenth century on the one hand, and the respective mass of the rural population on the other? What was the average vocabulary and syntactic range available to the Castilian peasant at the time of Cervantes and Góngora?

What, moreover, are the causalities of change, the agencies of transformation which affect the 'locutionary total' of a given culture? The complexity of factors and uncertainty of evidence are such that it is difficult even to phrase one's questions plausibly. Even as it is among the most constant and ubiquitous of human acts, so speech is among the most susceptible to the modifications of the biological and social environment (it is probably an error to keep these two apart). There are intricate, deep-felt contiguities between obscurity and silence on the one hand and loquacity and light on the other. One of the principal metamorphoses in human affairs has been that brought on by the altering equation between the hours spent in darkness and those spent in light. To an extent often unnoticed by social historians, the great mass of mankind passed a major portion of its life in the varying shades of opacity between sundown and morning. The history of artificial lighting, from the palaeolithic hearth-fire to the neon of the modern metropolis, with its virtual mutation of night into a 'counter-day', cannot be separated from that of consciousness itself. In what ways have the conventions and statistics of linguistic exchange been modified by the voluntary prolongation of the lit portions of existence? Correlatively, in what respects has the evolution of the habitat, from open and collective spaces to the closed and even individual room – an evolution itself subject to crucial climatic, economic, sexual and ideological variants – affected the occasions, critical mass, volume and styles of discourse?

All these and a host of analogous questions pertain to what the French historians now call *l'histoire des mentalités* and of which Febvre's investigation of the sense of smell in sixteenth-century sensibility or Vovelle's attempt to map changing attitudes towards the remembrance and commemoration of death in a given community and religious-economic *milieu*, are pioneering examples. Because it is itself the dominant instrument of any such inquiry, the linguistic text and what can be gathered from oral traditions is often taken as an axiomatic constant. In fact, the modalities of language vary as complexly in dimension, form and distribution as do the data of human experience and conception which they embody. And if this is true of external speech, it is equally true of inner and inward speech. In short, the phenomenology of self-address is itself historical. If the audible speech acts of cultures, social classes, genders, age-groups and epochs change under the pressures of inheritance and environment (inheritance *is* environment), so do the inaudible, the internalized, the autistic. Even more than that 'historical theory of inner speech' asked for by Vygotsky, we need some idea of what the material for and towards such a theory would be.

This essay aims to initiate lines of thought on what appears to be a radical shift in the relative density and tenor of external and internalized speech-forms in the literate segments of western society between the seventeenth century and the present. It derives from the critical postulate that certain genres of writing are peculiarly related to inward discourse and give warrant to its prolixity. It might be profitable, on another occasion, to review this postulate in some detail.

The generation and emission of language by the individual both enacts and mirrors the power relations, the conventional and contingent hierarchies in the social unit. In middle- and upper-class families of the classic age, lines of force were manifestly concordant with primacies of age, gender and public station. Initiation of verbal activity, whether inquisitive, prescriptive or generally propositional, seems to have been one of the unexamined preroga-tives of men as distinct from women, of parents as distinct from children, of masters as distinct from servants (it is just the inversion of this latter code which creates the comic, challenging element in Molière's depictions of articulate, vocally peremptory servants and halting masters). The currency of words was largely minted and issued by the senior masculine presence in the given familial unit. The recurrent idealization, in poetry, in manuals of good conduct, in homiletic texts, of the softness of voice of 'good women', is a certain indicator of the privileged loudness of men. Conversely, we can document the suspicion largely held and enunciated in plays, satires and moral tracts that women, when among themselves, when out of masculine earshot, would literally erupt into conspicuous prodigalities of speech. The scenario is one of intense polarization by virtue of gender and setting. The hoard of words, the available resources of verbalization were essentially in paternal-masculine hands in the mixed familial situation; this same hoard could, as it were, be purloined and expended wastefully when women conversed among themselves and privily. The *salon*, as it begins during the seventeenth century, exactly defined a neutral ground: one on which men and certain elect women (such election being, however, ambiguous, in that it pointed to the blue-stocking, to the *frondeuse*, or to the 'emancipated' female) could claim and exercise equal rights of verbal instigation and response. The appeal for such rights is made poignant in *The Taming of the Shrew*, Act IV, scene iii, when Kate says:

> Why sir I trust I may have leave to speake,
> And speake I will. I am no childe, no babe,
> Your betters have indur'd me say my minde,
> And if you cannot, best you stop your eares,
> My tongue will tell the anger of my heart,
> Or else my heart concealing it will breake,
> And rather than it shall, I will be free,
> Even to the uttermost as I please in words.

The restriction here is subtle: the sole freedom possible to women in the classic order of familial-social primacies is, precisely, *in words*. But even Shakespeare, in terms charged with valuations of reciprocal speech-rights as old as the Pauline epistles, seems to give authority to Kate's final capitulation. And this capitulation once more underlines the dialectic of speech:

> Come, come, you froward and unable wormes,
> My minde hath bin as bigge as one of yours,
> My heart as great, my reason haplie more,
> To bandie word for word, and frowne for frowne;
> But now I see our Launces are but strawes ...

In *The Silent Woman*, Shakespeare's contemporary, Ben Jonson, drastically conjoins suggestions of sexual and verbal incontinence: 'She is like a conduit-pipe that will gush out with more force when she opens again.'

What is unmistakable is the general sense of the compression of speech-energies in women by virtue of masculine-imposed criteria of decorum. Such compression must be equilibrated by compensatory modes of release ('or else my heart concealing it will break'). It is, therefore, more than probable that the sum of utterance in the lives of women, notably of educated women, during the sixteenth and seventeenth centuries and almost until the partial collapse of the *ancien régime* of familial hierarchies in the late eighteenth century, was unequally divided between audible speech and various modes of self-address. Besides expending words on one another, with an inflationary abandon which men suspected and satirized, women were necessarily liberal of speech to themselves. But they also availed themselves of a second instrument of inaudible eloquence: the letter. Here, again, statistics are either roughly conjectural or fail us altogether. But the collation of evidence from direct witness, from personal memoirs, from the importance which education and prescriptive works on gentility and right conduct attribute to the epistolary arts, together with what survives of correspondence, points to a 'golden age' of letter-writing from the rise of feminine literacy during the latter sixteenth century to a period roughly preceding the First World War. And there is every reason to believe that in the totality of epistolary production and exchange, the feminine component was major. To a marked degree, the personal letter represented the most ready and acceptable guise in which women could act politically, socially, psychologically on society at large. The private escritoire, be it in the life of Madame de Sévigné or in that of any female character in the novels of Jane Austen, is the privileged locus of the linguistic industry and verbal dissemination of women. But in composing a letter one speaks first and foremost to oneself (nothing is more significant of the verbal destitution of the servile classes, particularly in small-town and rural circumstances, than the compelled resort to public letter-writers and their set formulas on even the most spontaneous, intimate occasions of erotic appeal or family sorrow). Thus the immense current of 'lettered discourse' embodies and represents, at only one remove, the concomitant richness of inner speech. The letters of the classic age are soliloquies *à deux*.

It is a sociological commonplace that ours is not or no longer a letter-writing culture. This observation does not bear on quantity (consider the plethora of administrative, commercial, bureaucratic mail), but on function and quality. An ancillary and complex factor is that of the decline in hand-writing. In ways which are not clearly analysable, the temporal and formative relations of hand-writing to inner speech are more harmonically co-ordinate and immediate than are those of impersonal mechanical transcription such as that of the typewriter. The silences, the quasi-ritual privacies which accompanied the constant and voluminous production of epistolary acts in former times are no longer a current part of personal usage. The modern personal letter is, except in special cases which are themselves often imitative of an archaic motion, ephemeral. An entire register of narrative, introspective, confessional, commemorative notation and articulation, of which the epistolary novel, which extends from the late Renaissance through *Pamela* and *La Nouvelle Héloïse* the whole way to Dostoevsky's *Poor Folk*, is the outward manifestation, has lapsed from normal awareness. It has been widely argued that the telephone call has replaced the personal written missive. Where one formerly wrote a letter, by hand, one now makes a telephone call. Quantitative studies, particularly with regard to the United States, show that in the total aggregate of telephone-speech of a personal category, the feminine component is paramount. Nor can there be any doubt as to the linguistic and gestural wealth and complication of the resultant communicative act. Investigations of the relevant range of volume, pitch, stress, speed and idiomatic adjustments indicate that there is a 'telephone language' with its own distinctive features and semiotic context (there are women who make up or dress before telephoning). The telephone has complex functions in courtship and sexual role-playing. It helps to codify the linguistic devices of reciprocal identification, acceptance or refusal within and between peer and age-groups. But its relations to inner language and to the furnishings of silence which encompass inner language differ radically from those of the personal letter. Though this cannot be proved, the intuitive supposition is worth putting forward that the crucial distinction is one of time sequence. There is, especially in the case of hand-writing, a definite time-lapse between internalized enunciation − the *pre-scriptive* procedure of sentence or phrase-construction − and the externalizing movement of the hand. In the swift reciprocities of a telephone conversation, the temporalities of interior-exterior transfer are probably much more rapid and immediate. There may be an internalized rehearsal of reply by the listener (he is speaking his rejoinder to himself while listening to the voice of the caller); or there may be, particularly where teenage or feminine virtuosi of the medium are concerned, a near-abolition of the pre-scriptive plane. The language-stream is rapid, unmediated and semantically provisional − this is to say that meaning can at every moment be recalled, modulated, subverted by intonation. To anticipate the general finding of this essay, the personal letter in its classic phase cultivates and refines the inventory of inner discourse, whereas the telephone conversation consumes and vacates the reserves of inwardness (the telephone monologue, such as certain playwrights have used it for either tragic-solipsistic or comic purposes, would represent a problematic, fascinating intermediary between classic and modern types of self-expression).

The interactions of language and sexuality constitute one of the essential dynamics in the human condition. The plane of being on which these interactions occur is at once so vital and so complex that it negates the ordinary differentiations made between the psychological and the somatic, the spiritual and the neurochemical. The cardinal notion is that of a 'script'.[4] At any given instant, the composite of sexual behaviour is made up of an

4. cf. J. Gagnon: *Human Sexualities* (New York, 1977).

entire spectrum of determinants: there are implicit or explicit social conventions which will help to shape even the most private, seemingly instinctive
performance; there are physiological constants, but these too seem to have
their historicity and their social-psychological variants; there are super-
structures of expectation, fantasy, moral coding which precede, envelop
and classify the existential data. Together these form the script within or
against which men and women enact their sexualities. In this script, the
speech-components are pervasive and penetrating. A voluminous mythology, much of it verbally formulated and transmitted, precedes the fulfilment of homo- or heterosexual impulses. The scenario of excitement
which stimulates and focuses the libido is, to a large extent, verbal, and
there is every reason to suppose that there are structural analogies between
and interactions of onanism and unvoiced soliloquy (onanism is a mode of
autistic address). It is the sexual and the scatological in close contiguity, love
having 'pitched its mansion in the place of excrement', which energize a
substantial portion of taboo, underground and argotic parlance. It is, very
likely, one of the more sensitive markers of the differentiations in the speech
patterns of social classes, that this portion was, traditionally, externalized by
the lower and internalized by the more privileged strata of the community.
So close and mutually informing are the relations between sexuality and
language, that certain social anthropologists categorize both as being
branches of an encompassing semantic. The fundamental possibilities of
sexual relations, together with the concomitant prohibitions (incest), would
have developed inseparably from the terminological and grammatical means
of requisite designation (the exchange of words and that of women constitute analogous grammars, through them social consciousness is made
articulate).

We know little of the history of successive sexual scripts. Evidence is
suspect just because it is evidence – so much of the critical material being,
almost by definition, private and even subconscious. Were middle-class
young women in the nineteenth century as ignorant of sexual terminology
and facts as romantic and Victorian homilies, novels, memoirs would have
us believe? Is it conceivable, as some social psychologists have maintained,
that female orgasm is itself a relatively late, historically-coded phenomenon,
brought on not by inevitable physiology but by the gradual development
of 'neuro-sociological' (we lack the proper term of compaction) expectations
and awareness? To what degree is the relative distribution of sexual discourse
between private and public, between socially-licit and clandestine, between

genteel and argotic, a reliable guide to the study of erotic behaviour? At best, one proceeds tentatively.

For reasons which may be related to the new modes of domestic hygiene, to the contraction and economic formalization of the 'nuclear' family, to the fascinating and widespread reorientation of personal existence from the outside (the street, the common) to the interior of the house, the late sixteenth and early seventeenth centuries witness a sharp diminution in the area of permissible erotic speech and gesture. The Reformation is simultaneously a cause and beneficiary of this reduction. Rabelais, who still knew the old festive order, Montaigne and Shakespeare are the foremost observers of this modulation towards gestural and verbal constraint. Articulate bawdy becomes the ambiguous prerogative of the anarchic and servile elements in society. The official script is one of reticence or professed ignorance. The manufacture of pornography is so vital and inventive – notably during the eighteenth and nineteenth centuries – precisely because 'surface' discourse operates within a generally enforced contract of denotative and inferential propriety. If the pragmatics and fantasy-life of sexuality are allowed overt linguistic expression, such expression is almost neutralized by the ritual of occasion: the military mess, the gentlemen's smoker, the bachelor's pre-nuptial *souper*. On open ground, between adult men and women, the script is one of silence or edulcorating paraphrase (the 'language of flowers', the lexicon of pastoral, the blushful idiom of the valentine). Sensibility is expurgated, often masking the economic motives and brutalities of treatment which characterize the facts of married life (*Daniel Deronda*, *The Portrait of a Lady* are masterly documents of the dissociation between spoken and felt life, between roseate idiom and crass circumstance). When this script alters, it does so at surprising speed. Though any such dating is absurd, one would want to single out the tea-time in Bloomsbury when Lytton Strachey, observing a stain on Vanessa Bell's gown, threw out the immense single query: 'Semen?'

We are too near to the sources of this revolution in word and feeling, we are too intimately a part of it, to arrive at any confident aetiology. The breakdown of the high bourgeois-mercantile order in Europe, under stress of world war and economic crisis, is obviously a part of the cause. But more subterranean currents of revolt and positivity were at work. Among these psychoanalysis and the behavioural sciences are pre-eminent. We know now that psychoanalysis is, inescapably, a branch of applied linguistics. Freud, and Lacan after him, are 'meta-linguists', claiming to elicit the true meaning of meaning. We need not be concerned here with the growing realization that the Freudian theory and *praxis* of semiology was founded on an absurdly restrictive material base: that of the speech-script, extreme literacy, allusive conventions of middle-class diction among Central Europeans (mainly women) in the brief period from the 1880s to the 1920s. Nor need we engage the problem of the therapeutic undecidability of the analytic process (when is analysis 'completed', in what way could a cure be verifiably defined?). The paramount fact remains: psychoanalysis, directly and through its saturation of the climate of educated discourse and imagining, has radically shifted certain speech-balances. Revelation, audible utterance, externalization of even the most inward intentionalities and occlusions, either to the analyst-auditor or to others in society, or to oneself, has been made an instrument and validation of authenticity ('frankness as never before', wrote Pound). Free association is a device exactly calculated to pierce the membrane between inner and outer speech, to deflect into the diagnostic light and echo-chamber the unpremeditated rush and shadows of self-colloquy. It is a Freudian postulate that the motor-energies and referential tactics of the inward speech thus externalized and glossed will be primarily sexual. Even though this postulate has been qualified or partly abandoned by subsequent analytic schools, its effects on the erotic-semantic script have been decisive. So far as middle-class usage is concerned, particularly in the United States, the taboos enforced since the Renaissance have been lifted. If anything, explicitness of sexual pronouncement carries with it positive markers of adult poise and candour. The media have led and reflected the way. Some four centuries of assumed or explicit censorship have collapsed nearly overnight in the domain of printed texts, stage-plays, films and the entire gamut of mass media. It is not easy to suggest any class of linguistic material or depiction which would still be subject to effective inhibition. The news-stand, the sex-emporium and the art of the novel after the failed prosecution of *Lady Chatterley's Lover* in 1962 represent a profound innovation (or reversion) in the psychosomatic environment, in the spaces of feeling and expression in which we conduct our affairs or dreams.

The consequences for the history of inner speech are, most probably, those of a drastic reapportionment. This would be most dramatically so in the case of middle-class women, many of whom will have passed within a generation from zones of near-silence or total inwardness in respect of sexual language to a *milieu* of permissiveness and, indeed, of competitive display. But the change would be scarcely less marked in the experience of the middle-class adolescent, and of numerous adult males (especially those lacking experience in the army barrack). Words, phrases, carnal exactitudes which were formerly unvoiced or which were reserved, kept numinous and pristinely exciting for occasions of utter intimacy and initiation (the lover teaching the beloved certain expressions, asking him or her to repeat them in a litany of complete trust), are now loud from every page, film-screen and hoarding. The night-words are the jargon of morning and noon. The statistically oriented investigation into sexual behaviour, from Havelock Ellis to Kinsey and Masters and Johnson, has brought with it a fundamental impetus to publication, to making public in the full sense of the term. No less than the psychoanalyst, though within an entirely different methodological framework, the sociological interviewer, the social worker, the marriage counsellor, the spokesman in group therapy, elicit and reward the emission, the detailed externalization of what was once inchoate and private.

These mutations in script and value, in sense and sensibility, are far too manifold to judge peremptorily. What is involved is the pivotal concept of the economy of self. This economy depends on the allocation of mental and nervous resources as between the private and the public, the interior and the exterior, the autonomous and the collectively focused aspects of our being. It involves the complex equations of solitude and gregariousness, of silence and of noise which seem to regulate the 'tuning', the *Stimmung* as Heidegger would say, of identity. In this economy, the relative densities of inner and outer discourse and the dialectics of tension between these densities, play a significant part. Unquestionably, the proportions have altered massively, and in favour of the outside.

The receptor of the interior vocative can be one of the multitudinous fictions of the self: 'conscience', the 'sardonic narker', the 'empathic witness', 'the encourager', or any of a great range of accomplice or monitory personae (in the Thai language there is a special pronoun used when addressing oneself). It can be a presence drawn from either the living or the dead, or a composite of real and imagined figures. Customarily this lodger and listener inside will answer back. There is one significant exception in which the most intense of soliloquies and unvoiced speech-currents can assume a dialectical structure: the address of the self to God, whether it be in the mode of prayer, meditation or report. Except in the case of the illuminate and the mystic, no articulate reply is expected. But the implicit discourse is not unfocused, it is not freely associational as in the therapy situation. On the contrary, it is highly structured and historically coded. Unvoiced invocation to the deity is, presumably, a primal and universal element in all religious experience. But in the history of religions, as in that of language itself, there have been variations of stress as between externalized collective utterance and the inaudible colloquy of the individual and the numinous presence. The energies of domesticity (the turn towards and into the private room), the emphasis on individuation, the notion of psychic resources as being a capital worth amassing and investing prudentially, mark the movements of religious reform and the concurrent emergence of the modern middle classes during the sixteenth and, especially, during the seventeenth centuries. The seventeenth century can be documented as having been the classic period of inward religious address. We cannot dissociate virtuoso performances of sustained inward concentration such as the meditations of Pascal, the analytic introspections of Descartes or the monologues of ecstasy in St John of the Cross, from a much wider executive form and practice. Within a mould of silence and privacy, the sensibility of the seventeenth century, in both its Reformation and Counter-Reformation guise, trained itself to achieve extraordinary intensities, durations and translucencies of autonomous, unspoken eloquence. This training has its deliberate pedagogic aspects. There is a considerable literature consisting of manuals of meditation, of progressively more arduous and prolonged exercises in silent concentration and exact focus. Baruzzi's magisterial study shows how the transcendent flights of ecstatic immediacy in St John of the Cross, the augment of mortal speech into the 'grammar of light' before God, are generated by strict, perfectly rational drills and disciplines.[5] The exercises prescribed by Ignatius of Loyola aim to make of the wilful and disseminated bursts and eddies of interior speech a sharply vectored, unwavering thrust. The analogy would be that of a laser beam so rigorously directed to the object of meditation — a sentence in a text, an iconic presentment of the saintly or divine presence, some precise feature of the Deity — as to allow no scatter. The spaces of introspective notice are to be cleansed of all except the chosen target. Such elimination of interference, of the phenomena of scatter and waste which characterize the normal streams of consciousness can only be achieved by severe training and conscription of will. Where it is accomplished, there occurs that phenomenological reduction to pure apprehension, to absolute grasp (Husserl's phenomenological exercises are explicitly related to the disciplines of Cartesian meditation) which enables the individual to engage in an authentic 'dialogue of one', between 'self and soul' as the baroque often phrases it, between self and God.

5. Jean Baruzzi: *Saint Jean de la Croix et le problème de l'expérience mystique* (Paris, 1924).

Linguistically, this mode of address is paradoxically public. Though stringently private and solitary in its setting, and solipsistic in its psychological means, the internalized rhetoric of the mystic, of the meditator, of the Puritan ponderer on Scripture is precisely that: a rhetoric. We know from the exercises proposed for purposes of training, as well as from the numerous testimonials of 'inner pilgrimage' (of which Bunyan's is exceptional only in regard to narrative richness), that inner discourse has its tropes, its topics, its taxonomies of pathos, no less than does voiced address and eloquence. The ultimate intimacies of the speaking ego, the self in its final nakedness, are semantically formal. There is, so far as word and syntax go, a confessional propriety, a decorum *in extremis* which distinguishes the acceptable styles of invocation and self-analysis from the anarchic, vainglorious falsities of unmediated discourse indulged in by 'enthusiasts' of every breed (the Ranters, the babblers in Adamic tongues). In his chamber the silent soliloquist with and towards God, is soberly attired; his 'privity' aims at awesome communion. His unvoiced idiom, too, is garbed. It has, even in 'the spirit's lamentation', its logical armature which, notably in the reformed and Puritan worlds, was that taught by Ramus's *Dialectic*.

Again, quantification is impossible. One knows that in monastic orders and during periods of secular retreat, such as were widely practised throughout the sixteenth and seventeenth centuries, silence and its accompaniment of internal exegetic, examinatory or meditative speech predominated. One has grounds for supposing that the weight of quiet in the Calvinist, Puritan and Pietist households and the consequent inflection towards internalized modes of articulation, was considerable and may, in many instances, have tipped the balance of the day. This would also have been the case in the quasi-monastic conditions of Spanish courtly and genteel existence (of which the exercises of Loyola seem to have been a close reflection). The Pauline injunction to women's silence *in ecclesia* may have been matched by the sparsities of speech of the Puritan *pater familias* and the notorious taciturnity of the *hidalgo* (both strategies are ironized in Shakespeare's Malvolio). We do not have enough reliable evidence to tell. But what cannot be overemphasized is the effect of generations of schooled introspection, of self-probing discourse, on the subsequent development of modern literature and of the modern typologies of personality. If the numbing silences of Scottish, Victorian and Lutheran Sundays are a direct legacy of seventeenth-century linguistic autism, so are the modern novel and the lyric of self-revelation. With the very gradual decline of formal religiosity in common life or, more exactly, with the partial metamorphoses of this religiosity into more generally 'humanistic' and worldly configurations of feeling, came a shift in the focus of self-address. Throughout the later seventeenth century we find a deepening fascination with the complexities of the ego, complexities not to be disciplined or even negated in the interest of immediacies of religious encounter, but on the contrary to be mapped and cultivated for their own sake. The prose novel, whose beginnings are so characteristically those of the fantasy-journey or of the epistolary dialogue, is the product of this fascination. And many of its early triumphs, such as the fictions of Rousseau, of Jane Austen, of the Brontës, directly embody the techniques and rhetorical conventions developed in previous periods of religious-ethical introspection and confessional notation. Concomitantly and against express prohibition (the reading of fiction on the Sabbath being deemed, in protestant households, a direct breach of the divine compact, almost to our own day), the novel takes over those functions and instrumentalities of analysis, of moral-psychological mapping and discrimination, of silent converse, which were once the staple of the sermon, of the exegetical tract, of the manual of spiritual exercises. It is the genius of the Joycean interior monologue to make articulate within itself the entire moral and technical history of self-discourse, and it is no accident that Joyce works out his idiom with specific reference to Jesuitical procedures of meditational, unvoiced elocution.

The concentration on what Gerard Manley Hopkins called 'inscape' found transcription into another textual register even more immediate to the pulse of inner speech than is the novel. We have no count of the millions, of the tens of millions of words set down by men and women in private diaries and journals during the golden age of the genre, from the early seventeenth century to the years just after the First World War (this terminal date is bound to be conjectural). The implicit or explicit, subconscious or conscious orders of motivation, of receptive intention can vary the whole way from a journal such as that of the Goncourts, conceived to be read by the world at large 'one day', to the self-dramatizing privacies of diaries set down in cipher. The styles of address, of titular location between writer and reader exhibit the same variousness. Dorothy Wordsworth's journals are brilliant trials of perception and notation, endeavours of the transported, sensorily sharpened self to submit to the reflecting and critical ego the data of ecstatic experience. The inward dialogue in Henry James is pursued between the restive, recalcitrant persona of the baffled or disenchanted craftsman, often imagined as *mon vieux*, and the super-id, as it were, of moral-aesthetic commitment and material compulsion. Kafka's diaries are part of an extremely complex, almost patho-logical discipline of self-distancing, of self-estrangement, in which the man and the writer construe between themselves those modes of haunted imper-sonality which organize Kafka's parables and tales. The massive journals kept by Cosima Wagner are a ritual self-dedication to the Master's arduous service, yet also an ambiguous ritual in that they presume an unknown but sympa-thetic reader who will, in future, bear witness to the depth of the writer's sacrifice, to the expense of spirit in abnegation. All these are public peaks of a literally incommensurable hidden industry. When fully published, Amiel's mid-nineteenth-century journal, almost certainly meant only for his own eyes, will run to some sixteen thousand closely-printed pages. The diaries of Virginia Woolf are reputed to comprise some twenty volumes. Wars, accident and social dislocation have certainly destroyed a mass of documentation; a comparable mass remains unpublished, in the family attic, in the bank-vault, in the never-looked-at Regency or Victorian personal album with its marbled boards or tooled leather and clasps. Again, the role of women diarists in the total aggregate may well have been paramount. The young girl's journal, the often stylized mirror of guarded intimacies (whose exchange with that of the husband on or just before marriage constitutes so obvious a sexual-semantic equation) appears to have been a staple of genteel upbringing. It is in her most secret diary, as Balzac, George Eliot, Turgenev narrate, that the young wife and mother voices the epiphanies, disappointments or raw sorrow of her condition. Barred from public expression of political, ideological and psychological conviction or discovery, the intelligent woman in the *ancien régime* and nineteenth century makes her journal the forum, the training ground of the mind. The man, in turn, may confide to the trusteeship of his diaries material of an as yet socially inadmissible category, particularly in respect of sexual experience, whether actual or fictive (Michelet's intimate journals are a striking but by no means isolated case). The point is worth stressing: methodologically and in substance, much of what still passes for social history and for the scholarly reconstruction of the climate of sentiment, of the literacies of psychological awareness before Freud and modern 'emancipation' is, probably, inaccurate: it overlooks the sophistications of social-psychological insight and data contained in the fantastically loquacious world of the diary. This is so especially of the analyses of dreams set down voluminously in this private mode.

Loquacity, copiousness and temporal duration characterize the idiolects of diary-writers. But here, as in the intimate records of self-correction, of the keeping of private accounts before God common to the seventeenth century (the massive diaries of Kierkegaard exactly mark the transition from the heuristic-meditational to the modern vein), the stream of speech is inward. The rhetorical structures are unvoiced, the acts of self-address are performed in silence (innumerable journals tell of the privileged nocturnal hours in which the writer turns from the tumult of the domestic or public day to the healing silences of the self). Once more, we are dealing with linguistic production whose lexical and grammatical conventions may closely mirror those of external, audible utterance – this is not always the case, as we know from coded diaries and from journals set down in partly infantile, partly 'made-up' vocabularies – but whose statistical extent and intentionality belong to the shadow-side of discourse. And once again, separations by gender and social class seem to have been critical: the productivity of women in this sphere was probably preponderant, and that of the lower classes, even where individuals were technically literate, seems to have been very scant (the 'diary of the chambermaid' is, with very few known exceptions, a fiction of male erotic fantasy). Thus we find a distribution of discourse with a strongly internalizing factor.

It is impossible to say with any confidence whether or not the diary habit has declined generally. For what it is worth, it is one's impression that this is indeed so. The tempo of the middle-class day, the new licences and positive valuation given to every kind of intimate 'publication' and self-expression, the decay of hand-writing – a phenomenon whose socio-psychological implications have been little explored – the complex but radical changes in the whole theory and *praxis* of privacy – all these point towards the gradual erosion of the diary medium. Great twentieth-century diaries, such as Gide's, are highly self-conscious, even archaicizing gestures (in Gide's case, reference to the Pascalian precedent is constant). The diaries of modern politicians and diplomats are, in fact, public papers which observe a convention of temporary discretion. Techniques of therapeutic externalization have essentially replaced the role of the diary in the conservation of interior poise, in the defusing of potentially contagious elements of fantasy-life and psychic suggestion. Here again, a covert but consequential alteration has taken place in the respective dimensions and authority of outer and inner speech.

One further aspect of this change needs mention. A hierarchical order, a classic social structure defines itself and articulates its power relations in reference to a shared syllabus of texts. These can, as in the case of republican

Rome, be prophetic and juridical; they can, as in the Enlightenment, be stylistic and philosophical; the shared syllabus of the Victorian ruling caste is that of the Authorized Version, of certain Latin classics, notably Horace and Virgil, of the Book of Common Prayer and of the axis of national poetic genius as it runs from Shakespeare and Milton through Gray to Tennyson. But in each case, the crucial device is that of a consensual echo formed by generally available citation from, allusion to, inference of, one or more of the canonic texts. This device depends, in large part, on a mnemonic base. We have alluded to the *ars memoriae* used by late medieval and Renaissance disciplines in the mental ordering and retention of knowledge. It can be said that the education of the European lettered men and women, particularly of men, from the grammar and monastic schools of the sixteenth century, through the *lycées*, *gymnasia* and public schools of the nineteenth century, almost to the present, was also an *ars memoriae*. In it, learning *by heart* (an idiom worth thinking about) was the dominant method and aim. The almost implausible mnemonic feats of a young Macaulay, who knew a fair measure of the western classics by heart before entering university, have biographical notoriety. But something approaching this degree of trained recall was, in fact, the norm of middle-class political and intellectual literacy. Recall by heart of extensive tracts of classical verse and biblical narrative or prophecy was the assumed guarantor of civil, intellectual and even private exchange. The profound effects of this training and usage of memory on the architecture of sensibility and on the organization of speech have never been investigated adequately. But they were, quite obviously, considerable. To take only the English case, we know from diaries, journals, private memoirs, correspondence and reports of conversation, how deeply the habits of perception and reference drawn from Horace or Virgil, from Scripture or Shakespeare, reached into the life and utterance of the mind. Again and again, though the diarist or speaker may be unconscious of the fact, apparently native and unpremeditated testimonies of personal feeling take on a canonic guise (domesticity and old age are voiced in the manner of Horace or Catullus, men wax jealous to the cadence of Othello; when the Brontës or George Eliot record their innermost tribulations and resolutions they do so, often unawares, in the precise idiom of Ecclesiastes, the Psalms or the Pauline epistles). In short: inner consciousness and speech are made dense with, are charged by, the specific imprint of literacy on remembrance (and it is on this referential literacy, as it reaches to the very roots of the subconscious, that so much of Freudian decoding relies).

Nowhere has the change in the values and practices of western middle-class culture been more readily observable. Progressive and populist ideals of education can nearly be defined by virtue of their opposition to 'learning by heart'. The electronically expressed and inventoried 'information explosion' has been such as to make the mnemonic means of the ordinary brain inadequate and unreliable. There is no longer, moreover, a widely agreed canon of exemplary texts, dates or recognitions. Mappings of what it is that a man or woman must know, must know well enough to call at once to mind to refer to, imply manifestly or cite, are now as diverse and reciprocally polemic as are ideologies or ethnic-political identifications. Even where vestiges of such an agreed syllabus and echo-repertoire exist, the changes in the structures of leisure and attention, the magnified exposure of individual attention to the information-avalanche and synchronic immediacies of the media, leave little time and little natural space for the cultivation of memory. In many politically ecumenical and technologically oriented school systems, notably in the United States, the education of the young is planned amnesia (for reasons of censorship, of vital oral tradition, and of the relatively backward state of the electronic mass-media, the Soviet Union and eastern Europe represent a challenging exception; that which is known by heart, from literature, from history, plays a crucial part in the survival of individual and social integrity). In the West, we carry far less inner ballast than did the literate caste, the shapers of spirit and of speech, in preceding generations. Here again, the material and moral desolation of the First World War and its aftermath seem to mark a watershed.

To summarize: the totality of human linguistic production, the sum of all significant lexical and syntactic units generated by human beings, can be divided into two portions: audible and inaudible, voiced and unvoiced. The unvoiced or internal components of speech span a wide arc: all the way from the subliminal flotsam of word or sentence-fragments which, presumably, are a perpetual current or currency of every phenomenology of consciousness, sleeping and waking, to the highly defined, focused and realized articulacy of the silent recitation of a learned text or of the taut analytic moves in a disciplined act of meditation. Quantitatively, there is every reason to believe that we speak inside and to ourselves more than we speak outward and to anyone else. Qualitatively, these manifest modes of self-address may enact absolutely primary and indispensable functions of identity; they test and verify our 'being there'. Taken together, internal and external discourse constitute the economy of existence, of our presentness, in a way which philosophers, from Heraclitus to Heidegger, have characterized as quintessentially human.

This paper has suggested that there is a history, a morphology, a rhetoric of inner speech as there is of outer. The relationships of internal language to the environment are dialectical, precisely as are those of voiced utterance; they help to create the world of experience and, at the same time, reflect it. The very notion of history entails that of change. In the case of inward speech, this change can be twofold: the relative proportions of inner and outer address within the semantic whole can alter, and there can be transformations in the functions and composition of the internalized mode. As would be the case in any dynamic composite, these two sorts of change will tend to be congruent. Function and structure will alter with proportion. But the point needs refinement: the total quantity of internal speech acts, their mean rate and frequency may well be a constant of the entropy of the psyche. What has changed will be the relative intensity and significance of these acts in proportion to outward discourse, and their morphology.

There is evidence that such a change has taken place between the late sixteenth and seventeenth centuries, which may have been the classic age of soliloquy, and the speech-sensibility of the present. Certain absolutely key aspects of the relative distribution of psychological and social identity and value as between private and public, unvoiced and declared, religious and secular, have been more or less drastically modified. The contribution of women, of the young, of the economically and socially less advantaged levels of the community to the aggregate of enunciation, has sharply increased. Seminal areas of self-enclosure, of a social contract of mutually agreed taciturnity, on sex, on the life of fantasy and nervous tension, but also on monetary affairs (the taboo on the discussion of one's earnings or real wealth), have been opened up to examination and avowal. Today, the stress is on 'saying all', on telling 'how it is', in explicit rebuttal to what are regarded as archaic, class-determined, uptight atavisms of censorship and decorum. Concurrently, there has been a marked decline in those techniques of concentrated linguistic internality which went with religious meditation, methodical introspection and learning by heart (it is striking to what extent the pseudo-oriental practices of meditation now in vogue in the West, and among the children of a pulverized middle class, aim at ideals of verbal minimalism, of image rather than word, of sonorous vacancy; in current sensibility this part of Asia is remote from the scholastic nicety and discursive wealth of Cartesian, Pascalian or Kierkegaardian descent into the self). The approved loquacities of psychoanalysis, of mundane confession, as they are practised in modern therapy, in modern literature, in competitive gregariousness and in the media, go directly counter to the ideals of communicative reticence or autonomy represented by the private letter, diary or journal. The telephone consumes, with utter prodigality, raw materials of language of which a major portion was once allocated to internal use or to the modulated inwardness of the private, silently conceived written correspondence. One is tempted to conclude that where much more is, in fact, being heard, less is being said.

The concept of an economy of and within personal identity is teleological, this is to say that it implies aims of equilibrium. The creative well-being of an organic system depends on intricate balance between stimulus and repose, between use and recuperation. This balance, in turn, derives from adjustments between inner and outer environment. Language constitutes both in the most immediate and dynamic sense. It is the pulse and skin of conscious being. It draws its energies from interactions of silence and noise, of emission and retention, of containment and disclosure, far more complex and topologically ingenious than any we can imagine, let alone map. Rudimentary as they are, our diagnoses of autism, of aphasia, of speech disorders that range from extreme inhibition to ungovernable flow, tell us that these interactions are acutely vulnerable. Arguably, the most crucial of these reciprocities is that between outer and inner discourse, between the inter-personal and intra-personal dimensions in the linguistic whole. If this is so, a change of relative weight is one that would affect the personality of the individual and his stance in the world.

This essay has put forward the thought (the variousness and ambiguous tenor of the evidence are such as to allow no categorical or conclusive formulation) that the shift in the balance of discourse since the seventeenth century has been *outward*. There would seem to have been a concomitant impoverishment in the articulate means of the inward self. We have lost a considerable measure of control over the fertile ground of silence. Expending so much more of our 'speech-selves', we have less in reserve. In a sense that fully allows the play on meaning, the centre of gravity has been displaced, and we bend outward, mundanely, from the roots of our being. One might almost define the decline of a classic value-structure, as felt in the Renaissance and seventeenth century, and active still among the literate until the great crises of world war and social revolution, as being a shift from an internalized to a voiced convention of personality and utterance. Whether it is this shift, rather than any political-economic crises, that underlies the widely debated but little-understood phenomena of anomie, of alienation, of anarchy of feeling and gesture in the current situation, is a question worth raising.

➤ *Speech as Translation* ➤

Since Saussure, linguists distinguish between a diachronic (vertical) and synchronic (horizontal) structure of language. This distinction applies also to internal translation. If culture depends on the transmission of meaning across time — German *übertragen* carries the exact connotations of translation and of handing down through narrative — it depends also on the transfer of meaning in space.

There is a centrifugal impulse in language. Languages that extend over a large physical terrain will engender regional modes and dialects. Before the erosive standardizations of radio and television became effective, it was a phonetician's parlour-trick to locate, often to within a few dozen miles, the place of origin of an American from the border states or a north-country Englishman. The French spoken by a Norman is not that of the Touraine or the Camargue. *Hoch-* and *Plattdeutsch* are strongly differentiated. Indeed, in many important languages, differences of dialect have polarized to the degree that we are almost dealing with distinct tongues. The mutual incomprehensibility of diverse branches of Chinese such as Cantonese and Mandarin are evident. A Milanese has difficulty in understanding the Italian spoken in neighbouring Bergamo. In all these cases comprehension demands translation along lines closer and closer to those of inter-lingual transfer. There are dictionaries and grammars of Venetian, Neapolitan, and Bergamasque.

Regional, dialectal disparities are the easiest to identify. Any body of language, spoken at the same time in a complex community, is in fact rifted by much subtler differentiations. These relate to social status, ideology, profession, age, and sex.

Different castes, different strata of society use a different idiom. Eighteenth-century Mongolia provides a famous case. The religious language was Tibetan; the language of government was Manchu; merchants spoke Chinese;

classical Mongol was the literary idiom; and the vernacular was the Khalka dialect of Mongol. In very many cases, such as the sacred speech of the Zuni Indians, such differences have been rigorously formalized. Priests and initiates use a vocabulary and formulaic repertoire distinct from everyday language.[1] But special languages — hieratic, masonic, Ubuesque, mandarin, the semi-occult speech of the regimental mess or fraternity initiation — pose no essential difficulty. The need for translation is self-evident. Far more important and diffuse are the uses of inflection, grammatical structure, and word-choice by different social classes and ethnic groups to affirm their respective identities and to affront one another. It may be that the agonistic functions of speech inside an economically and socially divided community outweigh the functions of genuine communication. As we shall see throughout this study, languages conceal and internalize more, perhaps, than they convey outwardly. Social classes, racial ghettoes speak *at* rather than *to* each other.

Upper-class English diction, with its sharpened vowels, elisions, and modish slurs, is both a code for mutual recognition — accent is worn like a coat of arms — and an instrument of ironic exclusion. It communicates from above, enmeshing the actual unit of information, often imperative or conventionally benevolent, in a network of superfluous linguistic matter. But this redundancy is itself functional: one speaks most completely to one's inferiors — the speech-act is most expressive of status, innuendo, and power — when a peer is in earshot. The ornamental irrelevancies and elided insinuations are not addressed so much to the tradesman or visitor as to one's fellow officer or clubman who will recognize in them signals of complicity. Thackeray and Wodehouse are masters at conveying this dual focus of aristocratic semantics. As analysed by Proust, the discourse of Charlus is a light-beam pin-pointed, obscured, prismatically scattered as by a Japanese fan beating before a speaker's face in ceremonious motion. To the lower classes, speech is no less a weapon and a vengeance. Words may be appropriated and suborned, either by being given a clandestine significance or by being mocked through false intonation (in tribal warfare a captured fetish will be turned against its former owners). The pedantic decorum of 'menial' parlance in Molière, in Jeeves, is

1. For a classic study of secret speech forms, cf. Michel Leiris: *La Langue secrète des Dogons de Sanga (Soudan Français)* (Paris, 1948). In this case, the special, occult language arises both from reasons of mythical initiation and from the differentiation between men and women. cf. also M. Delafosse: 'Langage secret et langage conventionnel dans l'Afrique noire' (*L'Anthropologie*, XXXII, 1922). Though obviously dated, A. Van Gennep's 'Essai d'une théorie des langues spéciales' (*Revue des études ethnographiques et sociologiques*, I, 1908) remains of interest.

a stratagem of parody. Where there is no true kinship of interests, where power relations determine the conditions of meeting, linguistic exchange becomes a duel. Very often the seeming inarticulateness of the labourer, the thick twilight of Cockney speech, or the obeisant drag of Negro response are a well-judged feint. The illiteracy of the trooper or the navvy were porcupine quills, calculated to guard some coherence of inner life while wounding outward. The patronized and the oppressed have endured behind their silences, behind the partial incommunicado of their obscenities and clotted monosyllables.[2]

This, I suspect, makes for one of the radical differences between upper- and lower-class language habits. The privileged speak to the world at large as they do to themselves, in a conspicuous consumption of syllables, clauses, prepositions, concomitant with their economic resources and the spacious quarters they inhabit. Men and women of the lower class do not speak to their masters and enemies as they do to one another, hoarding what expressive wealth they have for internal use. For an upper- or middle-class listener, the authentic play of speech below stairs or in the proletarian home is more difficult to penetrate than any club. White and black trade words as do front-line soldiers lobbing back an undetonated grenade. Watch the motions of feigned responsiveness, menace, and non-information in a landlord's dialogue with his tenant or in the morning banter of tally-clerk and lorry-driver. Observe the murderous undertones of apparently urbane, shared speech between mistress and maids in Genet's *Les Bonnes*. So little is being said, so much is 'being meant', thus posing almost intractable problems for the translator.

Polysemy, the capacity of the same word to mean different things, such difference ranging from nuance to antithesis, characterizes the language of ideology. Machiavelli noted that meaning could be dislocated in common speech so as to produce political confusion. Competing ideologies rarely create new terminologies. As Kenneth Burke and George Orwell have shown

2. cf. the following for examples of the social stratification and social-strategic uses of speech: Felix M. and Marie M. Keesing: *Elite Communication in Samoa* (Stanford University Press, 1956); J. J. Gumperz and Charles A. Ferguson (eds.): *Linguistic Diversity in South Asia* (University of Indiana Press, 1960); Clifford Geertz: *The Religion of Java* (Illinois, 1960); Basil Bernstein: 'Social Class, Linguistic Codes and Grammatical Elements' (*Language and Speech*, V, 1962); William Labor, Paul Cohen, and Clarence Robbins: *A Preliminary Study of English Used by Negro and Puerto Rican Speakers in New York City* (New York, 1965); Robbins Burling: *Man's Many Voices: Language in its Cultural Context* (New York, 1970); Peter Trudgill: *The Social Differentiation of English in Norwich* (Cambridge University Press, 1974).

in regard to the vocabulary of Nazism and Stalinism, they pilfer and decompose the vulgate. In the idiom of fascism and communism, 'peace', 'freedom', 'progress', 'popular will' are as prominent as in the language of representative democracy. But they have their fiercely disparate meanings. The words of the adversary are appropriated and hurled against him. When antithetical meanings are forced upon the same word (Orwell's Newspeak), when the conceptual reach and valuation of a word can be altered by political decree, language loses credibility. Translation in the ordinary sense becomes impossible. To translate a Stalinist text on peace or on freedom under proletarian dictatorship into a non-Stalinist idiom, using the same time-honoured words, is to produce a polemic gloss, a counter-statement of values. At the moment, the speech of politics, of social dissent, of journalism is full of loud ghost-words, being shouted back and forth, signifying contraries or nothing. It is only in the underground of political humour that these shibboleths regain significance. When the entry of foreign tanks into a free city is glossed as 'a spontaneous, ardently welcomed defence of popular freedom' (*Izvestia*, 27 August 1968), the word 'freedom' will preserve its common meaning only in the clandestine dictionary of laughter.

That dictionary, one supposes, plays a large role in the language of children. Here diachronic and synchronic structures overlap. At any given time in a community and in the history of the language, speech modulates across generations. Or as psycho-linguists put it, there are 'phenomena of age grading' in all known languages. The matter of child-speech is a deep and fascinating one. Again, there are numerous languages in which such speech is formally set apart. Japanese children employ a separate vocabulary for everything they have and use up to a certain age. More common, indeed universal, is the case in which children carve their own language-world out of the total lexical and syntactic resources of adult society. So far as children are an exploited and mutinous class, they will, like the proletariat or ethnic minorities, pilfer and make risible the rhetoric, the taboo words, the normative idioms of their oppressors. The scatological doggerels of the nursery and the alley-way may have a sociological rather than a psychoanalytic motive. The sexual slang of childhood, so often based on mythical readings of actual sexual reality rather than on any physiological grasp, represents a night-raid on adult territory. The fracture of words, the maltreatment of grammatical norms which, as the Opies have shown, constitute a vital part of the lore, mnemonics, and secret parlance of childhood, have a rebellious aim: by refusing, for a time, to accept the rules of grown-up speech, the child seeks to keep the world open to his own, seemingly unprecedented needs. In the event of autism, the speech-battle between child and master can reach a grim finality. Surrounded by incomprehensible or hostile reality, the autistic child breaks off verbal contact. He seems to choose silence to shield his identity but even more, perhaps, to destroy his imagined enemy. Like murderous Cordelia, children know that silence can destroy another human being. Or like Kafka they remember that several have survived the song of the Sirens, but none their silence.

The anthropology or, as it would now be called, ethno-linguistics of child-speech is still at a rudimentary stage. We know far more of the languages of the Amazon. Adults tend to regard the language of children as an embryonic, inferior version of their own. Children, in turn, guard their preserve. Among early explorers were the novelists of the second half of the nineteenth century. Behind them lay certain tenacious eighteenth-century notions. Diderot had referred to 'l'enfant, ce petit sauvage', joining under one rubric the nursery and the natives of the South Seas. The sense of a dubious Eden, with its implications of a lost linguistic innocence and immediacy, colours our entire image of the child: we speak still of the *jardin d'enfants*, the *Kindergarten*. The passage from the transitional into the exploratory model is visible in Lewis Carroll. *Alice in Wonderland* relates to voyages into the language-world and special logic of the child as Gulliver relates to the travel literature of the Enlightenment. Both are subversive considerations of the general venture, and statements of limitation: they inform the voyager that he will, inevitably, find what he has brought with him and that there are blanks on the map beyond the reach of his survey.

Henry James was one of the true pioneers. He made an acute study of the frontier zones in which the speech of children meets that of grown-ups. *The Pupil* dramatizes the contrasting truth-functions in adult idiom and the syntax of a child. Children, too, have their conventions of falsehood, but they differ from ours. In *The Turn of the Screw*, whose venue is itself so suggestive of an infected Eden, irreconcilable semantic systems destroy human contact and make it impossible to locate reality. This cruel fable moves on at least four levels of language: there is the provisional key of the narrator, initiating all possibilities but stabilizing none, there is the fluency of the governess, with its curious gusts of theatrical *bravura*, and the speech of the servants so avaricious of insight. These three modes envelop, qualify, and obscure that of the children. Soon incomplete sentences, filched letters, snatches of over-heard but misconstrued speech, produce a nightmare of untranslatability. 'I said things,' confesses Miles when pressed to the limit of endurance. That tautology is all his luminous, incomprehensible idiom can yield. The governess seizes upon 'an exquisite pathos of contradiction'. Death is the only plain statement left. Both *The Awkward Age* and *What Maisie Knew* focus on children at the border, on the brusque revelations and bursts of static which mark the communication between adolescents and those adults whose language-territory they are about to enter.

The speech of children and adolescents fascinated Dostoevsky. Its ferocious innocence, the tactical equivocations of the maturing child, are reproduced in *The Brothers Karamazov*. St Francis's ability to parley with birds is closely echoed in Alyosha's understanding of Kolya and the boys. But for all their lively truth, children in the novels of James and Dostoevsky remain, in large measure, miniature adults. They exhibit the uncanny percipience of the 'aged' infant Christ in Flemish art. Mark Twain's transcriptions of the secret and public idiom of childhood penetrate much further. A genius for receptive insight animates the rendition of Huck Finn and Tom Sawyer. The artfulness of their language, its ceremonies of insult and kinship, its tricks of understatement are as complex as any in adult rhetoric. But they are unfailingly re-creative of a child's way. The discrimination is made even more exact by the neighbouring but again very different 'childishness' of Negro speech. For the first time in western literature, the linguistic terrain of childhood was mapped without being laid waste. After Mark Twain, child psychology and Piaget could proceed.

When speaking to a young boy or girl we use simple words and a simplified grammar; often we reply by using the child's own vocabulary; we bend forward. For their part, children will use different phrasings, intonations, and gestures when addressing a grown-up from those used when speaking to themselves (the iceberg mass of child language) or to other children. All these are devices for translation. J. D. Salinger catches us in the act:

> Sybil released her foot. 'Did you read "Little Black Sambo"?' she said.
> 'It's very funny you ask me that,' he said. 'It so happens I just finished reading it last night.' He reached down and took back Sybil's hand. 'What did you think of it?' he asked her.
> 'Did the tigers run all around that tree?'
> 'I thought they'd never stop. I never saw so many tigers.'
> 'There were only six,' Sybil said.
> '*Only* six!' said the young man. 'Do you call that *only*?'

'Do you like wax?' Sybil asked.

'Do I like what?' asked the young man.

'Wax.'

'Very much. Don't you?'

Sybil nodded. 'Do you like olives?' she asked.

'Olives – yes. Olives and wax. I never go anyplace without 'em.'
. . .
Sybil was silent.

'I like to chew candles,' she said finally.

'Who doesn't?' said the young man, getting his feet wet.

This is the *'perfect* day for bananafish', the swift passage from Pentecost to silence. Being so near death, Seymour, the hero of the story, translates flawlessly. Usually, the task is more difficult. There is so much we do not know. Even more than the illiterate and the oppressed, children have been kept in the margin of history. Their multitudinous existence has left comparatively few archives. How, for instance, do class-lines cut across age gradients? Is it true that the current revolution in the language of sex is entirely a middle-class phenomenon, that sex-talk of the most anatomical and disenchanted kind has always been in use among children of the working-class? One thing is clear. The entry of the child into complete adult notice, a heightened awareness of its uniquely vulnerable and creative condition, are among the principal gains of the recent past. The stifled voices of children that haunt Blake's poetry are no longer a general fact. No previous society has taken as much trouble as ours to hear the actual language of the child, to receive and interpret its signals without distorting them.

In most societies and throughout history, the status of women has been akin to that of children. Both groups are maintained in a condition of privileged inferiority. Both suffer obvious modes of exploitation – sexual, legal, economic – while benefiting from a mythology of special regard. Thus Victorian sentimentalization of the moral eminence of women and young children was concurrent with brutal forms of erotic and economic subjection. Under sociological and psychological pressure, both minorities have developed internal codes of communication and defence (women and children constitute a symbolic, self-defining minority even when, owing to war or special circumstance, they outnumber the adult males in the community). There is a language-world of women as there is of children.

We touch here on one of the most important yet least understood areas of biological and social existence. Eros and language mesh at every point.

Intercourse and discourse, copula and copulation, are sub-classes of the dominant fact of communication. They arise from the life-need of the ego to reach out and comprehend, in the two vital senses of 'understanding' and 'containment', another human being. Sex is a profoundly semantic act. Like language, it is subject to the shaping force of social convention, rules of proceeding, and accumulated precedent. To speak and to make love is to enact a distinctive twofold universality: both forms of communication are universals of human physiology as well as of social evolution. It is likely that human sexuality and speech developed in close-knit reciprocity. Together they generate the history of self-consciousness, the process, presumably millenary and marked by innumerable regressions, whereby we have hammered out the notion of self and otherness. Hence the argument of modern anthropology that the incest taboo, which appears to be primal to the organization of communal life, is inseparable from linguistic evolution. We can only prohibit that which we can name. Kinship systems, which are the coding and classification of sex for purposes of social survival, are analogous with syntax. The seminal and the semantic functions (is there, ultimately, an etymological link?) determine the genetic and social structure of human experience. Together they construe the grammar of being.

The interactions of the sexual and the linguistic accompany our whole lives. But again, much of this central area remains unexplored. If coition can be schematized as dialogue, masturbation seems to be correlative with the pulse of monologue or of internalized address. There is evidence that the sexual discharge in male onanism is greater than it is in intercourse. I suspect that the determining factor is articulateness, the ability to conceptualize with especial vividness. In the highly articulate individual, the current of verbal–psychic energy flows inward. The multiple, intricate relations between speech defects and infirmities in the nervous and glandular mechanisms which control sexual and excretory functions have long been known, at least at the level of popular wit and scatological lore. Ejaculation is at once a physiological and a linguistic concept. Impotence and speech-blocks, premature emission and stuttering, involuntary ejaculation and the word-river of dreams are phenomena whose interrelations seem to lead back to the central knot of our humanity. Semen, excreta, and words are communicative products. They are transmissions from the self inside the skin to reality outside. At the far root, their symbolic significance, the rites, taboos, and fantasies which they evoke, and certain of the social controls on their use, are inextricably interwoven. We know all this but hardly grasp its implications.

In what measure are sexual perversions analogues of incorrect speech? Are there affinities between pathological erotic compulsions and the search, obsessive in certain poets and logicians, for a 'private language', for a linguistic system unique to the needs and perceptions of the user? Might there be elements of homosexuality in the modern theory of language (particularly in the early Wittgenstein), in the concept of communication as an arbitrary mirroring? It may be that the significance of Sade lies in his terrible loquacity, in his forced outpouring of millions of words. In part, the genesis of sadism could be linguistic. The sadist makes an abstraction of the human being he tortures; he verbalizes life to an extreme degree by carrying out on living beings the totality of his articulate fantasies. Did Sade's uncontrollable fluency, like the garrulousness often imputed to the old, represent a psycho-physiological surrogate for diminished sexuality (pornography seeking to replace sex by language)?

Questions crowd upon one. No sphere of the *sciences de l'homme* is more compelling or nearer the core. But how much have we added to firm knowledge since Plato's myth of a lost, androgynous unity?

The difference between the speech of men and of women is one aspect, though crucial, of the interactions of language and eros. Ethno-linguists report a number of languages in which men and women use different grammatical forms and partially distinct vocabularies. A study has been made of men's and women's speech in Koasati, a Muskogean language of south-western Louisiana.[3] The differences observed are mainly grammatical. As they bring up male children, women know men's speech. Men, in turn, have been heard using women's forms when quoting a female speaker in a story. In a few instances, and this is an extraordinarily suggestive point, the speech of women is somewhat more archaic than that of men. The same obtains in Hitchiti, another Creek Indian tongue. The formal duality of men's and women's speech has been recorded also in Eskimo languages, in Carib, a South American Indian language, and in Thai. I suspect that such division is a feature of almost all languages at some stage in their evolution and that numerous spoors of sexually determined lexical and syntactical differences are as yet unnoticed. But again, as in the case of Japanese or Cherokee 'child-speech', formal discriminations are easy to locate and describe. The far more important, indeed universal phenomenon, is the differential use by men and women of identical words and grammatical constructs.

3. cf. Mary R. Haas: 'Men's and Women's Speech in Koasati' (*Language*, XX, 1944).

No man or woman but has felt, during a lifetime, the strong subtle barriers which sexual identity interposes in communication. At the heart of intimacy, there above all perhaps, differences of linguistic reflex intervene. The semantic contour, the total of expressive means used by men and women differ. The view they take of the output and consumption of words is not the same. As it passes through verb tenses, time is bent into distinctive shapes and fictions. At a rough guess, women's speech is richer than men's in those shadings of desire and futurity known in Greek and Sanskrit as optative; women seem to verbalize a wider range of qualified resolve and masked promise. Feminine uses of the subjunctive in European languages give to material facts and relations a characteristic *vibrato*. I do not say they lie about the obtuse, resistant fabric of the world: they multiply the facets of reality, they strengthen the adjective to allow it an alternative nominal status, in a way which men often find unnerving. There is a strain of ultimatum, a separatist stance, in the masculine intonation of the first-person pronoun; the 'I' of women intimates a more patient bearing, or did until Women's Liberation. The two language models follow on Robert Graves's dictum that men do but women are.

In regard to speech habits, the headings of mutual reproach are immemorial. In every known culture, men have accused women of being garrulous, of wasting words with lunatic prodigality. The chattering, ranting, gossiping female, the tattle, the scold, the toothless crone her mouth wind-full of speech, is older than fairy-tales. Juvenal, in his Sixth Satire, makes a nightmare of woman's verbosity:

> cedunt grammatici, vincuntur rhetores, omnis
> turba tacet, nec causidicus nec praeco loquetur,
> altera nec mulier; verborum tanta cadit vis,
> tot pariter pelves ac tintinnabula dicas
> pulsari, iam nemo tubas, nemo aera fatiget:
> una laboranti poterit succurrere Lunae.

[The grammarians yield to her; the rhetoricians succumb; the whole crowd is silenced. No lawyer, no auctioneer will get a word in, no, nor any other woman. Her speech pours out in such a torrent that you would think that pots and bells were being banged together. Let no one more blow a trumpet or clash a cymbal: one woman alone will make noise enough to rescue the labouring moon [from eclipse].]

Are women, in fact, more spendthrift of language? Men's conviction on this point goes beyond statistical evidence. It seems to relate to very ancient perceptions of sexual contrast. It may be that the charge of loquacity conceals resentment about the role of women in 'expending' the food and raw material brought in by men. But Juvenal's allusion to the moon points inward, to the *malaise* which distances men from crucial aspects of feminine sexuality. The alleged outpouring of women's speech, the rank flow of words, may be a symbolic restatement of men's apprehensive, often ignorant awareness of the menstrual cycle. In masculine satire, the obscure currents and secretions of woman's physiology are an obsessive theme. Ben Jonson unifies the two motifs of linguistic and sexual incontinence in *The Silent Woman*. 'She is like a conduit-pipe', says Morose of his spurious bride, 'that will gush out with more force when she opens again.' 'Conduit-pipe', with its connotations of ordure and evacuation, is appallingly brutal. So is the whole play. The climax of the play again equates feminine verbosity with lewdness: 'O my heart! wilt thou break? wilt thou break? this is worst of all worst worsts that hell could have devised! Marry a whore, and so much noise!'

The converse are men's professions of delight in women's voices when their register is sweet and low. 'Comely speech' is, as the Song of Solomon affirms, an ornament to woman. Of an even greater and more concordant beauty is silence. The motif of the woman or maiden who says very little, in whom silence is a symbolic counterpart to chasteness and sacrificial grace, lends a unique pathos to the Antigone of *Oedipus at Colonus* or Euripides' Alcestis. A male god has cruelly possessed Cassandra and the speech that pours out of her is his; she seems almost remote from it, broken. Though addressed to an inanimate form, Keats's 'unravish'd bride of quietness' precisely renders the antique association of feminine quality with sparseness of speech. These values crystallize in Coriolanus's salute to Virgilia: 'My gracious silence, hail!' The line is magical in its music and suggestion, but also in its dramatic shrewdness. Shakespeare precisely conveys the idiom of a man, of a personage brimful with overweening masculinity. No woman would so greet her beloved.

Not that women have been slow to answer. Elvira's

> Non lo lasciar più dir;
> il labbro è mentitor ...

has rung down through history. Men are deceivers ever. They use speech to conceal the true, sexually aggressive function of their lips and tongues.

Women know the change in a man's voice, the crowding of cadence, the heightened fluency triggered off by sexual excitement. They have also heard, perennially, how a man's speech flattens, how its intonations dull after orgasm. In feminine speech-mythology, man is not only an erotic liar; he is an incorrigible braggart. Women's lore and secret mock record him as an eternal *miles gloriosus*, a self-trumpeter who uses language to cover up his sexual or professional fiascos, his infantile needs, his inability to withstand physical pain.

Before the Fall, man and woman may have spoken the same tongue, comprehending each other's meaning perfectly. Immediately after, speech divided them. Milton identifies the moment and its unending sequence:

> Thus they in mutual accusation spent
> The fruitless hours, but neither self-condemning:
> And of their vain contest appear'd no end.

The grounds of differentiation are, of course, largely economic and social. Sexual speech variations evolve because the division of labour, the fabric of obligation and leisure within the same community is different for men and for women. In many cases, such as the exclusively male use of whistle speech among the Mazateco Indians of Oaxaca, men mark their sociological and physical 'superiority' by reserving to themselves certain forms of communication. *Taceat mulier in ecclesia* is prescriptive in both Judaic and Christian culture. But certain linguistic differences do point towards a physiological basis or, to be exact, towards the intermediary zone between the biological and the social. This is the area in which the problem of the relations of linguistic conventions to cognitive processes is most difficult. Are there biologically determined apprehensions of sense data which precede and generate linguistically programmed conceptualizations? This is a question we shall come back to. E. H. Lenneberg states: 'I have data on sex difference, and some colors are unanimously called by girls something and by men something else.' Using anthropological material, F. G. Lounsbury comments: 'I feel sure that a woman's color vocabulary is quite a bit greater than a man's.'[4] Both observations must have a social as well as a psycho-physiological foundation. The sum of difference in the language habits of men and of women makes for two ways of fitting speech to the world: 'When all's done,' said Lady Macbeth to negate the fierce reality of Macbeth's vision of Banquo, 'You look but on a stool.'

4. H. Hoijer (ed.): *Language in Culture* (University of Chicago Press, 1954), p. 267.

Whatever the underlying causes, the resultant task of translation is constant and unfulfilled. Men and women communicate through never-ending modulation. Like breathing, the technique is unconscious; like breathing also, it is subject to obstruction and homicidal breakdown. Under stress of hatred, of boredom, of sudden panic, great gaps open. It is as if a man and a woman then heard each other for the first time and knew, with sickening conviction, that they share no common language, that their previous understanding had been based on a trivial pidgin which had left the heart of meaning untouched. Abruptly the wires are down and the nervous pulse under the skin is laid bare in mutual incomprehension. Strindberg is master of such moments of fission. Harold Pinter's plays locate the pools of silence that follow.

By far the greater proportion of art and historical record has been left by men. The process of 'sexual translation' or of the breakdown of linguistic exchange is seen, almost invariably, from a male focus. The relevant anthropology — itself a term charged with masculine presumptions — distorts evidence as does the white traveller's edge of power over his native informant. Few artists, though they are among the greatest, have rendered the genius of women's speech and seen the crisis of imperfect or abandoned translation from both sides. Much of the concentrated richness of the art of Racine lies in his 'ear' for the contrasting pressures of sexual identity on discourse. In every one of his major plays there is a crisis of translation: under extreme stress, men and women declare their absolute being to each other, only to discover that their respective experience of eros and language has set them desperately apart. Like no other playwright, Racine communicates not only the essential beat of women's diction but makes us feel what there is in the idiom of men which Andromaque, Phèdre, or Iphigénie can only grasp as falsehood or menace. Hence the equivocation, central in his work, on the twofold sense of *entendre*: these virtuosos of statement hear each other perfectly, but do not, cannot apprehend. I do not believe there is a more complete drama in literature, a work more exhaustive of the possibilities of human conflict, than Racine's *Bérénice*. It is a play about the fatality of the co-existence of man and woman, and it is dominated, necessarily, by speech-terms (*parole, dire, mot, entendre*). Mozart possessed something of this same rare duality (so different from the characterizing, polarizing drive of Shakespeare). Elvira, Donna Anna, and Zerlina have an intensely shared femininity, but the music exactly defines their individual range or pitch of being. The same delicacy of tone-discrimination is established between the Countess and Susanna in *The Marriage of Figaro*. In this instance, the discrimination is made

even more precise and more dramatically different from that which characterizes male voices by the 'bisexual' role of Cherubino. The Count's page is a
graphic example of Lévi-Strauss's contention that women and words are
analogous media of exchange in the grammar of social life. Stendhal was a
careful student of Mozart's operas. That study is borne out in the depth and
fairness of his treatment of the speech-worlds of men and women in Fabrice
and la Sanseverina in *The Charterhouse of Parma*. Today, when there is sexual
frankness as never before, such fairness is, paradoxically, rarer. It is not as
'translators' that women novelists and poets excel, but as declaimers of their
own, long-stifled tongue.

I have been putting forward a truism, but one whose great importance and
consequences usually go unexamined.

Any model of communication is at the same time a model of trans-lation,
of a vertical or horizontal transfer of significance. No two historical epochs,
no two social classes, no two localities use words and syntax to signify
exactly the same things, to send identical signals of valuation and inference.
Neither do two human beings. Each living person draws, deliberately or in
immediate habit, on two sources of linguistic supply: the current vulgate
corresponding to his level of literacy, and a private thesaurus. The latter is
inextricably a part of his subconscious, of his memories so far as they may
be verbalized, and of the singular, irreducibly specific ensemble of his somatic
and psychological identity. Part of the answer to the notorious logical
conundrum as to whether or not there can be 'private language' is that aspects
of every language-act are unique and individual. They form what linguists
call an 'idiolect'. Each communicatory gesture has a private residue. The
'personal lexicon' in every one of us inevitably qualifies the definitions,
connotations, semantic moves current in public discourse. The concept of a
normal or standard idiom is a statistically-based fiction (though it may, as we
shall see, have real existence in machine-translation). The language of a
community, however uniform its social contour, is an inexhaustibly multiple
aggregate of speech-atoms, of finally irreducible personal meanings.

The element of privacy in language makes possible a crucial, though little
understood, linguistic function. Its importance relates a study of translation
to a theory of language as such. Obviously, we speak to communicate. But
also to conceal, to leave unspoken. The ability of human beings to misinform
modulates through every wavelength from outright lying to silence. This
ability is based on the dual structure of discourse: our outward speech has
'behind it' a concurrent flow of articulate consciousness. 'Al conversar

vivimos en sociedad,' wrote Ortega y Gasset, 'al pensar nos quedamos solos.' In the majority of conventional, social exchanges, the relation between these two speech currents is only partially congruent. There is duplicity. The 'aside' as it is used in drama is a naive representation of scission: the speaker communicates to himself (thus to his audience) all that his overt statement to another character leaves unsaid. As we grow intimate with other men or women, we often 'hear' in the slightly altered cadence, speed, or intonation of whatever they are saying to us the true movement of articulate but unvoiced intent. Shakespeare's awareness of this twofold motion is unfailing. Desdemona asks of Othello, in the very first, scarcely realized instant of shaken trust, 'Why is your speech so faint?'

Thus a human being performs an act of translation, in the full sense of the word, when receiving a speech-message from any other human being. Time, distance, disparities in outlook or assumed reference, make this act more or less difficult. Where the difficulty is great enough, the process passes from reflex to conscious technique. Intimacy, on the other hand, be it of hatred or of love, can be defined as confident, quasi-immediate translation. Having kept the same word-signals bounding and rebounding between them like jugglers' weights, year after year, from horizon to horizon, Beckett's vagrants and knit couples understand one another almost osmotically. With intimacy, the external vulgate and the private mass of language grow more and more concordant. Soon the private dimension penetrates and takes over the customary forms of public exchange. The stuffed-animal and baby-speech of adult lovers reflects this take-over. In old age the impulse towards translation wanes and the pointers of reference turn inward. The old listen less or principally to themselves. Their dictionary is, increasingly, one of private remembrance.

I have been trying to state a rudimentary but decisive point: inter-lingual translation is the main concern of this book, but it is also a way in, an access to an inquiry into language itself. 'Translation', properly understood, is a special case of the arc of communication which every successful speech-act closes within a given language. On the inter-lingual level, translation will pose concentrated, visibly intractable problems; but these same problems abound, at a more covert or conventionally neglected level, intra-lingually. The model 'sender to receiver' which represents any semiological and semantic process is ontologically equivalent to the model 'source-language to receptor-language' used in the theory of translation. In both schemes there is 'in the middle' an operation of interpretative decipherment, an encoding–

decoding function or synapse. Where two or more languages are in articulate interconnection, the barriers in the middle will obviously be more salient, and the enterprise of intelligibility more conscious. But the 'motions of spirit', to use Dante's phrase, are rigorously analogous. So, as we shall see, are the most frequent causes of misunderstanding or, what is the same, of failure to translate correctly. In short: *inside or between languages, human communication equals translation.* A study of translation is a study of language.

The fact that tens of thousands of different, mutually incomprehensible languages have been or are being spoken on our small planet is a graphic expression of the deeper-lying enigma of human individuality, of the bio-genetic and bio-social evidence that no two human beings are totally identical. The affair at Babel confirmed and externalized the never-ending task of the translator — it did not initiate it. Logically considered, there was no guarantee that human beings would understand one another, that idiolects would fuse into the partial consensus of shared speech-forms. In terms of survival and social coherence such fusion may have proved to be an early and dramatic adaptive advantage. But, as William James observed, 'natural selection for efficient communication' may have been achieved at a considerable cost. This would have included not only the ideal of a totally personal voice, of a unique 'fit' between an individual's expressive means and his world-image, pursued by the poets. It meant also that the 'bright buzz' of non-verbal articulate codes, the sensory modes of smell, gesture, and pure tone developed by animals, and perhaps extra-sensory forms of communication (these are specifically adduced by James) all but vanished from the human repertoire. Speech would be an immensely profitable but also reductive, partially narrowing evolutionary selection from a wider spectrum of semiotic possibilities. Once it was 'chosen', translation became inevitable.

Thus any light I may be able to throw on the nature and poetics of translation between tongues has concomitant bearing on the study of language as a whole. The subject is difficult and ill-defined. Regarding the possible transfer into English of Chinese philosophic concepts, I. A. Richards remarks: 'We have here indeed what may very probably be the most complex type of event yet produced in the evolution of the cosmos.'[5] He may be right. But the complexity and range of implication were already present in the first moment of human speech.

---

5. I. A. Richards: 'Towards a Theory of Translating', in Arthur F. Wright (ed.): *Studies in Chinese Thought* (University of Chicago Press, 1953), p. 250.

➤ *Privacies of Speech* ➤

In a short, uncannily dense lyric, Celan speaks of 'netting shadows written by stones'. Modern literature is driven by a need to search out this 'lithography' and *écriture d'ombres*. They lie outside the clarity and sequent stride of public speech. For the writer after Mallarmé language does violence to meaning, flattening, destroying it, as a living thing from the deeps is destroyed when drawn to the daylight and low pressures of the sea surface.

But hermeticism, as it develops from Mallarmé to Celan, is not the most drastic of moves counter to language in modern literature. Two other alternatives emerge. Paralysed by the vacuum of words, by the chasm which has opened between individual perception and the frozen generalities of speech, the writer falls silent. The tactic of silence derives from Hölderlin or, more accurately, from the myth and treatment of Hölderlin in subsequent literature (Heidegger's commentaries of 1936–44 are a representative instance). The fragmentary, often circumlocutionary tenor of Hölderlin's late poetry, the poet's personal collapse into mental apathy and muteness, could be read as exemplifying the limits of language, the necessary defeat of language by the privacy and radiance of the inexpressible. Rather silence than a betrayal of felt meaning. Or as Wittgenstein wrote of his *Tractatus*, in a letter to Ludwig Ficker dated, it is thought, late October or early November 1919: 'my work consists of two parts: the one presented here plus all that I have *not* written. And it is precisely this second part which is the important one.'

The classic statement of the paradox is Hofmannsthal's 'Letter of Lord Chandos' of 1902. The young Elizabethan nobleman has been fired by poetic and philosophic dreams, by the design of penetrating art and mythology to their hidden, Orphic centre. The whole of natural creation and of history have seemed to him an articulate cipher. But now he finds that he can scarcely speak and that the notion of writing is an absurdity. Vertigo assails him at the thought of the abyss which separates the complexity of human phenomena from the banal abstraction of words. Haunted by microscopic lucidity – he has come to experience reality as a mosaic of integral structures – Lord Chandos discovers that speech is a myopic shorthand. Looking at the most ordinary object with obsessive notice, Chandos finds himself entering into its intricate, autonomous specificity: he espouses the life-form of the wheelbarrow in the garden shed, of the water-bug paddling across the ocean of the pail. Language, as we know it, gives no access to this pure pulse of being. Hofmannsthal's rendition of this paralysing empathy is cunning:

> Es ist mir dann, als geriete ich selber in Gärung, würfe Blasen auf, wallte und funkelte. Und das Ganze ist eine Art fieberisches Denken, aber Denken in einem Material, das unmittelbarer, flüssiger, glühender ist als Worte. Es sind gleichfalls Wirbel, aber solche, aber solche, die nicht wie die Wirbel der Sprache ins Bodenlose zu führen scheinen, sondern irgendwie in mich selber und in den tiefsten Schoss des Friedens.

We shall come back to this description of a matrix of thought more immediate, more fluid and intense than is that of language. Stemming from a writer who was steeped in music, the notion of introspective vortices, 'leading' to foundations deeper, more stable than those of syntax, is of great interest. Clearly, however, no earthly language can rival this vehemence of vision and repose. Chandos seeks a tongue 'of which not a single word is known to me, a tongue in which mute objects speak to me and in which I shall one day, perhaps, and in the grave, have to give account of myself before an unknown judge'. So far as the natural world goes, it is the language of total privacy or of silence.

The disasters of world war, the sober recognition that the finalities of lunacy and barbarism which occurred during 1914–18 and the Nazi holocaust could neither be adequately grasped nor described in words – what is there to *say* about Belsen? – reinforced the temptations of silence. A good deal of what is representative in modern literature, from Kafka to Pinter, seems to work deliberately at the edge of quietness. It puts forward tentative or failed speech-moves expressive of the intimation that the larger, more worthwhile statements cannot, ought not, to be made (Hofmannsthal came to speak of the 'indecency of eloquence' after the lies and massacres of world war). An entry in Ionesco's diary summarizes the ironic, crippled posture of the writer when words fail him:

> It is as if, through becoming involved in literature, I had used up all possible symbols without really penetrating their meaning. They no longer have any vital significance for me. Words have killed images or are concealing them. A civilization of words is a civilization distraught. Words create confusion. Words are not the word (*les mots ne sont pas la parole*) ... The fact is that words say nothing, if I may put it that way ... There are no words for the deepest experience. The more I try to explain myself, the

less I understand myself. Of course, not everything is unsayable in words, only the living truth.

No writer can arrive at a more desolate conclusion. Its philosophic implications, the 'negative creativity' which it has exercised in recent literature, are of great importance. An *Act Without Words*, Beckett's title, represents the logical extreme of the conflict between private meaning and public utterance. But so far as a model of language goes, silence is, palpably, a dead end.

There is a second alternative. So that 'words may again be the word' and the living truth said, a new language must be created. For meaning to find original untarnished expression, sensibility must shake off the dead hand of precedent as it is, ineradicably, entrenched in existing words and grammatical moulds. This was the programme set out by the Russian 'Kubofuturist', Alexei Kručenyx, in his *Declaration of the Word As Such* (1913): 'The worn-out, violated word "lily" is devoid of all expression. Therefore I call the lily *éuy* — and original purity is restored.' As we have seen, this notion of a language made pure and veritable again as the morning light has a theological provenance. But it springs also from a specific historical conjecture prevalent in the late eighteenth and nineteenth centuries. Considering the innocent finality of Hebrew poetry and of Greek literature, the paradox of freshness combined with ripeness of form, thinkers such as Winckelmann, Herder, Schiller, and Marx argued that Antiquity and the Greek genius in particular had been uniquely fortunate. The Homeric singer, Pindar, the Attic tragedians had been, literally, the first to find shaped expression for primary human impulses of love and hatred, of civic and religious feeling. To them metaphor and simile had been novel, perhaps bewildering suppositions. That a brave man should be like a lion or dawn wear a mantle of the colour of flame were not stale ornaments of speech but provisional, idiosyncratic mappings of reality. No western idiom after the Psalms and Homer has found the world so new.

Presumably, the theory is spurious. Even the earliest literary texts known to us have a long history of language behind them.[1] What we notice of the formal building-blocks in even the most archaic of Biblical passages and what we understand of the formulaic composition of the *Iliad* and *Odyssey* point to a lengthy, gradual process of selection and conventionality. No techniques

1. The most recent anthropological and linguistic hypotheses put at *c.* 100,000 years ago the emergence of 'characteristically human speech'. The breakthrough would coincide with the last Ice Age and the manufacture of new types of elaborate stone and bone implements. cf. Claire Russell and W. M. S. Russell: 'Language and Animal Signals', in N. Minnis (ed.); *Linguistics at Large* (London, 1971), pp. 184–7. Our earliest literatures are very late forms.

of anthropological or historical reconstruction will give us any insight into the conditions of consciousness and social response which may have generated the beginnings of metaphor and the origins of symbolic reference. It could be that there was a speaker of genius or manic longing who first compared the magnitude of his love to that of the sea. But we can observe nothing of that momentous occasion. Nevertheless, factitious as it is, the model of a lost *poiesis* has a powerful negative influence. It spurs on the intuition, widespread after the 1860s, that there can be no progress in letters, no embodiment of private and exploratory vision, if language itself is not made new.

This making new can take three forms: it can be a process of dislocation, an amalgam of existing languages, or a search for self-consistent neologism. These three devices do not normally occur in isolation. What we find from the 1870s to the 1930s are numerous variants on the three modes, usually drawing on some element from each.

Nonsense poetry and prose, nonsense taxonomies, and nonsense alphabets of many sorts are an ancient genre often active just below the surface of nursery rhymes, limericks, magic spells, riddles, and mnemonic tags.[2] The art of Edward Lear and of Lewis Carroll, however, is probably cognate with the new self-consciousness about language and the logical investigations of semantic conventions which develop in the late nineteenth century. An obvious force and sophistication of psychological conjecture lie behind Lewis Carroll's disturbing assertion that nonsense languages, however esoteric, would be totally understandable to 'a perfectly balanced mind'. As Elizabeth Sewell points out, the dislocations of normal vocabulary and grammar in nonsense have a specific method. The world of nonsense poetry concentrates 'on the divisibility of its material into ones, units from which a universe can be built. This universe, however, must never be more than the sum of its parts, and must never fuse into some all-embracing whole which cannot be broken down again into the original ones. It must try to create with words a universe that consists of bits.'[3] None of these bits can be allowed to engender external references or accumulate towards a final manifold. In other words: nonsense-speech seeks to inhibit the constant polysemy and contextuality of natural

2. Throughout this section I am drawing on the great study by Alfred Liede: *Dichtung als Spiel: Studien zur Unsinnspoesie an den Grenzen der Sprache* (Berlin, 1963). The best analyses of the language of nonsense with special reference to English may be found in Emile Cammaerts: *The Poetry of Nonsense* (London, 1925), and Elizabeth Sewell: *The Field of Nonsense* (London, 1952).

3. Elizabeth Sewell, op. cit., pp. 53–4.

language. The grammar of nonsense consists primarily of pseudo-series or alignments of discrete units which imitate and intermingle with arithmetic progressions (in Lewis Carroll these are usually familiar rows and factorizations of whole numbers).

The idiom of Jabberwocky, says Miss Sewell, aims at 'making no direct connection for the mind with anything in experience'. On closer inspection, however, this does not turn out to be the case. Eric Partridge's witty gloss on the four new verbs, ten new adjectives, and eight new nouns in Jabberwocky shows how near these coinages lie to the resonance of familiar English, French, and Latin constituents.[4] It is not enough to adduce some 'half-conscious perception of verbal likeness'.[5] That perception is more often than not immediate and inescapable. Hence the fact that the feats of the Dong and of the Snark can be and have been brilliantly translated into other tongues.

> 'Twas brillig, and the slithy toves
> Did gyre and gimble in the wabe:
> All mimsy were the borogroves,
> And the mome raths outgrabe

haunts us by analogy. Thoroughly familiar phonetic associations and sequences from English ballads lie in instant, explicit reach. In Celan's terms, the echoes are not 'splintered' but knit in mildly unexpected ways.

From the point of view of the renewal of language, there lies the weakness of the whole undertaking. The material is too pliant, the translation too immediate. It draws too readily on counters of feeling and of imagery long-established in the sound-associations of English or any other public speech. The best of Lear, in particular, is Victorian, post-Blakeian verse delicately out of focus, as is a solid shape when the air beats about it, blurring it faintly, on a hot day.

'I said it in Hebrew – I said it in Dutch – / I said it in German and Greek –' proclaims Lewis Carroll in 'The Hunting of the Snark', 'But I wholly forgot (and it vexes me much) / That English is what you speak!' There has been poetry made of this oversight. Bilingual and multilingual poetry, i.e. a text in which lines or stanzas in different languages alternate, goes back at least to the Middle Ages and to contrapuntal uses of Latin and the vulgate. The minnesinger Oswald von Wolkenstein composed a notorious *tour de force*

4. cf. Eric Partridge: 'The Nonsense Words of Edward Lear and Lewis Carroll', in *Here, There and Everywhere: Essays upon Language* (London, 1950).

5. Elizabeth Sewell, op. cit., p. 121.

incorporating six languages, and there are combinations of Provençal, Italian, French, Catalan, and Galician-Portuguese in troubadour verse. In his monograph on *The Poet's Tongues,* Professor Leonard Forster cites a delightful poem of the fifteenth century made up of alternating lines of English, Anglo-Norman, and Latin. A simpler, well-known example is provided by a German Christmas carol also of the fifteenth century:

> Ubi sunt gaudia?
>> Niendert mehr denn da,
>> Da die Engel singen
> Nova cantica
>> Und die Schellen klingen
> In Regis curia
> Eia wärn wir da!

The finest instance I am aware of, from both a literary and linguistic point of view, is modern. Meeting in Paris in April 1969, Octavio Paz, Jacques Roubaud, Edoardo Sanguineti, and Charles Tomlinson produced a *renga.* This is a collective poem or set of poems modelled on a Japanese form which may date back to the seventh or eighth century. But this *renga* is more than a collective act of composition: it is quadrilingual. Each poet wrote in his own tongue echoing, countering, transmuting through sound-play and masked translation the lines written immediately before him, in turn, by the three other authors. The resulting English–French–Italian–Spanish texts are of extreme imaginative density and raise issues of language and of translation to which I will return. Even one example (II.i) will show something of the interactive energies released:

> *Aime criaient-ils aime gravité*
> *de très hautes branches tout bas pesait la*
> *Terre aime criaient-ils dans le haut*
> (*Cosí, mia sfera, cosí in me, sospesa, sogni: soffiavi, te-*
>> *nera, un cielo: e in me cerco i tuoi poli, se la*
> *tua lingua è la mia ruota, Terra del Fuoco, Terra di Roubaud*)
> *Naranja, poma, seno esfera al fin resuelta*
> *en vacuidad de estupa. Tierra disuelta.*
> *Ceres, Persephone, Eve, sphere*
> *earth, bitter our apple, who at the last will hear*
> *that love-cry?*

A good measure of the prose in *Finnegans Wake* is polyglot. Consider the famous riverrounding sentence on page one: 'Sir Tristram, violer d'amores, fr'over the short sea, has passencore rearrived from North Armorica ...' Not only is there the emphatic obtrusion of French in *triste, violer, pas encore* and *Armoric* (ancient Brittany), but Italian is present in *viola d'amore* and, if Joyce is to be believed, in the tag from Vico, *ricorsi storici*, which lodges partly as an anagram, partly as a translation, in 'passencore rearrived'. Or take a characteristic example from Book II: 'in deesperation of deispiration at the diasporation of his diesparation'. In this peal a change is rung on four and, possibly, five languages: English 'despair', French *déesse*, Latin *dies* (perhaps the whole phrase *Dies irae* is inwoven), Greek *diaspora*, and Old French or Old Scottish *dais* or *deis* meaning a stately room and, later, a canopied platform for solemn show. In Joyce's 'nighttalk' banal monosyllables can knit more than one language. Thus 'seim' in 'the seim anew' near the close of 'Anna Livia Plurabelle' contains English 'same' and the river Seine in a deft welding not only of two tongues but of the dialectical poles of identity and flux.

Joyce represents a borderline case between synthesis and neologism. But even in *Finnegans Wake*, the multilingual combinations are intended towards a richer, more cunning public medium. They do not aim at creating a new language. Such invention may well be the most paradoxical, revolutionary step of which the human intellect is capable.

We have no real history of these enigmatic constructs. They turn up in the apocrypha of heresy trials, alchemy, and occultism. The inquisitor will report or the heretic profess the use of a secret, magical idiom impenetrable to the outsider. The orthodox investigators – Gottfried von Strassburg denouncing the great poet Wolfram von Eschenbach for his resort to *trobar clus*, the secret diction of the courts of love, the pursuers of Paracelsus – assign a Satanic origin to the hidden words. The initiate, such as the early prophets of the Mormon Church, on the other hand, claims angelic inspiration or a direct Pentecostal visitation by 'words robed in fire'.[6] In the nature of the case, the evidence is either puerile or lost.

The same is, on the whole, true of the new and private tongues invented by individuals for their own singular use. But it is probable that many writers, certainly since Rimbaud and Mallarmé, have at some point and, perhaps, to an intense degree, shared Stefan George's wish 'to express themselves in a

---

6. For the theological and social problems posed by claims to direct instruction in Divine or angelic speech during, for example, the seventeenth century, cf. L. Kolakowski: *Chrétiens sans église* (Paris, 1969).

language inaccessible to the profane multitude'. In George's own case, the thirst for hermeticism was compelling. He made an orphic exercise of his personal life and art so far as modern circumstance would allow. His language-artifacts include at least two poems in a *lingua romana* made up of transparent elements drawn from French, Spanish, and Italian.[7] Pursuing his search for untainted purity and originality of statement, George constructed an entirely secret speech. Reportedly, he translated Book I of the *Odyssey* into this 'neology'. If George's disciples are to be trusted,[8] the master had this translation destroyed before his death lest vulgar scholarship ransack its secrets. The tale is, very likely, a *canard*, but the theoretic design of deepening and renewing the authority of a classic text by 'translating it forward' into a language hitherto unknown and itself innocent of literature, is astute and suggestive. Two somewhat haunting verses of this alleged translation survive. They are embedded in 'Ursprünge', a poem which deals, appropriately, with the persistence of antique, necromantic energies under the ascetic surface of early Christianity:

> Doch an dem flusse im schilfpalaste
> Trieb uns der wollust erhabenster schwall:
> In einem sange den keiner erfasste
> Waren wir heischer und herrscher vom All.
> Süss und befeuernd wie Attikas choros
> Ueber die hügel und inseln klang:
> CO BESOSO PASOJE PTOROS
> CO ES ON HAMA PASOJE BOAÑ.

'A song which none can grasp yet which makes us riddler and master of All.' I have seen something indistinctly like these syllables only once, on a Maltese inscription. It might be worth imagining just which two lines in *Odyssey* I George is 'translating'. The formulaic pattern is unmistakable.

By far the most interesting exercises in neologism in western literature are those performed by Russian futurists and by Dada and the Surrealists and *lettristes* who derive from the Dada movement after 1923. This is not the place

---

7. For examinations of Stefan George's views on a synthesis of romance languages and classic German to renew the vitality of European poetry, cf. H. Arbogast: *Die Erneuerung der deutschen Dichtersprache in den Frühwerken Stefan Georges. Eine stilgeschichtliche Untersuchung* (Tübingen, 1961), and Gerd Michels: *Die Dante-Übertragungen Stefan Georges* (Munich, 1967).

8. The story is told by both Ernst Morwitz and Friedrich Gundolf in their memoirs of George.

to go into the extensive, intricate literary aspects of Dada.[9] But it now seems probable that the entire modernist current, right to the present day, to minimalist art and the happening, to the 'freak-out' and aleatory music, is a footnote, often mediocre and secondhand, to Dada. The verbal, theatrical, and artistic experiments conducted first in Zurich in 1915–17 and then extended to Cologne, Munich, Paris, Berlin, Hannover, and New York, constitute one of the few undoubted revolutions or fundamental 'cuts' in the history of the imagination. The genius of Dada lies less in what was accomplished (the very notion of 'finish' being in question) than in a purity of need and disinterestedness of creative and collaborative impulse. The slapstick and formal inventions of Hugo Ball, Hans Arp, Tristan Tzara, Richard Huelsenbeck, Max Ernst, Kurt Schwitters, Francis Picabia, and Marcel Duchamp have a zestful integrity, an ascetic logic notoriously absent from a good many of the profitable rebellions that followed.

Many instigations, themselves fascinating, lie behind the Dada language-routines as they erupt at the Cabaret Voltaire in 1915. It seems likely that Ball chose the name of the cabaret in order to relate Dada to the Café Voltaire in Paris at which Mallarmé and the Symbolists met during the late 1880s and 1890s. For it was Mallarmé's programme of linguistic purification and private expression which Ball and his associates sought to carry out.[10] The notion of automatic writing, of the generation of word groups freed from the constraints of will and public meaning, dates back at least to 1896 and Gertrude Stein's experiments at Harvard. These trials, in turn, were taken up by Italian Futurism and are echoed in Marinetti's call for *parole in libertà*. The crucial concept of 'randomness' (*Zufall*) applied to language referred itself not

9. The field has reached an extension and complexity such that there is nearly need for a 'bibliography of bibliographies'. The following are of particular use: R. Motherwell (ed.): *The Dada Painters and Poets* (New York, 1951); Willy Verkauf (ed.): *Dada. Monographie einer Bewegung* (Teufen, Switzerland, 1957); the catalogue on *Cubisme, Futurisme, Dada, Surréalisme* issued by the Librairie Nicaise in Paris in 1960; Hans Richter: *Dada — Kunst und Antikunst. Der Beitrag Dadas zur Kunst des 20. Jahrhunderts* (Cologne, 1964); Herbert S. Gershman: *A Bibliography of the Surrealist Revolution in France* (University of Michigan Press, 1969). Valuable material on Dada poetry is contained in G. E. Steinke: *The Life and Work of H. Ball, founder of Dadaism* (The Hague, 1967), and in Reinhard Döhl's authoritative monograph, *Das literarische Werk Hans Arps 1903–1930* (Stuttgart, 1967). But wherever possible, it is best to refer to the letters, documents and memoirs written by those actually involved in Dada. Hugo Ball's *Briefe 1911–1927* (Cologne, 1957), Ball's autobiographical novel *Flametti oder vom Dandysmus der Armen* first published in Berlin in 1918, and Otto Flak's *roman à clef, Nein und Ja. Roman des Jahres 1917* (Berlin, 1923), remain indispensable.

10. cf. R. Döhl, op. cit., p. 36.

only to Mallarmé's *Igitur* but to the 'trance poetry' attempted by the decadent movement of the 1890s. The techniques of *collage* in the plastic arts show a parallel development with Dada verse and had a direct influence on Arp's treatment of language. Sound-poetry and *poésie concrète* were very much in the air; witness Kandinsky's *Klänge* published in Munich in 1913. The Zurich milieu at the time was rootless and polyglot. German, French, Italian, Spanish, Rumanian, and Russian were current in and around the Dada circle. The idea of syncretism and of a personal *patois* lay close at hand.

Yet these several strains would, I believe, have remained loose and modish but for the shock of world war. It was from that shock and its implications for the survival of human sanity that Dada derived its morality. The 'neologies' and silences of Ball, of Tristan Tzara, of Arp have affinities of despair and nihilistic logic with the exactly contemporaneous language-critiques of Karl Kraus and the early Wittgenstein. 'We were seeking an elemental art', recalls Hans Arp, 'which would cure man of the lunacy of the time.'[11] As Dada sprang up, 'madness and death were competing ... Those people not immediately involved in the hideous insanity of world war behaved as if they did not understand what was happening all around them ... Dada sought to rouse them from their piteous stupor.'[12] One of the instruments of awakening was the human voice (Giacometti running along the Limat and shouting into the houses of solid Zurich citizens). But the sounds uttered could not, as Hugo Ball urged, belong to languages corrupted to the marrow by the lies of politics and the rhetoric of slaughter. Hence the endeavour to create 'poetry without words'.

The most penetrating record of this attempt is contained in Ball's memoir, *Die Flucht aus der Zeit*, issued in 1927. The 'flight from the times' could only succeed if syntax, in which time is given binding force, could be broken. Ball's account is of extreme interest to both literature and linguistics:

> I do not know whence came the inspiration for the cadence. But I began to chant my rows of vowels in the manner of a liturgical plainsong and sought not only to maintain a serious mien but to enforce seriousness on myself. For a moment it seemed to me as if the pale, distraught face of a young boy had emerged from my cubist mask, the half-terrified, half-inquisitive face of a ten-year-old hanging, tremulous and eager, on the lips

11. Hans Arp, *Unsern täglichen Traum. Erinnerungen, Dichtungen und Betrachtungen aus den Jahren 1914–1954* (Zurich, 1955), p. 51.

12. Ibid., p. 20.

of the priest during the requiem masses and high masses in his home parish.

Before speaking the lines, I had read out a few programmatic words. In this kind of 'sound-poetry' (*Klanggedichtung*) one relinquishes – lock, stock, and barrel – the language which journalism has polluted and made impossible. You withdraw into the inmost alchemy of the word. Then let the word be sacrificed as well, so as to preserve for poetry its last and holiest domain. Give up the creation of poetry at second-hand: namely the adoption of words (to say nothing of sentences) which are not immaculately new and invented for your own use.

A quotation from Ball's *Elefantenkarawane* gives some idea of the intended effect:

> jolifanto bambla ô falli bambla
> grossiga m'pfa habla horem
> égiga goramen
> higo bloika russula huju
> hollaka hollala
> blago bung
> blago bung
> bosso fataka
> ü üü ü
> schampa wulla wussa ólobo
> hej tatta gôrem
> eschige zunbada
> wulubu ssubudu uluw ssubudu ...

What is here onomatopoeic foolery (*blago*) can, in the famous *Totenklage*, become enigmatic and strangely suffocating.

Ball's programme, like Khlebnikov's attempt to create a 'star-language', calls for absolute linguistic renovation. They lead directly to the principles enunciated in the *lettrist* manifestos of the mid-1940s: 'elevation beyond the WORD', 'the use of letters to destroy words', 'the demonstration that letters have a destiny other than their incorporation in known speech'. Surrealism, *lettrisme* and 'concrete poetry' have gone forward to break the association not only between words and sense, but between semantic signs and that which can be spoken. Poetry has been produced solely for the reading eye. Take, for instance, Isidore Isou's

Larmes de jeune fille
— poème clos —

M dngoun, m diahl Θhna îou
hsn îoun înhlianhl M pna iou
vgaîn set i ouf! saî iaf
fln plt i clouf! mglaî vaf
Λ o là îhî cnn vîi
snoubidi î pnn mîi
A gohà îhîhî gnn gî
klnbidi Δ blîglîhlî
H mami chou a sprl
scami Bgou cla ctrl
gue! el înhî nî K grîn
Khlogbidi Σ vî bîncî crîn
cncn ff vsch gln iééé . . .
gué rgn ss ouch clen dééé . . .
chaîg gna pca hi
Θ snca grd kr di.

The result is a disturbing sensation of possible events and densities (Heidegger's *Dichtung*) just below the visual surface. No signals, or very few apart from the title, are allowed to emerge and evoke a familiar tonal context. Yet there is no doubt in my mind that we are looking at a poem, and that it is, in some way, oddly moving. The wall is at the same time blank and expressive.

Whether such devices unlock 'the inmost alchemy of the word' or preserve the sanctum of poetry is a moot point. With Isou's confection we are at the limits of language and of semantic systems about which anything useful can be said. This latter restriction — the impossibility of cogent metaphrase — may not be as conclusive or condemnatory as it seems. There are other expressive modes which also defy useful comment.[13] Moreover, what occurs at the

13. One of the most instructive border areas between 'normal' and 'private' linguistic practices is that of schizophrenia. As L. Binswanger and other psychiatrists have pointed out, the distinction between schizophrenic speech-patterns and certain forms of Dada, Surrealist, and *lettrist* literature lies mainly in the fact of historical and stylistic context. The inventions of the patient have no external aetiology and he cannot comment on them historically. cf. David V. Forrest: 'The Patient's Sense of the Poem: Affinities and Ambiguities', in *Poetry Therapy* (Philadelphia, 1968). But as Augusto Ponzio shows in his essay, 'Ideologia della anormalità linguistica'

limits, in the region where linguistic structures shade into arbitrary 'non-significance', is not trivial. One need only recite Ball's *Klanggedichte* to a child to realize that a great deal of meaning, of presence – partly musical, partly kinetic, partly in the form of subliminal or incipient imagery – is being communicated. The problem consists in locating the point at which contingent, increasingly private signals cease emitting any coherent stimulus or any stimulus to which there could be a measure of agreed, repeatable response. Obviously, there is no general rule. In 'Larmes de jeune fille', some of the signs will convey to a mathematician possible specificities of intent, possible relevancies to the sound and theme of the poem which other readers may miss altogether. The self-defeating paradox in private language, be it the *trobar clus* of the Provençal poet or the *lettrisme* of Isou, lies in the simple fact that privacy diminishes with every unit of communication. Once utterance becomes address, let alone publications, privacy, in any strict sense, ceases.

But the 'frontier zone' need be neither one of the literary striving after personal style nor one of experimental strangeness. It is a constant of natural language. This is the overriding point. Private connotations, private habits of stress, of elision or periphrase make up a fundamental component of speech. Their weight and semantic field are essentially individual. Meaning is at all times the potential sum total of individual adaptations. There can be no definitive lexicon or logical grammar of ordinary language or even of parts of it because different human beings, even in simple cases of reference and 'naming', will always relate different associations to a given word. These differences are the life of normal speech. Few of us possess the genius needed to invent new words or to imprint on existing words, as the great poet or thinker does, a fresh value and contextual scope. We make do with the worn counters minted long since by our particular linguistic and social inheritance. But only up to a point. As personal memory ramifies, as the branches of feeling touch deeper and nearer the stem of the evolving, irreducible self, we crowd words and phrases with singular sense. Only their phonetics, if that, will remain wholly public. Below the lexical tip – a dictionary is an inventory of consensual, therefore eroded and often 'sub-significant' usages – the words

---

(*Ideologie*, XV, 1971), the very definition and perception of speech-pathology are themselves a social and historical convention. Different periods, different societies draw different lines between permissible and 'private' linguistic forms. cf. also B. Grassi: 'Un contributo allo studio della poesia schizofrenica' (*Rassegna neuropsichiatrica*, XV, 1961), David V. Forrest: 'Poiesis and the Language of Schizophrenia' (*Psychiatry*, XXVIII, 1965), and S. Piro: *Il linguaggio schizofrenico* (Milan, 1967).

we speak as individuals take on a specific gravity. Specific to the speaker alone, to the unique aggregate of association and preceding use generated by his total mental and physical history. When memory or occasion serve, we may externalize and make explicit certain levels of private content. In his self-analysis, *L'Âge d'homme*, Michel Leiris observes that the *s* in 'suicide' retains for him the precise shape and whistling sibilance of a *kris* (the serpentine dagger of the Malays). The *ui* sound stands for the hiss of flame; *cide* signifies 'acidity' and corrosive penetration. A picture of oriental immolation in a magazine had fixed and interwoven these associations in the child's mind. No dictionary could include them, no grammar formalize the process of collocation. Yet this is precisely the way in which all of us put meaning into meaning. The difference is that, more often than not, the active sources of connotation remain subconscious or outside the reach of memory.

➤ *Creative Falsehood* ➤

My conviction is that we shall not get much further in understanding the evolution of language and the relations between speech and human perform-ance so long as we see 'falsity' as primarily negative, so long as we consider counter-factuality, contradiction, and the many nuances of conditionality as specialized, often logically bastard modes. *Language is the main instrument of man's refusal to accept the world as it is.* Without that refusal, without the unceasing generation by the mind of 'counter-worlds' – a generation which cannot be divorced from the grammar of counter-factual and optative forms – we would turn forever on the treadmill of the present. Reality would be (to use Wittgenstein's phrase in an illicit sense) 'all that is the case' and nothing more. Ours is the ability, the need, to gainsay or 'un-say' the world, to image and speak it otherwise. In that capacity in its biological and social evolution, may lie some of the clues to the question of the origins of human speech and the multiplicity of tongues. It is not, perhaps, 'a theory of information' that will serve us best in trying to clarify the nature of language, but a 'theory of misinformation'.

We must be very careful here. The cardinal terms are not only elusive; they are so obviously tainted with a twofold indictment, moral and pragmatic, Augustinian and Cartesian. 'Mendacium est enuntiatio cum voluntate falsum enuntiandi' ('A lie is the wilful utterance of an articulate falsehood'), says Saint Augustine in his *De mendacio*. Note the stress on 'enunciation', on the point at which falsity is enacted through speech. It is very nearly impossible to make neutral use of 'mis-statement', 'deception', 'falsehood', 'misprision', or 'unclarity', the latter being the special object of Cartesian criticism. The unclear, the ambiguously or obscurely stated is an offence both to conscience and reason. Swift's account of the Houyhnhnms compacts an ethical with a pragmatic and a philosophical condemnation:

> And I remember in frequent Discourses with my Master concerning the Nature of Manhood, in other parts of the World; having occasion to talk of *Lying*, and *false Representation*, it was with much Difficulty that he comprehended what I meant; although he had otherwise a most acute Judgment. For he argued thus; That the Use of Speech was to make us understand one another, and to receive Information of Facts; now if anyone *said the Thing which was not*, these Ends were defeated; because I cannot properly be said to understand him; and I am so far from receiving Information, that he leaves me worse than in Ignorance; for I am led to believe a Thing *Black* when it is *White*, and *Short* when it is *Long*. And these were all the Notions he had concerning that Faculty of *Lying*, so perfectly well understood, and so universally practised among human Creatures.

Again we observe the close juncture of speech with verity, the view of truth as being a linguistic responsibility. Falsity, miscorrespondence with the actual state of affairs, results from the enunciation of 'the Thing which was not'. The 'impropriety' — Swift's terminology is at once psychologically flat and adroitly comprehensive — is simultaneously moral and semantic. A lie 'cannot be properly said to be understood'. Of course there can be 'error', a colour-blindness, a smudge on the spectacles. Discriminations must be allowed according to a scale of intent, of sustaining or inhibiting circumstance. Nevertheless, though mistake and deliberate falsehood are differentiated, both are seen from the outset as privations, as ontological negatives. The entire gamut from black lie to innocent error is to be found on the left and shadow-side of language.

Yet how vast that side is and, *pace* Swift's irony, how imperfectly understood. The outrightness of moral and epistemological rebuke in Saint Augustine, in Swift — whose argument is cognate to that of Hume on

'chimeras' — is itself historical. The Greek view was far more qualified than
the Patristic. One need only recall the enchanted exchanges between Athene
and Odysseus in the *Odyssey* (XIII) to realize that mutual deception, the swift
saying of 'things which are not' need be neither evil nor a bare tactical
constraint. Gods and chosen mortals can be virtuosos of mendacity, con-
trivers of elaborate untruths for the sake of the verbal craft (a key, slippery
term) and intellectual energy involved. The classical world was only too ready
to document the fact that the Greeks took an aesthetic or sporting view of
lying. A very ancient conception of the vitality of 'mis-statement' and 'misunderstanding', of the primordial affinities between language and dubious
meaning, seems implicit in the notorious style of Greek oracles. In the *Hippias
minor* Socrates enforces an opinion which is exactly antithetical to that of
Augustine. 'The false are powerful and prudent and knowing and wise in
those things about which they are false.' The dialogue fits only awkwardly
in the canon and its purpose may have been purely 'demonstrative' or
ironically *a contrario*. None the less, Socrates' case stands: the man who utters
falsehood intentionally is to be preferred to the one who lies inadvertently
or involuntarily. In the *Hippias minor*, the topic is referred to what was
probably an allegoric commonplace, to a comparison between Achilles and
Odysseus. The effect is, at best, ambivalent. 'For I hate him like the gates of
death who thinks one thing and says another', declares Achilles in Book IX
of the *Iliad*. Opposed to him stands Odysseus, 'master deceiver among
mortals'. In the balance of the myth it is Odysseus who prevails; neither
intellect nor creation attenuate Achilles' raucous simplicity.

In short, a seminal, profound intuition of the creativity of falsehood, an
awareness of the organic intimacy between the genius of speech and that of
fiction, of 'saying the thing which is not', can be traced in various aspects of
Greek mythology, ethics, and poetics. Gulliver's equation of the function of
language with the reception of 'Information of Facts' is, by Socratic standards,
arbitrary and naive. This 'polysemic' awareness survives in Byzantine rhetoric
and in the frequent allusions of Byzantine theology to the duplicities, to the
inherently 'misguiding' texture of human speech when it would seek the 'true
light'. But from Stoicism and early Christianity onward, 'feigning', whose
etymology is so deeply grounded in 'shaping' (*fingere*), has been in very bad
odour.

This may account for the overwhelming one-sidedness of the logic and
linguistics of sentences. To put it in a crude, obviously figurative way, the
great mass of common speech-events, of words spoken and heard, does not

fall under the rubric of 'factuality' and truth. The very concept of integral truth – 'the whole truth and nothing but the truth' – is a fictive ideal of the courtroom or the seminar in logic. Statistically, the incidence of 'true statements' – definitional, demonstrative, tautological – in any given mass of discourse is probably small. The current of language is intentional, it is instinct with purpose in regard to audience and situation. It aims at attitude and assent. It will, except on specialized occasions of logically formal, prescriptive, or solemnized utterance, not convey 'truth' or 'information of facts' at all. We communicate motivated images, local frameworks of feeling. All descriptions are partial. We speak less than the truth, we fragment in order to reconstruct desired alternatives, we select and elide. It is not 'the things which are' that we say, but those which might be, which we would bring about, which the eye and remembrance compose. The directly informative content of natural speech is small. Information does not come naked except in the schemata of computer languages or the lexicon. It comes attenuated, flexed, coloured, alloyed by intent and the *milieu* in which the utterance occurs (and *'milieu'* is here the total biological, cultural, historical, semantic ambience as it conditions the moment of individual articulation). No doubt there is a large spectrum of degree, of moral accent, between the imprecise shorthand of our daily idiom, the agreed falsity of social conventions, the innumerable white lies of mundane co-existence at one end and certain absolutes of philosophic, political non-truth at the other. The shallow cascade of mendacity which attends my refusal of a boring dinner engagement is not the same thing as the un-saying of history and lives in a Stalinist encyclopedia. Gnostic finalities of falsehood are not in common play. But between them these two polarities delimit what is, by all evidence, the larger part of private and social speech.

Linguists and psychologists (Nietzsche excepted) have done little to explore the ubiquitous, many-branched genus of lies.[1] We have only a few preliminary surveys of the vocabulary of falsehood in different languages and

1. Otto Lipmann and Paul Blaut: *Die Lüge in psychologischer, philosophischer, sprach- und literaturwissenschaftlicher und entwicklungsgeschichtlicher Betrachtung* (Leipzig, 1927) remains a pioneering work. There are points of considerable psychological and philosophic interest in René Le Senne: *Le Mensonge et le caractère* (Paris, 1930), and in Vladimir Jankélévitch: 'Le Mensonge' (*Revue de Métaphysique et de Morale*, XLVII, 1940), and *Du Mensonge* (Lyons, 1943). Jankélévitch returned to the theme, from a more epistemological point of view, in an article on 'La Méconnaissance' (*Revue de Métaphysique et de Morale*, new series, IV, 1963). Harald Weinrich's *Linguistik der Lüge* (Heidelberg, 1966) is a lucid but restricted introduction to an as yet unmapped field. The most recent treatment is that of Guy Durandin: *Les Fondements du mensonge* (Paris, 1972).

cultures.[2] Constrained as they are by moral disapproval or psychological *malaise*, these inquiries have remained thin. We will see deeper only when we break free of a purely negative classification of 'un-truth', only when we recognize the compulsion to say 'the thing which is not' as being central to language and mind. We must come to grasp what Nietzsche meant when he proclaimed that 'the Lie – and *not* the Truth – is divine!' Swift was nearer the heart of anthropology than he may have intended when he related 'lying' to the 'Nature of Manhood' and saw in 'false Representation' the critical difference between man and horse.

We need a word which will designate the power, the compulsion of language to posit 'otherness'. That power, as Oscar Wilde was one of the few to recognize, is inherent in every act of form, in art, in music, in the contrarieties which our body sets against gravity and repose. But it is pre-eminent in language. French allows *altérité*, a term derived from the Scholastic discrimination between essence and alien, between the tautological integrity of God and the shivered fragments of perceived reality. Perhaps 'alternity' will do: to define the 'other than the case', the counter-factual propositions, images, shapes of will and evasion with which we charge our mental being and by means of which we build the changing, largely fictive *milieu* of our somatic and our social existence. 'We invent for ourselves the major part of experience', says Nietzsche in *Beyond Good and Evil* ('wir erdichten ...' signifying 'to create fictionally', 'to render dense and coherent through *poiesis*'). Or as he puts it in *Morgenröte*, man's genius is one of lies.

We can conceive of a signal system of considerable efficacy and scanning range which lacks the means to 'alternity'. A number of animal species possess the expressive and receptive equipment needed to communicate or exchange elaborate and specific information. Whether acoustically or by coded motion (the dancing bees) they can initiate and interpret cognitive, informative messages. They can also use camouflage, ruse, and beautifully exact manoeuvres of misdirection. Miming injury, the mother bird will try to lead the predator away from her brood. The line between such tactics of counter-factuality and lies or 'alternity' looks fluid. But the difference is, I think, radical. The un-truths of animals are instinctual, they are evasive or sacrificial reflexes.

2. cf. Samuel Kroesch: *Germanic Words for Deceiving* (Göttingen–Baltimore, 1923); B. Brotheryon: *The Vocabulary of Intrigue in Roman Comedy* (Chicago, 1926); W. Luther: *Wahrheit und Lüge im ältesten Griechentum* (Leipzig, 1935), an important, neglected beginning; Hjalmar Frisk: *Wahrheit und Lüge in den indogermanischen Sprachen* (Götenborg, 1936); J. D. Schleyer: *Der Wortschatz von List und Betrug im Altfranzösischen und Altprovenzalischen* (Bonn, 1961).

Those of man are voluntary and can be wholly gratuitous, non-utilitarian, and creative. To the question 'where is the water-hole?', 'where is the source of nectar?', an animal can give an answer in sound or motion. The answer will be a true one; it is a strictly constrained response to an 'information-stimulus'. Though making use of words, the Houyhnhnms will do likewise: they can only emit or interpret 'information of facts'. Swift's emblem remains one of elemental centaurs, of an instinctual ethic across the borders from man. It may be that the rubric of camouflage extends to silence, to a withholding of response. At a higher level of evolution, in the primate stage perhaps, the animal will refuse an answer (there is something less than human in Cordelia's loving reticence). But even here only a complex reflex is involved. Full humanity only begins with a reply stating 'the thing which is not': i.e. 'the water-hole is a hundred yards to my left' when it is actually fifty yards to my right, 'there is no water-hole around here', 'the water-hole is dry', 'there is a scorpion in it'. The series of possible false answers, of imagined and/or stated 'alternities' is limitless. It has neither a formal nor a contingent end, and that unboundedness of falsehood is crucial both to human liberty and to the genius of language.

When did falsity begin, when did man grasp the power of speech to 'alternate' on reality, to 'say otherwise'? There is, of course, no evidence, no palaeontological trace of the moment or locale of transition – it may have been the most important in the history of the species – from the stimulus-and-response confines of truth to the freedom of fiction. There is experimental evidence, derived from the measurement of fossil skulls, that Neanderthal man, like the newborn child, did not have a vocal apparatus capable of emitting complex speech sounds.[3] Thus it may be that the evolution of conceptual and vocalized 'alternity' came fairly late. It may have induced and at the same time resulted from a dynamic interaction between the new functions of unfettered, fictive language and the development of speech areas in the frontal and temporal lobes. There may be correlations between the 'excessive' volume and innervation of the human cortex and man's ability to conceive and state realities 'which are not'. We literally carry inside us, in the organized spaces and involutions of the brain, worlds other than the world, and their fabric is preponderantly, though by no means exclusively or uniformly, verbal. The decisive step from ostensive nomination and tautology – if I say that the water-hole is where it is I am, in a sense, stating

3. cf. Philip H. Lieberman and Edmund S. Crelin: 'On the Speech of Neanderthal Man' (*Linguistic Inquiry*, II.2, 1971).

a tautology — to invention and 'alternity' may also relate to the discovery of tools and to the formation of social modes which that discovery entails. But whatever their bio-sociological origin, the uses of language for 'alternity', for mis-construction, for illusion and play, are the greatest of man's tools by far. With this stick he has reached out of the cage of instinct to touch the boundaries of the universe and of time.[4]

At first the instrument probably had a banal survival value. It still carried with it the impulse of instinctual mantling. Fiction was disguise: from those seeking out the same water-hole, the same sparse quarry, or meagre sexual chance. To misinform, to utter less than the truth was to gain a vital edge of space or subsistence. Natural selection would favour the contriver. Folk tales and mythology retain a blurred memory of the evolutionary advantage of mask and misdirection. Loki, Odysseus are very late, literary concentrates of the widely diffused motif of the liar, of the dissembler elusive as flame and water, who survives. But one suspects that the adaptive uses of 'alternity' reached deeper, that the instrumentalities of fiction, of counter-factual assertion were bound up with the slowly evolving, hazardous definition of self. There is a myth of hand-to-hand encounter — a duel, a wrestling bout, a trial by conundrum whose stake is the loser's life — which we come across

4. While reading proofs of this chapter, I came across the following passage, also in galley, by Sir Karl Popper ('Karl Popper, Replies to my Critics' in *The Philosophy of Karl Popper*, ed. Paul Arthur Schilpp, La Salle, Illinois, 1974, pp. 1112–13):

The development of human language plays a complex role within this process of adaptation. It seems to have developed from signalling among social animals; but I propose the thesis that what is most characteristic of the human language is the possibility of story telling. It may be that this ability too has some predecessor in the animal world. But I suggest that the moment when language became human was very closely related to the moment when a man invented a story, a myth in order to excuse a mistake he had made — perhaps in giving a danger signal when there was no occasion for it; and I suggest that the evolution of specifically human language, with its characteristic means of expressing negation — of saying that something signalled is not true — stems very largely from the discovery of systematic means to *negate* a false report, for example a false alarm, and from the closely related discovery of false stories — lies — used either as excuses or playfully.

If we look from this point of view at the relation of language to subjective experience, we can hardly deny that every genuine report contains an element of decision, at least of the decision to speak the truth. Experiences with lie detectors give a strong indication that, biologically, speaking what is subjectively believed to be the truth differs deeply from lying. I take this as an indication that lying is a comparatively late and fairly specifically human invention; indeed that it has made the human language what it is: an instrument which can be used for misreporting almost as well as for reporting.

in almost every known language and body of legend. Two men meet at a narrow place, often a ford or thin bridge, at sundown, and each in turn tries to force or bar a crossing. They fight till morning but neither prevails. The outcome is an act of naming. Either the one combatant names the other ('thou art Israel' says the Angel to Jacob), or each of the two discloses his name to the other – 'I am Roland', 'I am Oliver brother of the fair Aude', 'I am Robin of Sherwood forest', 'I am Little John'. Several primordial themes and initiatory rites are implicit. But one is the crux of identity, the perilous gift a man makes when he gives his true name into the keeping of another. To falsify or withhold one's real name – the riddle set for Turandot and for countless other personages in fairy-tales and sagas – is to guard one's life, one's *karma* or essence of being, from pillage or alien procurement. To pretend to be another, to oneself or at large, is to employ the 'alternative' powers of language in the most thorough, ontologically liberating way. The Houyhnhnms and the Deity inhabit a tautology of coherent self: they are only what they are. As e. e. cummings put it:

> one is the song which fiends and angels sing:
> all murdering lies by mortals told make two.

Through the 'make-up' of language, man is able, in part at least, to exit from his own skin and, where the compulsion to 'otherness' becomes pathological, to splinter his own identity into unrelated or contrastive voices. The speech of schizophrenia is that of extreme 'alternity'.

All these masking functions are familiar to rhetoric and to the conventions of social discourse. Talleyrand's maxim 'La parole a été donnée à l'homme pour déguiser sa pensée' is a pointed commonplace. As is the philosophic belief, concisely argued in Ortega y Gasset's essay on translation, that there is some fundamental gap or slippage between thought and words. Lies, says Vladimir Jankélévitch in his study of 'Le Mensonge', reflect 'the impotence of speech before the supreme wealth of thought'. A crude dualism is at work here, an unanalysed notion of 'thought' as previous to or distinct from verbal expression. The identical point – language seen as a garment cloaking the true forms of 'thought' – is put forward in Wittgenstein's *Tractatus* (4.002): 'Die Sprache verkleidet den Gedanken. Und zwar so, dass man nach der äusseren Form des Kleides, nicht auf die Form des bekleideten Gedankens schliessen kann; weil die äussere Form des Kleides nach ganz anderen Zwecken gebildet ist als danach, die Form des Körpers erkennen zu lassen.' The simile is not only epistemologically and linguistically misleading; it

betrays a characteristic moral negative. Language commits larceny by concealing 'thought'; the ideal is one of total equivalence and empirical verifiability (cf. the Houyhnhnms). 'What is said is always too much or too little,'
observes Nietzsche in the *Will to Power*, 'the demand that one should denude
oneself with every word one says is a piece of naïveté.' Even here the
pejorative image of disguise, of the false garb over the true skin is operative.
Undoubtedly the linguistic resources of concealment *are* vital. It is difficult
to imagine either the 'humanization' of the species or the preservation of
social life without them. But these are, in the final analysis, defensive adaptations, body-paint, the capacity of the leaf-moth to take on the coloration of
its background.

The dialectic of 'alternity', the genius of language for planned counter-
factuality, are overwhelmingly positive and creative. They too are rooted in
defence. But 'defence' here has a quite different meaning and gravity. At the
central level the enemy is not the other drinker at the water-hole, the torturer
seeking your name, the negotiator across the table, or the social bore.
Language is centrally fictive because the enemy is 'reality', because unlike the
Houyhnhnm, man is not prepared to abide with 'the Thing which is'.

Can we particularize T. S. Eliot's finding that mankind will only bear
small doses of reality? Anthropology, myth, psychoanalysis preserve dim
vestiges of the ancient shock man suffered at his discovery of the universality
and routine of death. Uniquely, one conjectures, among animal species, we
cultivate inside us, we conceptualize and prefigure the enigmatic terror of our
own personal extinction. It is only imperfectly, by dint of strenuous inatten-
tion, that we bear the knowledge of that finale. I have suggested that the
grammars of the future tense, of conditionality, of imaginary open-endedness
are essential to the sanity of consciousness and to the intuitions of forward
motion which animate history. One can go further. It is unlikely that man,
as we know him, would have survived without the fictive, counter-factual,
anti-determinist means of language, without the semantic capacity, generated
and stored in the 'superfluous' zones of the cortex, to conceive of, to articulate
possibilities beyond the treadmill of organic decay and death. It is in this
respect that human tongues, with their conspicuous consumption of subjunctive, future, and optative forms, are a decisive evolutionary advantage.
Through them we proceed in a substantive illusion of freedom. Man's
sensibility endures and transcends the brevity, the haphazard ravages, the
physiological programming of individual life because the semantically coded
responses of the mind are constantly broader, freer, more inventive than the

demands and stimulus of the material fact. 'There is only *one* world,' proclaims Nietzsche in the *Will to Power*, 'and that world is false, cruel, contradictory, misleading, senseless ... We need lies to vanquish this reality, this "truth", we need lies *in order to live* ... That lying is a necessity of life is itself a part of the terrifying and problematic character of existence.' Through un-truth, through counter-factuality, man 'violates' (*vergewaltigt*) an absurd, confining reality; and his ability to do so is at every point artistic, creative (*ein Künstler-Vermögen*). We secrete from within ourselves the grammar, the mythologies of hope, of fantasy, of self-deception without which we would have been arrested at some rung of primate behaviour or would, long since, have destroyed ourselves. It is our syntax, not the physiology of the body or the thermodynamics of the planetary system, which is full of tomorrows. Indeed, this may be the only area of 'free will', of assertion outside direct neuro-chemical causation or programming. We speak, we dream ourselves free of the organic trap. Ibsen's phrase pulls together the whole evolutionary argument: man lives, he progresses by virtue of 'the Life-Lie'.

The linguistic correlates are these: language is not only innovative in the sense defined by transformational generative grammar, it is literally creative. Every act of speech has a potential of invention, a capacity to initiate, sketch, or construct 'anti-matter' (the terminology of particle physics and cosmology, with its inference of 'other worlds', is exactly suggestive of the entire notion of 'alternity'). In fact, this *poiesis* or dialectic of counter-statement is even more complex, because the 'reality' which we oppose or set aside is itself very largely a linguistic product. It is made up of the metonymies, metaphors, classifications which man originally spun around the inchoate jumble of perceptions and phenomena. But the cardinal issue is this: the 'messiness' of language, its fundamental difference from the ordered, closed systematization of mathematics or formal logic, the polysemy of individual words, are neither a defect nor a surface feature which can be cleared up by the analysis of deep structures. The fundamental 'looseness' of natural language is crucial to the creative functions of internalized and outward speech. A 'closed' syntax, a formally exhaustible semantics, would be a closed world. 'Metaphysics, religion, ethics, knowledge — all derive from man's will to art, to lies, from his flight before truth, from his negation of truth', said Nietzsche. This evasion of the 'given fact', this gainsaying is inherent in the combinatorial structure of grammar, in the imprecision of words, in the persistently altering nature of usage and correctness. New worlds are born between the lines.

Of course there is an element of defeat in our reliance on language and

the imaginary. There are truths of existence, particularities of material substance which escape us, which our words erode and for which the mental
concept is only a surrogate. The linguistic pulse of perception and counter-
creation, of apprehension and 'alternity' is itself ambivalent. No one has come
nearer to identifying the reciprocal motion of loss and creation in all utterance,
in all verbalized consciousness, than Mallarmé in a compressed sentence in
his preface to René Ghil's *Traité du Verbe* (1886): 'Je dis: une fleur! et, hors
de l'oubli où ma voix relègue aucun contour, en tant que quelque chose d'autre
que les calices sus, musicalement se lève, idée même et suave, l'absente de
tous bouquets.' But as Mallarmé himself notes, in a preceding sentence, it is
this absence which allows the human spirit its vital space, which enables the
mind to construe essence and generality – *la notion pure* – beyond the narrows
and shut horizons of our material condition.

In the creative function of language non-truth or less-than-truth is, we have
seen, a primary device. The relevant framework is not one of morality but
of survival. At every level, from brute camouflage to poetic vision, the
linguistic capacity to conceal, misinform, leave ambiguous, hypothesize,
invent is indispensable to the equilibrium of human consciousness and to the
development of man in society. Only a small portion of human discourse is
nakedly veracious or informative in any monovalent, unqualified sense. The
scheme of unambiguous propositions, of utterances as direct pointers or
homologous responders to a preceding utterance, which is set out in formal
grammars and in the extension of information theory to language study, is
an abstraction. It has only the most occasional, specialized counterpart in
natural language. In actual speech all but a small class of definitional or
'unreflective-response' sentences are surrounded, mutely ramified, blurred by
an immeasurably dense, individualized field of intention and withholding.
Scarcely anything in human speech is what it sounds. Thus it is inaccurate
and theoretically spurious to schematize language as 'information' or to
identify language, be it unspoken or vocalized, with 'communication'. The
latter term will serve only if it includes, if it places emphasis on, what is *not*
said in the saying, what is said only partially, allusively or with intent to
screen. Human speech conceals far more than it confides; it blurs much more
than it defines; it distances more than it connects. The terrain between speaker
and hearer – even when the current of discourse is internalized, when 'I' speak
to 'myself', this duality being itself a fiction of 'alternity' – is unstable, full
of mirage and pitfalls. 'The only true thoughts', said Adorno in his *Minima
Moralia*, 'are those which do not grasp their own meaning.'

Possibly we have got hold of the wrong end of the the stick altogether when ascribing to the development of speech a primarily informational, a straight-forwardly communicative motive. This may have been the generative impulse during a preliminary phase, during a very gradual elaboration and vocalization of the truth-conditioned signal systems of higher animals. One imagines a transitional 'proto-linguistic' stage of purely ostensive, stimulus-determined 'speech' of the kind which recent investigators have taught a chimpanzee.[5] Then, it may be towards the end of the last Ice Age, occurred the explosive discovery that language is making and re-making, that state-ments can be free of fact and utility. In his *Einführung in die Metaphysik* (1953), Heidegger identifies this event with the true inception of human existence: 'Die Sprache kann nur aus dem Ueberwältigenden angefangen haben, im Aufbruch des Menschen in das Sein. In diesem Aufbruch war die Sprache als Wortwerden des Seins: Dichtung. Die Sprache ist die Urdichtung, in der ein Volk das Sein dichtet.' There is, to be sure, no evidence that this discovery, with which language as we know it truly begins, was explosive. But inter-related advances in cranial capacity, in the making of tools, and, so far as we can judge, in the lineaments of social organization do suggest a quantum jump. The symbolic affinities between words and fire, between the live twist of flame and the darting tongue, are immemorially archaic and firmly en-trenched in the subconscious. Thus it may be that there is a language-factor in the Prometheus myth, an association between man's mastery over fire and his new conception of speech. Prometheus is the first to hold Nemesis at bay by silence, by refusing to disclose to his otherwise omnipotent tormentor the words which pulse and blaze in his own visionary intellect. In Shelley's *Prometheus Unbound* Earth celebrates this paradoxical victory, the articulation through silence of the powers of word and image:

> Through the cold mass
> Of marble and colour his dreams pass;
> Bright threads whence mothers weave the robes their children wear;
> Language is a perpetual Orphic song,

---

5. cf. Philip H. Lieberman: 'Primate Vocalizations and Human Linguistic Ability' (*Journal of the Acoustical Society of America*, XLIV, 1968); J. B. Lancaster: 'Primate Communication Systems and the Emergence of Human Language', in P. C. Jay (ed.): *Primates* (New York, 1968); Allen R. and Beatrice T. Gardner: 'Teaching Sign Language to a Chimpanzee' (*Science*, CLXV, 1969). All the evidence, together with a powerful argument on the evolution of language out of the use of tools, is summarized in Gordon W. Hewes: 'An Explicit Formulation of the Relationship Between Tool-Usings, Tool-Making, and the Emergence of Language' (*Visible Language*, VII, 1973).

Which rules with Daedal harmony a throng
Of thoughts and forms, which else senseless and shapeless were.

(412–17)

If we postulate, as I think we must, that human speech matured principally through its hermetic and creative functions, that the evolution of the full genius of language is inseparable from the impulse to concealment and fiction, then we may at last have an approach to the Babel problem. All developed language has a private core. According to Velimir Khlebnikov, the Russian futurist who thought more deeply than any other great poet about the frontiers of language, 'Words are the living eyes of secrecy.' They encode, preserve, and transmit the knowledge, the shared memories, the metaphorical and pragmatic conjectures on life of a small group – a family, a clan, a tribe. Mature speech begins in shared secrecy, in centripetal storage or inventory, in the mutual cognizance of a very few. In the beginning the word was largely a pass-word, granting admission to a nucleus of like speakers. 'Linguistic exogamy' comes later, under compulsion of hostile or collaborative contact with other small groups. We speak first to ourselves, then to those nearest us in kinship and locale. We turn only gradually to the outsider, and we do so with every safeguard of obliqueness, of reservation, of conventional flatness or outright misguidance. At its intimate centre, in the zone of familial or totemic immediacy, our language is most economic of explanation, most dense with intentionality and compacted implication. Streaming outward it thins, losing energy and pressure as it reaches an alien speaker.

✦ *Theme and Variations* ✦

We have seen Horace asserting that the poet's work is the sole guarantor of immortality for other men. There is, therefore, a special poignancy in the fact that the poet himself is mortal, that the singer who ensures survival for others should fall prey to death. In William Dunbar's 'Lament for the Makers', which scholars assign to the period between 1510 and 1520, the terror of the theme is unconcealed. Neither clerk nor theologian can escape, and the poets also are doomed:

I se the makaris amang the laif
Playis heir ther pageant, sine gois to graif;
Sparit is nocht ther faculte;
   Timor mortis conturbat me

He has done petuously devour
The noble Chaucer, of makaris flowr,
The Monk of Bery, and Gower, all thre;
   Timor mortis conturbat me.

There follow ten hammering stanzas enumerating other poets gone. Then the vice closes on Dunbar himself:

Sen he has all my brether tane,
He will nocht lat me lif alane,
On forse I man his nixt pray be;
   Timor mortis conturbat me.

The Renaissance takes up the topic but introduces a dialectic of negation: the poet must die, yet either in his own spiritual person or through the poetic lineage of which he is a part, he will know rebirth. In this treatment of the theme there are obvious complications of adjustment to a Christian view. How is Orpheus' return from the underworld, which is used emblematically throughout the whole tradition of elegy and celebration, to be reconciled to the Christian interpretation of death?[1] The conventions of pastoral serve as an ingenious compromise. By transposing into the landscape and idiom of Theocritus and Virgil, the Christian elegist achieves two effects: he gives to the conceit of the poet's immortality an allegoric distance, and he hints subtly at symbolic concordances between the Apollonian–Orphic tradition and that of the Good Shepherd. Pastoral and paschal interact. A number of subsidiary motifs appear in each variant. With the death of the particular poet, the art of the Muses is itself on the point of extinction. The mourning poet, moreover, feels threatened. How much time is there left for *him*? His lament, therefore, has both a public and a private echo. But this lament must cease. The master is not truly gone. The genius of his verse, the reflection of this genius, pallid as it may be, in the elegy now being composed, initiate a

1. In his remarkable study of *Orpheus in the Middle Ages* (Harvard University Press, 1970), John Block Friedman has shown how late-antique thought, Neoplatonism, and Christian iconography lead to the gradual evolution of an 'Orpheus–Christus figure'. From the twelfth century on this syncretic conception influences art and literature.

counter-current of hope. The mourning landscape modulates into spring. These motifs and the general motion of the argument become formulaic. They allow us to read five major English poems as members of a set related by explicit permutations (each poet in turn takes into account the ways in which his predecessors have organized the invariants).

The tension in Thomas Carew's 'Elegy on the Death of Dr Donne' (1640) stems from a need to accord pagan with Christian counters. The need was the more acute because of Donne's ecclesiastical status and the notorious distance between Donne's profane and sacred poetry. The death of the Dean of St Paul's has left poetry 'widdowed'. Carew doubts that there is sufficient inspiration left to produce even an adequate lament:

> Have we no voice, no tune? Did'st thou dispense
> Through all our language, both the words and sense?

Donne had found poetry in a barren state:

> So the fire
> That fills with spirit and heat the Delphique quire,
> Which kindled first by thy Promethean breath,
> Glow'd here a while, lies quench't now in thy death . . .

Through Donne's verse the Muses' garden has been purged of 'Pedantique weedes'. Donne had opened up for English poets a 'Mine of rich and pregnant phansie'. This image of subterranean venture leads naturally to Orpheus. But Carew gives Orpheus' formulaic presence a critical twist. Such was the wealth and masculine energy of Donne's exploitation that even the Thracian singer would have found in Dr Donne an 'Exchequer', a treasure-trove of invention. Donne's merit was the greater as he accomplished these feats in 'our stubborn language' and at a time when the primacy of the classics and the long labours of their imitators had left only 'rifled fields' (the Proserpine theme with its many affinities with that of Orpheus and with the symbolic drama of seasonal change is not far off). Yet although Donne's demise and Donne's own treatments of the topic of universal decay bear witness to 'the death of all the Arts', some impulse to creation remains. Carew's simile is a fine one: a swiftly turning wheel stays in motion for a time even when the hand which spun it is withdrawn. In a final stringency Carew binds together the formulaic strands of classical mythology and Christian vocation. 'Delphique quire' exactly prepares for the necessary conjunction. Donne was

> Apollo's first, at last, the true God's Priest.

This twofold consecration and the ambiguities it entails are, of course, the substance of *Lycidas* (1645). More readers than Dr Johnson have been left uncomfortable by the poem's uncompromising stylization of grief, by the ways in which mythological–pastoral conventions are made to carry the moral weight and logical progress of Milton's meaning. But this is the point. No major poem in English literature depends more rigorously on implicit citation, on the postulate of a repertoire of allusion, echo, and counterpoint. The flora of the opening lines directs us to Horace's Ode I.1 and to Spenser's *Shepheards Calendar* for September and January. 'Hard constraint' (Milton's 'Bitter constraint') had moved Spenser to write his *Pastoral Eclogue* on Sidney. Lycidas is the name of the shepherd in Theocritus' seventh Idyll and also that of one of the pastoral speakers in the ninth Eclogue of Virgil. Spenser's *Astrophel* and a long-established device of augmentative pathos lie behind Milton's threefold reiteration of Lycidas' name. 'Who would not sing for Lycidas' is a rewording of 'Carmina sunt dicenda; neget quis carmina Gallo?' from Virgil's tenth Eclogue (Pope will use the formula in *Windsor Forest*: 'What Muse for Granville can refuse to sing?'). There is hardly a line in *Lycidas* which does not solicit, and so far as immediacy of effect goes, presume the reader's awareness of relevant classical and Elizabethan constants.

It is Milton's achievement to use the formulaic and the conventional with such control and confident self-projection, that he appears to go behind the conventions, behind the Horatian, Virgilian, Ovidian variants to an original pressure of experience. He intimates, as it were, and brings to bear on personal feeling those facts of death, of desolate and reborn landscape, of the poet's sense of mystery and doubt as to the nature of his calling, which underlie, which at some time out of historical reach generated the structure of pastoral. Milton can do so just because the 'sincerity' of his lament for Edward King is a qualified and opportunistic one. The anguish of the poem in regard to unfulfilled promise and to the menace of the contemporary political–religious situation points, obviously, to Milton himself. But this egotism is, as we noted, a part of the convention; it is a set element in a poet's mourning for a fellow poet. The stylized, entirely expected character of Milton's material everywhere multiplies the resonance of his statement. Orpheus enters inevitably but to supreme effect:

> What could the Muse her self that *Orpheus* bore,
> The Muse her self, for her enchanting son
> Whom Universal nature did lament,

When by the rout that made the hideous roar,
His goary visage down the stream was sent,
Down the swift *Hebrus* to the *Lesbian* shore.

The motif of resurrection is present in Carew, but Milton gives it a new splendour. Melding Orphic and Christian annunciations of rebirth, *Lycidas* completes its parabolic motion in joy:

Weep no more, woeful Shepherds weep no more,
For *Lycidas* your sorrow is not dead ...

The paradox is theological but also strictly formulaic. It is first stated by Pindar, then rephrased by Horace and by Ovid in the *Metamorphoses*. The act of poetic lament is itself a proof that poetry shall endure.

By 1821 the machinery of pastoral was a stale sham. Yet *Adonais* invests it with a vitality which goes well beyond the rhetorical flourish, beyond the sheer prosodic drive of the poem. This is because Shelley's literalism in the handling of the mythological-antique conventions (at the service, to be sure, of his own highly idiosyncratic allegoric *personae*) is as intense, as personal as is that of Milton, though in a totally opposed direction of thought. '*Adonais*', writes Harold Bloom, 'is in a clear sense a materialist's poem, written out of a materialist's despair at his own deepest convictions, and finally a poem soaring above those convictions into a mystery that leaves a pragmatic materialism quite undisturbed.'[2] Shelley's despair at Keats's death, at the organic finality of that death, is deliberately in excess of the facts so far as the acquaintance of the two poets goes. But this excess is integral to Shelley's realization — a realization which we know to be formulaic in this pattern of elegies — of his own threatened condition and of the profoundly ambiguous nature of the poet's existence on earth. In a closing movement beyond philosophic or pragmatic evidence, *Adonais* breaks free of earth and envisions a Platonic–apocalyptic radiance wholly extrinsic to man. The echoes of *Lycidas*, the parallelisms of rhetorical structure are everywhere apparent. But the type of permutation applied to the traditional constants and to Milton's particular format is that of a radical critique. Shelley's text is a rebuttal of Milton's the more focused because it operates by means of intentional echo.

Exactly as in Milton, the name of the dead poet sounds over and over at

2. Harold Bloom: 'The Unpastured Sea: An Introduction to Shelley', in H. Bloom (ed.): *Romanticism and Consciousness* (New York, 1970), p. 397.

the start of the lament. And with reference not to Keats but certainly to *Lycidas*, Shelley hints at a death by drowning:

> Oh, weep for Adonais — he is dead! ...
> For he is gone, where all things wise and fair
> Descend; — oh, dream not that the amorous Deep
> Will yet restore him to the vital air;
> Death feeds on his mute voice, and laughs at our despair.

From line 19 to line 190 the bleak reality of organic and individual death is reiterated: '*He* will wake no more, oh, never more.' The surge towards transcendence, with its precise echo to Milton, begins with the opening verse of Stanza XXXIX:

> Peace, peace! he is not dead, he doth not sleep —
> He hath awakened from the dream of life ...

Orpheus is present though unnamed:

> He is made one with Nature: there is heard
> His voice in all her music, from the moan
> Of thunder, to the song of night's sweet bird ...

But the mourner leaves behind earthly reality even though it is now animate with Adonais' genius. The sphere of man is too corrupt a vessel to contain the ultimate energies of poetic–metaphysical vision. The last stanza concentrates a sum of mastered inheritance and self-recognition so great that it erupts — no other word will do — into numbing clairvoyance. Proceeding from a final allusion to *Lycidas* and the drowning of Edward King via the Platonic and Petrarchan simile, always precious to him, of the soul's bark, Shelley foretells his own death:

> The breath whose might I have invoked in song
> Descends on me; my spirit's bark is driven,
> Far from the shore, far from the trembling throng
> Whose sails were never to the tempest given ...

Rejecting both the pastoral and the Christian contract with immortality, yet drawing largely on the formulaic tradition in which both are instrumental, Shelley's lament, like Dunbar's, rounds on its maker.

In *Thyrsis* (1866) the permutation of canonic features is consciously parasitic. When Matthew Arnold calls on Thyrsis, Corydon, Bion, and their

Sicilian 'mates', he does so at second and third hand. The invocation is, patently, one to Milton and Shelley. But the resulting academicism and touch of self-mockery are apt. They communicate the scholastic ambience, the elevated bookish tenor of Arnold's relations with Clough. Fragile as they are, moreover, the pastoral formulas draw a paradoxical integrity from the fact – it is the key fact – that Arnold's sorrow has a private truth present neither in *Lycidas* nor *Adonais*. The elegy keeps in delicate poise a self-conscious pathos and gentle irony neither of which cancels out grief or agnosticism. The placing of Orpheus illustrates Arnold's method. A Sicilian shepherd would have followed Thyrsis into the underworld

> And make leap up with joy the beauteous head
>   Of Proserpine, among whose crowned hair
>   Are flowers first open'd on Sicilian air,
> And flute his friend, like Orpheus, from the dead.

Today no such dispensation is allowed. In Clough's early death Arnold, who is at this point entirely formulaic, sees his own prefigured:

> Yes, thou art gone! and round me too the night
>   In ever-nearing circle weaves her shade ...

Then, in deliberate rephrasing of Milton and Shelley, the singer turns from desolation:

>   yet will I not despair.
>   Despair I will not, while I yet descry
>   'Neath the mild canopy of English air
>   That lonely tree against the western sky.

And Thyrsis' voice, here the *genius loci* of the Virgilian eclogue and landscape, confirms:

> *Why faintest thou? I wander'd till I died.*
> *Roam on! The light we sought is shining still.*

That Thyrsis' words contain an allusion to a well-known passage in Clough's own poetry again illustrates the balance between formal convention and intimacy in Arnold's 'monody' (Milton uses the same technical term to designate *Lycidas*).

  This elegiac 'set' to which one could add, but only I think with some qualifications, Swinburne's 'Ave atque Vale' and Tennyson's *In Memoriam*, is simultaneously implicit and examined in Auden's 'In Memory of W. B. Yeats' who had died in January 1939. Auden exploits the pathetic fallacy knowing it to be suspect yet fundamental to the interplay of landscape and mourning throughout the pastoral genre:

> He disappeared in the dead of winter:
> The brooks were frozen, the airports almost deserted,
> And snow disfigured the public statues;
> The mercury sank in the mouth of the dying day.
> O all the instruments agree
> The day of his death was a dark cold day.

Orpheus enters. It is not, this time, or in the first instance, the Orpheus of resurrection but as in Milton the singer dismembered: 'Now he is scattered among a hundred cities'. 'The rout which made the hideous roar' in *Lycidas*, the philistine mob which hounded Adonais to his doom, the vulgar positivists who threaten the Parnassus of Thyrsis and the Scholar-Gypsy, are neatly transmuted into brokers 'roaring like beasts on the floor of the Bourse'. But poetry endures:

> it flows south
> From ranches of isolation and the busy griefs,
> Raw towns that we believe and die in; it survives,
> A way of happening, a mouth.

Auden's passage is a permutation, highly personal yet also firmly traditional, of corresponding motifs in Ovid and Milton. It is not poetry as abstraction but Orpheus' head which journeys south 'to the *Lesbian* shore'. It is the slain Orpheus who, as Ovid reminds us, does not cease from song:

> membra iacent diuersa locis, caput, Hebre, lyramque
> excipis: et (mirum!) medio dum labitur amne,
> flebile nescio quid queritur lyra, flebile lingua
> murmurat exanimis, respondent flebile ripae.

[The poet's limbs lay scattered far and wide. But, Oh Hebrus, you received his head and his lyre, and (oh miracle!) while they floated in midstream, the lyre sounded desolate notes, the lifeless tongue murmured mournfully, and the river-banks replied sorrowingly.]

(Metamorphoses, XI. 50–53)

Finally Auden reflects on the whole exercise of poets mourning poets. He observes its moral ambiguity. He worries over the central paradox of linguistic immortality. There is something strangely disturbing, even distasteful in the fact that

> Time that is intolerant
> Of the brave and innocent,
> And indifferent in a week
> To a beautiful physique,
>
> Worships language and forgives
> Everyone by whom it lives;
> Pardons cowardice, conceit,
> Lays its honours at their feet.

In the scandal of that forgiveness, however, lie the larger obligation and promise. No less than Carew, Milton, Shelley, and Arnold before him, Auden closes bracingly. Orpheus' unconstraining voice must follow man 'To the bottom of the night'. It must persuade us to rejoice even in the black and winter of history. The coda is pure pastoral:

> In the deserts of the heart
> Let the healing fountains start,
> In the prison of his days
> Teach the free man how to praise.

'Permutation' organizes many other 'sets' in western poetry and poetic drama, as it does also in music and iconography. It enters into play wherever formulaic elements are at once broad enough to shape a literary form and specific enough to produce identifying, lasting verbal expressions peculiar to that form. This is the case in the family of poets' elegies on poets which runs unbroken in English from Sidney and Spenser to Auden. The formulaic elements of pastoral setting, of self-recognition, of transition from despair to hope, were based on the classical idyll and eclogue. They generated stylizations so supple and efficacious as to serve poets of profoundly different temper and outlook over four centuries. Each mourner in turn drew on the formal structure and on the verbal detail of his predecessors' work. It is the constancy not only of verbal turns but of a genre as a unit which makes 'permutation' more comprehensive and wide-ranging than 'substitution' though both are, as we saw, closely related. The line of descent from Cowley's treatment of the 'coy mistress' theme to that of Donne and of Herrick is immediately verbal; it organizes a topic rather than a genre. 'In Memory of W. B. Yeats' marks the further development, with all the stress on organic cohesion which 'development' can carry, or possibly the concluding statement, of a major form.

Let me propose one further heading under the general class of partial transformations; this class extends, as we have seen, from most literal translation to parody and oblique, even unconscious, echo or allusion. In 'The Extasie' Donne advanced the thesis that there occurs in the spiritual and carnal union of authentic love a commingling, an osmotic confluence of two souls:

> When love with one another so
> Interinanimates two soules
> That abler soule which thence doth flow
> Defects of loneliness controules.

There is manuscript authority also for a simpler form of the key term: we can read 'interanimates'. And it is this variant which I would use. 'Interanimation' signifies a process of totally attentive interpenetration. It tells of a dialectic of fusion in which identity survives altered but also strengthened and redefined by virtue of reciprocity. There is annihilation of self in the other consciousness and recognition of self in a mirroring motion. Principally, there results a multiplication of resource, of affirmed being. 'Interanimated', two presences, two formal structures, two bodies of utterance assume a dimension, an energy of meaning far beyond that which either could generate in isolation or in mere sequence. The operation is, literally, one of raising to a higher power.

If we consider these attributes, it will be immediately apparent that they reproduce the terms proposed throughout this study to define and characterize translation itself. Intensely focused penetration, the establishment of mutual identity through conjunction, the heightening of a work's existence when it is confronted and re-enacted by alternate versions of itself — these are the structural features of translation proper. Even where it relates works remote from one another in language, formal convention, and cultural context, 'interanimation' will show itself to be one further derivative from, one further metamorphic analogue of translation. If this has not always been obvious, the reason may be that the area of relations covered by this rubric is so immediate to and so ubiquitous in our culture.

➤ English Tomorrow ➤

The threat of dispersal, of a crisis in the organic coherence between language and its cultural content, could stem from another and paradoxical direction. Here the argument bears crucially on English.

'At countless points on the earth's surface, English will be the most available language – English of some sort.'[1] I. A. Richards's prediction, made in 1943, has proved accurate. Like no other tongue before it, English has expanded into a world-language. It has far outstripped its potential competitors. A large part of the impulse behind the spread of English across the globe is obviously political and economic. In the aftermath of the Second World War, and building on earlier colonial–imperial foundations, English acted as the vulgate of American power and of Anglo-American technology and finance. But the causes of universality are also linguistic. There is ample evidence that English is regarded by native speakers of other languages, whether in Asia, Africa or Latin America, as easier to acquire than any other second language. It is widely felt that some degree of competence can be achieved through mastery of fewer and simpler phonetic, lexical, and grammatical units than would be the case in North Chinese, Russian, Spanish, German, or French (the natural rivals to world status). Today, English is being taught as a necessary skill for modern existence not only throughout continental Europe, but in the Soviet Union and China. It is the second language of Japan, and of much of Africa and India. It is estimated that 88 per cent of scientific and technical literature is either published in English initially or translated into English shortly after its appearance in such languages as Russian, German, and French. The novelist, the playwright, whether his native tongue be Swedish, Dutch, Hebrew, Hungarian, or Italian, looks to English translation for his window on the world. Though figures are very uncertain, the community of English-speakers has been reckoned at 300 million, and is growing rapidly. But statistics, however dramatic, do not make the main point. In ways too intricate, too diverse for socio-linguistics to formulate precisely, English and American-English seem to embody for men and women throughout the world – and particularly for the young – the 'feel' of hope, of material advance, of scientific and empirical procedures. The entire

---

1. I. A. Richards: *Basic English and its Uses* (London, 1943), p. 120.

world-image of mass consumption, of international exchange, of the popular arts, of generational conflict, of technocracy, is permeated by American-English and English citations and speech habits.

Doubtless there are opposing trends. Threatened at their most vulnerable point of self-definition, other language communities are resisting the Anglo-Saxon tide. Witness the politically organized struggle of French to maintain itself in the Middle East and French Africa, and to halt the inroads of *franglais* at home. There is evidence also that the very pressures for social, technological uniformity generated by the Anglo-American model are producing reactions. The bitter struggles between Walloons and Flemings, the language riots which plague India, the resurgence of linguistic autonomy in Wales and Brittany point to deep instincts of preservation. Norway now has two standard languages where it had only one at the turn of the century. Dialect and variant forms of speech are tending towards autonomy. Nevertheless, English dominates as a world-language whose reach far exceeds that of Latin in the historical past, and whose efficacy has all but nullified such schemes as Esperanto.

The consequences lie outside the scope of this study. They are, at many points, contradictory. American English, West Indian English, the idiom of Australia, of New Zealand, of Canada, the varieties of English spoken and written in West Africa have immensely enriched the total spectrum of the mother-tongue. It can fairly be argued that the energies of innovation, of linguistic experiment, have passed from the centre. Has there been an 'English English' author of absolutely the first rank after D. H. Lawrence and J. C. Powys? The representative masters of literature in the English language, since James, Shaw, Eliot, Joyce, and Pound have been mainly Irish or American. Currently, West Indian English, the English of the best American poets and novelists, the speech of West African drama demonstrate what can be called an Elizabethan capacity for ingestion, for the enlistment of both popular and technical forms. In Thomas Pynchon, in Patrick White, the language is fiercely alive. The metropolitan response has been, in several respects, one of fastidious retrenchment. Much of contemporary verse, drama, fiction written in England is spare, minimalist, and thoroughly distrustful of verbal exuberance. The techniques of Philip Larkin, Geoffrey Hill, Harold Pinter, and David Storey enact a hoarding of old treasures by means of incisive austerity. It is too early to tell. But the question of the future influence of English at large on English 'at home' is one of the most interesting to face the linguist and historian of culture.

If there is enrichment, moreover, there is also loss. 'English of some sort' said Richards, meaning a basic, orthographically rationalized version. But the simplifications may be of an even more damaging order. The externals of English are being acquired by speakers wholly alien to the historical fabric, to the inventory of felt moral, cultural existence embedded in the language. The landscapes of experience, the fields of idiomatic, symbolic, communal reference which give to the language its specific gravity, are distorted in transfer or lost altogether. As it spreads across the earth, 'international English' is like a thin wash, marvellously fluid, but without adequate base. One need only converse with Japanese colleagues and students, whose technical proficiency in English humbles one, to realize how profound are the effects of dislocation. So much that is being said is correct, so little is right. Only time and native ground can provide a language with the interdependence of formal and semantic components which 'translates' culture into active life. It is the absence from them of any natural semantics of remembrance which disqualifies artificial languages from any but trivial or *ad hoc* usage.

The internationalization of English has begun to provoke a twofold enervation. In many societies imported English, with its necessarily synthetic, 'pre-packaged' semantic field, is eroding the autonomy of the native language-culture. Intentionally or not, American-English and English, by virtue of their global diffusion, are a principal agent in the destruction of natural linguistic diversity. This destruction is, perhaps, the least reparable of the ecological ravages which distinguish our age. More subtly, the modulation of English into an 'Esperanto' of world-commerce, technology, and tourism, is having debilitating effects on English proper. To use current jargon, ubiquity is causing a negative feedback. Again, it is too soon to judge of the dialectical balance, of the reciprocities between profit and loss which accrue to English as it becomes the lingua franca and shorthand of the earth. If dissemination weakened the native genius of the language, the price would be a tragic one. English literature, the penetrating yet delicate imprint of a uniquely coherent, articulate historical experience on the vocabulary and syntax of English speech, the supple vitality of English in regard to its unbroken past – these are one of the excellences of our condition. It would be ironic if the answer to Babel were pidgin and not Pentecost.

← *Future Literacies* →

We have seen something of the collapse of hierarchies and of the radical changes in the value-systems which relate personal creation with death. These mutations have brought an end to classic literacy. By that I mean something perfectly concrete. The major part of western literature, which has been for two thousand years and more so deliberately interactive, the work echoing, mirroring, alluding to, previous works in the tradition, is now passing quickly out of reach. Like far galaxies bending over the horizon of invisibility, the bulk of English poetry, from Caxton's Ovid to *Sweeney Among the Nightingales*, is now modulating from active presence into the inertness of scholarly conservation. Based, as it firmly is, on a deep, many-branched anatomy of classical and scriptural reference, expressed in a syntax and vocabulary of heightened tenor, the unbroken arc of English poetry, of reciprocal discourse that relates Chaucer and Spenser to Tennyson and to Eliot, is fading rapidly from the reach of natural reading. A central pulse in awareness, in the language, is becoming archival. Though complex in its causes and consequences, this dimming of recognitions is easy to demonstrate:

> Yet once more, O ye laurels, and once more,
> Ye myrtles brown, with ivy never sere,
> I come to pluck your berries harsh and crude,
> And with forced fingers rude
> Shatter your leaves before the mellowing year.
> Bitter constraint, and sad occasion dear,
> Compels me to disturb your season due;
> For Lycidas is dead, dead ere his prime,
> Young Lycidas, and hath not left his peer.
> Who would not sing for Lycidas? he knew
> Himself to sing, and build the lofty rhyme.

Laurel, myrtle and ivy have their specific emblematic life throughout western art and poetry, and within Milton's own work. We read, in his fine tribute to Giovanni Manso:

> Forsitan et nostros ducat de marmore vultus,
> Nectens aut Paphiâ myrti aut Parnasside lauri
> Fronde comas ...

The ivy stands for poetry when it is particularly allied to learning: Horace's *Odes*, I.i.29, and Spenser's *Shepheards Calendar* for September tell us that, as they told it to Milton. *Odes* I is at work also in 'myrtles brown' (*pulla myrtus*). The *Shepheards Calendar* for January and *Macbeth*, obviously, are resonant in the use of 'sere'. And the echo moves forward to Tennyson's *Ode to Memory* and 'Those peerless flowers which in the rudest wind / Never grow sere' (*rude* has, as it were, carried over into Tennyson's ear from Milton's next line). 'Hard constraint' had moved Spenser to write his *Pastoral Eclogue* on Sidney, and the entire trope of compulsion is summarized in Keats's *Ode to Psyche*:

> O Goddess! hear these tuneless numbers, wrung
> By sweet enforcement and remembrance dear.

The Spenser and the Keats phrasings both temper and heighten the special coil of Milton's word-order: *sad occasion dear*, in which 'dear' signifies whatever affects us most directly, be it in love or in hatred, in pleasure or in grief (cf. *Hamlet*, 'my dearest foe in heaven', or *Henry V*, 'all your dear offences'). Lycidas is, of course, the name of the shepherd in Theocritus' seventh Idyll and that of one of the speakers in the ninth Eclogue of Virgil. The immediate reiteration of the name, particularly at the start of the line, is a long-established convention of pathos, a musical augment of sorrow. Spenser's *Astrophel* was probably in Milton's mind –

> Young Astrophel, the pride of shepheards praise,
> Young Astrophel, the rusticke lasses love.

Both 'repeats', the Spenserian and the Miltonic, will sound in Shelley's *Adonais*. 'Who would not sing for Lycidas?' is almost translation: from Virgil's tenth Eclogue, II.iii – 'Carmina sunt dicenda; neget quis carmina Gallo?' cf. the *reprise* in Pope's *Windsor Forest*:

> Granville commands; your aid, O Muses, bring!
> What Muse for Granville can refuse to sing?

And so on.

All these are surface markings. We find them in dictionaries and concordances. They can be put at the bottom of the page in what might be called 'first-level footnotes'. But the information they provide is only the outward of literacy.

Fullness of response depends on an accord, almost intuitive because so thoroughly schooled, with the whole nature of Milton's enterprise, with the context of intent and agreed emotional, designative reflexes on which the poem is built. A natural reading implies an apprehension, generalized but exact, of what is meant by Idyll and Eclogue, and of the millennial interplay, at once symbolic and conventional, between images of Arcadia and of death. It is an apprehension which includes, for supporting or contrastive reference, not only something of Greek pastoral and a reasonable amount of Virgil, but Giorgione and Poussin. Milton's *monody*, itself a term charged with precise intimations of range and tone, is nearly impossible to get into right focus if one has no acquaintance with that mode of Italian elegiac pastoral, often composed in Latin, in which the world of Arcadia comprises problematic, philosophically resistant elements of contemporary politics and religion. Is any naturalness of response to the text plausible without familiarity, again unobtrusive because long-established, with the grid of seasonal, botanical, and celestial markers that direct the motion of the argument and allow its vital economy (the amaranth, the day-star, the agricultural and liturgical overtones of May)?

To 'read' *Lycidas*, to seize its purpose at any level but that of vague musicality, is to participate, and not only with one's brain, in the central equivocation between death and poetic glory. Milton's is one of the archetypal statements of the trope of transcendence, of that cast for immortality beyond 'the parching wind'. This is a poem about fame and the sacrificial gamble which 'scorns delights and lives laborious days'. The pulse of allusion that beats steady in almost every line, back to Greek, to Latin, to Scripture, and which echoes forward to Dryden, to Arnold, to Tennyson's *In Memoriam*, is no technical ornament. It is a full-scale pronouncement of accord with the value-relations of personal genius and menacing time which underlie a classic culture. The lament for the poet gone is always autobiographical: the mourner tenses his own resources against the ubiquitous blackmail of death. The 'sincerity' of his grief is intense but reflexive. Dissent from this code of moral, psychological conduct, be deaf to its particular idiom, and you will no longer be able to read, to hear, the great tradition of elegy and poetics, of meditation between language and death, which led unbroken from Pindar and Virgil to *Thyrsis* and to Auden's commemoration of the death of William Butler Yeats.

Here, too, there could be footnotes. Conceivably, such 'second-level' annotation could refer the reader of *Lycidas* to all the requisite classical, scriptural and contemporary material. It could tell him of the history of elegiac modes and of Milton's notion, old as Hesiod, of the civilizing and sacramental functions of the shepherd-singer. In fact, of course, such annotation would soon run to incommensurable absurdity (it is this which distinguishes it, though not always sharply, from what I called 'first-level footnotes'). To be genuinely informative, contextual annotation would soon amount to little less than a history of the language and of culture. We would find ourselves involved in a process – familiar to information theory – of infinite regress. The total context of a work such as *Lycidas* or the *Divina Commedia*, or *Phèdre* or Goethe's *Faust* – is 'all that is the case', or the active wholeness of preceding and sequent literacy. The thing cannot be done.

But suppose that it could. Suppose that some masterly editorial team devised a complete apparatus of explanation, by virtue of glossaries, concordances, biographical and stylistic appendices. What will have happened to the poem?

This is the decisive point.

As the glossaries lengthen, as the footnotes become more elementary and didactic, the poem, the epic, the drama, move out of balance on the actual page. As even the more rudimentary of mythological, religious or historical references, which form the grammar of western literature, have to be elucidated, the lines of Spenser, of Pope, of Shelley or of *Sweeney Among the Nightingales*, blur away from immediacy. Where it is necessary to annotate every proper name and classical allusion in the dialogue between Lorenzo and Jessica in the garden at Belmont, or in Iachimo's stealthy rhetoric when he emerges in Imogen's chamber, these marvellous spontaneities of enacted feeling become 'literary' and twice-removed (in part, of course, the problem is one of time, of the mere fact that meaning is no longer grasped as quickly, as directly as it is articulated). How is Pope's *Essay on Man* to register its delicate precision and sinew when each proposition reaches us, as it were, on stilts, at the top of a page crowded with elementary comment? What presence in personal delight can *Endymion* have when recent editions annotate 'Venus' as signifying 'pagan goddess of love'?

These are no rhetorical, futuristic questions. The situation is already on us. In the United States, there have appeared versions of parts of the Bible and of Shakespeare in basic English and in strip-cartoon format. Some of these have circulated in the millions. The challenge they represent is serious and credible. It will not be brushed off. We are being asked to choose. Would we have something, at least, of the main legacy of our civilization made accessible to the general public of a modern, mass-society? Or would we rather see the bulk of our literature, of our interior history, pass into the museum? The question cannot be evaded by consoling references to paperback sales or to presentations of classic material – excellent as such presentations sometimes are – on the mass media. These are only surface noises and salutations to a past whose splendour and authority are still atavistically recognized.

The issues are compelling and demand the most honest possible response. Already a dominant proportion of poetry, of religious thought, of art, has receded from personal immediacy into the keeping of the specialist. There it leads a kind of bizarre pseudo-life, proliferating its own inert environment of criticism (we read Eliot *on* Dante, not Dante), of editorial and textual exegesis, of Narcissistic polemic. Never has there been a more hectic prodigality of specialized erudition, in literary studies, in musicology, in art history, in criticism and that most Byzantine of genres, the criticism and theory of criticism. Never have the meta-languages of the custodians flourished more, or with more arrogant jargon, around the silence of live meaning.

An archival pseudo-vitality surrounding what was once felt life; a semi-literacy or sub-literacy outside, making it impossible for the poem to survive naked, to achieve unattended personal impact. Academy and populism. The two conditions are reciprocal, and each polarizes the other in a necessary dialectic. Between them they determine our current state.

The challenge is: was it ever different?

The answer is not as straightforward as current abrasiveness would suggest. Despite pioneering studies, particularly with regard to the nineteenth century in England, our knowledge of the history of reading habits, of the statistics and quality of literate response at different moments and in different communities of western Europe, is still rudimentary. Such well-attested but local facts as the wide dissemination and collective study of Godwin's *Political Justice* during the 1790s, or what we know of the sales and circulation of such writers as George Sand and Tennyson, may or may not be more generally indicative. The evidence is hard to come by and harder to assess. One deals with impressionistic notions of 'climate' and 'tonality'.

Nevertheless, certain contours do emerge. Scriptural and, in a wider sense, religious literacy ran strong, particularly in Protestant lands. The Authorized Version and Luther's Bible carried in their wake a rich tradition of symbolic, allusive, and syntactic awareness. Absorbed in childhood, the Book of Common Prayer, the Lutheran hymnal and psalmody, cannot but have marked a broad compass of mental life with their exact, stylized articulateness and music of thought. Habits of communication and schooling, moreover, sprang directly from the concentration of memory. So much was learned and known *by heart* — a term beautifully apposite to the organic, inward presentness of meaning and spoken being within the individual spirit. The catastrophic decline of memorization in our own modern education and adult resources, is one of the crucial, though as yet little understood, symptoms of an after-culture.

As to knowledge of the classics, here again the evidence varies and is susceptible of different interpretations. But exposure to the forms and conventions active in *Lycidas* was certainly part of a sound education from the seventeenth century until very recently. Different curricula and different social settings obviously entailed varying degrees of depth: but the Homeric and Virgilian epic, the poetry of Ovid and of Horace, the theory of genres in Aristotle and Longinus, were no recondite topics. With a few exceptions (mainly those bearing on the Italian and renaissance-Latin corpus), none of Milton's imitations and pointers would have been outside the scope of my father's schooling in a Vienna *Gymnasium* before the First World War, or indeed outside my own in the *section lettres* of the French *lycée* system of the 1930s and 1940s.

The organized amnesia of present primary and secondary education is a very recent development. There is irony in the fact that one associates the main impetus of this change, its frankest theoretic justifications, with the United States. For it was in the North America of the late eighteenth and nineteenth centuries that the ideal, both Puritan and Jeffersonian, of a general biblical and classical literacy was most widely aimed at.

Concentric to these spheres of 'book-knowledge' lies a personal, unforced intimacy with the names and shapes of the natural world, with flower and tree, with the measure of the seasons and the rising and setting of the stars. The principal energies of our literature draw constantly on this set of recognitions. But to our housed, metallic sensibilities, they have become largely artificial and decorative. Do not, today, inquire of the reader next to you whether he can identify, from personal encounter, even a part of the flora, of the astronomy, which served Ovid and Shakespeare, Spenser and Goethe, as a current alphabet.

Any generalization in these matters is suspect. But the fundamental 'poly-semic' texture of poetry, drama, fiction, certainly since the seventeenth century, the writer's deployment of meaning at many simultaneous levels of directness or difficulty, does imply the availability, perhaps utopian yet perhaps realistic also, of a wide literate public. Heremeticism, the strategy of the incomprehensible, as we find it in so much of art and literature after

Mallarmé, is a reaction, haughty and desolate, to the decay of a natural literacy:

> We were the last romantics — chose for theme
> Traditional sanctity and loveliness;
> Whatever's written in what poets name
> The book of the people; whatever most can bless
> The mind of man or elevate a rhyme;
> But all is changed, that high horse riderless,
> Though mounted in that saddle Homer rode
> Where the swan drifts upon a darkening flood.

But let us assume that Yeats's picture is idealized, that Pegasus has gone more often than not bareback. Let us suppose that the Victorian public-school boy, the *Gymnasiast* or *lycéen* to whom the text of Homer, of Racine, of Goethe, offered natural purchase, were always but a small number, a conscious élite. Even if this was so, the case stands. Restricted as it may have been, that élite embodied the inheritance and dynamics of culture. Its social, economic predominance and confident self-perpetuation were such that the model of a culture — whose values may, indeed, have been specialized and minority-based — served as general criterion. This is the point. Power-relations, first courtly and aristocratic, then *bourgeois* and bureaucratic, underwrote the syllabus of classic culture and made of its transmission a deliberate proceeding. The democratization of high culture — brought on by a crisis of nerve within culture itself and by social revolution — has engendered an absurd hybrid. Dumped on the mass market, the products of classic literacy will be thinned and adulterated. At the opposite end of the spectrum, these same products are salvaged out of life and put in the museum vault.

Again, America is the representative and premonitory example. Nowhere has the debilitation of genuine literacy gone further (consider recent surveys of reading-comprehension and recognition in American high schools). But nowhere, also, have the conservation and learned scrutiny of the art or literature of the past been pursued with more generous authority. American libraries, universities, archives, museums, centres for advanced study, are now the indispensable record and treasure-house of civilization. It is here that the European artist and scholar must come to see the cherished after-glow of his culture. Though often obsessed with the future, the United States is now, certainly in regard to the humanities, the active watchman of the classic past.

It may be that this custodianship relates to a deeply puzzling fact. Creation of absolutely the first rank – in philosophy, in music, in much of literature, in mathematics – continues to occur outside the American *milieu*. It is at once taken up and intelligently exploited there, but the 'motion of spirit' has taken place elsewhere, amid the enervation of Europe, in the oppressive climate of Russia. There is, in a good deal of American intellectual, artistic production (recent painting may be the challenging exception), a characteristic near-greatness, a strength just below the best. Could it be that the United States is destined to be the 'museum culture'? There is no more fascinating question in the sociology of knowledge, none that may touch more intensely on our future. But it lies outside the scope of this essay.

These changes from a dominant to a post- or sub-literacy are themselves expressed in a general 'retreat from the word'. Seen from some future historical perspective, western civilization, from its Hebraic-Greek· origins roughly to the present, may look like a phase of concentrated 'verbalism'. What seem to us salient distinctions may appear to have been parts of a general era in which spoken, remembered and written discourse was the backbone of consciousness. It is a commonplace of current sociology and 'media-study' that this primacy of the 'logic' – of that which organizes the articulations of time and of meaning around the *logos* – is now drawing to a close. Increasingly, the word is caption to the picture. Expanding areas of fact and of sensibility, notably in the exact sciences and the non-representational arts, are out of reach of verbal account or paraphrase. The notations of symbolic logic, the languages of mathematics, the idiom of the computer, are no longer meta-dialects, responsible and reducible to the grammars of verbal cognition. They are autonomous communicatory modes, claiming and expressing for themselves an increasing range of contemplative and active pursuit. Words are corroded by the false hopes and lies they have voiced. The electronic alphabet of immediate global communication and 'togetherness' is not the ancient, divisive legacy of Babel, but the image-in-motion.

Many aspects of this analysis (which was, in fact, put forward some years before McLuhan gave it explosive currency) may well be mistaken or exaggerated. Transmutations of this order of magnitude do not occur overnight and at the immediately graphic surface. But the general 'feel' of the argument is persuasive. There *is* a comprehensive decline in traditional ideals of literate speech. Rhetoric and the arts of conviction which it disciplines, are in almost total disrepute. Pleasure in style, in the 'wroughtness' of expressive forms, is a mandarin, nearly suspect posture. More and more of the informational energy required by a mass-consumer society is being transmitted pictorially. The proportions of articulate charge between margin and column of print is being reversed. We are moving back to a layout of the 'spaces of meaning' in which the pictorial bordure pre-empts more and more of the whole. Often now, it is the shred of text which 'illustrates' (here also, the premonitory presence is that of Blake).

If my previous suggestions are at all valid, it will be obvious where the principal connections lie.

The classic speech-construct, the centrality of the word, are informed by and expressive of both a hierarchic value-system, and the trope of transcendence. These nodes of sensibility are interactive and mutually re-enforcing at every point. Indo-European syntax is an active mirroring of systems of order, of hierarchic dependence, of active and passive stance, such as have been prominent in the fabric of western society. The cliché tag regarding the capacity of Latin grammar to reproduce characteristic attitudes in Roman feeling and conduct, is true in a more acute and general sense. An explicit grammar is an acceptance of order: it is a hierarchization, the more penetrating for being enforced so early in the individual life-span, of the forces and valuations prevailing in the body politic (the tonalities of 'class', 'classification' and 'classic' are, naturally, cognate). The sinews of western speech closely enacted and, in turn, stabilized, carried forward, the power relations of the western social order. Gender differentiations, temporal cuts, the rules governing prefix and suffix formations, the synapses and anatomy of a grammar – these are the *figura*, at once ostensive and deeply internalized, of the commerce between the sexes, between master and subject, between official history and utopian dream, in the corresponding speech community.

The affinities between the pre-eminence of the word and the classic gamble on and against death are even more central and complex. The ontological and hermeneutic aspects of the modulations between a language-culture and death, explored, for example, in Heidegger and Paul Ricoeur, are too demanding to be touched on here. The point is that the very verb-systems of Indo-European languages are 'performative' of those attitudes towards act and survival which animate the classic doctrine of knowledge and of art. What the poet terms 'glory' is a direct function of the felt reality of the future tense. The ordered density of remembrance hinges on the prodigal exactitudes of Indo-European praeterits. Thus the time-death copula of a classic structure of personal and philosophic values is, in many respects, syntactic, and is inherent to a fabric of life in which language holds a sovereign, almost magically validated role. Diminish that role, subvert that eminence, and you will have begun to demolish the hierarchies and transcendence-values of a classic civilization. Even death can be made mute.

The counter-culture is perfectly aware of where to begin the job of demolition. The violent illiteracies of the graffiti, the clenched silence of the adolescent, the nonsense-cries from the stage-happening, are resolutely strategic. The insurgent and the freak-out have broken off discourse with a cultural system which they despise as a cruel, antiquated fraud. They will not bandy words with it. Accept, even momentarily, the conventions of literate linguistic exchange, and you are caught in the net of the old values, of the grammars that can condescend or enslave.

Changes of idiom between generations are a normal part of social history. Previously, however, such changes and the verbal provocations of young against old have been variants on an evolutionary continuum. What is occurring now is new: it is an attempt at a total break. The mumble of the drop-out, the 'fuck-off' of the beatnik, the silence of the teenager in the enemy house of his parents, are meant to destroy. Cordelia's asceticism, her refusal of the mendacities of speech, proves murderous. So does that of the autistic child, when it stamps on language, pulverizing it to gibberish or maniacal silence. We empty of their humanity those to whom we deny speech. We make them naked and absurd. There is a terrible, literal image in 'stone-deafness', in the opaque babble or speechlessness of the 'stoned'. Break off speech to others and the Medusa turns inward. Hence something of the hurt and despair of the present conflict between generations. Deliberate violence is being done to those primary ties of identity and social cohesion produced by a common language.

But are there no other literacies conceivable, 'literacies' not of the letter?

This is being written in a study in a college of one of the great American universities. The walls are throbbing gently to the beat of music coming from one near and several more distant amplifiers. The walls quiver to the ear or to the touch roughly eighteen hours per day, sometimes twenty-four. The beat is literally unending. It matters little whether it is that of pop, folk or rock. What counts is the all-pervasive pulsation, morning to night and into night, made indiscriminate by the cool burn of electronic timbre. A large segment of mankind, between the ages of thirteen and, say, twenty-five, now lives immersed in this constant throb. The hammering of rock or of pop creates an enveloping space. Activities such as reading, writing, private communication, learning, previously framed with silence, now take place in a field of strident *vibrato*. This means that the essentially linguistic nature of these pursuits is adulterated; they are vestigial modes of the old 'logic'.

The new sound-sphere is global. It ripples at great speed across languages, ideologies, frontiers and races. The triplet pounding at me through the wall on a winter night in the north-eastern United States is most probably reverberating at the same moment in a dance-hall in Bogota, off a transistor in Narvik, via a juke-box in Kiev and an electric guitar in Bengazi. The tune is last month's or last week's top of the pops; already it has the whole of mass society for its echo-chamber. The economics of this musical esperanto are staggering. Rock and pop breed concentric worlds of fashion, setting and life-style. Popular music has brought with it sociologies of private and public manner, of group solidarity. The politics of Eden come loud.

Many contexts of the decibel-culture have been studied. What is more important, but difficult to investigate, let alone quantify, is the question of the development of mental faculties, of self-awareness, when these take place in a perpetual sound-matrix. What are the sweet, vociferous hammers doing to the brain at key stages in its development? We have no real precedent to tell us how life-forms mature and are conducted at anywhere near the levels of organized noise which now cascade through the day and the lit night (rock, in particular, bends and colours the light around it). When a young man walks down a street in Vladivostok or Cincinnati with his transistor blaring, when a car passes with its radio on at full blast, the resulting sound-capsule encloses the individual. It diminishes the external world to a set of acoustic surfaces. A pop régime imposes severe physical stress on the human ear. Some of the coarsening or damage that can follow has, in fact, been measured. But hardly anything is known of the psychological effects of saturation by volume and repetitive beat (often the same two or three tunes are played around the clock). What tissues of sensibility are being numbed or exacerbated?

Yet we are unquestionably dealing with a literacy, with codes of recognition so widespread and dynamic that they constitute a 'meta-culture'. Popular music(s) have their semantics, their theory of genres, their intricate play-offs of esoteric against canonic types. Folk and pop, 'trad music' and rock, count their several histories and corpus of legend. They show their relics. They number their old masters and rebels, their betrayers and high priests. Precisely as in classical literacy, so there are in the world of jazz or of rock-'n-roll degrees of initiation ranging from the vague empathies of the tyro

(Latin on sun-dials) to the acid erudition of the scholiast. At the same time there is an age-factor which makes the culture of pop more like modern mathematics and physics than the humanities. In their execution of and response to popular music, the young have a tension-span, a suppleness of appropriation denied to the old. Part of the reason may be a straightforward organic degeneracy: the delicate receptors of the inner ear harden and grow opaque during one's twenties.

In short, the vocabularies, the contextual behaviour-patterns of pop and rock, constitute a genuine *lingua franca*, a 'universal dialect' of youth. Everywhere a sound-culture seems to be driving back the old authority of verbal order.

Classical music has a large part in this new presence of sound. Increasingly, I believe, it is penetrating the lives, the habits of attention and repose of men and women who were once 'bookish'. In numerous homes, the hi-fi components and the rack for long-playing records occupy the place of the library. High-fidelity reproduction and the L.P. are more than a mechanical gain. They have opened up, brought into easy range, a large territory of music, of tonality and lost form, accessible before only to the eye of the archivist. In many respects, the quality of the modern phonograph makes of the private sitting-room an idealized concert-hall. It allows a new fastidiousness of listening: no alien coughs disturb, no shuffling of wet feet, no false notes. The long-playing record has changed the relations of the ear to musical time. Because they can be put on at one go, or with a minimum of interval, works in a large format – a Mahler symphony – or meshed sequences such as the *Goldberg variations*, can now be listened to integrally, at home, and also repeated or segmented at will. This flexible interplay between time-notation in the musical piece, and the time-flow in the listener's personal life, can be at once arbitrary and illuminating. As is the entirely novel fact that *all* music can now be heard at any hour and as domestic background. Tape, radio, the phonograph, the cassette will emit an unending stream of music, at any moment or circumstance of the day. This probably accounts for the industry in Vivaldi and the minor eighteenth century. It explains the prodigality of the baroque and of the pre-classical chamber ensemble in the L.P. catalogue. So much of this music was, in fact, conceived as *Tafelmusik* and aural tapestry around the busy room. But we now tend to employ the great modes also as if they were background. If we choose, we can put on Opus 131 while eating the breakfast cereal. We can play the *St Matthew Passion* any hour or day of the week. Again, the effects are ambiguous: there can be an unprecedented intimacy, but also a devaluation (*désacralization*). A Muzak of the sublime envelops us.

Habits of the bibliophile, of the library-cormorant as Coleridge called him, have shifted to the collector of records and performances. The furtive manias, the condescensions of expertness, the hunter's zeal which bore once on first editions, colophons, the *in-octavo* of a remaindered text, are common now among music-lovers. There is a science and market in old pressings, in out-of-stock albums, in worn 'seventy-eights', as there has long been in used books. Catalogues of recordings and rare tapes are becoming as exegetic as bibliographies. Particularly in America, the record- and music-store will be where the bookstore was, or books will hang on, in uneasy co-existence, as part of a music emporium. Where the Victorians published pocket-books for lovers, garlands of prose and rhyme for lovers to read aloud to one another, or in whispered exchange, we issue records to seduce by, to spin when the fire is low in the grate. If Dante wrote the line now, crystallizing total passion and the world shut out, it would, I think, read: 'and they listened no more that day'.

The facts behind this 'musicalization' of our culture, behind the shift of literacy and historical awareness from eye to ear (only some, even among serious listeners, can read the score), are fairly obvious. But the underlying motives are so complex, one is so much a part of the change, that I hesitate to put forward any explanation.

The new ideals of shared inner life, of participatory emotion and leisure, certainly play a part. Except in the practice of reading aloud, pater familias to household, or of the tome passed from hand to hand and read aloud from in turn, the act of reading is profoundly solitary. It cuts the reader off from the rest of the room. It seals the sum of his consciousness behind unmoving lips. Loved books are the necessary and sufficient society of the alone. They close the door on other presences and make of them intruders. There is, in short, a fierce privacy to print and claim on silence. These, precisely, are the traits of sensibility now most suspect. The bias of current sentiment points insistently towards gregariousness, towards a liberal sharing of emotions. The 'great good place' of approved dreams is one of togetherness. The harsh hoarding of feelings inside the reader's silence is out. Recorded music matches the new ideals perfectly. Sitting near one another, in intermittent concentration, we partake of the flow of sound both individually and collectively. This is the liberating paradox. Unlike the book, the piece of music is immediate common ground. Our responses to it can be simultaneously private and social. Our delight banishes no one. We draw close while being, more compactly, ourselves. The mutual tide of empathies can be dishevelled and frankly lazy. The sheer lustre, the *fortes* or *pianos* of stereophonic reproduction in a private room, can be narcotic. A good deal of classical music is, today, the opium of the good citizen. Nevertheless, the search for human contact, for states of being that are intense but do not shut out others, is real. It is a part of the collapse of classic egoism. Often music 'speaks' to that search as printed speech does not.

Perhaps one may conjecture further. The lapse from ceremony and ritual in much of public and private behaviour has left a vacuum. At the same time, there is a thirst for magical and 'transrational' forms. The capacity of organized religion to satisfy this thirst diminishes. Matthew Arnold foretold that the 'facts' of religion would be replaced by its poetry. Today, one feels that in many educated but imperfectly coherent lives that 'poetry of religious emotion' is being provided by music. The point is not easy to demonstrate; it pertains to the interior climate of feeling. But one does know of a good many individual and familial existences in which the performance or enjoyment of music has functions as subtly indispensable, as exalting and consoling as religious practices might have, or might have had formerly. It is this indispensability which strikes one, the feeling (which I share) that there is music one cannot do without for long, that certain pieces of music rather than, say, books, are the talisman of order and of trust inside oneself. In the absence or recession of religious belief, close-linked as it was to the classic primacy of language, music seems to gather, to harvest us to ourselves.

Perhaps it can do so because of its special relation to the truth. Neither ontology nor aesthetics have satisfactorily enunciated that relation. But we feel it readily. At every knot, from the voices of public men to the vocabulary of dreams, language is close-woven with lies. Falsehood is inseparable from its generative life. Music can boast, it can sentimentalize, it can release springs of cruelty. But it does not lie. (Is there a lie, anywhere, in Mozart?) It is here that the affinities of music with needs of feeling which were once religious, may run deepest.

Conceivably, an ancient circle is closing. In his *Mythologiques*, Lévi-Strauss has asserted that melody holds the key to the *'mystère suprême de l'homme'*. Grasp the riddle of melodic invention, of our apparently imprinted sense of harmonic accord, and you will touch on the roots of human consciousness. Only music, says Lévi-Strauss, is a primal universal language, at once comprehensible to all and untranslatable into any other idiom. Speech comes later than music; even before the disorder at Babel, it was part of the Fall of man. This supposition is, itself, immemorial. It is fundamental to Orphic and Pythagorean doctrines, to the *harmonia mundi* of Boethius and the sixteenth century. It guided Kepler and was inferred, almost as a commonplace, in Condillac's great *Essai sur l'origine des connaissances humaines* of 1746. It is no accident that the two visionaries, most observant of the crises of the classic order, Kierkegaard and Nietzsche, should have seen in music the mode of pre-eminent energy and meaning. With the mendacities of language brought home to us by psychoanalysis and the mass media, it may be that music is regaining ancient ground, wrested from it, held for a time, by the dominance of the word.

In part these are metaphors and discursive myths. But the condition of feeling which they reflect is real. The literacies of popular and classical music, informed by new techniques of reproduction no less important than was the spread of cheap mass-printing in its time, are entering our lives at numerous, shaping levels. In many settings and sensibilities, they are providing a 'culture outside the word'. This movement will, I expect, continue. We are too close to the facts to see them whole. The test of objectivity is, still, bound to be personal. In ways which are simple-minded but difficult to paraphrase, the 'motion' of these lectures seeks to echo, to parallel by other means, a musical figure: a tentative upward arc and descent in the orchestra – it holds one's breath – towards the close of Bartók's *Bluebeard's Castle*. We seem to stand, in regard to a theory of culture, where Bartók's Judith stands, when she asks to open the last door on the night.

For Matthew Arnold, the touchstones of supreme civilization, of personal feeling in accord with the highest moral and intellectual values, were passages of Greek, Shakespearean or Miltonic verse. One suspects that for many of us, now, the image of decisive recourse would be less a touchstone than a tuning-fork. *Musique avant toute chose.*

If music is one of the principal 'languages outside the word', mathematics is another. Any argument on a post-classic culture and on future literacy will have to address itself, decisively, to the role of the mathematical and natural sciences. Theirs may very soon be the central sphere. Statistics can be shallow or ambiguous in interpretation. But those which tabulate the growth of the sciences do, in plain fact, map a new world. More than ninety per cent of all scientists known to human record are now living. The number of papers which may be regarded as relevant to an advance in chemistry, physics, and the biological sciences, i.e. the recent, active literature in these three fields alone, is estimated as being in excess of three and a quarter million. The critical indices in the sciences – investment, publication, number of men trained, percentage of the gross national product directly implicated in research and development – are doubling every seven to ten years. Between now and 1990, according to a recent projection, the number of monographs published in mathematics, physics, chemistry, and biology will, if aligned on an imaginary shelf, stretch to the moon. Less tangibly, but more significantly, it has been estimated that some seventy-five per cent of the most talented individuals in the developed nations, of the men and women whose measurable intelligence comes near the top of the curve in the community, now work in the sciences. Politics and the humanities thus seem to draw on a quarter of the optimal mental resources in our societies, and recruit largely from below the line of excellence. It is almost a platitude to insist that no previous period in history offers any comparable growth in the rate, multiplicity and effects of scientific-technological advance. It is equally obvious that even the present fantastic pace (interleaved, as it may be, by phases of disillusion or regrouping in certain highly developed nations) will at least double by the early 1980s. This phenomenology brings with it wholly unprecedented demands on information absorption and rational application. We stand less on that shore of the unbounded sea which awed Newton than amid tidal movements for which there is not even a theoretic model.

One can identify half a dozen areas of maximal pressure, points at which pure science and technological realization will alter basic structures of both private and social life.

There is the galaxy of bio-medical 'engineering'. Spare-part surgery, the use of chemical agencies against the degeneration of ageing tissues, pre-selection of the sex of the embryo, the manipulation of genetic factors towards ethical or strategic ends – each of these literally prepares a new typology of man. So does the direct chemical or electro-chemical control of behaviour. By implanting electrodes in the brain, by giving personality-control drugs, the therapist will be able to programme alterations of consciousness, he will touch on the electro-chemistry of motive to determine the deed. Memory-transfer through bio-chemical transplant, for which controversial claims are now being made, would alter the essential relations of ego and time. Unquestionably, our current inroads on the human cortex dwarf all previous images of exploration.

The revolutions of awareness that will result from full-scale computerization and electronic data-processing can only be crudely guessed at. At some point in 1969, the information-handling capacity of computers – i.e. the number of units of information which can be received and stored – passed that of the 3.5 billion brains belonging to the human race. By 1975, computers will be leading by a fifty-to-one ratio. By whatever criterion used, size of memory, cost, speed and accuracy of calculation, computers are now increasing a thousandfold every fifteen years. In advanced societies, the electronic data-bank is fast becoming the pivot of military, economic, sociological and archival procedures. Though a computer is a tool, its powers are such that they go far beyond any model of governed, easily limited instrumentality. Analogue and digital computerization are transforming the relations of density, of authority, between the human intellect and available knowledge, between personal choice and projected possibility. Connected to telephone lines or to more sophisticated arteries of transmission, multipurpose computers will become a routine presence in all offices and most homes. It is probable that this electronic cortex will simultaneously reduce the singularity of the individual and immensely enlarge his referential and operational scope. Inevitably, the mathematical issues of electronic storage and information-retrieval are becoming the focus for the study of mind.

The fourth main area is that of large-scale ecological modification. There is a good deal of millenarian naïveté and recoil from adult politics in the current passion for the environment. Nevertheless, the potentialities are formidable. Control of weather, locally at least, is now conceivable. As are the economic exploitation of the continental shelves and of the deeper parts of the sea. Man's setting or 'collective skin' is becoming malleable on a scale previously unimaginable. Beyond these fields lies space-exploration. Momentary boredom with the smooth histrionics of the thing ought not to blur two crucial eventualities. There is the establishment of habitable bases outside a polluted, overcrowded or war-torn earth, and, remote as it now seems, the perception of signals from other systems of intelligence or information. Fontenelle's inspired speculations of 1686, *Sur la pluralité des mondes*, are now a statistical function.

We cannot hope to measure the sum and consequence of these developments. Yet all but the last-mentioned are in definite sight. That not one of these exploding horizons should even appear in Eliot's analysis of culture indicates the pace of mutation since 1948. Our ethics, our central habits of consciousness, the immediate and environmental membrane we inhabit, our relations to age and to remembrance, to the children whose gender we may select and whose heredity we may programme, are being transformed. As in the twilit times of Ovid's fables of mutant being, we are in metamorphosis. To be ignorant of these scientific and technological phenomena, to be indifferent to their effects on our mental and physical experience, *is to opt out of reason*. A view of post-classic civilization must, increasingly, imply a vision of the sciences, of the language-worlds of mathematical and symbolic notation. Theirs is the commanding energy: in material fact, in the 'forward dreams' which define us. Today, our dialectics are binary.

But the motives for trying to incorporate science into the field of common reference, of imaginative reflex, are better than utilitarian. And this is so even if we take 'utilitarian', as we must, to include our very survival as a species. The true motives ought to be those of delight, of intellectual energy, of moral venture. To have some personal *rapport* with the sciences is, very probably, to be in contact with that which has most force of life and comeliness in our reduced condition.

At seminal levels of metaphor, of myth, of laughter, where the arts and the worn scaffolding of philosophic systems fail us, science is active. Touch on even its more abstruse regions and a deep elegance, a quickness and merriment of the spirit come through. Consider the Banach-Tarski theorem whereby the sun and a pea may be so divided into a finite number of disjointed parts that every single part of one is congruent to a unique part of the other. The undoubted result is that the sun may be fitted into one's vest pocket and that the component parts of the pea will fill the entire universe solidly, no vacant space remaining either in the interior of the pea, or in the universe. What surrealist fantasy yields a more precise wonder? Or take the Penrose theorem in cosmology which tells us that under extreme conditions of gravitational collapse a critical stage is reached whereby no communication with the outside world is possible. Light cannot escape the pull of the gravitational field. A 'black hole' develops representing the locale of a body of near-zero volume and near-infinite density. Or, even more remarkably, the 'collapse-event' may open 'into' a new universe hitherto unapprehended. Here spin the *soleils noirs* of Baudelaire and romantic trance. But the marvellous wit is that of fact. Very recent observations of at least two bodies, a companion to the star Aur and the supergiant star Her 89, suggest that Penrose's model of a 'hole in space' is true. 'Constantly, I seek a poetry of facts', writes Hugh MacDiarmid:

Even as
The profound kinship of all living substance
Is made clear by the chemical route.
Without some chemistry one is bound to remain
Forever a dumbfounded savage
In the face of vital reactions.
The beautiful relations
Shown only by biochemistry
Replace a stupefied sense of wonder
With something more wonderful
Because natural and understandable.

That 'poetry of facts' and realization of the miraculous delicacies of perception in contemporary science, already informs literature at those nerve-points where it is both disciplined and under the stress of the future. It is no accident that Musil was trained as an engineer, that Ernst Jünger and Nabokov should be serious entomologists, that Broch and Canetti are writers schooled in the exact and mathematical sciences. The special, deepening presence of Valéry in one's feelings about the after-life of culture is inseparable from his own alertness to the alternative poetics, to the 'other metaphysics' of mathematical and scientific pursuit. The instigations of Queneau and of Borges, which are among the most bracing in modern letters, have algebra and astronomy at their back. And there is a more spacious, central instance. Proust's only successor is Joseph Needham. *À la recherche du temps perdu* and *Science and Civilization in China* represent two prodigiously sustained, controlled flights of the re-creative intellect. They exhibit what Coleridge termed 'esemplastic powers', that many-branched coherence of design which builds a great house of language for memory and conjecture to inhabit. The China of Needham's passionate re-composing – so inwardly shaped before he went in search of its material truth – is a place as intricate, as lit by dreams, as the way to Combray. Needham's account, in an 'interim' essay, of the misreadings and final discovery of the true hexagonal symmetry of the snow-crystal has the same exact savour of manifold revealing as the Narrator's sightings of the steeple at Martinville. Both works are a long dance of the mind.

It is often objected that the layman cannot share in the life of the sciences. He is 'bound to remain / Forever a dumbfounded savage' before a world whose primary idiom he cannot grasp. Though good scientists themselves rarely say this, it is obviously true. But only to a degree. Modern science is centrally mathematical; the development of rigorous mathematical formalization marks the evolution of a given discipline, such as biology, to full scientific maturity. Having no mathematics, or very little, the 'common reader' is excluded. If he tries to penetrate the meaning of a scientific argument, he will probably get it muddled, or misconstrue metaphor to signify the actual process. True again, but of a truth that is half-way to indolence. Even a modest mathematical culture will allow some approach to what is going on. The notion that one can exercise a rational literacy in the latter part of the twentieth century without a knowledge of calculus, without some preliminary access to topology or algebraic analysis, will soon seem a bizarre archaism. These styles and speech-forms from the grammar of number are already indispensable to many branches of modern logic, philosophy, linguistics and psychology. They are the language of feeling where it is, today, most adventurous. As electronic data-processing and coding pervade more and more of the economics and social order of our lives, the mathematical illiterate will find himself cut off. A new hierarchy of menial service and stunted opportunity may develop among those whose resources continue to be purely verbal. There may be 'word-helots'.

Of course, the mathematical literacy of the amateur must remain modest. Usually he will apprehend only a part of the scientific innovation, catching a momentary, uncertain glimpse of a continuum, making an approximate image for himself. But is this not, in fact, the way in which we view a good deal of modern art? Is it not precisely through intervals of selective appropriation, via pictorial analogies which are often naive in the extreme, that the non-musician assimilates the complex, ultimately technical realities of music?

The history of science, moreover, permits of a less demanding access, yet one that leads to the centre. A modest mathematical culture is almost sufficient to enable one to follow the development of celestial mechanics and of the theory of motion until Newton and Laplace. (Has there been a subtler re-capturer of motive, of the dart and recoil of mind, than Alexandre Koyré, the historian of this movement?) It takes no more than reasonable effort to understand, at least along major lines, the scruple, the elegance of hypothesis and experiment which characterize the modulations of the concept of entropy from Carnot to Helmholtz. The genesis of Darwinism and the subsequent re-examinations which lead from orthodox evolutionary doctrine to modern molecular biology are one of the 'very rich hours' of the human intellect. Yet much of the material, and of its philosophical implications, are accessible to the layman. This is so, to a lesser degree, of some part of the debate between Einstein, Bohr, Wolfgang Pauli and Max Born – from each of whom we have letters of matchless honesty and personal commitment – on the issue of anarchic indeterminacy or subjective interference in quantum physics. Here are topics as crowded with felt life as any in the humanities.

The absence of the history of science and technology from the school syllabus is a scandal. It is an absurdity to speak of the Renaissance without knowledge of its cosmology, of the mathematical dreams which underwrote its theories of art and music. To read seventeenth- and eighteenth-century literature or philosophy without an accompanying awareness of the unfolding genius of physics, astronomy and algebraic analysis during the period, is to read only at the surface. A model of neo-classicism which omits Linnaeus is hollow. What can be said responsibly of romantic historicism, of the new mappings of time after Hegel, which fails to include a study of Buffon, Cuvier and Lamarck? It is not only that the humanities have been arrogant in their assertions of centrality. It is that they have often been silly. We need no poet more urgently than Lucretius.

Where culture itself is so utterly fragmented, there is no need to speak of the sciences as separate. What does make them so different from the present state of the humanities is their collectivity and inner calendar. Overwhelmingly, today, science is a collective enterprise in which the talent of the individual is a function of the group. But, as we have seen, more and more of current radical art and anti-art aspires to the same plurality. The really deep divergence between the humanistic and scientific sensibilities is one of temporality. Very nearly by definition, the scientist knows that tomorrow will be in advance of today. A twentieth-century schoolboy can manipulate mathematical and experiential concepts inaccessible to a Galileo or a Gauss. For a scientist the curve of time is positive. Inevitably, the humanist looks back. The essential repertoire of his consciousness, the props of his daily life as a scholar or critic are from the past. A natural bent of feeling will lead him to believe, perhaps silently, that the achievements of the past are more radiant than those of his own age. The proposition that 'Shakespeare is the greatest, most complete writer mankind will ever produce' is a logical and almost a grammatical provocation. But it carries conviction. And even if a Rembrandt or a Mozart may, in future, be equalled (itself a gross, indistinct notion), they cannot be surpassed. There is a profound logic of sequent energy in the arts, but not an additive progress in the sense of the sciences. No errors are corrected or theorems disproved. Because it carries the past within it, language, unlike mathematics, draws backward. This is the meaning of Eurydice. Because the realness of his inward being lies at his back, the man of words, the singer, will turn back, to the place of necessary, beloved shadows. For the scientist, time and the light lie before.

Here, if anywhere, lies the division of the 'two cultures' or, rather, of the two orientations. Anyone who has lived among scientists will know how intensely this polarity influences life-style. Their evenings point self-evidently to tomorrow, *e santo è l'avvenir.*

Or is it really?

This is the last question I want to touch on. And by far the most difficult. I can state it and feel its extreme pressure. But I have not been able to think it through in any clear or consequent manner.

That science and technology have brought with them fierce problems of environmental damage, of economic unbalance, of moral distortion, is a commonplace. In terms of ecology and ideals of sensibility, the cost of the scientific-technological revolutions of the past four centuries has been very high. But despite anarchic, pastoral critiques such as those put forward by Thoreau and Tolstoy, there has been little fundamental doubt that it ought to be met. In that largely unexamined assurance, there has been a part of blind economic will, of immense hunger for comfort and material diversity. But there has also been a much deeper mechanism: the conviction, centrally woven into the western temper, at least since Athens, that mental inquiry must move forward, that such motion is natural and meritorious in itself, that man's proper relation to the truth is one of pursuer (the 'haloo' of Socrates cornering his quarry rings through our history). We open the successive doors in Bluebeard's castle because 'they are there', because each leads to the next by a logic of intensification which is that of the mind's own awareness of being. To leave one door closed would not only be cowardice, but a betrayal — radical, self-mutilating — of the inquisitive, probing, forward-tensed stance of our species. We are hunters after reality, wherever it may lead. The risks, the disasters incurred are flagrant. But so is, or has been until very recently, the axiomatic assumption and *a priori* of our civilization, which holds that man and the truth are companions, that their roads lie forward and are dialectically cognate.

For the first time (and one's conjectures here will be tentative and blurred), this all-governing axiom of continued advance is being questioned. I am

thinking of issues that go far beyond current worries in the scientific community about the environment, about weaponry, about the mindless applications of chemistry to the human organism. The real question is whether
certain major lines of inquiry ought to be pursued at all, whether society and
the human intellect at their present level of evolution, can survive the next
truths. It may be – and the mere possibility presents dilemmas beyond any
which have arisen in history – that the coming door opens on to realities
ontologically opposed to our sanity and limited moral reserves. Jacques
Monod has asked publicly what many have puzzled over in private: ought
genetic research to continue if it will lead to truths about differentiations in
the species whose moral, political, psychological consequences we are unable
to cope with? Are we free to pursue neuro-chemical or psycho-physiological
spoors concerning the layered, partially archaic forms of the cortex, if such
study brings the knowledge that ethnic hatreds, the need for war, or those
impulses toward self-ruin hinted at by Freud, are inherited facts? Such examples can be multiplied.

It may be that the truths which lie ahead wait in ambush for man, that the
kinship between speculative thought and survival on which our entire culture
has been based, will break off. The stress falls on *'our'* entire culture because,
as anthropologists remind us, numerous primitive societies have chosen stasis
or mythological circularity over forward motion, and have endured around
truths immemorially posited.

The notion that abstract truth, and the morally neutral truths of the sciences
in particular, might come to paralyse or destroy western man, is foreshadowed in Husserl's *Krisis der europäischen Wissenschaften* (1934–7). It
becomes a dominant motif in the theory of 'negative dialectic' of Horkheimer,
Adorno and the Frankfurt School. This is one of the most challenging, though
often hermetic, currents in modern feeling and in the modern diagnosis of
the crisis of culture. Tito Perlini's long essay, 'Autocritica della ragione
illuministica' (in *Ideologie*, IX/X, 1969), is not only a lucid introduction to this
material, but a stringent statement of the case.

Reason itself has become repressive. The worship of 'truth' and of autonomous 'facts' is a cruel fetishism: *'Elevato ad idolo di se stesso, il fatto è un tiranno
assoluto di fronte a cui il pensiero non può non prosternarsi in muta adorazione'.*
The disease of enlightened man is his acceptance, itself wholly superstitious,
of the superiority of facts to ideas. *'La spinta al positivo è tentazione mortale
per la cultura.'* Instead of serving human ends and spontaneities, the 'positive
truths' of science and of scientific laws have become a prison-house, darker

than Piranesi's, a *carcere* to imprison the future. It is these 'facts', not man, which regulate the course of history. As Horkheimer and Adorno emphasize in the *Dialektik der Aufklärung*, the old obscurantisms of religious dogma and social caste have been replaced by the even more tyrannical obscurantism of 'rational, scientific truth'. 'Reality has the better of ideology', writes Perlini, meaning that a myth of objective, verifiable scientific evidence has over-whelmed the utopian, fundamentally anarchic springs of humane conscious-ness: *'In nome di un'esperienza ridotta al simulacro di se stessa, viene condannata come vuota fantasticheria la stessa capacità soggettiva di progettazione dell'uomo.'*

The vigour of the indictment, its moral and intellectual attractions, are evident. But so are its weaknesses. It is no accident that Horkheimer and Adorno were unable to complete the *Dialektik*. Nowhere do we find sub-stantive examples of how a liberated, 'multi-dimensional' man would in fact re-structure his relations to reality, to that 'which is so'. Where is the actual programme for a mode of human perception freed from the 'fetishism of abstract truth'?

But the argument is flawed at a more elemental level. The pursuit of the facts, of which the sciences merely provide the most visible, organized instance, is no contingent error embarked on by western man at some moment of élitist or bourgeois rapacity. That pursuit is, I believe, imprinted on the fabric, on the electro-chemistry and impulse-net of our cortex. Given an adequate climatic and nutritive *milieu*, it was bound to evolve and to augment by a constant feed-back of new energy. The partial absence of this questing compulsion from less-developed, dormant races and civilizations does not represent a free choice or feat of innocence. It represents, as Montesquieu knew, the force of adverse ecological and genetic circumstance. The flower-child in the western city, the neo-primitive chanting his five words of Thibetan on the highway, are performing an infantile charade – founded on the surplus wealth of that same city or highway. We cannot turn back. We cannot choose the dreams of unknowing. We shall, I expect, open the last door in the castle even if it leads, perhaps *because* it leads, on to realities which are beyond the reach of human comprehension and control. We shall do so with that desolate clairvoyance, so marvellously rendered in Bartók's music, because opening doors is the tragic merit of our identity.

There are two obvious responses to this outlook. There is Freud's stoic acquiescence, his grimly tired supposition that human life was a cancerous anomaly, a detour between vast stages of organic repose. And there is the Nietzschean gaiety in the face of the inhuman, the tensed, ironic perception that we are, that we always have been, precarious guests in an indifferent, frequently murderous, but always fascinating world:

> Schild der Notwendigkeit.
> Höchstes Gestirn des Seins!
> – das kein Wunsch erreicht,
> – das kein Nein befleckt,
> ewiges Ja des Seins,
> ewig bin ich dein Ja:
> denn ich liebe dich, o Ewigkeit!

Both attitudes have their logic and direction of conduct. One chooses or alternates between them for uncertain reasons of private feeling, of authentic or imagined personal circumstance. Personally, I feel most drawn to the *gaya scienza*, to the conviction, irrational, even tactless as it may be, that it is enormously interesting to be alive at this cruel, late stage in western affairs. If a *dur désir de durer* was the mainspring of classic culture, it may well be that our post-culture will be marked by a readiness not to endure rather than curtail the risks of thought. To be able to envisage possibilities of self-destruction yet press home the debate with the unknown, is no mean thing.

But these are only indistinct guesses. It is no rhetorical move to insist that we stand at a point where models of previous culture and event are of little help. Even the term *Notes* is too ambitious for an essay on culture written at this moment. At most, one can try to get certain perplexities into focus. Hope may lie in that small exercise. 'A blown husk that is finished', says Ezra Pound of man and of himself as he, the master-voyager of our age, nears a homecoming:

> A blown husk that is finished
>   but the light sings eternal
> a pale flare over marshes
>   where the salt hay whispers to tide's change.